A History of Religion in Britain

*Practice and Belief
from Pre-Roman Times
to the Present*

Edited by
Sheridan Gilley and W. J. Sheils

BLACKWELL
Oxford UK & Cambridge USA

Copyright © Basil Blackwell Ltd, 1994

First published 1994

Blackwell Publishers
238 Main Street
Cambridge, Massachusetts 02142
USA

108 Cowley Road
Oxford OX4 1JF
UK

Library of Congress Cataloging-in-Publication Data
A History of religion in Britain: practice and belief from pre-Roman
  times to the present / Sheridan Gilley and W. I. Shiels [i.e. Sheils].
      p. cm.
    Includes bibliographical references and index.
    ISBN 0–631–15281–4 (alk. paper). – ISBN 0–631–19378–2
  (pbk. alk. paper)
      1. Great Britain–Church history. 2. Great Britain–Religion.
  3. Great Britain–Religious life and customs. I. Gilley, Sheridan.
  II. Sheils, W. J.
  BR743.H55 1993
  200'.941–dc20   93–39083
                                                                 CIP
British Library Cataloguing in Publication Data
A CIP catalogue record for this book is available from the British Library.
Typeset in 11 on 13 pt Plantin by Photoprint
Printed in Great Britain by TJ Press Ltd, Padstow, Cornwall

A History of
Religion in Britain

This book is due for ret:

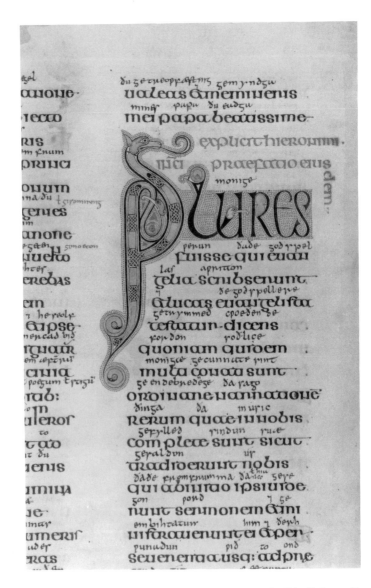

Frontispiece   The opening of St Luke's Gospel from the Lindisfarne Gospels

For Meg and Sarah

Contents

List of Plates   ix
Notes on Contributors   x
Preface   xiv

Introduction   Sheridan Gilley and W. J. Sheils   1

Part I   Conversion and Christendom   11

1   **Religion in Roman Britain**   Martin Henig   13
2   **Religion in Anglo-Saxon England**   Gerald Bonner   24
3   **From the Conquest to the Black Death**   Rosalind Hill   45
4   **Piety in the Later Middle Ages**   Norman Tanner   61
5   **Medieval Wales and the Reformation**   Glanmor Williams   77
6   **Religious Life in Medieval Scotland**   Michael Lynch   99

Part II   Reform, Revival and Enlightenment   127

7   **The Church in Scotland from the Reformation
     to the Disruption**   James K. Cameron   129
8   **Reformed Religion in England, 1520–1640**
     W. J. Sheils   151
9   **Anglicanism in Stuart and Hanoverian England**
     Ian Green   168
10 **Radical Sects and Dissenting Churches, 1600–1750**
     Michael Mullett   188
11 **Rational Religion in England from Herbert of Cherbury
     to William Paley**   David A. Pailin   211
12 **Catholicism in England from the Reformation
     to the Relief Acts**   W. J. Sheils   234

13   The Evangelical Revival in Eighteenth-Century Britain
     W. R. Ward   252

Part III   Industrialization, Empire and Identity   275

14   Church and State since 1800   Edward Norman   277
15   The Church of England in the Nineteenth Century
     Sheridan Gilley   291
16   Religious Life in Industrial Britain, 1830–1914
     David Hempton   306
17   Hebrews Hellenized? English Evangelical Nonconformity
     and Culture, 1840–1940   Clyde Binfield   322
18   The Roman Catholic Church in England, 1780–1940
     Sheridan Gilley   346
19   Religion and Community in Scotland and Wales
     since 1800   Keith Robbins   363
20   British Religion and the Wider World: Mission and
     Empire, 1800–1940   C. Peter Williams   381
21   Secularists and Rationalists, 1800–1940   Edward Royle   406

Part IV   Modern Britain   425

22   The Jewish Community in Britain   Jonathan G. Campbell   427
23   Religious Life between the Wars, 1920–1940
     Stuart Mews   449
24   The Christian Churches in England since 1945:
     Ecumenism and Social Concern   Alan M. Suggate   467
25   Religious Pluralism in Modern Britain   Paul Badham   488
26   Secularization and the Future   Alan D. Gilbert   503

Chronology   523
Selected Further Reading   534
Index   566

List of Plates

Frontispiece   The opening of St Luke's Gospel from the Lindisfarne Gospels ii

Plate 1   The conventual church of the Cistercian monastery at Tintern (Monmouth), viewed from the north 10

Plate 2   The monument of Sir William Gee (d. 1637), with his first and second wives, and his children, in York Minster 126

Plate 3   Caledonia Road Church, Glasgow (architect Alexander Thomson, 1856) 274

Plate 4   Pope John Paul II meets Salvation Army Commissioner Eva Burrows at the house of Cardinal Gray during his visit to Great Britain in 1982 424

Notes on Contributors

Paul Badham is Professor and Head of Department of Theology and Religious Studies in the University of Wales, Lampeter, where he teaches modern church history and modern theology. Most of his writing has been in the area of contemporary Christian thought but he has also edited *Religion, State and Society in Modern Britain*.

Clyde Binfield is Reader in History at the University of Sheffield where he has taught since 1964. He is editor of the *Journal of the United Reformed Church History Society*, is a past President of the Ecclesiastical History Society, and is President of the Chapels Society and Chairman of the National Council of YMCAs. His publications focus on the social, cultural and architectural contexts of Nonconformity.

Gerald Bonner, formerly of the University of Durham, is Distinguished Professor of Early Christian Studies at the Catholic University of America, Washington DC, which has recently awarded him the Johannes Quasten Medal for Excellence in Scholarship and Leadership in Religious Studies. He is the author of *St Augustine of Hippo: Life and Controversies*, and has delivered the Jarrow Lecture for 1966 and the Durham Cathedral Lecture for 1970 on the Venerable Bede, both of which have been published. He has written widely on Bede, St Cuthbert and Anglo-Saxon spirituality.

Revd James K. Cameron FBA is Emeritus Professor of Ecclesiastical History in the University of St Andrews where he has held a chair since 1970, having previously been a lecturer at King's College, Aberdeen. He edited *The First Book of Discipline* in 1972 and has contributed a number of articles on Scottish church history and on the European Reformation to journals in Britain and abroad.

Jonathan G. Campbell is Lecturer in Theology and Religious Studies in the University of Wales, Lampeter, where he teaches Biblical Studies, Hebrew and Judaism. He maintains a strong interest in issues in contemporary Judaism. His other main area of research is Second Temple Judaism, and his doctoral thesis on the Dead Sea Scrolls will appear as a book in 1995.

Alan Gilbert is Vice-Chancellor and Principal of the University of Tasmania, having previously been on the staff at the University of New South Wales. He did his research degree at Oxford and has written two books, *Religion and Society in Industrial England* and *The Making of Post-Christian Britain: A History of the Secularization of Modern Society*, as well as being a co-author of a study of churchgoing in modern Britain.

Sheridan Gilley is Reader in Theology in the University of Durham. His publications include *The Irish in the Victorian City* and *The Irish in Britain 1815–1939*, both edited jointly with Roger Swift, and *Newman and his Age*. He has published extensively on the Church in the modern era.

Ian Green is Reader in Modern History at the Queen's University, Belfast and the author of *The Re-establishment of the Church of England 1660–1663* in addition to a number of articles on the early modern Church. He is currently completing two monographs, on catechisms and catechizing and on other means of religious instruction in England between 1540 and 1740.

David Hempton is Professor of Modern History in the Queen's University of Belfast where he has taught since 1979. He is the author of *Methodism and Politics in British Society 1750–1850*, co-author of *Evangelical Protestantism in Ulster Society 1740–1890* and contributor of a number of articles on the religious history of Britain and Ireland in the modern period.

Martin Henig is a Research Associate of the Institute of Archaeology, Oxford University. His books include *Religion in Roman Britain* and *Art in Roman Britain*. Since 1985 he has been editor of the *Journal of the British Archaeological Association*.

Rosalind Hill is Professor Emerita in the University of London, having retired from teaching at Queen Mary and Westfield College. She has edited the registers of medieval English bishops and written several articles on medieval church history. She is the editor and translator of the *Gesta Francorum*.

Michael Lynch taught at University College, Bangor before coming to Edinburgh University, where he is now Professor of Scottish History.

Formerly editor of the ecclesiastical history journal, the *Innes Review*, he is presently joint literary secretary of the Scottish History Society. His books include *Edinburgh and the Reformation* and *Scotland: A New History*, and he is currently engaged as general editor of the forthcoming *Oxford Companion to Scottish History*.

Stuart Mews became Reader in Religious Studies at Cheltenham and Gloucester University in 1993, having previously taught the history and sociology of religion at Lancaster University. He has been Visiting Fellow at St John's College, Oxford and has edited several books, including *Religion and National Identity*, *Religion in Politics* and *Modern Religious Rebels*, in addition to the journal *Theology*.

Michael Mullett teaches history at Lancaster University and is the author of studies of radical Christianity, popular culture, Luther, Calvin, James II and Nonconformist archives. He is currently preparing a collection of essays on George Fox and a book on John Bunyan.

Edward Norman, an Anglican priest, is Dean at Christchurch College Canterbury. Among his many books is *Church and Society in England 1770–1970*. He was formerly a Lecturer in History at Cambridge University.

David Pailin studied in Cambridge, Dallas and Manchester, where he is Reader in the Philosophy of Religion. In addition to articles he has written the following books: *The Way to Faith, Attitudes to Other Religions: Comparative Religion in Seventeenth- and Eighteenth-century Britain, Groundwork of the Philosophy of Religion, God and the Processes of Reality: Foundations of a Credible Theism, The Anthropological Character of Theology: Conditioning Theological Understanding* and *A Gentle Touch: From a Theology of Handicap to a Theology of Human Being*.

Keith Robbins is Vice-Chancellor of the University of Wales, Lampeter. A former President of the Ecclesiastical History Society and of the Historical Association, he has written extensively on political, diplomatic and ecclesiastical topics. His collected essays have been published under the title *History, Religion and Politics*.

Edward Royle is Reader in History at the University of York where he specializes in the social and political history of modern Britain. His publications include *Victorian Infidels: Radicals, Secularists and Republicans, Chartism*, and a general study entitled *Modern Britain: A Social History 1750–1985*.

W. J. Sheils is Provost of Goodricke College in the University of York, where he teaches economic and social history. He has published books on puritanism and on the English Reformation and edited a number of texts. He was editor of **Studies in Church History** from 1981 to 1990 and is on the editorial board of the *Journal of Ecclesiastical History*.

Alan M. Suggate is Lecturer in the Department of Theology, University of Durham. He is the author of *William Temple and Christian Social Ethics Today*, and has published a number of articles on contemporary Christian social ethics as well as on Japanese Christianity and society.

Norman Tanner is a Jesuit priest who teaches medieval church history at Campion Hall, Oxford and Heythrop College, London. He has written various books and articles on medieval religion and is the editor of *Decrees of the Ecumenical Councils*.

W. R. Ward is Emeritus Professor of Modern History in the University of Durham. Most of his seventeen books deal with religious practice and belief, notably his *Protestant Evangelical Awakening*, *Faith and Faction* and (with R. P. Heitzenroter) a new edition of *Wesley's Journals and Diaries*, of which six volumes have appeared.

Glanmor Williams CBE, FBA, was Professor of History at the University College of Swansea from 1957 until his retirement, and is the author of several books and articles, particularly on the religious history of Wales.

C. Peter Williams is Vicar of Ecclesall, Sheffield. He was for many years on the staff at Trinity College, Bristol, latterly as Vice-Principal, and has published widely on aspects of the nineteeth-century missionary move-ment.

Preface

There is usually a gap between an aim and its achievement, and seven years have elapsed since we first conceived the idea of a comprehensive survey of the history of religion in Great Britain within the compass of a single volume. Any endeavour of this nature arises out of friendship and also makes demands upon it. We are very grateful to our contributors for the learning and enthusiasm which they have brought to the project, for the efficiency with which they wrote their chapters, and for the good-natured patience with which they awaited its completion.

We owe a particular debt to Blackwell for the first approaches in the matter and for their continuing support since. We would especially like to thank Gillian Bromley for the care and thoroughness of her copy-editing, and Dr Elizabeth Varley for compiling the index so expeditiously. We must also thank Professor J. P. Mackey for giving us permission to republish Professor Glanmor Williams' essay which first appeared in a collection edited by him, *An Introduction to Celtic Christianity* (Edinburgh, 1989).

A book such as this could not have been written without the extraordinary body of recent research about the history of the Church and of religion in this country. This has both transformed our understanding of the subject and shown us how much there is still to learn. We trust that this volume is both a record of the present state of knowledge and a point of departure for future discovery.

Sheridan Gilley and W. J. Sheils
Laetare Sunday, 1994

Introduction

Sheridan Gilley and W. J. Sheils

THE AIM of this book is to provide a comprehensive survey of the principal concerns of much recent writing and research on the history of religion in Great Britain from its origins to the present day. Few themes in the history of this island can claim to have been of such importance to the life of its people from the earliest inhabitants; and as the influence of British religion grew with that of Britain itself, its reach extended around the world.

The earliest surviving evidence for religious practice in Britain pre-dates the written record, and its interpretation must be conjectural or rely on the archaeological evidence. A mass of such material is deployed in the opening chapter of this book, in which Martin Henig demonstrates the syncretic fusion of pre-Roman Celtic religion with that of the Roman conquerors, and goes on to show that subsequently there was continuity, as at Lullingstone, as well as discontinuity, between those ancient gods and their shrines and the new God at the coming of Christianity.

With the Anglo-Saxon invasions, the origins of England properly so called, the break in continuity was more marked. Gerald Bonner describes not only the conversion of the new English population to Christianity, by missions from Ireland and from Rome, but also the brilliant cultural flowering of Anglo-Saxon Christianity in the Lindisfarne Gospels and the writings of the Venerable Bede. This achievement led to missionary activity itself, with men like Boniface and Willibrord preaching on the continent, before the Viking invasions destroyed much of that earlier growth. Recovery was achieved in the tenth-century monastic revival of Dunstan and Ethelwold, and the career of St Wulfstan, the most attractive of the Anglo-Saxon episcopal saints, eloquently expresses the very best of the pre-Conquest Church.

Wulfstan was the only one among the Anglo-Saxon Church hierarchy to survive the Conquest in person, but the Normans built on the foundations laid by those administrators to strengthen the diocesan structure of the Church they inherited. In other respects, however, the Normans were innovators and reformers, and Rosalind Hill describes their contribution to canon law and to the organization of cathedral churches. These reforms were carried out chiefly by clerics, but in other respects royal patrons and their powerful clients were the agents of change, especially in fostering the growth of the monastic orders. The Benedictines were brought into closer contact with reformed practices on the continent and, in the twelfth century, new orders, especially the Cistercians, were promoted. The arrival of the friars in the following century revitalized urban religion and the world of learning, and many of them achieved great influence in the Church through their sermons and writings. The decrees of the Fourth Lateran Council of 1215 secured the structures of parochial life, and much else besides, and they were given a ready reception in England where, by the mid-fourteenth century, the Church was distinguished by its orthodoxy and fidelity to the traditions of western Christendom.

The strength of those inherited structures of diocesan and parochial life, and the work of the religious orders, carried over into the late medieval Church. New institutions and types created a rich variety of orthodox practices in response to lay piety; fraternities, chantries, mystery plays, anchorites and mystics flourished in most parts of the country, despite the discordant note sounded by Wyclif and the Lollards. The period saw a great deal of ecclesiastical building, on both great and small scales, the results of which continue to adorn the towns and countryside of Britain; and Norman Tanner stresses that, as far as the religious practice of the mass of the population is concerned, its inner content and meaning are best understood in terms of its outer forms, especially the liturgy, which expressed both a vigorous local diversity and a richness of texture at every level of late medieval culture.

The account of Welsh Christianity given by Glanmor Williams takes us back to Romano-British Christianity, aspects of which persisted through to the Norman invasion. That invasion brought brutal discontinuity to the Church in Wales, a disjuncture reflected in the very different parts played by the Benedictine and the Cistercian abbeys in the medieval Welsh Church, whose diocesan structure had been placed within the province of Canterbury during the twelfth century. The arrival of the Reformation, secured on a lasting basis during the reign of Elizabeth I, brought further disruption, but also led to the translation of the Bible into Welsh. This vernacular text found its way into the hearts, language and culture of the people, and eventually restored to them some of the achievements of the pre-Conquest Celtic Church which had been overlain by the Normans.

In Scotland, too, a revival of interest in the traditional saints of the country was the catalyst for religious revival, this time in the twelfth century, a period that also saw the introduction to Scotland of new religious orders, most of which had close links with France. The piety which resulted was fostered and encouraged by the royal court, whose influence in religious affairs remained of central importance throughout the middle ages. By the end of the fifteenth century the cult of the Passion, which was particularly associated with the Observant Franciscans, the favourite religious order of the House of Stewart, had penetrated the spiritual and cultural life of the towns and linked Scotland to many strands of the new devotional climate emerging in the Low Countries and Germany. As Michael Lynch shows, by the end of the middle ages Church and Court stood jointly at the centre of a cultural renaissance in Scottish society.

By the beginning of the sixteenth century the various national churches of Great Britain had developed the main institutional structures of western Christendom in their mature forms and had come to play an integral part in the lives of the people. Orthodoxy was their distinguishing characteristic, and vigorous local traditions of lay piety provided a rich cultural background. In Scotland that piety drew on traditions associated with new movements on the continent, but the humanist scholarship of the English universities also shared in the renewed biblical devotion. That devotion, which also formed part of the beliefs of the Lollards, led to the translation of the Bible into the vernacular languages of the island, which not only reinvigorated the Welsh Church but played a prominent part in the changes associated with the Reformation both north and south of the border.

Reform in Scotland had started within the Church under Archbishop Hamilton, but the failure of the Catholic reform movement and the influence of Lutheran ideas and scholars were merely a prelude to the triumph of Calvinism. At first, however, that triumph was both ambiguous and uncertain, and the retention of superintendents in the new, and otherwise Presbyterian, church order was to prepare the way for the restoration of episcopacy under James VI and its enforcement under his son. The Prayer Book imposed in 1638 resulted in a National Covenant and a Scottish rebellion, followed by a period of upheaval under Cromwell, and a mixed episcopal and quasi-Presbyterian Church from the 1660s until the abolition of episcopacy in 1690. Episcopacy lay outside the Established Church in Scotland from that time onwards and a tradition of secession, in part under the influence of the evangelical movement, produced a number of seceder churches during the eighteenth century. Meanwhile the national Church divided between the old-fashioned Calvinists and the new-style rationalists, the Moderates, who while not questioning the articles of the Reformed faith held them with a liberal temper. Buttressed by patronage, it was this group which came increasingly to dominate the Church during the later part of the eighteenth century.

The decline of traditional piety in England was as sudden as it was north of the border, but its replacement by Reformed religion took a great deal longer. The Reformation was neither as successful as the early evangelists claimed, nor as limited in its outreach as the sermons of the Puritan divines suggest, but it was only in the seventeenth century that reform can be said to have reached most of the country, and even then the character of that reform was disputed. The Church was undeniably Calvinist in theology, but opinions differed over the central doctrine of grace, as well as over other issues such as the liturgy, ecclesiastical discipline and the nature of the ministry. These disputes are discussed in later chapters, but Sheils also reminds us here of the common elements in the Reformed Christianity shared by the people and revealed to us through the catechisms and other popular forms of religious writing.

This theme is also pursued in the chapter by Ian Green to offer a perspective on the pastoral effectiveness of the seventeenth-century Church of England. He argues that the mainstream of Anglican religious practice was less affected by such currents as Laudian churchmanship or Latitudinarian moralism than the traditional narrative of the Church's fortunes might suppose, and explains what might otherwise seem puzzling: the sources of strength in a Church suddenly thrown down by force of arms and then triumphantly restored to a vital place in the nation's life.

That place was, however, to exist alongside a number of Protestant Dissenting churches which were eventually granted toleration in 1689. The tradition of Dissent had its origin in the disputes of the Elizabethan and Jacobean churches, and its adherents were to grow in number in response to the Laudian Arminianism of the 1630s. The range of belief increased greatly in the proliferation of sects following the failure of the Presbyterian covenanted Commonwealth during the Interregnum, and grew again with the alienation of moderate Presbyterians in response to the full-blown Anglicanism of the Restoration. The legacy of Protestant Dissent in these circumstances, with its many varieties and sub-divisions, was a major strand in English Christianity, beside those churches owing allegiance to Canterbury and Rome, which has made a powerful contribution to the shape of international Protestantism.

In such a context of dissension, where rival groups often claimed the 'inner light' as their authority, it may be no surprise to see a resort to reason as the ultimate authority in religion, the more so as scientific method also began to engage the energies of the educated classes. In his chapter David Pailin traces that approach from the late seventeenth to the early nineteenth century, discussing both heterodox Deists, with their proofs of natural religion and denial of revelation, and the orthodox, who sought to show that revealed religion was also reasonable. This is a tradition which has retained an influence both in modern forms of opposition to Christianity and within Christianity itself.

While the search for a rational basis for religion was contemporary with the legislative acceptance of Dissenters, Roman Catholics remained excluded from the provisions of the Act of Toleration. The history of Catholicism since the Reformation has engendered a lively debate among historians over whether the Catholic body was a mere survival of the medieval Church or a revival in its own right. Between its re-formation by seminary priests in the 1570s and the first Relief Act of 1778 English Catholicism underwent a transformation from a gentry-dominated community – at its strongest in Lancashire but with an important metropolitan dimension – to one of large urban congregations over which the clergy exercised an increasing degree of control.

Also during the eighteenth century mainstream Dissent, along with a portion of the Established Church, was revitalized by the evangelicals, committed ministers and charismatic preachers supported by their lay adherents. This revival was a British phenomenon which also reflected the strengths and strains of international Protestantism evinced in the 'Great Awakening'. W. R. Ward analyses its differing experiences in all three countries; each was rooted in seventeenth-century Puritanism, but the Welsh revival was also grounded in the Welshness of the Church in Wales while its Scots counterpart had a difficult relationship with the seceder tradition and with the mission to convert the popish or prelatical or (some would say) pagan Highlands. English evangelicalism, on the other hand, and especially Wesley's, can best be explained as a resort to voluntary effort in an attempt to achieve the sort of spiritual revival that appeared to many to be beyond a hamstrung, law-bound, official Church.

Thus, by the beginning of the nineteenth century, the religious climate of all three countries had changed radically, each containing vigorous Dissenting traditions alongside the Established Church. Differing degrees of toleration had been extended to these churches, and in all of the countries an increasingly urban population had found in voluntarism a source of religious revival.

The paradox enunciated in Norman's chapter on Church–State relations since 1800 is that the weakening of that connection has more to do with the strength of voluntarism within Dissent than with secularization. Where disestablishment did take place, in Ireland and Wales, this reflected the vigour of rival religious traditions rather than any weakness of religion itself, and in England attachment to the Established Church survived even among those who would not claim to be especially religious. Indeed, when the privileges, powers and property of the Established Church came under fire in the nineteenth century, its defence, as Sheridan Gilley shows, sparked one of the most remarkable institutional and spiritual revivals in its history, resulting in liveliness and creative tension as well as division between the Protestant, Catholic and liberal traditions within Anglicanism.

That revival was, however, largely conservative and middle-class, and the great failure of the Church was its inability to win the loyalty of the new industrial proletariat in the world's first industrial nation. The social limitations of Victorian Christianity provide the theme of Hempton's chapter, which describes the intensity and strength of pockets of working-class religion in Britain, in Cornwall, Wales, the Durham coalfield, among the urban Irish poor, in smaller backstreet Bethels and round popular and devoted priests and pastors. Yet the working class in general was neither churchgoing nor Secularist, regarding religion as a matter of ethics rather than of worship. Its members were selectively influenced by Christian elites and by Christian values rather than by Christian institutions (with the possible exception of schools and Sunday schools) or by Christian doctrine.

Christian values, almost as much as doctrine, also set the context for the development of that middle-class Nonconformity which emerged in nineteenth-century Britain. Derived from a largely self-conscious exclusion from the mainstream of Victorian society, the integrated system of values developed by the leadership of churches such as the Congregationalists eventually gained for their members a more central place in national life. Tracing the ministerial careers of the Vaughans, father and son, and the histories of four congregations, Binfield's chapter presents a portrait of a community of individuals, high-minded and forward-looking, but with a strong regard for tradition; socially concerned on questions of rights and citizenship; suburban rather than civic in its interests; and sure of the rightful but modest contribution to history, or God's plan, required from each of its members.

If this was a story of transition, then that of the Catholics described by Sheridan Gilley was one of transformation, in which the English tradition was radically reshaped by Irish immigrants from below and from above by a wave of Oxford-educated converts, drawn to the Ultramontane movement stemming from Rome. The combination of Irish ethnic exclusiveness and English Romanizing militancy caused strains within the Catholic Church, but together they sustained a massive expansion and reassertion of Catholicism in Britain continuing to the eve of the Second Vatican Council.

Religion in Wales and Scotland during the nineteenth century was also a vital affair, charted here by Keith Robbins. In Scotland the Disruption of

1843, leading to the formation of the Free Church of Scotland, and the union of the Relief and Secession churches in 1847 as the United Presbyterians, resulted in the existence of three major Calvinist churches with national pretensions; in the present century the majority of their members have reunited. In Wales the Established Church had been overwhelmed by the growth of Nonconformity, and especially Calvinistic Methodism, by 1850, but had made something of a recovery by the end of the century. This did not avert disestablishment in 1920, however, and in the later years of this century both countries have faced a secularization, the more dramatic for being delayed.

The growth of British influence worldwide during the course of the nineteenth century led to foreign missionary enterprise on an enormous scale. The initial impulse of the Protestant churches to create indigenous native-led churches in the colonial territories was soon defeated, and resulted in the triumph of white-led missionary churches by 1900, a system still in place until the Second World War and dismantled only with the empire. This development, however, owed as much to missionary theology as to the complex and sometimes discordant relations between the missionary impulse on the one hand and imperialism, racialism and western commerce on the other.

Alongside these great religious changes there existed in Victorian Britain an admittedly small but none the less influential Secularist movement which, as Edward Royle shows, owed its strength to the opposing strength of religion. Like some religions it too had its warring factions, led by Holyoake and Bradlaugh, which corresponded ideologically and sociologically to the categories of denomination and sect, with similar practices, such as Sunday schools and hymn-singing, to those of the Dissenting chapels they set out to combat. As secularization has progressed in the course of this century, so the avowedly Secularist societies have declined.

Secularism is not confined to the history of Christianity but also figures in Campbell's survey of the history of the Jews in Britain, who trace their ancestry to the small number of Jews who settled in England after the Norman Conquest, suffering bouts of persecution until their expulsion by Edward I in 1290. They were readmitted to England under Cromwell, and developed their distinctive forms of organization through the eighteenth and nineteenth centuries before the arrival of full emancipation. The community was transformed by the huge influx of pauper refugees from Russia after 1881 – in a manner not dissimilar to the earlier transformation of Catholicism by the Irish poor – and they made a significant contribution to left-wing politics in the first half of this century. More recently there has been a shift to the right among many adherents, and the community has become increasingly polarized between associations of synagogues on traditional and liberal lines. Externally the identity of British Judaism is threatened by the effects of out-marriage as well as secularization.

In his chapter on the inter-war years Mews points to the renewed focus on sacramental religion in the early 1920s and describes the ways in which churchmen of all denominations sought to broaden their appeal to the laity, whose increased spending power had led to the emergence of a leisure industry, aspects of which caused dismay in some ecclesiastical circles. To others, however, sacramentalism acted as a stimulus, and several attempts were made to renew the social and political witness of the churches. As the 1930s progressed the problems of unemployment at home and of the rise of fascism abroad tempered the optimism of Church leaders, many of whom were also troubled by the changing attitudes to sexual morality which they associated with the spread of contraception. The 1930s witnessed a dramatic decline in churchgoing among the mass of the population so that, at the outbreak of the Second World War, there was a vacuum in national spiritual leadership which, somewhat surprisingly, the Roman Catholics sought to fill.

In the post-war years described by Alan Suggate, faced with the decline in church attendance, there has been a convergence of the churches in the areas of ecumenism, eucharistic worship, ethics and social responsibility, and political activism, but despite these initiatives the path to the conclusion of more formal schemes of unity, including that sought by the Anglicans and Methodists, has proved more difficult.

As the mainstream churches have declined, so there has been an expansion of 'fringe' religious movements, with a somewhat paradoxical growth in the new conservative and usually fundamentalist Dissenting churches – Afro-Caribbean, charismatic, Jehovah's Witnesses, and Mormons – whose members will be more numerous than those of the traditional Protestant churches by the end of the century. Yet levels of identification with Christianity remain high among non-churchgoers, while convinced atheists and agnostics remain an undogmatic minority. On the other hand, new religions (such as the 'Moonies' and Hare Krishna) have attracted attention out of all proportion to their numbers, while immigration in the past three decades has made Islam and Sikhism great popular religious movements in this country for the first time.

These changes do not, in the view of Professor Badham, amount to secularization, which is the theme of Alan Gilbert's chapter. He argues that in spite of its complexity secularization is a process which occurs on a number of levels – cognitive, instrumental and expressive – in connection with modernity, and marginal or sectarian religion may flourish as a counter-culture to it. The expanding Pentecostal and house churches and the Muslim community may dispute this analysis of their recent growth, but it challenges mainstream Christianity to consider its strategies for survival. No religion, not even Christianity, has received a guarantee from its founder of its perpetuity in any one country; and with the approach of the second millennium of Christianity, a question mark stands over the British churches and the shape in which they are destined to survive.

Plate 1   The conventual church of the Cistercian monastery at Tintern (Monmouth), viewed from the north
Photograph: Keith Ellis.

PART I

Conversion and Christendom

1

Religion in Roman Britain

Martin Henig

R ELIGIOUS ACTIVITY in Britain is traceable at least as far back as the fourth millennium BC; the construction of impressive ceremonial monuments, of which Stonehenge is the grandest, and of elaborate tombs for the dead suggest that the lives of people living in the Neolithic and Bronze Ages were dominated by beliefs in gods and divine powers. Archaeologists working from analogy with 'primitive' cultures of our own time and from intelligent guesswork based on surviving structures and excavated artefacts have made some attempt at reconstructing these lost beliefs, for lost to us they really are. We have no writings or even traditions going back to these times in Britain and thus no names of gods, goddesses or festivals.

A history of religion in Britain has to start much later, in the Iron Age, a century or so before Christ. Classical sources do tell us a little about the Celts, who at this time inhabited much of north-western Europe as well as Britain, and their beliefs, though even here there are great difficulties, for Posidonius, Diodorus Siculus, Julius Caesar and other writers consciously or unconsciously interpreted the religion of the Celts in the light of Greek and Roman ideas. Thus, for example, the druids, who seem to have had priestly functions and officiated at sacrifices, were sometimes seen as philosophers with sophisticated Pythagorean views on the transmigration of souls. (Ancient writers did, however, note the less elevated side of Celtic religion, including human sacrifice: their accounts of ritual killings were certainly founded in fact, as is illustrated by the recent discovery of the body of a man who had been killed by garrotting and by having his throat cut before being thrown into a pool at Lindow in Cheshire.) Veneration for springs and groves is mentioned, testimony borne out by the evidence of placenames of Roman date; for example, *Aquae Arnemetiae* (Buxton) records a spring sacred to a native goddess whose name includes the word *nemet* (sacred grove). A few deities, such as Esus, Taranus and Teutates, are cited in writings on Iron Age religion elsewhere, but there is nothing to connect them specifically with Britain. Nevertheless, to judge from the great variety of divine names on inscriptions of post-conquest date, in Gaul as well as Britain, there were many gods; but most of them were very local, for contacts between peoples were inevitably uncertain at a time of poor communications.

Although the Romans were not missionaries in any religious sense, the governing classes of the empire were imbued with the desire to pacify, civilize and reduce to order, and religion was involved in all these processes. As the druids provided the focus for British resistance to Rome they were suppressed, although it is quite clear from excavations on the sites of native sanctuaries such as those at Harlow in Essex, Hayling Island in Hampshire and Uley in Gloucestershire that cults continued without a break. The only specifically recorded native attack on a Roman religious sanctuary in Britain in the first century concerns the great temple of the divine Claudius (*Divus Claudius*) at Colchester. When emperors died, the Senate might decree their deification; this practice accorded with the belief that the souls of the truly great would join the gods at the end of their mortal lives. Julius Caesar, Augustus and the conqueror of Britain, Claudius, achieved this honour. The rebel queen of the Iceni, Boudicca, and her followers saw the great new temple as an affront, the *arx aeternae dominationis*, 'citadel of everlasting subjugation', as Tacitus (*Annals*, xiv. 31) puts it. In AD 61 they burnt it to the ground. Although the veneration of imperial *divi* can have had no roots in Iron Age Britain, the reason for this hostility was political and not religious, just as were Rome's clashes with the druids. This arose from the arrogance of the Roman settlers and not from resistance to a foreign cult. In the course of time, when the power of Rome came to be seen in a kindlier light, it became natural to make obeisance through prayer and sacrifice to a symbol of its might. Gods were after all most visible in their power, and self-evidently the Roman emperor was powerful. For many people the imperial cult was manifest simply as a part of everyday religion, and it became the universal practice for the divine power (*numen*) resident in the reigning emperor to be invoked in association with other deities.

Religion was romanized in its outward forms in ways which inevitably had profound effects on the mode of both cult practice and thought about the gods. First, the Latin language became the medium of polite expression. It was the language of culture and, indeed, the only common literate tongue in the Roman West. Dedications to the gods now frequently took the form of votive altars inscribed in Latin. The native names of deities were conflated with Latin ones, and hence every god and goddess acquired a classical persona and a mythology. Secondly, as Tacitus records (*Agricola*, 21) the building of temples was encouraged as a necessary part of the development of the province; he lists *templa* before *fora* (administrative and market complexes) and *domos* (Roman-style houses for the British gentry). Some of these temples were in a fully Roman style while others followed a native style of square or circular *cella*, often with a surrounding ambulatory, but whatever their plan all were constructed of stone (or at least had stone footings) and were embellished with the same sorts of architectural ornaments, such as columns, pilasters and pediments, that Graeco-Roman temples were given throughout the Mediterranean world. This is suggested by representations of deities standing within shrines stamped on votive plaques of bronze or silver and carved on stone reliefs.

Images of the gods comprise a third aspect of romanization, in their effects perhaps the most important of all. When a sculptor produced a cult image in the form of one or other of the Roman deities he, or rather his patrons, effectively ensured the continued veneration of that god at the sanctuary. Thus at Uley pre-Roman material is suggestive of a warrior god, and even after the Roman conquest small votive spears continued to be given. However, the cult image is of Mercury, following a statue by Praxiteles, and votive images on altars and bronze figurines also depict that god. It is clear from inscriptions, including invocations to the deity scratched on lead 'curse' tablets, that in the Roman period this long-established Celtic deity was known as Mercury. His earlier name is lost.

The very important temple at Bath was built beside a hot spring dedicated to a native goddess called Sulis. In this case the name was preserved and even took precedence over the Roman Minerva, with whom she was equated. The gilt-bronze head of what is probably the cult image remains and shows that she was conceived in classical guise, as a type of Minerva Medica. A silver-gilt patera handle from Capheaton in Northumberland is ornamented with a figure of Minerva presiding over springs and a temple; it is tempting to associate this with Bath (though the goddess had springs elsewhere in the empire) and it certainly expresses the Roman conception of religion in which the divine powers, envisaged in anthropomorphic form, entered into contractual relationships with their votaries.

Gifts, both animate and inanimate, were lavished on the gods by the Celts, but the legally minded Romans conceived of a highly formal style of bargaining. First came the announcement or *nuncupatio*, a prayer beseeching the god or goddess for favours, reminding him or her of divine virtues such as justice, and promising to pay a reward if the deity should heed the request. If the prayer was answered the *solutio* became due: a sacrifice, a carved stone altar or some other gift. It is not in the least surprising to find these thoroughly Roman practices performed by soldiers in the Roman army, for instance in the altars set up to Jupiter by the commanders of units each January, thanking him for his protection over the previous year and asking for his aid in the year ahead. The sacrifice of a bull, ram and boar (*suovetaurilia*) depicted on a relief from Bridgeness on the Antonine Wall in south Scotland is identical to the ceremony shown on many reliefs from Rome, except that the ceremony is presided over by the commander of the second legion, based in Britain, rather than the emperor. Excavation of temple sites, together with the evidence of inscriptions, has shown us that the cult practices of Rome had also become thoroughly accepted by the civilian population.

Bath, again, provides the clearest evidence. It had priests, one of whom was buried at Bath by his wife, and other officials, such as *haruspices* (the name *haruspex* was evidently Etruscan and means 'gut-gazer') who pronounced on the will of the gods by examining the entrails of sacrificial animals. (Incidentally, the cattle bones recovered from the temple precinct are virtually all of cows, showing that the practice of dedicating female animals to goddesses was observed.) There is likely to have been a dream-interpreter here as at Lydney Park in Gloucestershire, for at least one person set up a statue after having had a dream or vision of the goddess – presumably elucidated by the *interpres*. The people who came to the temple included soldiers seeking health, such as the centurion Marcus Aufidius Maximus, whose freedman set up an altar with the usual formula for a *solutio*, v(otum) s(olvit) l(ibens) m(erito) (freely and deservedly paid his vow); a Gallic stonemason who also gave an altar; and a woman who dropped an ivory amulet in the form of a pair of breasts into the spring. Ordinary people are well represented by the lead tablets from the spring supplicating Sulis to recover stolen property from malefactors, and by masses of coins thrown in as dedications. The Bath sanctuary was very large and wealthy. As well as the main temple and its accompanying altar, it was embellished with baths, probably a theatre, a circular rotunda or *tholos*, and a monumental carved screen, the last given by a religious guild.

The sanctuary at West Hill, Uley was very simple by comparison, but here too there were ancillary buildings as well as votive altars and, as at Bath, requests to the deity scratched on lead tablets. Sacrifices must have been controlled by an efficient priesthood which ensured that only goats or rams and cockerels, Mercury's cult animals, were sacrificed. The temple may have had only local importance, but the remains of sacrifices and the art objects recovered from the site show that it must have been a flourishing concern. There is still an allusion to its former fame in the name of the parish of Nympsfield, the first part of which derives from *nemet* (sacred grove).

Every temple excavated shows diversity in architecture, dedication and cult. It is very tempting to see such epithets as *Cunomaglos* (hound prince), bestowed on Apollo at Nettleton in Wiltshire, or *Rigonemetos* (king of the sacred grove), applied to Mars near Lincoln, as suggesting only superficial romanization, but such an attitude should be resisted. There was a very fine balance between the perception of deity inherited from the Iron Age and that of Roman ideology. In the two examples quoted above we should recall that Apollo enjoyed hunting and that Mars was first and foremost an agricultural god. Even the prominence of a Celtic name such as Sulis does not mean that the cult remained backward; the extreme sophistication of Bath belies that. The sanctuary of the god Nodens, sometimes equated with Mars, at Lydney is on a considerably smaller scale, though it too had baths and a large guest-house. Nodens seems to have been a healing deity, as a few anatomical votives suggest, and his cult animal was the hound, represented in a number of figurines. In the Mediterranean world the hound was sometimes associated with Aesculapius, and it is noteworthy that Lydney shares one specialized type of building with Epidaurus, an *abaton* (literally meaning 'inaccessible' – that is, to anyone who had not undergone the requisite purification) where the sleeping votary received visitations from the god. A late mosaic from the *cella* of the temple at Lydney was laid from the proceeds of worshippers' offerings by the priest who styled himself *praepositus religionum*, though the supervision of the workmen was left to the dream-interpreter (*interpres*). It is, of course, true that our evidence is heavily weighted in favour of the relatively well-to-do (who could afford to make dedications) and the educated (who could express themselves in Latin), but this is inevitable. Nevertheless, the variety of religious observance in Britain was due not to lack of romanization but to lack of central organization. The same local complexity can be savoured in Roman Greece from the pages of Pausanias's guidebook.

What did people want from the gods? The evidence of sculpture and inscriptions suggests that the fertility of the land, of animals and of one's own family was immensely important. Images of three mother goddesses with baskets of fruit on their knees, sometimes accompanied by children, and of Fortune with her horn of plenty (*cornucopia*), rudder and wheel as well as the *genius loci*, also with a cornucopia, suggest this. Mars also protected the crops and woodlands; Diana and Silvanus took care of hunting. The new Roman world of commerce made Mercury very popular, though he too was concerned with pastoral fertility. Minerva was a healer, but also concerned with craft, and the guild of smiths at Chichester built a temple to Neptune and Minerva as early as the reign of Nero when Chichester was formally part of a client kingdom. Jupiter Greatest and Best (*Optimus Maximus*) presided over all.

The occasional record of a dream or vision, as of Sulis Minerva at Bath, and the example of an *abaton* or sleep-house at Lydney (and probably at Nettleton) point to the sort of warm, personal relationship with a deity such as Aelius Aristides enjoyed with Asklepios in the Greek east. Although literary sources are lacking for Britain, we have no right to dismiss as either mercenary or mechanical the sense of awe and reverence felt by many a worshipper before a cult image or even in front of a small figurine of a deity in a household shrine. It is clear that some gods and goddesses invited such an emotional response to a marked degree. Many of them originated in the east but one of them, Bacchus, seems to have been present in the Greek world in the Mycenean age and in Rome from early in the Republic. There is no clear line of religious demarcation between these 'mystery' or 'saviour' gods and other deities. Jupiter Dolichenus, who came from Asia Minor, was especially venerated by army personnel and their associates, but apart from a particular tendency to vouchsafe visions to his worshippers, there is no real evidence for a developed mystery cult.

Bacchus could offer more. As the god of the vine he brought the gift of intoxication; thus he was present at every drinking party, and satyrs, maenads and sileni occur again and again in genre art. Readers of Euripides' terrifying play *The Bacchae* will realize that his advent might be catastrophic, and the Roman Senate knew what it was doing when it tried to suppress Bacchanalia in 186 BC, although if there was any intention to do away with worship of the wine-god entirely, it was doomed from the start. Discrete *collegia*, like that which met at the Villa of the Mysteries outside Pompeii in the first century BC, continued to exist. In Britain the evidence for such *collegia* is late (from the fourth century) and includes three marbles from the *Mithraeum* site beside the Walbrook in London, which seem to date from a period after the temple had ceased to be used by devotees of Mithras (i.e. after the truly Mithraic sculptures were buried). The most remarkable of these is a group of Bacchus and his followers inscribed *Hominibus bagis bitam* – '(thou givest) life to wandering men'. A silver canister containing an infusor, concealed in the wall of the temple, may have been associated with Mithras or with Bacchus – I suspect the latter. It is very likely that the infusor was used to lace wine with drugs in order to induce hallucinations or a state of ecstasy. Another more or less contemporary meeting-place of Bacchic devotees has been recognized at Littlecote in Wiltshire, where the mosaic of a tri-conch building alludes to Bacchus and to his follower Orpheus. The deep seriousness with which Bacchus was taken as a personal saviour is reinforced by his depiction on the lid of a lead coffin from Holborough in Kent and especially in the presence of a marble statuette in a grave near the villa of Spoonley Wood in Gloucestershire. To the wider world Bacchus was a great and beneficent power of nature: he and his followers are carved in high relief on the capital of an enormous free-standing column at Cirencester. He is also shown, with other deities, on the altar which stood in front of the temple of Sulis Minerva at Bath.

The same range of experience is manifest in the cult of the Great Mother, Cybele, and her paramour Attis, imported into Rome from the east in the late third century BC. Although the festivals of this cult were incorporated into regular state observances, they displayed a number of orgiastic features very much at odds with traditional religion. For instance, on 24 March each year, the *Dies Sanguinis*, men lashed themselves in honour of the goddess and even castrated themselves in memory of Attis, who performed this act of self-mutilation when driven mad by his infidelity towards her. Roman citizens were forbidden to castrate themselves, but the need was felt for a guild of supporters who were devoted to the cult but stopped short of sacrificing their virility. These *dendrophori*, as their name implies, had the task of carrying a pine tree, the tree under which Attis died, into the cult temple (*metroon*) on 22 March, but they also operated as a burial guild. A probable temple of Attis and Cybele is known at Verulamium (St Albans); they were certainly worshipped here, for the inscription on a pot from a burial at Dunstable mentions the *dendrophori* of Verulamium. In London, too, there was a *metroon*: a bronze figurine of Attis was found in the Thames, as was a pair of bronze castration clamps, elaborately decorated and including busts of Attis and Cybele, providing graphic evidence of one of the more lurid cult rites. So far, however, there is no evidence from Britain of the *taurobolium* in which the devotee could literally bathe in the life force, the blood of a sacrificed bull.

As with Bacchus, there seems to have been a more acceptable, public face of the cult of Cybele and Attis, interestingly confined to Britain, where it must have been conflated with the veneration of a local hunter-god. According to one version of the myth Attis was a Phrygian prince killed by a boar when out hunting. Statues and reliefs apparently showing Attis (identified by his Phrygian cap) dressed as a huntsman have been discovered in London and in Gloucestershire.

Isis and the other Egyptian deities were also present in Britain. Readers of Apuleius's *Golden Ass* will be familiar with the very deep relationship which Isis could maintain with her votaries through dreams and visions. An engraved gem from Wroxeter showing Isis may have belonged to a particular devotee, while another, a birth-charm from Welwyn in Hertfordshire, may be interpreted as an approach to the saving goddess at a crisis; but the altar at London dedicated to her by a governor of Britain surely belongs to the realm of public religion. The same goes for the temple of Serapis built at York by the commander of the sixth legion.

The one cult which truly corresponds to the model of a closed community of worshippers was Mithraism, which in Britain has left its fullest archaeological record outside army camps in the north, although the most splendid example known in Britain was beside the Walbrook in London, where it attracted patronage from soldiers (as witnessed by an ex-voto set up by a veteran of the second legion) and probably also from merchants. The cult was practised by initiates, who had to be male, in buildings (Mithraea) designed to resemble caves and recalling the cave in which, at the beginning of time, the young god Mithras killed the primeval bull from whose blood all life came. In order to achieve enlightenment, the postulant had to pass through various grades, access to each of which involved initiation ceremonies and trials. This must have inculcated a sense of fulfilment as adherents embarked on a spiritual journey towards the light. A hint at the sort of practice which Mithraists had to undergo is provided by a grave-like pit at Carrawburgh where a symbolic burial and rebirth could have been enacted. At Rudchester an altar simply dedicated *Deo* (to the god) within a wreath is a reminder of a ceremony for the grade of *Miles* (soldier), in which the initiate rejected a wreath handed to him on the point of a sword with the words 'it rests in the god!' At Housesteads a splendid relief shows Mithras being born from a cosmic egg (more usually he emerges from a rock), and accompanying inscriptions hail him as *Saecularis*, 'Lord of Ages'. At the Walbrook Mithraeum, so rich in marble sculpture, an inscription uses the phrase *ab Oriente ad Occidentem*, 'from the east to the west', which can be compared with the well-known formula used by Christians (but not necessarily originating with them), 'from Alpha to Omega'. Central to Mithraism was the meeting together for sacred meals on benches laid along the aisles of Mithraea. These feasts made Mithraism especially obnoxious to Christians, who saw the practice as a parody of the Eucharist. In London there is evidence that the Mithraeum was attacked, perhaps in the second decade of the fourth century, not long after the inscription mentioned above was set up.

Christianity shared many features with these cults. If 'bathing in the blood of the Lamb' was taken in a purely metaphorical sense, the language is suggestive of the *criobolium* (of the cult of the Magna Mater); 'castration for the Word's sake', also a feature of oriental religion, was taken literally by Origen, while much more generally the commemorative liturgy and sacred meals of all these cults had their great Christian counterpart in the Eucharist. An aspect less often stressed is that Christianity shared in the public side of religion, in the presentation of votive gifts (so clearly seen in the dedication of plate at Water Newton) and, after the Peace of the Church in AD 312, in formal public ceremony.

What made Christianity unique was its Jewish heritage, which firmly separated it from polytheistic religion. Jewish diaspora communities –

mainly in the east and in Rome – were evidently of importance in the initial spread and development of Christianity. Britain, it is clear, was not of any significance in this formative stage, though the name of a third-century martyr at Caerleon, Aaron, is suggestive of a Jewish convert. Unlike Judaism, Christianity was not the religion of a national group, and as Christians separated themselves from the general veneration of the gods on which the prosperity of the empire depended, they were liable to sporadic persecution as an anti-social element in society.

Julius and Aaron, the martyrs of Caerleon, are shadowy figures; more is known of St Alban, whose death and burial on or near the site of the abbey church is beginning to find confirmation in archaeological excavation. The date of his martydom is not known. John Morris's thesis that it took place under the Severans early in the third century is now being questioned, and he may have died in the middle of the century or even at the orders of Constantius Chlorus, at the time of the Diocletian persecutions. Although Eusebius implies that Constantius did not rigorously pursue Christians, it must be remembered that he was writing his history for Constantius' son, who before his conversion was, like his father, a devotee of the Unconquered Sun, and therefore unlikely to have been neutral in religious matters!

Most peoples in antiquity regarded dead bodies with disgust, but for Christians graves, especially the graves of what Professor Peter Brown has called 'the very special dead', were centres for devotion. Thus the cult of St Alban on the site of a Verulamium cemetery, and other possible cemetery churches, as at Colchester and London, would suggest a fundamental religious shift. Perhaps the most extensive Christian cemetery excavated to date is at Poundbury, outside Dorchester, where some tombs seem to have been elaborate and may have been *cellae memoriae*. The number of graves here and elsewhere that are aligned east–west and lack grave goods, and are therefore probably Christian, is valuable evidence of the spread of the new religion.

None of the archaeological evidence in Britain is earlier than the fourth century, but from that time it is more extensive than is often believed. However, although there are places that may be definitely identified as sites of Christian worship (such as the House Church at Lullingstone in Kent, with its paintings of *Orantes* and of the Christogram) and also unequivocally Christian objects (such as the silver vessels from Water Newton), much of the evidence from Britain is very peculiar, showing curious compromises of practice and perhaps even shared belief with surrounding pagans. Not only is the language used in the Water Newton dedications to God similar to that used by others in making offerings to pagan deities, but silver-gilt leaves of a form familiar from many temple sites were also offered, though here each was embellished with the chi-rho, representing the first two letters of Christ's name, rather than with the image of a deity. At Hinton St Mary, a bust of Christ appears on a mosaic floor backed by a chi-rho. It is flanked by four lunettes, one of which shows a tree of life and three hounds chasing deer, evoking the Psalmist: 'For dogs have compassed me: the assembly of the wicked have inclosed me' (Ps. 22:16). The adjoining room, also with scenes of hounds and deer at the sides, has a central motif of Bellerophon on Pegasus, slaying the Chimaera. If this example can be explained as simple allegory, it is less easy to give the same explanation for a floor at Frampton, where as well as a chi-rho there are many other motifs, including two appearances of the great saviour god Bacchus.

It is possible that the Frampton mosaics, from an establishment which does not seem to be a normal villa, simply reveal the patron's religious confusions, but it is more likely that he was attempting to 'paganize' Christianity. Such a symbiotic situation is also suggested by a leaden tablet from Bath containing the words *seu gentilis seu Christianus* (whether pagan or Christian), a phrase which implies the coexistence in the same community of two sets of people with the same expectations. A certain Senicianus owned a gold ring, discovered at Silchester, which bears an inscription around the hoop adjuring him to 'live in God', but also has a head of Venus on the bezel; and again, at Uley, part of a casket bearing scenes *en repoussé* of Abraham about to sacrifice Isaac, of Jonah and the whale (shown as a *ketos* or sea-monster), of Christ and the centurion and Christ and the blind man was carefully folded and presented, like many other offerings here, to Mercury. While the House Church flourished at Lullingstone, offerings continued to be placed in front of two old marble busts in the cellar below it.

Although Christianity was the official religion of the empire for most of the fourth century, and although temples lost their lands and, in the mid-century, their treasures too, much of the most remarkable evidence for religion in late Roman Britain is pagan. Many of the great villa owners retained their traditional allegiances. Their mosaic floors show Orpheus surrounded by the beasts, most magnificently at Woodchester, or Bacchus, at Stonesfield in Oxfordshire. At Littlecote both Bacchus and Orpheus seem to be present in the rich and esoteric imagery on the floor of a house shrine. The ranges of myth-covered floors at Frampton and at Brading on the Isle of Wight belong to the same sort of cultivated society with neo-platonic leanings which Macrobius shows us in his *Saturnalia*. On the Brading pavement we see Orpheus, Bacchus and also a strange figure with the head of a cockerel, probably a Graeco-Roman version of the Jewish God, known as Iao. At Brading too is that most typical figure of late pagan piety, the holy man, practitioner of theurgy, who could raise himself to the level of the divine by means of meditation and trance.

The recent discovery of a treasure of silver spoons and strainers and of gold jewellery at Thetford in Norfolk reminds us of the highly traditional nature of this world. Inscriptions on the spoons show that the treasure was dedicated to Faunus, a very ancient god from Latium. Faunus seems to have been celebrated in feasts analogous to those practised by members of the mystery cults, or by Christians at the Eucharist, by aristocratic devotees who called themselves by cult *signa* such as Agrestius (countryman) or Persevera (she who has persevered). Faunus belongs to the same world of nature as Bacchus; a satyr appears in relief on the splendid gold belt-buckle from the hoard and it may be that this was regarded as a figure of Faunus. It seems likely that the Thetford treasure was made in the last decade or so of the fourth century; it demonstrates that, to the very end of Roman Britain, traditional beliefs were not confined to ill-educated backwoodsmen.

The speed with which the Christian Church triumphed in the first years of the fifth century may be in large part attributable to the remarkable organization of bishoprics (which is known to have existed in Britain even as early as the Council of Arles in 314), providing a sense of security and continuity which no other religion and no secular authority could offer. There are indications that the Church in Britain may sometimes have been heterodox: Pelagius, who pursued his controversy with St Augustine in the Mediterranean world, was himself a Briton. Christians in Roman Britain, living alongside pagan neighbours, perhaps found the doctrine of grace rather esoteric. In 429 St Germanus came to Britain, apparently to Verulamium, and showed the local notables the error of the Pelagian 'heresy' which had taken hold there by winning a skirmish against a band of barbarians. The world was becoming dangerous, and another Briton, Patrick, was carried into servitude in Ireland; later he converted many of the inhabitants, who had never been citizens of Rome. In the middle of the fifth century Saxons and other barbarians effectively demolished the structure not only of Roman government but of Roman culture too. It seems that much of western Britain was later rescued by men who felt some allegiance to Rome and to Christianity. The spokesman for this Arthurian age, writing in the sixth century, is Gildas. He writes in Latin for a universal Christian Church, but unlike Germanus or Patrick he can hardly be regarded as a Roman.

2

Religion in Anglo-Saxon England

Gerald Bonner

IF, BY AN arbitrary but convenient choice of dates, we regard the arrival of the Roman mission led by Augustine in King Ethelbert's kingdom of Kent in 597 as constituting the beginning of Anglo-Saxon Christianity, and the defeat and death of King Harold Godwinson at Hastings on 14 October 1066 as marking its close, we shall be considering a period of four and a half centuries – a longer span of time than that which elapsed between the accession of Henry VIII and the end of the Second World War. No serious historian would attempt to describe the religious history of the latter period in a single chapter, yet this is what is here proposed in respect of the former. It may well be true that change, both social and cultural, was slower in earlier times. The Englishman of 1066 was probably less culturally differentiated from his ancestor of 597 than the Englishman of 1945 from his predecessor of 1509; but he had changed – radically, in respect of his religion. Our discussion must therefore be impressionistic, dwelling on general features and omitting much which is, considered in itself, historically important.

While the year 597 is undoubtedly decisive in English history, it marked neither the coming of the English to England, which began in the fifth century, nor the beginning of religion among them. The English had a religion before they were Christians, a branch of that wider Teutonic religion existing in various forms in Germany and Scandinavia. We know of deities like Woden (the Odin of Scandinavia); Thunor (Thor), the hammer god of Indo-European tradition; and Tiw or Tiwaz, a god whose name is derived from the Indo-European root *deiw*, 'to shine', and who was the ancient sky god, of greater antiquity than Woden or Thunor. We know too of a goddess Friga or Frigg, consort of Woden and patron of marriage and childbirth. Old English charms, although recorded by Christian scribes, show traces of sun worship and of a fertility cult of Mother Earth, perhaps to be identified with Friga. The goddess of spring, Eostre, has by a strange anomaly given her name to the greatest of Christian festivals. Bede, in his work *De Temporum Ratione* (s.15), gives some valuable details about the English pagan year, including the information that it began on 25 December, 'when we celebrate the birth of the Lord', and that the night which preceded it, 'now reckoned most holy among us', was known as *Modranect*, 'the night of the Mothers' – a group perhaps to be identified with a triad of mother goddesses venerated in Roman Britain and on the continent of Europe. Again, in his *Ecclesiastical History*, Bede describes the restrictions imposed on a pagan priest: he might not ride a stallion or carry weapons. Place-name evidence reveals where individual gods were worshipped: Woden all over England, Thunor predominantly in the south. Bede refers to temples, like the one in which King Redwald maintained two altars, one for Christian worship and the other for pagan sacrifice; or that at Goodmanham, near York, where Coifi, the former pagan priest converted to Christianity, demonstrated his new allegiance by hurling a spear into the shrine, perhaps as a ritual challenge to Woden. Place-name evidence also indicates the sites of pagan temples, with derivations from elements like *ealh*, a temple; *hearh* or *hearg*, a temple, altar, idol or sanctuary; and *weoh*, an idol or sanctuary (found respectively in place-names like Alkham, Harrow-on-the-Hill and Weyhill). Archaeological excavation at Yeavering, in Northumberland, has uncovered one such temple. Archaeology again has provided evidence of pagan burial practices, by both cremation and inhumation; and the fact that the dead were commonly provided with grave goods, of which the greatest and most famous example is the ship burial at Sutton Hoo in Suffolk, with its mixture of pagan and Christian artefacts, suggests a belief in an afterlife. Finally, Old English literature and art, although the work of Christians, preserve the memory of pagan heroes like Wayland the Smith (who figures in Kipling's *Puck of Pook's Hill*), whose name occurs in poems like *Deor* and *Waldere* and whose exploits are depicted, in company with classical and Christian scenes, on the famous Franks Casket, a product of early eighth-century Northumbria, now in the British Museum.

Our knowledge of Anglo-Saxon paganism is limited. We have no direct accounts from the pagans themselves, while a Christian author like Bede, though he may refer to paganism, cannot be expected to show the same sympathy and understanding which is revealed on every page of his references to Christianity. What in particular we do not know, and would very much like to know, is the character of the average individual's attachment to paganism: was there an element of real devotion towards his or her religion, or was religious observance essentially formal and designed to insure the worshipper's well-being in this life and the next, if any? The problem becomes particularly acute in discussing the manner of the conversion of the English to Christianity. On the surface it would appear that paganism rapidly gave way whenever an English king decided to become Christian, but could revive on his death if his successor upheld the old religion. Thus, when King Saeberht of the East Saxons died in 616/17 his three sons, who during his lifetime had 'in some measure', says Bede, abstained from idolatry while remaining heathen at heart, openly proclaimed their hostility to Christianity and drove out their bishop, Mellitus, with the result that for nearly forty years his see of London was vacant and the East Saxon kingdom lost to Christianity, which had to be proclaimed afresh by St Cedd in 654. However, the outbreak of the Yellow Plague in 664 caused a further relapse on the part of King Sigehere, then reigning jointly with his brother Sebbi, who remained a Christian, and part of his people. Sigehere, says Bede,

> together with his part of the nation, deserted the sacraments of the Christian faith and apostasized. For the King himself and the majority of both commons and nobles loved this present life, seeking no other and not even believing in any future existence; so they began to restore the derelict temples and to worship images, as if they could protect themselves by such means from the plague.

At an earlier time King Redwald of East Anglia – a premature exponent of inter-faith dialogue – having been baptized at the Court of King Ethelbert of Kent, found on his return home that he could not convert either his wife or his nobles and was driven to the humiliating expedient of maintaining in the same building a Christian and a pagan altar, to satisfy both his own convictions and those of his subjects. Finally, although the greater part of England was at least nominally Christian by the time of the Synod of Whitby in 664, the kingdom of the South Saxons (Sussex) was converted only by the preaching of St Wilfrid, during his exile there from 681 to 686.

Thus, though the story of the conversion of England gives the impression of a people as ready to change its religion on the command of a king as were its descendants in the sixteenth century, closer examination of the evidence suggests that the process of conversion was more complicated. Christianity prevailed and became the official religion of the English nation. Nevertheless, the process was a long one, and even after the Christian victory pagan practices lingered, to the distress of the Church and of conscientious secular rulers, to find expression in the use of charms and practices, some of which may have survived to modern times, their origins having been forgotten.

The defeat of Old English paganism may well have been brought about by its fundamental character. Unlike Christianity it was not so much a religion as a collection of religions. Individual gods were venerated in particular areas, but without a common creed. In contrast to Christianity, paganism lacked any theological foundation and on the intellectual level it was particularly vulnerable to a rival religion based on a theological and philosophical world-view and representing the Roman order and the classical tradition which the northern barbarians admired while they destroyed it.

Again, some pagans may have taken a utilitarian attitude to their religion, like that ascribed by Bede to the pagan priest Coifi who, when King Edwin of Northumbria and his council debated the pros and cons of accepting Christianity, declared:

> None of your followers has devoted himself more earnestly than I have to the worship of our gods, but nevertheless there are many who receive greater benefits and greater honour from you than I do and are more successful in their undertakings. If the gods had any power they would have helped me more readily, seeing that I have always served them with greater zeal.

(It is significant in this context that, according to Bede, the reversion of the East Saxons to paganism in 664 was due to the Yellow Plague. The new religion did not seem to offer any protection; perhaps the old would.) But utilitarianism apart, paganism lacked an answer to the deeper problems of human existence, as is well expressed by the words Bede ascribes to the unknown Northumbrian thegn whose speech follows that of Coifi in the debate before King Edwin, in which human life is compared to the flight of a sparrow through a banqueting hall on a winter's night.

> For the few moments it is inside, the storm and wintry tempest cannot touch it, but after the briefest moment of calm, it flits from your sight, out of the wintry storm and into it again. So this life of man appears but for a moment; what follows or what went before, we know not at all. If this new doctrine brings us more certain information, it seems right that we should accept it.

For the thoughtful and sensitive mind, Christianity offered a better explanation of the mystery of human life and death than did the old religion.

Nevertheless we may suspect that the anonymous thegn was not typical of the average Englishman. Perhaps more indicative of the mind of the masses during the process of conversion is the attitude revealed in an episode described in Bede's *Life* of St Cuthbert, which occurred during Cuthbert's youth when five rafts on the River Tyne, manned by monks, were in danger of being swept out to sea by a sudden gust of wind. A crowd of rustics, standing on the bank, began to jeer at the monks and when Cuthbert remonstrated with them retorted: 'Let no man pray for them, and may God have no mercy on any one of them, for they have robbed men of their old ways of worship, and how the new worship is to be conducted, nobody knows.' One may guess that these nameless peasants spoke for a good many converts in the middle of the seventh century. They had rejected their old gods and received baptism, no doubt following the wishes of the reigning king – Edwin, Oswald or Oswiu, whichever it might be – but were then left very much to their own devices on account of a shortage not merely of ordained ministers but even of competent catechists. It was no wonder that they felt bitter. If the words given by Bede represent the substance of their remarks, they may not have been devotedly attached to their old faith but, at the same time, they were not irreligious. They wanted something to put in its place and the new religion had not supplied it. For such people the temptation to revert to paganism at a time of personal crisis is understandable. Better the gods you know than the unknown God of Christianity.

It is impossible to assign to any one Christian church, whether the Roman, the Irish or the Frankish, the credit for evangelizing England, but one individual stands out: Pope Gregory the Great, the Apostle of the English. The famous story of his encounter with a group of English boys in the slave market at Rome, told by an unknown monk of Whitby who was Gregory's first biographer and, with some variations, by Bede in the *Ecclesiastical History*, has passed into legend. Gregory's elevation to the supreme pontificate in 590 prevented him from undertaking the English mission himself and his choice of Augustine as leader appears in the light of history to have been a poor one, since Augustine seems to have been regrettably lacking in initiative and powers of leadership. Fortunately Ethelbert, King of Kent, in whose kingdom the Roman mission landed early in 597, proved sympathetic, being already acquainted with Christianity through his marriage to a Christian Frankish princess who was permitted, by the terms of the marriage contract, to practise her religion and to maintain a chaplain. In the event the conversion of Ethelbert, together with a large number of his subjects, took place with surprising ease. In the autumn of 597 Augustine was able to go to Gaul, there to be consecrated the first bishop of the English, and at Christmas, according to the report of Pope Gregory in a letter to the Patriarch of Alexandria in July 598, ten thousand converts were baptized in and around Canterbury.

King Ethelbert was the most powerful ruler in England in his day and it was under his influence that his nephew Saeberht, King of the East Saxons, and Redwald, King of the East Angles, received baptism – though, as we have seen, after Saeberht's death in 616/17 his sons relapsed into paganism and drove out their bishop, Mellitus, while Redwald was forced to compromise his Christianity in the face of opposition from his wife and nobles. Then in 625 – or possibly earlier, in 619 – a fresh opportunity for missionary activity in the north arose from a request by Edwin, King of Northumbria, to have the Kentish princess Ethelburga, Ethelbert's daughter, as his wife. Ethelburga was provided with a chaplain in the person of Paulinus, who had come to assist Augustine in 601, and who was now consecrated bishop in order that he might pursue an authoritative ministry in Northumbria. His preaching and conversation caused King Edwin, grateful for his preservation from an attempted assassination, to offer his newly born daughter Eanfled for baptism at Easter 626. Edwin was now considering the possibility of being himself baptized, but only after the matter had been debated by his council – evidence that even a successful king might find it expedient to seek a measure of popular support before embarking on so portentous a step as to change his religion. The council responded favourably; as already described Coifi, the former high priest, deliberately desecrated the pagan shrine of Goodmanham and ordered it to be set on fire; and Edwin was baptized at York on Easter Day, 12 April 627.

According to Bede there was such great enthusiasm for Christianity among the people of Bernicia, the more northern of the two kingdoms which made up Northumbria, that when Paulinus spent a period of thirty-six days at the royal palace of Yeavering, he devoted the whole time to catechizing and baptizing from morning to night. This raises the question as to the possibility of some Christian survival from sub-Roman times in English-occupied parts of Britain, which would mean that in some areas at least Christian missionaries did not have to address themselves to a completely ignorant audience. Any answer to this question will depend on the character ascribed to the English conquest. If one holds, as nineteenth-century historians generally did, that the English either slaughtered the Romano-British population or drove it into the western parts of Britain, the question does not arise. More recent study has, however, raised doubts about so wholesale an extermination of the natives. It is questionable whether the English came in such large numbers as to need to destroy their predecessors for the sake of acquiring land. Certainly the northern kingdoms of Bernicia and Deira were originally very small and it was possible for the British kingdom of Elmet, situated to the south-west of York, to maintain its independence until it was annexed by Edwin of Northumbria soon after 617. Elsewhere there are hints of British survival. There is the village of Withington in Gloucestershire, where British and English populations apparently lived side by side, though with the English as the dominant partner. We know of Englishmen bearing Celtic names, of whom Caedmon of Whitby, the first English Christian poet, is the most famous example, suggesting intermarriage in which the British mother was able to name the child. There is even a tradition in Welsh circles that the baptizer of King Edwin was Rhun, son of Urien, a Briton; and while there is no reason to prefer this tradition to the statement of Bede, who was not likely to be misinformed on such a matter, that the baptizer was Paulinus, more friendly relations may have existed between Christian Celt and pagan English than one would gather from the pages of Bede. It is therefore quite possible that the population of Northumbria, and perhaps of some other English kingdom, may not have been so ignorant of Christianity as is often assumed.

Nevertheless, while the tradition of Christianity may have survived in some areas, notably in the north and west, there is no reason to suppose that it was in an organized form. Furthermore, whatever evidence may be adduced for the survival of the Romano-British population, the fact that the English language wholly replaced Celtic in areas where the English were politically dominant – in striking contrast to the persistence of English under Norman rule – makes it clear that the English victory was cultural as well as military. In that sense the conversion of the English was a missionary, and not a revivalist, enterprise.

The apparent success of Paulinus in Northumbria was brought to an end by the defeat and death of King Edwin at the battle of Hatfield Chase, near Doncaster, in 632, at the hands of Caedwallon (Caedwalla), the Christian ruler of Gwynedd in north Wales, in alliance with Penda, an able military leader, subsequently king of the midland English kingdom of Mercia and always a strong pagan. The aftermath of this disaster was a reversion to paganism on the part of Edwin's successors, Osric and Eanfrith, both of whom were put to death by Caedwallon in 633. A year later Eanfrith's brother, Oswald, gained a decisive victory over Caedwallon at Heaven-field, on the Roman Wall, not far from Hexham, having first set up as his standard a wooden cross and prayed for divine help in his hour of need. During Edwin's reign Oswald had been in exile among the Irish in what is now south-west Scotland, acquiring from them both Christianity and a knowledge of the Irish language. Himself a devout believer, he desired to continue the policy of his predecessor, Edwin. For this he needed a bishop; but the services of Paulinus were not available, since the latter had, after the disaster of Hatfield Chase, taken the princess Eanfled to safety in Kent and apparently remained there (he was to finish his career as Bishop of Rochester), leaving behind him at a village near Catterick his deacon, James – 'the one heroic figure in the Roman mission', as Sir Frank Stenton called him – to keep alive a Christian presence in the north. Oswald, in these circumstances, preferred to look for a bishop to St Columba's foundation of Iona, and from it came the Irish St Aidan, one of the most endearing figures in the history of English Christianity. Aidan established himself on the tidal island of Lindisfarne, which provided him with a base from which he could set out on his missionary journeys round his huge diocese. Oswald and Aidan worked together in perfect harmony and Bede provides a happy picture of the King on occasion acting as interpreter for the Irish preacher, whose knowledge of English was limited.

Because of the introduction of the Irish mission from Iona, the religious situation in Northumbria was for a long time complicated by a diversity of practice, notably with regard to the form of the monastic tonsure and the manner of calculating the date of Easter. The latter was the essential ground of contention, because it provided the most obvious sign of disunity among the Christians of Northumbria. Everyone agreed that Easter, the festival of light, should be celebrated on the Sunday during the week of the first full moon after the vernal equinox so that, in theory at least, Easter Day should be flooded with light, both by day and by night. The question was: when did this week start? The Irish, following a tradition which looked back to the very early Church, allowed as permissible days the fourteenth to the twentieth of the first lunar month after the equinox. However, the ecclesiastical day begins not at dawn but at dusk. Accordingly, in the view of the Roman Church, the fourteenth day of the lunar month began on the evening of the thirteenth day. This meant that if Sunday fell on the fourteenth day, the Paschal ceremonies would be held on the night of the thirteenth, when the moon was not yet full. Therefore, said the Romans, the permitted days should be from the fifteenth to the twenty-first.

Later readers are inclined to be impatient with such scruples as being mere hair-splitting (and not only later readers; already, in the fifth century, the Greek Church historian Socrates Scholasticus had said roundly: 'The Saviour and His Apostles have enjoined us by no law to keep this feast, nor in the New Testament are we threatened with any penalty or punishment or curse for the neglect of it, as the Mosaic Law does the Jews'), but such an outlook was wholly foreign to the seventh century. Everyone agreed that Christians ought to keep Easter at the same time; most people believed that you imperilled your immortal soul by failing to observe the right date. In Oswald's Northumbria the presence of James the Deacon (who, of course, followed the Roman practice), combined with the tendency of Northumbrian kings to seek their brides from southern English kingdoms where the Roman usage prevailed, ensured the continuance of a division in the northern Church over the date on which Easter should be celebrated.

Aidan's monastery on Lindisfarne was destined to become one of the most famous religious houses in England. In it Aidan trained a number of

English youths, including two brothers: Chad, afterwards Bishop of York and then of Lichfield; and Cedd, the apostle of the East Saxons. Nor did he overlook the vocations of women. It was he who in 648 summoned St Hild, a great-niece of King Edwin, to preside over a small convent on the north bank of the Wear, from which she moved in 649 to Hartlepool, as successor to the Abbess Heiu, and from which in 657 she founded the famous double monastery of Whitby, housing both monks and nuns, over which she presided as abbess. Bede, who anxiously assures his readers that he does not approve of Aidan's failure to observe the correct (Roman) date of Easter, was nevertheless full of admiration for his sanctity, humility and pastoral devotion.

Lindisfarne was not, however, to be famous simply as a house of prayer. It was also to be a centre for the production of Christian art in the form of illuminated manuscripts of the highest quality, including the famous Lindisfarne Gospels (now in the British Library), the work of the Englishman Eadfrith, Bishop of Lindisfarne from 698 to 721, and the Durham Gospels (now in the Chapter Library of Durham), the work of an unknown scribe, possibly the Irishman called Ultán. Both these manuscripts are written in the Irish half-uncial hand, destined to develop into the English national hand (Anglo-Saxon minuscule) for writing the vernacular, and are sumptuously decorated. Both are expressions of the extraordinary cultural flowering produced in Northumbria by the impact of Irish and Italian Christianity on the English people.

Meanwhile Christianity was making progress in other parts of Britain. In East Anglia it had little chance of success under the compromising Redwald, or under his son Eorpwald who, although converted to Christianity, was soon afterwards (627/8) killed by a heathen called Richberht, after which the kingdom relapsed into paganism for three years. However, in 630 or 631 Eorpwald's half-brother Sigeberht, who had been converted to Christianity in Gaul, became king and invited a Burgundian bishop named Felix to settle in his kingdom to preach the faith. Felix accepted the invitation and established his see at Dunwich in Suffolk; the name of Felixstowe, near Ipswich, perpetuates the memory of a ministry which lasted some seventeen years. Felix was assisted by an Irish ascetic named Fursey or Fursa, who came to East Anglia and was presented by King Sigeberht with a derelict castle (probably Burgh, in Suffolk) in which to settle. Fursey was a successful missionary, making many converts, but his fame rests principally on his visions of the other world, which anticipated Dante's: they were so impressive as to cause him to sweat whenever he remembered them and spared him the need to wear any but the thinnest garments, however cold the weather.

The conversion of Wessex was begun by an Italian bishop named

Birinus, who came to England, apparently at the command of Pope Honorius I (625–38), to preach the Gospel in the midlands. However, when he found on his arrival that the people of Wessex were still heathen he preferred to start work on the spot without losing time in travel. Cynegils, King of Wessex, was baptized by him in 635, having for godfather his prospective son-in-law, Oswald of Northumbria. When Birinus died in about 650, Cynegils' son and successor, Cenwahl, invited a Frankish bishop named Agilbert to succeed him. Agilbert, although consecrated in Gaul, had spent some years in Ireland, at that time a centre for learning, and seemed well qualified to become Bishop of Wessex. Unhappily Agilbert had a distaste for speaking foreign languages and in 660 King Cenwahl, wearied with having to deal with a bishop who would not speak English, divided his kingdom into two sees, appointing an Englishman named Wini to be Bishop of Winchester and leaving Agilbert as Bishop of Dorchester-on-Thames. In high dudgeon at losing half his see Agilbert went back to Gaul, where he subsequently became Bishop of Paris. At a later date Wini had to be deprived of his see of Winchester for reasons unknown to us, and Cenwahl then appealed to Agilbert to return. Agilbert, however, declined to abandon Paris and in his place sent his nephew Leuthere, who was consecrated Bishop of Winchester in 670. The Church in Wessex was by now firmly established and destined to have a great future in later Saxon times.

The large central English kingdom of Mercia was, from some date between 626 and 632 until 654, ruled by Penda, the last great pagan monarch in England. It was Penda who, in alliance with the Christian prince Caedwallon of Gwynedd, had defeated and killed Edwin of Northumbria in 632 – an example of the way in which political necessity reconciles divergent religious beliefs. Although himself a committed pagan, Penda was not implacably hostile to Christianity and – perhaps for diplomatic reasons – was prepared to allow his son, Peada, to marry Alchfled, the daughter of King Oswiu of Northumberland, and to become a Christian. Penda's dislike and contempt were reserved for those who professed Christianity and then failed to live up to the standards of their profession – an honest attitude and not untypical of a good many later Englishmen. (It is possible that these feelings were provoked by the behaviour of his British ally Caedwallon who, after his victory over Edwin, ravaged Northumbria with such ferocity as to suggest that he desired to exterminate the whole English race.) Mercian fear of Northumbria meant that there could never be permanent peace between the two kingdoms. In 641 Penda defeated and killed King Oswald at the battle of Maserfelth – Oswestry, in Shropshire – where the Northumbrian king was campaigning in an attempt to prevent a junction between British and Mercian forces against Northumbria. Oswald's death in battle fighting against the pagans caused him to be venerated as a martyr and his cult eventually extended from Northumbria to the rest of England and even to the European mainland. Thirteen years later, in 654, Penda was again at war with Oswald's successor, King Oswiu, but his luck had run out and he was defeated and killed at the battle of the River Winwaed (the site has not been precisely identified, but was in the region of the modern Leeds).

King Oswiu celebrated his victory by devoting his infant daughter, Aelflaed, to God, together with a large grant of land, and entrusting her to the care of St Hild, at Hartlepool. Aelflaed was one of those – Bede was another – who found herself provided with a vocation without any opportunity to decline; again like Bede, she contrived to make a success of it, becoming Abbess of Whitby in succession to Hild in 680. She represents a type common among Anglo-Saxon royalty of a woman who made a career in the cloister, either by her own choice or by that of her parents, and so achieved a distinction which she probably would never have enjoyed if she had remained in the secular world. Anglo-Saxon Christianity, like medieval Christianity in general, was dominated by the monastic ideal.

The controversy between the Irish and the Roman parties in the Northumbrian Church over the calculation of the date of Easter came to a head in 664. As long as Aidan lived, no one cared to force the issue because of the love and esteem which he enjoyed, and peace was maintained, with some difficulty, after his death in 651 under his successor, Finan. Finan died in 661 and a campaign to adopt the Roman reckoning was then launched by Alchfrid, son of Oswiu and sub-King of Deira, urged on by St Wilfrid, a much-travelled Northumbrian aristocrat, then Abbot of Ripon and a vehement defender of the Roman use. No doubt King Oswiu was glad to have the opportunity to settle the Easter question once and for all, since he observed the Irish calculation while his wife Eanfrid, brought up in Kent, adhered to the Roman, with the result that on occasion one royal partner might be celebrating Easter while the other was still keeping the Lenten fast. A synod held at St Hild's abbey at Whitby gave both parties the chance to put their case, with Bishop Colman advocating the Irish practice and Wilfrid the Roman. In the end King Oswiu decided in favour of Rome, saying with a smile that he preferred to follow St Peter, to whom the keys of the Kingdom of Heaven had been entrusted, rather than Columba the Irishman. So the Northumbrian kingdom came to conform to the practice of the greater part of Christendom. Bishop Colman felt that he could not abandon the custom of his predecessors and, after having arranged for a successor, left Northumbria and returned to Ireland, accompanied by a number of supporters, both Irish and English. Tuda, who took over from Colman, had been educated by the southern Irish, who observed the Roman use, and may thus have seemed a suitable man to unite the divided traditions in Northumbria. Previous adherents of the Irish Easter, like St Hild and St Cuthbert, now accepted King Oswiu's decision.

In 669 there arrived in England a new Archbishop of Canterbury in the person of Theodore, a Greek monk of Tarsus. His appointment was due to a decision of Pope Vitalian (657–72). The original English candidate Wigheard, chosen by the joint action of King Egbert of Kent and King Oswiu of Northumbria, had died at Rome, where he had been sent for consecration owing, it would appear, to a lack of bishops in England as a result of deaths from the Yellow Plague. Wigheard reached Rome safely but there succumbed to the plague, together with most of his companions. Rather than waste time sending to England for another candidate, Vitalian decided to use his own initiative. His first choice was a native of Africa named Hadrian, then abbot of a monastery at Naples; but Hadrian declined the office. Vitalian's choice eventually fell on Theodore, already aged 66 but strong and healthy and endowed with a great reputation for learning. Theodore set off in May 668, accompanied by Hadrian, who was not allowed to escape going to England, and Benedict Biscop, a Northumbrian nobleman and former monk of the famous island monastery of Lérins, who was at that time on his third visit to Rome as a pilgrim for Christ's sake.

For Bede, the long reign of Theodore as Archbishop of Canterbury – he lived until 690 – was a golden age for the English Church. Besides his learning, which made Canterbury famous, Theodore was an able and energetic administrator, who effectively made himself primate of all England, in anticipation of the claims which later Archbishops of Canterbury made to authority over their colleagues of York. His personality is dramatically exemplified in his dealings with St Chad, Bishop of York (not Archbishop; that title came only later with Egbert [732/4–766]), whom he deposed from his see on the grounds of possibly invalid consecration and then, impressed by his humility, conditionally reconsecrated and sent off to be Bishop of the Mercians. Chad was accustomed to travel about his diocese on foot, in accordance with Irish ascetic practice which he had learned from St Aidan. Theodore wanted him to ride, presenting him with a horse for that purpose, and when Chad demurred, lifted him bodily into the saddle with his own hands – no mean feat for a man in his late sixties.

Theodore's masterful personality was, however, a source of trouble as well as of benefit for the English Church, as was shown in the long-drawn-out struggle between him and St Wilfrid. Unquestionably there were faults on both sides and Wilfrid, unlike Chad, was not the man to take deposition tamely; but the story of his repeated efforts to regain control of the see from which he had been arbitrarily removed in 678, while they reveal an obstinate tenacity on Wilfrid's part not in accordance with the highest ideals of Christian forbearance, also show Theodore in no very amiable light. It is something that the two men were reconciled before Theodore's death in 690, though Wilfrid never recovered York, dying in 709 or 710 as Bishop of Hexham and Abbot of Ripon. He was a great monastic founder and claimed the credit for having introduced the Benedictine Rule into England; but perhaps his noblest achievement was the conversion of Sussex to Christianity during his exile there between 681 and 686.

In marked contrast to Wilfrid is the ascetic figure of St Cuthbert, successively a monk at Old Melrose and Ripon, Prior of Lindisfarne, and later hermit on the Farne Islands, before being consecrated Bishop of Lindisfarne in 685. His episcopate was a short one and he resigned in 687, dying on the Inner Farne on 20 March of that year. The apparently miraculous preservation of his body from decay ensured his popularity as a saint in later ages; but a sympathetic reading of his *Lives*, two by Bede and one by an anonymous monk of Lindisfarne, suggests that his reputation for sanctity was well deserved and that his austerity was combined with a pastoral concern of the highest order. He, like St Hild, is an example of one trained in the Irish tradition who was able to accept the decision of the Synod of Whitby without abandoning those traits of asceticism and care for others which represent Irish Christianity at its best.

The later seventh and the eighth century witnessed a great cultural flowering in Christian Northumbria. To St Aidan's foundation of Lindisfarne was added a large number of religious houses, of which the most famous was Benedict Biscop's twin foundation of Wearmouth-Jarrow, the home of Bede, which stood in relation to the Roman tradition of book-copying as Lindisfarne did to the Irish. Its scriptorium, which used the Italian uncial hand and brought it to a pitch of perfection unsurpassed elsewhere, produced the famous Latin Bible called the Codex Amiatinus, written at the command of Abbot Ceolfrith for presentation to Pope Gregory II and now in the Laurentian Library at Florence.

The magnificent library of Wearmouth-Jarrow, built up by Benedict Biscop from repeated visits to the European continent, made possible the later achievements of Bede, the crowning intellectual glory of Anglo-Saxon England, without whose *Ecclesiastical History* no history of the country in this period could be written. Bede stands alone, without a peer; but he was not the only Anglo-Saxon Latinist. Apart from his elder contemporary St Aldhelm (639–709), Abbot of Malmesbury and Bishop of Sherborne, we have the anonymous monks who composed the Whitby life of Pope Gregory the Great; the Lindisfarne life of St Cuthbert; and the Wearmouth-Jarrow life of Abbot Ceolfrith. Furthermore, in evaluating the cultural achievement of Christian Northumbria, account must be taken of its stone-carving, of which the great crosses at Ruthwell (Dumfriesshire) and Bewcastle (Cumbria) are the supreme examples. The Ruthwell Cross bears inscriptions in Latin and Old English, the latter being an apparent quotation from the poem *The Dream of the Rood*, in which the poet beholds Christ's cross and hears it recount the story of the God–man's victorious encounter with death and hell on Calvary. This short citation is a reminder of another cultural achievement of Anglo-Saxon England: the composition of a Christian vernacular literature, the oldest original writing in a Germanic language, of which the poems of Caedmon are the earliest-known example. Furthermore, it was a Christian milieu, perhaps Northumbrian though more probably East Anglian, that produced *Beowulf*, the greatest early English epic poem.

By the time Bede died in 735 a diocesan system had been established over the whole of England. The northern province consisted of four dioceses: York, Hexham, Lindisfarne and Whithorn in Wigtonshire (this last having been founded shortly before 731 on the site of Candida Casa, the monastery of the fifth-century British missionary St Ninian). The southern province contained twelve sees: Canterbury, Rochester, Selsey, Winchester, Sherborne, London, Dunwich, Elmham, Worcester, Hereford, Lichfield and Lindsey (in north Lincolnshire). The see of Dorchester-upon-Thames, which had been occupied by Birinus and Agilbert, had a bishop named Aetla, a former pupil of St Hild, in about 680, but after him the succession seems to have lapsed and was not effectively established until the tenth century, being subsequently removed to Lincoln in the eleventh. Archbishop Theodore also established a see at Leicester during his primacy, but here too there was apparently no continuance and the see was refounded in 737.

By 735 too the religious life had developed, with monasteries for men and double houses, which sheltered both sexes under the rule of an abbess. These communities included Canterbury, Lyminge, Lindisfarne, Melrose, Minster-in-Thanet, Gilling, Whitby, Ripon, Hexham, Lastingham, Peterborough, Chertsey, Barking, Monkwearmouth-Jarrow and Wimborne Minster. The picture was not entirely a bright one. When the monastery of Coldingham was accidentally burnt down some time after 681, Bede regarded the fire as a punishment for the worldliness and corruption of its inmates, and in his famous letter of 734 to Bishop Egbert of York he deplored the existence of fraudulent monasteries, set up by unscrupulous noblemen to avoid taxation and military service; but the general impression is of a vigorous and flourishing monasticism.

Furthermore, at the time of Bede's death the English mission to the continent, designed to bring their Germanic kinsmen to faith in Christ, was already under way. Having its origin in Ireland, with its principal architect the Northumbrian abbot Egbert, its first target was Frisia. Here the great leader was St Willibrord (658–739), apostle of Frisia and subsequently Archbishop of Utrecht, who had been trained under Wilfrid at Ripon and subsequently under Egbert in Ireland. Willibrord was responsible for the foundation of the monastery of Echternach, in Luxembourg, famous as a centre for book-copying. Even more famous than Willibrord is the West Saxon Winfrith, better known as St Boniface, the apostle of Germany, Archbishop of Mainz and martyr (c.675–754), distinguished alike as a preacher and as an organizer, who not only established the episcopal system in Germany, but also brought about reform in the Frankish Church. Of the English mission to the continent it may be said that it represents an attempt by the English to give back to their pagan kinsmen what they themselves had received from Christian Europe and also, by the readiness of Willibrord and Boniface to place themselves under the patronage of the Pope in their mission, that it helped in the development of the medieval papacy.

Our knowledge of worship as conducted in the Anglo-Saxon Church is, at one and the same time, both considerable and limited. We can be fairly sure about the types of liturgy used; we have some evidence of the personal devotions of the educated; but with regard to the mind of the ordinary worshipper, we can only conjecture. Public worship was conducted in Latin and resembled the rites which were, until quite recently, in use in the Roman Catholic Church. Augustine and his companions would presumably have used prayers of a Roman character, and these would have been introduced into Northumbria and other kingdoms where the Roman missionaries penetrated. The liturgy used by St Aidan and the Irish mission would have been similar in essentials, but would have included non-Roman features taken from the liturgies used in Gaul and Spain. It is reasonable to suppose that similar additions and variations would have been admitted by the Roman party, since Pope Gregory had authorized Augustine to draw upon Gallic, as well as Roman, practices, if he thought them suitable for the English Church.

The conduct of the services would again have been like that familiar to modern Roman Catholics, at least until quite recently. The vestments would likewise have been similar: there is a famous miniature in a tenth-century manuscript at Corpus Christi College, Cambridge (MS 183), showing St Cuthbert vested in a chasuble and alb of very modern appearance. Incense was used – we have a vivid account by Bede of Abbot Ceolfrith of Wearmouth-Jarrow taking leave of his brethren at a farewell service, thurible in hand, before setting off on his journey to Rome – while St Boniface's reference to Bede as 'a candle of the Church' reminds us that a great basilica, like that of St Wilfrid at Hexham, would have been ablaze with light. An English peasant, ignorant of Latin, who attended a service at Hexham might well have been moved to a sense of awe and devotion by the splendour of the architecture, the elaboration of the ritual, and the chanting of the liturgy in a sonorous and unknown tongue – rather like a modern visitor, ignorant of Church Slavonic, who is nevertheless intensely moved by the liturgy of the Russian Orthodox Church.

What the peasant's feelings would have been in some small church, the ancestor of the later parish church, built on the estate of his overlord and served by a local priest with an imperfect command of Latin, is harder to say. Perhaps the very unintelligibility of the liturgical language would have made an impression, like that made by a charm-formula upon his pagan ancestors. If devout, the peasant would know his way about the service and understand its various stages, even if the words remained a mystery. If he were lucky enough to have as his priest one capable of teaching and preaching effectively – and there certainly were good preachers in Anglo-Saxon England – he might have had a good knowledge of the doctrines of the religion which he professed; but in the end his inner feelings and deepest convictions must remain forever closed to us.

There is, however, one important source of information about the religious feelings of the better-educated Anglo-Saxon Christians in the various private prayers and devotions in both Latin and Anglo-Saxon which, by good fortune, have survived in manuscripts to reveal something of the character of religion in early England. These include the Books of Nunnaminster (British Library, Harley MS 2965) and Cerne (Cambridge University Library, MS Ll.I.10), together with a prayer collection composed in the eighth century or earlier, preserved in the British Library (Royal MS 2.A.XX) and another of the eleventh century contained in the Cottonian manuscripts in the British Library (Galba A.XIV and Nero A.II, fos. 3–13). In these prayers one finds both the unemotional brevity of Rome and the intense (and wordy) devotion often associated with Irish piety. In the Book of Nunnaminster and in the Cotton manuscripts there is a Christocentricity which anticipates that devotion to the divine humanity so typical of later Western spirituality. Interestingly, we also find it in Bede, in the prayer which closes the *Ecclesiastical History* (V, 24):

> And I pray Thee, merciful Jesus, that as Thou hast graciously granted me sweet draughts from the Word which tells of Thee, so wilt Thou, of Thy goodness, grant that I may come at length to Thee, the fount of all wisdom, and stand before Thy face for ever.

We may compare with this prayer of Bede, composed in the eighth century, one from the eleventh-century British Library Cotton manuscript:

> O Lord Jesus Christ, who hast passed from this world to the Father and didst love them that were in the world; make me in my mind to pass from earthly things to the things above; to despise what is transitory and to desire only the heavenly; and to burn with the flaming fire of Thy love. And do Thou, O God, who didst deign with Thy most holy hands to wash the feet of Thy holy apostles, purify my heart by pouring upon it the radiance of Thy Holy Spirit, that I may be able, in all things and above all things, to love Thee, our Lord Jesus Christ.

The flourishing English Christian culture of the eighth century was effectively destroyed in the ninth by the Danish invasions. The sack of Lindisfarne in 793 was a foretaste of what was to be the fate of the greater part of England in the next hundred years. In 835 the Danes overran the Isle of Sheppey and in 842 they sacked London. They spent the winter of 854–5 on Sheppey, revealing a threat of permanent settlement, as opposed to intermittent raiding, and in 865 a great Danish army landed in England, occupying York in 866. It was then, it would appear, that the famous library of the school of York, celebrated by Alcuin (c.735–804), spiritual disciple of Bede and friend of Charlemagne, the English schoolmaster and biblical reviser of the Frankish empire, perished. From Yorkshire the Danes marched southwards and in 869/70 defeated and killed King Edmund of East Anglia, who was subsequently honoured as a martyr. Then in Wessex they came upon unexpected resistance from King Ethelred I and his brother Alfred, who succeeded him in 871. Alfred's struggle against the Danes has passed – deservedly – into the realm of heroic legend. Our concern here is with his work as a restorer of the Church. His great achievement politically was to prevent the Danes from settling in Wessex, and in the years which followed the treaty between Alfred and the Danish leader Guthrum in 886, the English king set himself to rebuild in Wessex the civilization which the Danes had destroyed elsewhere. A tradition of Christian learning survived in Northumbria at the town of Chester-le-Street in County Durham, where, in 883, the Lindisfarne community had established itself, with the remnants of its library and some books from Wearmouth-Jarrow; but as a creative cultural force, Northumbria was finished.

Wessex itself was hardly in a better case. Even if we allow for an element of exaggeration in Alfred's celebrated complaint that in 871, when he became King of Wessex, 'there were very few on this [south] side of the

Humber who could understand their [Latin] service books in English or translate a letter from Latin into English, and I believe there were not many beyond the Humber,' it would seem that by the year 900 regular monastic life had almost wholly come to an end in central and southern England. The heroic temper of Alfred's character, which caused him, after his victory over the Danes, to learn Latin in order to translate into English works which he judged to be of value, becomes the more admirable if we remember the intellectual wasteland in which he found himself.

We know hardly anything about the English Church in the first half of the tenth century. It seems likely that such monasteries as remained passed into the possession of secular clergy, not following any rule. The monastic revival of the second half of the century, which brought new life to the English Church, is associated particularly with three men: Dunstan (*c.*909–88); Ethelwold (*c.*912–84) and Oswald (d. 992). Of these Dunstan was appointed Abbot of Glastonbury in 943, where he formed a community following the Rule of St Benedict, and was subsequently made Bishop of Worcester in 957, to which he added London, held jointly, in 959, before becoming Archbishop of Canterbury in 960. Ethelwold, who had made Abingdon a model house under his abbatial rule, became Bishop of Winchester in 963 and, after expelling the secular clergy from the Old and New Minsters there, installed Abingdon monks in their place. Oswald, who had studied the reformed monasticism of the continent at the monastery of Fleury-sur-Loire and had thereafter been abbot successively of Westbury-on-Trym and Ramsey, succeeded Dunstan at Worcester in 961, becoming Archbishop of York in 972 but holding the two sees together until his death in 992.

With three monastic bishops thus installed in well-endowed sees, King Edgar (King of Mercia and Northumbria 957; King of all England 959; d. 975) was able to press ahead with Church reform. This included the establishment of a uniform monastic observance common to all England, embodied in the famous *Regularis Concordia*, a supplement to the Benedictine Rule observed in common by all English monasteries, compiled by Ethelwold and promulgated by the decision of a council which met at Winchester, probably around 973. The long reigns of Dunstan, Ethelwold and Oswald enabled them to train a second generation of monks who, established in monasteries in southern and central England – for in the north the monastic revival, inaugurated by Aldwine of Winchcombe, did not begin until after the Norman Conquest – were able to survive the second Danish invasion, which began in the years following the accession of Ethelred II (the Unready) in 978 and was accomplished thirty-eight years later by the accession of the Danish King Cnut in 1016.

Cnut, although one of the greatest Scandinavian war leaders, was also the first Viking chieftain to enter the fraternity of civilized Christian kings. He was himself much influenced by Wulfstan, Archbishop of York from 1003 to 1023. Cnut's outlook is fittingly symbolized in a famous drawing in the *Liber Vitae* (a record of benefactors for whom prayers are to be offered) of Hyde Abbey (earlier the New Minster, Winchester), showing him and his first wife, Queen Aelgyfu, presenting an altar cross to the New Minster. Cnut visited Rome in 1027, where he attended the coronation of the Roman emperor, Conrad, and as a result of this visit, made a law requiring the full payment by all his subjects of what was owed to God, including the famous Peter's Pence, a gift to Rome, which had been sent by Alfred when circumstances permitted, and of which the payment had been enforced by Alfred's successors, Edmund and Edgar.

The monastic revival of the tenth century helped to make the later Anlgo-Saxon period one of high Christian cultural achievement. England did not, it is true, produce another Bede; but men like Bede are exceptional in any age. On the other hand, the arts flourished – the period 966–1066 has been called the golden age of Anglo-Saxon art. Of architecture we know less than we would like, since the English tended to build in wood rather than stone and the Norman passion for building meant that many existing churches were pulled down and replaced by others built in stone. Nevertheless one famous example survives in the church of St Andrew at Greensted-by-Ongar in Essex, a 'stave church', built in the Scandinavian fashion in the early years of the eleventh century, which may be compared with surviving examples of building in stone of an earlier epoch, like Earls Barton, Northamptonshire, or Escomb, County Durham, and later ones like Derehurst, Gloucestershire and Barnack, Northamptonshire.

In the field of book-copying and book-painting the artists of the last century of Anglo-Saxon England reached a very high standard. No longer was Northumbria the source of the great masterpieces of writing and illumination. The Vikings had destroyed the northern centres of book production, and it is in the south that we find works of brilliant quality like the Bosworth Psalter, possibly designed for St Dunstan himself; the Sherborne Pontifical; the Benedictional of St Ethelwold; and the Grimbald Gospels. These – the Bosworth Psalter apart, which is in an insular hand – are written in the so-called Caroline minuscule, imported from the continent, like the uncial hand at an earlier epoch. If to book-painting we add the allied art of embroidery – the Bayeux Tapestry seems to have been the work of English artists and its achievement was anticipated in the famous stole and maniple, made at Winchester between 909 and 916 and subsequently presented to the shrine of St Cuthbert at Chester-le-Street, County Durham – together with ivory-carving, metal-work and sculpture, we can confidently assert that no contemporary state in western Europe could claim a higher degree of artistic brilliance than England, while the English might, with some justification, have regarded themselves as the people who made possible the continental cultural revival of the eighth and ninth centuries, with its sequel in the achievements of German artists under the Ottonian emperors in the tenth and eleventh.

To all this may be added a vigorous vernacular literature. Between 990 and 994 Aelfric, the Abbot of Eynsham, Oxfordshire, composed his *Catholic Homilies* – two sets of sermons translated from the Latin Fathers and compiled to help parish priests in their duties, somewhat in the manner of the later *Book of Homilies*. A few years later Aelfric followed this with his *Lives of the Saints*. His contemporary Wulfstan, Archbishop of York, was responsible for the most powerful piece of writing of the age – the *Sermo Lupi ad Anglos*, an appeal to the English people calling them to repentance in the crisis of 1014, when Cnut and Ethelred the Unready were striving for mastery. The number of manuscripts in which these and other writings in Old English have survived shows that there was a welcome for works in the native language. In addition, the fact that some of these manuscripts were copied as late as the twelfth century is evidence that Englishmen retained a respect for their native learning, long after English had been driven from a position of honour and replaced by Anglo-Norman as the language of court and society.

When Cnut died in 1033 he was succeeded by his son, Harold, who died in 1040, being followed by his half-brother Harthacnut, Cnut's son by his second wife, Emma of Normandy. Harthacnut, however, died in 1042 and was succeeded by his own half-brother, Edward the Confessor, the son of Cnut's widow Emma by her first husband, Ethelred the Unready. So the old Wessex royal line was restored in the person of the devout Edward, who had spent twenty-five years in Normandy and has become notorious for his Norman sympathies. Perhaps oddly, it was this pious king who introduced the practice, to be followed by William the Conqueror, of appointing secular clergy rather than monks to the episcopate, and his reign saw some decline in monastic fervour, despite the existence of distinguished houses like that of Evesham in Worcestershire, under Abbot Aethelwig, and Worcester, under St Wulfstan, later bishop of the city from 1062 to 1095, whose reputation was such that he enjoyed the favour and respect of King William I and was one of the few Englishmen to retain high office under both William and his son, William Rufus. He was also the subject of numerous miracle stories after his death, in a tradition which looks back to the saints' lives recorded by Bede. It is said that when King John was asked where he wished to be buried he replied: 'To God and St Wulfstan I commend my body and my soul.'

Wulfstan remained a popular saint in England throughout the middle ages, and it therefore seems fitting to conclude this account of the Anglo-Saxon Church with him. Conservative in temperament and untravelled – he does not appear to have left England during his lifetime – he was animated, both as an abbot and as a bishop, with the same reforming zeal as the Hildebrandine movement was producing on the continent in this period. He was conscientious in the visitation of his diocese; encouraged church-building; and – a more questionable expression of reforming zeal in modern eyes – sought to promote clerical celibacy by dismissing his married clergy. In this he agreed with the decision of a Roman council held by Pope Gregory VII in 1074, but showed himself harsher than Lanfranc's Council of Winchester of 1076, which required celibacy only of canons, and not of parish priests and chaplains in castles and manor-houses. More attractive to contemporary opinion is his successful campaign to end the slave trade with Ireland, which disgraced the port of Bristol. Slavery had always been an accepted institution among the English, though often forbidden by Church and State alike, and neither the love of God nor the fear of King William I had been able to stop the Bristol merchants from shipping their own countrymen to slavery in Ireland. Wulfstan made repeated visits to Bristol of two or three months' duration at a time and eventually, by his preaching, not only abolished the Bristol trade but inspired other ports to do the same. Although not himself a scholar, under his rule the diocese of Worcester became a centre for Old English literature and culture. (His biography – since lost – by his chaplain and chancellor Coleman, adapted in Latin by William of Malmesbury, is the last piece of consecutive writing in Old English known to us.) Wulfstan had, appropriately, a special reverence for Bede, and for his predecessors at Worcester, St Dunstan and St Oswald.

Altogether, this last bishop of Anglo-Saxon England was a worthy representative of the tradition which formed him and which was now to undergo a sea change by the coming of the Normans.

3

From the Conquest to the Black Death

Rosalind Hill

IN THE PERIOD between AD 1000 and 1350 the Church was everyone's concern. It christened, married and buried people, and through the Mass it gave assurance of forgiveness of sins and opened the gates of eternal life. It provided sanctuary and, through the practice of oath and ordeal, played a great part in the administration of justice; its clergy were almost the only source of learned, and indeed of literate, men; its buildings were the only place where you could be sure of meeting all your neighbours; its wealth contributed extensively to the royal treasury and even supplied a large part of the available army. It is therefore meaningless to draw an arbitrary line between Church and State, or to consider such incidents as Henry II's quarrel with Becket or Edward's resistance to the papal bull *Clericis Laicos* as if they were symptoms of some deep antagonism between royal and ecclesiastical power. They were nothing of the kind. Bishop and king alike stood for order and authority in a society which, like our own, could easily slip back into barbarism and lawlessness, and for this reason they looked to one another for mutual support. Without this alliance, the achievements of the high middle ages would have been impossible. 'Assuredly', say the laws of Cnut, 'God will be gracious to him who is duly loyal to his lord,' and Aethelred II orders his officials to protect the clergy 'as they wish to have God's friendship and mine'. In pre-Conquest England there was no division between the secular and ecclesiastical courts, and royal law codes laid down enactments about such things as the behaviour of priests, the conditions of marriage, and the prohibition of idolatry and superstition, while the Church administered the oath and ordeal without which the King's justice could not work.

The pre-Conquest Church was organized in two provinces (Canterbury and York) and sixteen bishoprics (Carlisle was not founded until 1133). Some of these were later reorganized, the *cathedra* being removed to a notable city, as, for example, Crediton to Exeter, Selsey to Chichester or

Thetford to Norwich. Bishops met from time to time in synods to discuss matters of common interest or to issue injunctions, but their regular place of meeting was in the King's Council, where they were among his most influential advisers. St Wulfstan was not only Archbishop of York and the author of *Sermo Lupi ad Anglos,* a terrific denunciation of the sins of contemporary society, but also the man chiefly responsible for framing the secular laws of Cnut.

Bishops were often, although not invariably, monks. A tradition, stretching right back to the time of the conversion, made it clear that monasteries and bishops' households were the two great centres of education. Sometimes, as in the cathedral churches of Winchester and Worcester, they were by the eleventh century synonymous, although the bishops always needed the help of some administrators drawn from the ranks of the secular clergy. In others, such as York and, before 1083, Durham, the chapter consisted of secular clergy, even though the bishop might himself be a monk. By 1014 it was laid down in a synod that candidates for ordination must bring testimonials from their teachers, and undergo an examination in learning and doctrine. If by necessity they had to be ordained before they were judged fully proficient, they must swear to complete their education as soon as possible. The rule of clerical celibacy was not yet binding except upon the regular clergy, and however much strict reformers might have deplored the fact, it is clear that many secular clergy, from the cathedral to the humblest parish, were married, and that their wives were both respectable and respected. But, although reformers are notoriously apt to exaggerate, some bishops must have lived in a way little to be distinguished from that of lay nobles, since Archbishop Wulfstan found it necessary to exhort them to shun minstrels and hard-drinking feasts, and to take no part in judgements involving sentences of death or mutilation.

Parochial life as we understand it hardly existed in England before the end of the tenth century. The earliest English churches had been 'minsters', which were not monasteries in the strict sense but groups of clergy sent out by the bishops and protected by the local landowners, originally as centres of evangelism. A few people built private chapels. From the time of Alfred onwards it became increasingly common for rich men to found churches on their estates (to have a private church was one of the marks which differentiated the thane from the socially inferior free peasant). Such churches varied in importance from the head minster, which was staffed by several priests and had a graveyard attached to it, to the humble field church, which was a small chapel, often built of wood. The patron, in any case, chose and maintained his own priest, and was in a position to bully him, in one case insisting on almost blocking up the church door by a large nut-tree, under which he liked to sit and drink.

Bishops, assisted by their own clergy (including, at least in some dioceses, an archdeacon), did their best to encourage the outlying clergy to lead orderly lives and carry out a thorough ministry, but clearly their work involved an uphill struggle. The Northumbrian Priests' Law, issued between 1006 and 1023, forbids, among other things, the celebration of Mass with ale instead of wine, or in a wooden cup, and instructs the priest that he must not come armed into church, take a second wife while the first is alive, or condone heathen worship among his parishioners. It is easy to understand how these practices had grown up in the state of poverty and insecurity that prevailed during the Danish invasions.

The instruction which a good priest had to give his people was of necessity fairly simple. They must learn the Creed and the Lord's Prayer, 'in which there are seven petitions, with which he who says it inwardly applies to God for every single necessity . . . either for this life or the next'. The priest should keep and use at least a Missal, a Gospel book, a Psalter and Penitential (a list of sins with appropriate penances), and he should exhort, and if possible preach. Scholars like Aelfric wrote books of suitable homilies, but it is uncertain how widely they were used. Babies were to be baptized on pain of a heavy fine. The priest was to learn and teach a manual craft (the influence of St Dunstan is clearly apparent here), and he was to give an example of public decency by avoiding secular dress, eschewing taverns, and keeping the altar clear of mice, and the graveyard free of dogs, horses and most especially pigs.

It would be wrong to think of England in the earlier eleventh century as a religious backwater. Edward the Confessor was building his splendid new abbey at Westminster, and works of art such as the Romsey rood and the Chichester panels reflect the beautiful artistic tradition of the period. Churches were not only built, they were richly endowed. William I is said to have despatched twenty-eight waggon-loads of English ecclesiastical treasures to enrich the churches of Normandy, and English embroidered vestments were famous as far afield as Sicily. Nevertheless, the Church in England was a little old-fashioned. The developments in canon law associated with the law schools of Lotharingia, and with the reformed papacy after the Synod of Sutri in 1046, found no immediate echo on the north side of the Channel. Stigand, Archbishop of Canterbury at the time of the Conquest, had been consecrated by an anti-pope. The Church was still strongly proprietary, and lay patrons, from the King downwards, expected to be responsible for bestowing a benefice, which in English law was simply a piece of real property. When William I invested his bishops with ring and staff, as he consistently did, he was, in his own eyes, handing over a valuable fief to a tenant-in-chief. That the bishop was also his spiritual father in God he would readily have admitted, for he was a devout man and, according to his lights, a reformer. He took it for granted, however, that it was he, and not the Pope or the Archbishop, who had the final authority to enforce the decrees of ecclesiastical councils such as those held at Winchester or Windsor by Archbishop Lanfranc. It was the King who, by his decree, separated the spiritual from the temporal courts and he did it rather as a matter of administrative convenience than because he felt it improper for a layman to meddle with canon law. He was prepared to pay Peter's Pence to Rome as a matter of ancient and respected tradition, but he quite firmly refused to admit that it was a custom which allowed any claim to papal overlordship. Gregory VII, who recognized a reformer when he saw one, did not press the matter. William may have flouted every reformist decree of the papal curia when he high-handedly deposed Stigand from the see of Canterbury, and himself chose and invested his successor; but that successor was, after all, Lanfranc, famous as a strict reformer and as one of the greatest canonists of the age. Moreover, although the battle of Hastings was won under a banner blessed by the Pope himself, the Conqueror and his followers had demanded from the papal legate, and had duly performed, a suitable penance (extending even to those who 'intending to slay, had not succeeded in slaying any') for shedding Christian blood. New religious foundations grew up all over the country to attest to the fulfilment of this penance by Norman landowners, from the King himself downwards.

It was in the reign of William I that the first clearly defined step was taken to assert the primacy of Canterbury over the province of York. Gregory I had laid it down in a letter to St Augustine of Kent that priority should alternate between the two provinces on the basis of the seniority of each individual archbishop. In practice the unification of the English kingdom by the royal house of Wessex and the impoverishment of the north by continual warfare had made the ascendancy of Canterbury inevitable in the late Anglo-Saxon period. After the Conquest the claims of York were raised again and maintained with some tenacity. In 1072 Archbishop Thomas of York made a profession of canonical obedience to Lanfranc and his successors in the see of Canterbury, but this was not at once accepted in the north, and the dispute rumbled on. It was not until the middle of the fourteenth century that the last ecclesiastical foray into the southern province was made by the Archbishop of York with his cross carried before him erect, while His Grace of Canterbury pronounced sentence of interdict upon every place in which his presumptuous brother prelate might dare to display this sign of equal authority.

William I was a friend to the clergy and a reformer, albeit a conservative one, but his successor was nothing of the kind. William II quarrelled with his archbishop, Anselm, one of the greatest of medieval theologians, and drove him into exile. It was while he was abroad in Italy that Anselm absorbed the ideas which have been called 'High Gregorian' – namely, the acknowledgement of the supreme authority of the Pope over all earthly rulers, the independence of the clergy from secular control and the repudiation of lay investiture. These ideas Anselm brought back with him when Henry I recalled him to England, and they were to have a lasting effect upon the English Church from the beginning of the twelfth century until the Reformation. Yet the English Church never became completely High Gregorian. Successive kings liked to begin their charters of liberties with some such phrase as 'I will make the Church free', and to promise that they would refrain from interfering in the election of bishops, and from exacting from the clergy any payment or service except such as might reasonably be claimed from their temporal possessions. In practice it is clear that although cathedral chapters were instructed to make a perfectly free election, they normally chose the candidate for whom the King had indicated a preference, and that, although the King renounced the right to invest with ring and staff, he retained that of receiving homage from a bishop before his consecration. Any clerical landowner who broke his fealty or failed to provide his *servitium debitum* was liable to run into serious trouble in the King's court.

This system of royal patronage did, in fact, work rather well. Although the normal route to a bishopric was apt to lie through the tenure of high office in the royal household, or the rule of a great abbey of royal foundation, such places were no bad training ground. English bishops between 1107 and 1350 were, on the whole, a thoroughly hard-working body of men, highly capable as administrators and judicious in their choice of subordinates. The publication of a large number of episcopal *acta* and registers has shown us how much the English Church owes to this truly remarkable, and often underestimated, body of men. They had their detractors. The St Alban's chronicler, Matthew Paris, who disapproved on principle of all foreigners (although his ideas of what constituted a foreigner were somewhat peculiar), might complain that some of Henry III's bishops, who owed their position to relationship with the royal house, were 'detestable in dress and speech; they had faces like play-actors and wore indecent boots,' but his remarks can never have applied to more than a few, and one of his most detested foreigners, Boniface of Savoy, seems in practice to have been an excellent archbishop.

The organization of the cathedral chapter in the nine 'secular' cathedrals (York, London, Lincoln, Chichester, Wells, Exeter, Salisbury, Hereford and Lichfield), where the church was not organized as a monastery, dates from the reign of William I. It remained almost unaltered (despite the doctrinal changes of the Reformation) until the nineteenth century. The arrangements owed something to Norman custom, although they were not imported wholesale but evolved, largely from practical experience, in the three great centres of York, London and Lincoln. A corporate body of canons was established to supervise, through their four great offices, dean, precentor, chancellor and treasurer, the running of the cathedral and the training of clergy, and to act as a kind of advisory council to the bishop. Each canon was maintained from the cathedral revenues by means of a prebend, usually an appropriated church but occasionally a special fund, such as the prebend *consumpta per mare* in St Paul's, London. Some of the canons, including always holders of the four great offices, were bound to keep residence for at least two-thirds of the year. Others were not. A prebend could quite lawfully be used to provide a stipend for a man whose duties lay in another part of the diocese, as for the Archdeacon of Richmond in the diocese of York, or even in another part of the world, as for Stephen of Tathwell who was the Bishop of Lincoln's official proctor in the papal curia. Vicars as representatives were instituted to stand in for the canons in the duties connected with the cathedral and their prebendal parishes.

The remaining dioceses (Canterbury, Winchester, Rochester, Norwich, Ely, Worcester, Durham and Carlisle) were monastic cathedrals – Benedictine or, in the case of Carlisle, Augustinian. In them the duties of the chapter were fulfilled by the prior and senior obedientiaries of the monastery, of which the chancel of the cathedral was in a sense the private chapel. (Such cathedrals as Canterbury and Winchester illustrate clearly, by the existence of a heavy and solid chancel screen, the difference which existed between the regulars within it and the secular world in the nave.) The bishop, though not a member of the community, held the titular position of abbot. After the Reformation these 'regular' cathedrals were refounded upon the 'secular' pattern.

Throughout the twelfth century the authority of the Pope and the Roman curia was steadily growing, and by the time of such popes as Alexander III and Innocent III it was very powerful indeed. But Rome was a long way from England (it was exceptional for the journey to be completed in less than six weeks). The English Church was extremely orthodox in doctrine, and accepted the Pope as Vicar of Christ and universal ordinary, from whom all ecclesiastical power was derived. But in practice he lived far away, and although this century saw the election of the only Englishman to become Pope (Adrian IV) Rome, as a rule, knew little of conditions in England. The Pope could, and sometimes did, appoint legates *a latere* whose authority over-ruled that of the *legatus natus*, the

Archbishop of Canterbury. Appeals from ecclesiastical courts went to Rome and could be settled there, but the results were referred back to English bishops for practical application. The Pope normally delegated to these bishops some of his powers of interpreting and administering canon law, so that, for example, a man born in bastardy but otherwise qualified for ordination did not have to undertake the expensive journey to Rome, but could obtain a dispensation from his own diocesan. When serious disputes arose involving English clerics, the Pope increasingly made use of judges-delegate, senior and responsible ecclesiastics who were empowered to act in the Pope's name in particular cases. Although in the last resort papal authority had to be upheld, the English province enjoyed a good deal of practical independence. Alexander III was extremely reluctant to intervene in the quarrel between Henry II and Becket, and even after the spectacular murder of the archbishop he did not press the King to extremes. Innocent III intervened in the dispute between John and the monks of Canterbury over the election of an archbishop, and eventually, when John proved stubborn, excommunicated him. But, again, the Pope acted diplomatically. His nominee for Canterbury was Stephen Langton, a Lincolnshire man with an outstanding reputation for scholarship as well as a remarkable capacity for administration, and the King, after his rather ungracious submission, was restored to papal favour.

The growth of canon law between the publication of Gratian's *Decretum* and the fourth Lateran Council was bound to have a great effect upon the theory and practice of English common law, and incidentally upon the daily life of every man and woman. The study of law was intensely interesting to twelfth-century scholars. Vacarius had been lecturing on the subject at Oxford as early as the reign of Henry I, and had written a textbook for his students. As the work of Gratian was extended, glossed and worried over by successive canonists in the papal curia and the law schools of Paris and Bologna, English ecclesiastical courts extended and developed their competence. They claimed cognizance of all matters concerning the clergy, their persons and their spiritual (as opposed to their temporal) possessions, and over the whole field of matrimonial and testamentary disputes. This naturally brought them into conflict with common law and feudal custom, and could raise difficult problems. What was to happen when a cleric (and the minor orders of the Church covered a very mixed collection of persons) committed such an offence as murder or burglary or poaching the royal deer, more especially if he did it in the company of laymen who would be tried in the King's court and probably hanged? How far could a lay patron maintain his rights over a church or monastery which he had founded and endowed at his own expense? If a valuable heiress were betrothed to the King's enemy, could anything be done to annul the arrangement and precipitate her and her possessions into the arms of his friend? These and similar problems, especially that of the 'criminous clerk', were apt to bedevil relationships between the lay and ecclesiastical powers. Moreover, since the church courts could not inflict sentences of death or mutilation, it was clearly in the interests of accused persons to prove themselves, if possible, to be clerics, and thus to escape from lay clutches – a practice which university students found it highly advantageous to exploit. On the whole the boundaries between the two jurisdictions had, by the end of the twelfth century, been worked out with a good deal of common sense. The Church courts kept cognizance of all cases involving clerics, but tacitly allowed the royal courts to proceed in matters of treason or breach of the forest laws. Civil cases involving real property normally went to the royal courts, even when they involved a patron's right to present a candidate to the living of a church. The bishop, however, could reject the man if he proved upon examination to be unworthy or illiterate. The practice of ordeal by water or hot iron, normal in twelfth-century royal courts, ended in 1219 as a direct result of a decree of the Fourth Lateran Council forbidding priests to officiate at such a ceremony.

The century which followed the Norman Conquest saw a remarkable increase in the number of English monasteries. Successive kings, with the exception of William II, followed the tradition of their Anglo-Saxon predecessors in supporting and endowing the great Benedictine houses already in existence, such as St Alban's and Westminster. They also established new foundations, such as William I's abbey of Battle. Their followers copied them, and a number of new houses grew up from the pious foundations of Norman barons and their wives. Lanfranc, by the reforming constitutions which he designed for Christ Church, Canterbury, tried to bring the customs of the English houses into line with the reformed practices of continental monasteries and especially of Bec, but these constitutions were not generally adopted, and most English houses remained autonomous until the development of the Benedictine general chapters in the thirteenth century. Some English foundations were, however, directly colonized from the great French houses, and these became what were later known as 'alien priories', dependent daughter-houses of such abbeys as Bec or Fleury. Others were established as priories directly dependent upon a motherhouse in England, such as Tynemouth which was, rather surprisingly, a daughter of St Alban's.

After the beginning of the twelfth century the influence of the new, reformed orders began to be felt in England. Cluny was never popular; its constitution was probably too strongly centralized in Burgundy, and Lewes and Bermondsey remained the only two outstanding Cluniac priories. The Cistercians, however, had an enormous influence on the

English Church, and their first foundation at Waverley in 1128 was followed by many others. An Englishman, Stephen Harding, had played a great part in the growth of the order, and although St Bernard never came to England himself he had many friends here, notably Ailred, who became Abbot of Rievaulx. Cistercian houses were not only famous for austere holiness; they were also relatively cheap to establish, since they would accept no property which had already been developed and no feudal dues, but asked instead for 'desert' land on which they could live in peace. This led to the foundation of the great northern abbeys on lands which either were uncultivated or had been laid waste in the Conqueror's harrying of the north. Such sites, like those on the Welsh border, were often extremely beautiful, and the Cistercian reaction against the elaborate ornaments of Romanesque churches led to their enhancement by the eventual building of Gothic abbeys, remarkable not only for the austere beauty of their architecture but also for the efficiency of their domestic arrangements.

Another order which became popular in twelfth-century England was that of the Augustinian Canons. These were not, strictly speaking, monks, although their pattern of life was cenobitic. They aimed at imitating the corporate life of the Apostles, and had considerable influence in education and in the founding of hospitals. They had a few great houses such as Merton, St Mary de Pratis in Leicester and the cathedral priory at Carlisle, but the great majority of their houses were small, and as time went on not very clearly distinguishable from monasteries.

Other orders such as the Carthusians and the Premonstratensian Canons settled in England, but their houses were not very numerous. The one purely local order, the Gilbertines, was founded by St Gilbert of Sempringham about 1131, and never spread beyond eastern England. The original house was a small community of nuns, to which St Gilbert added canons regular, to act as priests, and lay brothers and sisters to do most of the domestic work and run the farms. Men and women did not, as in the early Anglo-Saxon houses, work together, but lived in separate cloisters, and had virtually no corporate life; nor did the women ever attain membership of the house of student canons eventually established at Cambridge. English nuns in this period were in any case far fewer than monks, and their only great houses were those of pre-Conquest foundation, such as Amesbury, Romsey and Shaftesbury.

A monastery was intended to be a place of prayer and contemplation, a place where people might pursue unhindered the true end of mankind, 'to glorify God and to enjoy him for ever'. From this life there might spring, incidentally, many good works, but it was no part of a monk's essential duty to educate, relieve, heal or shelter his fellow-Christians in the world, still less to devote himself to the efficient running of the abbey's estates,

although all these things had to be done and were often done well. The real
contribution of monastic life to the world is seen not in social benefits but in
the new devotional movement associated with St Anselm, bringing the
believer into a deeper understanding of the humanity of Christ as well as of
his Godhead, or in the writings of St Ailred, who links the idea of a deeply
spiritual love with the practical considerations of community life ('How is
it that you say that you would give your life for me, when you will not lend
me a needle and thread when I need one?'). Yet from the peripheral
activities of a monk's life much of social advantage might flow. Monastic
schools catered almost exclusively for novices, but of the large numbers of
secular schools which grew up in twelfth-century England, many were
situated in towns which already possessed a monastery. The monastic
scriptoria copied and multiplied books, and most of the narrative sources
which we possess were written in them. Monastic guest houses sheltered a
mixed multitude of travellers, ranging from kings on royal progresses to
pilgrims seeking distant shrines or indigent people looking for work, and
the monks' almsgiving was a considerable, though not the only, strand in
the relief of poverty. It is possible that this charity extended into the field of
medical work, since some houses are known to have contained
distinguished doctors whose reputation caused such people as Henry I to
borrow their services, and some founded dependent hospitals, such as St
Bartholomew's in London for poor, sick persons, or St Paul's in Norwich
as a refuge for the aged. Private patrons were encouraged by these
examples, as witness the leper hospital in Brackley, founded by the Zouche
family. Finally, monastic farming had a considerable influence upon the
economy of England, notably upon the wool trade.

Both before and after the Conquest the life of a hermit or of an enclosed
anchorite was popular and greatly respected. It is difficult to estimate the
number of such solitaries, but it is clear from scattered references that there
were many of them, and that their influence was considerable. Contemporar-
ary biographies of such people as Christina of Markyate, Godric of
Finchale and Wulfric of Haselbury provide an illuminating picture, not
only of the lives of the recluses themselves, but also of those who relied on
them for advice and guidance in all sorts of affairs, mundane as well as
spiritual. Most of the recluses of whose lives we have detailed knowledge
were English or Anglo-Scandinavian rather than Norman, and most came
from fairly prosperous middle-class families (Christina was the daughter of
a substantial burgess and his socially ambitious wife, and Godric had been a
successful merchant), although a few aristocratic ladies, like Ailred's sister
and Loretta the widowed Countess of Leicester, appear among their ranks.
The possession of a hermitage or anchorhold added distinction to a local
community. Hermits, who were free to go out of their cells, often

maintained themselves by work such as road-mending, the repair of bridges or the tending of beacons in return for their keep, although they also received charitable alms, and some had private patrons. Enclosed anchorites were maintained by patrons or by alms from the community, and there is evidence that some of them copied books, or sewed clothes for the poor. Their advice was eagerly sought. Christina was befriended by the Abbot of St Alban's, and seems to have become his spiritual counsellor. Wulfric's reputation brought people from all over southern England to ask for his advice, and he was credited with miraculous powers. It is reported that he once cured a dumb man so thoroughly that the patient was thereafter able to speak fluently not only in English but also in French, to the great vexation of the monolingual parish priest.

Such popularity could sometimes lead to trouble. The *Ancren Riwle*, written as a guide to three young women desiring to live as anchoresses, warns them against peering out of their windows, listening to gossip and entangling themselves in local feuds. In order to avoid disputes with the hayward they were advised to 'keep no beasts, but only a cat'.

Any study of the religious life in England in the period between the accession of Henry III and the middle of the fourteenth century is bound to take into account the Fourth Lateran Council of 1215, one of the major reforming councils of western Christendom. It was by the decrees of this council that the practice of confession and communion at least once a year was made binding upon all adult Catholics, that every vacant office or benefice in the church was to be filled within three months by a man whose fitness was to be tested by examination and checked by proper supervision, that church buildings and furnishings were to be properly maintained, that all marriages were to be celebrated in the presence of a priest and after due notice, and that regular provision was made for diocesan synods and visitations to maintain good order. Moreover, from 1198 onwards the papal registers had been regularly kept. This fact seems to have encouraged archbishops and bishops to arrange for the keeping of their own records according to the precedent set by Rome, employing in their chanceries trained scribes, and storing their archives in boxes and baskets. While it is possible, as the work of recent scholars has shown, to recover a great many *acta* of twelfth-century bishops, such material has to be painstakingly collected from widely scattered sources. From the time of Hugh of Wells, Bishop of Lincoln 1209–35, registers of the official *acta* of each bishop began to be kept. In their fully developed form these registers contained lists of ordinands and of persons instituted to prebends, benefices and headships of non-exempt religious houses, as well as copies of official letters and mandates sent out in the bishop's name. It is no accident that the list of incumbents of a parish church usually begins in the thirteenth century. Moreover, copies of synodal statutes were distributed to the senior clergy who assisted the bishop, and many of these have survived.

As a result of all this record-keeping, we know a good deal more about the English Church in this period than at any earlier time, and this very knowledge may bias our historical judgement. Reformers tend to bring to light what is wrong with a society; they ignore the silent, decent and unremarkable majority. They also tend to under-rate the work of their predecessors. Provincial and diocesan synods were now held more regularly, and episcopal visitations carried out more frequently than before, but they were not new. Archdeacons and rural deans had been holding their local courts to deal with sins and squabbles in the twelfth century, and if some marriages had been contracted with more gaiety than solemnity in taverns and other unsuitable places, most were already celebrated at the church door, and in the presence of a priest, before this practice became obligatory in 1215. It used to be thought that the Fourth Lateran Council was the landmark in safeguarding the livelihood of the parish priest; it is now known that vicarages were being properly established as early as 1170. Yet it is still true to say that the thirteenth century was a notable period of reform in diocesan history, and that this reform was the work of a remarkable series of bishops, supported by a large number of highly trained and usually very able administrators.

These bishops were an extremely hard-working body of men. Some, like Langton and Peckham of Canterbury and Grosseteste of Lincoln, were by any standard outstanding scholars; others, like Sutton of Lincoln and Martival of Salisbury, had distinguished themselves in university administration. A few owed their promotion to the kings' desire to provide for such men as Burnell, who had served them well in high offices of state. Such training did not mean that they were obsessed by mundane preoccupations. Rather, the experience of their earlier careers seems to have given them a particular degree of energy and thoroughness when dealing with their dioceses. Even when called away to play their part in the King's service or attend his councils they seem to have established, in suffragans, officials, vicars-general and archdeacons or their officials, thoroughly competent subordinates to carry on their work.

While the dean looked after the cathedral, the bishop's work took him out into the diocese. Ideally he was supposed to visit, examine and correct every part of it, beginning with his cathedral, once in three years. This was easier in small dioceses like Rochester than in very large ones such as York or Lincoln, or in Carlisle or Durham which lay upon a dangerous frontier. Since the contents of visitation records were of more ephemeral interest than synodal statutes few have survived. Still, it is clear from the registers

that bishops were constantly on the move, making a temporary base in one
of their manor houses or a convenient abbey, and going out three or more
times a week to one of the neighbouring churches, to which they had
caused all the local clergy, and representatives of the reliable laity, to be
summoned. Here they heard complaints, and investigated local standards
of faith and morals. They also visited all religious houses in the diocese
which were not, like the Cluniacs, covered by papal exemptions. Lists of
corrigenda were drawn up, and the bishop would appoint commissaries to
see that his instructions were properly carried out.

In the case of a parochial visitation, the enquiry would concern first the
priest and his church. He must be devout and diligent in his work, and
sufficiently literate to understand the Latin of the Gospels, Breviary and
Psalter, and to expound the relevant portions in the vernacular. It was
desirable that he should preach, and little books of homilies, with such
pleasant titles as *Dorme Secure*, existed to help him. He must also be able to
understand the instructions delivered to him in the diocesan or
archidiaconal synods, and to explain them to his people in the course of the
Sunday Mass, which was the only occasion when most of them would be
present. At such times not only moral exhortations and warnings were
delivered, but also public announcements, sentences of excommunication,
recommendations for charitable collections for good causes, and warnings
not to leave wells uncovered or fires unguarded, for the better preservation
of infants' lives. The priest should live as a celibate (in fact some cases of
faithful if unofficial concubinage and a few of profligacy came to light), and
he must keep his chancel, his church books and furnishings and his own
dwelling in good repair, provide the candles and incense, keep the Host
and the holy water under lock and key, and see that the churchyard was
properly fenced and that fairs, unlawful games and grazing animals were
kept out of it. Patrons and parishioners sometimes helped by providing
new vestments and books, or by setting up candle funds for the
maintenance of lights, for which the offerings of candles often demanded
from penitents must have been helpful. The rector's livelihood was
provided from his tithes, his glebe lands, and the traditional offerings at
Mass, the churching of women and funerals (the last often taking the form
of the dead man's second-best beast or chattel). There were often small,
supplementary presents sanctioned by custom, such as eggs at Easter or
loaves of bread. In a prebendal or appropriated church the vicar's portion
of the income was determined by the bishop at not less than five marks a
year. Old and sick incumbents were not retired (except by their own wish),
but were provided with coadjutors responsible for them and their parishes.
The enquiry covered also private chapels held under licence from the

bishop, and chantries established to provide a perpetual service of prayer for the dead.

The lay parishioners were bound to know by heart the Lord's Prayer, the Hail Mary and the Creed, and to be able to make the sign of the cross. They were to attend Mass on Sundays and great feast days, and to come regularly to communion and confession, for which purpose the priest was to explain to them the Ten Commandments, the three theological and four cardinal virtues, the seven deadly sins and the seven works of mercy. They were also to pay their tithes, bring their babies for baptism (or in emergency baptize them themselves, using the proper formula), and marry at the church door in the sight and hearing of witnesses. Three or four times a year, at the so-called 'cursing seasons', the priest would publicly denounce as excommunicate all unknown sinners who had committed such crimes as murder, robbery, sacrilege, removal of a neighbour's landmark or, after 1281, breach of the provisions of Magna Carta. It is impossible to say whether these blanket excommunications provoked many people to confession and repentance, but they would hardly have remained a regular part of the church's life had they been entirely ineffective. People were also warned against afflicting their children, especially girls, with frivolous or unsuitable names, and against superstitious practices such as the veneration of trees or unauthorized holy wells. Of serious heresy there was very little trace in England.

The thirteenth century saw the rise of religious orders of a new type: the friars, whose most notable examples in England were the Dominicans and Franciscans. Unlike monks, they were not bound by the vow of stability; their profession was dedicated to the reform of the secular world. Their houses were normally established in towns, not as centres of the contemplative life but as bases from which to sally out on their lawful business (a fact which made them immediately suspect to established monks). Dominicans aimed at fighting the devil and refuting heretics by their high standard of orthodox learning, and by training good preachers. The Franciscans' original aim was to convert and serve the urban poor by implicating themselves in a life of equal poverty, but later they modified their customs and paid greater attention to learning. Both orders were immediately subject to the Pope, and cosmopolitan in their recruitment. Not subject to diocesan control, they could preach anywhere except in churches to which they had not been directed by the bishop, and their sermons, often delivered at market crosses, seem to have been popular. As trained preachers they knew the art of keeping people awake, and many of the odder stories in which medieval literature abounds come from the friars' *exempla*.

Friars gained influence in high places. It became customary for the royal family to choose them as confessors. Some became archbishops. Grosseteste, the learned Bishop of Lincoln, was a friend of such notable scholar-friars as Adam Marsh, and was himself lector to the Franciscans at Oxford while Chancellor of the university.

English cathedral schools had been notable since the early twelfth century, although Englishmen tended to gravitate to Paris. Oxford and Cambridge, which achieved university status in the thirteenth century, were not cathedral cities, but each possessed a bridge on a notable trade route, and each lay in territory fertile enough to maintain a population of clerks who, while 'seeking the pearl of wisdom in the field of learning,' made no immediate contribution to the economy. The fact that the cathedral chancellor was somewhat remote seems to have encouraged their independent growth. Oxford was already notable in the early twelfth century. Cambridge, originally rivalled by Northampton, developed after a migration from Oxford in 1209, and achieved fame before 1250. Both were universities of the magisterial type, ruled by a congregation of regent (teaching) and non-regent masters. At their head was a chancellor, elected, according to the regents, by themselves, and appointed, according to the bishop, by himself. The curriculum was of the normal medieval type, with four faculties, of arts, law, medicine and theology, the mastership of arts being required as the basis for work in any of the others. Students matriculated young (at about sixteen) and were expected to be already fluent in Latin, the language of instruction. Since books were expensive, teaching was by lecture and disputation. Lodgings were at first precarious, but later some of the regent masters rented halls, and lodged in them along with their students. After the middle of the thirteenth century colleges began to be founded, either as charitable or chantry bequests, and these soon included houses of study for members of religious orders. The Chancellor had jurisdiction over all members of the university, and was assisted by two proctors, whose chief function seems to have been to keep the scholars out of the clutches of the lay courts.

The English Church in this period was an essentially orthodox body, holding fast to the traditions of western Christendom. Heresy was almost non-existent, and any resistance to the Pope's pronouncements arose rather from a dislike of foreigners, and especially of tax collectors, than from any questioning of papal authority. Great scholars such as John of Salisbury, Robert Grosseteste and William of Ockham took a high place in the intellectual life of the time. But the outstanding quality which distinguished the English province was the strongly practical nature of its organization. With few exceptions, the clergy commanded the respect of contemporaries – and command ours also: they worked hard, and in difficult circumstances they usually did very well. The Church in England was a faithful part of Catholic Christendom, and the practice of its people reflected that, but it was already showing some of those qualities which would lead in later centuries to the Anglican tradition.

4

Piety in the Later Middle Ages

Norman Tanner

THE *OXFORD ENGLISH DICTIONARY* gives as one of its definitions of piety 'devotion to religious duties and observances; godliness, devoutness, religiousness'. The emphasis is on inner religious life rather than on the externals of ecclesiastical organization – rightly so for this chapter, partly because the whole book is a history of religion, not of ecclesiastical organization, and partly for a reason special to the years between 1350 and 1520 (the period covered in this essay). That is to say, the external structures of the medieval English Church were largely established by the thirteenth century; there were relatively few changes thereafter and it would be tedious to repeat what has already been said in earlier chapters. In the area of popular piety and devotions, on the other hand, there were important developments in the late medieval period, and these will be our principal concern.

It is important to begin with an overview of the religious outlook in late medieval England because only if we understand the overall framework and mentality of the period will the details make sense. The starting point is that England was part of Western Christendom. This fact provides the basic context. The split between the Eastern Church, centred on Constantinople, and the Western Church, centred on Rome, had become formal in 1054 with the mutual exchange of anathemas by the leaders of both churches. Thereafter the two churches went their more or less separate ways. At the end of the period, with the sixteenth-century Reformation, the Western Church itself became fragmented into Catholics and Protestants. In the meantime, and therefore throughout our period, England was an integral part of Western Christendom. It is necessary to remember this, because there has been much discussion among historians about the independence of the English Church in the late middle ages.

It is certainly true that the Church in England enjoyed a considerable measure of autonomy in the fourteenth and fifteenth centuries, as indeed did other national churches. It was to be seen in the areas of liturgy,

spirituality and devotional life, intellectual matters, Church government
and law, and it was accompanied by a certain distancing from the papacy.
In many ways Western Christendom was a federation of national and
regional churches, but this did not mean that the individual churches were
cut off from each other. They were parts of a whole, semi-autonomous but
sharing basic things in common and in communion with each other.

In area Western Christendom was approximately the same as Western
Europe today, plus some parts of central Europe. In other respects it was
very different. In population we may guess that it comprised around 60
million people shortly before the beginning of the period, with somewhat
less than half that number in Eastern Christendom. The number was
dramatically reduced by the Black Death of 1348–9 and its subsequent
outbreaks, perhaps by as much as a third or even more, and the earlier peak
had probably not been reached again by 1520. Western Christendom,
moreover, occupied a small corner of the world. Today Christianity is a
global religion with adherents in almost every part of the world. This state
of affairs has brought a certain self-confidence, a sense that Christianity is
an expanding religion. But the situation is relatively new, largely the result
of the discovery of the new world in the sixteenth century and Europe's
colonial expansion in the nineteenth. The late middle ages did not share
this optimistic mood. At that time Christianity had existed for well over a
millennium and yet seemed to be making little progress. Indeed, in many
ways it was a shrinking religion. That is to say, Christianity, and a *fortiori*
Western Christendom, was probably smaller in geographical extent than it
had been a thousand years earlier, in the last century of the Roman empire.
Gains in north and central Europe had been offset by massive losses,
mostly to Islam, in the near east and north Africa. Islam, although a much
younger religion than Christianity, was already more widespread. It
continued to advance, except in Spain, and to threaten Christendom,
culminating in the capture of Constantinople in 1453. There was also the
threat from the north-east. Mongols had captured Budapest in 1242 and
the memory of them was still fresh. The final defeat and extinction of
Christendom must have seemed a real possibility.

There was also a sense of cultural inferiority. Four cultures or
civilizations were felt to be, in various ways, superior to Christianity. The
first of these was Judaism, a much older religion than Christianity, which
possessed in many ways a richer culture and whose people were renowned
for their skills in business and other walks of life. The second was Islam,
which, as we have seen, was expanding faster and more widely than
Christianity; its architects and artists were at least as skilled as Christians,
as travellers to Spain and the near east could see, and its philosophers,
notably Avicenna and Averroës and other commentators on Aristotle, were

the envy of western scholars. The third was Byzantium, the heir and preserver of the ancient world, with its great city of Constantinople; and the fourth, the ancient world of Greece and Rome, long since vanished except in Byzantium, yet surviving vigorously in people's memory and still largely unsurpassed by the west in its achievements in philosophy, literature, art, government and law. In these respects too, then, our period pre-dates the intellectual self-confidence, at times arrogance, which became associated with Christianity as it developed into a dominant world religion from the sixteenth century onwards. The underlying mood was rather one of unease and defensiveness. Many of the attitudes and responses of the period, which may appear to us today as strange or unnecessarily aggressive, such as the crusades, the obsession with heresy or the expulsion of Jews, must be seen in this context. People who are ill at ease or threatened often act in such ways.

These feelings of insecurity were compounded by the disasters and crises of the fourteenth and fifteenth centuries, making the late middle ages a period of more acute and pressing problems than the period covered by the previous chapter. The consequences of the Black Death and its recurrences have already been mentioned. There were also some unusually severe famines, and there was probably a climatic change for the worse, reflected in the fact that England stopped growing grapes for making wine in the fourteenth century. From 1337 to 1453 England and France were locked in the Hundred Years War, with its associated political insecurity and economic demands. Then there were ecclesiastical and intellectual crises. In 1305 the papacy was transferred from its traditional home in Rome to Avignon in France, where it remained until 1377. This change was especially objectionable to England, which was at war with France for the latter half of that period. It was followed by the Great Schism from 1378 to 1417, when Western Christendom was divided in its allegiance between two and later three popes, and then by the Conciliar Movement lasting until 1449, when a reunited papacy quarrelled with a succession of general councils over supremacy in the Church. Our period ends with some worldly and immoral popes such as Alexander VI and Julius II.

This institutional fragmentation was accompanied by a breakdown in the intellectual synthesis of the twelfth and thirteenth centuries. That is to say, the harmonizing of the Christian faith with philosophical reason, apparently achieved with remarkable success by Thomas Aquinas and others in the thirteenth century, was called into question and eventually shattered. Duns Scotus from Scotland and William of Ockham from Surrey, both Franciscan friars and both students and teachers at Oxford University, were important figures in this process.

There was also the re-emergence of heresy: John Wyclif and the Lollards in England and John Hus and his followers in Bohemia. Other aspects of the late medieval crisis could be mentioned: apparent stagnation in the religious orders, the obsession with death in art, and an anti-intellectualism in devotional life, to be found in Thomas à Kempis's *Imitation of Christ*. Some writers talk of almost unmitigated gloom: French historians often speak of a *conjoncture de crise* – a coming together of many elements to produce a fundamental crisis of identity. But this may be to exaggerate. Human beings are remarkably resilient and, as we shall see, there was great vigour and activity in late medieval England. Insecurity, mostly subconscious, seems to me more characteristic of the period than pessimism, but the contrast with the expansionist mood that prevailed in the sixteenth century and after is striking. This was the world in which England found itself after 1350, and it forms the essential framework for the rest of this chapter.

England was a country of somewhere around five million inhabitants in 1300, reduced to perhaps three million by the Black Death and its recurrences, and slowly rising again after about 1450. Of those people nine-tenths lived in the countryside, only one-tenth in towns; the opposite of today. We are therefore dealing with a basically agrarian society, not an urban one, and this has important implications for popular religion. Also important was the fact that Christianity was already an old religion in England by the beginning of our period. It had existed in the country since the Roman occupation and had been almost the only religion since the conversion of the Danish settlers in the tenth century; the Jews were expelled from the country in 1290. Two significant points follow from this: first, we are dealing with an inherited religious situation, with all the complexity and weight that this inevitably brings; and second, we are treating of a single-religion society, not a pluralist society like modern England, in which Christianity is only one religion among others and in which religion is merely one facet of life among many others – sport, education, politics, work. Christianity was effectively the only religion in late medieval England, and it permeated every aspect of life. Its role was more akin to that of Catholicism in Poland or northern Portugal until recently, or even to that of Islam in a modern Islamic state.

What was this Christianity like? A beginning may be made to answering this question by describing the main religious institutions and activities of the time, and of these the parish must be the starting point. In the countryside the parish would have been the religious institution with which most people came into contact most immediately. Its importance has been described in the previous chapter, and what was said there applies to our period too. Its continuing vitality is shown by the remarkable programme of rebuilding parish churches all over the country between the fourteenth and the early sixteenth century. During this period, most parish churches were extensively rebuilt on a larger and grander scale, usually in what is called the Late English Gothic or Perpendicular style. Indeed, most of what we actually see today of our medieval parish churches dates from this period. The rebuilding was of course a work of piety in itself, but it also attested to the importance of all that went on inside the church. This meant first of all the official round of services and sacraments, but also a wide range of other activities. Pious confraternities, craft guilds and chantries were often attached to particular parish churches. Hermits and anchorites, too, were often based on them. In all these ways the parish church was a major focus of the local community. It was quite a hive of activity including sometimes secular activity, though the ecclesiastical authorities tried to restrict that. It would probably also have been a blaze of colour, especially in the late medieval period – a point worth emphasizing, because we tend to think of medieval churches as simple and bare. That austerity, however, was largely the result of the Reformation and afterwards, when so many of the statues, wall paintings and stained-glass windows were destroyed. When whitewash is removed, as is the case at Chaldon in Surrey or at South Leigh or Chalgrove in Oxfordshire, we are sometimes able to see just how much of the walls was formerly covered with religious paintings depicting biblical scenes or lives of the saints. Similarly, a reading of William Dowsing's *Journal* reveals in great detail the iconoclasm wreaked by him on English churches during the Civil War period. Even so, much remains visible to the discerning eye, such as the painted rood panels in many Norfolk churches. These works of art were not only an expression of piety and a decoration for the church, but also a means of religious education through the biblical and other scenes which they depicted. Finally, at the apex of the parochial system, there were the great cathedrals, one or occasionally two for each of the seventeen dioceses into which England was divided. The cathedrals contained everything mentioned above, plus a certain amount more at the episcopal level, conducted on a grander but probably a rather less personal level than in the parish churches.

Every parish had, or ought to have had, at least one priest who had the official spiritual care of his parishioners – the 'cure of souls' as it was sometimes called. This brings us to a second major feature of the religious scenery of late medieval England: the clergy and religious orders. They too have already been discussed in earlier chapters, and what was said there mostly applies to our period also. There were no major changes in organization. England continued to be divided into the two ecclesiastical provinces of Canterbury and York, each with its own archbishop and comprising fourteen and three dioceses respectively; these dioceses in turn were sub-divided into archdeaconries, deaneries and finally some 9,000 parishes. The religious orders founded in the previous centuries continued: the absence of any new religious order might be regarded as a weakness of the period. The only significant growth point was the increase in the number of monasteries of the Carthusian order, which was generally regarded as the most austere of all the orders, from three to nine between the end of the thirteenth century and the fifteenth. As for overall numbers, it has been estimated that the number of men in religious orders in England stood at around 14,000 (in about a thousand houses) in 1300, declined by at least a third from the time of the Black Death onwards, and later grew slowly to about 10,000 in 1520. To this total should be added perhaps twice as many members of the secular clergy (called 'secular' to distinguish them from members of religious orders, who lived under a 'rule' and therefore were called 'regular' clergy): that is, perhaps an average of two priests attached to each of the 9,000 or so parishes, plus a number in ecclesiastical administration, in the universities and serving as schoolmasters, as private chaplains to families or to craft guilds and pious confraternities, a considerable number as chantry priests, a few freelance priests, and a number of clerics who were waiting to be ordained priests. According to these figures, approximately one in fifty of the male population of England, and a correspondingly higher proportion of the adult men, were clerics or members of religious orders. For women the figures were very much smaller, in contrast to recent times; the number of nuns has been estimated at about 3,000 in 1300, falling sharply after the Black Death, and later slowly rising to around 2,000 in 1520.

The clergy and religious orders were an integral part of popular religion, both as ways of life chosen by a significant proportion of the population and through the influence they exercised on the laity. We should therefore be wary of stressing an artificial contrast between clerical religion on the one hand and lay piety on the other. All clerics and religious, after all, had spent the first fifteen or twenty years of their life as lay people, and most of them kept close contacts (some would say too close) with the lay world throughout the rest of their lives. In this sense they were an expression and intensification of lay Christianity, not ranged in opposition to it. There has, however, been considerable debate among historians about whether their ways of life were in decline in our period. We have noted the decline in numbers, but there is no reason to think that it was significantly sharper, proportionally, than in the population as a whole. As for a decline in morals and discipline, visitation records reveal many faults of all kinds. This evidence cannot be ignored, but we should remember that we are dealing with a large number of frail human beings in difficult callings, so that a certain amount of failure is to be expected; it is far from clear that the faults were graver or more widespread than in either the earlier or the later periods. Anticlericalism was certainly a significant feature in late medieval England, as can be seen from these visitation records and from the works of Chaucer and Langland, and more violently from the killings of clerics in the popular revolts of 1381 and 1450, but overall it seems to have been less intense than in most parts of the European continent. The protest tended to have as its aim the reform of the clergy and religious orders, rather than their abolition. In general there was co-operation in England at many levels between the laity and the clergy and religious, and their relationship was one more of complementarity than of opposition.

The parishes, the clergy and religious orders represented the 'old order' of Christianity in late medieval England: that is to say, the religious institutions that were already well established in the country before 1350. They continued to remain very influential and to retain vitality during the late middle ages. Nevertheless, the period also saw new religious developments. Some of these were wholly new in the late middle ages; others had existed before but flowered in this period and were specially characteristic of it. In most of them England was following developments elsewhere in Europe, emphasizing the extent to which the country was part of Western Christendom. In some cases, however, there were particularly English characteristics. Most of these new movements were focused on the laity, underlining the point that in England, as elsewhere in Europe, the late middle ages was especially an age of lay piety.

Perhaps the best-known of the newer institutions were craft guilds and pious confraternities. Some had existed in England well before 1300, but their golden age was the fourteenth and fifteenth centuries. Craft guilds were associations of the members of a particular craft or trade in a particular town. Their primary purpose was the social and economic regulation of the craft or trade, but almost all of them had a religious dimension. Pious confraternities had similar religious activities but were normally centred on a parish church or a religious house, rather than on a craft or trade. A central feature was the annual 'day' of the guild or confraternity, usually the feast day of the saint to whom it was dedicated. The day comprised a mixture of religious and social activities: usually a Mass for all living and dead members, other religious devotions, and finally a banquet for the members. Many guilds and confraternities made provision for members in need, whether from sickness or poverty, and a few had their own hospitals. They took part in civic and religious processions, and the craft guilds were normally responsible for the mystery plays. We still have four almost complete texts of these cycles of plays – from Coventry, York, Chester and one unknown location – and we know that there were many more. Each of the cycles contained between twelve and about fifty plays giving a remarkably full representation of the stories of both the Old and the New Testament. The whole cycle was performed on one day, usually at Whitsuntide or on the feast of Corpus Christi. The plays were often performed on movable carts, so that each play would be performed several times in different parts of the town. Each craft was normally responsible for a particular play. It must have been a colourful day in the town's life, and the plays would have acted as a tourist attraction, drawing in many from the surrounding countryside. Probably some of the plays were subsequently performed in smaller towns and villages of the area, many of which, like Ashburton in Devon, had their own interludes performed by parish guilds. In these and other ways guilds and confraternities would have influenced the countryside, but they were primarily urban institutions.

Chantries were another institution particularly characteristic of the late middle ages. In essence they were the saying or 'chanting' of Masses and other prayers for various people, especially souls in purgatory. They were based on the belief that God allowed the benefit of Masses and prayers to be given to various people in these ways. As institutions, they could be an entire college of priests, sometimes a university college, such as All Souls College at Oxford, which was founded by the Archbishop of Canterbury in 1438 for forty priests, with the object of their praying for the souls of King Henry V and those Englishmen who had died in the wars in France, as well as of forming an academic institution. Less grandly, they might be a single priest saying a daily Mass in perpetuity (hence called a 'perpetual' chantry) for the founder of the chantry and his or her family, often in a specially constructed chapel within the parish church or cathedral, like the ornate Beaufort chapel in Warwick or the simpler Holme chapel in Holy Trinity, Goodramgate at York. Or they might be simply half a dozen Masses which a tradesman asked in his will to be said for his soul. Priests said the Masses but the laity, as founders and benefactors of the chantries, could exercise much control in other respects, determining the number and even the times of the Masses as well as various supplementary prayers to be said at them and at other times. Chantries were thus an aspect of lay piety expressing a form of eucharistic devotion which increased greatly throughout Western Christendom at this time. In London, on the eve of the dissolution of the chantries under Henry VIII, there were forty-four perpetual chantries in St Paul's Cathedral alone and a further 186 of them in the city's parish churches; and there appear to have been at least 200 chantry priests in York in the mid-fifteenth century. The institution was obviously open to abuse, as reformers were quick to point out – the unnecessary multiplication of Masses, the appearance of buying and selling Masses; but a chantry also expressed much beauty and good theology in its worship. Founded on the Eucharist, it witnessed to the centrality of the suffering, death and resurrection of Jesus Christ, and was normally an act of spiritual charity to the founder's friends and neighbours as well as being of benefit to him or her. Finally, chantries were a way of beautifying and diversifying the worship in cathedrals and parish churches, and the priests assigned to them often assisted with parochial duties.

Hermits and anchorites had existed in England at least since the seventh century but appear to have become significantly more numerous in the late middle ages. Indeed, their number appears to have been unusually large in comparison with most continental countries. Anchors and anchoresses (known collectively as anchorites) lived a solitary life in a cell (called an anchorage), which was usually attached to a parish church or a religious house, and devoted themselves principally to prayer, though they would do some work and many acted as counsellors. Hermits were also solitaries primarily devoted to a life of prayer, but they were not fixed to a particular abode, and almost all were men. Some of them performed civic tasks such as looking after a gate in the city wall or a bridge; others seem to have felt free to move from place to place. Sometimes the journey was an act of penance for others: a hermit called Richard Ferneys was bequeathed £40 in the will of a wealthy Norwich merchant in 1429, 'to make a pilgrimage for me to Rome, going round there fifteen times in a great circle, and also to Jerusalem, doing in both places as a true pilgrim does'. Unfortunately we are not told whether he accepted the challenge! In large cities like London, York and Norwich there were probably half a dozen hermits and anchorites living there at any given time. Altogether we know of several hundred of them between 1350 and 1520, about half of whom were women and half men. Most of them were lay people, but some were nuns, monks, friars or priests, as it were on loan from their religious houses or parishes. The many anchoresses were an important aspect of female religion, and they partly offset the small number of women who became nuns. Indeed, the most famous of all these recluses was a woman, Julian of Norwich, the anchoress and author of the spiritual classic, *Revelations of Divine Love*. They were normally expected to take a vow to persevere in their way of life until death. It was obviously a very difficult vocation, and most individuals probably embarked on it in middle age. But a few were young: Richard Rolle, also a renowned writer of devotional works, appears to have become a hermit at the age of 18.

Hermits and anchorites represent an attempt to lead a committed Christian life outside the traditional framework of religious orders. Beguinages were another way of doing this, but in a community rather than by a solitary life. These communities of lay women (called 'beguines' after their alleged founder, Lambert le Bègue), originally living in ordinary houses rather than in convents, were very popular in the Low Countries and the Rhineland. In England, however, they appear to have been virtually non-existent; only two or three possible communities in Norwich are known to us. This absence is remarkable and suggests, when taken with the unusually large number of hermits and anchorites, that there was already a solitary and reserved element in English piety.

Pilgrimages in late medieval England have been immortalized by Chaucer's *Canterbury Tales*. They remained a popular and important devotion for most of our period, though they were probably in decline in the early sixteenth century, and the fortunes of individual shrines varied considerably. A mixture of religious devotion and a social outing, they were typical of medieval religion and of the way in which religion was interwoven with the rest of life. The journey might be to the shrine of a local saint, to one of the national shrines such as St Thomas of Canterbury or Our Lady of Walsingham, or to one of the great shrines abroad, principally Jerusalem, Rome and St James of Compostela in Spain. Margery Kempe, the eccentric but very devout wife of a (King's) Lynn merchant, travelled to all three shrines abroad as well as to others in Germany and Norway, and to many others in England, between 1413 and 1433. The registers of St Thomas's Hospice in Rome, which was a hostel for English pilgrims in the city, recorded more than 200 pilgrims a year between 1479 and 1514. Another form of holy journey, the crusade to recapture the Holy Land, on the other hand, was undoubtedly in decline. It seems to have retained some importance as an ideal, but with the fall in 1291 of Acre, the last Christian stronghold in the Holy Land, its success became increasingly unlikely. Crusades continued to be called, even into the sixteenth century, and a few people from England participated, but they were more of a dream than a reality. The years of the capture of Jerusalem and of King Richard I were long since past. Both the need to call crusades and their failure formed part of Christendom's sense of insecurity in this period.

These were the principal religious activities and institutions of late medieval England. There were others which we would classify as educational or charitable or social, but which for medieval people included an essentially religious element. In education, Oxford and Cambridge remained the only two universities in the country, with about 1,000–1,500 students in each. They continued to be principally for the education of the clergy, although laymen were coming in increasing numbers in the fifteenth and early sixteenth centuries. In addition, we know of several hundred schools and there were probably considerably more. In these, learning for a lay career was becoming more important, but religion remained a central element and many of the schoolboys would have gone on to become priests. For girls the possibilities were more limited. Charity towards one's neighbour was a basic religious duty, and we know of over 500 hospitals in the country. Most of them were in towns and had been founded in the twelfth and thirteenth centuries, when urban growth had made these institutions necessary. Medical knowledge was primitive, so that we should think of hospitals as being for the care of the sick, the elderly and the marginalized in society, rather than for the cure of illnesses in our modern sense. Finally, we turn to daily work, the family and everyday life. These too, as we have seen from the parishes, the craft guilds and other things, were influenced by Christianity at many levels, from the solemnization of marriage and the other rites of passage to the organization of holy days and other communal celebrations.

This outline of the religious institutions and activities of the time is a necessary prelude to consideration of the inner aspect of religion which is our main concern. For medieval people there was far less of a distinction between the outer and the inner aspects of religion than for us today. This was partly because people were largely unlettered and therefore did not think conceptually to anything like the same extent as we do now, and partly because their actions were much more unified and public, less compartmentalized and private, than those of people today, reflecting the fact that late medieval England was a single-religion society. Medieval people thought and expressed themselves largely by what they did, and therefore their external activities were the key to, indeed for the most part *were*, their inner piety. It is therefore important to take seriously their institutions and activities, and to realize that these for the most part summarized the piety of the age.

Only in a very secondary place was there a private and intellectual piety in our modern sense. This is not to disparage medieval religion in any way, but simply to say that it was learnt and practised in significantly different ways from today. The extent of this more intellectual piety depended much on the level of literacy. Among the clergy, at least among the minority who had studied at a university, we may assume a certain level of learning. Among the laity, literacy was undoubtedly increasing in our period, but it still pertained only to a minority. As for the books they read and used for prayer, there is the basic and sad fact that no complete Bible in an English translation was generally available. The only one, the 'Wycliffite' Bible, was banned by the ecclesiastical authorities because of its associations with John Wyclif. It is true that the Bible was present in many ways: there was the Latin Vulgate version; many books contained extracts in English from the Bible; reference was made to it in most other religious works; and its message was communicated through the liturgy, paintings and stained-glass windows in churches, the mystery plays, and many other ways. So it would be wrong to think of late medieval Christianity as non-biblical. Nevertheless, the absence of an approved English translation of the Bible had a major and detrimental influence on English piety. The most popular books were missals, breviaries containing the Divine Office, and other prayer books. These could be used for a combination of vocal and meditative prayer as well as for following the liturgical services. Lives of saints were also popular, as were works of mystical writers; we know that such books were often read aloud to a group of people. Here we may note that England produced four of the most important mystical writers of the period: Richard Rolle and Julian of Norwich have already been mentioned, and to these we must add Walter Hilton and the unknown author of *The Cloud of Unknowing*. There was also the world of university learning. How far the universities influenced popular piety is much debated. Indeed, a common criticism of the time was that university theology was too abstract and academic, insufficiently in contact with everyday religion; there was a certain split between faith and reason, as mentioned earlier, and an element of anti-intellectualism in religion, though this should not be exaggerated.

So far England has been considered in a rather uniform way, but it is important to remember the differences within the country. Those between town and countryside have already been mentioned. There were also regional differences, though these are more difficult to define. That is to say, England was in many ways still a federation of regions, each with its own characteristics, and this was apparent in religious matters. There were the regional liturgical rites of Salisbury, York, Hereford, Norwich and Lincoln, though by our period the first-named (normally called the 'Sarum' rite, after the Latin name of the town) was becoming predominant over the whole country. The various cycles of mystery plays were centred on different regions. Each region had its own provincial capital, which acted as a religious metropolis for the area: York for the north, Norwich for East Anglia, London for the south-east, and so on. And each region seems to have had characteristic elements in its piety: a type of High Church, almost baroque, religion in East Anglia and parts of the north, typified by Norwich and York; a more reserved, Puritan religion in the south-east and the midlands, illustrated by the Lollard centres in London, Coventry and Leicester. Within a region there would be marked differences between one village and another, depending on the interests and abilities of the parishioners and the parish priest, and on other factors. Finally, there were the perennial differences between human beings – of age, temperament, condition of life and personal choice.

These personal differences merit further attention. The wide range of religious institutions and activities provided much for most tastes and temperaments: there were some things for more active and exuberant characters, others for more contemplative characters and a strong place for feminine features. People responded in a correspondingly wide variety of ways to these opportunities. Nobody could engage in everything, nor was he or she expected to. There was a certain minimum – mainly parochial duties – to which all were expected to conform, but beyond that there was much freedom of choice. At one end of the spectrum came Margery Kempe, who engaged with amazing energy in almost every aspect of the religion of her day: distant pilgrimages, frequent attendance at sermons and religious services, wide knowledge of religious books (by having them read to her), a vow of celibacy, taken together with her husband, but only after rearing a family of fourteen children; yet even she was accused of heresy, partly because she was considered to be too actively engaged. Others engaged deeply but in a more restricted range of things, such as the hermit Richard Rolle or the anchoress Julian of Norwich. Yet others were deeply committed to certain things but were critical of others, such as John Wyclif or William of Ockham. There is not much evidence of outright rejection of Christianity, but it is likely that there was some, and clearly people would avoid leaving around evidence of views for which they might be prosecuted; certainly witchcraft and occult practices continued to exist, and the mystical elements of traditional religion were sometimes erroneously invested with magical connotations. The sheer range and intensity of religious activities – all for a population of at most about five million – show this to have been a remarkably religious period. None the less, this activity must be seen in terms of people: piety overall means in actuality many very different and complex individuals, who cannot be simplified into an average man or woman in the street.

Any account of late medieval piety would be incomplete without some further mention of John Wyclif, who was probably the most influential person produced by the English Church during the late middle ages and who, with his followers, produced the only indigenous heretical movement to be prosecuted by the authorities. Wyclif was born around 1330, probably in Yorkshire. He studied at the University of Oxford, was ordained a priest, and spent almost all the remainder of his life as a teacher at that university, retiring in 1381 to the rectory of Lutterworth in Leicestershire, where he died three years later. He was the leading English philosopher of his time, but he is known to us chiefly because of his breach with the Church. This began with his attacks on various abuses in the Church, such as excessive clerical wealth and the holding of political power by bishops and priests, but he went on to attack a number of doctrines, notably regarding the Eucharist and other sacraments and the authority of the Church. It was his doctrinal attacks that resulted in his official condemnation, though this was muted until after his death. He emphasized the importance of the Bible and encouraged an English translation of it, though it is now thought unlikely that he took a direct hand in the version that was later produced. A group of followers gathered round him, subsequently called Lollards as a term of abuse (the word was apparently derived from the Dutch *lollen*, 'to mumble', and meant a vagabond or religious eccentric). At first they were mostly Oxford dons, but even in his lifetime he had a wider influence. Subsequently the movement spread to most parts of England and to almost all ranks of society, but degrees of support varied greatly and it always remained a minority position. Lollardy got caught up in an unsuccessful revolt led by Sir John Oldcastle in 1414, and thereafter the movement lost direct influence, though there is some evidence of a limited revival from about 1490 onwards.

Wyclif and the Lollards showed both the strengths and the weaknesses of the Church of their day. The fact that the English Church was hesitant to condemn him shows that there was more tolerance, and a wider range of acceptable opinions within the framework of orthodoxy, than we might have expected. Indeed, when William Sawtry became the first Lollard martyr in 1401, he was the first English man or woman to be put to death for heresy since 1216 – a remarkable gap and one of which England may be proud, inasmuch as it stands in contrast to almost every other European country of the time and provides a medieval ancestry for its much later and just reputation for religious toleration. But Wyclif and many Lollards went too far, becoming strident and extreme in their attacks, and unfortunately the Church authorities reacted too far in the other direction. Over a hundred Lollards were burnt in the fifteenth and early sixteenth centuries, and religious opinion became somewhat polarized between supporters and opponents of Wyclif. This led to a certain stagnation in religious life, with healthy reforms and new movements not being sufficiently encouraged or even tolerated by the ecclesiastical authorities; much of the range and variety noted above derived from local or individual initiatives rather than from officially organized movements for reform. Wyclif was not the direct cause of the Reformation in England, but he played an indirect role. Relatively few were willing to accept his extreme views, but the whole climate of opinion was influenced by what he had said; in this way he prepared the ground and is rightly called the 'morning star' of the English Reformation.

To attempt to conclude this chapter is difficult. Piety in late medieval England was a varied and complex phenomenon and we have been dealing with a long period of time. I hope that at least I have shown something of its variety and complexity, and demonstrated that any attempt to simplify matters would be to trivialize the people of the time. I would like to close by indicating some recent trends in research and in debates among historians.

Two of the oldest debates have been about the independence of the English Church and whether the alleged decadence of the late medieval period caused and justified the Reformation. Sometimes these debates have been rather *parti pris*, with both Protestant and Roman Catholic historians having certain axes to grind. Recent historians, however, have widened both debates. In the first case, they have emphasized that there were many other points of reference and loyalty for English people besides the papacy, such as Western Christendom as a whole, the region, town or countryside, and the parish, so that too much concentration on relations with the papacy distorts the true situation. In the second case, they have shown that there was remarkable vitality within popular religion, even if there were areas of decadence within the institutional Church, so that England's religion in the sixteenth century, both Reformation and Counter-Reformation, must be seen as springing out of late medieval religion as much as in reaction against it. Certainly most historians would now agree with William Pantin's judgement on fourteenth-century England and extend it to the fifteenth and early sixteenth centuries: 'With all the faults and scandals of the times, and there were many, it was at the same time a profoundly religious period.' Indeed, most historians would argue that the Church was in much better shape in England than in most other countries of late medieval Europe. Cardinal Wolsey, for example, with his immorality and glaring abuses, was exceptional in England, whereas he would have been quite a common figure in France, Germany or Italy at the time.

Another recent trend among historians has been to move away from the study of the institutional Church and towards the study of popular religion, called 'traditional religion' by its recent and distinguished historian, Eamon Duffy. It is an attempt to investigate 'inner' rather than 'outer' religion, and is usually accompanied by a 'from below' approach to Church history; that is to say, a method which begins at the grass-roots level of ordinary Christians and what religion meant to them, as distinct from an earlier convention of beginning with the institutional Church of bishops and ecclesiastical authorities, and then more or less trying to deduce from this the religion of the faithful. This chapter reflects that trend, but two caveats must be stressed, both of which have already been mentioned. In both cases the distinction must not be drawn too sharply, as if the two aspects were in opposition to each other: that is to say, for mostly unlettered people, such as in late medieval England, piety chiefly consists of their external religious activities, not something beyond or different from them; and the older and more clerical religion was for the most part complementary, not in opposition, to the newer and more lay-oriented religion of the period.

Late medieval England, which still stands about us in its splendid legacy of great churches and cathedrals, remains in part a *terra incognita* to the modern mind. To recapture the spirit of that rich and varied world, with its many mansions of the spirit and its heights of intellectual, literary, mystical and artistic achievement, is a challenge to our sensibilities, but no one contemplating the spiritual and material remains of the period can doubt the value of the exercise.

5

Medieval Wales and the Reformation

Glanmor Williams

THE CELTIC CHURCH

CHRISTIANITY, IT HARDLY needs saying, formed no part of the original Celtic heritage of the Welsh. It was first brought to Britain by Roman merchants and soldiers and, during the era of imperial rule, remained very much a religion of the towns and the civilian settlements, of which there were relatively few in Wales. When the legions finally departed, Christianity undoubtedly survived, as may be gleaned from the archaeological record of a Roman town like Caerwent or the Roman villa at Llantwit Major, and also from the accounts of missions by St Germanus of Auxerre, who came to Britain in the fifth century AD and combated with devastating success such followers of the British-born heretic, Pelagius, as he found there. Furthermore, the sixth-century writings of Gildas, the only contemporary native author whose work survives, make it plain that he was addressing an audience that had long been mainly Christian, even if some of them – notably their rulers – were outrageously sinful and near-pagan in their practice.

Nevertheless, one of the most striking and long-lived features of the religious history of the Welsh was the profound impact made upon them by 'Celtic Christianity'. This was the legacy of the activities of the 'Celtic saints' among them from the fifth to the seventh/eighth centuries AD. These enthusiastic, peripatetic evangelizers, mainly monks, were associated with a number of lands which then spoke Celtic languages – Ireland, western Scotland and the Isles, the Isle of Man, parts of northern England, Wales, Cornwall and Brittany – and most of which we still think of as the Celtic countries and regions. It was the impetus given by these monks as itinerant preachers and missionaries which did a great deal to extend and strengthen Christian belief and worship among the population. They not only inherited the existing Christian tradition but were candescently inspired by the infusion into their midst of the ascetic ideals of Eastern Christianity, which spread into Britain via France; a religious and cultural importation that seems to be confirmed by archaeological finds of high-quality pottery of eastern Mediterranean origin. Their ranks may also have been augmented by the arrival among them of Christian compatriots moving westwards from those parts of Britain which were coming under pressure from pagan Anglo-Saxons. Certainly, there survived long afterwards an intense awareness of what the Britons believed to be their Christian superiority over the pagan and barbarian origins of the Anglo-Saxons.

Information concerning the Celtic saints is sparse and uncertain. Most of those *vitae* which purport to recount their deeds, with one or two rare exceptions like the seventh-century life of St Samson of Dol in Brittany, were not committed to writing until five or six hundred years after their lifetime. Though, like the *Life* of St David by Rhigyfarch (1056–99), they may contain fragments of early material transmitted down the centuries by oral tradition, they are interspersed with so many legends, miraculous stories and hagiographical myths that it becomes extremely difficult to establish the truth concerning the genuine deeds of the saints. Some, especially those of south-east Wales, such as Illtud or Dubricius, were associated with traditions of learning. A few, like Cadog or David, were well known, widely venerated and have a number of churches dedicated to them in more than one Celtic country. Others were much more localized in their appeal and are remembered in no more than a single dedication, like Crallo, recalled now only at Llangrallo (Coychurch). But the widespread general appeal of these saints is impressively borne out by the large number of ancient Welsh place-names which are made up of the element *Llan* (meaning church) together with the name of the saint to whom it is dedicated, e.g. Llandeilo ('the church of Teilo'), or Llantrisant ('the church of three saints'). Not all of these names go back as far as the lifetime of the saint(s) whose name is preserved, and many of these churches were dedicated to them after they themselves were dead – saintly dedications being somewhat unstable in the middle ages. But all the same the nomenclature brings out the popular attraction of the saints; a popularity which survived throughout the middle ages and well beyond. Though they were not formally canonized, these saints acquired for themselves an illustrious reputation as men of exceptional sanctity on the basis of their dedicated leadership, their moral qualities and their power to work miracles.

Many of them had chosen the monastic way of life. Reliable evidence exists to show that there were men living according to the monastic rule from the fifth century onwards. The number of monastic foundations appears to have increased substantially between *c*.AD 550 and 650 and that period was distinguished by an increased impetus to travel abroad and found new churches in fresh territories. Some devotees went as far as to live a life of unworldly holiness in eremitical isolation or in the company of a small select group of associates, often on island sites such as Caldey off the Pembrokeshire coast or St Seiriol's Island off Anglesey. Testimony from early sources right down to Rhigyfarch's eleventh-century *Life* of St David suggests that many of these men, whether living in community or not, set great store by austerity and self-renunciation. The ascetic ideals of these early monks, and especially of the hermits, were held up for centuries afterwards as the very mirror of Christian perfection. There is no doubt, either, that for a long period after the fifth and sixth centuries the monastery had a more important and prominent role in the Welsh Church, even if it was less significant than it was in Ireland, than was usual in many other countries.

In spite of the importance of the monastic element, however, there remained considerable scope for the influence and authority of bishops also. Some of the leading monasteries, like St David's or Llandeilo Fawr, housed a bishop as well as an abbot. 'There was no incongruity in placing the seat of a bishopric in a monastery,' says Professor Wendy Davies; 'no distinction of type was seen between the two communities; and there may have been no actual distinction between the two, particularly by the ninth and tenth centuries.' From the bishops downwards, it was usual for the clergy to take wives, and the practice of clerical marriage remained widespread in Wales right down to the Reformation, when legislation permitted it again. Among the Welsh clergy, before the Norman Conquest it was common enough for sons to succeed to their fathers' benefices by hereditary right, although it is also only fair to recall that remarkable gifts of learning and character might be transmitted in some clerical families along with ecclesiastical position and material possessions, as such gifted bodies of men as the family of Bishop Sulien (1011–91) of St David's, or the family of Llancarfan in the diocese of Llandaff, remind us.

The administration and jurisdiction exercised by these bishops are not easily determined. Neither is the number of pre-Conquest dioceses; there may have been as many as seven bishops' seats in south Wales, including centres like Llandeilo Fawr and Llanbadarn, as well as St David's and Llandaff, though only two – Bangor and Llanelwy (St Asaph) – have been traced in the north. The bishops of St David's may have enjoyed a place of some pre-eminence among their brethren, judging by some slight indications in the writings of Asser and elsewhere; but it is almost certain that this did not constitute an institutionalized archbishopric but was merely a recognition of greater prestige and distinction. Over most of the pre-Norman period the links between the bishops and those clergy who recognized their authority took the form of an association between 'mother' churches, founded mostly by major saints, and 'daughter' churches, founded later by the same saint or one of his followers and acknowledging a state of 'filial' dependence on the 'mother' churches. Thus, for instance, many churches in Glamorgan regarded Illtud's foundation at Llantwit Major as their mother church; others in mid-Wales looked to Padarn's church at Llanbadarn; while those of the north-west were dependent on Beuno's foundation at Clynnog. Nevertheless, by the end of the 'Celtic' period, i.e. the tenth and eleventh centuries, there are signs of a gradual shift towards a more territorial organization of diocesan arrangements. A number of monasteries continued to exist, but all were under the overarching authority of bishops.

Some of the larger and better-known churches exercised extensive privileges of protection (*nawdd*) over those who fled to them for sanctuary. They zealously upheld and guarded such powers, since they were among the most efficacious weapons they had at their disposal when contending with lay powers. The *Life* of St David, for example, went to the length of claiming that all the bishops of the British Church acknowledged that David's protection 'should apply to every ravisher and homicide and sinner, and to every person flying from place to place in every kingdom and each region where there may be land consecrated to holy David'. And, it added, 'let no kings or elders or governors or even bishops, abbots, and saints dare to grant protection in priority to holy David.' Closely associated with such moral authority was the formidable talent for cursing their enemies attributed to some of the Celtic saints; Cadog, for one, was credited with having caused robbers to be swallowed by the earth and King Rhun and his followers to be blinded.

Comparatively little can be established with certainty concerning the extent to which the Church was able to maintain its tradition of learning and scholarship during the dark ages. But there are pointers indicating that some of its achievements in this field were well kept up in spite of all the detrimental pressures from ignorant laymen and the savage onslaughts of Scandinavian raiders, whose attacks wrought havoc on many leading churches from the eighth to the eleventh century. Early on in the period, the erudite Illtud (475–c.525) had founded a famous school at Llanilltud Fawr (Llantwit Major) in that part of south-east Wales which had come under the most pervasive civilizing influences of Rome. Illtud was reputed to have a profounder knowledge than any other Briton of the Old and New Testaments and of every other kind of scholarship and art, and he succeeded in attracting to his academy disciples from far and near, including St Samson of Dol (*c*.485–565), Gildas (*flr*. sixth century), and possibly even the redoubtable Maelgwn Gwynedd (d. *c*.547), prince of north Wales. The churches and monasteries of south-west Wales, on the other hand, do not seem to have shared in this exceptional level of attainment. Even so, it ought not to be forgotten that it was a man from west Wales, Asser (d. 909), a son of the diocese of St David's, whom Alfred the Great chose to summon to his court to raise the standards of learning there. Similarly, the clergy of Gwynedd in the north-west maintained close contacts with scholars in Ireland and on the continent. The intellectual achievements of a distinguished family like that of Bishop Sulien provide further impressive evidence of how brilliantly the best clerics of the age succeeded in keeping alive the highest traditions of ecclesiastical learning in spite of all the difficulties and discouragements.

Not surprisingly, there were close links between the Church and literature – in Latin and in Welsh. Among the very earliest writing in the Welsh language which has survived to us are the *englynion* (quatrains) penned by a Welsh cleric in honour of the Trinity on the tenth-century Juvencus manuscript. Again, the ancient Welsh prophetic poem of the tenth century, *Arymes Prydain* ('Presage of Britain'), presents St David as the focus of patriotic unity and religious zeal for his compatriots. Illustrated manuscripts and other examples of early Christian art are comparatively rare, though the Gospel of St Chad, now at Lichfield, has undoubted connections with Wales. Much the most important survivals of this kind are the 450–500 stone monuments of the early Christian period (fifth to eleventh century AD). The earlier ones, dating from the fifth and sixth centuries, show the influences of the Latin alphabet and Roman styles of writing, but some are in the Ogam alphabet and Irish style. The later monuments of the ninth to the eleventh centuries are magnificent examples of tall, sculptured stone crosses revealing a Celtic fondness for geometrical patterns and elaborate stone carving, though they are not uninfluenced by Hiberno-Saxon models.

The nature of Christian belief and practice among the population at large is not at all easy to determine in the light of the scanty evidence available to us. Over the centuries emphases may no doubt have changed significantly. It is also possible that there were marked differences of approach as between one region of Wales and another; south-east Wales, for instance, was inclined to maintain much more intimate contact than other parts of the country with neighbouring regions of England, whereas Gwynedd tended to preserve closer links with Ireland and Irish clerics. However, in so far as it is possible to generalize on the subject of Christian faith and custom, we may perhaps be justified in singling out for special emphasis the following traits.

It seems probable that the most enticing attraction held out by the

Christian Church was its promise to the faithful, beset by the hardships and uncertainties of brief existence on earth, of the reward of life eternal. In this respect, the Juvencus *englynion* provide us with a vivid evocation of the power of God as mediated through his Church: 'The world cannot express in song bright and melodious, even though the grass and trees should sing, all thy glories, O true Lord . . . He who made the wonder of the world will save us, has saved us. It is not too great toil to praise the Trinity.' Those moral qualities which ought to typify the true Christian were increasingly emphasized. Among them were resistance to the deadly sins prompted by the three cardinal enemies of mankind – the world, the flesh and the devil – and adoption of the central Christian virtues of commitment, humility and charity. By the time that the lives of the saints came to be written, these were pre-eminently the merits which those heroes of the faith were said to have manifested. The same qualities would also be heavily underscored in the later literature of the Court poets of the twelfth and thirteenth centuries and the *cywydd* poets from the fourteenth to the sixteenth century.

The saints themselves tended to dominate popular religion. Although the more famous figures in the Christian pantheon such as the Blessed Virgin Mary, or Peter, or Michael, were as well known in Wales as in other European countries, the saints who loomed particularly large in the people's mind were the home-grown variety like David or Beuno or Cadog, and many others little known or even unknown outside their own particular locale. In an age which set such enormous store by secular heroes and demigods and attributed to them superhuman qualities on which the leadership and security of the country depended, it was hardly to be wondered at that the Christian Church should produce its own champions, on especially favoured terms with the Almighty and endowed by him with miraculous authority. The saints were normally the scions of royal or aristocratic lines, possessing the same characteristics of leadership, fortitude and determination being shown by their secular brethren in this formative age when the future of the Welsh people was being shaped out of the debris of the Roman empire. The saints had the added advantage over laymen of being willing to place their talents unreservedly at the disposal of the King of Heaven. When, in return, he showed them marks of his special regard, it was thought only natural that in the exercise of their God-given attributes they would remember particularly their own people who held them in such high regard.

Long after a saint was dead, his *mana* was firmly believed to live on in the place(s) he had adorned with his holy life. Relics associated with him became the objects of intense pride and veneration in those localities where they were preserved. The bones of a saint were especially highly regarded. Cadog's were attributed with far-reaching powers of being able to perform miracles, expel demons, and procure abundance and fertility. A saint's bones were not only the 'spiritual title-deeds' of a church but also represented his 'continuing presence and the protection which he afforded to his community and its possessions'. From at least as early as the sixth century, as we know from Gildas's testimony, shrines were constructed so as fittingly to contain and protect the saintly remains, and such shrines became of greater consequence than the churches associated with them. Not surprisingly, many ordinary men and women wished to be buried as near as possible to the aura of the saint in the hope of benefiting from his favour after death. Some of the excavations of early sites, carried out at places like Arfryn near Bodedern in Anglesey, have revealed a large number of burials concentrated around a central focus. Nor were the bones of a saint the only objects held in honour. Other possessions closely linked with him, such as bells, croziers, altars, wells, or even books, were also treasured. Cadog's bell, said to have been made by Gildas, was preserved at Llancarfan, as was another, also reputedly made by Gildas, at Llantwit Major, and both had supernatural properties attributed to them. The brass head of a crozier, preserved at Baglan, was commended to Edward Lhuyd as late as 1690 as a 'sacred relic which had wonderful effects on the sick'. Holy wells associated with the saints were, for centuries, resorted to by those seeking a cure for physical ailments, and some, like Winifred's Well at Holywell, still command the loyalty of present-day pilgrims.

Such places sanctified by connections with saints and their relics naturally attracted a large concourse of those who came to venerate the holy men's memory, or to seek health for their own bodies and souls, or even from more mundane motives of curiosity and a desire to see wonders. Journeys by Welsh votaries to foci of Christian remembrance as distant and celebrated as Jerusalem or Rome were not uncommon; traditionally, one of David's most famous peregrinations was his visit to Jerusalem, where he was believed to have been created archbishop by the patriarch. But there were other revered shrines within easier reach for would-be worshippers, like St David's, or Bardsey, hallowed as the burial-place of thousands of saints, which attracted large numbers of pilgrims.

Parishes do not seem to have been carved out in Wales until the twelfth century, after the coming of the Normans. It may well be, however, that in the lowland and more populous areas of Wales, as in Cornwall, there were a considerable number of churches and chapels founded in the pre-Norman period and probably transformed into full-scale parishes in the twelfth century. Of the relationship between priests who served these churches and their people during the earlier period it is difficult to speak with any certainty. Little has survived to show that there was much in the way of close pastoral or instructional contact between them or to indicate how frequently or regularly the populace attended for worship at church services. Care does appear to have been taken, however, to ensure that infants were baptized by the clergy and the dead buried by them – two aspects of the priestly function to which we might have expected singular importance to be attached. There also seems to have been considerable emphasis on the need for giving alms and doing penance. But in general, as might be anticipated amid a population that was small, scattered, poor and illiterate, and subject to frequent internal wars and raids as well as invasions and attacks from outside, the people were, as far as can be judged, 'collective Christians'. That is to say, they reposed their trust in the prowess of their saints and in the ritual performed by their clergy to do all that was necessary to safeguard them from evil and ensure their salvation in the world to come.

There are some other prevailing attitudes in the Celtic Church in Wales on which attention should be focused. First, the Welsh cherished unqualified pride in what they held to be their early conversion in apostolic times and the independent origin of their Christianity, regarding both as tokens of the signal approval bestowed on the early British by God. Second, they believed strongly in the superiority of their own indigenous British tradition, as contrasted with that of the Anglo-Saxons who had for so long been pagan barbarians. Third, they associated with their distinctive past the glorious achievements of their own native saints, accounts of whose holiness and supernatural feats were firmly interwoven into the history, folklore and legends of the various regions of Wales. Fourth, they were unshakably convinced of their orthodoxy and loyalty to the faith throughout their history; they believed themselves to have been proof against Roman persecution, Pelagian and other heresies, and pressure from Anglo-Saxon oppressors and Scandinavian raiders. Finally, they continued to harbour a hope that, as a people, they had been preserved by the hand of God to carry out some major sacred mission which he had in store for them. In the centuries following the Norman Conquest all these convictions were to be subjected to severe erosive forces; but, although in some respects weakened or changed, they continued to survive, buckled but unbroken, to the end of the middle ages and beyond.

THE NORMAN CONQUEST AND THE MEDIEVAL CHURCH

When, from the end of the eleventh century onwards, the Normans began to encroach on parts of Wales, it was inevitable that they should seek to exercise control over the Church in the interests of their own expansion. What they found was an ecclesiastical polity still markedly Celtic in character, its discipline and institutions differing widely from those with which they were familiar. This constituted a state of affairs which the intruders would tolerate no longer than they had to. Accustomed to a Church ruled over by warrior-aristocrat bishops of Norman origin and upper-class abbots of Latin-style monasteries which had come under the inspiration of a reforming papacy, the Normans were pious according to their lights, as well as practical. Brutal and worldly as they often were, they could cloak their pugnacious instincts and their political need to control the Church with an agreeable sense of a mission to introduce ecclesiastical reform. Individual Norman lords carried out their conquest of the south and east – the 'marches' of Wales – in piecemeal fashion; but they were not the only ones to appreciate the need for getting their hands on the Church. Behind them stood the Norman kings of England and their archbishops of Canterbury, who were at least as aware of the strategic importance of bringing the Welsh Church under their sway.

One of the first steps in the process of subordination, from which complete subjection might be expected to follow, was to gain direction over the choice of bishops and secure their allegiance to the archbishops of Canterbury. Hitherto, bishops in Wales had been independent of his authority; but in 1107 Urban, the first Norman bishop of Llandaff, was induced to make the initial profession of obedience to the primate of England. It was a decisive step which set the pattern for the future. By the middle of the twelfth century the bishops of all four Welsh dioceses had been pressurized into making a similar profession. Thus had the first and crucial step for bringing the Church under the control of king and archbishop been accomplished. It was a shift pregnant with consequences for Church and people, not incomparable in scope and magnitude with those later to be brought about by the Protestant Reformation and the Methodist Revival.

The new-style prelates introduced far-reaching modifications into the organization, possessions and discipline of their dioceses. They replaced authority exercised on the basis of 'mother' and 'daughter' affiliation with a pattern of territorially demarcated dioceses having fixed geographical boundaries; a tactic not carried through without fierce disputes and controversies over possessions and jurisdiction between rival bishops. Within the newly defined territorial bishoprics other ecclesiastical boundaries were also mapped out for the first time. Rural deaneries and archdeaconries came into being, the former based on civil administrative units, the commote (*cwmwd*) or cantref, the latter on earlier kingdoms or provinces like Meirionnydd (Merioneth) or Brycheiniog (Brecknock). Parishes were carved out, too – a slow and complicated procedure, not completed in north Wales until well into the fourteenth century. For the maintenance of the clergy in these parishes, tithes were introduced on a regular basis for the first time.

In this process of reconstruction and reorganization, some of the most distinctive features of the life of the Celtic Church were rudely thrust aside. The Normans found dedications to Celtic saints strange and unacceptable and proceeded to eradicate them and rededicate the churches to saints with whom they were familiar. The old Celtic *clas*, or body of canons, usually hereditary and attached to a mother church, was destroyed wherever possible. Its endowments were then transferred to monasteries in England or on the continent which found favour with the conquerors. Churches in south-east Wales, which came early under Norman rule, suffered especially badly, and by this process the venerable *clasau* founded by Illtud at Llantwit Major and by Cadog at Llancarfan were suppressed and their possessions handed over to the abbeys of Tewkesbury and Gloucester.

Closely connected with the steps taken to break up the *clasau* was the introduction of Latin-style monasteries into Wales. The first to be founded were daughter priories of English or continental houses approved of by the Normans. Planted only along the normanized fringes and built in the shadow of Norman castles in lordship capitals like Chepstow, Monmouth, Brecon or Cardiff, they were almost as much an instrument of conquest as the castle or the borough. Not one Benedictine house flourished in those parts of Wales held for any length of time by the Welsh princes. Throughout the middle ages the Black Monks' houses were alien colonies, recruiting their members from a non-Welsh population.

Another of the purposes of the new territorial organization was to pave the way for the introduction of stricter canons of ecclesiastical discipline, in the enforcement of which archdeacons and rural deans were to be the key officers. These officials were normally men of Welsh origin and in close touch with priests and people. But theirs was no easy task; progress was slow, and compromise and failures inevitable. A notorious stumbling-block was the celibacy of the clergy. Many of the Welsh priests, in accordance with time-honoured custom and in defiance of canon law, continued to take wives right down to the Reformation. Such notable sixteenth-century bishops as the Catholic William Glynn (1555–8) or the Protestant Richard Davies (1560–81) were both sons of married priests.

One of the more beneficial consequences of the Norman Conquest was that it ended the tendency on the part of the Welsh Church to be somewhat isolated from the Church in general; the price of earlier autonomy had been the peril of stagnation. The advent of the Normans helped decisively in throwing the Welsh Church open to fresh and invigorating streams of reform flowing briskly from the continent. One of the most momentous consequences of this was to bring clerics in Wales into a more intimate relationship with the fountain-head of medieval religion, the reformed papacy. To Rome the most active and zealous clerics, Welsh and Norman alike, turned for leadership and guidance; from Rome came much of the driving force underlying the transformation of ecclesiastical organization and government.

Yet, profound and far-ranging as were the changes brought about by the Normans, they did not by any means completely submerge earlier characteristics. Older ways were tenaciously defended and novelties stubbornly resisted. The overlordship of Canterbury, for instance, was not accepted without tense and embittered struggles to uphold the autonomy previously enjoyed by Welsh prelates. In the northern principality of Gwynedd the princes, following a precedent set by Owain Gwynedd (1137–70), regarded the diocese of Bangor as their own preserve, and were unwilling to allow the authority of Canterbury to be extended over the see. In south Wales the claims of St David's to be regarded as an archbishopric were an even more crucial source of controversy. Gerald of Wales, himself three parts a Norman, was to stand forth as the most vigorous of all champions of St David's alleged rights to be considered the metropolitical see of Wales. For a quarter of a century, from 1176 onwards, he fought a desperate though ultimately vain campaign to have those pretensions upheld, pleading his case in season and out of season, in St David's and in England, at royal court and papal curia, amid the clergy and the laity, with all the resources of one of the swiftest pens and most fluent tongues known to the middle ages.

Moreover, however much the Normans might dominate some of the upper echelons of the hierarchy, they were simply too few in number to be able to dispense with the option of having to make extensive use of native-born clergy at the grass-roots level and also on some of the more exalted planes within the Church. Many Welshmen were not unwilling to participate in changes which they recognized as being in the best interests of religion. Among other things they accepted papal leadership readily, and in due course were successful in enlisting papal support for Welsh claims to more sympathetic treatment. In 1274, for example, seven Welsh Cistercian abbots wrote to Pope Gregory X seeking, with some success, his sympathy on behalf of Prince Llywelyn ap Gruffydd.

Again, in the face of the Norman intention to drive out or downgrade dedications to Welsh saints, the Welsh contrived to cling on to them with rare and dogged determination. St Andrew might have been introduced by the Normans to a place alongside St David in the dedications of the latter's cathedral, but it was Welsh Dewi who survived as the magnet for popular pilgrimage and patriotic loyalty, almost completely eclipsing St Andrew in the people's devotion. Similarly, at Llandaff – the cathedral and see which came most completely under Norman domination – the shrine which proved to be its most specific and enduring attraction was that of the three Welsh saints: Teilo, Dyfrig and Euddogwy.

Not even in the sphere of Latin-type monasteries did the Normans have it all their own way. In contrast with the failure of the Norman-sponsored Benedictines, the Cistercian order was conspicuously successful among the Welsh. Admittedly, the White Monks were first introduced into Wales under the Norman aegis, and a small minority of their houses, like Tintern or Basingwerk, always remained Anglo-Norman in sympathy. But as an order the Cistercians were not associated in Welsh minds with alien conquest. Far from being the timid henchmen of the conquerors who clung to the skirts of castle and borough, the sons of Cîteaux sought out the undeveloped solitudes of mountain and moorland, especially in *pura Wallia*, i.e. the area not encroached upon by the Normans. Their emphasis on retreat into the wilderness, manual labour, austere discipline and rigorous self-renunciation seemed to reincarnate the pristine ideals of the monastic life of the Celtic saints. Their adoption of pastoral ways of farming on the whole fitted smoothly into prevalent agrarian patterns in Wales, though there was more friction between them and the native population in this context than has often been recognized. Cistercian houses became havens of ordered prayer and worship, cradles of learning, patrons of literature, literary chroniclers and active agents of historic and patriotic aspiration, pioneers in the arts of agriculture and stock breeding, flock management and wool production, and even embryonic industry and metal working. Contributions of this kind won them a unique place in the affections of prince and people. The names of their houses – Strata Florida, Aberconway, Valle Crucis, Margam, Hendygwyn-ar-Daf – are among the most hallowed in the history of religion in medieval Wales.

The newer religious orders of Franciscan and Dominican friars were likewise taken warmly to the Welsh bosom when they appeared in the thirteenth century. From their ranks sprang some of the foremost scholars and bishops of the age. Typical of them was the Dominican, Anian Ddu, bishop of St Asaph (1268–93). Scion of a royal line of princes and warriors, he was prepared to proclaim his rights as a prince of the Church against Welsh abbots or English bishops, King Edward I or Prince Llywelyn the Last. Another leading friar, John Wallensis, was an outstanding Franciscan regent-master at Oxford and Paris, a prolific author whose sermon collections were among the most popular compendia of their kind in medieval Europe. John was one of a number of young Welsh clerics fired with an insatiable thirst for learning. Members of the religious orders and secular clergy alike, they found their way in growing numbers to the universities, particularly to Oxford.

The learning of the clerics was not confined to the small and highly educated élite who were at ease in the Latin language and literature. One of the most striking achievements of the medieval Welsh Church was to produce a substantial body of literature in the vernacular, which the less-educated clergy and laity might understand. Parts of the Bible were translated into Welsh; so were the Creed, the more popular hymns and prayers, the lives of the saints, and works of devotion and mysticism. These prose recensions were well known to the bards of Wales and left a pronounced impress on their verse, much of which was devoted to religious subjects. Their themes were few and simple, recurring again and again. Chief among them were praise of the Trinity, the sufferings of Christ, and terror at the prospect of the last judgement and hell – perhaps the most persistent and awe-inspiring motif, accompanied by unrelenting insistence on the brevity and brittleness of human life and the vanity of men's preoccupation with worldly honour and possessions, the need for regular confession of sins, and the merit of devotion to the Blessed Virgin and the saints. All of these are refrains which serve to demonstrate the marked continuity between the values of the medieval era and those commented upon earlier in considering the mentality of the Celtic Church.

THE LAST PHASE OF THE MEDIEVAL CHURCH

From the fourteenth century until well on into the fifteenth, the Church passed through a prolonged series of upheavals which had detrimental consequences for it. Some of the most important causes of this 'time of troubles' affected the Western Church as a whole and can be mentioned only briefly in passing. Among the most serious were the decline in the moral, spiritual and practical authority of the papacy as a result of the Babylonish Captivity and the Great Schism; the break-up of the thirteenth-century synthesis of philosophy and religion and the emergence of deeply divisive controversies and heresies; the cooling ardour of the religious orders; and the economic and social disruption caused by demographic crisis and economic decline.

Other causes affected England and Wales more immediately. First among them was the final conquest of Wales, effected by Edward I in 1282–3. The tendency thereafter – much speeded up in the fourteenth century – was to subordinate the interests of the Welsh Church to those of the English State even more intensively than before. In the fourteenth century the King of England recruited virtually all his leading civil servants from among the clergy. He rewarded them with bishoprics and other valuable preferment in the Church. This tended to turn them more and more into administrators and politicians, absent from their sees and incapable of giving them pastoral care and direction. In Wales the deficiency was made all the worse by the King's exclusion of Welsh clerics from the most lucrative benefices there. For a time, the papacy sought to protect the native interest by promoting Welshmen by means of papal provisions. But before the end of the fourteenth century papal influence had been effectively negated in practice, though not in name, as a result of the pope's need to placate the English monarchy in order to gain its support during the Schism. This exclusion of Welsh clerics from the upper ranks of the hierarchy built up a strong sense of resentment and frustration which was to find expression in the Glyndŵr Rebellion (1400–c.1415).

Another major source of upset was the seemingly interminable campaigning of the Hundred Years War with France. This led the King to exploit clerical appointments and tap the financial resources of the Church still more thoroughly in the interests of the State. The wars also had a damaging effect on the leading religious order in Wales, the Cistercians, who were now cut off from their mother house in France for long periods and whose discipline and standards suffered in consequence.

To add still further to the woes of the Church came the Black Death (1348–50) and a number of subsequent visitations of epidemic disease in 1361, 1369 and later. Landed possessions and the income of the clergy were hit hard. Even more serious, the numbers of the clergy were sharply reduced and the replacements hastily drafted in were of very mixed quality. The religious orders suffered extremely badly and, as the numbers of monks and friars fell drastically and afterwards remained well below their former levels, their contributions to scholarship and literature slumped markedly.

All these disasters could not but aggravate the severe economic difficulties of the age. By the end of the fourteenth century the Church and its clergy had become much poorer, and there is widespread evidence of the acute financial problems and reduced resources confronting them. To adjust to their added liabilities and diminished income they were obliged to resort to a variety of devices, most of which were not in the best interests of the Church even if they temporarily palliated economic embarrassment. Pluralism and non-residence became increasingly common among the secular clergy, while the monasteries resorted to acquiring appropriations of parishes and leasing out rectories and temporal estates, as well as deliberately restricting their intake of monks. Clergy of all kinds found it increasingly necessary to depend upon the more unrestricted sale of indulgences to make ends meet. Like the laity, they found themselves under grinding pressure from deteriorating social and economic circumstances. Many of the Welsh clergy were in as bitter and rebellious mood as their lay kinsfolk and were inclined, like them, to attribute their problems almost wholly to their English overlords. It needed only a spark to touch off rebellion.

That spark came when Owain Glyndŵr raised the standard of revolt in September 1400. In his approach to the problems of the Church as well as those of the State, Owain could appeal to age-old and elemental layers of patriotism among the clergy as well as the laity. In his 'Pennal Programme' of 1406 he resurrected the immemorial claim to the autonomy of the Welsh Church and the role of a Welsh archbishop of St David's, independent of Canterbury and controlling all the higher clerical appointments in the interests of Wales – and, of course, its independent prince! He also sought to re-establish earlier Welsh links with a sympathetic papacy – in his case the pontiff at Avignon – to use it as an ally against England in the creation of a separate province and two independent Welsh university institutions. He succeeded, moreover, in harnessing the patriotic energies and ambitions of a variety of Welsh clerics in the interests of his principality. The success of his appeal to his principal allies bound all the recognized upholders of the Welsh heritage to him: higher clergy like Bishop John Trefor and Gruffydd Young, along with many of the parish and lesser clergy and students, and their counterparts among the Cistercian and Franciscan orders. He even managed to secure support from that notable Lollard critic of the English establishment, Walter Brut.

For a brief, intoxicating year or two it looked as if Glyndŵr's heady and high-flying prospectus for an independent State and autonomous Church might be implemented; but by 1408–9, at the latest, his whole ambitious enterprise could be seen to be unravelling fast into ignominious failure. Meantime, in the course of his insurgency the Church had suffered untold losses. Its buildings and estates were severely damaged, in some instances destroyed; worship was badly disrupted and discipline shattered; learning and literature were at their lowest ebb. The monastery of Margam was in 1412 described as 'utterly destroyed so that abbot and convent were obliged to go about like vagabonds'. Such destitution was not untypical of much of the life of the Church when the rebellion ended. Even a century and a half later, in the preface to the first Welsh New Testament of 1567, its appalling consequences were still remembered. Bishop Richard Davies could deplore in tones of deep distress the damage caused by Glyndŵr and his enemies: 'What destruction of books [i.e. manuscripts] Wales suffered . . . from the townships, bishops' houses, monasteries and churches that were burnt throughout all Wales at that time.'

And yet, painful and devastating as had been the troubles of the fourteenth century, and especially those of the fifteenth, the Church was able to stage a remarkable recovery. By 1500 the process of material recuperation was largely complete. Income from clerical possessions was more or less back to normal, and the adjustments needed to meet a changing age, already begun in the fourteenth century, had been taken much further. It was now normal for the higher clergy to hold a number of preferments simultaneously and for most of them to be non-Welsh and non-resident. Monasteries were content to lease out most of their temporal and spiritual assets and live in comfortable and relaxed fashion on the proceeds. Their charitable functions – care of the sick and elderly, hospitality for travellers and alms-giving to the poor – though still undertaken, were sharply diminished in scale. Friars tended to be far more confined to their houses and much less concerned with itinerant preaching than they had earlier been.

The revived material fortunes of the Church were visible, too, in the great wave of church-building, in the shape of extensions, refurbishing and embellishments which characterized the period from the second half of the fifteenth century down to the Reformation. This was an age of building new Lady chapels, aisles and towers; extending and glazing windows; and erecting new images and, especially, graceful and elaborate rood screens and lofts. Much of this activity was connected with and financed by fresh or revived activity in encouraging devotees to resort to the new attractions set up in the churches. Famous roods, like the ones at Tremeirchion or Brecon, or images such as that of the Virgin at Pen-rhys in the Rhondda or of Gwenfrewi at Holywell, developed into sources of magnetic appeal for worshippers from far and near.

Another symptom of contemporary recovery was the upsurge of religious verse and prose, which constituted a striking feature of the efflorescence of literature in general. Although earlier concepts of the deity as a remote, majestic and omnipotent ruler and judge of the universe are not absent from this literature, greater emphasis was now placed on the humanity of the second person in the Trinity and the agony of his sufferings on behalf of sinful and frequently ungrateful mankind. The same human touch may also be seen in the approach to the Virgin Mary, whose womanly qualities of tenderness and affection, and compassion for sinners at the last judgement, are prominently highlighted. As much to the fore as ever, also, are the *mana* of the saints and sacred places, especially those of Welsh origin, and their continuing capacity to work miracles on behalf of their votaries and shower blessings upon them. Along with these familiar motifs goes an increased emphasis on the need to resist the insidious temptations of wealth and self-indulgence and to eschew the grosser sins of carnality, pride and sensuality, all of which are unsparingly denounced after the fashion of those versified medieval sermons made so popular by Siôn Cent (?1367–?1430), the poet of puritanical restraint, austerity and other-worldliness, and his many followers. Attendance at church, regular payment of tithes and respect for the sacraments are also warmly advocated. But perhaps the most persistent refrain of all is still the overwhelming concern with the four last things – death, judgement, heaven and hell – and the ineradicable dread of the possibility of an eternity spent in indescribable torment as punishment for sins unpardoned.

On the threshold of the Reformation, although to outward appearances the Church had recovered well from the trials and tribulations of the fourteenth and fifteenth centuries, there were aspects of its condition which left it in a vulnerable state. First, there were manifest weaknesses among its clergy. Almost all the bishops in Welsh dioceses and a majority of the higher clergy were servants or favourites of the Crown, owing their preferment to royal goodwill, and men who would hesitate to act in opposition to the King's commands and wishes, whatever they might be. Customarily not Welsh by origin and absent from Wales, most were graduates in law, not theology, and administrators rather than pastors of souls. Between them and most of the parish clergy, as well as between them and the native population, yawned a wide gap of wealth, interest, attitude, culture and language. Oversight of the dioceses, with their poor, thinly populated, dispersed and inaccessible parishes, was fitful and inadequate. Nor was the state of belief and morals amid the largely illiterate and monoglot Welsh-speaking population improved by the presence among them of an ill-educated and badly remunerated lower clergy, scarcely capable of setting a moral example or imparting doctrinal instruction to their parishioners. It was hardly to be wondered at that in his preface to the first Welsh printed book of 1546, *Yny Lhyvyr Hwnn*, the devout and learned Erasmian humanist, Sir John Price of Brecon, should pointedly denounce the Welsh clergy for their failure to teach their charges even the rudiments of religious belief; a state of affairs which had made it necessary for him to publish his primer.

Shortcomings in Church life such as these occasioned by the indifferent quality of the secular clergy were further aggravated as a result of the reduced state of the religious orders, once the spearheads of devotion and learning. Friars, formerly so active in preaching, hearing confession and promulgating Latin and Welsh literature, were now much more inert and less effective. The monks, also, for a century or more stringently reduced in numbers, had lost most of the zeal and vitality which had fired their orders in earlier centuries, and appeared content to lead the leisurely, comfortable, quiescent life of *rentiers*. Neither they nor the friars seemed any longer desirous or capable of awakening religious enthusiasm or offering a conspicuous example to the laity. In view of this lack of vision and dynamism among the clergy much of the creative drive in religious life and literature seemed to have passed from them to a minority of educated and pious laymen.

As far as popular belief and devotion were in question, there was a disturbing dependence on the externalities of the means of grace, many of which appeared to be divorced from considerations of morality and genuine understanding. Men and women depended on practices like the multiplication of Masses, lifeless repetition of prayers, unthinking veneration of the saints and quasi-idolatrous addiction to their relics, participation in pilgrimages and commercial transactions in indulgences, rather than to a more committed adherence to Christian behaviour and belief, to save them from the consequences of their misdeeds. The more enlightened trends of contemporary piety, like the *devotio moderna*, or Catholic humanism, or reformed monastic life, found little echo in Wales. The overwhelming majority of its population remained collective Christians, content to leave it to the priesthood, many of whose members were no better than the laity, to minister the sacraments and perform the ritual on their behalf. Religion consisted for most of a body of traditional practices and assumptions, unquestioningly accepted but dimly appre- hended. Habit, not conviction, was the strongest element in their faith, as it had been down the centuries. It left them nearly as ill-prepared to defend the old as to accept the new in the face of the Reformation storm soon to break on them.

THE REFORMATION

When the Reformation came to Wales, it fell into two distinct phases, separated by the five-year intermission (1553–8) of the Catholic Mary's reign. The first phase, from c.1527 to 1553, witnessed the innovations introduced into the life of the Church during the reigns of Henry VIII and Edward VI, while the second, from 1558 to 1603, ensured that the Reformation was secured on a lasting basis by Elizabeth I.

Widely ranging and weighty in consequence for the future as Henry VIII's policies were – in so far as they destroyed the links binding England and Wales to the papacy, established the King as supreme head of the Church, dissolved the monasteries, broke up many of the centres of pilgrim devotion, and tentatively introduced some cautious measures of religious and doctrinal reform – on the whole they made surprisingly little difference to the everyday practice of religion. Medieval rites continued largely intact, conducted in Latin by a priesthood still celibate in theory. It could almost be said to be papism without the Pope. In Wales, Henry was a strong and popular king, his actions were acceptable to the gentry, and by and large met with very little opposition. Even such conservative poets as Siôn Brwynog, later to attack the Reformation with vehemence, greeted Henry's changes with some approval.

The same could not be said of the Edwardian changes, which proceeded more radically in several directions. First, they swept away much that was accustomed and dearly loved in the fabric and appearance of parish churches. Altars, images, shrines, vestments, ornaments, treasures, rood lofts and screens, chantries, guilds, fraternities, candles and incense, now disappeared, leaving the churches cold and bare, 'like barns', as one indignant poet protested. Customary practices, such as the veneration of the saints, carrying rosaries, kneeling at Mass and beating the breast, praying for the dead, or 'creeping to the Cross' on Good Fridays, and other similar observances, were forbidden. Second, medieval services were replaced by the Reformed rites embodied in the transitional Prayer Book of 1549 and the even more distinctly Protestant services of the Book of 1552. The fact that English was the language of the Prayer Books gave added offence in Wales, where over most of the country it was no more intelligible than Latin and far less revered. The Welsh, having always prided themselves on their loyalty to the Church, now believed that they were being turned by *force majeure* into heretics, and English heretics at that. *Ffydd Saeson* – 'faith of Saxons' – was how one poet contemptuously dismissed the hated new regime. Third, the clergy were officially allowed to take wives, though formal permission to do so may have made very little practical difference in Wales, where many were already accustomed to maintain wives, or at least 'hearth companions'.

Edward's reign had brought about nothing less than a religious revolution. It was a transformation that proved to be deeply unpopular in Wales, where a number of poets voiced uncompromising opposition to the innovations as they affected churches and their furnishings, clergy, altars, saints, the language of worship, and other alterations in celebration and practice. The Protestant bishop of St David's, Robert Ferrar (1548–54), was only one of those who commented on the adherence of the people to their old ways and their impenitent resistance to rapid and brusque change. He feared that what he called 'the grudge of the people' was so impassioned that it might irrupt into open rebellion. A minority, admittedly, accepted the new fashion; but the greater number by far appeared to welcome the return to the papal fold led by their royal shepherd, Queen Mary, in 1554.

For much of Elizabeth's long tenure of power, too, a mass of conservatism and time-serving was reported to be obstinately lingering on. Right down to the end of her reign, and even after, there were eloquent comments by Protestant observers on the people's ignorance, lack of conviction and reluctance to abandon ingrained habits. The Welsh clergyman and Protestant author, Huw Lewys, could comment as late as 1595 that many of his fellow-clergymen had been 'like bells without clappers or a candle under a bushel', with the result that even old people of sixty and upwards could give no more account of their faith than newborn children. Nevertheless, it is also true that the Elizabethan Church made a more profound and lasting impact, especially on the literate sectors of the population, than has usually been acknowledged. It succeeded for a number of reasons. Some of these were political and social and depended on its appeal to the ruling elite, the landed gentry; but, important as they were, we shall not pursue them here. For our particular purpose, more relevant are the two chief religious and cultural considerations: the reinterpretation of Welsh religious history put forward by the Reformers; and the translation of the Bible and Prayer Book into Welsh.

The most complete and skilful revision of Welsh history was the version of it outlined by Bishop Richard Davies in his highly influential 'Letter to the Welsh Nation' (*Epistol at y Cembru*), with which he prefaced the first translation into Welsh of the New Testament (1567), undertaken by William Salesbury, Thomas Huet and himself. The 'Letter' was an imaginative adaptation to the particular needs of Wales of the general tenor of Reformation historiography. Like Reformers elsewhere, Davies was convinced that the Reformation was no new-fangled heresy but represented a return to that purity of teaching and worship established by Jesus Christ and his immediate followers in the Early Church and unsullied by corruptions later introduced by the papacy and its agents. As far as Wales was concerned, he rehearsed a number of firmly held convictions but gave them a strongly Protestant twist. He referred lovingly to the belief that Britain had first been converted to Christianity by Joseph of Arimathea, who had planted the faith in all its gospel immaculacy. This had subsequently been maintained by the people of Wales intact and uncontaminated in spite of Roman persecution, the heresies of Pelagius and others, Anglo-Saxon paganism and, most crucial of all, in the face of that brand of Christianity tainted by papal superstition which Augustine of Canterbury had brought to England as the emissary of Rome. Only as a result of being forced to accept the adulterated papism of England at the point of the sword had the Welsh eventually been dragged down into the mire of Roman superstition and idolatry. Now, after centuries of benighted ignorance and idolatrous superstition, Davies argued, by virtue of what he called 'the second flowering of the Gospel', they were being led back to the realm of truth and light. His reconstruction of history proved to be compellingly influential and appealing among many of his fellow-countrymen on three counts. It bonded the Reformation to some of the oldest and most venerable themes of Welsh history. It bluntly refuted the commonly made suggestion that Reformation teaching was a neoteric, upstart heresy, lacking roots in earlier faith and history, and sought to show, on the contrary, that it was grounded in the earliest and most glorious phase of Christianity in Britain. Finally, it met, head-on, the criticism that Reformed teaching was an alien, English creed, imposed on the Welsh by the insensitive *diktat* of an unsympathetic government; in Davies' book it was *papist* beliefs which had originally been forced on the Welsh by their Saxon enemies. Implicit in all that he wrote was the idea that it was the Reformation that was the great purpose for which God had preserved the Welsh people and their language.

The potential seductiveness for the Welsh of this revamping of their history was not lost on defenders of Catholicism. The anonymous author of *Y Drych Cristnogawl* (1585), the most notable Catholic book to be published in Welsh during Elizabeth's reign, was not slow to repay Davies in his own coin. He directed his efforts to showing how all earlier Christian history in Wales had been betrayed by the treachery of the Reformation. He agreed that one of the most memorable aspects of the past had been the early conversion by Joseph of Arimathea. But he proceeded to point out also that another early pioneer in Britain had been King Lucius son of Coel, who had sent to the Pope for missionaries to come to Britain to convert the people. In addition, the first Christian emperor of Rome, Constantine, had been a Briton, who had been received into the faith by the Pope. He then went on to show how the early saints of the Welsh, in whom they took such justifiable pride, had all been firmly in the Catholic tradition. Such had been the glorious state of Wales in the past. Alas! how dramatically circumstances had been changed for the worse by the 1580s, when there were whole shires in Wales where some of the inhabitants lived like animals, knowing little more of Christ and his religion than brute beasts. So much for the Reformers' concept of the great things for which the Welsh had been preserved! Literary duels like this one between Davies and his anonymous antagonist make it plain that the two sides viewed the battle for the soul of Wales past as an integral part of the struggle for its soul present.

One of the central contentions of the Reformers was that the faith of the early Britons had been unshakably founded on scriptural authority and that a vernacular Bible had been an essential and much-loved possession among them. To restore a Welsh version of the Scriptures was their first priority. In the first decade of Elizabeth's reign Richard Davies and William Salesbury exerted themselves with unresting vigour and purpose to secure a new translation for their people. An Act of Parliament of 1563 laid down that the Bible and Prayer Book should be translated into Welsh by 1567 and thereafter used in public worship in all those parishes where Welsh was the language normally used by the inhabitants. Translations of the New Testament and Prayer Book were duly published in 1567. Twenty-one years later William Morgan produced his classic version of the whole Bible. These translations represented an epoch-making triumph for the Reformation and, in the long term, proved to be of incalculable worth to the life of Wales. In the religious sphere, they gave meaning and reality to Reformation doctrine and worship for the largely monoglot population of Wales. As for the Welsh language, they accomplished more than any other single factor in keeping the language alive and vigorous into the twentieth century. Welsh literature, too, benefited just as much from being provided with a standard and model on which to base itself in the future. Bible and Prayer Book contributed no less powerfully to buttressing the sense of a separate and distinctive nationality in Wales.

Scriptural translation, as in other countries, proved to be the key to the success of the Reformation in Wales. At the end of the sixteenth century it had a long way to go but was now firmly on the road to its ultimate triumph. The Reformers had, with brilliant success, grafted their ideals into the ancient stock of patriotic instincts and emphasized the essential continuity of the Reformation with all that was earliest, best and most specific to Wales. They had appealed to the belief in its links with the earliest roots of Christianity in the country. They confirmed that the Reformation, like the initial conversion, was a renewed token of God's continuing favour. They underlined that the Reformation meant a return to the pristine purity of Christianity based on scriptural authority. They upheld the autonomy of the early Celtic Church and the virtues of its leading figures. They stressed the long-standing belief in the purpose which God had had in reserve for the Welsh and confidently implied that its fulfilment had been the 'second flowering of the Gospel' in their own tongue; a translation authorized by the restored British (i.e. Welsh) kingship of the Tudor dynasty. It was here, if anywhere, and now, if at all, that the true rebirth of the ancient glories of the British race was taking place. It was a striking and, on the whole, successful revitalization of Celtic ideals, and one eagerly taken to heart by many of the educated classes; not least because it merged so smoothly into the political stance of loyalty to the Tudor dynasty and State being encouraged by the monarchy. Yet, as we have seen, there was little in all this that could not have been given an equally convincing Catholic adaptation and complexion by those Catholic reformers determined to work through the vernacular tongue as well as Latin, or by a Catholic political régime desirous of winning over Welsh loyalty. What has subsequently made the Protestant version look 'inevitable' has been the continued existence down the centuries of a Protestant establishment in Church and State.

6

Religious Life in
Medieval Scotland

Michael Lynch

IN 1565 THE BISHOP of Dunblane, in Rome on a mission to raise a papal subsidy to aid a Catholic Restoration under Mary, Queen of Scots, gave Pope Pius V a long history lecture. For 1,364 years, ever since the pontificate of Victor I, he argued, a long and unbroken line of Kings of Scots had protected the Church and defended the faith on behalf of the papacy. It was much the same text as that written by the immensely learned canon lawyer Master Baldred Bisset in 1301, when he had advised the Pope that the Scots had been converted to Christianity some 400 years before the English and that no fewer than thirty-six kings had ruled over the Scots while the English languished in paganism. At least 400 years of this history were apocryphal, as was Pope Victor, but there was an essential truth amidst these durable historical myths. The papacy and the Scottish Crown had long enjoyed a special relationship, and the emergence of a Scottish Church had owed as much to successive Kings of Scots as they had relied on it to underpin their own authority.

The first duties of holy men were as the magicians and clerks of kings. Magic was demonstrated at the inauguration of a king or at his victory in battle; Aedan macGabhrain prospered after he was ordained by Columba as king of Dalriada in 574 but his grandson Domnall Brec met with a series of catastrophes ending in his death in 642 because, it was said, he had breached the promise made by his own kindred to remain faithful to Iona. By the eighth century, holy men had become the cultivators of kingship. It is no coincidence that the appearance of legends of a line of kings coincided with the emergence of an active clergy around the King. Clerics brought to the person of kings a heightened sense of the old ways, as the bringer of benefits and victories, but they also promulgated a new view of kingship. This mandarin class forged a role for itself as the advocates and interpreters of high kingship. Columba and Adomnan concerned themselves with overkings, of Dalriada and of Picts, who were worthy of Christian record, like kings of Judah and Israel. The merging of different peoples under an overking of Picts in the eighth and ninth centuries was accompanied by the cultivation of different traditions of saints as well as by the compilation of genealogies of kings by the learned orders.

Saints are not born, they are created. More powerful in death than in life, they become, once acclaimed, the servants of future generations of the servants of Christ. Ninian, Columba, Adomnan (the most important of Columba's hagiographers) and Kentigern, probably the four best-known early Scottish saints, all became subjects of a cult within a few decades of their deaths, but they were all also later recast, both in the twelfth or thirteenth centuries and again in the fifteenth, as born-again saints to fit new fashions of hagiography or the demands of contemporary ecclesiastical politics. Our information about them and other early apostles of Scotland is entangled with the assumptions and motives of many generations of biographers and hagiographers. Medieval Scottish chroniclers were intent on tracing the long genealogy of present kings to demonstrate their status. Medieval chroniclers of the Early Church were concerned with subsuming the long, difficult and doubtless uneven story of the progress of Christianity into a cult of the personality of a few holy men. Religious centres, as they gathered in prestige, needed a foundation legend, and often saints were rediscovered – as was Kentigern, within a century of his death in 612, in the case of Glasgow. He and Ninian would be reinvested with a new sanctity in the fifteenth century, as Glasgow's cathedral church was reconstructed and extended.

THE EARLY CHURCH

The first missionary was Ninian, who had brought Christianity to the south-west, probably in the late fifth century, and it was at Whithorn that this bishop's seat was established at the celebrated *Candida Casa* ('white house'). The seventh century would see the first revival of the cult of Ninian, but in the east rather than the west, for much of it was the product of a mission of the neo-Northumbrian Church, anxious to find or invent spiritual roots in Lothian so as to placate local opinion. By the time of the reign of the Pictish king Nechtan (706–24), the native cult of Ninian was being used to prepare the way for a new cult of St Peter. Dedications to Ninian stood beside others to St Peter, especially in Angus and the Mearns and in Mar and Buchan, and some churches were already built 'after the Roman manner', in stone.

The progress of Columba, originally an apostle of the Dalriadic Scots, based in modern Argyll and the southernmost of the Western Isles, was more spectacular still: within two centuries of his death in 597 he would reach the stature of a saint of the confederation of peoples – Picts, Scots, Britons and others – that would come to be encompassed in the 'kingdom of the Scots'. In his own lifetime the efforts of Columba, kinsman of an Irish royal family, who had come to Scotland from Ireland in 563 but had probably not settled on Iona until the early 570s, were narrowly concentrated along the western seaboard of Scotland, from Loch Awe in the south to Skye in the north. He was at once client and protector of the Kings of Dalriada, but he was never, as Bede later claimed, an apostle of the Picts; his one visit to the court of Bridei, king of the northern Picts, near Inverness, was an expedition to impress a pagan king by magic and tribute rather than a mission to preach the gospel. In Adomnan's *Life*, written *c*.690, some ninety years after his death, Columba was portrayed as both abbot and pilgrim. Iona fitted both roles to perfection. This busy transit camp of the Columban *paruchia*, a 'small and remote island of the Britannic ocean', was recast as the backdrop for Adomnan's picture of a simple holy man, giving it a timelessness and universality which rings deep chords even to this day. Prophet, apostle and pilgrim – his vision of Columba is a compelling one, which was designed to elevate its subject among the saints not just of the Irish Church but of Western Christendom as a whole.

Adomnan's *Life* of Columba, itself an exercise in piety, was also a skilfully disguised political tract for its times, written only twenty-five years after the Synod of Whitby, where the leadership of Iona had been challenged by one of its own converts, the infant church of Northumbria which had begun on Lindisfarne in the 630s. Adomnan, as a result, would within a few decades of his death also achieve saintly status. As early as 727, his relics had begun to be transported across the Ionan *paruchia* in a portable shrine. The official adoption of a cult of Adomnan, marked by the conservation of his relics, directly copied the pattern of the original cult of Columba. The famous *Brecbennach* of Columba, a house-shaped portable shrine for his relics, which later somehow became associated with Monymusk in Aberdeenshire, became the most visible and potent symbol of the post-Columban Church. The Monymusk reliquary and other emblems of Columba would be carried into battle not only by Kings of Dalriada but also by later Kings of Scots. His crozier or *bachall* would accompany the armies of Kings of Scots against their Viking enemies in 903 and 918. The *Brecbennach* would even be carried before the army of Robert Bruce at Bannockburn in 1314. But in 1314 the Scots went with not one patron saint but two, for they also carried with them the banner of St Andrew. This cult of twin national saints had begun five centuries before Bannockburn, amidst the complicated politics of the kingdom of the Picts.

By the early eighth century the Pictish Church had the customs and saints of not one tradition but three to exploit: a Romano-British tradition which went back to Ninian; a new Roman cult of Peter; and the powerful, fast-growing reputation of Columba's Iona. In the course of that century a new, still more exotic addition would be added to the communion of saints of the Pictish Church – Andrew, the Apostle. A legend was cultivated that St Rule or Regulus was told by an angel to take the relics of St Andrew to Scotland; they along with the relics of Columba would become the twin emblems of a Church of the Scots which would emerge out of the Church of the Picts. The long reign of the Pictish king Constantine (789–820) saw a flowering of officially sponsored ecclesiastical art of various kinds. It is not surprising that Pictish kings should begin to see themselves as God-given patrons of the Church after the fashion of the Roman Christian Emperor Constantine. The adoption by Pictish kings of the cult of Constantine (with no fewer than four kings so called between 789 and 997) mirrors its growing popularity after *c*.750 in western Europe, where the majesty of kingship and its nearness to God became increasingly intertwined, especially with the reign of Charlemagne.

The most striking religious image sponsored by a Pictish king is the St Andrews tomb shrine, which (in similar vein to another at Meigle showing Daniel in the lions' den) depicts David holding open the jaws of a lion. It has similarities, too, with motifs in the *Book of Kells*, which was begun probably on Iona in the late eighth century. The purpose of this stone-built shrine or sarcophagus, nearly six feet in length with elaborately carved panels and corner posts, which was found by workmen digging in the precincts of the later cathedral in 1833, is unclear; perhaps it was to hold the relics of a saint such as Andrew himself or Regulus, legendary carrier of the Apostle's bones to Scotland. There is a crucial difference between it and the *Brecbennach*. Columba's shrine in this form was portable, designed to be carried throughout the Ionan *paruchia*. The bewildering journeys of Columba's relics back and forward across the Irish Sea from their base on Iona in the seventh and eighth centuries were part of a saint's progress among the faithful. The St Andrews sarcophagus, in contrast, suggests a Church based firmly in an established royal centre rather than a missionary one. It hints at a Church of kings of joint peoples, Picts and Scots, rather than a pan-Celtic one.

In 807, Iona had been abandoned in the face of the Viking threat, but the cult of Columba was still too powerful to be cast aside. In the 840s, in the reign of Kenneth macAlpin (*c*.843–58), the various emblems of Columba were split, going west or east to safer parts of the old Ionan *paruchia*. What is now known as the *Book of Kells* went from Iona to the new monastery at

Kells; the fragmentary psalter known as the *Battler* also went to Ireland. The *Brecbennach* went east, as did Columba's crozier. His relics themselves were divided up in 849 to what in effect were now almost separate daughter churches, at Kells and Dunkeld. In Scotland, the cult of Columba followed Kenneth macAlpin eastwards, to the royal and religious centre which he established at Dunkeld.

What Kenneth was doing was no more than a continuation of a process begun by previous kings of Picts. The two religious centres of the emerging kingdom of the Scots under Kenneth and his successors were at Dunkeld and St Andrews, carefully dedicated to different traditions of saints. It was a distinctively Scottish solution to a Scottish problem. The very nature of ninth- and tenth-century kingship was composite; so was its Church. It was a mandarin class of churchmen who must have developed the cults of St Peter and Constantine which had marked the reigns of the last of the Pictish kings. By contrast, cultural achievements of the new macAlpin dynasty are curiously absent; no great ornamental sculpture or manuscripts comparable to the *Book of Kells* survive from this period. The image cast for the macAlpin dynasty and its realm between 840 and 1050 must largely have been the creation of a written culture. Not surprisingly, the dual imagery of this Church – of Picts and Scots – was also reflected in its organization. The revival in the Irish Church in the eighth century of the cult of asceticism, a return to the purity of the Columban-type pilgrim, was also felt in Pictland. In the next two centuries, new communities of *Céli Dé* (servants of God) were established, but they were no longer confined to minor centres such as the island at Loch Leven; they were now also attached to major royal and religious centres such as Kilrimont and Dunkeld. The Culdees, as they are usually called, are the symbol of a Celtic revival in a post-Columban Church, which had survived the dismemberment of the Ionan *paruchia*. The firm foundations of a distinctive, national Church had already been laid. A close link between Church and King, the merger of two cults of national saints and a new vision of the duties of Christian kings had all been established in the eighth century and consolidated in the ninth. In this, the Church of a confederate people, Roman and Celtic traditions, abbot and bishop co-existed, as did the cults of Columba and Andrew, Adomnan and Ninian.

The next recasting of the image of a national Church came in the twelfth and thirteenth centuries, again with a new royal dynasty, the heirs of Malcolm III (1058–93). The conventional view of Malcolm's reign rests heavily on the influence wrought on the King by his second wife. With Margaret, the subject of the first 'official' biography of a Scottish monarch, written by her confessor, the Benedictine abbot Turgot, the difficulty is to separate cult – indeed, two cults – from contemporary reality. Shortly after her arrival a small Romanesque church was built at Dunfermline, the royal residence where she and Malcolm were married, and three Benedictine monks were sent at her request from the great mother house at Canterbury to form the nucleus of a Benedictine priory. It was a modest but none the less important first step, though in a direction which was not followed to any extent in Scotland. The beginnings of the huge, austere building (which still survives) are to be traced to its refoundation in 1128 in the reign of her youngest son, David. Yet the expansion of European monasticism, which so distinguished twelfth-century Scotland, drew not on the Benedictine impulse but on other religious orders – most notably the Augustinians or the Cistercians and Tironensians, both reformed Benedictine orders. The *Life* written by Turgot, some twenty years after Margaret's death, touches on Dunfermline only briefly, as one of the many venues illustrating the faith and works of a deeply pious woman. Dedicated since her childhood – spent in recently converted Hungary – to 'a life of soberness' and meditation 'day and night upon the law of the Lord', her personal devotions found outlets in a renewed royal cult of St Andrew and in the patronage of eremitic monks of Loch Leven as well as in Dunfermline. Turgot describes how she supported twenty-four poor people all year round, ministered daily to nine abandoned young orphans, washed the feet of six of the poor during the seasons of Lent and Advent and had 300 more fed in the royal hall before herself.

The impact of a queen who knew no Gaelic, unlike her bilingual husband, must have been muted beyond the immediate circles of the royal court. The reforms with which Turgot credits Margaret – re-establishment of more regular observation of the Lenten fast, the discouragement of celebration of the Mass with 'I know not what barbarous rite' and prohibitions on marriage within forbidden degrees – all brought Scotland into closer line with established practice elsewhere in the Church Universal, but other, probably more important issues, such as clerical celibacy and observance of a strict rule in monastic communities, were left untouched. There can be little doubt, however, of the depth of the mark which Margaret left on her children. A firm believer in the axiom of not sparing the rod, her real legacy lay in the conspicuous piety of her sons. Yet it was the work of the manufacturers of a second cult of Margaret, some 150 years after her death, that first laid stress on the pious David as son of Margaret. To acclaim the queenship of Margaret as a fundamental turning point in the history of Scotland or its Church is to risk reading history backwards from 1250 – which was what the chroniclers of the royal house of macMalcolm intended when Margaret, now canonized as a saint, was formally reburied in Dunfermline in a great set-piece occasion which accompanied the inauguration of Alexander III.

THE MEDIEVAL CHURCH

On 19 June 1250, the body of Queen Margaret, wife of Malcolm Canmore, was moved from its resting place in Dunfermline Abbey to a new shrine nearer the great altar. After almost five years of petitions to Rome, Margaret had been canonized as Scotland's first (and only) royal saint. Although he did not live to see it, the ceremony was a notable triumph for Alexander II, in whose reign the Scottish Church had reached its mature form. The cleric who had organized the campaign was David Bernham, royal client and confidant and the first native-born Scot to be Bishop of St Andrews (1239–53) since 1093. The inauguration of Alexander's eleven-year-old son five days after his father's death in July 1249, which came close to a formal rite of anointing and coronation (which first took place only in 1331 on the accession of David II), Margaret's canonization two months later and her investiture in the following year were all testimony to a coming of age not only of the macMalcolm dynasty but also of the Scottish Church and a new maturity in the relationship between Church and State.

The Scottish Church had been given new status in 1192 when Pope Celestine III (1191–8), in a bull *Cum universi,* declared that all the Scottish sees except Galloway (which was under the jurisdiction of York) should enjoy the status of 'special daughter' of Rome, immediately subject to the papacy rather than to Canterbury, Durham or York. Yet popes had been consistently reluctant to grant to kings of Scots the full rites of anointing and coronation or to confer metropolitan status on St Andrews, despite petitions in the reigns of David I (1124–53) and Malcolm IV (1153–65). It was no accident that the reign of William the Lion (1165–1214) saw a revival of the legends of the origins of kings of Scots and a further elaboration of the cult of St Andrew. Visible evidence of the heightened dependence of the macMalcolm dynasty and the Church on each other were the *Pictish Chronicle,* which was copied during the reign, with its tracing of the common origin of Scots, Picts and Britons to Scota, daughter of the Pharaoh, and the beginnings of the building of a new cathedral at St Andrews in the 1160s, at 320 feet in length and 168 feet across its transepts far larger than any other church in the realm. The intertwined identity of King, Church and people – originating in the children of Israel, linked ever since the time of Columba by a royal priesthood, and now given alternative form in a second national saint – was nearly complete.

The cult of Andrew, which had steadily grown in the tenth and eleventh centuries, was given fresh elaborations in the course of the twelfth. By the 950s, more than a century before Queen Margaret instituted the celebrated free transport across the Forth at Queensferry for pilgrims to St Andrews, there is ample evidence that the shrine of St Andrew at what was still called 'Kilrymond' was already a popular pilgrimage centre, whose fame had spread throughout Scotland and further afield. Constantine II had retired to the monastic life there in 952 and an Irish prince called Aed is known to have died there 'in pilgrimage' in 965. By the eleventh century, that older place-name was being superseded by the name of the Apostle himself.

Although St Andrew was to become the patron saint of the macMalcolm dynasty – just as Columba had been that of the macAlpin line before it – the substitution was never total. Queen Margaret enjoyed a reputation long after her death as the rebuilder of Iona as well as the patron of pilgrims of the Apostle. Malcolm Canmore's son Donald Ban had his bones moved from Dunkeld to Iona *c.* 1105, and the usual burial place for kings of Scots from 1107 onwards was at Dunfermline rather than St Andrews. Thus the identification of Columba with the Celtic Church and St Andrew with the new practices of Western Christendom introduced in their various forms in the twelfth century was never absolute. It was significant that the establishment of a second route for pilgrims to St Andrews across the Forth, between North Berwick and Ardross, known as the Earl's Ferry, was the work of the premier native noble of the mid-twelfth century, Duncan Earl of Fife. As in secular politics, a balance between old and new was struck within the Church – in piety and in its saints as much as in its organization. It was a hybrid Church for a hybrid people.

Just as the staff of Columba had allowed a mixed army of Picts and Scots to fight together in 918 as 'Albanaich' (men of Scotland) against a common enemy, so the authority of the Apostle was gradually cultivated: by the time of William Fraser, Bishop of St Andrews (1279–97), the legend insisted on the suzerainty of the Apostle over all the peoples of Scotland, 'the Picts, Scots, Danes and Norwegians'. By 1279 the seal of the Bishop of St Andrews bore the image of St Andrew crucified, and in 1286 it also appeared on the seal of the Guardians of the Kingdom, accompanied by the legend, 'Andrew be leader of the compatriot Scots'. By 1318, when St Andrews Cathedral was consecrated in a service of national thanksgiving 'for the notable victory granted to the Scottish people by blessed Andrew, protector of the realm' four years earlier at Bannockburn, the identification of apostolic saint and nation was complete.

In the Declaration of Arbroath of 1320, the identity of the Scottish nation was taken one stage further. The reputation of Bruce as well as the status of the Scots was proven by the touchstone of 'our patron and protector', Andrew. This was a document written for the eyes of the Pope, but at home both the Church and kings of Scots were aware of their identities as shepherd and leader of what was still acknowledged to be a confederation of peoples. Robert Bruce, a Gaelic-speaking Celtic king as well as a feudal ruler descended from an Anglo-Norman family, had taken both symbols of the Scottish Church, the *Brecbennach* of Columba and the cross of Andrew in the form of the saltire flag, to the field of Bannockburn.

The twelfth century, which was, in terms of building and the introduction of new religious orders, the most dynamic century in the history of the medieval Church, also saw the introduction of many new biblical and continental saints. Nowhere was the change more obvious than in the King's newly founded burghs, where the new parish kirks were dedicated to such as St Mary (at Berwick, Dundee, Glasgow and Haddington), St Nicholas (Aberdeen, Lanark and Renfrew) or St Giles (Edinburgh and Elgin). Yet some older dedications, such as that to St Clement (seen in both Dundee and the fishing port of Footdee close to Aberdeen), which was popular along the seaboard of northern Europe in the eleventh century, remained. Elsewhere dedications were considerably more mixed, encouraged by the number of native saints' lives written or rewritten in the twelfth century. In rural parish kirks, Andrew, brother of Peter, had to compete with Kentigern, Ninian, St Machar and St Serf. Local cults of Celtic or other early saints were as much a part of the early medieval Church as was the veneration of Andrew as a national saint.

The composite identity of the Scottish Church in the twelfth and thirteenth centuries mirrored the shifting, hybrid character of both the macMalcolm dynasty and the nobility. It also masked the clash of continuity and change going on within the Church itself, especially among the secular clergy. Fothad, who had died in 1093, the same year as Malcolm and Margaret, had been followed by an unbroken line of distinguished Anglo-Norman bishops, of whom the greatest were Robert (1124–59), an Augustinian canon of Scone who had supervised the enlargement of St Rule's as a cathedral and priory church and had perhaps also planned the creation of a new cathedral before his death, and William Malvoisin (1202–38), who had brought the reorganization of the huge diocese to a conclusion. Native Scots were a rarity among the twelfth-century episcopate, which was largely Anglo-French in origin.

In this period, Scottish cathedrals had naturally turned to their English counterparts to provide a model for their organization and constitutions: Moray, perhaps prompted by the example of its first effective bishop, Richard of Lincoln (1187–1203), looked to Lincoln Cathedral for its constitutions in 1212; Glasgow had already adopted those of Salisbury, and Dunkeld followed suit in the 1250s. The influence of English diocesan reform on St Andrews did not come to a sudden end in 1238, for Bernham had been a member of Malvoisin's household and had modelled the development of a small group of professional administrators to run his diocese on the work of Robert Grosseteste, Bishop of Lincoln. The Sarum use in worship, as a result, had gained widespread, if not complete, acceptance by then. By 1250, however, a new breed of churchmen had emerged. Bishops were increasingly likely to be either royal servants or the kin or clients of noble families; the favour of Alexander III (1249–86) and the tentacles of Comyn patronage extended far into the benefice structure of the late thirteenth-century secular Church. By the reign of Alexander III, the *ecclesia Scoticana* was staffed largely by Scots.

The new reformed religious orders established in the course of the twelfth century – Augustinians, Cistercians and Premonstratensians – were all French in origin but had been introduced via daughter houses already set up in England. Only the Tironensians among the first generation of monastic incomers came directly from the mother house in France – at Tiron near Chartres. Whether the parentage was direct or indirect, there is an important truth in the saying that every Scottish monastery was 'a little bit of France'. Like Tironensian abbots, heads of Cistercian houses were obliged to attend the regular meetings of all abbots of the order, at Cîteaux in Burgundy. In turn, it was the duty of abbots of mother houses in all orders to inspect daughter houses every year. The monastic world knew no frontiers, although few orders were as systematic in their contacts as the Cistercians, which by 1273 had no fewer than eleven houses ranging from Melrose in the Borders to Saddell in Argyll and Kinloss in Moray, each with at least thirteen monks and ten or more lay brothers. Often granted large tracts of uncultivated land ideal for sheep farming, the Cistercians accounted for four of the fifteen different religious houses which had warehouses in Scotland's premier port of Berwick in the thirteenth century; their organization, which controlled some 5 per cent of the Scottish wool clip, allowed them to act as a virtual trading consortium. The absence of restrictions on the holding of lands by religious orders within towns made the economic links between society and the religious in Scotland rather closer than in England.

The involvement with society of the Augustinian canons took a different form. Not an enclosed order like Cluniacs, Tironensians or the thirteenth-century arrivals, the Valliscaulian monks, the primary mission of the Augustinians was to go out into the world of the laity, usually serving the parish churches which were appropriated to their house. They also had a strong eremitical character, which suited their takeover and reform of a number of old *Céli Dé* communities. These were often situated in remote sites, like Inchcolm in the Firth of Forth or Inchmahome on the Lake of Menteith. If the Tironensians were the proprietary order of David I, it was the Augustinians who had succeeded to this mantle before the end of the twelfth century, based in or near royal centres such as Holyrood near

Edinburgh, Cambuskenneth across the Forth from Stirling, and St Andrews itself. No order was as close to the royal house between 1200 and 1450.

The introduction, again as a result of royal patronage, of two mendicant orders – the Dominicans (Black Friars) and Franciscans (Grey Friars) – in the reign of Alexander II (1214–49) was a further sign of the vitality of the Scottish medieval Church. Each was brought to Scotland within two decades of its foundation as an order. By the end of the century there were already a dozen Dominican houses and six Franciscan, mostly sited on the edge of major towns, where they might practise their work of preaching, teaching and charity. Other friars – notably the Carmelites (White Friars) and the Trinitarians (Red Friars) – followed. These orders conformed to the pattern already becoming apparent in other branches of the thirteenth-century Church, being consciously international in outlook but staffed for the most part by local men. The 1250s saw the beginning of a campaign for the establishment of a separate Franciscan province, which had a chequered history until its final establishment in 1483. The Dominicans, although nominally part of the English province until 1481, showed from an early date strong devolutionist tendencies. In 1289 a papal indulgence acknowledged the growing sense of nationalism among the religious by forbidding the appointment of foreigners as heads of any religious houses in Scotland.

The thirteenth century brought changes, too, for many of the ordinary secular clergy, and not all of them were welcome. By 1300 more than 60 per cent of parish kirks had their teinds (tithes) appropriated, in whole or in part, to another ecclesiastical foundation – usually a religious house or cathedral chapter. This figure would rise to 85 per cent by the sixteenth century. Already by 1250 part of the price of magnificent buildings such as the abbeys of Kelso or Dryburgh or the new cathedral churches and growing diocesan administration of sees like St Andrews and Glasgow was becoming apparent: instead of beneficed parish priests, many parishes were beginning to be served by vicars. This was almost certainly not yet as damaging as it would be on the eve of the Reformation, by which time much of the ordinary business of the Church was carried out by curates for absentee benefice-holders. Yet the process had already begun by which the 'foot soldiers' of the later medieval Church would be chaplains of various sorts, underpaid, lacking in job security and forever on the move. It is as well to remember that within most great ecclesiastics – ranging from William Wishart, a bishop of Glasgow in the late thirteenth century who is alleged to have amassed twenty-two rectories and prebends by the time of his election, to the celebrated Bishop Elphinstone who employed a race of Elphinstones in his Aberdeen diocese in the late fifteenth century – there lurked either a pluralist or a nepotist, and that behind them was a transient and poorly paid workforce.

THE LATER MEDIEVAL CHURCH: CLERGY AND CROWN

The descent of the parish clergy into real poverty belonged to the late fourteenth and the fifteenth centuries. In the thirteenth century, vicars-pensioner (who were paid only a fixed pension rather than a share of the teinds of the parish) were allowed ten merks a year (a merk was two-thirds of a pound) and chaplains five pounds. By the fourteenth century such vicars were supposed to be paid a minimum of ten pounds, but often were not. It is likely that the intention of the Church authorities was to keep the income of the parish clergy on a par with that of freeholders or husbandmen, the backbone of rural society who, if they had an income of ten pounds, were required by Parliament to be armed and horsed for military service. Their status was not unlike that of seventeenth-century ministers of the Reformed Church, whose income matched that of the lairds (gentry), feuars and greater tenant farmers in their congregations. But increasingly the income of the parish clergy fell in real terms as price inflation gripped late medieval Scotland. Long before the Church was faced by a spiritual crisis, it was confronted by an economic one.

The shortcomings of the medieval Church were slow to emerge and responsibility for them is difficult to assign with any precision. Nepotism was the natural reflection of a society in which kinship counted for so much. Pluralism was endemic to an ecclesiastical system which had in the twelfth and thirteenth centuries sunk so many of its assets, in manpower as well as in stone and finance, into centres of excellence, in the form of the cloister or the cathedral chapter. Prestigious building schemes amid poverty were not unique to the medieval period. The dramatic beauty of Elgin Cathedral deserved its description as 'the ornament of the realm, the glory of the kingdom, the delight of foreigners'. There can also be little doubt that such bishops were concerned above all else with bringing the teachings of Christ to ordinary members of society; the thirteenth-century statutes of the Scottish Church, which provide the bulk of what evidence there is of ordinary parish life, are filled with a concern to administer the sacraments and teach the faith that would not be out of place in the sixteenth century or the twentieth. The parish clergy were enjoined to celebrate the sacraments 'with devout solemnity in the Catholic faith according to the precise form handed down by the holy fathers and the holy Scriptures' and parishioners were in their turn to be urged 'to explain that same faith to their children and to teach them to keep the Christian faith'.

Such indications as there are show that the vast bulk of them performed their duties with reverence. There can be little doubt, however, that there was a drastic loss of status of the clergy in minor orders, linked to their falling income, in the fifteenth and early sixteenth centuries. Responsibility for this rests primarily with a hierarchy which failed to divert enough resources into the ordinary parish system, but it also belongs to the lay patrons who employed chaplains on minimum wages in collegiate churches, hospitals or other lay foundations. The laity expected more to be done for the salvation of their souls, but were unwilling or unable to pay as much for it as before.

The continuing anomaly of a national Church, specifically under papal protection but lacking a metropolitan – which lasted until the elevation of St Andrews into an archbishopric in 1472 – had two effects. It encouraged an unusually close liaison between Scotland and the papal court, and representatives of both the Scottish Church and Crown grew adept in the complex arts of lobbying in Rome; but it also resulted in a close interest expressed by Scottish kings in Church appointments. The development after 1225 of a national provincial council of the Scottish Church, headed by a conservator rather than an archbishop, had the effect of accelerating both tendencies. It is likely that these provincial councils developed a higher notion of their powers than Rome may have expected – a development which has lured some historians into thinking the pronouncements of the pre-Reformation councils of 1549, 1552 and 1559 to be 'anti-papal'.

These councils also generated a clear sense of group solidarity among the hierarchy, which would be given practical effect in pleading the Scottish cause at Rome and elsewhere during the Wars of Independence. The long struggle with England tested many loyalties, but the Scottish bishops for the most part held to a fairly consistent view which was unusual among other groups in Scottish society. It may seem surprising that churchmen proved to be those most willing to turn a blind eye to the sacrilegious murder of John Comyn by Robert Bruce in the Greyfriars' kirk in Dumfries in February 1306; but they had more to lose than most from English hegemony. It was the cause they backed rather than the man, who was until at least 1314 on trial as much among the clergy as in other sections of the political community. Their nationalism was both informed and self-interested; it stemmed from two centuries and more of intermittent claims of various parts of the English Church to jurisdiction over them. The close-knit ties of kin and clientage which bound together the middle ranks of most dioceses meant that few broke ranks.

The shift of the papal court from Rome to Avignon after 1309 encouraged a trend which had already begun with the Anglo-Scottish wars: in the thirteenth century many Scottish students had gone to Oxford or

Cambridge, but in the fourteenth they preferred the universities of Paris, Orleans, Louvain or Cologne. A new cosmopolitan nationalism affected the leading Scottish clergy as a result. The increasing control exerted by the Avignon papacy over appointments fuelled contests over benefices, encouraged ambitious young Scots to court patrons at Avignon, raised costs and reduced the income enjoyed by new benefice-holders. The results reverberated through the clerical system: the increased costs were passed on; more parish kirks had their revenues appropriated; the vicar with a 'perpetual vicarage', enjoying some share in the teinds, might find himself a vicar-pensioner, with a fixed stipend in a period of rising prices and a falling pound, forced to resort to other devices to scrape a living. The combined effect of a country struggling to recover from the impact of a century of intermittent warfare, the slump in trade after a brief recovery in the 1370s and the new costs of papal provision to benefices did not impoverish the whole Scottish Church, but it did drastically accentuate the gap between appropriators and appropriated.

The Great Schism (1378–1417) which followed, with rival popes in Avignon and Rome, initially strengthened the links between Scotland and France. The steadfast loyalty of the Scottish Church to the Avignon popes – Scotland was the only kingdom in Europe to remain single-mindedly loyal to Benedict XIII (1394–1417) – had a number of important consequences. The most notable was the founding of Scotland's first university. The exile of Benedict from France in 1408 had resulted in the return to Scotland of a number of masters who had formerly taught in French universities. By 1412 they had founded a school at St Andrews, which a year later was granted the necessary six bulls of protection and privilege by Benedict, according it university status and the right to confer degrees. The liberal patronage of the Avignon popes, anxious to sustain support in Scotland for their cause, had encouraged inflated expectations among both churchmen and laity; these were deflated after 1417 by the restored Martin V, who was anxious to reassert his accustomed rights to papal provision and full common services. This was the background to the sharp friction after 1424 between James I, a restored Scottish king anxious to make his mark, and a Pope determined to defend his authority against general councils. The pattern which would last for more than a century was set. Every king from James I to James V would complain about the exactions which emanated from Rome, probe the technicalities of the ecclesiastical appointments system and seek to exploit its loopholes. Parliament, once given a taste of a new secular authority over the Church, would act still more aggressively; it, even more than Stewart kings, was the advocate of the rights, both accustomed and novel, of the Crown over the Church.

The year 1472 saw the appointment of the first Archbishop of St Andrews. The sudden appearance of a Scottish metropolitan in the unlikely form of Patrick Graham, who was also granted legatine powers, paradoxically brought about a far more serious crisis in relations with the papacy than that of the 1420s. His deprivation in 1478, a discredited and somewhat pathetic figure, was a major, if distasteful, victory for the Crown. His replacement by William Scheves (1478–97), a royal placeman noted for his competence as an administrator rather than his scholarship or reputation as a pastor, was as cynical an appointment in a Church which was brimming with talent as that of Graham by Sixtus IV had been. The reality of the situation in which both James III (1460–88) and the popes found themselves in the 1470s and 1480s was that neither could afford to risk losing control over the Scottish Church. The Crown, with its other sources of income faltering, was increasingly reliant on its revenue from the Church; and the recasting of royal authority in the fifteenth century brought about an increasing dependence of the Crown on a class of skilled administrators and jurists, among whom William Elphinstone, trained in both canon and civil law at Paris and Orleans and chancellor under James III, was *primus inter pares*.

The jostling between king and papacy was resolved by the succession of a more conciliatory pope, in the shape of Innocent VIII. Within a year a golden rose, the traditional mark of papal favour, had arrived, and in 1487 a face-saving compromise was arranged. The Indult (privilege) of that year did not bind the Pope to accept the King's 'humble supplications' regarding provision to benefices, but it accepted that the Crown should enjoy the revenues of all major benefices and abbacies for fully eight months after they fell vacant. The right of nomination by the Crown was not conceded, but the door was left firmly ajar for future kings and parliaments to exploit. In 1535 the Pope, with the spectre of another Henry VIII in prospect, conceded the *ius nominandi* and extended the period of delay in making appointments to a full twelve months.

THE LATE MEDIEVAL CHURCH: LEARNING AND THE LAW

There were no Scottish universities before the founding of St Andrews in 1412. The next century would see a college (St Salvator's) erected at St Andrews in 1450 to teach theology and philosophy, a college of arts founded at Glasgow in 1451, and the setting up at Aberdeen in 1495 of the College of St Mary in the Nativity (or King's College), which in its second foundation of 1505 ambitiously proposed four faculties. Further colleges shortly followed at St Andrews: St Leonard's, erected in 1513 as a 'college of poor clerks' based on the austere model of the College of Montaigu in Paris, was fuelled by Augustinian piety; St Mary's, first mooted in 1525, given formal foundation in 1538 and reorganized in 1544, would become the centre of the movement for internal reform of the Church in the late 1540s and 1550s. All these foundations were the acts of bishops, who placed them at the centre of their dioceses, and were clerically endowed.

The impact of what amounted to a national programme for higher learning – Elphinstone referred to his university as being built for the 'glory of the fatherland' – was both wider and narrower than it may first seem. It had long been university graduates who filled most of the ranks of the higher clergy and they also staffed the burgeoning departments of the royal administration under Stewart kings. Yet the curriculum of the new universities, despite ambitious plans, remained narrowly concentrated in faculties of arts. The study of theology was patchy, and that of medicine or the law negligible. The numbers of graduates were still modest – not many more than ten a year graduated from the new University of St Andrews before 1450, perhaps thirty came out of it and Glasgow in the later part of the century, and the total annual crop of graduates of all the universities was not likely to have been more than a hundred in the 1540s. The bulk of them were still churchmen; St Leonard's, like the others, saw itself as a 'holy college'. The most talented or ambitious who wished to pursue their studies further – usually by specialization in those passports to ecclesiastical preferment, canon and civil law – continued to go abroad, to the great universities of western Europe.

This was not a new trend: Scots had travelled to foreign seats of learning for centuries. It is known that more than thirty Scots studied at the great legal centre of Bologna between 1265 and 1294, and larger numbers probably went to both Oxford and Paris. By the fourteenth century, however, with the papacy established at Avignon, France had become the obvious mecca for Scottish churchmen and students. Both the Italian and English universities fell from favour. The French connection laid down firm roots in the century after 1350, and no group did more to encourage the flowering of its multifold aspects than the clergy, who trained, studied, petitioned and lobbied at Paris, Orleans and Avignon. By the second quarter of the fifteenth century, encouraged by the foundation of Louvain University and the continuing importance of Bruges as a staple port, a strong Flemish cultural connection had also taken root.

Many university men made their mark elsewhere because, like the most celebrated philosopher of his age, John or Duns Scotus (d. 1308), they chose to follow a career outside Scotland, in his case at Oxford and Paris. Not the least of the achievements of the fifteenth and early sixteenth centuries was that the new university foundations went a long way towards reversing the academic brain drain: Hector Boece, lured home by Elphinstone from the College of Montaigu to become the first Principal of Aberdeen University, was a close friend of the great Erasmus and a devotee of the new learning; and John Mair (or Major), who had gained a European-wide reputation while at Paris, returned to become Provost of St Salvator's College in 1534.

Far less is known of the other two sectors of the medieval education system: the grammar schools and the variety of 'little', song and vernacular schools. Duns Scotus had gone to a grammar school at Haddington, and it seems likely that the upsurge in university education reflected a parallel increase in the number of grammar schools, most of which were based in towns. Many were associated with cathedrals or with collegiate churches of different kinds, which were sharply increasing in number from the 1380s onwards. Some religious houses, too, had monastic schools which opened their doors, like the Cistercian abbey at Kinloss, to a wider intake of boys. Some friaries had their own 'lector' in theology or arts, and the Dominican house at Ayr had a tutor in grammar in 1420. By the time of the Education Act passed by Parliament in 1496, which encouraged the attainment by the sons of barons and freeholders of 'perfyte latyn', it seems likely that the growing demands of the state for administrators and lawyers may have been threatening to outstrip supply. The course of the sixteenth century would see the increasingly heavy hand of state intervention in both the grammar schools and the universities, but the curriculum taught in these schools remained much the same as it had been in 1500 or 1400.

There were many other kinds of schools in medieval Scotland, although they were not necessarily parish schools. The most easy to trace are the song schools attached to both cathedral and collegiate churches, reflecting the reviving interest in the fifteenth century in church music. There were also reading or 'English' schools, situated in rural areas as well as in towns and intended to give only a rudimentary education, probably mostly to boys. There were probably also some small schools designed for girls, sometimes run by women or by nuns, often described as sewing schools. It is likely that many lairds ran private schools for their children and perhaps also those of their kin or tenants. The schoolmasters in most of these rudimentary schools were usually chaplains of various kinds, eager to supplement a meagre income by taking on extra work. The effect of the Protestant Reformation was felt most keenly in this area of schooling. The generations after 1560, however, saw the consolidation rather than the establishment of an elementary national system of education; in many cases, schools were refounded or recast rather than created as new foundations.

Most of the leading figures in the later medieval Church had had a legal education, and it seems likely that they were the instigators of a number of attempts in the fifteenth century to codify the law. The gradual emergence of a central civil law court, the Court of Session, which was eventually established in 1532 with fifteen paid judges or senators, had been going on for more than a century. The mixed composition of this body, which comprised eight ecclesiastics and nine laymen, was symptomatic of its times. In many areas – relief of the poor, provision for education, patronage of new ecclesiastical corporations and chaplaincies, and not least the law – the expertise and long experience of churchmen remained vital, but the laity was making increased demands and exercising a new level of patronage and control. It was ironic that the bulk of these extra demands, which made Church and State as well as clergy and society more intertwined than ever, had to be financed through the system of appropriation of the teinds of parish kirks. Although as yet hardly faced with a serious challenge from heresy, the parish system was bleeding from a thousand cuts, either self-inflicted or caused by the new demands made of it by society.

A Church in Decline?

The later fifteenth century was an age of paradoxes. It saw the Crown more in control of appointments to benefices than ever before, but it also witnessed a chorus of criticisms of the papacy in Parliament and elsewhere, especially in the 1490s. The creation in 1492 of a second archbishopric, of Glasgow, had provoked Parliament into protests about the 'unestimable dampnage to the realme' inflicted by the costs of rival prelates pursuing actions at Rome against each other. Yet it was a rivalry which was largely of the Crown's own making, for James IV had been the primary supporter of the claims of Glasgow. It was also an age of a great spiritual awakening, even though the Church was enmeshed in economic crisis.

The fourteenth century had seen a slackening of interest in local or early saints, but they experienced a marked revival from the second quarter of the fifteenth century onwards. This was the age of Walter Bower, whose *Scotichronicon* combined an anti-English patriotism with the revival of a cult of native saints. Bower, an Augustinian abbot of Inchcolm, turned his island abbey into a devotional centre dedicated to Columba. James Haldenstone, another Augustinian prior (of St Andrews) of the same period, was an early campaigner for the canonization of St Duthac of Tain as well as a restorer of the cathedral church dedicated to the Apostle. Bishop William Lauder of Glasgow was at the same time, in 1420, petitioning the Pope for permission to move the feretory of St Mungo to a more prominent place in his cathedral church.

The revival of interest in lesser saints, such as St Thenew at Glasgow, St Triduana at Restalrig near Edinburgh and St Ebba at Coldingham later in the same century, all marked the opening up of new archives of the historical memories of a nation. This movement reached its climax in what has been called a national liturgy, the *Aberdeen Breviary* assembled by Bishop William Elphinstone of Aberdeen – one of the earliest surviving Scottish printed books, produced in Edinburgh by Walter Chepman and Andrew Myllar in 1510. In it are to be found more than seventy native saints, all assigned feast days and each a history lesson in itself. Yet Elphinstone's liturgy, which was intended to supplant the English Sarum use, was far more than a narrow propaganda tract for its times; it included most of the major new devotions current in Europe, such as St Mary *ad Nives*. The *Breviary* was not a new development; it was the culmination of a century which had seen first the revival of native saints and later the new European Marian cults, such as Our Lady of Consolation, and the cult of the Holy Family. It also summed up the new fashion in the later fifteenth century for continental devotions centring on the Passion of Christ, such as the Five Wounds and the Most Holy Name of Jesus. Many of these, like the Holy Blood (still to be seen in the Fetternear Banner, which belonged to the Edinburgh merchant guild) were imported direct from Flanders. The history of Scottish worship, like much of the history of medieval Scotland, was a blend of two sets of influences – nationalist and continental.

This quickening of spiritual life had many threads, and not all of them led in the same direction. The Mass was meant to be, as the chronicler Walter Bower had explained earlier in the same century, for 'the salvation of the living and the redemption of the dead'. The primary function of fifty or so collegiate churches founded between 1400 and 1550 was the saying of votive Masses for the dead, in order to shorten their time in purgatory. This was, however, a deeply felt need which affected all orders of society. Two of these foundations – Restalrig and Holy Trinity, Edinburgh – were the work of the Crown. A few – St Giles' in Edinburgh and Holy Trinity in St Andrews being the outstanding examples – were burgh parish churches awarded collegiate status as the result of substantial rebuilding, lengthy petitioning and considerable investment by townspeople, and more would follow in the sixteenth century, including St Mary's in Haddington and the Holy Rude at Stirling. Most collegiate kirks, however, were the tangible results of the patronage of nobles or barons; such were Kilmaurs, founded in 1403 by the local Cunningham family before it acquired an earldom, or Crichton, founded in 1449 by Lord Crichton, chancellor of James II.

Roslin, the most celebrated of these churches, was typical for the fact that its foundation in 1446 was only the prelude to a century of investment but unique in its elaborate architecture and sometimes fantastic internal decoration, such as its carving of the dance of death and the enigmatic 'Prentice Pillar'. Yet the existing chapel was merely the first stage of plans for a much larger building which were cut short by the Reformation. Most of these foundations were conventional expressions of piety in an age of austerity. St Giles', in the largest burgh in the realm, had an establishment of about twenty clergy in 1466, but more typical was Kilmaurs in rural Ayrshire which had six chaplainries in 1413, each costing somewhere between five and ten pounds a year.

Can the wave of collegiate foundations be taken as a sign that the Mass had come to be 'above all else a Mass for the dead'? That would be to take a narrow view of the trends of late medieval piety. The votive Mass for the dead needs to be placed beside the appeal of two other sets of devotions. A new popularity of the rosary, in itself part of a series of devotions dedicated to the Virgin Mary, spread across northern Europe and reached Scotland, like so much else in the period, via Flanders: the exquisite Arbuthnot *Book of Hours*, composed for the parish church of Arbuthnot by its own vicar, James Sibbald, about 1480, shows an image of *Sancta Maria in sole* surrounded by a five-decade rosary of red beads and pink roses. Books of hours were usually the precious private psalters of the rich (and especially of noblewomen), but the rosary itself was a set of devotions popular in all sections of society: both James III and James IV had expensive sets of beads of gold made for them; the Fetternear Banner, the elaborate tapestry made for the Holy Blood Confraternity of the Edinburgh merchant guild about 1520, also featured a rosary; and cheap, illicit rosaries were being sold at Turriff fair in Banffshire in 1579. The cult of the Virgin Mary, which has long been a particular feature of Scottish Roman Catholicism, can be traced to the fifteenth century.

The other important devotion of the period was the Passion: 'Devoit remembrance of the passion is better than our Lady and all the sanctis prayit for him', claimed one late-fifteenth-century work. It is no coincidence that the three opening pieces in the most important surviving manuscript collection of pre-Reformation Scottish devotional verse, Arundel MS 285, are all penitential works on the Passion: the *Tabill of Confessioun* of the Court poet and chaplain, William Dunbar; the *Contemplacioun of Synnaris* of the Observant Franciscan William of Touris, probably a member of the family of Touris of Inverleith near Edinburgh; and the *Passioun of Crist* of Walter Kennedy, a graduate of Glasgow. But the cult of the Passion was not a Protestant devotion before its time, although it would – unlike Marian devotions – later be adapted for

Protestant use. The *Contemplacioun* was written specifically for James IV (1488–1513), probably as part of his annual retreat at Eastertide when, girded with an iron belt, he would seek expiation for his involvement in the death of his father in the revolt of 1488. These devotional poems, however, were part of a wider spiritual movement, exemplified too by the cults of the Holy Blood and the Five Wounds of Christ, which also originated in the Low Countries. The preparation through the long season of Lent for what was probably for most ordinary men and women an annual celebration of Communion at Easter depended on populist representations of the Passion: the Passion plays adopted in a number of burghs in the later fifteenth century; paintings depicting the crucifixion and last judgement on church walls, such as those which survive from the kirk of Foulis Easter in Angus; the private ritual of the rosary – all were versions of the same obsession, with the salvation of souls of the living.

The late medieval Catholic mind would not usually try to erect a mental barrier between devotions to the Passion and to the Virgin Mary. In collegiate churches, it was common for services to begin, at five or six in the morning, with a Mass of the Blessed Virgin, celebrated by the Lady priest; various votive Masses would follow, over the course of the next ten or twelve hours. In the *Aberdeen Breviary*, there was a regular commemoration of the Blessed Virgin on Saturdays, no doubt to act as a counterpoint to the custom, in larger churches, to have a Mass of Corpus Christi each Thursday morning at the Holy Name, Holy Blood or Corpus Christi altars. Here was a regular reminder of the two greatest feast days of the year – Corpus Christi and the Assumption of Our Lady.

More regular still, however, was the practice of exposing the Holy Eucharist for veneration. New feasts, such as the Crown of Thorns, the Five Wounds and also the Compassion of the Virgin, pointed in the same direction. This might be done in various ways: one, also common in England, for it reflected the use of the Sarum rite, was to suspend the Eucharist in a small box or pyx above one of the altars. Another, widely used in Europe and especially in the Low Countries, was the use of a decorated wall cupboard or aumbry, known in Scotland as a sacrament house, which allowed continuous exposure of the Eucharist. It is likely that this was the most common practice in Scotland by the fifteenth century. Here was a liturgical practice which could be used in different kinds of churches, ranging from the ornate example erected in the 1460s in memory of Bishop Kennedy in the collegiate church of St Salvator at St Andrews to the smallest parish kirk. Some thirty-five examples have been traced, mostly in the east and to the north of the Tay, all dating from 1446 onwards; half of them, remarkably, were constructed after 1500. It is the best evidence that exists of a popular devotion to the Blessed Sacrament,

similar to that in Flanders and the Rhineland, which was still in full flow in
the first half of the sixteenth century. The remarkable survival of large,
painted oak panels at the small collegiate church of Foulis Easter, dating
from *c.*1453, which include scenes of both the crucifixion and the
Annunciation, gives a clue as to the intimate link between the various cults
of the Passion and the veneration of the Eucharist, which was the central
feature of late medieval devotions in Scotland. Its aumbry would have been
the focal point of the whole church.

What was the main stimulus and who were the main agents of the new
liturgical revival which marked this period? Bishops, such as Blacader of
Glasgow and Elphinstone of Aberdeen, were prominent, and in Elphinstone's case the stimulus extended beyond his cathedral church to a
number of small parish kirks within his diocese. Lay patrons, ranging from
'new' nobility of the fifteenth century to newly incorporated burgh guilds,
were much more prominent than ever before. The examples upon which
many of them drew came from the Low Countries, the natural point of
reference both for merchants, who traded through the staple ports of
Bruges, Middelburg or Veere, and for clerics, *en route* to Louvain or
Cologne.

Urban society was changing rapidly in this period, and nowhere more
obviously than in the burgh church. Each burgh still had only one parish
church, but population was on the increase – Dundee had a congregation of
4,500 souls in the 1480s, accommodated within St Mary's, the largest of
Scotland's burgh churches. Many urban parishes also stretched far into the
surrounding countryside and linked town and country intimately; the size
of St Mary's in Haddington surely reflected the large rural segment of the
'urban' parish. The incorporation of craft guilds was late in Scotland,
taking place in the major towns between 1474 and 1530, and this
development also found expression in both the new collegiate churches and
the cults of purgatory and individual saints. The single *corpus christianum*,
which comprised the whole community of the burgh, remained, but each
of the new components of urban society was given its own niche. The sense
of an ordered hierarchy in urban society was symbolized by the new Corpus
Christi procession, which can first be identified in Aberdeen in the 1440s,
with all the guilds taking part, the most senior having the position closest to
the Blessed Sacrament. Although little is known about the detail of plays
and pageants, they undoubtedly figured prominently in the new civic cult
which marked the half-century after 1475.

Within the large burgh churches, the guilds would be expected to
finance a chaplain serving an altar dedicated to a particular saint as a mark
of their new incorporated status. The supervision exercised over chaplains
by civic authorities was virtually total, and extended even to the

dedications, number and times of Masses. The elaboration of a civic cult was still flourishing on the very eve of the Reformation: as late as 1557, the skinners of Perth commissioned a new painting of their patron saint, Bartholomew; it was the only altarpiece which escaped the attention of the mob which ransacked the burgh church two years later, after a sermon preached by John Knox. Far from being moribund by the early sixteenth century, the burgh church probably came closest in the *ecclesia Scoticana* to meeting the growing demands of its flock. The case for sharply increasing numbers of Protestants from the 1530s onwards is – with the exception of Dundee and perhaps also Perth – at its weakest in the towns. As was the case with Norwich, Edinburgh, where Protestants comprised less than a fifth of the population in 1561, would move in the course of one or two generations *after* the Reformation from being a centre of conspicuous late medieval Catholic piety to being a testbed of radical Protestantism.

Although the burghs provide the fullest evidence of popular devotions, there is enough known about pilgrimages to show that this form of piety also persisted in strength, even in the sixteenth century. Before 1400, it had been common for royal or noble pilgrims to visit the celebrated shrines of western Europe, such as Compostela or Rome itself. The fifteenth century, the age of the rediscovery of Scottish saints, saw royal patronage turn to the domestic shrines at St Andrews, Ninian at Whithorn and St Duthac at Tain. This trend, however, should not necessarily be taken to signify new, inward-looking devotions, for prominent in it were the foreign queens of James II, III and IV. It was Margaret of Denmark who, in thanksgiving for the birth of her son in 1473, seems to have set the fashion for Whithorn, which he, after his accession as James IV, regularly followed, sometimes on foot from as far away as Stirling. The journey from Tain to Whithorn, the marathon among Scottish pilgrimages, seems to have acquired new status among ordinary pilgrims in his reign. Few clues exist to indicate the degree of popularity of these or other well-known shrines, of which there were a score or more. In 1413, the shrine of Our Lady of the Hamer, at Whitekirk in East Lothian, a holy well founded in the late thirteenth century, which was probably in the second rank of popularity, is supposed to have been visited by no fewer than 15,653 pilgrims. Whatever the precise numbers, it is certain that James I had houses built to accommodate pilgrims there in 1430. The continuing thirst of the pilgrims for new outlets is also confirmed by the attacks made by Protestant critics like the Earl of Glencairn on the shrine at Musselburgh, dedicated to Our Lady of Loreto, founded in 1532. Much of the evidence for the pre-Reformation period similarly suggests the growth rather than the slackening of popular piety.

In a complex period which seems to point in opposing directions, William of Touris, author of the *Contemplacioun*, is a useful pattern-case of his age. His poem would be used, after 1560, in a Protestant form – another example of orthodox Catholic piety being turned to novel use. Probably the product of a family of lairds, he belonged to the Observants, a new, breakaway branch of the mendicant Franciscan friars, which had the reformist centre of Cologne as its mother province in northern Europe. Only one major monastic foundation – the Charterhouse at Perth (1429) – had been established since 1300, but within fifty years of their introduction to Scotland by Mary of Gueldres in *c.*1455 no fewer than nine Observant Franciscan houses were set up. With friaries at royal centres such as Edinburgh, Perth, St Andrews and Stirling, the Observants became the favourite religious order of the house of Stewart. Mary of Gueldres founded at least four of the houses and her grandson, James IV, described himself as their 'son and defender'. Based in all three university centres as well as in the major burghs, situated beside the massive building programme going on at Stirling Castle from the reign of James IV onwards, and also enjoying links with important noble families such as the Oliphants and Setons, their position suggests that they were probably the most important stimulus of the age. Here was an order which kept faith with its ideal of an apostolate of work carried out while living a life of spartan simplicity, and its brethren kept in close touch with all three estates of the realm, linking learning, the royal court, and both aristocratic and urban patronage.

The Observant Franciscans were only one of many channels through which the cultural and religious influences of Flanders, the Rhineland and France flowed into Scotland. Ecclesiastical architecture (seen most obviously in the collegiate churches), saints, devotional cults, the new sophistication in church music and the continuing influence of studies at the universities of Louvain, Cologne and Paris all testify to the importance of the connections with France and the Low Countries. The Church still did most of all the institutions in Scottish society to nurture Scotland's links with continental Europe. With little evidence of late medieval heresy in Scotland, it was, ironically, along those long-established conduits of European influence that Protestant ideas first flowed.

REFORM AND REFORMATION

Despite the lack of co-ordination among the higher clergy, there was from the last quarter of the fifteenth century onwards a renewed closeness between Rome and its 'special daughter'. The relationship was in part about the ordinary, almost daily stream of business – dispensations, indulgences, appointments to benefices – which continued unchecked until 1559. It was also in part a contest of rival sets of power-brokers, vying for revenues and control of benefices. Yet the 1540s and 1550s saw a steady stream of queries from Rome about the state of the Scottish Church and a series of papal visitors to inspect it – in 1543, 1556 and 1559. By the 1550s two sets of proposals for internal reform of the Church had materialized. One, seen in councils of 1549, 1552 and 1559, was the product of efforts by the Scottish province itself, emanating from St Andrews which must by then have been widely recognized as a Catholic reform centre. The other, drawn up by Cardinal Sermoneta in 1556, was the product of the *curia*. Both were overtaken by the events of 1559–60. Whatever the undoubted faults of the Church, it was far from blind to its own shortcomings.

It is difficult to make easy generalizations about the condition of the pre-Reformation Church, for it was a patchwork of endemic faults and new initiatives. The health of the religious – monks, canons regular and friars – tended to vary from one order to another, and at times even from one religious house to another. The monasteries, so often criticized as being moribund and out of touch with the needs of sixteenth-century society, were dealt a telling double blow by one modern historian: as an institution, he concluded in two memorable phrases, each survived only as a 'property-owning corporation' and the 'most damning fact' about their inmates was that they 'played hardly any part in the Reformation, on either side'. This may cast a novel role for monks, who were not trained as shock-troops in religious controversy. They were as unfitted for Catholic evangelism as for Protestant. It was the friars, and especially the Friars Preachers (the Dominicans) who took up the weapons of evangelical preaching. They were far more formidable opponents, for they took on the Protestant preachers on their own ground. And this may have been the reason why so many friaries were targeted for sacking by the Congregation in 1559.

In England, Thomas Cromwell's agents had scoured the monastic houses for spiritual corruption and sexual immorality to find pretexts for the dissolution of the monasteries in 1536. They found more than enough to fuel an accompanying Protestant propaganda campaign. Scottish monasteries, in contrast, seem to have largely escaped the worst moral vices. They were, however, in difficulty. The greatest recent change in monastic life was the rise of commendators as heads of religious houses. The trend, which began in the early part of the century but reached its height in the twenty years before 1560, may not have scarred the religious houses as grievously as was often thought; even the most scandalous of James V's appointees – the four bastard sons provided to five monasteries between 1534 and 1541 – were all at least technically clerics. Commendation did not result, as most historians used to maintain, in the widespread secularization of the monasteries, for more than half the commendators were bishops. More significant was the fact that the new commendators, whether sons of nobles or products of the prolific loins of James V, were all faced with the same economic pressures which induced them to secularize monastic property to keep their houses in being. Although commendation did little to lend a new sense of urgency to the religious, it probably did not fatally wound them either. There were, on the contrary, signs that traditional devotions were flourishing in many houses and the number of novices was on the increase. Young men were flocking into the monasteries in the 1550s rather than flocking out. All of this might be summed up as a modest monastic revival. If there was a monastic crisis, it was one of economics rather than of spirituality.

The price of these achievements, as with many of those of the fifteenth century, was the same – the further bleeding of the ordinary parish system. All the new university foundations and many of the collegiate churches were financed by the system of appropriating parish teinds. By now 85 per cent of all parishes had some or all of their revenues appropriated. The system had been with the medieval Church almost since a new parish structure had emerged in the twelfth century, but it meant that the sixteenth-century quest for reform created a vicious circle. It established a cycle of poverty from which the only escape was into further abuses: parish priests, in order to augment their falling incomes, resorted to pluralism and absenteeism or to imposing unpopular charges on their parishioners. The effects were possibly not so bad as they might have been. Underpaid vicars and curates did, for the most part, attend to their pastoral duties diligently and, as a result, there was little of the aggressive anticlericalism directed against the parish clergy which marked other parts of Europe at this period. Even so, the Church was in dire need of fundamental overhaul. The Reformation overtook and absorbed a series of orthodox but largely ineffectual efforts at reform.

Plate 2 *The monument of Sir William Gee (d. 1637), with his first and second wives, and his children, in York Minster*
Reproduced courtesy of the Dean and Chapter of York; photographer: Jim Kershaw.

PART II

Reform, Revival and Enlightenment

7

The Church in Scotland from the Reformation to the Disruption

James K. Cameron

THE GROWTH OF PROTESTANTISM: 1525–1559

IN HIS *History of the Reformation in Scotland* John Knox, writing towards the end of his life, traced the origins of the Reformation to the Scottish followers of the English Lollards, and saw in the repressive efforts of the inquisitors of heretical pravity evidence of the emergence of opposition to the medieval Church that one day was to sweep it away. Nevertheless, the generalization 'that Scotland was a country of orthodox beliefs before 1520' cannot be gainsaid. There was, as in other parts of Western Christendom, mounting dissatisfaction with the lives of churchmen and the growing burden of ecclesiastical exactions, but little or no sign of a lack of concern for the consolation that religion can bring. A harbinger of impending danger can be detected in the weakening of the Church at the parochial level by the near-complete appropriation of parish churches for the support of large and somewhat lax monastic houses, which were often held *in commendam* by members of the royal family and the nobility; of collegiate churches, which initially signified a new but short-lived spiritual awareness; and of the universities and colleges which in the previous century had been born of the Church's realization of the need to raise education standards among the clergy. Consequently, at the parish level the Church was ill served; the vicar-priests were often illiterate and of necessity greedy; the poor were neglected and oppressed; and apart from the burghs, where the merchants' religious interest had found expression in some fine church buildings, as in Perth, Stirling, Dundee and Aberdeen, parish churches were often in a neglected, even a ruinous state.

If the condition of the Church at parochial level demanded reformation, the same could be said of the higher clergy and especially of the bishops who, in accordance with an agreement with the papacy, were effectively appointed by the Crown; they were largely drawn from the influential families, were often pluralist and their moral conduct frequently ill befitted their high calling. They devoted the greater part of their energy to politics rather than religion and were accustomed to wield extensive power. This was especially true of the archbishops of St Andrews and Glasgow, who held for much of the second quarter of the sixteenth century dominant positions in both Church and State.

What was true of the general spiritual decline in the monastic and mendicant orders on the continent held good also in Scotland. The border abbeys had suffered much from repeated military invasion, and those in other parts of the country were often lacking in spiritual vitality. The Grey Friars had also declined, but among the Dominicans, although they were comparatively few in number, there had been signs of revival. It was, however, the Augustinians who were to show perhaps the keenest interest in contemporary religious affairs and who were to give to the reforming movement not only some of its leaders but also a considerable proportion of its first parish ministers.

As the Lutheran movement gained momentum on the continent, a growing awareness of the new doctrines began to be detected in Scotland and to cause alarm. Acts of Parliament in 1525 and subsequent years prohibited the importation of Luther's writings at the sea ports, but did little to stem that tide or to suppress the growing interest in reform in academic and commercial centres on the east coast. In 1528 Patrick Hamilton suffered martyrdom in St Andrews as a Lutheran heretic. He had previously studied at Paris and Louvain, then had left St Andrews, where he had possibly been influenced by the local interest taken in the Lutheran affair, to study at the new University of Marburg, where he publicly defended theses embodying the essence of Luther's doctrine, which are evidence of the extent of his new theological understanding. Hamilton's death profoundly affected religious life in Scotland, and won for the cause of reform a number of converts. Some suffered persecution, others fled the country, yet the cause of Reformation continued to make progress, fostered by the dissemination of Tyndale's *New Testament* as well as pamphlets such as John Johnson's *Confortable Exhortation*, John Gau's *Richt Vay to the Kingdom of Heuin* and other Protestant propaganda supplied by exiles from printing presses on the continent.

The political strategy of the country's leaders which brought the Church and the government closer together and allied their fortunes with those of France had, despite the fact that Henry VIII's retaliatory invasion of the country in 1542 had deprived it of its young king, the effect of encouraging the emergence of a pro-English party among sections of the nobility, who in time were to emerge as the defenders of Protestantism. For a brief moment at the beginning of the reign of the infant Queen Mary there was a vague possibility that a Henrician type of Reformation might be carried out. Those who controlled the government permitted by Act of Parliament the possession of the Scriptures in the vernacular as part of their pro-English policy. Whatever the aims of the government were, and it is unlikely that they could be described as Protestant, its action gave considerable encouragement to those who sought reform and disseminated 'heretical' books and pamphlets. These seemingly favourable political developments provided the background for renewed Protestant activity, centred on Dundee and Angus in the east, Ayr in the south-west and certain parts of Lothian, which was carried out in 1544 and 1545 with remarkable freedom. This activity was severely challenged by the execution of George Wishart in March 1546 as part of a fresh round of persecution instigated by Cardinal David Beaton, at whose hands a pro-French policy had once again been adopted by the government. The mission of Wishart, who had experienced Protestantism in England and on the continent, particularly in Switzerland, marks the phasing out of Lutheran influences and the emergence of a more militant Reformed outlook and programme subsequently associated with the name of John Knox, a close companion of Wishart in the last year of his life.

The murder of the cardinal in the same year (1546), partly the result of a 'deadly feud' and religious opposition, the uneasy 'truce' that existed particularly in St Andrews during the protracted settlement of Beaton's successor as Archbishop of St Andrews, John Hamilton (half-brother of the head of the house of Aran), together with events that had been taking place in England and on the continent, aroused among the churchmen an awareness of the dangers that lay ahead if some measure of reform were not undertaken. There had already been a number of iconoclastic outbursts throughout the country. Archbishop Hamilton undertook the re-foundation of St Mary's College, which had been begun by his immediate predecessors, and in which the Dominican presence was strong, in an effort to raise the educational standard of the clergy and stem the swelling tide of heresy. At the same time he appears to have been influenced by the Catholic reforming programme that had been pursued by Hermann von Wied, Archbishop of Cologne, and also by the Council of Trent. He may have been following the German example in holding a number of provincial councils (in 1549, 1552 and 1559), the primary objective of which was the removal of clerical abuses and the adoption of a programme of reform in line with that currently being advocated at Trent. He had also, with the support of his councils, drawn up a Catechism in the vernacular to help the clergy in their instruction of the people. This work, which probably emanated from St Mary's College, owed something to Grooper's

Enchiridion (printed along with the Canons of the Councils of Cologne), and although the Catechism is orthodox in its sacramental teaching, it is significantly silent on the papacy.

These efforts towards conservative reform, which had the support of theologians and other leaders among the friars and canons regular, along with those of the scholarly Robert Reid, Bishop of Orkney, came, as it turned out, too late. If the canons of the Scottish councils, together with some of the contemporary literature, for example the poems of Sir David Lyndsay, truly reflect conditions among the clergy and the extent of ecclesiastical oppression of the poor, then indeed it is hard to believe that a more drastic reform could be long delayed. Yet it would be a mistake to hold that all hope of a conservative, Catholic Reformation, even in the 1550s, was vain.

The progress of the Protestant reformers, despite continuing (if less intensive) persecution, was maintained in the fifteen years following Wishart's death. At the same time political opposition to the pro-French rule exercised from 1554 by the Queen Mother, Mary of Guise, with the aid of a foreign army, was steadily mounting. Parties were beginning to take shape. The cause of the Protestants, supported by many among the barons and the merchant class, was merging with that of the politically discontented nobility, some of whom had accepted Protestantism, and who were beginning to realize the consequences of the 'usurpation' by the Queen Mother of their traditional rights to govern during the absence of their young Queen in France. In the interests of France, the Queen Mother at first pursued a policy of religious toleration. John Knox, who had in 1546 joined Beaton's murderers in St Andrews Castle, who had been captured by the French, and who had during the reign of Edward VI spent some time in the service of the Church of England before going into exile on the continent, visited Scotland briefly in 1555 and put new heart into the reforming movement. Two years later, some of the leading Protestant nobility, later called 'the Lords of the Congregation', united in a solemn 'Common Band' or 'Covenant' by which they undertook 'with their whole power, substance, and our very lives to maintain, set forward and establish the most blessed word of God' and 'to labour at our possibility to have faithful Ministers purely and truly to minister Christ's Evangel and Sacraments to his people'. W. Croft Dickinson summed up the position as follows: 'The face of a Reformed Church was revealing itself. Some of the Protestant lords openly associated themselves with the preachers; some maintained preachers in their own households; and the leading preachers found that more and more they could rely upon temporal support.'

The year 1558, with the marriage of the Queen of Scots to the Dauphin, brought nearer the possibility of Scotland being ruled as a province of France. At the same time the accession of Elizabeth and the revival of the fortunes of Protestantism in England brought hopes of political aid to the anti-French party in Scotland, especially as Francis and Mary had lost no time in asserting Mary's claim to the English throne. But internationally the future of Protestantism was critical. With peace between France and Spain it seemed as if their united forces would be directed towards the elimination of Protestantism both on the continent and in Great Britain. The possibility of Scotland being used as a second front for a joint Franco-Spanish Catholic attack upon England was keenly realized, especially in England. However much she disliked it, Queen Elizabeth was constrained in her own interest to help the Scots Protestant nobility and their supporters among the barons and from the burghs in their opposition to French Catholic domination, which became decidedly anti-Protestant. John Knox had returned at the request of the nobility. By the early summer of 1559 the Reformation had become a Revolution. Protestant congregations complete with kirk sessions had been set up with the full support of the local magistrates in the prominent burghs such as Dundee and Montrose in the east and Ayr in the west. The renewed economic and social liveliness of the burghs and changes in the structure of society provided the conditions in which Reformed opinion took root and from which it found the support it needed. Even in St Andrews, the metropolitan city and the seat of the country's oldest and largest university, many among town and gown alike were won over and a Reformed congregation established. Churches were 'cleansed', and religious houses ransacked wherever the army went. Political power was taken out of the hands of the Queen Mother and transferred to a 'Great Council' of the realm. But it required the presence of English forces on land and at sea to bring victory and the end of hostilities, secured by the Treaty of Edinburgh between England and France in July 1560. Elizabeth obtained recognition from France; France agreed to withdraw its forces from Scotland; a meeting of the Estates was to be held – but the question of religion was left unmentioned and undecided. Along with other matters it was to be remitted to commissioners who were to be sent from the Estates to Francis and Mary in France.

Much had no doubt been gained by the Protestants, but much remained to be done. As a political, anti-French party, the Lords of the Congregation had even before 1560 been preparing the way for change. An absent Queen would be unable to aid the severely shaken Catholic Church, but the cause was not yet lost. The future would largely depend on the support each party could muster throughout the country, and particularly among those who would attend the forthcoming Parliament.

THE CHURCH REFORMED: 1560–1638

In preparation for the Parliament, the Great Council, even before the Anglo-French treaty had been concluded in July 1560, commissioned six of the church's religious leaders to draw up a Confession of Faith and a Book of Discipline in which they were invited to put forward proposals for the Reformation of the Church. Two of this commission had been faithful to the old Church until 1559 – John Wynram, sub-prior of the St Andrews Augustinians, and John Douglas, Provost of St Mary's College and Rector of the University of St Andrews – and had been supporters of the programme of conservative reform advocated by the provincial councils between 1542 and 1559. Under the new arrangement in the Church and in the university, both were to retain much of their former influence. John Spottiswoode and John Willock had experience of the Reformation in England and probably thought of the Scottish Reformation following lines not too dissimilar from those of the Church of England. John Row had recently returned from Rome and had been strongly influenced by the new learning. John Knox, who since 1559 had by his preaching exerted a powerful influence, brought with him an intimate knowledge of Protestantism in England, France, Germany, Switzerland and especially Geneva, where he had been pastor to a congregation of English exiles. All six collaborators produced their plans within a few days.

Parliament met in August 1560. It was unusually well attended. The titular leader of the Lords of the Congregation was the Duke of Châtelherault, the head of the house of Hamilton, who was also heir presumptive to the throne. His half-brother, John Hamilton, was primate and Archbishop of St Andrews, but he was undecided and appeared unable to make up his mind to throw in his lot with one side or the other. As it was highly probable that the Queen would never return to rule in person, it was in the interests of the Hamilton family that progress towards ecclesiastical reorganization should be kept under control. Parliament, with its larger than usual representation of barons and burgh representatives, had, however, no difficulty in sweeping away the authority and jurisdiction of the Pope, and removing from the statute book all acts prejudicial to 'heretics'. Nor indeed did it hesitate to forbid, with severe penalties, the celebration of Mass. The Confession of Faith, owing much to the teaching of Calvin and something to Bucer, was approved section by section without opposition even from the sparsely filled bench of bishops, and was entered in the statute book. But when it came to the Book of Discipline, which aimed at reorganizing the administration of the Church largely on the basis of the 'reformed Genevan' polity already established in a number of the burghs, and being followed by Protestants in France, there was vigorous opposition and rejection. The extensive claims to much of the Church's patrimony, in particular the tithes or teinds, is usually given as the primary reason for referring the First Book of Discipline for further consideration. But there was probably an unwillingness to dismember the old structure at this early stage. At least some of the leaders thought of reformation along the English pattern, which would have retained government control over ecclesiastical developments, and would not have run the risk of alienating English support. The Book of Discipline, revised in the autumn and early winter, was again presented to the government and signed by a number of the nobility and others in January 1561. In this new form nothing of the earlier claims was relaxed, but it is probable that the plan to divide the country into ten areas, each with its superintendent, was now put forward, that plan which was some years later to make easier a reversion to the former episcopal and diocesan structure. In the meantime, the Reformed Church, despite severe financial constraint, proceeded to organize itself according to the Book of Discipline.

Alongside this new structure much of the old edifice remained. Bishops and other clergy who refused to conform (and many did not conform), retained possession of their benefices and were not deprived; but in accordance with the Acts of Parliament they were forbidden to exercise any spiritual office – a fact that makes the Reformation in Scotland very different from that of England. Those priests and prelates who conformed were not automatically retained in their offices, and had first to satisfy the Reformed Church before admission to any cure. Nevertheless, the Reformed Church did draw many of its ministers from the former priesthood, especially from members of the Augustinian order, as well as from the educated laity. The future of the Reformed Church organization was in fact far from secure in 1561, and had not the Queen returned that year a widow much would have depended on the Hamiltons and others of the nobility, whose policy tended towards that of more conservative reform and alignment with England.

The six troubled years of Mary's unhappy reign brought many a conflict for the Reformed Church and its leaders, whom the Queen and her advisers failed either to win over or adequately to restrain. Although dependent for the most part on meagre financial resources granted by the Queen from a share of the third part of the income from benefices which were assigned to her, the Reformed Church continued to make ground. Congregations, with either ministers or readers, were subsequently established in the other burghs and in many of the rural parishes. A polity that was essentially Reformed was taking shape, largely on account of the advances that had been made before 1560. National or general assemblies, representative of all sections of the nation, were meeting at regular intervals to carry through much of the general business and legislation of the Church. At the same time the Church in the General Assembly repeatedly sought parliamentary recognition of the Book of Discipline and of its polity, and requested a demarcation of the boundaries of its spiritual jurisdiction which it claimed as an inherent possession. Although only five superintendents were appointed, a serious attempt was made with the election by the General Assembly of annual visitors to exercise spiritual oversight of much of the country from one of the leading towns of each area, and to plant congregations wherever necessary. Worship was completely reorganized by the adoption of the Book of Common Order, which closely followed the pattern used by Knox in the English Congregation in Geneva. Ecclesiastical discipline was strictly enforced on all sectors of the community by kirk sessions, comprising annually elected elders and the minister, with at times the help of the superintendent or visitor. Further, a beginning had been made towards the accomplishment of one of the most far-reaching proposals of the reformers – namely, the provision of education at all levels throughout the country for everyone who could benefit from it: a schoolmaster for every parish, and in the superintendent's town an 'arts college' that would prepare boys for admission to higher faculties in the universities; and a complete reorganization of the three medieval universities. Nevertheless, uncertainty about the future remained, even after Mary had fled the country to England and had been succeeded by her infant son, James VI of Scotland, the future James I of England.

In the new reign the most pressing needs of the monarchy and the government after a period of Civil War were of strength and stability, and those of the Church recognition by the State and financial security. Among the first decisions of Parliament was the re-enactment of the Protestant legislation of 1560, including the re-engrossment in the registers of the Confession of Faith; but once again the Book of Discipline failed to win approval. There was, not surprisingly, concern that the development of ecclesiastical claims to exercise an independent spiritual jurisdiction, which its acceptance implied, could lead to the weakening of government and even to conflict. The intention was to provide the much-needed financial support in return for a form of ecclesiastical government that was more acceptable to the State. As we have seen, the ancient ecclesiastical structure had remained in place, and as the incumbents of benefices (who were not Reformed ministers) were removed by death there was a growing demand that benefices, particularly those of parish churches, be returned to the Church and used to support ministers. Steps were taken by Parliament whereby, when a vacancy occurred, the patron presented a qualified candidate to the superintendent, who then had him admitted to both the cure and the benefice. As the Crown was the patron of the largest number of churches by far, the exercise of this statutory right of patrons would have the effect of reducing the control which the Church, in particular the congregations, had exercised over the ministry.

The needs of both State and Church led in 1572 to an agreement, never fully ratified, known as the Concordat of Leith, whereby episcopal sees on becoming vacant were to be filled by ministers nominated by the Crown as bishops, and thereafter examined and admitted by a reconstituted chapter of ministers. Efforts were made to ensure that the 'bishops' would be subject to the General Assembly of the Church in things spiritual, but at the same time would be able to take their traditional place as the spiritual estate in Parliament. The scheme had on paper the obvious benefit of retaining for the Church the sources of at least some of its former income, and thereby promising it a considerable measure of financial security. It had, nevertheless, the possibility of providing the means whereby the Crown through the bishops could exercise control over the Church and prevent further development in the exercise of spiritual independence in its courts, in particular in the General Assembly which regularly met immediately before Parliament and was accustomed to take a keen interest in national affairs.

The Concordat might have had a successful outcome had it not become obvious almost immediately that the reintroduction of episcopacy was being used by the government as a means of draining off much of the episcopal revenues for its own benefit. Further, it became clear to many that the Church was departing from its fundamental Reformed principles, especially on the question of the ministry. A number of exceedingly unwise nominations, not to say blatant abuses, were made by the Crown, which provided the Church in its General Assembly with the opportunity to raise the fundamental question of 'bishops as they now are' in a Reformed Church. As a result of discussion and debate the Church drew up and accepted a Second Book of Discipline in 1578. Bishops, as they existed in the Church, it was stated, had no basis in the Word of God. Further, the Book set down as its fundamental principle of Church organization the four offices of pastors, doctors, elders and deacons. Government of the Church was to reside in its graded system of courts comprising pastors, doctors and elders, and it would derive its authority not from the State but directly from Christ, the Church's head. To the moral and spiritual discipline of the courts of the Church all were 'in matters of conscience and religion' subject without distinction of person. At the same time the Church laid claim to its ancient patrimony.

For the State to have given wholehearted approval to such a scheme, with its far-reaching possibilities and theocratic tendencies, would have been at the very least dangerous, even though it did give its approval to the setting up of presbyteries, largely transferring the 'exercises' or 'prophesy-ings', which had existed in many parts in accordance with the provisions of the First Book of Discipline. It looked as if the return to the Reformed principles of 1560 would result in the setting up of a Presbyterian system (similar to that in France) which had no place for bishops and which was through its courts, and especially its General Assembly, in danger of providing a parallel government to that of the State, if indeed not a dominant one. In 1596 Andrew Melville did not shrink from telling the King that there were 'two kings' and 'two kingdoms' in Scotland, and that in Christ's kingdom, the Kirk, the King was 'but a member'. Twelve years earlier the young King had sought to restrain the Church by having Parliament pass the Black Acts, which aimed at checking the growing power of the Church by asserting the royal authority over the spiritual estate, subjecting all judgements of the Church to royal approval and forbidding the holding of assemblies except with the King's permission. The King's long-term plan was to establish the government of the Church in the hands of bishops. But in the meantime, on the advice of Chancellor Maitland, he acceded to the Church's demands to have its form of government recognized and this was done by parliamentary act in 1592. The Chancellor believed that in this way the King would be in a stronger position to assert his rights to the English throne, of which he was now the heir apparent.

For the next decade the Church had the opportunity to strengthen its presbyterial structure. Considerable advances were made in planting churches and erecting presbyteries. Nevertheless, the royal policy, which seemed over-lenient to Roman Catholics, alarmed the Church, whose outspoken criticism by some of its ministers in the pulpit resulted in the King's determination to restrict its power, by seeking to control the General Assemblies and by silencing Andrew Melville and others of the Presbyterian party. When securely on the English throne, King James succeeded in 1610 in having the General Assembly acknowledge the royal supremacy 'in the conservation and purgation of religion', and accept the introduction of a hierarchy together with the responsibility of the King for summoning General Assemblies. It was his intention to govern the Church and, to a certain extent, the Scottish realm, through the newly appointed bishops, who tended to regard the Church 'as a divine instrument of a divinely appointed civil authority'.

From 1610 to 1638 the Church had some notable bishops, among whom were John Spottiswoode, William Cowper and John Forbes of Corse, whose writings had in their day a continental reputation, and whose Calvinism has been described as 'not so rigid as that of their Puritan brethren'. For a time episcopal rule was tolerated, but when it was seen to acquiesce in the King's intention of bringing the Church into still closer conformity with England, the opposition so long silenced began to be heard again. Dear to the King's heart was the union not only of the crowns but of his two kingdoms, and with that objective he had the Scottish Parliament enact in 1618 the Five Articles of Perth, which prescribed kneeling at communion (hitherto communion had been received sitting at tables), private communion for the sick, private baptism in cases of necessity, confirmation by bishops, and the observance of the five festivals – Christmas, Good Friday, Easter, Ascension Day and Whitsunday. These 'innovations' were not unnaturally regarded as 'Romish', but in addition were seen as subversive of, indeed contradictory to, the Church's spiritual claims. They were put forward for acceptance in accordance with what was described in the Act as 'the innate power which we [the King] have by our calling from God by which we have power to dispose of things external in the Church as we shall think them to be convenient and profitable for advancing true religion among our subjects'. This application of the doctrine of the divine right of kings in matters spiritual could have far-reaching effects. Many objected not to the new requirements in themselves, but only to the basis for them and the way in which they were introduced.

Within a decade new leaders had begun to appear to take up the challenge on behalf of the Church and its claim to an innate independent spiritual jurisdiction. Thus, King Charles I found himself faced with nothing short of religious and political rebellion when, following his father's plan to rule the Church, he took steps to have the Church accept and use, on the authority of a royal warrant alone, a Book of Canons and a new liturgy. Earlier, he had on behalf of the Church sought to put the ecclesiastical finances on a more secure basis (from which the Church still derives some benefit), but in his liturgical programme he had followed the advice of William Laud, later Archbishop of Canterbury, who was devoid of sympathetic understanding of the Scottish scene. The Canons and Constitutions Ecclesiastical of 1636 were aimed in the main at controlling the life of the clergy and at introducing ceremonies long discarded as unbiblical and 'popish'. *The Book of Common Prayer* (1637) owed much to the English Prayer Book, was similarly considered 'popish' by some and was to be forced upon the Church as 'the only form which *We* [the King] . . . think fit to be used in God's Public Worship in this our Kingdom'. Undoubtedly, in the popular mind anti-popish sentiment and fear of a Romeward trend were uppermost. But for others, such as Alexander Henderson, George Gillespie and Samuel Rutherford, the exercise of the royal power in matters spiritual without any attempt to obtain the sanction of the Assembly contained a threat to both ecclesiastical and parliamentary government.

THE CHURCH AND THE COVENANTS: 1638–1689

Reaction to the royal ecclesiastical policy was swift and dramatic. In times of crisis, as in the late 1550s, in their own interests and those of public peace, recourse was had by the country's leaders to the practice of entering into a solemn 'band' or Covenant. Archibald Johnston of Warriston, a lawyer, and Alexander Henderson, a minister, on the invitation of those opposed to the royal policy, in 1638 drew up as their counter-blast the famous National Covenant. The strongly anti-Roman Negative Confession of 1581 which had been signed by King James VI was put in the forefront and reaffirmed, then the Acts of Parliament since 1560 passed against the Roman Church and in favour of the Reformed faith, and finally the solemn obligation assumed by those who signed it to resist the recent innovations and to maintain the 'True Reformed Religion'. At the same time readiness to uphold the 'King's Majesty, his Person and Authority' was promised. On 28 February, 1638, and the following days, the Covenant was signed amid popular enthusiasm by nobles, barons, ministers, burgesses and commons in Edinburgh, and copies were carried to other parts of the country. The King agreed to the summoning of a free General Assembly which met in Glasgow in November. Those of Presbyterian and Puritan inclination dominated. Those of the opposing faction were soon deposed or excommunicated. With only one dissenting voice, the Assembly rejected 'all episcopacy different from that of a Pastor over a particular flock'. Despite the attempt of the King's commissioner to dissolve the Assembly, it continued to sit and went on in its various 'acts' to assert the basic principle of the Reformed Church in its relations to the state, namely that the Church is independent of the state, has its own systems of government and has its own authority, in accordance with the Word of God, to pronounce on spiritual (i.e. moral and religious) issues and cannot be assimilated into the civil government. As a final act of defiance the Assembly declared that 'this national kirk hath power and liberty to assemble and convene in her yearly General Assemblies' and then went on to fix the date of the next meeting 'unless his Majesty should otherwise appoint'. The line between loyalty and rebellion was not yet severed; it was still possible for the King to find a way out by rejecting his advisers. Any idea that the Covenanters were separatists would have been roundly rejected, but in the eyes of King Charles they were rebels who must be overcome by force of arms.

The history of the conflict that culminated in the execution of the King at the hands of the English Parliament belongs perhaps more to political than to ecclesiastical history. Those defending the rights of the Scottish Church, unconvinced that the King could be trusted when in 1641 he accepted the abolition of episcopacy in Scotland, were drawn into supporting the King's political opponents in England. By the Solemn League and Covenant in 1643, in return for a promise of Presbyterianism in England, help was given to the English Parliament.

At the same time the English Parliament had determined on a revision of the doctrinal and governmental basis of its Church: to this end it had summoned an Assembly of Divines to meet at Westminster and to make proposals for parliamentary legislation. On receiving an invitation to attend, the General Assembly sent as its commissioners some of its ablest leaders and theologians, including Alexander Henderson, Robert Baillie, Samuel Rutherford and George Gillespie. From this Assembly emanated the Westminster Confession of Faith, the Larger and Shorter Catechisms, the Directory for the Public Worship of God and the Form of Church Government. The Confession and Catechisms, which are strongly Calvinist, were accepted by the General Assembly in Scotland – though not without hesitation – and thereafter replaced the Confession of Faith of 1560 and the Heidelberg Catechism which had hitherto formed the basis of much of theological education. The Directory replaced the Book of Common Order of 1564. In accepting the Westminster Confession the General Assembly maintained that the Church could hold assemblies 'by the intrinsical power received from Christ' and without the consent of the magistrate. When the Scottish Parliament ratified the Confession in 1690, this fact was not recalled. Over the succeeding centuries these documents were to exert a profound influence on the Church and on religious life in Scotland. The Confession still forms its subordinate standard of faith.

From 1643 Scottish affairs, ecclesiastical and civil, were in the hands of the Covenanting leaders, whose extreme Puritan demands began to provoke dissension. Weakened by drastic purges of those who had in 1646 entered into an engagement to restore Charles I when he sought refuge in Scotland, they were no match for Cromwell's retaliatory invasion when in 1649 Charles II was proclaimed King in Edinburgh in succession to his executed father. The courts of the Church were bitterly divided. The 'Protesters' wished to have all non-Covenanters debarred from all positions of trust in Church and State, and insisted upon the signing of the Covenants by all in authority. The 'Resolutioners' were to make more moderate demands. Cromwell's victory over Charles II at Worcester, and the King's flight to the continent, allowed the forces of the Commonwealth to carry through their military occupation of Scotland. The Church remained faction-ridden. The 'Protesters' stoutly contended for the Church's independence. The government intervened and prohibited the holding of General Assemblies. At this stage the Covenanting movement was burning itself up in party strife. Contention over the privileges of the Church, and the power of its courts and judicatories, was to make ecclesiology of paramount importance to the Scots, at the expense of other central doctrines of the faith. In much of the national literature and in the minds of many for years to come this was 'the heroic period in the history of the national church'.

In restoring Charles II to his throne in 1660 some of the more moderate 'Resolution' party played a prominent role, among them James Sharp, subsequently Archbishop of St Andrews. At first it was understood that the King would allow Scotland to retain its Presbyterianism. But it soon became apparent that he was of another mind. Those who had been prominent in opposition were tried and executed, among them James Guthrie, minister of Stirling and leader of the 'Protesters', and Johnston of Warriston, who had drawn up the National Covenant and had been clerk of the General Assembly in 1638. Samuel Rutherford, author of *Lex Rex* and principal of St Mary's College, St Andrews, a stout defender of the Church's claims and those of the rule of law, would have shared the same end had not natural death intervened. The restoration of supreme monarchical power, it was soon realized, meant not the acceptance of a Presbyterian polity, but the return to 'the true reformed protestant religion in its purity of doctrine and worship' as it had been 'established within this Kingdom during the reigns of his royal father and grandfather'. Episcopacy was restored; but the King was prepared to allow 'the present administration by sessions, presbyteries and synods'. General Assemblies were not called, although Parliament in 1663 established a purely clerical national synod of archbishops, bishops, deans, archdeacons and moderators of presbyteries. The rights of patrons in presenting ministers, which had been abolished by Parliament in 1649, were once again restored. The royal supremacy was put into effect. For a brief spell it looked as if an experiment of bishops with presbyteries might succeed. Support from those of less narrow, less fanatical views was on the increase, and might have triumphed had not the tide been turned by the state's insistence on persecution in the interests of conformity.

Hundreds of ministers of strongly Puritan leanings resigned their benefices rather than accede to the government's plans. In strongly Presbyterian areas of the south-west many took to holding services in the hills. Troops were sent against these conventicles, which in turn prepared for armed resistance. The bishops, for the most part, backed the government's policy of repression. The murder by 'distracted Covenanters' of Archbishop Sharp in 1679 signalled the outbreak of rebellion, which was ruthlessly put down. The possibility of the King's brother and heir, James, Duke of York, a Roman Catholic, acceding to the throne alarmed the Presbyterian south, who rallied round Richard Cameron in defence of the Covenants and the divine right of Presbyterian Church government. War again broke out, bringing with it cruel persecution that lasted for almost a decade – 'The Killing Time' of 1680–8 – which left an 'indelible mark on the soul of Scotland'. The extremist views of the Cameronians were not, however, representative of all Presbyterians.

King James VII, a Roman Catholic, was proclaimed King of Scotland on the death of Charles II in 1685, the year in which Louis XIV of France had revoked the Edict of Nantes. James was bent on removing the penal laws against his co-religionists in Scotland. By royal proclamations of indulgences he granted some concessions to the Presbyterians who would not worship under the episcopal clergy and suspended the laws against Catholics – but not the laws against conventicles. The collapse of James II's rule in England brought rejoicing to many in Scotland and unleashed the pent-up hostility towards the bishops, who were regarded as the foremost supporters of the Stuart tyranny.

In March 1689 a Convention of Estates declared William and Mary King and Queen of Scotland. At the ensuing Parliament the bishops stayed away. 'Prelacy and the superiority of any office in the Church above presbyters', it was maintained, 'is and has been a great and insupportable grievance to this nation and contrary to the inclinations of the generality of the people, they having been reformed from Popery by presbyters, and ought to be abolished.' The end of the long struggle to put the relations between Church and State on a mutually acceptable basis was in sight, and was to be the most important issue facing the new rulers in Scotland.

For almost 130 years much of the Church's energies had been consumed in defending its claims to spiritual independence. At the same time, continuous progress had been made in establishing the Reformed faith throughout the country, in providing parishes with ministers and schoolmasters, in repairing and erecting church buildings, and in exercising a strong ecclesiastical discipline at local and national levels. Considerable progress had been made in the area of university education, primarily to satisfy the needs of the Church but also to meet those of the government. Scotland's three medieval universities were frequently visited by joint civil and ecclesiastical commissions. Glasgow University (founded in 1450) was completely reorganized and revitalized in 1577, mainly under the direction of Andrew Melville. The University of St Andrews (founded in 1411) was also reconstituted two years later. Its newest college (St

Mary's, founded in 1538) was transformed into a college of divinity and was intended to provide the Church with a highly educated ministry skilled in the languages of the Bible as well as in theology. Andrew Melville was brought from Glasgow to be its principal in 1580. The University of Aberdeen was also reorganized, and two new 'universities' or colleges, along the lines of the academy of Geneva and of the Protestant academies of France, were founded primarily on the initiative of the Church: the College of Edinburgh in 1588, and Marishal College in New Aberdeen in 1593.

Many in the Church took a prominent part in the development of Protestant learning and won international recognition by their writings. Robert Rollock, the first Principal of Edinburgh University, was well known for his books on Covenant theology and for his commentaries, which won praise from Theodore Beza. Robert Boyd of Trochrig was widely read, particularly in France, and Rutherford was highly thought of in the Low Countries. Among the episcopal leaders pride of place must go to the saintly and scholarly Bishop Leighton, who won for himself lasting recognition, especially for his commentary on 1 Peter. John Forbes of Corse was among the most eminent of the very distinguished group of northern scholars known as 'The Aberdeen Doctors'. Apart from his *Institutiones*, he was the author of an interesting *Irenicum*, in which he followed the example of his teachers on the continent, David Paraeus and Franciscus Junius, in seeking to bring about a reconciliation of Presbyterians and Episcopalians. Many Scottish scholars, philosophers and theologians, as well as studying on the continent in this period, played a prominent part subsequently as teachers, particularly in the French Protestant academies, the most notable and influential scholar among these being John Cameron.

Andrew Melville was primarily responsible for introducing Ramism in the Scottish universities, where it was to exercise a profound but not exclusive influence. At an early stage Calvin's *Institutes*, the Genevan Catechism and then the Heidelberg Catechism were fundamental in theological instruction. Covenant theology, as expounded by Piscater at Herborn, was taught by his pupil Robert Howie, Melville's successor in St Andrews. On the Arminian question the Presbyterian party maintained that the Episcopalians were not upholders of the Orthodox Calvinist position. In the theological debates at the Westminster Assembly of Divines, the Scottish commissioners took a prominent part in drawing up its Confession and Catechisms. A strong Reformed foundation had been laid. In the years ahead much of the Church's attention was to be directed towards maintaining its witness in the face of opposition from Deism and Rationalism.

THE CHURCH IN THE AGE OF THE ENLIGHTENMENT 1689–1843

As in 1567, so in 1690 the primary needs of the monarchy in Scotland under William III were for strength and stability in order to maintain its position – at home in the event of a Catholic Jacobite reaction, and abroad in the face of domination from France. The King's chief Scottish adviser in ecclesiastical affairs, William Carstairs, who had received part of his theological education at Utrecht, has been described as 'the architect of the Church by Law Established'. The rejection of the Revolution by the Scottish bishops gave the King no option but to turn to the Presbyterians and to establish, by Act of Parliament in 1690, that system of Church government. His abandonment of strong action in the interest of Presbyterians and his insistence in his message to the first General Assembly of his reign that 'Moderation is what religion enjoins,' and what 'neighbouring churches expect of you' must have disappointed many. A new attitude towards religious controversy was, however, being encouraged and as a result fanaticism of a sectarian kind was beginning to be confined to small groups which later formed a strong element in the Secession Churches. There began to be less and less talk of the Covenants. Many of the parish incumbents who upheld the episcopal order and who would not take the oath of allegiance to the new sovereign were removed by the Church authorities. After 1705 those non-jurist bishops who remained in the country supported the Old Pretender, James VIII, as the legitimate King. To them the Scottish Episcopal Church of today traces in part its separate existence. It was not fully organized until 1766.

The Revolution Settlement had given back to the Church its General Assemblies, and therewith a growing sense of its national responsibility which became one of the most notable marks of its subsequent history, and which was demonstrated in the early eighteenth century by the efforts made to provide a sufficient number of ministers in every part of the country. But the nation itself did not immediately prosper, particularly in its trading adventures overseas. Economic pressures and the desire to have a Protestant succeed to the throne on the death of Queen Anne are regarded as the primary factors in the union of the English and Scottish Parliaments in 1707. By the Treaty of Union, Scotland was assured in the retention of its distinctive legal system and in its Protestant religion and Presbyterian Church government, as 'the only government of the church within the Kingdom of Scotland'. Henceforth the question of Church and State in the old form of royal attempts to dominate and to direct could no longer arise, although alarm was raised and the seeds of future conflict were sown by the restoration of patronage, for which there had been no request, by the United Kingdom Parliament in 1712.

The Revolution Settlement had fixed the Church's doctrine in the Calvinist theology of the Westminster Confession of Faith, to which a literal obedience was demanded from ministers and teachers. Within a few years, however, the Church began to exhibit considerable anxiety. In the southern kingdom Calvinism was in eclipse and new schools of thought hostile to it, having gained ground in England, were now penetrating the northern kingdom. In 1696 the General Assembly passed an act against those 'who maintain and disseminate pernicious principles tending to scepticism and atheism'. Church members were warned against 'Deists' and those who made it 'their business to overturn and ridicule true and pure religion'. Rationalism had begun to make its presence felt. There was still sufficient strength in the Presbyterian Church to curb those who might be tempted, in the developing international climate of Enlightenment, to attempt a modification of the accepted standards of orthodoxy. In the second decade of the eighteenth century a controversy arose in connection with the popularity of Edward Fisher's *Marrow of Modern Divinity* in which faith was defined largely in terms of experience and emotional response. Contemporary Orthodox Calvinism, on the other hand, in the words of John Haddow, Principal of St Mary's College, St Andrews, and professor of divinity, defined faith in purely intellectual terms: 'an intellectual assent unto a divine truth, upon the divine testimony recorded in Scripture'. Haddow and others claimed that 'the Marrow men' or 'Evangelicals' as they were beginning to be called, tended towards antinomianism, and therefore secured their condemnation by the Assembly in the interests of orthodoxy, unaware that by emphasizing the intellectual and ethical requirements as 'necessary acts of salvation', they were preparing the way for developments towards rationalism. Within a matter of years John Simson, a divinity professor in the University of Glasgow, who had been educated in Edinburgh and at Leyden, was charged with heresy. After protracted investigations, during which the courts of the Church engaged in metaphysical speculation hitherto unknown to them, Simson, 'the true pioneer of constructive liberalism in the church', was found not guilty of heresy but was prevented from continuing to teach. He was considered to have attributed 'too much to natural reason' at the expense of 'revelation and efficacious free grace'. Simson regarded theology as a continuing activity of the Church and maintained that with the aid of reason the Church must ever be seeking new forms for the expression of its beliefs. In failing to condemn him outright as a heretic, the Church provided evidence of the two parties existing within it, one tending towards a liberalizing of Calvinism, the other towards a hardening of it.

Further evidence of the emergence of a new theological temper was provided in the works of one of Simson's pupils, Archibald Campbell, professor of divinity and ecclesiastical history in St Andrews. In his *Discourse Proving that the Apostles were no Enthusiasts* (London, 1730) he aimed at presenting a reasoned defence of the necessity of revelation in opposition to the attacks of the English Deists, especially Tindal. It is significant that he does not at any point appeal to the authority of an infallible book or an infallible tradition, or to an infallible institution, but to 'the manly principles of Reason and Religion'. Attempts to convict him of heresy failed, thus providing clear indication of the strength of 'enlightened' views within the Church, of a pronounced shift in emphasis away from dogmatism in the direction of rationalism. Nevertheless, the Church in its Assemblies continued to be on guard and recommended ministers to stress in their sermons the doctrines of the faith and the necessity of conformity to the moral duties of the law, 'not from principles of reason only but also and more especially of revelation'.

The theological disputes of the first half of the eighteenth century are indicative of the various parties within the Church, which was having to cope with the effects of the Toleration Act and the Patronage Act. Those who opposed the new intellectual trends were usually to be found among those who opposed the Patronage Act. From the date of its passing in 1712 until 1784 the Church in its General Assembly every year denounced it as 'grievous and prejudicial to the Church'. It was in the minds of many associated with the evil days that had passed. Potentially, its operation could limit the Church's freedom, and in particular the freedom of the individual congregation to exercise an element of choice in securing a minister. The presentee could not easily be rejected by the congregation or by the presbytery and consequently the congregation's call lost much of its significance. But whenever the presbytery did reject, it was possible for the General Assembly to step in and appoint an 'overriding' committee to carry through the induction. In 1732 the General Assembly passed, with very little approval at other levels of the Church, an Act that left the members of the congregation with virtually no say whatever in calling their pastor – evidence that the Church was failing to recognize the changes in the social and economic climate. Ebenezer Erskine, one of the ministers of Stirling, was strongly censured by the courts of the Church for continued outspoken opposition to this Act. Eventually, he and three fellow ministers left the Church to form an independent presbytery; they were joined in 1737 by four others. In a 'Judicial Testimony' they provided their defence, which included their dissatisfaction with the prevailing intellectual climate as revealed in the recent unsuccessful 'heresy' cases. Deposition from their charges was made definite three years later. Once again, issues of Church and State were re-emerging as a result of the operation of the revived

Patronage Act, and were being embittered by concern over the waning
interest in the Covenants and the growing support for liberalizing
tendencies in theology.

Throughout the second half of the eighteenth century the Church
continued to be disturbed by both issues, patronage and theological
development. The strict upholding of patronage by the Moderates led in
1762 to a further secession which resulted in the formation of the
'Presbytery of Relief'. Such disputes could only disrupt the life of the
Church. The party of 'moderates' which exercised a dominant influence in
its cultural, academic and social life was deeply influenced by the
Enlightenment and more particularly developments in Scottish philosophy. In the face of bitter criticism they prevented the passing of a sentence
of excommunication on David Hume, the distinguished philosopher, and
thereby encouraged the freedom of philosophical enquiry. Indeed, in
contemporary philosophical studies the leading role was taken by ministers
– William Leechman, Thomas Reid, George Campbell, James Beattie,
Alexander Gerard and William Robertson. Robertson is best remembered
for his *History of the Reign of the Emperor Charles V* (1769), and for the
eminent place he occupied in the history of historiography. For twenty-five
years he was the acknowledged leader of the moderate party in the Church
and the most distinguished ecclesiastic of his day.

The spirit of the age also deeply influenced the Scottish pulpit. Of the
considerable number of preachers renowned for the elegance and urbanity
of their sermons, the most influential was Hugh Blair. In his sermons,
which were regarded as 'polished, well-compacted and regular didactic'
orations, particular stress was put on moral themes and the cultivation of
the prudential virtues. Those in the pew were exhorted to 'cultivate
humanity' and to 'remember the natural equality of men'. Appeals to the
'eye of reason', and stress upon the importance of religious knowledge, are
often repeated. Moderation is a recurring theme: 'Satisfy yourselves with
what is rational and attainable.' 'Train your minds to moderate views of
human life and happiness.' There was, however, no attempt to call in
question the Church's attachment to the Calvinism of the Westminster
documents, of which, towards the end of the century, George Hill of St
Andrews was the leading exponent. His *Lectures in Divinity*, posthumously
published in 1825, became the standard textbook of theological instruction, replacing the old Dutch compendia. Hill welcomed 'extensive
information and enlightened criticism' as the 'hand maids of religion',
regarding the increase in human knowledge not as grounds for alarm, but
as a means of establishing and defending the faith. Hence, biblical criticism
as a 'rational exposition of the Word of God' was welcomed as 'the true
foundation of human knowledge'. Together with the advocates of natural

religion, he went a considerable way in regarding the Gospel as a 'republication of the religion of nature', although he maintained that the religion of nature was admittedly defective in that it only set out general grounds of hope to those who transgress. The Enlightenment had undoubtedly exercised a profound influence on theological thinking, but had not shaken the Church's adherence to its confessional standards.

There were, nevertheless, those within the Church who considered that moderatism, allied with the system of patronage, was endangering the evangelical nature of the faith. Indeed, in several parts of the country there was clear evidence of 'revivalism', as in Cambuslang in 1742. Pietistic Praying Societies began to be formed. George Whitefield, the English evangelist, visited Scotland and from 1741 to 1768 paid frequent visits to the main towns. John Wesley also toured the country, but with less success, due in large measure to his Arminianism. These 'missionary' visits stimulated the native evangelicalism which was increasing in strength and beginning to challenge the dominant intellectualism of the Moderates. Evangelical societies, similar to those in England, were springing up, but without official commitment from the Church. The Haldane brothers, James and Robert, aided by their financially secure family background, undertook evangelical tours throughout the country, engaging in 'unlicensed' preaching which in 1799 aroused complaints in the Church courts. The Church on all sides resented their mission, which seemed to have little regard for the existing ecclesiastical polity and discipline, and sought to have it curtailed. The future of the Haldanes' endeavour was to lie outside the Church of Scotland in Congregationalism and in Baptist churches; but within the Church the flame of evangelicalism was beginning to burn even brighter under the leadership of Andrew Thomson of St George's Church, Edinburgh. From 1810, by means of the magazine *The Christian Instructor*, he brought into being an Evangelical party that was soon bidding for the leadership in the national Church.

The century that was to follow, encompassing the new industralism, a rapid increase in population and extensive urban development, and the changing economic climate would present many new challenges to the Church. Problems that had shaped its past would re-emerge in contemporary dress. Issues that were so fundamental in the sixteenth and seventeenth centuries, especially in the matters of the Church's relations with the State and its innate freedom to order its own affairs, were to bring it to the point of disruption. In matters of doctrine, developments in philosophy and theology and the rise of the new critical approach to the interpretation of Scripture were, thanks to the impact of the Enlightenment, to be more easily accommodated. While upholding its national characteristics and responsibilities, the Scottish Church would begin to take on a more tolerant attitude to the rise and progress of other churches and denominations. It would become more expansionist and undertake leadership in overseas missionary endeavour. By the first half of the twentieth century it would have gone far towards restoring unity among Scottish Presbyterians and in taking a leading role in ecumenical discussions. In the forefront of all its endeavours it would aim to uphold what it regarded as its fundamental heritage, namely, its responsibility for the religious, educational and moral welfare of the nation.

8

Reformed Religion in England, 1520–1640

W. J. Sheils

T HE VIGOROUS VARIETY of pious practices in late medieval
England, which had produced regional traditions in architecture,
painting, and drama, was beginning to show signs of strain by 1520. Not
only were vocations to the religious life declining, but popular local
expressions of piety, such as the religious plays and processions in cities
like Coventry, were losing support. These trends owed something to
prevailing economic conditions; in the case of vocations the widening
opportunities for careers in secular professions available to the literate, and
in the case of the processions the severe financial pressures on urban
merchants were significant. More important than these factors, however,
were the changing religious aspirations of some sectors of society. Among
the peasantry these changes had been heralded by Wyclif, and implicitly
acknowledged by the hierarchy in the years following 1490 when their
collective defensive posture resulted in a renewed bout of persecution of
the Lollards. Among the more substantial landowners and merchants the
widening educational opportunities of the early sixteenth century created a
more literate laity increasingly aware of the humanistic and evangelical
criticism of much of conventional piety which was emerging from the great
continental centres of learning.

Conventional piety was, therefore, under scrutiny, but it still retained a
strong hold on the population at large, whose attachment to the Eucharist
and to Masses for the dead was eloquently expressed in their wills. The
monies left by the laity for pious purposes did much to sustain pastoral
provision in the parishes by securing the means for additional priests, often
serving chantries or fraternities, to support the beneficed clergy. It did,
however, mean that the laity, as providers of such services, sought a greater
say in parochial affairs and, in this respect, even orthodox piety was a
source of potential conflict with a Church intent on protecting its
institutional privileges. It was indeed the privileges of the Church, rather

than its piety, which provided the motor of reform when Henry VIII, unable to secure a divorce, decided to break with the papacy on matters of jurisdiction. The institutional changes of the 1530s, which resulted in the Crown assuming the supreme headship of the English Church, were accompanied by an attack on some of the traditional expressions of piety. This policy was fostered by a small but influential group at Court around the persons of the new queen, Anne Boleyn, and Thomas Cromwell, who patronized evangelical and humanist critics of the Church. Some of these had been at Cambridge, where they had been acquainted with Lutheran ideas in the 1520s, and a few had spent time on the continent, but most, like Thomas Starkey, voiced their criticism from an essentially orthodox doctrinal position.

In the climate of the early 1530s this was to be expected, for the King adopted an aggressively orthodox stance in matters of theology. Outspoken early Protestant leaders like Thomas Bilney were put to death for heresy, the occasion of his burning being his involvement with the distribution of the writings of another Protestant, William Tynedale, who had fled to the continent from where he was producing an English translation of the Bible. Tynedale was also to suffer martyrdom, in 1536, but the question of a vernacular Bible was indicative of change. By 1537 a translation had appeared which gained royal approval, and the royal injunctions of the following year required a copy to be placed in every parish church. In 1539 an official translation was published and in 1540 a cheap edition, suitable for private use, was issued. This Bible represented a considerable achievement for the evangelicals who had also, in the person of Thomas Cranmer, emerged as a force, albeit a shadowy one, within the Church itself. Indeed, the Convocation sermon of 1536 was preached by one of the most renowned evangelicals, Hugh Latimer, and in it he attacked some of the cornerstones of traditional piety: purgatory and Masses for the dead were challenged, as were the efficacy of saints' days and non-eucharistic ceremonial, while images and pilgrimages were dismissed thus: 'But to believe that God will be sought more in one place than in another, or that God will hear thee more in one place than in another, or more where the image is than where it is not is a false faith and idolatry, or image service.'

The reformers took the first steps in redefining doctrine at this Convocation with the publication of the Ten Articles. The Articles were strictly orthodox except in two important respects: the sacraments were reduced in number from seven to the three considered essential to salvation – baptism, penance and the Eucharist – and the article on the Eucharist was phrased ambiguously so that it was open to both orthodox and Lutheran interpretation. The royal injunctions of that year endorsed the articles and

Latimer's criticisms of traditional piety. The clergy were required to discourage the laity from the more extravagant acts of piety, and to preach the virtues of what amounted to a social gospel by stressing the spiritual efficacy of acts of charity towards the poor. However, these injunctions, and those of 1538, mark the high point of the reformers' achievements in the reign of Henry. The conservatives were always numerically superior and were soon able to overturn most of the reformers' successes. In 1537 they restored the sacraments to the traditional seven in *The Bishops' Book*, and in 1539 the Act of Six Articles reinstated the traditional eucharistic doctrine of transubstantiation, denied the need for Communion in both kinds for the laity, required clerical celibacy, and promoted the use of private Masses and auricular confession. This Act was a victory for the conservatives and provided the framework for official religion for the rest of Henry's reign.

Despite defeat at governmental level, the tensions of the 1530s and, above all, the presence of an English Bible had created a climate of speculative questioning in matters of religion among some sectors of the laity. For most, the dissolution of the religious orders would have had the most dramatic impact, not only in the countryside, where great institutions such as Fountains Abbey were swept away, but also in towns, where the friars had often been a focus for local piety. The disappearance of these powerful corporations must have diminished the Church in the eyes of many and called into question the life of prayer and worship which they represented, but its immediate effect may have been as keenly felt in the social as in the spiritual sphere. The campaign against images had resulted in the destruction of some notable ornaments, such as the rood screen at St Margaret Pattens in London, but in general these devotional objects were sources of local pride and had more defenders than critics. Masses for the dead continued to be requested in wills, even in London, but the endowment of chantries and obits on a more permanent basis declined dramatically by 1540. This marked some change in devotion, but the sacramental life, and the ceremonial by which it was transmitted to the laity, remained the same both in form and in language so that the parish churches, the centre of worship for the vast majority, and the clergy which served them represented continuity.

In the first half of the sixteenth century, therefore, Reformed religion existed for the most part outside of the formal structures of the Church. Lollard congregations survived in particular localities scattered throughout the south-east, most notably in the Chilterns, Kent, East Anglia and London, which provided a contact point between the separate groups. The Lollards' beliefs found echoes in the criticisms which the Christian humanists were making of the Established Church, and the infamous treatment of Richard Hunne, a London merchant accused of Lollardy by the bishop of London in 1516, did much to lend weight to such arguments. Humanists like Colet, however, remained orthodox; but from 1520 there is evidence of Lutheran literature arriving in the country and of heterodox views circulating in learned circles, particularly among a group of young scholars at Cambridge. Such views were also noted in East Anglia and, most importantly, in London where the evangelical tradition formerly sustained by Lollardy was maintained during the 1520s by a group of devotees known as the Christian Brethren. The kinship and commercial networks of the London merchants and, in particular, their apprentices helped to create a Protestant presence in the capital which existed independently of the formal parochial structure and which was to prove of crucial importance in providing continuity in those difficult years after 1540, when the dominance of the conservatives seriously threatened the embryonic Church. Outside of London it was less easy to circumvent ecclesiastical institutions, though careful use was made of preaching platforms by evangelical patrons in towns like Bristol and Canterbury. In such places and in ports like Rye and Hull, which had regular contact with the continent, Lutheran ideas had gained a foothold. In the countryside things were even more difficult; in Kent the influence of Cromwell and Cranmer bore some fruit among the gentry, and the universities, especially the Cambridge colleges of St John's and Trinity, stimulated evangelical allegiances in some of their gentry students from the provinces, but in the countryside generally known Protestants were spread very thinly indeed. That is not to say that things were not happening. Lively debate attracted the attention of the authorities, especially when it took place, as it often did, in inns, such as The Bell in Northampton, where interludes were performed mocking aspects of traditional piety; and the cumulative effect of the religious preambles to the surviving wills of the laity suggests that, in many counties, devotion to the Virgin and to the saints was in decline from the early 1530s.

The decline of traditional piety is not the same as the emergence of committed Protestantism, however, and it was not until the reign of Edward VI that an actively Protestant policy was espoused by government. The theological innovations of those six years were accompanied by sweeping changes in the outward forms of worship. Three of these must have caused even the least learned of the laity to take note: the dissolution of the chantries and the religious fraternities altered the appearance of church interiors as the chapels, altars, statues, and other ornaments associated with them were removed; the change in the language of worship to English must have increased the accessibility of the liturgy to the laity, if not necessarily their understanding of it; and the administration of the Communion in both kinds to the laity, together with the removal of the requirement for clerical celibacy, reduced the sense of separateness which the priestly life had acquired in the medieval Church. For the more thoughtful, these changes would have signified more substantial theological shifts expressing, first, the abolition of the notion of purgatory and denial of the efficacy of pious practices in mediating between the Church Militant on earth and the Church Triumphant in heaven; second, the stress on the scriptural basis of religion by putting biblical texts in the vernacular; and third, a change in the idea of ministry to one less sacramental and less distinct from a laity who had some share in the priesthood of all believers.

Such fundamental changes did not pass without comment, and there was some vigorous if localized defence of traditional practices, especially the Latin Mass, but the general picture is one of resigned acceptance. That owed something to the decline in attachment to traditional piety which has already been noted, but it owed more to the careful policy of the government in clothing these changes in traditional forms. Unlike the continental reforms, the liturgical structure of the First Prayer Book followed closely that of the Mass, and the central doctrine of the Eucharist, while denying transubstantiation, retained the idea of a 'mystical presence' in the sacrament, so that even a die-hard conservative like Stephen Gardiner could suggest that it implied, even if it did not fully express, traditional eucharistic doctrine. A less positive reason for acceptance of these changes rested in the limited ability of the government to enforce its religious policy in the localities, so that in fact the spread of Protestantism remained slow and piecemeal. The significant difference, however, was that it no longer needed to be clandestine, and this short reign saw significant advances. The universities played a crucial role in the dissemination of Protestantism, and it was at Cambridge that the Lancastrian gentleman John Bradford first came into contact with those Reformed ideas which he introduced to his family and locality. The influence of the university was also felt in East Anglia, not only among clerics and gentry but also in the towns, one of which, Ipswich, financed a civic preacher from 1551. Reformers at the universities received a boost with the arrival of two prominent continental Protestants, Peter Martyr at Oxford in 1548 and the great Strasbourg theologian Martin Bucer at Cambridge the following year. It was Bucer who pressed the English reformers further in the direction of the Swiss churches, initially through his revision of the Ordinal, in which he stressed the primacy of preaching for the ministry, and subsequently by the 1552 Prayer Book which did away with the traditional vestments, placed the altar among the people in the nave of the church, and removed any reference to a divine presence, real or mystical, in the Eucharist. The Prayer Book was introduced only in the last year of the reign and thus had little immediate impact; more important was the influence which Bucer exercised over younger scholars who were to rise to prominence in the Elizabethan Church. Contacts with theologians of such distinction internationalized English Protestantism in these years, but more direct knowledge was also gained through the presence of congregations of foreign refugees and merchants in London, where there were over 5,000, and in smaller towns such as Colchester and Southampton.

The reforms of Edward's reign were significant but short-lived. The accession of Mary in 1553 resulted in the restoration of Catholicism, but without much of the traditional institutional piety of the Church. The reformers were again excluded, but three features of their history in Mary's reign both reflected the advances already made under Edward and pointed to future developments. Contact with foreign theologians had given many of the educated, especially the younger, direct knowledge of the Reformed traditions of Europe, with the result that some 800 individuals, both lay and clerical, chose to go into exile at Strasbourg, Geneva and other places where they experienced for themselves a non-episcopal Church order and a more radical Protestant liturgy. At home, the tradition of congregational growth outside of the Church which had emerged under Henry, or even earlier with the Lollards, came into its own in a period of persecution. Groups of leading laity in London provided safe houses, and sometimes ships, like the *Jesus* in Rotherhithe, where Protestants could meet for sermons and worship. There were also groups in the countryside, in parishes in the Severn Vale; in Essex, where they met in 'woods, barns and other solitary places', though with a better-known headquarters at the King's Head in Colchester, where hounded clergy could get protection and visiting laity be put in contact with fellow-believers; and in Lancashire, where night meetings were organized by local gentry. Thus was strengthened that tradition of congregational independence which had been present from the beginnings of Protestantism. Finally, the years of Mary's reign were heroic ones for English Protestants, over 300 of whom suffered death for their beliefs. These included some of the great leaders of the early period such as Cranmer and Latimer, whose work had set their stamp on the new religion, but the majority were humble men and women, mostly from the southern and eastern counties. Such examples of constancy were testimony to the impact which Protestant ideas had made on the people in the first generation of reform, but were also important for the future in establishing a martyrology, ably chronicled by John Foxe in his *Actes and Monumentes*, first published in 1563.

Mary's death in 1558 brought the restoration of Catholicism to an end, and the new regime set about seeking a fresh settlement to the religious uncertainties of the previous twenty years. It was to be a Protestant settlement, but the character of that Protestantism had yet to be determined. Each element in the legacy of exile, martyrdom and congregationalism which the reformers inherited from Mary's reign was to have significant consequences for the new Church, but the immediate task was to establish its institutional and doctrinal structures. Both the nature of that settlement and the manner in which it was brought about have been the subject of debate. The political manoeuvring involved is not central to our concerns, except to say that it required a delicate balancing of conservative and reforming forces, with the former group appearing to have the greater power in terms of formal office. The settlement was therefore seen by many contemporaries as a compromise, as indeed it was, and by some of the more radical as temporary, which it proved not to be. Many of the tensions which the revived Church subsequently exhibited could be traced back to the circumstances of its original formulation.

Recent scholarship has restored the role of the Queen and her closest advisers, especially William Cecil, in the management of the settlement, in contrast to the earlier emphasis placed on the influence of radical MPs in the Commons. In the first month of her reign the Queen issued a proclamation promising reform 'in matters and ceremonies of religion' which also, however, forbade unlicensed preaching which had occasioned 'unfruitful dispute in matters of religion'. Much of this preaching was being done by Protestant speakers, especially in the capital. Having thus set out to control non-parliamentary discussion, the regime turned to Parliament to effect the changes and to give them the force of law. By April 1559 Acts of Supremacy and of Uniformity had been passed, but not without debate. First the royal title had to be settled. Henry VIII had adopted the title 'supreme head' and the original Bill followed this practice; but in response to more radical reformers as well as to appease conservative opinion, the title was changed to 'supreme governor' by the time the Act of Supremacy reached the statute book. The Act also repealed the heresy laws revived under Mary, and licensed the Protestant practice of receiving Communion in both kinds. The Act of Uniformity, setting out the form of worship to be adopted, was a direct descendant of the legislation of the reign of Edward VI. It differed, however, in two important respects from that of 1552: first, it retained the ornaments of the First Prayer Book of 1549, which radicals considered 'popish', and second, it effected a compromise between the two Edwardian Prayer Books in the wording of the Eucharist, attempting to combine Protestant memorialism with the traditional notion of a divine presence through the following formula: 'The body of Our Lord Jesus Christ, which was given for thee, preserve thy body and soul unto everlasting life: and take and eat this, in remembrance that Christ died for thee, and feed on him in thine heart by faith, with thanksgiving.' These compromises were opposed by the more committed reformers, especially those who had had contact with the continental churches, but retained sufficient traditional elements to gain majority support in the House of Lords – just. These two Acts, therefore, passed into law; but the seeds of future dissent were sown in the preamble to the Act of Uniformity which, in reference to the traditional ornaments, held out hope of further changes with the phrase that they should be used 'until other order shall be taken therein', a promise which was repeated in the preface to the published Prayer Book.

It was one thing to legislate for change, but another to bring it about. Despite its conservative tone, the Protestant direction of the settlement was clear enough to occasion the wholesale resignation of those bishops who had served under Mary. The government thus had the opportunity to appoint committed reformers to lead the Church, and the need was sufficient to override the doubts which some of them had about serving in an episcopal Church, though a few of the more radical exiles, like Thomas Sampson, preferred to take senior university posts rather than bishoprics. Among the rank-and-file clergy the situation was more confused, and the government had to use what was available. It hoped to retain most of the parish clergy and did so; but as many of these men were trained in a pastoral tradition not suited for Reformed ideas and retained a strong affection for their traditional worship, they were not likely to be the heralds of reform. For most of these, and for most of their parishioners, the pastoral services, supplying the sacraments, and giving comfort and support in times of difficulty, were the mainspring of the ministry. The strategy of the government was to try to keep this aspect of religion going until such time as a new generation of clergy, trained at the universities to preach the Gospel, could bring that Gospel to the people. Thus in the early years of Elizabeth's reign there was great diversity both within and between regions: when the reforming Archbishop Grindal was transferred to York from London in 1570 the strength of conservatism there made the north appear to him more like 'another church, rather than a member of the rest' in comparison to his experiences in the capital, where his main difficulty had been in dealing with Protestant radicals who wished to purify the liturgy of its remaining popish elements. Between such extremes, and perhaps more usual, was the ministry of William Sheppard, an ex-monk, who remained vicar of Heydon in Essex from 1541 until his death in 1586, and whose pastoral dedication to his flock, exhibited in modest works of charity towards individuals and small attempts to improve the social amenities of his parish, represented 'a series of conforming experiences' which helped to ease the transition from the old religious world to the new. Such may have been the case in many parishes, for the Reformation needed its midwives as well as its begetters.

Those begetters, however, needed to build upon the legislation of 1559, and to provide a fuller statement of the doctrinal framework of the Established Church. Royal injunctions in the same year made clerical marriage legal once again, required the removal from churches of statues and the liturgical trappings of the old religion, and insisted that altars be replaced by Communion tables. Such requirements emphasized the Protestant nature of the settlement, but still fell short of the hopes of some, and especially of men like Thomas Lever who had seen the Reformed churches of the continent. Lever was a man of ability and influence, who chose to work alongside rather than fully within the episcopal Church in its early years as town preacher of Coventry, a post which was financed by subscriptions from the congregation and which did not require him to perform the sacramental duties of the ministry. The needs of the Church were great, and in 1561 Lever was persuaded to take on the responsibilities of an archdeaconry, but still he remained aloof from the sacramental life of the Church, as did his fellow-exile William Whittingham, Dean of Durham. These two, and some others, became identified as 'godly preachers which have utterly forsaken anti-Christ and all his Romish rags' and were distinguished from the bishops, many of whom were also former exiles, 'That for worldly respects receive and allow them'. This distinction between the two strands of reform was made in 1564, following the formulation of the Articles of Faith which had been adopted by Convocation in 1563 as the doctrinal basis of the Church.

That doctrine owed more to the practice of the Swiss reformers than to Luther's ideas, which had been so important in the earlier years. In particular the Articles included a statement on 'predestination and election' which began as follows: 'Predestination to life is the everlasting purpose of God, whereby . . . he hath constantly decreed, to deliver from the curse and damnation, those whom he hath chosen in Christ out of mankind.' This fundamental doctrine commanded a wide measure of agreement, but dissension arose over the means by which this theological position should be given expression in matters of worship and Church order. It became clear that, despite the hints of future change in the legislation of 1559, the Queen was determined to stick with the terms laid down then. Attempts were made in Convocation to introduce further changes to the liturgy, but they were rebuffed and thirty-eight Articles were passed, based largely on the Edwardian model. One central issue, that of the Eucharist, remained unresolved, and it was not until 1571 that a form of words, admitting a spiritual presence in the sacrament but also stressing the faith of the communicant, was agreed and the Thirty-Nine Articles received the approval of Parliament.

Disagreement among reformers in the 1560s focused on worship, and especially on the use of the surplice in the service. For the bishops the wearing of the surplice was a matter of indifference, but one which, for the sake of decency and uniformity, should be required; for the more radical reformers the surplice was at worst part of the 'Romish rags' of Antichrist and thus to be rejected, or at best a matter of indifference which should not be imposed on tender consciences. In 1565, at the request of the Queen, Archbishop Parker decided to clamp down on the diversity of practice in ceremonial and, among other things, required that the surplice be worn. On the eve of Easter 1566, 110 clergy were summoned before the courts and asked to conform; thirty-seven, including such distinguished figures as the martyrologist John Foxe, refused to do so and were suspended from office. Thus at the principal festival in the liturgical calendar one-third of the parishes in London were deprived of their ministers, many of whom, in the eyes of their congregations, represented the most diligent preachers. There followed a pamphlet war between the parties, each of which appealed to leading continental divines; eventually the views of the bishops prevailed and eight beneficed clergy and a few curates were deprived, though some of these subsequently found livings away from the capital. Many of them, however, continued to hope for further reform, and these views found sympathy in influential quarters. Some of the bishops were themselves uneasy about enforcing the surplice and important provincial clergy such as Anthony Gilby, rector of Ashby de la Zouche, a town which he made a centre of instruction and advice for aspiring young ministers, also objected.

In the wake of the Vestiarian Controversy at least one London congregation followed the example of their Marian predecessors and withdrew from the Church, adopting a form of church order governed by pastors and elders which they had witnessed among the French Protestant refugees in the capital. This was the beginning of a separatist tradition which was to remain as an important minor theme in the religious history of the next half-century; for most, the question of separation rested on the issue of how far one could remain within a Church not yet fully reformed. Such people, like the Brownists of the 1580s, shared many of the criticisms of the establishment made by those Puritans who chose to remain within the Church, but held them either to a greater degree or with a higher sense of congregational independence. There were other small groups, however, like the clandestine Family of Love in Cambridgeshire, whose traditions were based on entirely different theological premisses. Separatism was condemned by all authorities, as much by the Puritans as by the bishops, and some of its leaders were put to death, but it was a tradition which grew as the seventeenth century progressed, particularly during the stress of the Civil War. In the immediate context, however, the importance of the Plumbers Hall congregation in the 1560s lay in the question of Church order, for it was on this issue that the central conflict between the bishops and their critics within the Established Church arose.

A series of lectures delivered at Cambridge in 1570 by Thomas Cartwright challenged episcopal orders as having no basis in Scripture, and advocated a Presbyterian form of Church order similar to the Swiss models and to that recently adopted in Scotland. Cartwright was forced to leave Cambridge, and removed to Geneva, but his ideas gained a following among younger divines and also from some of those who had suffered deprivation in 1566. These men, organized by John Field, gained support from influential laymen and introduced a Bill into Parliament in 1571 removing all objectionable ceremonial, including the surplice, from the *Book of Common Prayer*. No agreement was reached and the radical ringleaders were prosecuted before the courts, but the return of Cartwright and the calling of a new Parliament in 1572 encouraged the radicals to renewed effort, especially in the aftermath of Catholic plots involving the succession. The tone of the campaign was offensive, calling bishops 'Antichristian, devilish, and contrary to Scripture'. What was advocated was a system of ecclesiastical government in which the clergy were appointed by their congregations, in which the ministry was divided into pastors, who looked after the cure of souls, and doctors, who concentrated on the prime ministerial responsibility of preaching. These were to be supported in the parishes by elders, who supervised discipline, and deacons, who assisted with pastoral work. The ministers of a region would meet together regularly in *classes*, under the leadership of an elected moderator, to decide on weighty matters of policy, to determine knotty points of theology and to supervise each other's activities. Thus bishops, the Church courts and their officials, cathedral dignitaries and parochial officers such as churchwardens would be replaced by these orders. Presbyterianism, in varying degrees of completeness, failed to secure a majority in successive Parliaments, but continued to command support, albeit often qualified, among influential provincial clergy and gentry, as well as in the capital. Unofficial *classes* were established by the clergy in the midland shires for a short time during the 1580s, but there is little evidence of parochial elderships being set up. For the most part these *classes* confined themselves to regulating clerical affairs and fought shy of any disciplinary role. Among the more pressing ministerial matters dealt with by them was preaching, or more particularly the absence of it in some parishes.

From the time of Cranmer's *Ordinal* preaching had been placed high among ministerial functions, but until well into the 1570s the shortage of suitable clerical manpower had rendered this prominence more of an aspiration than a reality. As time passed, however, the absence of a preaching ministry in many parishes was a source of scandal to the Puritans and of regret to the bishops. Informal exercises or prophesyings, where clergy of a particular locality could meet for mutual support and exhortation, were established in many areas in the early 1570s, and were often attended by the laity who would hear sermons there. Initiated by the radicals, and allowed by the bishops, these meetings finally fell foul of the Queen, following the radical sermons preached at Southam, a celebrated Puritan meeting, in 1574, and were banned. Many continued a fitful existence thereafter in recognition of their usefulness in helping the clergy to acquire new skills and in combating conservatism and superstition among the laity, but they represented an uneasy compromise between the authorities and the radicals – the more so as the universities began to produce graduates in increasing numbers to take on the ministry. To the Puritans, preaching was an essential element of the Reformed ministry, and many laity withdrew from those parishes in which it was not performed, thus threatening the parochial nature of the Church on which so much of its law depended. Non-preaching ministers were condemned by their preaching colleagues as no ministers, and the issue became very divisive from the mid-1580s, often setting cleric against cleric. The failure of the institutional structures to provide sufficient preachers also gave the laity an opportunity to promote locally financed initiatives in religion which it had not had since the dissolution of the religious guilds. The examples of Ipswich and Coventry have already been mentioned, and from the 1570s many other town corporations set up lectureships, often in association with prophesyings in the early years. Sometimes these lectureships supported a particular individual, as in Northampton, but often the endowment provided for a series of lectures, usually delivered on market day, to be given by invited clergy from the neighbourhood. Thus by the 1590s in many places the main function of the Reformed ministry, preaching, depended for support not on the ecclesiastical hierarchy but on the laity, whether individuals, corporations or congregations. It is not surprising that such people demanded some say in what was being preached.

The Calvinist nature of the 1559 settlement was reinforced as time passed, so that the leading scholar of the English Reformation has described its importance in the early seventeenth century as follows: 'Calvinism can be regarded as the theological cement of the Jacobean church . . . a common and ameliorating bond uniting conformists and moderate puritans.' Central to that theology was the doctrine of predestination, and in discussion of this the age-old issue of the relation between the visible Church on earth and the invisible elect in paradise was reopened. In essence the fundamental difference of view on this was stated in the controversy between Cartwright and Archbishop Whitgift in the 1570s. Cartwright wished to restrict membership of the visible Church to those who could demonstrate their election through their godly lifestyle, whereas Whitgift, following a passage in Theodore Beza, stressed the impossibility of a division between the elect and the damned in this world and argued for a more comprehensive view of the Christian community. Both views could be sustained in Calvinist theology and have recently been distinguished by the terms experimental and credal predestinarianism. For the former it was essential that the adherents' view of salvation was exhibited in this world by a style of piety which separated the godly from the rest and, in its more rigorous formulations, to give concrete expression to that division by the exercise of ecclesiastical discipline. The logical destination of such a position was separatism, but few followed that route and, in the seventeenth century, the thrust of experimental predestinarianism focused on the piety of the individual rather than on that of the congregation. Thus the godly, be they gentlewomen such as Margaret Hoby of Hackness in Yorkshire, urban patricians like Ignatius Jourdain of Exeter, or humble London artisans like Nehemiah Wallington, could pursue their personal salvation, and that of their households, family and friends, at some distance, but not in total separation, from the multitude. They came to be known as, and called each other, 'the godly', a less pejorative term than the more usual 'Puritan', and it was their brand of reform which Tawney called 'the true English Reformation' and which scholars have more recently described as a 'Calvinist consensus'. It was a religion of discipline, as Wallington wrote in his notebooks: 'It is not an easy thing to be a Christian; it is not reading of Scripture, or boasting of faith in Christ, though these be good they cannot prove one to be an absolute Christian; there must be a conformity of life.' That conformity had to show in the outward actions of the individual, and was sustained by regular prayer and reading of the Bible, as Margaret Hoby did daily, and by frequent attendance at sermons followed by repetition and discussion of the preacher's themes and texts within the household or among friends, as was the case in Lord Montague's home at Boughton in 1637. The preachers of these sermons were more often than not subsidized by supporters among the local gentry, and it was those same individuals that the preachers charged with the responsibility, as magistrates, of bringing about the reformation of society. Thus in towns like Exeter and Northampton we see the council attempting to impose a sabbatarian discipline on the inhabitants, regulating the moral lives of the citizens and ensuring attendance at sermons. In the countryside, gentry magistrates like the Lewkenor family of Denham in Suffolk collaborated with their ministers to bring about a godly commonwealth in miniature, and in parishes where there was no resident squire, such as Terling in Essex, the more prosperous farmers sought to achieve much the same end, and to restrain the profligacy of the poor, especially in regard to the alehouse, through the exercise of parochial office.

Godly discipline became the hallmark of elites, at whatever level, in many communities after 1580, and the huge sermon literature published in those years testifies to its cultural dominance. It was an austere creed, uneasy with the visual and theatrical elements which had been such a prominent part of traditional belief and concentrating on the word as contained in the Bible, whether read or heard. As such, Reformed religion was not accessible to the uncommitted, and in consequence its arrival in many communities produced divisions in society which the Calvinist doctrine of grace, with its stress on election, served to reinforce. Much of the surviving sermon literature depicts the godly living an embattled life surrounded by a godless multitude lost in 'profanity and popery, those twin sisters in evil'. It had become clear by the 1580s that preaching alone was not going to bring the population to a true understanding of the Reformation, and that traditional beliefs retained a strong hold. The extent of ignorance and indifference among the people has been well chronicled in Keith Thomas's *Religion and the Decline of Magic*, which remains an elegant reminder of the limits of evangelization. There is no doubt that the early reformers held an optimistic view of the efficacy of their endeavours in preaching, and indeed this was a necessary tactic in seeking government support. That assessment also influenced the interpretations of generations of historians, who saw the Reformation as a natural, and fairly smooth, progression to a modern, Protestant state. Influenced by the work of Thomas and supported by extensive researches in local archives, recent studies have focused in contrast on the piecemeal and fragmentary nature of reform, and in some cases, as in the work of Scarisbrick and the recent important study by Duffy, on its failure to penetrate many local communities. Such a view is sustainable until the 1580s, but thereafter we must be careful not to accept too readily the laments of early Stuart divines about the godlessness of the people; their sermons were directed at the godly and their supporters in government and thus represent both a literature of complaint and an exhortation to further endeavour by the State. From the 1580s an alternative strategy to preaching was devised to reach the people, and the following half-century saw a flood of catechetical literature issue from the press. This literature concentrated on the basic tenets of belief, and its effect in creating, if not a learned, at least an informed Protestant people has been demonstrated by Ian Green. Moreover the catechisms, of their nature, concentrated on what was common within Reformed religion rather than on those issues which divided the Puritans from the establishment.

Those divisions have already been referred to in the distinction drawn between experimental and credal Calvinism, with the godly representing adherents to the former view. For the credal Calvinists, the division between the elect and the reprobate which existed in eternity was not reflected in the Church as it existed in the world. The Church had to contain the elements of true faith, certainly, but once those were present then other matters, such as ceremonies, which did not infringe its true vocation, should be left to the discretion of the magistrate, whom it was the duty of the Christian to obey. Just as the Church on earth could contain elements which were not necessary to salvation, so also it could contain those individuals whose activities did not manifest signs of their election. There were of course limits to this inclusiveness, and fornicators and the like would suffer the penalty of excommunication, but for Calvinists of this stamp the Church was potentially the servant of the whole nation. This inclusive tradition had always been present in the early Reformation, and was given fresh intellectual definition in the work of Richard Hooker, whose defence of the Establishment, *Of the Laws of Ecclesiastical Politie*, was published in the 1590s. Historians disagree over the extent to which this represented innovation, and about its relation to those Arminian doctrines of grace and of the Church which divided the early Stuart establishment. Defence of *iure divino* episcopacy and renewed emphasis on the sacramental elements in the service gained favour under James I, and an able and powerful group associated with William Laud captured control of the Church in the 1620s. It was their attempt during the following decade to impose their views on the parishes, in particular the urban ones, which led to the breakdown of the Reformed compromise. The rejection of Arminianism in the provinces, and the abolition of episcopacy in the 1640s, shows Laud and his associates to have been a small, if temporarily powerful, minority, but this must not obscure the fact that their views drew on a pastoral tradition which many moderate Puritans also shared. The pastoral emphasis of Reformed religion received its most eloquent defence in George Herbert's *The Countrey Parson*, with its characterization of the ideal minister as the source of neighbourliness and charity among his parishioners. Though Herbert was an Arminian himself, his book, written in the 1630s, became a popular manual for clergy of all persuasions.

These clergy, Hooker as much as the Puritans, all bemoaned the ignorance of the people; but, as has been suggested, they did not despair of them. The Calvinist Francis Inman, writing in 1622, described them as follows:

> There be manie poor servants and laborers; many that are of trades and manuall sciences; many aged persons of weak and deceived memories. Of these, some never learned so much as to reade, some very little and moste of them have or will have small leisure to learn long discourses: the world or other vanities taking their thoughts and cares. Yet all these have immortall souls, to remain after a few daies in eternall ioye or in endless paines. Of these care must be had . . .

Richard Baxter, in his autobiography, gives us pictures of both sides of the relationship between the godly and the multitude. A vivid account of his family life as a young man shows his parents being tormented by the rabble on account of their godly lifestyle, and has been used by historians to illustrate the central role of Puritanism in the polarization of early modern society. His reflections on his parishioners at Kidderminster in the 1640s, however, provides a more subtly differentiated analysis of their religiosity, in twelve categories ranging from 'learned Professors of religion' to those who 'spend their lives in vanity', with many intermediate distinctions. While Baxter considered that many of these remained woefully ignorant of the full implications of Reformed religion, he recognized that they knew the words of the Catechism and understood the need to mend their lives and serve God. Well down his list, in ninth place in fact, were those 'of tollerable knowledge . . . but yet they live in idle tipling company'. This was a matter of regret rather than of condemnation to Baxter, and the phrase 'of tollerable knowledge' illustrates both the success and the limitations of the Reformation among the populace. The religion of these people remains elusive to the historian, but it no doubt involved an attachment to the parish church and an acquaintance with the rudiments of faith. A recent attempt to recover it has been made by Eamon Duffy through the chapbooks which dealt with religious themes and had a ready market in mid-seventeenth-century England. His conclusions stress their firmly evangelical rejection of reliance upon works, the need for a lively faith and 'their attractive emphasis on social justice, charity, and the dignity of God's poor . . . and above all the gospel of penitence, forgiveness, and grace which was the centre and best of English puritanism'.

The testimony of Baxter and the evidence of the chapbooks show that Protestantism had penetrated deep into English society in the century or so after the break with Rome, even if the more committed Calvinists failed to recognize the fact. The heaven of Sir Thomas More was achieved by very different means from the paradise of John Milton; the berobed aldermen of York who attended civic lectures in the 1630s had a very different understanding of religion from their great-grandfathers who had taken part in the Corpus Christi processions of the 1530s; and the people looked to the Ten Commandments and the Bible rather than to the sacraments and the saints for guidance through the vicissitudes of life.

The settlement of 1559 had provided a framework for a Calvinist Church rather than a confession of faith and so, in the following century, divisions and tensions within that framework led ultimately to Civil War and the disestablishment of the Church. But those divisions, which exercised the literate and committed, should not obscure the slow process of evangelization which took place among the people. Traditional festivities, like blessings of ploughs, were still enjoyed and many churches still contained survivals of the old religion, such as the carved rood screens of Devon or the painted panels of East Anglia. But these, though they caused anxiety to the godly, were as much part of local pride and custom as of religion after 1600. Regional differences remained, with 'dark corners of the land' still to experience the full effect of the changes, but by 1640 it can be said that the nation and the majority of its people were unequivocally Protestant. Nevertheless, though the nation shared that experience, it had yet to agree on what that experience should mean and thus remained divided. However, the principal divisions within society were not, as many contemporaries would have had it, between Protestantism and popery or between the godly and the ungodly (though these, of course, existed) but within Protestantism itself.

9

Anglicanism in Stuart and Hanoverian England

Ian Green

THE TERM 'Anglicanism' did not become current until the mid-nineteenth century, when the role of the Established Church of England was being reappraised. Since then it has been applied to the early modern period in at least four different ways. In the late nineteenth and early twentieth centuries, conservative episcopalians used the term to describe what for them constituted the historic heart of their Church: devotion to the English liturgy, a high estimate of the sacraments, respect for tradition and assertive churchmanship. They were selective in focusing not on the confused period of the sixteenth century or what to them seemed the lowered standards of the Church in the eighteenth century, but on the era from Richard Hooker and Lancelot Andrewes to Jeremy Taylor and Thomas Ken. From the 1950s to the 1970s, however, a new usage developed which equated 'Anglicanism' with the beliefs and practices embodied in the Elizabethan settlement as distinct from those of the 'Puritans'. This interpretation faced problems in that on many points, not least their hostility to 'popery' and separatism, many bishops and moderate 'Puritans' stood shoulder to shoulder rather than face to face. More recently, two other views have been advanced, both returning to the older view, albeit in different ways. Peter Lake, supported by Conrad Russell, has argued that men like Hooker, Andrewes and others 'invented' an Anglicanism which was sacramentalist, authoritarian and isolationist (what would in the 1620s have been dubbed 'Arminianism'). They did so in conscious response to the rival claim to orthodoxy made by those 'godly', high Calvinist members of the Church of England such as William Perkins and George Abbot who instead stressed the importance of double predestinarian doctrine, preaching and edification. Since then, John Spurr has argued that it was the episcopalian sufferers of the Interregnum and Restoration, men like Henry Hammond, John Bramhall and Jeremy Taylor, who 'invented' a distinct Anglicanism characterized by a shift towards a more Catholic understanding of the historic nature of their Church, a new moral theology which reacted against the downgrading of the human role implicit in double predestinarian teaching, and a new stress on the rich devotional life available to the faithful through the devout use of the Church's liturgy and sacraments. However, after the 1689 Act of Toleration and the establishment of Whig hegemony after 1714, Spurr suggests, the Church became more pragmatic, its teaching more rational and its ritual less formal.

What one is to make of these different claims is not yet clear, but much depends on the kind of material one examines. If one looks at the sermons preached by Andrewes before the King took Communion at one of the major festivals, one does indeed find a high estimate of the sacrament, just as if one examines the polemical writing of established figures or the scholastic exercises of budding theologians at university, one tends to find even relatively small points of difference between fellow Protestants being magnified to the point where they seem to be separated by an unbridgeable chasm. If, on the other hand, one looks at the way in which the more educated clergy tried to explain to their less well educated flocks the basics of the Christian faith, as summarized in the Apostles' Creed, the Ten Commandments and the Lord's Prayer, one finds a far greater degree of consensus between conformists and 'Puritans', 'Calvinists' and 'Arminians', or 'High Church' and 'Latitudinarian'. And if one examines the balance between prayer, Word and sacrament embodied in the Church's liturgy, and the actual performance of ritual outside cathedrals and fashionable London churches, one tends to find a pattern which was somewhere between the 'godly' and the High Church ideals. Similarly, if one looks at the way in which the familiar cadences of the Prayer Book, the celebration of the Lord's Supper and the 'rites of passage' came to be regarded by the laity in many a rural parish, one can find signs of faith and piety, albeit of a humbler kind than that envisaged by a William Perkins or a William Law. In the pages which follow, an attempt will be made, first, to see what views the more highly educated members of the Established Church may have had in common in the seventeenth and eighteenth centuries, and second, to ask how far these published views corresponded with actual practice in the parishes.

The basic doctrines taught by the English Church in the seventeenth and eighteenth centuries were much the same as those inherited from the Edwardian Reformation and the Elizabethan settlement, as expressed in the *Book of Common Prayer*, the short Catechism of 1549, the Thirty-Nine Articles of 1571 and the two volumes of official homilies of 1547 and 1563. While the English Church was clearly well within the 'magisterial Reformation' on most matters, some of its views did mark it out to some degree from continental Protestantism: for example, its acceptance of much of the old system of hierarchy and discipline, and its idiosyncratic views on the nature of the sacraments. The official understanding of predestination and justification, as enunciated in these formularies and expounded by leading churchmen in the mid-sixteenth century, also straddled rather than exactly mirrored the views of Lutherans or Calvinists. It is tempting but perhaps not advisable to look to this mid-sixteenth-century body of doctrine for a definitive statement of later dogma. The formularies of 1547–71 were written at a time when continental as well as English reformers' ideas were still in flux: as elsewhere, it would be some time before the full implications of the English Church's position were elaborated. Thus the authors of the most explicit statement of doctrine, the Thirty-Nine Articles, had been concerned to state the fundamentals of the faith and to warn against what should *not* be believed rather than laying down what should be believed down to the last detail. The doctrines in the liturgy, Catechism, homilies and Articles should perhaps be viewed more as an anchor which restrained conformable churchmen from drifting too far from the position taken under Edward and Elizabeth. It cannot be denied that some otherwise strongly committed members of the English Church took pronounced exception to elements in these formularies, but if there was such a thing as an 'Anglican' in the period from 1550 or 1600 to 1800, it was someone who for the most part did not deviate too far from the norms laid down at the outset. Subsequent developments in the theology of the Established Church were mostly amplifications or refinements of these original norms, or represented relatively limited shifts.

It has been persuasively argued that what was distinctive about the early Protestant Church of England was not a systematic theology but a theological method which evolved between the late sixteenth and the late seventeenth centuries. This method had three elements: the authority of Scripture, the use of reason, and the appeal to antiquity. Scripture always had prime place, as was made abundantly clear by the early concern for an accurate translation of the Bible and the stress in the Church's official formularies on scriptural warrant and the importance of Bible reading. But where matters were not stated definitively or prescribed literally it was thought permissible to use the power of reason that God had given man, and also to look to the experience of the Church in the first six or seven centuries. The method used in the other major Protestant churches of the day was not very different, in that there was a similar interest in patristics and a distinct revival of scholastic technique among a number of theologians working in Germany and Switzerland; but English churchmen were perhaps less apologetic about their use of tradition and reason.

Individual English thinkers might have different emphases, for example Richard Hooker and Robert Sanderson on reason, and Lancelot Andrewes, Henry Hammond and John Cosin on antiquity; also, different challenges might provoke different emphases. But at all times a balance of sorts was preserved in that neither an unswerving biblical fundamentalism nor an excessive regard for scholastic methods of exposition or for tradition was allowed to dominate.

One of the results of this method, and of early attempts to defend the new teachings, was the practice of trying to distinguish between on the one hand the fundamentals of the faith, on which there could be no doubt or disagreement (and on which there would be a large measure of agreement with most other Protestants), and on the other hand *adiaphora* (or 'things indifferent') and questions of opinion – speculative matters on which it was advisable not to spend too much time, and to deal charitably with those who took a different view. This distinction between basics and inessentials was resisted by some, the logic of whose opinions tended to drive them to the margins of the Church or even outside it; and even for those who accepted it, the dividing line was often not easy to draw. But at least for those disposed to accept such a distinction, it permitted amicable differences of opinion on a number of topics not only between English episcopalians and some moderate Protestants abroad but also between most English conformists.

One area in which there was much debate in the Stuart period was on the doctrine of salvation. This debate had two main aspects: predestination, and the nature of justification. The first major challenge came from what has come to be known as 'Calvinism', though recent work by Kendall, Clifford, Weir and White suggests that on a number of issues, such as the nature of the divine decree, the extent of Christ's atonement, the best way to obtain assurance of election and the terms of the covenant of grace, there was no single or uniform 'Calvinist' position. Equally, at at a number of points late Elizabethan and early Stuart 'Calvinism' clearly owed more to the revived scholasticism of Theodore Beza, the Heidelberg theologians and William Perkins than to Calvin himself. From the 1580s to the 1620s, well-placed groups of academics and clergy did their best to modify the 1571 Articles in a high Calvinist direction, as in the Lambeth Articles of 1595. But these attempts to insist that everyone believe in a double predestination irrespective of faith or sin foreseen, and in irresistible and indefectible grace, were unsuccessful, partly because the Crown did not wish to be dictated to by pressure groups, and partly because other churchmen thought that there were, as John Hales put it, more 'maybes and peradventures' on such matters than the high Calvinists allowed. Undeterred, the high Calvinists fought back in the 1620s and 1630s by branding their opponents 'Arminians' – a term of theological abuse (based on the writings of the Dutch writer, Arminius, condemned at the Synod of Dort in 1619) on to which were grafted grave political charges: 'Arminians' were accused of being pro-Catholic, pro-Habsburg, absolutist and clericalist. Efforts to demonstrate the existence of English 'Arminianism' in those decades have been made, but are hampered by the portmanteau nature and indiscriminate application of the label at the time.

The situation was evidently more complex than a simple 'Calvinist'/ 'Arminian' divide, not least in that there were certain doctrines on which moderates could agree, and some practical considerations which inclined them to avoid the extremes; but in addition three observations may be made. First, an examination of the best-selling catechisms of the day suggests that the classic doctrines associated with high Calvinism were *not* taught much at elementary or even intermediate levels of instruction, a fact which ties in both with continental practice in the sixteenth century and with the English authorities' efforts to confine debates on double predestination to the university schools. Second, while it is unclear what importance the average parish priest or educated layman of the early Stuart period gave to these issues, to judge from their typical reading matter they seem to have been more interested in matters of a devotional and practical kind; even the significance of the marginal notes in the Geneva Bible in this respect has probably been much exaggerated. Third, it seems quite possible that on issues such as irrespective reprobation, the atonement and perseverance a majority of educated episcopalians had *never* been high Calvinists in a strict sense, and that by 1660 they had come to reject the other tenets of double predestinarianism as well. Some, like Peter Heylyn, rejected them openly and provocatively; others, like Tillotson and Burnet, seem to have felt that it was better to avoid the subject or attempt a balanced synthesis. To call 'Arminian' the teaching that Christ died for all, that grace was resistible and that those who with the help of the Holy Spirit responded to grace would be saved and those who did not would not, is acceptable in that it corresponds to Arminius' teaching (and later Lutheran thought). But it could also be called 'Anglican', in so far as it rested on the more literal interpretation of the views of Cranmer and other early English reformers.

The second area of soteriology that was much debated – again in print, at least – was the nature of justification. It has been suggested that one of the hallmarks of later Stuart and early Hanoverian religion was the rise of 'moralism' – a stress on 'holy living' which came dangerously close to undermining Christ's role in justification by returning to a works-righteousness approach to salvation. 'Moralists' are also said to have lowered the demands of the Gospel to produce a 'Christianity without tears'. In defence of this argument are cited supposedly 'moralistic' works by Henry Hammond, Jeremy Taylor and George Bull, in which it was stated that faith, repentance or obedience had to precede justification. Also cited are the so-called 'Latitude-men' (John Wilkins, Simon Patrick, Edward Stillingfleet, John Tillotson and others) who are said to have been persuaded by their more rational approach to theology to elevate the capacity of man to do good, and so to have reduced the role of Christ to that of a moral exemplar.

Restoration churchmen were certainly worried that people might conclude from the Calvinist idea that the elect were justified once and for all *before* they were sanctified that there was no need for them to be good thereafter. They were also anxious to counter what they saw as a tidal wave of sin and pride, with the result that there was undoubtedly a heavy emphasis in the second half of the seventeenth century on the moral law, as in works like Richard Allestree's *The Whole Duty of Man* and Jeremy Taylor's *Holy Living*. But the idea of a major shift in official teaching is overdrawn and misleading. The notion that the 'moralists' were challenging Reformation doctrine rests heavily on contemporary allegations from the declining corps of high Calvinists, charges which have been repeated too often by later authors with a theological axe to grind. In fact, on some points, such as the imputation of Christ's righteousness in justification, men like Hammond, Bull and Stillingfleet were probably nearer to early English Protestantism than their critics; on others they innovated only in seeking to reconcile the conflicting messages in Paul and James which had troubled generations of theologians. A close reading of these men's work suggests that they were just as convinced of the totally gratuitous nature of justification and the valuelessness of works in achieving salvation as their opponents.

Where such men *were* different was in doubting the doctrine of imputation and rejecting the idea of justification as an event followed by a lifetime process of sanctification. Instead they stressed that justification and sanctification were part of a continuum: those who through prevenient grace repented and believed would be justified and with further grace would seek to lead better lives; but when they sinned again they had to renew their pleas for forgiveness, as in the fifth petition of the Lord's Prayer. As for sanctification, English Protestantism, in both its formularies and its simpler forms of religious instruction, had always urged the need for a godly life and the performance of good deeds not as a means to salvation but as the fruits of faith, and it would continue to do so throughout the seventeenth and eighteenth centuries. Indeed, during the seventeenth century, both moderate Calvinists and many non-Calvinists came to place great emphasis on a doctrine of the covenant of grace which taught that God had promised Christ to spare those who were in covenant with him, and that those who were in the covenant were bound to try to obey God's will and worship him. The alleged 'moralists' may have suggested that in the covenant of grace the precepts of Christianity were not more grievous than man could bear, but they certainly did not pretend they were easy.

To those looking back from the mid-nineteenth century, especially those of a High Church or Anglo-Catholic persuasion, the 'Anglicanism' of men like Andrewes, Laud, Cosin, Thorndike and Taylor – often referred to as the 'Caroline divines' – seemed to be characterized by a higher estimate of the value of the sacraments, a deeper insight into the value of liturgical forms in the life of the Church, especially the 'incomparable' *Book of Common Prayer*, and a conviction of the value of ceremonial and church design and fittings as a means of helping men to worship God. Such ideas are certainly more evident in the writings and in the actions of some Stuart churchmen than in those of their late Tudor counterparts, but these views and practices were by no means universally adopted, at either official or parish level. Episcopalian teaching was capable of containing eucharistic views which leant towards (but fell short of) a doctrine of the real presence and views which tended towards commemoration; what all 'Anglicans' agreed was that Christ was present, and that the Eucharist was a sacrament, conferring benefits on those who received in faith, rather than a mere ceremony of remembrance. Similarly, the English Church could contain a moderate range of views on baptism, and could exploit ideas on ritual, church fittings and liturgy borrowed from other ages or other areas without compromising the aversion of the majority of members to Catholic 'superstition'. Indeed, in some rural areas, lay conservatism and shortage of funds probably hindered the introduction of new rituals and fittings.

'Anglican' self-awareness was also sharpened by the necessity of fighting off challenges from old foes and new rivals outside the Church of England. For much of the period under review here, but especially from the 1630s to the 1690s, Catholic teaching was still perceived as a major threat, and a considerable amount of Anglican apologetic was devoted to rebutting it, as can be seen in the sermons and writings of men like William Chillingworth, William Laud, John Bramhall, John Cosin, Daniel Brevint, William Lloyd, John Tillotson, William Sherlock and Thomas Comber. As late as 1738, with Jacobite invasions still a possibility, Bishop Edmund Gibson reprinted a selection of earlier tracts as *A Preservative against Popery*. There was little new in the great majority of these polemical works, but their production represented a continuing affirmation of precisely where 'Anglicans' stood on those points of Church government, doctrine and ritual at which some thought they stood closer to Catholicism than to Protestant Dissent. The Anglican response to continued challenges from the latter was only marginally less hostile. The anti-Dissenter equivalent of Gibson's *Preservative against Popery* was a large volume published in 1685 entitled *A Collection of Cases and Other Discourses Lately Written to Recover Dissenters to the Communion of the Church of England*. In an abbreviated form edited by Thomas Bennet and known as *An Answer to the Dissenters' Pleas for Separation* this was a modest best-seller between 1700 and 1728. Some of the 'cases' were restatements of the Elizabethan and Jacobean replies to old Puritan objections; others dealt with new challenges from groups such as the Baptists, over believers' baptism, and Quakers, over the inner light. What is interesting about these essays is not simply their quality or their popularity, but that their authors included both so-called 'Latitude-men' like Simon Patrick and Edward Stillingfleet and conservative churchmen such as Henry Compton, George Hickes and John Sharp. In practice, at least before 1689, most of the so-called 'Latitudinarians' were not in favour of compromising official views or practices in order to win over moderate Dissenters, any more than they differed significantly in theology from their fellow churchmen. Indeed, it may be suggested that, like 'Arminianism' earlier in the century, 'Latitudinarianism' existed mainly in the eye of the beholder. Initially, there was a group of men with similar backgrounds, experiences and views who on some issues incurred the wrath of both Dissenters and High Churchmen, and later on there were pragmatists prepared to work under the Whigs; but a better label might be the one suggested by a member of the original group – 'moderate divines'.

More serious problems were posed by the spread of ideas which were either relatively new or hitherto insignificant in England, such as atheism, Socinianism, Arianism and Deism, though even these may have been less dangerous than was once thought. It used to be common practice for historians to link the eighteenth-century 'Age of Reason' with the growth of secularism, anticlericalism and irreligion. In recent decades, however, it has been suggested that the 'Enlightenment' found a comfortable home *within* the Christian churches of Europe, and may, therefore, have to be seen, as Sheridan Gilley has suggested, 'not as a revolt against religion, but as a creative if ambiguous phase in the history of Christianity itself', a period when men 'could not do without religion or do with religion as it was'. As we have seen, reason had been an acknowledged element in the theological method adopted in the sixteenth and early seventeenth centuries, and a number of English churchmen during the seventeenth century, including members of the Tew Circle, the Cambridge Platonists and the so-called Latitudinarians, would view human reason as 'the candle of the Lord', a God-given gift which it was their duty to use to best effect.

But this did not lead them to conclude that human reason, unaided by grace, was capable of solving all problems, or that there was no longer a need for faith. Theologians and scientists could place a greater emphasis on the study of nature as a means of understanding God's purpose without having to abandon or discredit what had been revealed by other means. Scholars could adopt a more critical approach towards the study of scriptures or miracles without having to shed their belief in the essential truth of Christianity. This balancing act was not always easy to perform; some churchmen opted out and stayed with the older stress on faith and revelation, while other thinkers were led by their enthusiasm for rejecting the 'scholastic' and the metaphysical into doubting the divinity of Christ, the existence of the Trinity or any form of divine revelation, even the existence of God. But where the balance was tilted too far one way or the other, mainstream theologians stepped in to try to redress it. John Tillotson and Richard Bentley proved the existence of God against the atheists; Bentley and Daniel Waterland asserted the orthodox position on Christ's divinity and on the Trinity against the Socinians and Arians; while churchmen as diverse as George Berkeley, Bentley, Joseph Butler, Waterland and William Law refuted the extremes to which some Deists had gone, by stressing the need for an appeal to both revelation and reason. What had made Socinianism and Deism a serious threat was not the numbers of their adherents but the fact that many of them were within the educated elite of the Church: hence the scale of the effort to defeat them. There were further alarms because by 1800 other major shifts of attitude had begun, but at that stage many still felt that the more serious doctrinal challenges had been contained or defeated.

If we turn now to look at the official position on Church government and Church–State relations, we find that this was based on the unique blend of old and new which political and economic as much as religious circumstances had produced in England by the 1560s. However, as with the other areas already explored, English episcopalians proved to be conscientious exponents and inventive defenders in the face of a number of challenges. For its painstaking and persuasive defence of the Elizabethan Church settlement against its Puritan detractors, Richard Hooker's *Of the Laws of Ecclesiastical Politie* has often been hailed as the first and greatest work of 'Anglicanism'. Under the early Stuarts, and especially under Laud, defence was temporarily turned into attack: the leaders of the Church became more assertive over rights and property which, they felt, had been wrongly alienated during or after the Reformation. They also asserted the power of the Church in Convocation to decide on doctrine, and pushed claims not just for the convenience and historic nature but also for the necessity of episcopacy, which they argued was exercised by divine right. In the 1630s, when the Crown was asserting its power to the full in the interest of uniformity, the Laudians remained avowedly monarchical, while other churchmen and laymen, hitherto supporters of royal and episcopal power, were beginning to draw back. The price paid by the Laudians for their relative conservatism on matters of ecclesiology and ritual, and for their continued association with the proud and reserved Charles I during his growing troubles with the Scots and the Irish and at a time of acute fear (partly orchestrated) of 'Popery' among his English subjects, was to be a scapegoat for Charles's intransigence. Laud was executed, episcopacy and the Church courts abolished, hundreds of parish clergy ejected, the liturgy proscribed, and much of the Church's wealth seized, even before the true revolutionaries of the 1640s – the army and its radical allies – seized power and executed Charles I as 'a man of blood' who had provoked the Civil Wars and against whom the Lord had repeatedly witnessed in battle.

The period of Puritan supremacy did, however, help to focus the minds of the more committed episcopalians on precisely where they stood on matters of Church organization; and much of the apologetic produced by men like Henry Hammond, John Bramhall and Herbert Thorndike defended ideas, especially about the role and historic nature of episcopacy, that would be characteristic of the English Church for many decades to come. In merely physical terms the damage was soon made good in the early 1660s, but there were more enduring legacies, such as a greater inclination to regard all forms of Dissent as not merely unnecessary but unnatural. There was a greater caution about pushing the larger clerical claims of the 1630s, but also a readiness to preach the duty of obedience to God's anointed in even more forcible terms than before the Civil Wars. There was an abandonment of the prophetic brand of history which had bolstered the Elizabethan and early Stuart Church by portraying the Reformation as the decisive breakthrough of the forces of light against those of Antichrist. But in its place there appeared a powerful providentialism which saw the return of monarchy and episcopacy at the Restoration, and the country's subsequent deliverance from plagues and plots, as part of God's special concern for the English people. What is more, these views seem to have been held not merely by those who could have been described as 'Anglicans' before the wars, but also by many of those who had been suspicious of Laud but who had been appalled by the political, social and religious turbulence that had followed his fall.

A second crisis in Church–State relations occurred in 1685–9. This had two elements: James II's campaign to secure a measure of equal opportunity for his fellow Catholics, which was stubbornly resisted; and the consequences of James's unexpected departure, which were much more damaging. In 1689 a small but eminent and zealous minority of those who had taken oaths of loyalty to James since 1685 felt that they could not renege on the principle of obedience to a divinely instituted authority which they had conscientiously taught since the Restoration. As a result of their inability to take a new oath to William and Mary, these Non-Jurors resigned or were deprived of their posts, and for the next few decades a number of them formed a breakaway Church which acted as a pointed reminder to many of those who *had* taken the oath, albeit with reservations. The year 1689 witnessed another major blow to the Established Church: moderate Protestant Dissenters who had resisted James II's Trojan horse – freedom of worship if they accepted toleration for Catholics too – were rewarded by an Act of Toleration which permitted them limited freedom of worship outside the State Church.

Other problems in Church–State relations in the Stuart and Hanoverian period were less dramatic but more persistent: coming to terms with the fact that the supreme governor might not be a perfectly sincere member of the church's communion; coping with demands for concessions to religious minorities from monarchs and political pressure groups; the loss of the clergy's power of independent taxation at the Restoration; the suspension of Convocation in 1689 and 1717; and the reduction of the jurisdiction of the Church courts over a number of areas of everyday life. In the later Stuart period bishops also had to reconcile themselves to the paradox that, although their advice was heeded less than before, they were expected to become regular attenders in the House of Lords to help royal ministers get Crown business through, unless they had strong scruples about particular items of policy.

Some of the problems just listed, such as the Non-Juring schism of the 1690s, faded in time. Others were at least partly solved by parliamentary legislation such as the stipulation in the Act of Settlement of 1701 that no future monarch or his consort could be a Catholic – hardly a guarantee of total commitment to the Church of England. But there remained dilemmas with which the Church and its individual adherents had to cope. Should the Church continue to preach passive obedience to divinely instituted authority as it had done before James II sought to use that obedience against the Church itself? English churchmen remained fundamentally committed to divine right monarchy and opposed to rebellion, but were anxious to see a purposeful alliance of Church and State rather than erastianism. Should the Church regard the 1689 Act of Toleration as a permanent or a temporary arrangement? All episcopalians were firmly opposed to Dissent, but some, faced by an apparently rapid growth of Nonconformity after 1689, felt that it was essential to return to the principle of one State, one Church, and wage a vigorous new campaign against Dissent, while others felt that a policy of persuasion rather than coercion should be adopted to try to win over Dissenters. Those who took the former view were likely to be associated with the 'High Church' camp which, led by Francis Atterbury, agitated for the return of Convocation; they were also likely to support the Tories as a mark of approval for their firm stand in support of the powers of the Established Church in 1689 and subsequent decades. Those who adopted the latter position were often called 'Low Churchmen' or 'Latitudinarians', and were usually more sympathetic towards the Whigs for their unwavering support for the Protestant succession at a time when the Tory party was deeply tinged with Jacobitism.

At times the hostility between these groups exploded into rage, as during the trial of Dr Sacheverell in 1710 and during the Bangorian controversy of 1717. But 'High' and 'Low' Church are as potentially misleading as most labels in the early modern period. They may represent less the norm than the extremes to which the more aggressive or ambitious clerical politicians like Atterbury were driven, and paying too much attention to these 'parties' may obscure the large amount of common ground that united 'Anglicans' as diverse as Nottingham, Burnet, Sharp, Wake and Gibson, not least in their desire to defend a Church and State whose interests they sincerely thought were identical. Evidently a majority of the prelates appointed after 1714 on the recommendation of Whig ministers were acceptable to their masters, but most of the episcopal biographies written to date suggest that bishops, at least until the mid-eighteenth century, demonstrated a capacity to remain conscientious churchmen first and politicians or administrators second. In this they were helped by the fact that the differences between Whig and Tory views of Church–State relations were not as marked as they had been under Anne. It may also be the case that the parish clergy were not predominantly staunch Tories, as is often asserted. It is true that far more of those who took part in later Stuart and early Hanoverian parliamentary elections and in the elections to Convocation voted Tory, but this obscures the point that, at least in the case of many of the parliamentary elections, the majority of the clergy did not take part at all. Perhaps this majority was too poor to vote, or perhaps it persisted in the old belief, expressed in clerical diaries and correspondence of the period, that since clergy could not be MPs it was not fitting for them to get involved in secular politics. Even if the parish clergy were mainly Tory in the age of Walpole, it is also possible that this commitment faded as the bubble of old Dissent burst and the bitterness of older quarrels burnt itself out.

The eighteenth-century Church can, like the aristocracy of that period, be portrayed as one of the pillars of an *ancien régime* in England, as has been done by Jonathan Clark. Spurr has also recently suggested that 'by the time of George III, the Church of England enjoyed a greater identity of interest and outlook with the politically powerful, landed classes' than at any time since the early seventeenth century. Indeed, in terms of their social background, income and lifestyle, the upper echelons of the clergy of the later eighteenth century were closer to the aristocracy and gentry of the day than ever before. The Established Church also played a leading part in State rituals such as coronations and royal funerals; it preached sermons to commemorate the martyrdom of Charles I and the Restoration of Charles II; it defended the political order and the judicial system of the day, and taught that the social hierarchy and inequalities of wealth were God's will, though it also stressed the duties and responsibilities of superiors to inferiors. However, once again this position was in essence derived from the 'magisterial' – and, in the English case, rather erastian – Reformation of the sixteenth century. Stuart and Hanoverian churchmen merely refined, extended or adapted views about Church and State that had for the most part been current under Elizabeth. It is yet another example of what might be termed an 'Anglican' synthesis that rested on a shared basis of views on doctrine, worship and Church organization which originated in the mid-sixteenth century but had been modified in response to the many challenges it had faced over the following two and a half centuries.

To understand what 'Anglicanism' meant, we must look at the practice as well as the theory. This is not straightforward, in that for most of the early modern period there were marked differences between a diocese like Winchester or Canterbury and one like Carlisle or Chester: in the endowments available to the bishop and chapter to help them perform their duties, and in the number, size and wealth of the parish livings, the educational standards of the lower clergy, and the ratio of clergy to laity. There were also variations between the forms of worship, the frequency of services and the style of preaching found in the average rural church and those found in cathedrals, college chapels and fashionable urban churches; and there were often subtle but distinct differences between the message conveyed at elementary levels of instruction and that delivered to the better-educated. To compound the problem, there were variations in the main thrust of pastoral effort: in the 1630s, bishops and archdeacons were particularly concerned to ensure minimum standards of conformity in religious conduct and church fittings; from the Restoration to the reign of Anne there was a growing concern, especially in London, to curb immorality and defeat religious apathy, by preaching and setting up societies and schools; from the 1730s there was a small but growing band of clergy anxious to re-evangelize the nation; and at the end of the eighteenth century many bishops tried to increase the frequency of services as a means to greater piety. But these contrasts and variations should not be exaggerated: the hard core of what may be called parish or Prayer Book Anglicanism probably changed little during the Stuart and Hanoverian period.

The heart of that Anglicanism was the *Book of Common Prayer*, which itself was not altered much in the two and a half centuries after its creation. This liturgy embodied many Anglican principles: the perceived need for set forms of prayer and worship in the vernacular and the due administration of approved sacraments; the focus on Scripture in the set rota of Bible readings, psalms and canticles, 'comfortable words' and other scriptural texts which punctuated its services; and the repeated use of the Creeds which linked Anglicanism to the first centuries of Christianity. Week in, week out, parish Anglicanism revolved around this liturgy with its familiar forms, and perhaps above all the rites of passage: baptism, marriage and burial. By the 1640s, to judge from the opposition that met its proscription, it had already achieved acceptance among many of the laity.

Though less endowed with pictures or symbols than before the Reformation, the parish church and churchyard still contained a number of potent images reflecting Anglican priorities: the lectern on which rested a folio King James Bible; the pulpit from which the minister preached the Gospel; the reading desk with a large copy of the latest edition of the *Book of Common Prayer*; the panels on the walls on which were inscribed the Apostles' Creed, the Ten Commandments and the Lord's Prayer which everyone should have learnt in the Catechism; the new church plate to replace or supplement the old; the rail at which communicants knelt to receive both bread and wine in the sacrament; the simple font in which children were baptized; the suitably inscribed stones placed over a growing number of graves in the churchyard; and the new sets of bells in the tower which rang out to express parishioners' joy or grief. The remodelled medieval parish church, and not the beautified chapels of Laud and Cosin or the neo-classical gems of Wren and Hawksmoor, was the norm, and a visit to one of the churches the Victorians did not 'improve' will tell you more about parish Anglicanism than any verbal description can.

One can also get close to it through the catechisms, tracts, manuals and devotional aids which the more active members of the parish clergy prepared and which were sold or given away in huge quantities between the early seventeenth and early nineteenth centuries. In the simplest of these – basic oral instruction by question and answer, broadsheets with a religious message, dialogues combining entertainment with instruction, simple sermons published in a cheap format, and samplers with approved texts or moral precepts – official beliefs were distilled to their essence, and presented in ways calculated to have the greatest impact on those parishioners with few or no reading skills. In a range of more advanced but still intermediate forms – catechetical lectures and sermons to help catechists or more advanced students, collections of prayers and meditations to help the devout prepare for Communion, open letters on moral dilemmas or spiritual problems, improving thoughts, moralistic essays, and treatises on how to live a better life and make a good death – the basic tenets of Anglicanism were further explained in ways that would appeal to the better educated and more leisured sections of society. Few men and women would have been touched by all these forms of instruction, but owing to the growth of literacy in early modern times, the rapid expansion of printing and later the creation of a network of provincial booksellers and libraries, few would have escaped contact with at least some of them.

As Anglican catechists never tired of stressing, their work laid the foundations of religion in the next generation by inculcating the essentials of the faith in a way that all could grasp: the Apostles' Creed (a summary of theology), the Decalogue (a rule of duty), the Lord's Prayer (a model of prayer) and an explanation of the sacraments (as tokens of faith and signs and channels of God's grace to us). The short catechism printed in the first Edwardian Prayer Book, extended in 1604 and slightly modified in 1661, was the form most commonly used, being available not only in the *Book of Common Prayer* but also in two little works printed in tens of thousands of copies every decade: *The ABC with the Catechism* and *The Primer and Catechism*. This was the catechism that Shakespeare learnt, to judge from the appearance of some of its phrases in his writings; and we know that two centuries later Wordsworth mastered it at a precocious age. In some respects it was easy to learn, as in the simple account of faith in 'God the Father, who hath made me . . . God the Son, who hath redeemed me . . . and God, the Holy Ghost, who sanctifieth me'. But some of its answers were overlong, and technical terms like 'sanctify' were not explained, so that between 1600 and 1800 well over a hundred expositions, commentaries and supplements were published by zealous clergy to help overcome these problems; how many more were prepared in manuscript and not printed is not known. Two forms stand out: Bishop John Williams's *A Brief Exposition of the Church-Catechism with Proofs from Scripture*, published twenty-eight times between 1689 and 1804, and John Lewis's *The Church-Catechism Explain'd by way of Question and Answer and Confirm'd by Scripture Proofs* which in England alone was reprinted fifty-eight times between *c*.1701 and 1820 (there were also editions in Welsh and Irish). The unusually high sales of these forms may owe something to their being recommended for use in charity schools, but in other respects they were much the same as dozens of other works which achieved steady sales during this period.

Catechizing was also designed to prepare young people and adult converts for confirmation and participation in the Lord's Supper. Confirmation enjoyed greater favour among laity and clergy from the later seventeenth century, and was the subject of another clutch of explanatory tracts in the eighteenth century, while the Eucharist stimulated a much longer and larger outburst of special pre-Communion catechisms and manuals. Concern that the laity prepared properly for Communion was not a Laudian or High Church monopoly; most of these works were designed with more practical considerations in mind – to persuade people not to avoid the sacrament out of mistaken scruples or idleness, to assist self-examination, and to inform them how to behave before, during and after reception. Some of these little treatises adopted the technique popular in late Elizabethan and early Stuart times of an imaginary dialogue between a wise minister or educated layman and an ill-informed or puzzled parishioner, as in William Fleetwood's *The Reasonable Communicant* which was published twenty-four times between 1704 and 1807. More common were manuals for the better-educated. Jeremy Dyke's early best-seller, *A Worthy Communicant*, concentrated on instruction, but the type which later proved most popular was that which combined an element of teaching with a number of prayers, meditations, 'ejaculations', hymns and psalms for use over a period of several days before reception, for example G.B.'s *A Week's Preparation towards a Worthy Receiving of the Lord's Supper* which had sold fifty editions by the 1750s. Inscriptions on the flyleaves of surviving copies suggest that many were given by parents or godparents to young people, perhaps at confirmation, but the scale of sales and the behaviour of committed Anglicans like John Evelyn suggests that adults may have used them as well.

Prayer was seen as a regular daily duty, not just for the week before Communion. At its simplest level, this duty was equated with an ability to understand and use the Lord's Prayer, a skill developed through catechizing, schooling and regular use in the most frequently repeated services of the Church. Mastery of the Lord's Prayer (and the Creed and Decalogue) was supposed to be a prerequisite for getting married or acting as a godparent. For those members of the laity with more education and time, another flood of publications was made available, even larger in scale than the production of Communion manuals. There had been no shortage of devotional aids during the first century after the Reformation, a growing proportion of them being of native origin, like Henry Valentine's *Private Devotions* (twenty-seven editions between 1631 and 1706). Other consistently popular examples of this genre were the compact little work by William Howell entitled *The Book of Common Prayer the Best Companion in the House and Closet as well as in the Temple* (twenty-one editions by 1758) and the much larger volume prepared by Robert Nelson, *A Companion for the Festivals and Fasts of the Church of England* (thirty-six editions by 1826), of which an abridged form for use in schools was also produced. Devotional works associated with the *Book of Common Prayer* or with Anglican leaders like Andrewes, Laud and Cosin sold well in the later seventeenth century, but other best-sellers like Abednego Sellers's *The Devout Companion* and Benjamin Jenks's *Prayers and Offices of Devotion* (over twenty editions each in the eighteenth century) had no such connections. Relatively few of these manuals were inspired by High Church interest in ancient or Eastern liturgies; the pastoral impulse was paramount.

Many of these works were published in a handy-sized format, offered prayers for all the obvious occasions and some less obvious as well, and included prayers for use by orphans, servants, 'a country-man', soldiers and sailors, 'such as are poor and low in the world' and prisoners, as well as those in the higher ranks of society. A broad readership was clearly desired by John Rawlet in the *Christian Monitor*, which he composed 'for all sorts of people', while William Burkit's *Poor Mans Help*, the little SPCK pamphlets written for servants, the popular religious verses and approved texts and sentiments in sampler books were clearly aimed at the lower ranks. We are not yet in a position to be sure how much impact these and other techniques of instruction had, but at the least their ubiquity indicates a strong commitment on the part of many educated Anglicans, while their variety suggests a clear advance on the limited range of techniques available in the later sixteenth century.

In trying to get its message across, the Church of England was hampered by an antiquated parish system and a shifting population. In areas of rapidly increasingly population many churches were too small for all but a fraction of the laity to attend at the one time, but the owners of the tithes and patronage (including many senior clergy) often objected to the splitting up of existing parishes to create extra new parishes in which rival churches would be set up. In areas of declining population, on the other hand, many churches were too big, with too few parishioners to afford the upkeep of the fabric and provide a decent income or justify the services of a full-time incumbent. In such cases incumbents could either seek extra income from a reduced range of approved occupations such as schoolteaching, or they could hold two livings – 'the only way to make ends meet', as one eighteenth-century curate put it. There was undoubtedly a sharp increase in pluralism in the later eighteenth century, but while there was justified criticism of the type of pluralism which enabled the well born or well connected to hold two valuable livings in different areas, it seems likely from recent research that the more common practice in the seventeenth and eighteenth centuries was the pairing of two poor livings, usually close to each other and often adjacent. This system was obviously far from ideal, but damage was limited by the fact that rich pluralists had to put a resident curate into one of their parishes (who in some cases seem to have been well liked by their flocks, perhaps better than the pluralists), and by the fact that poorer pluralists might be ministering to two or more congregations whose combined size amounted to no more than an average parish elsewhere.

Recent studies have also suggested that the clergy's performance of their duties, especially in the later Stuart and early Hanoverian periods, was not as dilatory as was once thought, though there were almost certainly both regional and chronological variations. In the seventeenth century, the higher educational qualifications and standards of morality demanded of ordinands by their diocesans, and the many pastoral problems, increased administrative workload and limited incomes that many parish clergy faced, must have been sufficiently obvious to deter many of those who did not have a reasonably strong sense of vocation. By the later eighteenth century, with clerical incomes rising and the cost of university education confining graduate entry largely to the sons of the manor house or the parsonage, many may have entered the profession less from a strong sense of vocation than from parental pressure or the expectation of a rich post. Even so, there are relatively few well-documented cases of clerical misconduct or neglect, surprisingly so given the picture of port-swilling, fox-hunting 'squarsons' painted by some contemporaries and later critics. The norm over much of seventeenth- and eighteenth-century England seems to have been the performance of two services on a Sunday (one in each church in the case of a poor pluralist), the administration of Holy Communion four times a year (six to twelve times in urban parishes and some late eighteenth-century rural ones), the performance of the rites of passage on demand, and a series of sessions of catechizing for part or all of the period between Lent and Michaelmas. This may have been less than the nineteenth-century ideal, but early modern clerics had much more to do than minister to spiritual needs. In an age of often severe social problems, they were increasingly called upon – or chose – to act as agents of central and local government for collecting statistics or administering poor relief, or to act as JPs, agents of the many voluntary societies or charities of the day, school governors, money-lenders, unpaid notaries public, doctors and even (to judge from Parson Woodforde's experience) as vets. Ironically, the improved education, better birth, higher income and enlarged roles of some of the clergy may have had the effect by the later eighteenth century of erecting higher barriers between the more gentrified sections of the clergy and their flocks than had existed before, though how far this worked against lesser clergy like the curate in Richard Gough's Myddle in 1702 or Francis Kilvert in Radnorshire in the 1870s is less clear.

The laity's reponse to the efforts of the Anglican clergy is hard to gauge. The return of communicants in 1603, the Compton census of 1676 and recent calculations for the mid-eighteenth century all suggest that the great majority of the population conformed to the Church of England; but work on individual parishes indicates that in some cases only a minority attended church regularly and that as few as 10 per cent took Communion. As elsewhere in Europe, however, attendance could vary widely, according to the size and pattern of settlement (larger parishes with scattered hamlets usually had lower attendance), the mobility of the population (parishes with higher turnovers had smaller turnouts), the inhabitants' chief occupations (pastoral workers, sailors and miners were less regular attenders than arable workers) and the attitude of the village notables (while some encouraged their servants and tenants to attend, others did not). Moreover, irregular attendance did not mean a desire to do without the rites of passage or to be excluded from village festivities that centred on the church. Lay perceptions of religious duties may have been selective and pragmatic compared to the Church's ideal, but they were not necessarily insincere. Most couples appear to have accepted the need for a church wedding, even if it had to be a clandestine marriage in a nearby parish without the required calling of the banns in their own. Most parents, as far as we can tell, wanted their children to be christened, even if they were sometimes upset by the conditions laid down by the Church for the choice of godparents. Confirmation was regarded as desirable, even if for some it was less an assertion of faith than a means of receiving an episcopal blessing or sharing in the treats given to confirmands. Of those who made wills, most began with a brief statement of faith; and if the illness proved fatal, their relations were anxious for the deceased to be buried in the churchyard with all due ceremony, though again some may have chafed at the restrictions imposed by the clergy on older funeral customs. Perhaps the best example of differing lay and clerical perceptions was Holy Communion. From incumbents' comments and pamphlets issued to defuse the situation, it seems clear that the clergy had scared away many of the laity by their warnings about the dangers of receiving Communion without due preparation and by their stress on the importance of intending to lead a new life thereafter. Some laymen appear to have become convinced that receiving the sacrament involved not merely a resolution but a *promise* not to sin again, and, fearing hellfire for breach of this promise, waited till they were on their deathbed to receive Communion. It was not a lack of belief, therefore, but a conviction that the sacrament was too holy for sinners like them, that may explain some low levels of participation.

There are other indications of acceptance of or at least familiarity with parish Anglicanism: those congregations which reported ministers who omitted sections of Prayer Book services in the early Stuart period, or in the 1640s tried to defend their minister, Prayer Book and church fittings from Puritan attack; those who supported the efforts made through Queen Anne's Bounty to raise the value of poor livings, or, fired by political and social as well as religious grievances, joined a 'King and Church' mob; those humble churchgoers who in the seventeenth century sang the metrical psalms so raucously as to make the gentry shudder, or who in the next century joined the re-formed choir, the village band or the local team of bell-ringers. Even the language spoken by the people had also, students of English tell us, been coloured by the liturgy, the homilies and the catechism which had been repeated so regularly in church and school.

By the early nineteenth century, however, the difficulties facing the Church of England were growing apace. There had perhaps been a decline of zeal in some sections of the clergy in the second half of the eighteenth century. In some parts of the country the imbalance between the number of parishioners and the number of seats in the church had become intolerable. There was a rapid growth of rival groups such as the Methodists, and a revival of Catholicism aided by an influx of Irish immigrants; together these groups would tilt the balance of religious persuasion away from the Church in the first half of the nineteenth century. There were zealots within the Church demanding greater effort, and critics outside it attacking the whole basis of Anglican 'priestcraft' or demanding the reform of abuses such as pluralism. There were individual reformers and some collective improvements in the late eighteenth and early nineteenth centuries, but the Church was too disparate a body and lacked the machinery and perhaps the will to undertake major reform. When many Church leaders were seen to demur at granting greater toleration to Dissenters and Catholics in 1828–9 and to oppose parliamentary reform in 1832, they became the target of radical attack and Whig opprobrium on an unprecedented scale, and reforms were imposed upon them. The Church of England would find it difficult if not impossible to recover the position and influence which it had worked for, and to no small extent been accorded, at both national and parish levels in the preceding three centuries.

10

Radical Sects and Dissenting Churches, 1600–1750

Michael Mullett

A DOMINANT FEATURE of the churches and sects which are the subject of this chapter is the fact and act of schism, of separation, of plurality. In this period, church secession was in itself generally regarded as disruptive, subversive and radical, for religious groups which broke away from major state-supported churches threatened to dissolve the bonds of a social and political order held together by religious sanctions and by universal membership of a single Church in each political society. This interpenetration of Church, State and society was particularly marked in post-Reformation England and Wales, a polity with a highly developed state control of religion and a consequent mingling of the roles of subject and church member. Yet from the start, 'radical' dissidents abandoned the national Church in pursuit of the re-creation of the ideal Church described in the New Testament, especially in the Acts of the Apostles.

The Church of England set up by statute (the Acts of Uniformity and Supremacy) in 1559 was, in the eyes of some, not a replica of the New Testament Church. Today's historians are inclined to emphasize the Reformed and Protestant nature of the Elizabethan Church of England. To some contemporary observers, however, the institution called *Ecclesia Anglicana* was not a scriptural or apostolic Church, but one which retained features of recently abolished 'popery'. Critics of the English national Church were given intellectual coherence by the scriptural revival spearheaded by John Calvin (1509–64) and his creation of a widely admired neo-apostolic Church at Geneva, yet his influence on the emergence of English religious Dissent was indirect. He himself detested the idea of sectarian or separatist churches. However, his model of a Reformed Church acted as a standard by which to judge other churches. The Church of England, as established in 1559, soon came to be examined by 'godly' critics according to the scriptural norms fostered by Calvin and enshrined in the Genevan Church and its sister churches in France, Scotland, the

Netherlands and elsewhere, and was found wanting. Yet Calvinists abhorred the idea of schism in the Church and cherished inclusive, disciplinarian social churches. Therefore most of *Ecclesia Anglicana*'s fierce Calvinist watchdogs stayed with it, criticizing from within but never quitting a Church that, after all, was at least 'halfly reformed' and might one day become fully so.

Others were less patient, more exasperated. There was a tradition in England, going back to Wyclif and the Lollards, of sectarian nonconformity, of illegal conventicles. This tradition had been re-awakened in Mary's reign (1553–8), and the underground dissident Church of those years, especially in London, later became the exemplar of Elizabethan and Stuart Separatism. The influential dissident theorist Francis Johnson (1562–1617) claimed the mantle of the Marian Protestants – who were, of course, essentially separatists from a state-supported Church – on behalf of the sectarian dissenters: 'for they [the Marian martyrs] were then separated from the rest of the land; and voluntarily submitted to the Gospel of Christ'. Thus association with the secessionist example of these martyrs under Mary, revered as those martyrs were by all who claimed the name of Protestant, gave a moral authority to acts of separation that might otherwise have been avoided for dread of 'schism'.

Under Elizabeth, few of the intellectual architects of Separatism rushed into the radical and dangerous position of abandoning an imperfect but Established Church. The Calvinist principles that faulted the Church of England for its lack of thoroughgoing reformation also frowned on separation, and laid great emphasis on Church discipline, exercised with the aid of godly secular magistrates. There were also other, perhaps less theoretical, reasons for avoiding Separatist radicalism. Among the well-educated Cambridge dons who formed the intellectual power-house of early Separatism there were understandable misgivings about the sacrifice of good clerical career prospects; even worse was the prospect of imprisonment and execution, like those of the leading Separatists in 1593, or of exile. The gradual and reluctant nature of the transition from vocal Puritan criticism of the Church of England to separation from that Church can be seen in the careers of some of the pilots of late Elizabethan and Jacobean Separatism, after the giants of Elizabethan dissent Henry Barrow (executed 1593), John Greenwood (executed 1593) and Robert Browne (d. *c.*1632) had either been killed or, in Browne's case, had conformed to the Church. Because of the hazards and moral difficulties involved in separating from the Established Church – a typical Separatist church covenant used the phrase 'whatsoever it [separation] should cost them' – dissatisfaction with the Church of England was not in itself always enough to push a person or a group into severance. Those who did leave were motivated not just by repudiation of the national Church, but also by the positive attractions of voluntary 'gathered' churches, by the vision of 'the true primitive apostolic constitution' and communion of saints.

One of the most important and creative leaders of early English Separatism, bridging the Elizabethan and Jacobean periods and assuming the mantle of the executed Henry Barrow, was the Yorkshireman and Cambridge cleric Francis Johnson. According to one account, Johnson's progress towards Separatism from a position of criticizing the faults of the Church of England from within was certainly hesitant. In the vivid – and possibly apocryphal – story of Johnson's conversion to Separatist principles given by his disciple Governor Bradford, Johnson was intellectually coerced into Separatism by reading the works of Henry Barrow, which he had been commissioned to destroy. Subsequently, Johnson became the pastor of Barrow's small following and guided it through the exile in Amsterdam to which it resorted after the anti-Separatist Act of 1593. Elizabethan and Jacobean Separatists tended to be outspoken, opinionated, courageous and articulate men and women of decided views: it had, after all, been their strongly held opinions and high standards that had led to their departure from an imperfect Church in the first place. These traits made them difficult to govern, and Francis Johnson in particular had to steer a course through bitter personal quarrels with his brother George (largely over the alleged extravagances of Francis's wife), arguments with the congregation's Dutch hosts and, within the congregation, some of the earliest and sharpest debates in post-Reformation English religious radicalism, over authority in a congregation and the role of ministry.

The point that Separatism was often accepted reluctantly rather than embraced enthusiastically is clearly illustrated in the career of another major Separatist pioneer, John Smyth (?1570–1612). Beginning, like Johnson, as a Cambridge-educated critic of the Church of England, Smyth progressed to Separatism against his own inclinations: as late as 1606, he was still trying to remain a basically loyal, though far from complacent, member of the Established Church. With a background of civic preaching in Lincoln, Smyth became associated with a gathered church, meeting in the area of Lincolnshire, Nottinghamshire and south Yorkshire. This gathering had formed in the early years of the seventeenth century and was linked to the former Cambridge don John Robinson, with bases at Gainsborough and Scrooby. Pressure of persecution forced these midland Separatists into exile in the Netherlands.

By 1610 the Protestant, tolerationist Netherlands hosted a profusion of small communities of English Separatist refugees. In Leyden, John

Robinson presided in relative tranquillity over an expatriate English community of about 300, emphasizing the role of the rank and file in the life of the Church. In Amsterdam, Francis Johnson maintained firm Calvinist principles and the authority of ministers and elders in autonomous congregations; also in Amsterdam, as pastor of another group of exiles, themselves dissidents from Johnson's fellowship, John Smyth began to display ultra-radical tendencies, giving him a claim to be considered the father of seventeenth-century English left-wing religion. Smyth's rapidly developing radical churchmanship included the following features: the virtual elimination of a separate clerical pastorate; an entirely spiritual, spontaneous, bookless approach to worship; and a pure and restricted definition of church membership. Some time before 1609, Smyth's increasingly hostile attitude to historic churches led him to repudiate the baptism that he had received in the 'popish' Church of England and, in Amsterdam, to proceed – sensationally – to re-baptize himself. With that action a new dimension was added to English radical religion, and the British Baptist churches received their founding charter. Re-baptism, and even more auto-baptism, were viewed with deep suspicion in Reformation Europe, not least because of their association with the social and sexual radicalism that had overtaken the German city of Münster in the 1530s. John Smyth had little in common with those earlier zealots; yet his re-baptism *was* a revolutionary action, because it marked an extreme individualization of church membership and introduced into English dissident religion a more decisive statement than had hitherto been expressed of total segregation from the national Church. Believers' baptism set a sacramental seal on the principle of the voluntary, perfectionist Church, and thereby threatened to dissolve society as it was generally conceived in seventeenth-century Europe.

The first decades of the seventeenth century were a hectic, creative period in the life of the English Separatist churches in the Netherlands. By 1620 the vigorous branch at Leyden that had originated in Lincolnshire was sending out fresh shoots to form congregational communities in America: the 'Pilgrim Fathers'. The English Separatists in the Netherlands never really took to exile: they seem to have shared their contemporary compatriots' dislike of foreigners and, more to the point, some of them felt they had a duty to promote godly religion in England. Therefore we shall look for fresh developments in English radical religion not in the Netherlands but in England itself, with the establishment of the Baptists and the development of a modified Separatism.

The impact of John Smyth's advanced radicalism helped propel two major leaders of the émigré Separatist communities back into relative conservatism. Partly as a reaction to Smyth's exaltation of congregational democracy, before his death in 1617 Francis Johnson continued to emphasize the authority of ministers and elders, while at the same time recognizing the validity of historic churches – even that of Rome. Likewise, before his death in 1625 the veteran Lincolnshire Separatist pastor John Robinson upheld the propriety of joining with Anglican congregations to hear the word of God preached. This made way for the next important development in English religious radicalism – though in fact it was a somewhat regressive development: 'semi-Separatism'.

Before looking at that phenomenon, we may note that the English refugee Separatist communities in the Netherlands, established in the last years of the sixteenth century and flourishing in the early years of the seventeenth, made important contributions to the theory, practice and life of English radical Protestantism. In the first place, the very existence of the gathered communities in a place of exile gave tangible expression to the basic Separatist sense of apartness: 'Come out of her, my people' (Rev. 18:4). In the free environment of the Netherlands the English dissidents, few in number and strong in conviction, were able, especially in the years of intense radicalism down to about 1610, to carry out the most ambitious experiments in churchmanship. In particular John Smyth, in his startling act of auto-baptism – from whose radical implications even he drew back – announced to the world that historical continuity had no place in the life of the Church, that the logical conclusion of Reformation is separation and that ultimately the Church consists of the individual.

After his death in 1612, Smyth's disciples – who tended to be more 'radical' than Smyth himself in their rejection of historic churches – returned to England under the leadership of the Nottinghamshire squire, Thomas Helwys (d. 1616). This group, taking its theological stand on a non-Calvinistic, non-predestinarian view of salvation as available to all, became known as General Baptists. Statistically a tiny sect of perhaps 150, by 1625 they had a rudimentary federation linking groups in London, the midlands and the west country. As we shall see, such churches based on believers' baptism played a leading role in the re-awakening of English radical religion in the 1640s.

The more conservative tendency, associated with Francis Johnson and John Robinson, was carried on by Henry Jacob (*c*.1563–1624), an oxford graduate and erstwhile reluctant Separatist, who spent some time in the Netherlands and returned to England in 1616 to establish, with his fellows, a kind of compromise Separatism. This was based on recognition of the Church of England as an at least partially Reformed Church with which a true Church or religious fellowship, organized on congregational principles, could allow itself 'on occasion to communicate'. If we measure the relative radicalism or relative conservatism of dissident groups by their attitudes to the Church of England, then we might say that Jacob stands at the head of a more cautious tendency in English Protestant opposition to the Church of England, as distinct from the more uncompromising stance represented by Smyth, Helwys and their followers.

The relatively conservative attitudes of 'semi-Separatism' were affected by the changing character of the Church of England, especially under Land in the 1630s, so that the mother church of Henry Jacob's tendency splintered, some of its members adopting the uncompromisingly sectarian stance of believers' baptism. This group's theology of salvation was Calvinistic and elective, unlike that of the General Baptists noted above. Because of its narrower view of salvation, this new Baptist movement was known as Particular Baptist: a further addition to the expanding list of English radical religious groups.

The Particular Baptists exhibit another, and deeply interesting, trend of the 1630s – and of the 1640s and 1650s. So far, in examining the emergence of dissident groups, we have concentrated on the influence of university-educated clerics (especially those from Cambridge). Now we need instead to note the increasing role of laymen, often coming from relatively humble backgrounds and not highly educated. Examples of the new lay and plebeian initiative, anticipating the laicism of radical religion in the 1640s and 1650s, are the founders of the Particular Baptists: the button-maker Samuel Eaton and the cobbler John Spilsbury, both Londoners. In fact such laypeople, especially from the trades and handicrafts, had always been to the fore in the membership of English religious dissident communities, but had hitherto accepted clerical leadership. In the refugee Separatist communities, for example, academic and clerical leadership was unmistakable, with pastors such as John Robinson and William Ames holding university posts in the Netherlands. However, the anticlerical reaction against Laud in the 1630s helped produce, in the underground churches, a dawning antiacademicism which anticipated and helped to make possible the movement for political democracy in the 1640s.

By 1640 'moderate radicalism' in the semi-Separatist tradition of Henry Jacob was far from vanquished, and was to resurface, as we shall see, in the Independency of the 1640s and 1650s. However, it is clear that in the ideologically polarized England of the 1630s there was also a much less conciliatory religious radicalism that was to produce the profusion of sects characteristic of the Civil War decades. A survey of the country in the 1620s and 1630s shows Separatist cells in places such as Coventry, Great Yarmouth, Tiverton, Salisbury, Boston, Norwich and Lincoln, as well as, of course, London. Among them were interesting regional developments, such as the internalized, spiritual religion fostered by Roger Brearely of

Grindleton in the West Riding. The heavy reliance in these small and scattered Separatist conventicles on the New Testament, which formed the marrow of their intense and protracted worship, encouraged the emergence of views which were, in the seventeenth century, startling, though not unheard-of: these included (sometimes) pacifism, and the commitment to toleration that Smyth had tried to promote. Arguably, though, the major 'radical' contribution of the dissenting groups, derived from their emphasis on the New Testament, was in the theory of the Church itself, where a positive view of the Church as a covenanted fellowship rather than as a socially comprehensive institution was gradually becoming dominant among the secessionists themselves. Elizabethan Separatism tended to begin in estrangement, often unwillingly accepted, from one particular imperfectly Reformed Church; rejection in principle of inclusive, social Church membership coterminous with a political society was slow in coming. The Elizabethan Separatist founding fathers generally believed in state supervision and state reform of religion. Later, as it developed in the seventeenth century, Separatism was more concerned to see in the gathered, separate congregation the only model of the true New Testament Church, free of State control, founded on voluntary covenants and made up of 'visible saints'. The voluntary principle at work here shows how far Separatist churchmanship anticipated the principles of Church membership in modern societies, in ways that were profoundly shocking to most seventeenth-century opinion. Indeed, in some ways seventeenth-century Separatist ecclesiology would pose a challenge to some denominations even today, for, as shaped by John Smyth, ultra-Separatism viewed the Church as formed by covenant rather than by historic tradition, and placed authority in the consensus of the individual congregation rather than in the State, clerical hierarchies or Church assemblies.

As radicalism advances, it tends to leave yesterday's militants looking like today's conformists. In Elizabeth's reign, the Presbyterian platform of Thomas Cartwright (1535–1603) might have seemed to be placed in the forward posts of radicalism. However, in the 1640s, after decades of luxuriant growth in English Puritanism and with the Church of England collapsing into the ruins of the Civil War, English (or Anglo-Scottish) Presbyterianism, with its belief in one single recognized Church in England and Wales, Scotland and Ireland, with its insistence on religious monopoly and on clerical leadership in a pyramidically organized and socially comprehensive national Church, represented the epitome of Puritan conservatism. Demands for an exclusively Presbyterian Church order were to be withstood by an emergent centre party, the heirs of Henry Jacob's semi-Separatists: the 'Independents'. The dinding lines between 'Presbyterians' and 'Independents' are blurred; for example, both groups shared an essentially Calvinist theology and a commitment to some kind of national Church. However, contemporaries rightly recognized that the terms 'Presbyterian' and 'Independent' stood for sharply opposed principles of Church order.

The Presbyterians' opportunity, the one real chance for classic Calvinism to establish itself as England's official religion, came after the outbreak of Civil War in 1642. The possibility of a quick and early royalist victory forced Parliament to seek allies and, in line with the principle 'my enemy's enemy is my friend', it formed an agreement with the Scots, who had been at war with Charles I since 1638 in defence of their national Reformation. The price of this alliance was the English Parliament's commitment, in 1643, to the Scots' Solemn League and Covenant, pledging Parliament to adopt in England a rigid, Scots-style Presbyterian order, clerically dominated, disciplinarian and monopolistic. It is true that English anticlericalism, ably represented by Sir Henry Vane the Younger, watered down the Covenant, so that Robert Baillie, a Scots Presbyterian agent in London, complained that it was a 'lame erastian Presbyterie' – toothless and, in comparison with the Scottish model, subordinate to the State. Nevertheless, classic Presbyterianism undoubtedly enjoyed genuine support in England in the 1640s and 1650s, especially among conservative Puritans who hated Laud's ritualist reaction but who wished to see a purified national Church order pledged to establish 'godly rule'.

Under parliamentary auspices, from 1643 a Presbyterian-dominated conference, the Westminster Assembly of Divines, began putting in place an ecclesiastical system and forms of worship and belief that would, it was hoped, at long last make of England the kind of strict Genevan polity of which Thomas Cartwright might have dreamed: England should finally take its place among the 'best reformed churches'. However, the Presbyterian plan took no account of alternative forms of Puritanism that had been nourished in groups like the Jacob Church and its offshoots throughout the 1620s and 1630s. By 1643 English Puritanism was vastly more heterogeneous – doctrinally, organizationally and spiritually – than envisaged in the Presbyterian model. Tolmie, for instance, distinguishes quasi-Separatists, semi-Separatists, strict Separatists and Independents – themselves broad categories, including groups that had been pushed into a more outright alienation by the High Anglican church policies and repressions of the 'Laudian decade'. By the time the Civil War broke out, there were two clearly demarcated Baptist church federations, alongside fringe and ephemeral groupings such as the neo-Judaist 'Thraskists' and mystics like John Everard influenced by the medieval devotional tradition. But Presbyterianism's rigidities were in part designed to combat such plurality, aimed at the 'extirpation of . . . heresy, schism, profaneness, . . .'. In pursuit of this conformity, Presbyterianism aroused, first of all in a minority of the Westminster Assembly itself, a liberal protest movement with its roots in the earlier Separatist and semi-Separatist traditions.

The Independents' clerical leadership resided in a small group of members of the Westminster Assembly fighting a rearguard action against the apparently inexorable implementation of Presbyterianism between 1643 and 1647. The spokesmen of the Independent cause, the authors of the 1644 *Apologeticall Narration* (William Bridge, Jeremiah Burroughes, Thomas Goodwin, Philip Nye and Sidrach Simpson) were the heirs of Henry Jacob's moderate congregational Church polity. Former exiles in the Netherlands, these 'Apologists' consciously saw themselves as a middle party between absolute 'Brownist' Separatism and 'the authoritative Presbyterial government'. Sharing with the Presbyterians a basically clerical and academic orientation and upholding the common Calvinist theology, the Apologist school, while attempting to minimize their differences with the orthodox Presbyterians, stressed the identity of the individual congregation (within a wider Church) and the necessity for some latitude and tolerance of belief – at least for their own group.

Clearly, not all the 'Independents' represented by the Apologists were Separatists or 'Sectaries'. Yet all separatists were Independents. Separatist Independency must occupy our attention here since its adherents, rich in variety if poor in actual numbers, were the true 'radicals' of the 1640s and 1650s. The 'Brownists, Anabaptists, Arians, Thraskists, Familists, Sensualists, Antinomians and others', whether or not they all actually existed in any numbers, were the terror of conservatives, and especially of the more conservative Puritans labelled Presbyterians. The sects provided material for the authoritarian Puritan minister Thomas Edwards, whose *Gangraena* (1646) is a lurid and far from skimpy catalogue of sects and the social and doctrinal menace they represented. Among the propagandist allegations of Edwards and his ilk was the charge that the moderate radicalism of the Independents bred the extremist radicalism of a host of sects. It was a charge that Presbyterians would need to use with caution, given their own secessionist relationship with the Church of England.

The work of conservative polemicists like Edwards is a good example of the force of largely groundless fear and the effectiveness of the big lie in human affairs: events are steered as much by fantasy as by fact. The kind of propaganda of which *Gangraena* is only the best-known example depicted Separatism as (a) threatening because numerically significant and (b) dangerous because the sectarians were revolutionary extremists and moral libertarians. What truth or falsity is there in those projections?

The numerical point can be dealt with quite swiftly. The demography of religious Dissent contains a paradox: though groups were numerous and congregations multifarious, numbers of adherents were low. An examination of two major phases in the history of English Protestant dissent – the exiled communities in the Netherlands and the Jacob Church in London – shows clearly its continual fissiparous tendencies. The Jacob Church in particular had created no fewer than eight offshoots by 1642, and the rapid development after 1640 of part-time ministry in the radical sects allowed them to form small splinter groups without the necessity of gathering a quorum large enough to pay a full-time minister. The number of congregations might be impressive – the Particular Baptists had over 250 branches by 1660, doubtless enough to fuel the fears of a Thomas Edwards – but with congregations as small as eighteen, the total membership amounted, McGregor calculates, to less than one half of one per cent of the population. Even in the hotbed of Separatism, the capital, the dissenters were both numerically insignificant and unpopular with the inhabitants.

It might be countered that the 'sectaries' were considered dangerous not so much because of their numbers but because of their location, influence, commitment and extremism: anarchist fanatics swarming in the capital, entrenched in the New Model Army, holding bizarre doctrines, with a well-thought-out revolutionary game plan. Such charges made up the bulk of Edwards' propaganda. The sectarians, he wrote, threatened, through what he regarded as the curse of religious toleration, to sever the links between magistracy and religion; they undermined Christianity and championed atheism, endangered the family and upheld licence along with all forms of immorality.

Undoubtedly, there was some truth in such allegations. For one thing, it was true, as we shall see, that Separatism broke the bond between Church and State. Moral values are always likely to be called into question in wartime, especially, perhaps, during civil wars; in addition, the effective suspension of press censorship in England during the Civil War period allowed a rich variety of opinions to flourish, some of which were antinomian, that is, amounting to a denial that moral laws bind the Christian united to God. However, whether this often purely theoretical antinomianism amounted to much misconduct in practice is open to question; and when we turn to actual sects, with some kind of durable membership and organization, we find that the radical groups targeted by Edwards tended to be, if anything, ultra-moralist. True, their highly developed anticlericalism led them to decry figures like Edwards and to condemn tithes, as well as formalism in worship and excessive academic theologizing, but when it came to morals, as McGregor shows, doctrines such as 'free grace', which was a hyper-Calvinist conviction of indestructible election, did not lead in any way to moral collapse: quite the reverse. Regarded by many contemporaries as a gateway that opened on to all other forms of extremism, the Baptists, both Calvinistic ('Particular') and non-Calvinistic ('General') were dedicated disciplinarians.

Typical of Baptist ecclesiastical life and of the social recruitment characteristic of the sects was the Bedfordshire tinker John Bunyan (1628–88). To us Bunyan is still chiefly famous for his classic fusion of popular culture and Puritan doctrine, *The Pilgrim's Progress* (1678 and 1684). He was also, though – virtually from the time of his conversion in the 1650s – an active Baptist–Independent preacher, church organizer and pastor. In a majestic series of works, generally lacking the entertainment value of *The Pilgrim's Progress*, the largely self-educated Bunyan hammered out the definitive Calvinist and Reformation soteriology in all its unflinching rigour – justification by faith alone, the absolute redundancy of works as means to grace, and an extreme predestinarianism.

In their social and political principles, the Baptists – taking them as archetypes of contemporaneous sectarian radicalism – showed precisely the kind of views we might expect from a largely petit-bourgeois movement of the industrious 'middling sort' of craftsmen and small farmers struggling to keep their heads above water. They exhibited respect for property in small units, alongside suspicion of monopoly; contempt for the indolent and the self-indulgent, whether rich or poor; bitter anticlericalism (expressed chiefly in demands for the abolition of tithes) and antiacademicism. The programme of the Levellers, a party born in the Parliamentarian army out of the grievances and the democratic procedures of the sectarians and the social classes from which they were recruited, elaborated this basic political profile. Republicans calling for a freeholder democracy, the Levellers demanded frequent parliaments and a redistribution of the franchise in favour of the small producer/trader and independent working farmer. However, none of the Leveller programme amounted to a revolution.

Though Leveller democratic politics derived ultimately from the religious sects, in the 1640s the religious priorities of the gathered churches collided with the Levellers' secular goals. The restriction of the sects' political activism came about because fundamentally the sectarians never quite knew whether they were isolationists and introverts or Puritan militants dedicated to transforming England. Some on the religious left also seem to have been influenced away from the possibility of political militancy by the accumulated propaganda that tried to portray them as extreme revolutionaries. The Baptists, despite their involvement in radical action and messianic expectation, especially around the time of the Nominated Assembly (an extraordinary Parliament with a millenarian inspiration convened after the collapse in 1653 of the republican 'Rump' Parliament), remained haunted by one of the great bogeymen of early modern European polemic. What 'Antichrist' was to Protestants in their battle with Rome the sixteenth-century Anabaptist John of Leyden, a figure of demonic sexual licence who had turned the German city of Münster into a totalitarian commune in the 1530s, was to conservatives in their campaign against religious subversives. Dogged by their alleged predecessor, the leadership of the English Baptists tended to play safe within the politics of the expiring Puritan Revolution.

Yet the sects were always, and necessarily, to the fore in the real, underlying revolution that was on foot in England in the decades of Civil War and Interregnum: the destruction of the unanimous society; the secularization of the state; the 'privatization' of religion. Through legislation proposed in 1653, the climacteric year of the Puritan Revolution, and introducing, *inter alia*, civil marriage and the abolition of compulsory tithes, England was on course to become Europe's first non-confessional society. Had it come about, this remarkable transformation would not have taken place in the way it has in modern Europe – through 'de-Christianization' – but rather through the very intensity of Christian profession on the part of the 'saints'.

It is extraordinary to realize the extent to which religious uniformity prevailed in pre-Civil War Britain. To take only one example, in England and Wales all were required by law to repair for worship to the nearest parish church; this worship, as the complaints of the London radical Katherine Chidley reveal, could still look disconcertingly like the popular Catholic piety of the fifteenth century to some. But this religious uniformity had begun to dissolve in what was an increasingly diverse and complex society. This process of dissolution was heralded by the sects before 1640 and was accelerated in the 1640s and 1650s, and although attempts were made to rebuild society's religious unanimity after 1660, the monolithic confessional society was at least badly damaged with the 1689 Act of Toleration.

Toleration was, of course, a major solvent of the unanimous community, and also a legal recognition that that community no longer existed. In the 1650s, with a large measure of toleration actually obtaining, tithe was the issue over which the implicit battle for a secular society, in which religion was personal not social, was fought. In addition, the widespread sectarian demand for 'believers' baptism' – the logical outcome of Separatism – signalled the repudiation of the concept of a Christian society. It was not a threat to property, or political democracy, or moral anarchy or millenarianism that made religious dissent 'radical' in the middle decades of the seventeenth century; what made seventeenth-century religious radicalism truly revolutionary was the voluntarism of the sects, abandoning the centuries-old quest for a Christian society under a Christian State.

Religious diversity in the seventeenth century introduced a discontinuity with the past, a discontinuity not consequent on the English Reformation of the previous century. The Tudor Reformation had retained not only a fundamental assumption about credal uniformity, but also many of the practical details of ancient religious observance. The issue of baptism was particularly useful in focusing attention on these questions of continuity and discontinuity. Questions asked by Elizabethan Separatists about baptism, brought to a head by John Smyth and made even more urgent by some dissidents in the 1640s and 1650s, threatened to sever these links of continuity with the past. To accept the baptism that almost all had received in the Church of England muted the force of separation and implicitly endorsed the Church of England – and, logically, its progenitor, Rome – as valid churches. Conversely, there could hardly be a baptism (or ministry) devolved from the Apostles except through the historic churches. The only alternative – the truly radical alternative – would be for all to be remade, through a new Pentecost or the appearance of a new John the Baptist, and the suspension meanwhile of all existing Church 'ordinances'. To wait for such a new beginning of the Church was the stance of those hyper-radical individuals labelled by contemporaries 'Seekers'.

The 'Seeker' position of waiting for new and miraculous revelations was part of the mood of expectancy of the 1640s and 1650s, reaching its climax in the messianism that inspired the Nominated Assembly. Yet the Seeker outlook may have been the product of disillusionment as much as of expectation. There was certainly disappointment with the failure to establish Christ's kingdom in England after the negative achievement of the execution of Charles I in 1649, and disillusionment too with the suffocating rigidities and increasing insistence on minutiae within the sects and gathered churches. When an obsessive scripturalism and disputes over the propriety of laying on hands or of immersion versus aspersion in baptism threatened to shatter Baptist communities, the need for uncertainty seemed to some to have become pressing. It is here that the 'Seeker' position has to be considered, but its amorphous nature makes it hard to define it as a sect. Hostile contemporaries did indeed believe that Seekers existed as a sect, partly because, as McGregor says, they could not envisage an ideology without a supporting organization. Indeed, there is evidence of groups meeting in expectation of enlightenment, but some of it comes retrospectively from Quaker luminaries who discovered later that they had once been Seekers, seeking the truth they subsequently found in Quakerism. There was no 'Seeker Church': it would have been a contradiction in terms. Seeker individualism – its proponents tend to be identified as single individuals – was the logical outcome of Puritan Separatism, while Seeker uncertainty was the ultimate reaction to Separatism's myriad conflicting infallibilities.

There has been something of a tendency in recent historical writing to minimize the extent and organizational strength of radical dissent in the 1640s and 1650s. We certainly need to be aware of the force of traditional religion, linked to popular culture, especially in reaction to the Puritan austerities of the Civil War and Interregnum periods. I have tried here to point out the minority nature of the radical churches. Some, such as the Ranters, hardly existed at all as groups, except in the fevered imagination of hostile propagandists. However, statistical insignificance in no way detracts from the extraordinary variety and intellectual audacity of radical and marginal movements in England in its revolutionary decades. Though Ranters and Seekers may have virtually disappeared under scholarly scrutiny, except as bogeymen to contemporaries, other sects, such as the marvellously durable Muggletonians, clearly did establish a genuine existence. Above all, the Quakers became a lasting container for the radicalism of the revolutionary decades.

Christian churchmanship needs repeatedly to be rescued from its own authoritarianisms of belief and structure. The Separatism that moved into the light of day in the 1640s and 1650s was a protest against the tyrannies of bishop and presbyter. Yet even the Baptists' male lay eldership could be as autocratic as any clerical officialdom, expelling moral and doctrinal dissidents and using Scripture selectively to set strict limits on women's role in the Church. Often the lay elders were wealthy manufacturers and merchants, like the London Baptist chief, William Kiffin (1616–1701), who combined economic with ecclesiastical power to check radical trends among the Baptists. Furthermore, the power of literacy was all the more pronounced in sects like the Baptists who used, or claimed to use, Scripture as their sole warrant. Power in the congregations may have been concentrated in the hands of male elders whose literacy enabled them to invoke and deploy Scripture against dissidents. Doubtless, elective theology also reinforced the concentration of power among elites within those sects which subscribed to a predestinarian viewpoint; but I wish to concentrate here on the way the Bible had come to be used as a legitimating icon, as an instrument of authority deployed by sect elites against illiterate and semi-literate rank-and-file members, among whom women loomed large. The exasperation of ordinary church members at the use made of the Bible by scripturally learned sect leaders against the views and conduct of those ordinary members produced an anti-scriptural reaction which can be glimpsed, to take one instance, in a Baptist woman's trampling under her feet the text of Scripture which 'she looked upon . . . as nothing'. To those for whom Scripture had become a new tyranny, Quakerism was to be a new emancipation.

Quakerism was the most radical organized religious movement to appear in seventeenth-century Britain, though it is arguable that in its later stages it succumbed to the creeping paralysis that affects even dissenting churches – oligarchic leadership, crypto-clericalism, legalism and formalism. The early Quaker movement was different from other left-wing groups like the Baptists in that it had a wider regional distribution. Its flexible and cellular structure and its eschewal of ritual and of clergy made it eminently suitable to cater for the special needs of the hitherto religiously neglected north country. Early Quakerism had its sources of strength in London, and also in Bristol and other towns and cities, but was as much a rural as an urban phenomenon, at least until the eighteenth century when Quakers moved townwards, probably in part to escape the demands for tithes that they stoutly refused to pay.

Quakerism came nearer than any other sect of the Civil War period to the status and numbers of a mass movement: indeed, the authorities in the 1650s hysterically feared a Quaker takeover of the country and took action accordingly. With numbers perhaps as high as 60,000, the first Quakers shared the typical social background of other sectarians: they were the classic 'middling sorts' of industrious peasant farmers, craftsmen and small traders, with the merest smattering of gentry. They took up some of the social and political themes of their predecessors in the other sects, with an even more emphatic refusal to pay tithes. They shared, and extended, the open, anti-elective view of salvation characteristic of the General Baptists, offering a potential entrée to all men and women. Their main appeal, however, was to those godly and somewhat austere men and women dissatisfied with the theologizing and bibliolatry of other sects such as the Baptists, from whom the early Quakers picked up a large following. There was a democracy and an egalitarianism in the Quakers' dethronement of the Bible as the talisman of an interpreting caste. For Quakers like the movement's leading founder, George Fox (1624–91), the Bible was deeply known, yet it shared authority with other potential sources of inspiration, such as the direct illumination that could enlighten every man and woman.

The liberating possibilities of such doctrines did not remain inert with the early Quakers. They drew out the social implications of their basic assumptions in a wide range of testimonies, from sustained protests against tithes to demands for greater equalization of property-owning, calls for fair prices and wages, a dawning peace witness, contempt for the idle rich, if not for the idle poor, and a simple, straightforward, downright, rather blunt, rather northern way of treating everybody the same. Their uniform, unceremonious mode of address and pointed refusal to bow and scrape were particularly shocking in the highly mannered society of seventeenth-century England, where rigid social stratification was signposted in elaborate codes of speech and body language.

The 'authorities' – provincial magistrates, army officers, clerics of the broad-based 'Established' Church of the 1650s, Parliament – were profoundly disturbed at the Quaker threat, and their alarm intensified the conservative reaction of the decade set in motion by the Blasphemy Act of 1650 and coming to fruition in the Restoration of Anglican monarchy in 1660. A major shock to conservatives was the graphic way in which one prominent Quaker, James Nayler (1617–60), likened himself to Christ, in entering Bristol, in Palm Sunday style, in 1656. Whether or not there was a real possibility of a Quaker coup in 1659, 'conservatives', now including some Baptist spokesmen as well as the Independents and the Presbyterians, thought there was. These groups became resigned to, or welcomed or actively worked for, the return of the traditional symbol of order, the Crown. The revolution of the saints was over, broken on a fatal internal discord between religious radicals and social reconstructionists.

Within a matter of months around 1660, the Puritan sects moved from ascendancy to subjection; before the end of 1662, the Presbyterians, Calvinist custodians of the principle of an authoritative, non-sectarian national Church, were faced with the prospect of becoming one more of the sects they themselves had reviled. Their numbers enhanced by those more conservative Puritans who did not rejoin the national Church after 1660, the separate churches now had to abandon godly rule and seek instead permission to exist. In the next, crucial, period of their history, the three decades between two revolutions, 1659–89, the un-established churches underwent, heroically, persecution; obtained, fitfully, indulgence; and gained, ultimately, toleration – of a kind.

Arguably, Quakerism was the form in which religious dissidence was best equipped to cope with defeat. First, the Quaker conception of the coming of Christ in the spirit of the individual believer, the belief in a spiritual 'Lamb's War' against evil, and the complete acceptance by Quakers of pacifism from 1660 onwards show the abandonment, or rather interiorization, of what had become an impractical millenarianism and activism. Second, the Quakers' superb organization and determined, if passive, defiance of authority on grounds of conscience enabled them if not to resist then to withstand repression after 1660. Quakerism, which had made such massive inroads among the Baptists in the 1650s, became radical Dissent's survival mechanism between 1660 and 1689, largely through the adoption of techniques of passive resistance.

In the decades between Restoration and Revolution England tried a last, painful experiment in sustained religious intolerance and the pursuit of the unanimous society. Two European states, France and the United Provinces of the Netherlands, had formally acknowledged differences in religion, and the Netherlands had combined economic success with its positive espousal of religious variety. Religious freedom had a growing volume of support in Europe, and in England in particular. However, the prospects for tolerating dissidence in England after 1660 were spoiled, or postponed, by political considerations. Protestant religious radicals had, it appeared, launched a civil war which led to the killing of a king, the victimization of royalist gentry and, allegedly, moral and social anarchy. Consequently, systematic religious intolerance was an essential part of the conservative reaction in England after the Restoration of the monarchy in 1660 – a Restoration which the Presbyterians themselves had helped engineer so as to suppress the fringe sects. By 1662, however, the terms of the settlement forced the Presbyterians to choose between acceptance of a High Anglican Church order and expulsion and subsequent repression, and erected a formidable apparatus of parliamentary persecution of dissidence.

Part of a transitional phase between a period of centuries when the need for religious agreement in societies was regarded as axiomatic and a modern age of pluralism and indifference, the seventeenth century confronted all the theoretical and practical problems of toleration. Even under Cromwell's tolerant regime the Quakers showed, by their aggressive behaviour towards other confessions, the sometimes difficult relationship between religious toleration and public order. Further, English Protestants remained concerned lest religious liberty should open the door to 'popery'. A royalist-dominated Parliament, meeting in a spirit of Anglican euphoria at the Restoration, but also with bitter memories of Interregnum hardships, resolved all difficulties over toleration with a statutory programme designed, with the strongest incentives, to restore the Elizabethan dream of a society united in religion. Despite the hopes of Puritan-inclined ministers such as Richard Baxter, the Act of Uniformity of 1662 imposed a liturgy on the Church of England that took no account whatsoever of a century of Puritan complaints. This liturgy was to be unreservedly accepted by parish incumbents as the price of retaining their posts: as a result over 2,000 clergy left the Church by the end of 1662 and formed much of the clerical leadership of the organized denominational Dissent that appeared after that date. Further legislation of the 1660s, known as the clarendon code, sought to deprive Dissent of that leadership, especially in the towns.

In one respect, the classification of religious bodies in England becomes simpler for the years after 1660. There was only one body that could lay any claim to be a national Church, though its style and personality were now more narrowly defined than hitherto: the 'Established sect', as one nineteenth-century Nonconformist historian liked to call the Church of

England. Outside that establishment there were only sects, or at most denominations. The more conservative Puritans were faced in 1662 with a cruel dilemma: conformity to a ritualistic and hierarchical Church or schism and the status of a sect. The viewpoint of the most scrupulous of the godly – the men and women of the most 'tender consciences' – was put, learnedly and massively, in a string of works by Richard Baxter (1615–91). To the left of the Presbyterians – and of those, like Baxter, who refused even the label 'Presbyterian' – were groups which were generally more intellectually comfortable with a sectarian identity. Congregational Independency had its theorist in John Owen (1616–83), the Baptists in Benjamin Keach (1640–1704), the Quakers in Robert Barclay (1648–90). However, as each group now carved out its theological and ecclesiological territory, a major task for the future was that of forging a common front between the groupings and perhaps looking for whatever opportunities existed for mergers.

Merger between the two largest dissident bodies, Presbyterians and Independents, was to some extent assisted by the fact that both now shared unmistakably sectarian characters. Presbyterians who had chosen Reformed principles in preference to inclusion in a neo-Laudian national Church were forced into the same sectarian mould as Congregationals who must now renounce the halfway-house Independency that had enjoyed a vogue since the days of Henry Jacob. As even the more conservative heirs of the Puritans abandoned many of their reservations about secession from the Church of England, the great reformed groups started to edge closer together. Even so, it has to be said that Presbyterians continued to hanker for re-inclusion in an Established Church, as their openness to 'Comprehension' schemes and their practice of 'Occasional Conformity' show. Nevertheless, alliances between the Dissenters at large, and possibilities of coalition and of mergers between the largest units, were definitely on the agenda after 1660. Alliances might arise from expediency, as with the Bristol sects' agreed strategy of obstructing the authorities in 1675 by holding non-stop meetings. Indeed, the 1670s were a promising decade for close religious co-operation between Presbyterians and Independents, heralding the 'Happy Union' of 1691. Although this merger broke up at the national level, union survived in some regions, especially in Devon.

The years of persecution between 1661 and 1689, especially in its bitterest phases in the 1660s and the first half of the 1680s, saw the radical churches take on a new feature: heroism, and even a whiff of romance. Hitherto, the godly had not been particularly notable for escapades, but the Restoration period is full of hair-raising adventure stories from around the country, of close shaves and resourceful deeds. What the Dissenters' plight did for their public image is a matter largely for conjecture. By 1663 penal laws against Dissent must have seemed to many to be justified in the light of a string of hare-brained terrorist insurrections by radical Dissenters ranging from Venner's Fifth Monarchist rising in the capital in 1661 to the Farnley Wood conspiracy near Leeds in 1663. To many guardians of law and order such activities justified the special provisions of the Conventicle Acts of 1664 and 1670, since it was widely believed that conventicles provided cover for sedition. However, the harassment of Dissenters meeting for worship awakened the seventeenth-century English people's normal sympathy for victims of the law. There was understandable public revulsion at cruel fines and imprisonments, crippling distraints on the stock-in-trade of industrious craftsmen, the bullying of widows, the sufferings of children for their parents' beliefs. In towns such as Bedford, attempts to enforce the penal laws would see the borough empty of inhabitants. The dawning of public sympathy for the Dissenters' misfortunes – a kind of popular ideology of toleration – was accompanied by widespread disgust at the Conventicle Acts, which violated English liberties and enriched predatory and disreputable informers. More influentially, attempts to rescue the sectarians from the laws were made spasmodically by King Charles II. Why the King made these overtures to the Dissenters is uncertain: possibly because he cared nothing for religion, or because he felt honour-bound by a pre-Restoration commitment to toleration, or because he wished to broaden his political base by acting as the tribune of the sects, or because he hoped to introduce toleration for the Catholics through offering it to the Protestant Dissenters. Twice, in 1662 and again ten years later, Charles issued, on the no doubt constitutionally illegal basis of his prerogative alone, permission for the Protestant Dissenters at least to worship in peace.

Following this response from the Crown, though seldom from an Anglican-dominated Parliament, to the rising chorus of demands for toleration, the issue became uppermost in political life not only during the reign of Charles II (1660–85) but even more so during that of James II (1685–8) – though not without strings. Charles II was a Catholic fellow-traveller and James II a Catholic zealot, and their offers of indulgence to the Dissenters included toleration of the Catholics, the objects of the Dissenters' deepest fears. Some Dissenters looked on James's blandishments with at best inert suspicion and at worst grave misgivings, though others responded warmly and William Penn tried to persuade the Quakers to support the King. Finally, after James's abdication and dethronement, Parliament offered a legal, constitutional but limited toleration under the Act of 1689.

The Protestant Nonconformity, or Dissent, that won permission to exist through the 1689 Toleration Act had its origins in Elizabethan Calvinist

Puritanism. Originally, English Puritanism had set out to complete the reformation of the Church of England – and the reform of English society too. In Puritanism's period of power in the 1640s and 1650s, the movement was indeed presented with the opportunity to take charge of English society, to impose godly morals, to recast popular culture. After 1660 and the irrevocable sectarianization of Puritanism, the proponents of the 'good old cause' lost for ever the opportunity to take in hand public life; though the Societies for the Reformation of Manners which emerged in the 1690s show something of Puritanism's concern for ethics in society. However, the retreat of Puritanism in virtually all its forms from the public domain after 1660, and even more so after 1689, meant that the later seventeenth- and eighteenth-century Nonconformist tended to be more concerned with his or her own moral condition than with that of others. However, Puritanism did not lose all of its old interventionism when it became Nonconformity: the busy concern for others was rechannelled into the running of families as little churches and into the control by chapel elites of the errant in their congregations – a disciplinarianism that was particularly marked among the Quakers. However, the disciplinary vigilance of the authentic Nonconformist tended to be directed in the first place at the self, in a sustained campaign to control his or her own nature.

The Puritan/Nonconformist personality operated within a highly structured organization of time. A passionate care for time – Quaker traders introduced fixed prices perhaps as much as anything to save the time otherwise wasted on haggling – arose from an acute sense of the brevity of life. The week began with a demanding, strenuous Sabbath of worship and religious instruction: relaxation was not high on the Nonconformist list of priorities. The Nonconformist Sabbath raised the curtain on a week devoted to steady labour in a calling, interspersed with family prayers, pious reading, the recollection of sermons, care for time as a rationed commodity, constant review of one's conduct, and sparing use of pastimes, food, drink and sleep. It was surely not a 'joyless' lifestyle, for those to whom it gave a sense of autonomy in the rational ordering of their own private and working lives. The Nonconformist ability to take charge of one's own life possibly protected the membership psychologically from what we would identify as chance and accident. The powerful sense of divine omnipotence shared by all the groups descended from Puritan stock in fact ruled out belief in mere accident: a misfortune was a punitive providence. To avert calamity, a person's and a family's strict covenant with God had to be upheld: for instance, to avert plague, family prayers ought never to be omitted. In point of fact, important features in the Nonconformist covenant – application to business, care for time, prudence, sobriety, restraint on expenditure – surely did help ward off disaster, at least economic disaster. Seen in purely materialist terms, the 'Nonconformist outlook' – more than a little neurotic, un-resting, an endless sequence of anxieties seeking appeasement – was a kind of survival mechanism for an age of danger.

Under this kind of heading, it is worth looking at the Nonconformist approach to education, in both the narrower and the wider meanings of the word. After 1662 the Nonconformists were firmly shut out of the English (though not the Scots) universities. It was no great loss, as things then stood in unreformed Oxbridge. They subsequently opened their own Dissenting Academies, twenty-three of which were in business as early as 1690, besides the regional Quaker schools opening up around that time. Although the individual Academy might be under threat from the death or removal of a teacher, and though the whole system might come under attack as it did in the Tory reaction under Queen Anne, yet the Nonconformists had a flexible and virtually indestructible education system, inseparable from their piety. At its heart were those twin bases of the Puritan tradition, the Sabbath and the sermon. The recollections of the Essex Puritan John Roger may represent a typical, if extreme, version of the sermon cult of countless of the brethren: writing down every sermon he heard, memorizing them, and then going over this memorized argosy in a regular, slightly obsessive, weekly routine. Versions of this tradition were maintained in the programmes of Nonconformist families: Saturday night seminars to discuss sermons, note-taking during preaching, verbatim recall of contents, and answers to quizzes by visiting pastors. What Talmudic study was for the European Jewish community, the sermon was for English and Welsh Nonconformists: the heart of an impressive system of mental training.

The scrupulosity, introspection and sensitivity that are the hallmarks of so many Puritan and Nonconformist diaries and autobiographies may have helped people in that particular religious tradition to be responsive to the sensibilities and emotional needs of others. This in turn may have helped to civilize and equalize marriage, for we find in the autobiographical reminiscences of Nonconformist ministers such as Oliver Heywood (1630–1702) an often anguished sensitivity to the rights of their wives.

At the same time, if the Puritan family was a classroom and the father of the family the teacher, wives and daughters took a lead in prayer. Nowhere in Dissent was its movement in the direction of greater equality between men and women taken as far as it was in Quakerism – and although even among the Quakers the role of women tended to become stereotyped and restricted, they had their women's meetings and a women's ministry, as well as insisting upon women's consent in marriage. The advances made by the Quakers in women's rights were within the Puritan and Separatist tradition that had produced Katherine Chidley of London and Dorothy Hazzard of Bristol.

By about 1720, when the establishment of the Hanoverian dynasty had made toleration reasonably secure, we can measure the statistical position of Dissent. Its numbers were nowhere near Defoe's wildly enthusiastic estimate of two million, though there was more truth in his boast that Nonconformists cornered much of the nation's wealth – at least its financial and commercial wealth. With their numbers stabilizing at about this time, we have an estimated total for England of about a third of a million, or a little over 6 per cent of a total population of around five and a half million. The Presbyterians, with over 3 per cent of the total population, outnumbered all the other Dissenters put together; the Independents (Congregationals) made up just over 1 per cent of the total population, while none of the other 'major' denominations – Particular Baptists, General Baptists, and Quakers – amounted to as much as 1 per cent nationwide, though the Quakers, with their highly developed organization, had the largest number of meetings of all. The distribution of Dissent, and of its constituent groups, was uneven. In general, Dissent was emphatically urban, and becoming more so. The Presbyterians were strongest in the north-west and south-west, the Congregationals (apart from their fastnesses in mid- and south Wales) in the south-east and mid-Anglia, the Baptists (apart from Wales) generally south and east of the line from the Humber to the Bristol Channel, and the Quakers evenly and thinly spread around the country, with a stronghold in Cumbria.

Though the picture of Dissent as a minority movement certainly stands, Nonconformity could make an impressive presence in particular places, such as the Somerset clothing centres, Nottingham and Bristol. It was in one of Presbyterianism's most assured centres – Exeter – that crippling discord hit the major denomination at a time when Dissenters were counting up their numbers, preparing agitation to enlarge the Toleration Act and moving towards closer interdenominational co-operation. Indeed, the dissident churches were exhibiting vitality not just in numerical consolidation and political confidence but also in devotional creativity, notably with the hymns of Isaac Watts (1674–1748). However, Dissent could not remain insulated from an intellectual movement to 'rationalize' Christianity. The Toleration Act had excluded Unitarians from its provisions. Few would have predicted that the Presbyterians, guardians of literal orthodoxy through all the doctrinal confusion of the 1640s and 1650s, would at the last fall prey to the 'heresy' most destructive of Christianity – though the violently anti-Dissenting clergyman Henry Sacheverell (1674–1724) had forecast as much.

Outright Unitarian opinions winnowed Dissent – or at least the

Presbyterians and General Baptists – in the eighteenth century, starting with the non-Trinitarian theology of the Exeter minister James Peirce, developing from 1716 onwards. However, the progress of Unitarian opinions was gradual up to and beyond 1750, partly because pastors with Unitarian ideas were understandably reluctant to proclaim them. Falling short of absolute Unitarian or 'Socinian' doctrines were Arian opinions, casting Christ in a lesser relationship to God the Father; there was also a growing vogue for a neo-Arminian outlook, fostered by the authoritative Richard Baxter, which moved away from one of Calvinism's most distinctive features, predestination. This doctrinal crisis in English Dissent's largest denomination was the product not only of a retreat from Calvinism – the intellectual foundation of English religious radicalism – but also of a weakening of traditional Christology and even a perceptible decline in Christianity itself, with ancient features, such as belief in hell, under attack from the newly fashionable rationalism and humanitarianism.

In the last twenty years of the period covered by this chapter, Dissent was showing some signs of decay – a term used in contemporaneous works such as the 1730 *An Enquiry into the Causes of the Decay of the Dissenting Interest*. Part of the problem for Dissent was fashion. The 'zeal' that was its hallmark – the London Quakers in 1731 lamented their 'coldness of zeal' – was for the time being out of style in an age of reason which deplored the 'enthusiasm' that had caused so much trouble in the previous century. In respect of their numerical decline some of the sects were their own worst enemies, causing a haemorrhage of their members by an oppressive discipline, so that the Quakers suffered a steady erosion of membership figures in every decade from the 1670s to the 1790s. The 'decline' in Dissent during the eighteenth century can, of course, be exaggerated: the Quakers were not alone in seeking continued increase through vigorous missionary work. Yet it is indisputable that at least some of the life and creativity had gone out of Dissent by the Georgian years – despite the work of outstanding pastors like the Northampton Congregationalist Philip Doddridge (1702–51). When life returned, it came predominantly from an Establishment source, in the shape of the Evangelical Revival which is the subject of a later chapter.

11

Rational Religion in England from Herbert of Cherbury to William Paley

David A. Pailin

IN MATTERS OF religious belief an authority is authoritative only so long as it is accepted to be such. Once questions begin to be asked about why an alleged authority is to be accepted or about who finally decides what it lays down, it is no longer the final court of appeal, for those questions ask for some prior authority which can authorize it and authoritatively interpret it. In disputed cases, reference can then be made to something or someone which is (or ought to be) agreed by the parties to be unquestionably authoritative. In the seventeenth and eighteenth centuries reflective people in England increasingly looked to reason for such a final authority in matters of religious belief.

Three factors formed the background to the appeal to reason. In the first place, there was a growing sense of the need to control fanaticism and bigotry. Those who did not share the enthusiasts' convictions did not only doubt the justification of the latter's certitudes. Where they were not amused, they were liable to be offended by the apparently boundless pretensions of the enthusiasts. William Penn's refusal to uncover in the presence of the King might be regarded as an annoying eccentricity while, if the reports are correct, the sight of early Quaker prophets appearing naked in the streets would at least have caused surprise (cf. Leslie: II, 268f). More seriously disturbing, however, were claims to divine authority to instruct others as to belief and practice. When John Hunt, 'Minister of the Gospel', dedicated his *Doctrine of God's Eternal Decrees* to the one 'from Whom I receiv'd it', namely 'the KING of KINGS', he was clearly implying a high status for his work (Hunt: iii). In a similar spirit George Fox

A full list of contemporary texts referred to in this chapter is to be found at the end of the chapter, pp. 231–3.

published letters to 'the Turk' and 'the Emperor of China' as well as to 'all KINGS, Princes, Governours . . . in Christendom' that they may not be ignorant of their duties now that 'God is come to Rule' (Fox: 208). People were also aware, thankfully more from continental reports and from Huguenot and other immigrants fleeing persecution than from native experience (*pace* memories of the Marian and Elizabethan 'martyrs' and the 'Great Ejection'), that unbridled religious convictions could lead to physical persecution.

Secondly, at the other extreme intellectually, there was the challenge of scepticism and unbelief. In England the spread of such notions was very limited until after the 'Glorious Revolution'. Even then, in spite of critics like Hume and Gibbon and lesser lights such as Blount, Toland, Collins, Woolston and Paine, the more extreme forms were more often attacked than actually expounded. So far as people were aware of radical scepticism, it was on the whole through the works of continental authors such as Montaigne, Charron, Bayle, La Mettrie and Voltaire. Furthermore, even though such works were published as John Florio's translation of Montaigne's *Essayes* in 1603 (with its sceptical attack on the pretensions of human reasoning in 'An Apologie of *Raymond Sebond*'), Thomas Hobbes' *Leviathan* in 1651 and Thomas Creech's annotated translation of Lucretius' *De Rerum Natura* in 1682, many attacks on sceptical attitudes and 'atheistic' ideas rebut an anonymous bogey, probably the wilder ideas rumoured to be entertained in some coffee-shop circles, rather than identifiable publications. In any case, for many people open profession of an out-and-out rejection of prevalent beliefs could be socially disadvantageous. While the roués of a Hell-Fire Club might be protected from persecution by their connections as well as by a less enthusiastic social order in England, in Scotland as late as 1697 a morally sound but intellectually unwise student, Thomas Aikenhead, was hanged for blasphemy, being refused mercy by the ministers of Edinburgh.

The third background factor – and the most important for understanding the development of rational religion in England as well as one of the sources of questioning doubt about belief – was the way in which the religious controversies that had begun in the sixteenth century undermined confidence in the traditional authorities for deciding such matters. The apparent failure of appeals to such authorities to resolve many disputes led to enquiries into whether there was another, superior authority to which conclusive appeal could be made. Although most people continued to cite what they alleged to be the determinative authority, be it the teaching of the Bible, the statements of the Christian credal tradition, the decisions of ecclesiastical bodies or the witness of experience, the more percipient recognized that in many cases no agreement is to be found that way. Even where the parties to a dispute agreed on what was to be accepted as the normative authority and so had a common mind on the relative status of the Bible, the creeds, the Church and its leaders, and experience, troublesome disagreements could and did arise concerning what the accepted authority laid down and who was to determine its meaning. Agreement that Christ said 'This is my body' and that this text was central to the doctrine of the Eucharist was found to solve nothing: the problem was how the statement is to be understood.

In the case of the Bible, common agreement that it is the written expression of divine revelation was accompanied by disagreements, sometimes leading to violence, about who is authorized to decide its correct interpretation – whether the magisterium of the Church centred in Rome or some other body – and about how, without begging the question, that issue is to be settled. Within England few people and practically no self-conscious believers, whether Protestant or Roman Catholic, would have challenged Thomas Guyse's principle that the 'Scriptures are the instituted Means of Knowledge and Grace' and that *'we have no need of another Revelation from God'* to determine faith and morals besides that which is given in them (Guyse: 110). Some believers, however, perceived that it is far from easy to put this principle into practice. Thus Jeremy Taylor argued for 'a very great necessity in allowing a liberty in Prophesying without prescribing authoritatively to other mens consciences'. He justified this on the grounds that 'our pious endeavour' at exegesis shows that we have no infallible and certain way of determining the meaning of many passages in the Bible (Taylor: 73). John Locke was blunter. In practice each sect assumes the authority to interpret and use the Bible and to declare the fundamentals of Christianity. As a result 'the scripture serves but, like a nose of wax, to be turned and bent, just as may fit the contrary orthodoxies of different societies' (Locke: III, 190). This perception, however, did not prevent Locke from presenting in *The Reasonableness of Christianity as Delivered in the Scriptures* what he claimed to be an 'unbiassed' reading of 'the plain direct meaning' of 'the written word of God' (ibid.: 3). As with many other critics, he apparently did not consider that his strictures applied to his own work!

Reflective believers thus found themselves faced with disturbing challenges from fanatics with more zeal than apparent sense, from sceptics whose doubts threatened sensible belief, and from believers whose appeals to the traditional authorities were found to provide no satisfactory way of settling disagreements about faith and practice. The result was a growing conviction that it is to 'reason' that people must turn as a final court of appeal. In response, then, to fanatics, sceptics and controversialists (and while liable to seem sceptical to fanatics, fanatical to sceptics and certainly to be controversial in their conclusions), reflective believers in England engaged in a prolonged debate about the nature and contents of what might be justifiable as 'reasonable belief' – and about whether or not it is justifiable to judge belief by the canon of reason. This chapter will briefly consider some of the more important contributions to this sometimes confused, often lively and always important debate about the basis of theistic faith in the period from Herbert of Cherbury to William Paley.

Edward Herbert, First Baron Herbert of Cherbury (1583?–1648), was an adventurer, diplomat, historian, poet and theologian as well as one of the first English writers on metaphysics and on comparative religion. Deeply suspicious of the self-serving tendencies of priestcraft and troubled by his observation of religious struggles on the continent and of dissension in England, he presented a radical solution to the problems posed by scepticism and religious disagreement. By examining reason, he attempted to establish certain fundamental ideas which all people must recognize to be true and by means of which any individual (particularly any layperson) may decide about the doctrines promoted by ecclesiastical authorities.

The foundation of his position is established in *De Veritate* (On Truth). Completed while Herbert was ambassador in France and first published in Paris in 1624, this work is 'Dedicated to every sane and unprejudiced Reader' (Herbert 1937: title page). It is a metaphysical treatise, combining epistemological, psychological and methodological considerations, that seeks to unravel 'the common nature of the search for truth which exists in every normal human being'. It thus concerns 'those truths which are universally accepted' (ibid.: 71). As a result of his investigations Herbert maintained that there are certain 'common notions' which have been bestowed by divine providence on humanity and are consequently latent in each individual. When brought to consciousness, these common notions provide the normative principles by which the nature and contents of true understanding are to be determined. By relying on them people may therefore avoid the errors of scepticism, dogmatism and fideism. Towards the end of *De Veritate* Herbert states what he perceives to be the common notions of religious understanding. These are: (1) 'There is a Supreme God'; (2) 'This Sovereign Deity ought to be Worshipped'; (3) 'The connection of Virtue with Piety' is 'the most important part of religious practice'; (4) Evil 'must be expiated by repentance'; and (5) 'There is Reward or Punishment after this life' (ibid.: 291–300).

According to Herbert, these five points constitute the only essential doctrines 'of which the true Catholic or universal church is built'. This Church properly 'comprehends all places and all men', is the source of salvation for all, and 'alone reveals Divine Universal Providence, or the wisdom of Nature'. The experience of any sane person who is prepared to follow the instruction of reason will confirm that 'it is and always has been possible for all men to reach' these truths (ibid.: 303ff). Herbert does not deny the reality of revelation, but he is concerned to emphasize that 'great care' must be taken to 'discern what actually is revealed' (ibid.: 308). Accordingly he lays down certain tests by which the trustworthiness of revelatory experiences and of claims about teaching allegedly revealed in the past may be given rational warrant.

Herbert developed his understanding of the rationally discernible character of authentic religious belief in two ways. In *De Religione Laici* (On a Layperson's Religion) he argued that by using reason (aided by prayer) an individual can decide between the faiths that compete for allegiance. The one that is to be accepted is the one that most closely conforms to the common notions – a religion summed up in this work as 'love and fear of God, charity towards one's neighbour, repentance, and hope of a better life' (Herbert 1944: 101). Doctrines allegedly imparted by revelation, transmitted by tradition and taught by priests are to be accepted only if they are in accordance with what reason perceives. Both in *De Religione Gentilium* (On the Religion of Non-Christians) and in *A Dialogue between a Tutor and his Pupil* Herbert attempted to justify his claim that the truths perceived in the common notions of religion are universally acknowledged. What appears to provide evidence to the contrary is either misunderstood, held to be symbolic assertions of the truth or dismissed as corruptions due to priestcraft. He is confident that the '*Universal Providence*' of 'the *Most Good and Great GOD*' ensures that the means of salvation are available to all peoples (Herbert 1705: 6f).

Herbert, then, looked to reason for the discernment of truth about God and humanity which avoids the errors of bigotry and scepticism and the inconclusiveness of appeals to traditional authorities. With a confidence that later controversies may suggest to be rather more optimistic than realistic the 'tutor' declares to 'his pupil' that in matters of religious belief as elsewhere we are to base our understanding upon:

> the use of that reason, which God gave us as a common light, by which to direct ourselves, and which we have as little cause to forsake, as to shut our windows against the sun-beams to study by a candle. So it teaches us the way whereby God comes down to all mankind, and consequently shews us there can be no more infallible path . . . than . . . the same light which God hath given us in our reason to see and know him . . . and that all other approaches to the divine Majesty are not only dark but dangerous. (Herbert 1768: 2f).

It is an appeal to reason and a confidence in what reason can establish which, as we shall indicate, others were to develop in various ways in the following century and a half.

One form taken by the recognition of reason as the determining factor for authentic belief does not regard rational reflection as the source of all religious insights. Instead it maintains that the traditional sources of those insights provided by the Bible, tradition and the Church are to be warranted and interpreted by reason. In this way it may seem at one level that the basic importance of such 'authorities' continues to be recognized. Their status, however, has been undermined. They are no longer self-evidently the final court of appeal. It is reason which establishes what authority they have and what they may properly require to be believed.

An example of this understanding of reasonable belief is found in the work of William Chillingworth (1602–44). Chillingworth enjoyed arguing about religion. In his mid-twenties he left the Church of England for that of Rome on the grounds that the latter alone offered a single, supreme and infallible yet catholic authority in matters of religious belief. Correspondence with Laud and his experiences in a Roman Catholic seminary, however, soon turned him into what he called 'a doubting Papist' (Chillingworth: 220). Eventually he returned to the Church of England. He is probably best remembered for his statement in *The Religion of Protestants A Safe Way to Salvation* that 'the BIBLE, I say, the BIBLE only, is the Religion of Protestants' (ibid.: 271). Nevertheless, his position was far from that of an arational biblicist. Although he held that the Bible is 'God's Word' and has 'sufficient certainty' to be the basis of true faith (ibid.: 271f), he took a deliberately discriminating approach to its contents. He insisted that each person must believe according to what she or he judges to be its correct interpretation. In the end individuals must follow their own reason. There is no higher authority for them to submit to. Those who claim that we should submit to a different authority must show that there is 'greater Reason to believe that Authority' – but in doing this they too cannot avoid endorsing reason as the final arbiter (ibid.: 69). It is, furthermore, not only 'unjust and unreasonable' to expect people to believe things with greater assurance than the evidence justifies: it is also 'impossible' for them so to believe (ibid.: 240). This, in Chillingworth's judgement, is in accordance with the divine will. He is 'certain that God hath given us our reason, to discern Truth and Falshood'. He fears that those who refuse its direction will find that God does not accept the '*Sacrifice of Fools*' (ibid.: 69; cf. 71f).

A somewhat different form of the recognition of the final authority of reason characterizes the rather diverse group of theological and religious thinkers known as 'the Cambridge Platonists'. Flourishing in the middle decades of the seventeeth century, the several members of this group were linked by a basic confidence in the power and significance of human reason, particularly through reflecting on reason itself, to discern the basic contents of authentic religious understanding. This is reflected in their affirmation of reason as 'the candle of the Lord' to be found within every person. Benjamin Whichcote, for example, affirms that there are certain truths about God and humankind which are grounded in the reason of things (*veritates, quae fundantur in rationibus rerum*) and are 'demonstrable by reason' (Whichcote: [2]41, [2]46). Similarly, Nathanael Culverwel holds that by means of reason people do not make (*facere*) the 'Law of Nature' but rather, as God intends, discover (*invenire*) both the reality of God and what God has established (Culverwel: [1]56). Since, then, God acts 'according to *Reason*' and '*loves* to see such a *noble Creature*, as *Man* is, . . . *imitate* him in his *Reason*', we are to act 'in the *choicest points of Religion*' according to what reason dictates (ibid.: [1]98), particularly by acknowledging 'the *unquestionable Truth* of a *Deity*' (ibid.: [1]138).

Their affirmations of the role of reason in discovering and authorizing the proper content of theistic belief did not mean that the Cambridge Platonists considered there to be no place in such belief for truths made known by revelation. Whichcote, for instance, recognized that there are also truths presented by divine revelation which make known matters beyond the scope of human reason (cf. Whichcote: [2]41). Such truths do not contradict but extend what human reason can perceive. He thus described them as fully compatible with and 'satisfactorie to . . . unbiassed reason' (ibid.: [2]46; cf. [2]102). Culverwel, too, affirmed that '*Whatsoever God reveals must needs be true.*' He pointed out, however, that since God is the source both of the truths discerned by reason in '*Nature*' and of those made known by the '*Spirit*', there can be no contradiction between them (Culverwel: [1]138). Where contradictions appear to arise, error is clearly present and reason must be used to discern what is the truth. As another of the Cambridge Platonists, John Norris, put it, nothing can be '*Theologically* true, which is *Philosophically* False' because 'the Light of Reason is as truly from God as the Light of Revelation'. God, then, as the ground of truth, can neither reveal what is contrary to reason nor require us to believe what is not justified by reason. The belief required of such 'a Reasonable Creture' as humankind must itself be reasonable (Norris: 197).

Among other works which may be cited as illustrating how reason was increasingly considered in seventeenth-century England to be the touchstone for authentic belief are those by a Bishop of Chester who also speculated about the habitability of the moon and became the first secretary of the Royal Society, and by a Bishop of Worcester whose broad sympathies did not prevent him engaging in controversies with Roman Catholics and Socinians and challenging the Trinitarian satisfactoriness of

Locke's understanding of a reasonable Christian faith. The former, John Wilkins, responded to the conflicting arguments of sceptics and fanatics (whose disputes he considers to be the main cause of unbelief) by being a strong proponent of natural theology. The purpose of *On the Principles and Duties of Natural Religion* (published posthumously in 1678) was, as he stated, 'to prove *the Reasonableness and the Credibility of the Principles of Natural Religion*' – that is, of that recognition and service of 'the Divine' which every person 'might know . . . by the meer principles of *Reason*, improved by Consideration and Experience' but 'without the help of *Revelation*' (Wilkins: 39). In order to fulfil this aim, Wilkins first provides arguments for the existence and attributes of God (from 'the Universal consent of Nations', the origin of the world, the 'contrivance' which orders 'all natural things', and the experience that a wise providence 'governs all things'; cf. ibid.: 40ff). He then proceeds to point out 'the wisdom' of conforming to the 'duties' laid down in this 'natural religion' since such conformity brings with it the highest happiness both in this world and after death. While in the final chapter he stresses that his work does not undermine the value of the revealed doctrines of Christianity (cf. ibid.: 394ff), his primary interest is to show that reason leads us to assent to the principles, and self-interest presses us to fulfil the duties, of 'Natural Religion'. Only so will our understanding be satisfied and our 'true wellfare' promoted (ibid.: 392).

Edward Stillingfleet, whom William and Mary appointed to the see of Worcester, was similarly insistent that the assent of 'faith' is 'a rational act'. As such it 'can be no stronger' than the 'reasonable grounds' upon which it is based (Stillingfleet 1673: 377, 395). However, while Stillingfleet, like Wilkins, gave arguments to prove the reasonableness of basic beliefs about the reality of God and 'the manifest error' of atheism (Stillingfleet 1702: 252), the major concern in his numerous writings is to establish the reasonableness of the doctrines of the Christian faith as based on the Bible. On the one hand he argues against those who refuse to accept the 'Spiritual truth' made known by revelation and recorded in the Bible. In this respect he maintains that 'the Spirit of God' provides these insights into the divine with 'such strong and persuasive grounds' that it is unwarrantable not to give 'a firm assent' to them (ibid.: 161). Since these grounds mostly come from records about 'Matters of Fact reported in the New Testament,' he asks in *A Letter to a Deist* merely that his opponent give to 'the History of the Gospel' the same kind of assent that is given to the reports of ancient historians such as Caesar and Livy (Stillingfleet 1677: 27). On the other hand, against Roman Catholic claims to magisterial authority in determining the correct sense of Scripture, Stillingfleet argued that God has given people 'Faculties' so that they may be dealt with as 'Rational

Creatures'. Each individual accordingly has 'a Right and Liberty' as well as 'a Capacity of Judging' for herself or himself what Scripture declares to be 'the true Way to Salvation' (Stillingfleet 1688: 40, 71). Here again, then, reason is considered to be the controlling authority. Although revelation may, as in the case of the doctrine of the Trinity, disclose matters which are 'above' reason's comprehension and hence are properly to be classed as 'mysteries', Stillingfleet maintained that it is reason which must determine both what has been authentically revealed and what the revelation contains (cf. Stillingfleet 1697: 230ff, 262ff, 288ff).

It is John Locke, however, who classically laid down the canon of reason which had been developing in the previous decades and which was to dominate theological discussion for over a century. In his *Essay Concerning Human Understanding* he concludes the chapter 'Of Reason' by asserting that faith is 'a firm assent of the mind' which is to be regulated by what reason judges to be the case and hence cannot be opposed to reason:

> He that believes, without having any reason for believing, may be in love with his own fancies; but neither seeks truth as he ought, nor pays the obedience due to his Maker, who would have him use those discerning faculties he has given him . . . in doing his duty as a rational creature. . . . For he governs his assent right, and places it as he should, who in any case or matter whatsoever, believes or disbelieves, according as reason directs him. He that does otherwise, transgresses against his own light, and misuses those faculties which were given him to no other end, but to search and follow the clear evidence, and greater probability. (Locke: I, 435)

With few exceptions, which will be mentioned shortly, this view of the final authority of reason was regarded as self-evidently valid. As a result, the subsequent debates about belief largely concerned the question of how that canon is to be met and what results from its application.

Locke himself judged that a proper application of the canon of reason establishes the credibility both of the reality of God and of certain revealed truths. Earlier in the *Essay*, having rejected the view that people naturally have an innate idea of God (cf. ibid.: I, 33ff), he discusses how the idea of God is constructed by 'enlarging' our ideas of certain qualities ('which it is better to have than to be without') to the scale of 'infinity' or perfection (ibid.: I, 182). A later chapter discusses 'our knowledge of the existence of a God'. According to Locke, reflection on his version of what is now generally known as the cosmological argument shows that the reality of God is a 'certain and evident truth', its 'evidence' being '(if I mistake not) equal to mathematical certainty'. It is 'the most obvious truth that reason discovers' as opposed to those matters which 'our senses . . . immediately' make known to us (ibid.: I, 389f). Augmenting the truths about God thus discernible by rational reflection are others which God discloses to humankind by revelation. While, however, these latter rectify deficiencies in our natural understanding, they have to be warranted by rationally convincing evidence that they have been given by God. Furthermore, while they disclose matters which are 'above reason', they must be rejected as spurious if they purport to declare matters which are clearly contrary to what reason discerns to be the case (cf. ibid.: I, 439). God wills that 'reason must be our last judge and guide in everything'. Accordingly, 'when he illuminates the mind with supernatural light, he does not extinguish that which is natural' (ibid.: I, 445). Reason thus identifies and controls what is to be believed about the divine.

In *The Reasonableness of Christianity* Locke indicates what he considers to be the basic constituents of a Christian's faith. It consists of assent to the reality of 'one eternal, invisible God' as 'his Lord and King' and to the status of Jesus as 'the Messiah, his King, ordained by God'. Such assent, together with its practical expression in 'allegiance' to this King's commands, is all that is 'absolutely necessary' to be a Christian and to be sure of 'the reward' of 'eternal life' (ibid.: III, 148[a]f). It is an interpretation of the biblical witness which shows Christianity to be 'a plain, simple, reasonable thing . . . suited to all conditions and capacities' (ibid.: III, 122).

Locke's version of reasonable Christianity seemed to some to be seriously inadequate. Edward Stillingfleet, while accepting the canon of reason, accused Locke of denying the doctrine of the Trinity; John Edwards, who challenged that canon, accused him of being a Socinian. They were charges against which Locke sought to 'vindicate' his position (cf. ibid.: III, 101ff). During the succeeding decades the debate about the nature and contents of 'reasonable belief' was sometimes searching, more than occasionally vituperative and often lively – although, as may be expected, some long-winded divines also joined the fray!

One group of thinkers involved in the debate are commonly dubbed 'Deists'. While the term is nearly always used pejoratively, the description is vague. There are large overlaps with other groups and individuals not so labelled and considerable differences of opinion between those to whom the label is applied. In the former respect, John Tillotson, who was appointed Archbishop of Canterbury in 1691 on Sancroft's deposition, is a debatable case. He delivered sermons which enjoyed considerable popularity because of their reasonableness in expounding the Christian faith. Published after his death in 1694, they sold well. Their character, however, also led to him being claimed as a fellow-traveller by the radical critic, Anthony Collins. Only somewhat tendentiously, he referred to Tillotson as the acknowledged '*head*' of 'all *English freethinkers*' (i.e. Deists) (Collins 1713: 143). The latter point is well illustrated by the different ways in which the notion of 'Deism' was defined at the time.

Stillingfleet's *Letter to a Deist*, for example, is addressed to someone who recognizes '*the* Being *and* Providence *of* God' but has '*a mean Esteem of the* Scriptures, *and the* Christian Religion' (Stillingfleet 1677: A3), while John Reynolds' *Three Letters to the Deist* address those who are 'gone off from the Principles of supernatural, (or, as it's called, revealed) Religion' on the grounds that 'the Light of Reason' and 'the Works of God' are quite sufficient to disclose the reality of God and humanity's relationship to the divine (Reynolds: 1). Samuel Clarke, however, distinguished four sorts of Deist: one holds that God exists but 'does *not at all concern* himself in the *Government* of the World'; a second maintains 'the Being' and 'the Providence of God' but supposes 'that God takes no notice of the *morally good* or *evil* Actions of Men'; the third may seem to entertain 'right Apprehensions' of the attributes of God but in fact they turn out to be without material substance, and has 'a prejudice against the Notion of the *Immortality of Humane Souls*'; the fourth sort, which Clarke describes as 'the only *True Deists*', has 'just and right Notions of God' and of humanity, but will only believe what is 'discoverable by the Light of Nature alone', denying all revelation (Clarke: 159, 164, 167, 169f). Finally, we might mention Daniel Waterland's view (expressed in an Archidiaconal Charge delivered in 1732) that current Deism is in effect disguised atheism – 'little else but revived *Epicureism*, Sadducism, and *Zendichism*,' it provides a cover for '*libertinism* only and *irreligion*'. In his view it is so uncertain about belief in God, providence, immortality and future judgement that it is inferior to 'Mahometanism' and 'Paganism' (Waterland: V, 66ff).

The term 'Deism', then, served as a blanket epithet expressing disapproval. Those who were so labelled were considered by their critics to have been unjustifiably extreme in their application of the canon of reason and hence to be at least deficient in their religious beliefs. The so-called 'Deists' themselves, however, provide a wide and interesting range of understandings. Some used the canon of reason in a primarily negative manner to undermine traditional beliefs. In *A Discourse of Free-Thinking* Anthony Collins criticizes biblically based beliefs about the revelatory and salvific activity of God on such grounds as that they impute favouritism to God (cf. Collins: 30), while in the later *Discourse of the Grounds and Reasons of the Christian Religion* he highlights the unsatisfactory character of arguments for the authenticity of the biblical revelation which depend on alleged fulfilments of prophecies. Other radical critics challenged traditional belief at various points. Charles Blount attacked, among other things, the corruptions attendant on priestcraft; Thomas Woolston threw a series of fire-crackers into the believers' roost by expounding in a series of tracts the allegation that 'the literal History of many of the Miracles of Jesus, as recorded by the Evangelists, does imply Absurdities, Improbabilities, and Incredibilities' (Woolston: 4); Thomas Chubb, a glover from Salisbury, applied his common sense to the status of the Bible to conclude that 'the epistles of the Apostles *were not* written by divine inspiration' but are 'the *produce* of the *judgment*' of each writer' who was 'liable to error with other men' (Chubb: 46).

Others among the 'Deists', however, made more positive – but largely overlooked – contributions to theological thought. John Toland's *Christianity Not Mysterious* undermines a widespread defence of such Christian doctrines as the trinitarian nature of God. This defence argues that what is not conceivable may nevertheless be properly credible as a revealed 'mystery'. While not denying the revelatory origin of Christianity (cf. Toland: xxvi, 47), Toland points out that belief presupposes an apprehension of the contents as well as a perception of the warrantability of a supposedly revealed doctrine. It would make no sense, for instance, to assent to the proposition that 'something call'd *Blictri* had a Being in Nature' if it were not known 'what this *Blictri* was'. Orthodox believers were troubled – and some infuriated – by Toland's suggestion that '*Contradiction* and *Mystery* are but two emphatick ways of saying nothing' (ibid.: 128, 134). On the assumption that God has given him his '*reasoning* faculties' to be used, William Wollaston seeks to delineate the 'religion of *nature*' which any 'Heathen *philosopher* . . . may be supposed' to be capable of discerning without any aid from revelation (Wollaston: 210f). The result was a fundamentally ethical Theism. However, whereas Wollaston considered that what is so discovered may be suitably augmented by revelation, Matthew Tindal maintained that a proper appreciation of the unchanging wisdom, justice, and perfection of God entails that all that human beings need to know about the divine has always been available to them by rational reflection. 'There's a Religion of Nature & Reason written in the hearts of everyone of us from the first Creation.' By reference to it 'any instituted Religion' is to be judged (Tindal: 52). As the true faith, then, Christianity must be 'as old as the creation'; the Gospel which is supposedly its revealed essence is 'a republication of the religion of nature' (Tindal: title). Tindal thus seeks to understand faith in a way that accords with the universality of divine providence.

Many others who investigated the reasonableness of belief were, however, neither in intention nor in result hostile to traditional orthodoxy. One group of works, for instance, sought in various ways to establish the rational warrant for basic beliefs about the reality of God. In contrast to the ontological arguments presented on the continent by Descartes and Leibniz, in England arguments for the reality of God generally assumed an *a posteriori* form. John Ray canvassed the natural order from the stars to the tail of the mole and the foot of the camel for evidence of 'the Existence and Efficiency of an Omnipotent and All-wise Creator' (Ray:[1]14). In the case of human beings, 'the Benignity of the Deity' is seen in the way that each person is provided with two hands and two eyes not only for convenience but also for 'Security' in case one is lost, and with a distinctive face so that 'Malefactors' may be detectable! According to Ray, such observations provide 'no contemptible Argument of the Wisdom and Goodness of God' (ibid.: [2]14, [2]20). Similar arguments were presented by William Derham among numerous others. In his *Astro-Theology*, Derham not only claims to demonstrate 'the Being and Attributes of God from a Survey of the Heavens' but also finds moral instruction in the 'Consideration of the prodigious Magnitude and Multitude of the heavenly Bodies' disclosed by the latest scientific studies. Such consideration teaches us 'not to overvalue this World, nor to set our Hearts too much upon . . . its Riches, honours, or Pleasures' (Derham 1738: title, 238). On the other hand, in his *Physico-Theology* Derham concludes from a wide-ranging survey of 'our *Terraqueous Globe*' that it both shows the reality of an 'infinitely wise and powerful Creator' and should 'excite us to due Thankfulness and Praise' (Derham 1723: 3, 432).

More obviously metaphysical considerations are present in the arguments about the reality of God advanced by Samuel Clarke and Bishop Berkeley. In his Boyle Lectures for 1704 the former sought to show the reasonableness of basic theistic belief by arguments 'from the most uncontestable Principles of Right Reason' and as close to the clarity and conclusiveness of mathematical reasoning as may be possible (Clarke: 6; cf. preface). The foundation of his case is a form of the cosmological argument from contingency to the necessity that '*Something*' must have '*really Existed from Eternity*' (ibid.: 9). This necessarily existing 'something', however, cannot be identified with the material world (cf. ibid.: 23). It must be thought of as one, simple, eternal, immutable, independent, infinite and omnipresent (cf. ibid.: 45ff). Clarke then turns from the *a priori* reasoning which can only demonstrate the reality of 'a Blind and *Unintelligent* Necessity' to *a posteriori* reasoning which infers the perfections of a theistic God from the characteristics of the world as derived from this 'Self existent Being' (ibid.: 51). Berkeley began from an idealist version of the cosmological argument. On the basis of his thesis that to be is 'to be perceived or known' he maintained that all things must be recognized to '*subsist in the mind of some eternal spirit*' (Berkeley: I, 89). Berkeley, however, like Clarke, found it necessary to augment his cosmological argument with *a posteriori* considerations in order to show that the God whose existence has been demonstrated is also to be regarded as 'one, eternal, infinitely wise, good, and perfect' (ibid.: I, 143).

Another group of writings paid attention to the question of the rational warrantability of assent to allegedly revealed doctrines and precepts rather than to that of the reality of God and natural morality. It is on this question that the debates about the content and reasonableness of Christian belief in the debates after Locke were most heated, ranged most widely and involved the greatest number of authors. Three distinct issues are involved in these debates. In the first place, it was considered by some to be necessary to show the need for revealed insights into the divine nature and will. They thus presented various arguments in response to radical claims that revelation is unnecessary since all that a person needs to know about the divine and about the proper conduct of human life is discernible by natural reason alone. One reply is that even what is knowable about such matters in principle may not be perceived in practice because of the 'state of great darkness and corruption in matters of religion and morals' into which 'mankind' has 'been sunk' (Leland 1754–5: I, 413). Another is that a saving faith includes a knowledge of matters which are not naturally knowable. Samuel Clarke, for example, held that a saving faith needs a revelation of the divine will to 'supply the undeniable Defects of the Light of Nature' (Clarke: 317). Even the wisest philosophers could not discover by their own reasoning why God created the world, how God governs the world, the reasons for and nature of the corrupt state of humankind and, above all, '*The Method*' by which sinful people '*may yet again restore themselves to the Favour of God, and to the Hopes of Happiness*' (ibid.: 295). Authors who maintained that what is supposedly *naturally* knowable is itself the product of an 'original revelation' in which God made known the divine will 'from the beginning' also held that later and further revelations are needed. As John Leland put it, 'Man's being in his original design a religious creature' does not mean that he does not stand 'in need of divine revelation to instruct him in religion', since 'through the negligence and corruption of mankind' the 'true primitive religion' which was originally disclosed has been 'in a great measure lost' (Leland 1754–5: II, 348ff). Hence it is maintained that it is not a denial of God's creative perfection but a mark of divine grace that God has revealed these matters as and to whom God wills.

A second issue was that of the reliability of the records of divine revelation and of the evidence authenticating it. For most authors this meant primarily the question of the historical accuracy of biblical reports of what was done and said, especially of the reports in the canonical Gospels. John Conybeare, for example, responded to doubts cast on the trustworthiness of the canonical Gospels by arguing that 'the several *historical* books of the New Testament were written in *that* age, in which they are commonly said to have been written' and by persons who 'were either *eye-witnesses* of what they relate, or had their *information* from those that were so'. These writers were 'persons of the utmost *simplicity* and *virtue*' who 'could have *no manner* of temptation to *falsify*' their accounts. Their reports, furthermore, were originally published within 'a *few years*' of what they record and 'in the *very country* where these facts are said to have happened'. Nevertheless, while it cannot be doubted that 'the *strictest inquiry*' must have been made into their truth, since they threatened 'a considerable alteration in the *established* religion', no falsehood was detected in them but instead '*vast numbers* immediately *embraced* the Christian faith' because of them. Finally, 'we have the utmost reason to think' that what they wrote has been '*faithfully*' transmitted to the present 'without any material corruptions' (Conybeare: 14f). More dramatic is Thomas Sherlock's response to doubts cast by Woolston and others on the apostolic reports of the resurrection of Jesus: he arraigns the Apostles before a judge and jury on the charge of 'giving false Evidence in the Case of the Resurrection of Jesus'. After the case has been heard, the foreman of the jury announces their verdict: 'Not guilty' (Sherlock: 109). The arguments may not seem very convincing today, but debates about them contributed significantly to the development of modern biblical scholarship.

To show the need for revelation and the reliability of the biblical records was not, however, the end of the story. A third and crucial issue remained to be settled if assent to revealed doctrines and precepts was to be justified according to the canon of reason. It was necessary to find some way of authenticating the alleged revelations as having come from God through persons or events duly authorized to disclose them. The most popular and widely debated argument in this respect was that from miracles. On the grounds that miraculous powers are intrinsically beyond what is naturally achievable, it was argued that people displaying them must be endowed with them by God. In answer to the claim that demonic powers might similarly equip their servants, it was argued – as illustrated by the battles between Moses and Pharaoh's magicians – that the powers which God grants are manifestly superior to those stemming from other supernatural sources. On this basis people who work miracles – or, as was held to be supremely the case with the resurrection of Jesus, have a miracle worked on them – are considered to be shown thereby to have divine authorization for what they disclose about the divine nature and will. Two other arguments of a similar nature which were also employed were that from prophecy (persons who predicted future events must have received their insights from God) and that from the spread of Christianity (a rather romanticized view of the spread of Christianity is used to argue that this faith could have spread so far and so fast only with divine backing). These 'proofs' of the authenticity of revelation were, however, the source of extensive arguments, since both the principles and the evidence used in them are debatable. Questions were asked, not only about the reliability of the evidence for such authenticating events but also about the possibility of a satisfactory definition of the concept of 'miracle'.

Partly as a result of the doubts thus raised about these 'external proofs' of revelation and partly in order to augment them by other reasoning, three 'internal' proofs were also put forward. These were drawn from the character of Jesus (since he cannot be deemed to have been either bad or mad, he must be who he said that he was – the Christ of God), from the excellency of Jesus' teaching (such wonderful insights must have been divinely inspired) and from the great advantages bestowed upon humankind by the revealed teaching. Such arguments might seem much more convincing to believers than to doubters, but they apparently helped to persuade the former that their assent to revealed matters was rationally justified. It is noticeable, furthermore, that those who emphasized the internal quality rather than the external marks of what is revealed tended also to interpret what is made known more as a sensible morality than as a matter of doctrines about supernatural states.

Positively, then, rational defenders of the Christian faith in one way or another maintain with Samuel Clarke that

> The Christian Revelation is positively and directly proved, to be actually and immediately sent to us from God, by the many infallible *Signs and Miracles*, which the Author of it worked publickly as the Evidence of his Divine Commission. Besides the great Excellency and Reasonableness of the *Doctrine* considered in itself . . . God has given us all the Proofs of the Truth of our Religion, that the Nature of the Thing would bear, or that were reasonable either for God to give, or Men to expect. (Clarke: 372, 446)

Negatively, there was Joseph Butler's argument in *The Analogy of Religion* that it is inconsistent for radicals to refuse assent to the revealed component of the Christian faith because of difficulties with its contents but nevertheless to accept the insights of natural theology into the reality of God. On careful reflection it turned out that the problems found with the former are analogous to and no greater than those to be found with the latter. Holding, then, that 'Probability is the very Guide of Life', Butler concluded that it is 'unreasonable' for those who accept the reality of God 'to urge Objections against Revelation' when there are other objections 'of equal Weight against natural Religion' (Butler: iv, 406). It is an argument which might convince those who are sure that it is rationally justifiable to believe in the reality of God. It collapses when, as in the case of David Hume, the arguments for belief in the reality of God advanced by natural theology are also held to be rationally wanting.

Not everyone, however, was convinced that the application of the canon of reason was the proper way to determine what is to be believed and practised. For some the notion of a 'reasonable religion' was close to being a contradiction in terms; for others the legitimate scope of reason in matters of religious belief was to be carefully circumscribed. Considerations of the nature of religion, of the content of doctrine and of the competence of reason were thus variously advanced to question the propriety of submitting belief to the judgement of reason. While it was only a minority who thus challenged the final dominance of the canon of reason, their views are sometimes interesting and ought not to be ignored.

John Edwards wrote several vigorous attacks on the 'reasonable' Christianity presented by Locke, accusing him of 'introducing a *Clipt Christianity*' and of encouraging 'the men of this too Giddy Age to truck their *Old Christianity* for a New Notion . . . which he shapes to himself' (Edwards: 247). Edwards considered the only authority for Christianity to be the Bible. Those who hold that everything in Christianity is to be submitted to the test of reason both 'irrationally extol humane Reason' and 'vilifie the Author of' the 'Reveal'd Religion' communicated through the Bible (ibid.: 134). Human reasoning should be confined to finite and empirical matters: the realm of the divine is beyond its competence. The infallible revelation of 'God's bare Word' given in the Bible 'is sufficient to determine our assent and belief' (ibid.: 139). The role of reason in religion which Edwards recognized was that of asserting and locating what may be called the canon of revelation.

An extreme version of the assertion of the biblical revelation as the repository of truth and a denial of the normative authority of reason is to be found in the works of John Hutchinson. According to his 'scripture philosophy', Genesis gives all people what God revealed through Moses. Among other things it provides 'the Fountain of all their real Knowledge of what they call Nature' (Hutchinson: ^{1}2). It is, furthermore, written in a language which God 'form'd' to express 'perfect Ideas' and uses the particular words which God has 'infallibly chosen and employed' (ibid.: ^{2}xxix). As a result the Scriptures are 'sufficient for Philosophy as well as for Salvation' (ibid.: ^{2}50). Believers must rely on what God has declared through Moses, not on what Newton and others claim to have discovered by reason!

A less radical view of the relationship between faith and reason is to be found in the works of a number of theologians who advanced doctrinal considerations to question the competence of the canon of reason in matters of religious belief. Edmund Gibson, in his *Second Pastoral Letter* to the Diocese of London, maintains that whatever might be 'the Powers of Reason in a State of *Innocence*,' in practice 'the Powers and Abilities of Reason' are subject to 'the present *corrupt* State of human Nature', lack the basic evidence by which to determine spiritual questions, and cannot provide 'a sufficient Guide to Salvation' (Gibson: 94, 98). While in 'Strength of Reason' and desire for truth 'the ancient philosophers' seem not to have been inferior to people today, consideration of what they claimed to know, of what they did not discern and of their disagreements confirms the grave inadequacy of reason as a guide in religion (ibid.: 102; cf. 102ff).

Other theologians argue that the nature of the divine and the character of human knowledge limit the authority of reason in religious matters. William Law put it that God's actions are 'above our comprehension' because they are '*fit* and *reasonable*' according to 'the *incomprehensible perfections*' of the divine nature (Law: II, 65). While there is some likeness between the attributes of the human and of the divine, it is not such as to allow the reason of the former to fathom the nature and actions of the latter (cf. ibid.: II, 91). A similar understanding underlies Peter Browne's claim that the only justifiable way of speaking about God is indirectly, by means of the analogies by which God has chosen to make Godself known – and even then it is not legitimate to try to use these analogies as premises for speculative inferences about the divine nature (cf. Browne: 283f, 114f). While rational reflection thus perceives that there is no way by which the 'finite can comprehend Infinity', since there is no 'Proportion or Similitude' by which the latter can be grasped in terms of the former, faith nevertheless trusts that what God has chosen to reveal is appropriately 'adapted to our Intellect' (ibid.: 31f). John Ellis neatly tried to turn Locke against himself. He argued that if Locke is correct in holding that our ideas are derived from sensation and reflection, there is no way that even 'the most advanced Mind' could properly conceive of 'an Eternal, Omniscient, Omnipotent, Infinitely Wise and Happy Being'. Nevertheless, 'what Nature could not do, Grace and Mercy have supplied'. From the time of Adam onwards, by 'Revelation, Inspiration, and Instruction', God has made the divine known to our 'Finite Intellect' (Ellis 1743: 33; 1747: 438f).

While some thus attempted in various ways to safeguard authentic faith and practice from the fashionable criterion of the canon of reason, others considered that the application of that criterion showed the Lockean ideal of reasonable belief to be unattainable – so far, at least, as a more or less recognizably Christian Theism is concerned. In this respect David Hume's works, while rarely original in their views on religion, provide a lively compendium of criticisms of the arguments purporting to show the rational justifiability of assent to natural and revealed truths about God. In particular, Hume's *Treatise of Human Nature* and his *Inquiry Concerning Human Understanding* suggest that 'the disquisitions of speculative philosophy' are 'magnificent, but perhaps fruitless enquiries' (Hume 1962: 134) and that a realistic appraisal of reason will lead to a healthy scepticism about its competence to provide knowledge of the fundamental truth about reality; his *Dialogues Concerning Natural Religion* highlight numerous difficulties with the standard arguments for the reality of God and imply that the only reasonable position is 'a total suspense of judgment' (Hume 1935: 230); his *Natural History of Religion* concludes that religious belief may reasonably be regarded as 'sick men's dreams' or 'the playsome whimsies of monkeys in human shape' (Hume 1956: 75), and that monotheism inculcates a morality appropriate to 'slavery and subjection' (ibid.: 52); his essay 'Of Miracles' undermines the most popular and supposedly the strongest of the authenticating marks of a revelation by arguing that 'no human testimony' is sufficient 'to prove a miracle, and make it a just foundation' for a 'system of religion' (Hume 1962: 127); his essay 'Of a Particular Providence and a Future State' points out that even if the argument from effect to cause were valid, 'the present scene of things, which is so full of ill and disorder', could only justify the ascription of commensurate attributes to the deity which produced it (ibid.: 147); and the essay 'On Suicide' maintains that if it be not impious to interfere with nature by building houses, cultivating the earth and sailing upon the seas, it ought not to be thought wrong to end life when 'pain or sorrow' renders living no longer desirable (Hume 1903: 592).

Put together, Hume's analyses constituted a comprehensive threat to the arguments which had been advanced in the previous decades in attempts to show the rational justification of religious belief. In some passages Hume did state that his rational appraisal proves that 'our most holy religion is founded on *Faith*, not on reason' (Hume 1962: 130). Accordingly, philosophical scepticism is 'the first and most essential step towards being a sound, believing Christian' (Hume 1935: 282). These remarks are almost certainly ironic. Hume seems to have been too much a child of his rationalist age to be prepared to entertain a view of religious faith which divorces it from a basis in reason. Those who took his work seriously could not be satisfied that the reasonableness of belief in God and in the Christian revelation had been established. Whereas Locke is optimistic about the result of adopting the canon of reason, Hume's reappraisals of the character and scope of reason and of the purported justifications of religious belief seem to imply that the application of this canon solves religious controversy only by dissolving away all religious belief!

Hume's views, however, did not put an end to arguments purporting to show that the conclusions of natural theology and assent to revealed truths satisfy the canon of reason. Although Leland described Hume as 'an elegant and subtil writer, and one of the most dangerous enemies to Christianity that have appeared among us' (Leland 1756: 80), it was easier to dismiss him as unreasonably sceptical (cf. Leland 1754–5: II, 2, 15) and a wrangler seeking fame than to try to meet his arguments. Attempts to discern and justify the reasonableness of Christian belief thus continued to be presented and confuted – and in much the same way as before.

At the end of the eighteenth century Thomas Paine and William Paley were hard at it. In _The Age of Reason_ Paine denies that 'the Almighty ever did communicate anything to man . . . otherwise than by the universal display of himself in the works of the creation, and by that repugnance we feel in ourselves to bad actions, and dispositions to good ones'. Maintaining that claims to revelation have been used to justify great evils, he denounced Christianity: 'Of all the systems of religion that ever were invented, there is none more derogatory to the Almighty, more unedifying to man, more repugnant to reason, and more contradictory in itself, than this thing called Christianity. Too absurd for belief, too impossible to convince . . . it renders the heart torpid, or produces only Atheists or fanatics.' What Paine advocates is a 'pure and simple Deism' which finds its Bible in the Creation and grows in the knowledge of God by studying the works of God in the world (Paine: [1]128f, [1]133).

Paley presents a very different understanding of what it is reasonable to believe. In 1794 his _View of the Evidences of Christianity_ was published. In the first half of the book he seeks, in view of Hume's objections to the argument from miracles (cf. Paley: III, 3ff), to establish that those who claimed to be 'original witnesses of the Christian miracles' are uniquely trustworthy because they were prepared both to suffer for their testimony and to adopt new rules of conduct (ibid.: III, 9). The second half is taken up with what he calls 'auxiliary evidences' for the truth of Christianity – such as the arguments from prophecy, from the morality of the Gospel, from the character of Jesus and from the propagation of Christianity – and with replies to various popular objections to these arguments. Eight years later his _Natural Theology_ appeared. Beginning with the analogy of a watch, he argues that just as 'every indication of contrivance, every manifestation of design' in the watch implies an intelligent maker, so the vastly greater 'complexity, subtilty, and curiosity' of 'the contrivances of nature' point to the existence of God (ibid.: IV, 12). Although, like versions of the same argument advanced a century earlier, most of the work is taken up with extensive descriptions of natural history, the initial statement of the argument includes a brief attempt to meet the kinds of objection which Hume, for example, raises in his *Dialogues Concerning Natural Religion* (cf. ibid.: IV, 2ff). The inspection of the wonders of nature, however, is not intended merely to excite our curiosity and to indicate the reality of some remote deity. For Paley, examination of the finely wrought 'hinges in the wings of an earwig' should make us aware that God cares for 'even the minutest parts' of the Creation: accordingly we should realize that 'we have no reason to fear . . . our being forgotten or overlooked, or neglected' (ibid.: IV, 355).

With the comfort found in considering an earwig, it is time to end this chapter. It is a long way from Herbert of Cherbury to Paley – and an equally long way from Paley to today. For all the liveliness, variety and insights of those debates, the question of what it is reasonable to believe remains.

WORKS CITED

Berkeley, George, 1843, *The Works*, ed. G. N. Wright, 2 vols, London.

[Browne, Peter], 1737, *The Procedure, Extent, and Limits of Human Understanding*, London.

Butler, Joseph, 1765, *The Analogy of Religion Natural and Revealed to the Constitution and Course of Nature*, 5th edn, London.

Chillingworth, William, 1719, *The Works*, 7th edn, London.

Chubb, Thomas, 1734, *Four Tracts*, London.

Clarke, Samuel, 1732, *A Discourse Concerning the Being and Atributes of God, The Obligations of Natural Religion, and the Truth and Certainty of the Christian Revelation*, 8th edn, London.

[Collins, Anthony], 1713, *A Discourse of Free-Thinking*, London.

Conybeare, John, 1812, 'The Nature, Possibility, and Certainty of Miracles Set Forth; and the Truth of the Christian Religion Proved from Thence,' repr. in vol. II of *Enchiridion Theologicum*, ed. John [Randolf] Lord Bishop of London, new edn, Oxford.

Culverwel, Nathanael, 1661, *An Elegant, and Learned Discourse Of the Light of Nature: With several other Treatises*, London.

Derham, William, 1738, *Astro-Theology: Or, A Demonstration of the Being and Attributes of God, from a Survey of the Heavens*, 7th edn, London.

Derham, William, 1723, *Physico-Theology: Or, A Demonstration of the Being and Attributes of God from His Works of Creation*, 6th edn, London.

Edwards, John, 1697, *The Socinian Creed: Or, A Brief Account of the Professed Tenents and Doctrines of the Foreign and English Socinians*, London.

[Ellis John], 1743, *Some Brief Considerations upon Mr Locke's Hypothesis, That the Knowledge of GOD is attainable by Ideas of Reflexion. Wherein is Demonstrated Upon his own Principles, That the Knowledge of God is not attainable by Ideas of Reflexion*, London.

Ellis, John, 1747, *The Knowledge of Divine Things from Revelation, Not from Reason or Nature*, 2nd edn, London.

Fox, George, 1706, *Gospel-Truth Demonstrated, In a Collection of Doctrinal Books*, London.

[Gibson, Edmund], 1732, *The Bishop of London's Three Pastoral Letters*, London.

Guyse, John, 1724, *The Standing Use of the Scripture to all the Purposes of a Divine Revelation*, London.

Herbert, Edward, Lord Herbert of Cherbury, 1705, *The Antient Religion of the Gentiles, and Causes of their Errors Consider'd*, trans. William Lewis, London.

Herbert, Edward, Lord Herbert of Cherbury, 1768, *A Dialogue between A Tutor and his Pupil*, London.

Herbert, Edward, Lord Herbert of Cherbury, 1937, *De Veritate*, trans. and intr. M. H. Carré, Bristol.

Herbert, Edward, Lord Herbert of Cherbury, 1944, *De Religione Laici*, ed. and trans. H. R. Hutcheson, New Haven.

Hume, David, 1903, *Essays, Moral, Political and Literary*, London.

Hume, David, 1935, *Dialogues concerning Natural Religion*, ed. N. K. Smith, Oxford.

Hume, David, 1956, *The Natural History of Religion*, ed. H. E. Root, London.

Hume, David, 1962, *Enquiries Concerning the Human Understanding and Concerning the Principles of Morals*, ed. L. A. Selby-Bigg, 2nd edn, Oxford.

Hunt, John, 1704, *The Saints Treasury: Or, A Discourse concerning the Glory and Excellency of the Person of Christ*, London.

[Hutchinson, John], 1724, 1727, *Moses's Principia*, Part I 1724, Part II 1727, London.

Law, William, 1892, *The Works*, Brockenhurst.

Leland, John, 1754, 1755, *A View of the Principal Deistical Writers that have Appeared in England in the last and present Century; with Observations upon them*, 2 vols, London.

Leland, John, 1756, *A Supplement to the First and Second Volumes of the View of the Deistical Writers*, 3rd edn, London.

Leslie, Charles, 1721, *The Theological Works*, London.

Locke, John, 1768, *Works*, 4 vols, 7th edn, London.

Norris, John, 1728, *An Account of Reason and Faith: In Relation to the Mysteries of Christianity*, London.

Paley, William, 1837, *The Works*, 5 vols, London.

Paine, Thomas, 1891, *Complete Theological Works*, London.

Ray, John, 1692, *The Wisdom of God Manifested in the Works of the Creation*, 2nd edn, London.

Reynolds, John, 1725, *Three Letters to the Deist*, London.

[Sherlock, Thomas], 1729, *The Tryal of the Witnesses of the Resurrection of Jesus*, London.

Stillingfleet, Edward, 1673, *A Second Discourse in Vindication of the Protestant Grounds of Faith Against the Pretence of Infallibility In the Roman Church*, London.

[Stillingfleet, Edward], 1677, *A Letter to a Deist, In Answer to several Objections against the Truth and Authority of the Scriptures*, London.

Stillingfleet, Edward, 1688, *A Discourse Concerning the Nature and Grounds of the Certainty of Faith*, London.

[Stillingfleet], Edward Lord Bishop of Worcester, 1697, *A Discourse in Vindication of the Doctrine of the Trinity with An Answer to the Late Socinian Objections*, London.

Stillingfleet, Edward, 1702, *Origines Sacrae: Or, A Rational Account of the Grounds of Natural and Revealed Religion*, 7th edn, Cambridge.

Taylor, Jeremy, 1647, *A Discourse of the Liberty of Prophesying, Shewing the Unreasonableness of prescribing to other mens Faith, and the Iniquity of persecuting differing opinions*, London.

[Tindal, Matthew], 1731, *Christianity as Old as the Creation: Or, The Gospel, A Republication of the Religion of Nature*, London.

Toland, John, 1702, *Christianity not Mysterious: Or, A Treatise Shewing, That there is nothing in the Gospel Contrary to Reason, Nor Above it: And that no Christian Doctrine can be properly call'd A Mystery*, London.

Waterland, Daniel, 1843, *The Works*, ed. W. Van Mildert, 6 vols, 2nd edn, Oxford.

Whichcote, Benjamin, 1753, *Moral and Religious Aphorisms . . . now re-published . . . by Samuel Salter, to which are added Eight Letters: which passed between Dr. Whichcote . . . and Dr. Tuckney*, London.

[Wilkins], John, Bishop of Chester, 1678, *Of the Principles and Duties of Natural Religion*, London.

Wollaston, William, 1726, *The Religion of Nature Delineated*, London.

Woolston, Thomas, 1727, *A Discourse of the Miracles of our Saviour*, London.

12

Catholicism from the Reformation to the Relief Acts

W. J. Sheils

DESPITE ITS conservative tones, the Protestant nature of the religious settlement of 1559 meant that the Marian bishops, with one exception, were unable to accept its terms and resigned *en masse*. Thereafter, until the Emancipation Act of 1829, English and Welsh Catholics lived under a variety of religious and legal constraints, the structure of which was devised in the first half-century following Elizabeth's accession when the Protestant regime was uncertain of its domestic support and keenly aware of the possible military threat from Catholic powers on the continent. The legislation, therefore, reflected not only the deep antipathy of committed Protestants to 'popish superstition', but also their suspicions about the loyalty of Catholics. Before embarking on the history of Catholicism during this period or of the relations between its adherents and their Protestant governors and neighbours, it is necessary to set out the formal legal framework.

CATHOLICS AND THE LAW

The 1559 Act of Uniformity established the famous twelvepenny fine on those who failed to attend their parish church, but contained no specific legislation against the Mass. That came in 1563 with an Act making any priest who said Mass, or any layman who procured it, liable to the death penalty, while those in attendance faced a fine of 100 marks. This law remained something of a dead letter until the late 1570s, but the publication of the papal bull of excommunication against Elizabeth in 1570, along with plots around the person of Mary, Queen of Scots, produced anti-papal legislation in the Parliament of 1571. The Queen, however, resisted demands for harsher penalties on her Catholic subjects until the end of that decade, when the arrival of English exiles trained on the continent as seminary priests, and their success in making converts, aroused further concern. The Parliament of 1581 equated the activities of the priests with treason, and linked Catholicism with the same suspicion of disloyalty, as well as imposing the much heavier monthly fine of £20 on those who failed to attend church. Four years later any Catholic priest in England and Wales was declared, *ipso facto*, guilty of treason, and any of the laity harbouring priests faced execution. This Act represented the culmination of Elizabethan policy, though there was further tightening of the financial legislation later in the reign.

The hopes which Catholics had on the accession of James I were soon dashed, and by the end of 1604 recusancy fines had been reimposed. The fiasco of the Gunpowder Plot, 'the last fling of the Elizabethan tradition of a politically engaged Catholicism', in 1605 led to further legislation restricting the movements of Catholics, requiring an oath of allegiance and giving the Crown the right to confiscate two-thirds of a recusant's lands. This last clause, however, had little practical consequence and, by the end of James's reign, royal policy seemed once again more favourable to Catholics. Under Charles, and especially in the household of Queen Henrietta Maria, they gained favour at Court, where papal agents were received. Elsewhere, however, Catholics found themselves caught up in the conflict between King and Parliament. On the one hand the financial difficulties of the Crown led the King to seek out recusancy fines more vigorously, increasing the income from that source fivefold between 1631 and 1640; on the other, the influence of courtier Catholics with the King intensified anti-Catholic attitudes among the gentry and the people. Rumours of plots, often implicating the Jesuits, were commonplace in many localities in the 1630s and, in addition to the stereotypes produced in popular literature, resulted in attacks on recusants, especially in the larger towns, in the period of heightened tension between 1640 and 1642 following the Irish rebellion.

The anti-Catholicism of Parliament was reinforced by the involvement of recusants on the royalist side during the Civil Wars. Legislation in the late 1640s required a specifically anti-Catholic oath of abjuration and increased the financial penalties on landholders, who now faced confiscation of four-fifths of their property. Under the Protectorate the financial exactions were relaxed and the general improvement in the position of Catholics promised to advance further at the Restoration. Henrietta Maria returned with her son, Charles II, who married a Catholic queen in 1662. The King's tolerant religious attitude led to a Declaration of Indulgence in 1672, but this was repudiated in 1674 when Parliament imposed a Test Act, which required all office-holders to receive the Anglican communion and specifically to deny transubstantiation. By this date the King's brother and heir, James, was known to be a Catholic, and the late 1670s saw a revival of persecution in the wake of the alleged 'popish plot'. This was followed by a constitutional struggle over the exclusion of James from the throne which, nevertheless, he ascended in 1685. The new monarch set about removing those obstacles which prevented Catholics from entering public life, but in the face of fierce parliamentary opposition was forced to do this through Declarations of Indulgence using the royal prerogative, thus provoking a constitutional crisis which was resolved by the removal of James and the accession of his daughter Mary and her husband William, the Protestant Prince of Orange. During their reign further restrictions were placed on Catholics, who were excluded from the Act of Toleration in 1689. An Act of 1695 barred them from the professions, by which time Catholic landowners had been made subject to further financial penalties with the imposition of the double land tax in 1692.

The Jacobite Risings of 1715 and 1745 revived popular suspicion of Catholics, but no further substantive legislation was directed against them. Their lands had to be registered from 1716, and Hardwicke's Marriage Act of 1753 declared marriage before priests to have no force in law. The thrust of this last Act was to clarify the law and not to penalize Catholics, who by then could look forward to legislation designed to lift some of the restrictions under which they lived. The first Relief Act of 1778 incorporated an oath of allegiance, but rendered priests immune from prosecution by informers and allowed the laity to inherit lands in their own name. In 1791 Catholic places of worship could be registered and Catholics were readmitted to the professions: the first steps towards emancipation had been taken and the community could more freely address itself to its relations with the rest of society which for so long had been coloured, though not always dominated, by the formal framework of the law.

SURVIVAL OR GROWTH?

The Protestant Settlement of 1559 was a close-run thing in Parliament and in many parts of the country, especially in the north and west where loyalty to the old beliefs existed not only among the people but also among landholders and gentry. The problem was, however, that this loyalty covered a wide spectrum of belief ranging from a folkloric attachment to traditional ceremonial on the one hand to the intellectual commitment of the Marian bishops to a universal Church on the other. It is, therefore, difficult to define the nature of religious conservatism in the years up to 1580, but we can be confident that traditional views, of whatever sort, were widely held. What is a matter of debate is the relationship which such views had with the Catholicism that emerged at the end of the century under the first generation of missionaries trained on the continent.

The traditional history of Catholicism was depicted as one of gradual decline from a national religion in the 1530s to that of a minority, gentry-led and withdrawn from mainstream society, and served by clergy who in many cases endured heroic suffering for their faith. Such a view was not only common among Catholic historians but was also held by distinguished Reformation scholars such as A. G. Dickens, who saw Catholicism retreat rapidly in the face of Protestant evangelization. Thus was established the view of English and Welsh Catholics, often expressed in contemporary polemical literature, as the surviving remnant of the medieval Church. This stress on continuity was overturned in 1975 by the publication of John Bossy's *The English Catholic Community 1570–1850*, in which he argued that the disruption following the 1530s marked the end of the late medieval Church and that the religion of the Catholic mission represented a fresh initiative. Thus the history of post-Reformation Catholicism was one of growth and development, not one of decline, and the agents of that growth were the seminary priests trained at Douai and, from 1580, the Jesuits. These young men, in particular, the latter trained on the continent and fired with the missionary zeal and the pastoral priorities of the Counter-Reformation, brought to England a religion demanding a high degree of personal and household piety within the framework of a hierarchical Church. In many respects these priorities were not very different from those of Protestant reformers such as Whitgift, and thus the Catholics of the late sixteenth-century mission were almost as far removed from the religion of their grandparents as were their conformist Protestant neighbours.

This account of a fracture in the history of Catholicism has been challenged by McGrath and Haigh, each on rather different grounds. McGrath suggests that Catholic revival under Mary had produced a revitalized clergy, many of whom sustained traditional religion in the early years of Elizabeth's reign, not least by sending young men abroad, and prepared the ground for the missionaries. Thus continuity was greater than Bossy suggested, the more so as the young missioners were taught by English scholars, many of whom had held university posts in Mary's reign and gone into exile in the 1560s. From there they produced apologetic and controversial works to inform an international audience about events in England and to sustain their co-religionists at home. The effect of this ministry in the 1560s was to create a conforming Catholicism in which 'many laymen who believed the faith in their hearts and heard Mass when they could, frequented the schismatic church'. On these foundations the later mission was built.

Haigh also stresses the continuity provided by the Marian clergy, especially in Lancashire, from where many recruits for the seminaries came, but in addition he traces the subsequent history of the Catholic community to a fundamental misdirection of missionary effort, which concentrated on gentry households, especially in the south-east and London, to the neglect of other parts of the country, such as Lancashire, where the survival of traditional beliefs could have provided the basis for a revitalized popular religion. In this view, post-Reformation Catholicism was not a story of growth but one of withdrawal into a 'seigneurial sect' until demographic changes in the eighteenth century altered its pattern.

The main support for the argument for continuity comes from consideration of the geographical distribution of recusants in the early seventeenth century, when their numbers were strongest in those areas of the country which, to judge from the evidence of wills, had remained most attached to traditional piety in the early sixteenth century. Thus in the north of England, except for Cheshire where the paucity of priests was blamed for a decline in numbers, substantial Catholic communities could be found, often based on the estates or among the tenantry of major landowning families, as in Derbyshire, or among more humble gentry like the Blundells of Little Crosby, whose estate was famously described as consisting of 'forty houses or thereabouts, and there are not . . . any other but Catholics in it'. Even in the North Riding of Yorkshire, where gentry involvement had declined slightly by the 1630s, the size of congregations continued to increase. By common agreement these were not regions which were lavishly endowed with clergy, though they continued to provide recruits for the seminaries. By contrast, in the southern counties Catholic landowners like the Treshams found themselves at loggerheads with their tenants and by the late 1580s had, as in Suffolk, 'withdrawn into their own internalised community'. Thus where priests were most numerous Catholic withdrawal from public worship and public life was most pronounced. The efforts of the missionaries, it is claimed, made little impact on the distribution of recusancy.

The exception to this pattern was London, whose importance as the centre of organization of the mission grew as time passed. Its great population growth and its increasing importance in national life made London an important centre not only for Catholics but also for other nonconforming religious groups. Here the Inns of Court, the embassy chapels, and later the Court of Henrietta Maria all provided patronage for priests and opportunities for Catholic gentry to practise their religion. Also significant in providing continuity in the capital was the work of London tradesmen and their wives in maintaining the clergy and in providing contact between them and different groups of provincial recusants. From the late sixteenth century this metropolitan element was central to the support of the mission and the community.

Bossy, on the other hand, points to environmental factors rather than geographical distribution as contributing to the emergence of recusancy, stressing the importance of upland regions and remoteness in the formation of Catholic groups. In so doing he notes exceptions within the broad geographical pattern: the lack of recusancy among the urbanized textile regions of West Yorkshire or the lead-mining districts of Derbyshire in the north, and the tenacious hold of Catholicism in the New Forest and in West Sussex. The conversion of these patterns into numbers remains a speculative business – indeed, problems of definition and of recording make it virtually impossible before 1600 – but figures from the early seventeenth century suggest that those making habitual use of the services of the missioners numbered between thirty and forty thousand, rising to sixty thousand by 1641. 'Habitual use' is a key concept and central to the debate about growth or decline, for in addition to such people there were other Catholics who had little or no contact with priests or at best with deprived survivors from Mary's reign. Such people were part of an amorphous and varied phenomenon attending 'church ales', using Latin prayers, and maintaining devotions to saints whose relationship to the mission was ill-defined and ambiguous. By 1600, however, the mission had begun to define itself in the context of those who had more than a passing contact with the clergy, and it is with this more coherent group of adherents that the future of Catholicism lay. The character of that Catholicism was to be determined by the two chief partners in the mission, the clergy and the gentry.

THE CATHOLIC CLERGY

With the establishment of a seminary at Douai in 1568 under the leadership of William Allen the post-Reformation Catholic mission can be said to have begun. Priests arrived slowly at first: there were only eleven by 1575, but the pace soon quickened and the total passed one hundred by 1580. During these early years there was no organization and priests led a peripatetic and solitary existence, their activities largely confined to the support of already known sympathizers, and often undertaken in their native region. The arrival in 1580 of the Jesuits, and in particular Robert Persons, was to change this. First a synod of 1581 denounced attendance at Anglican services as sinful, thereby making clear the issue of recusancy as opposed to church-papistry among the laity. Second, the problems of conducting the mission were discussed, the immediate result of which was greater organization at the continental end where Persons arranged for the departure of missionaries for England from Rouen. This secured a steady stream of priests, but not their safety. By 1586 over thirty had been executed and another fifty imprisoned, and the Babington plot of that year was exploited by the government to impugn the loyalty of all Catholics, driving a wedge between those gentry who sought to remain at peace with the regime and their neighbours, and those who actively sought the overthrow of the Queen. The international situation led to intense activity against recusants in the late 1580s, at which time a clerical network, organized by the Jesuits, began to take shape.

London was at the centre of a regional organization which depended on the support of safe (usually gentry-owned) houses, especially at a time when priests were likely to be removed suddenly as a result of arrest and imprisonment. It was among imprisoned priests at Wisbech in 1588 that the first major conflict over organization took place. It revolved around the question of authority, with the Jesuits on one side and the secular clergy, for the most part, on the other. The seculars sought the establishment of episcopacy, as expressing continuity with the past; Persons originally shared this view, asking that the bishops appointed work with an archpriest also. Neither of these schemes got much support at Rome and eventually a further suggestion of Persons, that an archpriest be appointed with limited jurisdiction and working closely with the Jesuits, was accepted. George Blackwell was appointed to the post in 1598 and almost at once faced opposition from sections of the secular clergy. Some appealed to Rome and another small group of thirteen, seeking accommodation with the regime, signed a Protestation of Allegiance in 1603. They were numerically insignificant in the context of the mission, but the views they expressed were of central importance, touching as they did on the vexed question of the political allegiance of what was by then a recognizably distinct religious group within society. That distinctiveness was the result of the determination of the priests to ensure that their adherents did not compromise with the Established Church. From this date, though Catholics might hope for favours from the Stuarts and, indeed, found support and converts at the Court, the work of the clergy was to be with their own people, and to this end they organized.

We have noted that the number of recusants increased by over 50 per cent in the first half of the seventeenth century. This rise was more than matched by the increase in clergy, and especially among the Jesuits, who in 1641 had 171 priests in the country, almost two-thirds of them working in the midlands, the south-east or London. It was among the Jesuits that the drive towards organization was strongest. By 1623 their numbers were sufficient for a separate English province to be established under a

Superior, based in London, who had oversight of the finances of the mission, the deployment of priests and their spiritual formation. The province was divided into twelve districts, each under a supervisor, and this framework survived into the mid-eighteenth century with only minor alterations of district boundaries and names. The latter are of interest in that the original district names, such as St Aloysius in the north-west, reflected the internationalist thrust of the mission, whereas those named later, such as St Hugh in Lincolnshire, paid greater attention to local tradition and continuity, reflecting the increasing influence of the gentry on the Society.

Organization among the seculars was less easily achieved and, in the early years, was bedevilled by the uncertain status of the archpriest. He did not enjoy the same authority over the seculars as the Superior did over the Jesuits and fell foul of the rivalry between the two groups of clergy, with the Jesuits claiming exemption from his authority. Furthermore, the seculars were held in low esteem by influential sectors of the Catholic laity, many of whom retained Jesuits as their household chaplains. The fundamental question at issue was that of ecclesiastical authority, and that focused on episcopacy. George Birkhead, archpriest from 1607, sought authority from Rome to exercise control over the regular clergy and, in particular, over the financial aspects of the mission, but without success. In 1623, however, a bishop was appointed. William Bishop was nominated to the titular see of Chalcedon and in the few months which he spent in England was able to lay the foundations for the organization of the secular clergy, creating a chapter, supported by vicars-general and archdeacons in the regions, to govern the affairs of the 400 or so seculars. The bishop also made conciliatory gestures to the recently arrived Benedictine order, granting a loosely supervised autonomy to the sixty monks active in the country, some of whom stressed accommodation with government and even contact with Anglicans. Through men like Augustine Baker the Benedictines were to exercise a profound influence on contemplative life within the Catholic community. Relations with other religious orders remained difficult, not only with the Jesuits but also with the newly founded Institute of the Blessed Virgin Mary (IBVM), an order of nuns founded by a Yorkshirewoman, Mary Ward, which worked chiefly in London reconciling lapsed Catholics and running schools and catechetical centres. These difficulties reflected papal disfavour with the international success of the Institute, which was suppressed in 1630. More significant in the national context were relations with the Jesuits and with the laity.

A new bishop, Richard Smith, had arrived in 1625 and set about establishing his position as 'spiritual father and pastor' of all Catholics in the realm. He began his assault on the Jesuits' autonomy by invoking the

Council of Trent's decree on confession, which limited the power of binding and loosing to parish priests or those with episcopal permission. As no parochial structure now existed, this meant that Smith claimed control over all confessors, thus imposing his authority at the most intimate point of the relationship between the priests and the laity. By doing so he aroused opposition not only from the religious orders, but also from their lay patrons, who were faced with the prospect of not being allowed to choose their own confessors. Smith also reopened claims to the control of missionary finance, requiring the laity to make general contributions to the support of the mission, forbidding payments to individual clerics and placing the sums raised under the authority of local archdeacons for redistribution. These claims were firmly grounded in the decrees of the Council of Trent and, in theory, might have achieved an urgently needed redistribution of missionary finances, but in practice they were totally out of touch with the realities of the English situation which, over a generation, had been characterized by vigorous Jesuit autonomy and gentry independence. The latter was also challenged by Smith's claim, as bishop, to exercise 'ordinary' jurisdiction over marriage, probate and other areas of Church law. This threatened the *modus vivendi* which many recusants had established with the Anglican ecclesiastical machinery on which they depended for certain legal services. Opposition from leading Catholic laymen saw Smith accused of treason, occasioning his retreat to the French embassy in 1629, and eventually into exile in 1631.

Smith's departure signalled the end of attempts to construct conventional hierarchical discipline among English Catholics until the accession of James II. Although relations between leading Jesuits and seculars over questions of authority were still marked by conflict, it is important to stress that this did not reflect the experience of most priests working in the mission before 1685. The majority, working in gentry households like that of the Stonor family in Oxfordshire, or among scattered farming communities on the moors of north Yorkshire, suppressed institutional rivalries in the face of the more pressing pastoral demands of serving the spiritual needs of their people.

THE CATHOLIC LAITY

As has been suggested, circumstances ensured that the laity played a dynamic role in the survival, revival and character of Catholicism between 1560 and 1660. That there was a strong attachment to the traditional piety of the old religion in many parts of England is well established, and regional studies of western and northern areas have revealed societies in which a public Catholic culture, described by Haigh as a 'relaxed, peasant Catholicism' survived into the 1580s. It was marked by Latin prayers, traditional celebrations, pilgrimages to local shrines and curative magic, sometimes manifested in well-publicized exorcisms. Such Catholicism needed to be sustained by the clergy if it was to grow and the evidence suggests that, without the priests, it withered. This was certainly the case in the two strongly traditional counties of Cumberland and Durham; the feudal Catholicism of the latter, so pronounced in the 1560s, had died away by the end of the century, while in Carlisle the complaint of the early Elizabethan bishop about the number of Masses being said and the protection given to Catholics by the gentry was no longer relevant by the 1600s, when a modest eighty recusants were recorded in the diocese. In the face of such evidence it is difficult to share Haigh's view that such traditional piety was more typical of Catholicism in the years between 1560 and 1660 than the devotion fostered by the mission.

Nevertheless, traditional piety did have a part to play in the life of the community, especially in the matters of the observance of fast days and the celebration of feast days. On both questions the enthusiasm of the laity outstripped that of the clergy. In the early seventeenth century Lady Montagu was shocked by the suggestion, made to her in her last illness by her confessor and her doctor, that she should eat meat on Ash Wednesday 'which she never did in her life before', and Robert Persons criticized his lay co-religionists for over-reliance, as he saw it, 'on such external practices as living on bread and water on Fridays, vigils and most of Lent, and things like that'. Such self-denial was most strongly found among the gentry, who had food enough, and was exercised as a form of self-conscious household piety among recusants. Holy days also set Catholics apart, principally by the obligation of hearing Mass, but also in the manner of celebration. Here some of the clergy shared the sabbatarian ethic of their Protestant counterparts but, at least until the 1650s, feasts such as Christmas were usually accompanied by plays, music and dancing. Thereafter more sober disciplines took over on holy days themselves, though the tradition of merry nights continued on adjacent days.

Such distinctive forms of piety survived best when not in isolation and this fact, allied to the urgent need for financial support on the part of the clergy, made the gentry household the most obvious environment for Catholic growth. Thus from the early days of the mission Catholic gentry became accustomed to take a leading role, as employers and supporters of the clergy, in offering opportunities to their co-religionists for worship in their homes, in providing resting places to peripatetic clergy, and, in times of persecution, in giving protection to the priests. Both great houses, like that of the Vaux family at Harrowden, and lesser ones, like that of the

Blundells at Little Crosby, became synonymous with a tradition of Catholic loyalty passed down through several generations. This was important, but not typical; on the one hand persecution and the laws of inheritance ensured that individuals regularly returned to the Established Church, and on the other hand conversion brought new recruits to the recusant ranks. Changing religious allegiance between generations and divided religious loyalties among siblings were commonplace. Even a strongly recusant family like the Meynells in Yorkshire produced its Protestants as well as its priests and nuns. In considering vocations, at least in the years before 1620, Bossy has drawn attention to the importance of matriarchs like Dorothy Lawson in providing continuity, for many clergy came from families with conforming fathers and papist mothers. The role of such women emphasizes further the household nature of Catholicism in these years.

The gentry were the principal source of financial support for the clergy from the early days of the mission, usually employing individuals, like the first martyr Cuthbert Mayne, as household chaplains. By 1616 the pattern had become well established, but the life was often a lonely one for the priest, lying low and seeing only his allocated servant and those who came to him for Mass and confession. The relationship with the household was not an easy one, involving as it did a delicate balance between financial dependence and spiritual authority. Furthermore, such domestication did not sit very easily with the missionary vocation with which the seminaries inspired their students. Some priests, like John Gerard and James Pollard, did play a prominent part in reforming the households of their gentry patrons and in large establishments, like that of Lady Montagu, the priest could have the cure of as many as eighty souls. These, though, were exceptions; more common, certainly after 1660, were complaints of lack of respect shown to the clergy by their patrons who told them 'not to meddle in the ordering of their families, their deportment towards their kindred and neighbours, or their dealing in bargains'.

It was the Mass, of course, which was at the centre of Catholic life. In the early years of the mission it was not uncommon for papists to attend Anglican services, withdrawing from Communion, but as time passed the priests insisted on a more complete withdrawal from public worship. This tendency towards separation was reinforced among the gentry by government policy, which increasingly excluded Catholics from local office-holding and public life. Withdrawal was not complete, however, and the chapels established by the Vavasour and Stapleton families at Hazlewood and Carlton in Yorkshire also had Anglican parochial functions. In Lancashire in the 1620s the Catholics were said to organize their services so that, on the way home, they met their Protestant neighbours coming out of church. Despite this, Mass was most commonly a private occasion for a private congregation which outsiders could attend only by invitation, invitations which were often extended to include breakfast and other social contact according to rank. Thus the regime at Osgodby in the 1620s:

> On Sundays we locked the doors and all came to Mass, had our sermons, catechisms, and spiritual lessons every Sunday and Holyday. On the workdays we had for the most part two masses . . . one for the servants at six o'clock in the morning . . . the other we had at eight for those who were absent from the first.

Not all households had a priest available every Sunday, and in such circumstances it became customary for Catholics to reserve Mass time for the saying of private prayers or for communal devotion, for which special handbooks were published. Such activities, often requiring literacy and a degree of leisure, were particularly suited to a gentry-based piety.

Crucial as the gentry household was in the countryside, this was less true of London, from where the mission was organized and where Catholic numbers increased most rapidly. Of course the town houses of landowners often provided Mass centres, but the embassies and the homes of London artisans were also important. The embassies were in regular contact with the Court, and it is important to note that the wives of all the Stuart kings were Catholic. When a new chapel was opened for Henrietta Maria in 1632 the celebrations involved 2,000 people. At that date and again under Charles II, however, Court Catholicism proved a mixed blessing for the recusant community, doing little to alleviate the social restrictions applied to Catholics while at the same time touching on the strongly anti-papal feelings of Parliament. Suspicion of royal policy led to a few physical attacks on Catholics in the 1630s, while the 'popish plot' scares of the late 1670s ushered in a spate of persecution. Court Catholicism, therefore, was more likely to complicate the lives of provincial Catholics than to ease their circumstances and, apart from creating an awareness of the cultural and artistic impulses of the Counter-Reformation, was of little importance.

Below the ranks of the aristocracy and gentry were the farming and artisan communities. The influence of the gentry on their tenantry has already been mentioned, and local studies of areas like East Anglia in the mid-seventeenth century have shown that recusancy among town-dwellers and farmers was found only where there were also Catholic gentry. Thus the influence of the gentry remained dominant; but, that said, plebeian Catholicism was not numerically insignificant. A recent study of Durham and Northumberland recusants suggests that at least 60 per cent were non-gentle, but that it was the yeomanry rather than artisans or the poorer rural dwellers who made up that number. In Yorkshire, too, the commoners grew as a proportion of known recusants, and among them women were strongly represented. Of course, such people were not so numerous as to be able to provide a significant contribution to the support of the ministry, being numbered in tens or hundreds per county in 1641. Lancashire was the exception to this, with over 8,000 non-gentry Catholics listed. In the same county in 1639 there were fifty priests serving eighty-two Mass centres, seven of which were independent of gentry patronage. This was a modest number but by 1700 the independent Mass centre, often located in a farmhouse or a building specifically for that purpose, offered an alternative to the gentry household for some Catholics. In such places Mass became more of a social event: the minority of communicants would arrive at 8 a.m. and then go home to breakfast, while the others, dressed in their Sunday best, arrived for Mass at 10 a.m. and stayed on for lunch with the families who lived nearby; the afternoon was then taken up by catechism for the children, with the rosary and evening prayers said before returning home.

Though the gentry provided the mainstay of the Catholic community throughout the seventeenth century, both in financial support for the priests and in providing recruits for the priesthood, and though that dominance greatly influenced the milieu in which Catholicism operated, the picture would not be complete without some acknowledgement of the contribution of the farming communities, especially in the north, or of those London tradesmen and women who often gave first shelter to newly arrived missionaries and also provided a network of contacts for Catholic gentry visiting the capital.

STAGNATION AND TRANSITION

The growth in numbers achieved in the early seventeenth century was not sustained after 1650, despite the even greater presence of priests to serve the community. To some extent this reflects the triumph of the gentry household ideal over the original missionary impulse, but the decline in converts was not entirely due to factors within the Catholic community. The Civil Wars had seen a sizeable proportion of recusant landowners side with the King. Following the victory of Parliament the estates of these people, as both delinquent and papist, were subject to severe fiscal pressure which, together with the general religious upheaval, resulted in some gentry reverting to church-papistry or, eventually, to Protestantism. In addition, the financial difficulties of Catholics meant that support for the clergy and the seminaries in which they were trained dwindled, so much so that many of the latter found themselves in debt.

Problems within the mission were also important; the question of authority had never been satisfactorily resolved and, even after the departure of Smith in 1631, the chapter of the secular clergy still sought to press the claim for episcopal government within a restored Catholic Church. Such an impracticable scheme led to divisions among the seculars which undoubtedly weakened the mission, but the arguments for episcopacy were revived among some leading Catholics as a means of ensuring control and order among the laity following its abolition in the Established Church in 1646. In consequence the chapter, under the leadership of John Sergeant, embarked on a policy of co-operation with the Cromwellian regimes, a policy which further alienated the seculars from the largely royalist recusant gentry. Thus the Restoration saw the Catholic community passing through a period of upheaval marked by declining lay numbers and deep clerical division. Not surprisingly, it proved unable to take advantage of the opportunities offered by the new regime.

Charles II had spent much of his exile in Catholic France and his Court began to reflect that experience in the fashionable world of the capital. Among scientists as well as in the arts a number of prominent figures were Catholic, such as the dramatist William Wycherley and the statistician Major Gaunt. Around the Court itself an increasing number of French and Italian artists and craftsmen were employed and, while in exile, several members of the aristocracy had flirted with Catholicism or had taken Catholic wives. But this metropolitan and cosmopolitan Catholicism was both fickle and fragile, and the ethos of the Court, where the French Duchess of Portsmouth was mistress of the King, ran counter to the household piety of the gentry. The community appeared divided and leaderless.

Philip Howard, a member of an ancient aristocratic family with close links to the Crown and a priest of the Dominican order experienced in papal diplomacy, appeared to offer fresh hope of leadership to the community, but the failure of the King to secure toleration for Catholics led to his withdrawal from England in 1673. The fear of popery within the political nation and the persecution of the 'popish plot' years made the period between 1665 and 1685 the nadir of post-Reformation Catholic fortunes. Conversions were falling off and Bossy has suggested that, as it entered the 1680s, the community could have had little confidence in its future prospects. However, the removal of Sergeant and the accession of James II provided the opportunity to resolve the vexed question of authority. The role of the vicar-apostolic was revived in 1685 with the return to England of Bishop John Leyburn, a former president of Douai.

He reorganized the mission into four districts, each governed by a vicar-general, established rural deans to help administer the districts and improved the financial arrangements of the mission. The framework was in place before James's deposition in 1688 and the details were worked out over the next two decades. These organizational changes coincided also with a new, and refreshing, pattern of recruitment to the clergy, which became less gentry-dominated.

The years after 1660 were undoubtedly ones of stagnation, if not decline, but they were also ones of transition once the opportunities of James's brief reign were seized. Clerical divisions were healed, the question of authority resolved, the dominance of the gentry was on the wane, and new religious initiatives, such as the return of the IBVM, were encouraged. Finally, Catholicism began to penetrate the urban communities in the provinces. If the years following the Glorious Revolution did not offer Catholics much cause for optimism, the community itself had undergone a readjustment which contained the seeds of hope.

The Eighteenth Century

The contemporary judgement of a leading priest, Joseph Berington, that Catholicism had gone into decline since the Revolution of 1688, was given greater force by Newman's evocative description, in his famous 'Second Spring' sermon, of eighteenth-century Catholicism as a beleaguered remnant 'dimly seen as through a mist or in twilight'. There was certainly a decline in influence, marked by Protestantism at Court and by gentry defections which sometimes left local missions in difficulties, but numbers were on the increase, steadily if not dramatically. Precise figures are difficult to establish, but a community of between 60,000 and 70,000 around 1700 had grown to something in excess of 80,000 by the First Relief Act in 1778. That modest growth incorporated substantial changes in the character of the community, about a quarter of which lived in the capital during the middle years of the century. Those changes came about partly as a result of the organizational reforms mentioned above and partly in response to developments in society which affected other nonconforming groups as much as the Catholics.

The establishment of the four districts and the progress being made towards financial independence allowed the bishops in charge of the districts to deploy the falling numbers of clergy more effectively. That independence also reinvigorated the clergy, whose sense of mission was provided with a practical inspiration through the devotional and instructional writings of John Gother. Gother had ministered to London congregations in the 1680s, had been a leading controversialist under James II, and was forced into retirement at Warkworth after the Revolution. He used that time to good effect in producing catechisms and devotional writings based on the spirituality of St Francis de Sales, with its emphasis on living the devout life fully in the world. This was a spirituality which incorporated a striking compassion for the poor and was committed to conversion, but it fostered a religion which was eirenical and not expressive of the baroque Catholicism which had proved so attractive to the Stuart courts. It provided a chance to 're-formulate the Catholic way of life in terms appropriate to an age whose values were rationality, regularity, and work'. At a time when mention of Jacobitism could still revive fears about Catholic loyalty and when financial burdens and professional barriers against Catholics were being strengthened, this new vision of the mission was essential.

The vision, however, still required practical application. This was to be provided by Richard Challoner, who had grown up in the Warkworth household, where his mother was the housekeeper, and been sent off to Douai by Gother in 1704. Challoner's time at Douai was one of modest growth for the college, whose vice-president he became in 1720. Increase in size, however, was not matched by growth in intellectual distinction; involvement in the Jansenist controversies encouraged an atmosphere emphasizing the conservative virtues of diligence and obedience, producing a cast of mind well suited to the sober missionary objectives implicit in Gother's writings. Challoner did not return to England until 1730, when he settled in London. Here was to be found the widest range of Catholics: the gentry who attended the embassy chapels in the west end; tradespeople and professionals in the area around Covent Garden; and labourers, weavers and dockers, mostly Irish, in the East End and Southwark. The city contained both fashionable churches, which Protestants often visited to savour the music in the liturgy, and garrets, often above public-houses, which served as Mass centres for the very poor. Between the two extremes there were many intermediate stages, and between them also there flowed a regular supply of alms and charity, inspired by the practical devotion of Gother's writings and characteristic also of other denominations at that time.

Challoner's ministry, and that of his colleague Monnox Harvey, among the London poor contributed greatly to the 'extraordinary progress of popery' noted in the 1730s. Harvey's register of converts, over ninety in seven years, shows the milieu in which they worked. The largest group, numbering fifteen, was comprised of those converting on marriage; others were reconciled through kinship ties. Other links, of employer and employee or of landlord and tenant, were also effective, and the impression is left of a close-knit social and religious community in which 'the congregation' played an important part in supporting the convert. Collectively they formed devout societies, established schools and distributed alms to the poor and the sick. In this busy and ever-changing environment Challoner's organizational abilities soon made him one of the most important priests on the mission, 'frequently consulted by persons of all denominations'. In 1741 he was consecrated bishop and was the effective leader of the London district. His visitation of 1741–2 revived the practice of confirmation among the laity; he also removed and occasionally persuaded patrons to sack unsuitable priests, established weekly conferences of the clergy to help them maintain their studies and sustain their spiritual life, and for over fifty years observed a pastoral concern for individual consciences which made him a valued adviser to the laity, even when his conservative nature and lack of ease with the gentry placed him somewhat at odds with the needs of his flock.

Catholic congregations were emerging in provincial towns also. The fashionable centre of Bath was served by a Benedictine who catered for the gentry who resorted there, thus making the town a meeting-place for landowning Catholics from different parts of the country. From 1753 published guides mention the Catholic chapel as one of the amenities of the spa, where many humbler papists, mainly employed in trades serving the gentry, also lived. Congregations of artisans were recorded elsewhere: in Durham, where they lived undisturbed 'going publickly to Mass'; at Lincoln, where there was a 'very public meeting' every Sunday evening in the 1720s; at Birmingham, where the Franciscans recorded forty-three conversions between 1725 and 1737; and among the tailors and shoemakers of Bristol, the shopkeepers of Worcester and the metal workers of Wolverhampton. Increasingly Mass centres were based on towns, in gentry town houses if not in chapels, and the town mission not the country house became the focus for Catholics in the rural hinterland. The centre at Salisbury catered for the carpet weavers of nearby Wilton, and both the Bath and Bristol chapels brought in Catholics from as far as fifteen miles afield. The peripatetic mission, like that covering sixty-eight villages and hamlets in Yorkshire, remained a feature of Catholic life in the upland regions, but in many places the congregations were based in towns among the sort of people and with the social institutions identified with other Nonconformist groups. Thus by the second half of the century Catholics occupied an increasingly secure place in society at large, distinct but not significantly different from other minorities and with an organizational structure geared to both national and local needs. Their cultural life, sustained by the Mass, was served by the growing number of booksellers distributing devotional literature and by such works as Challoner's

Britannia Sancta, which provided the community with a sense of its own history and a means of explaining to itself its place in contemporary society.

That said, it must be remembered that Catholics differed from other Nonconformists in being excluded from the terms of the Toleration Act, and the shadows of the Stuarts hung over them. Certainly they were made scapegoats after 1715 and suffered confiscations of property. This retribution was not repeated after the rebellion of 1745, when Catholics were more likely to suffer from sporadic and uncoordinated attacks from the mob than from official persecution. A further period of harassment was faced by London Catholics between 1767 and 1771, when prosecutions were launched against fifteen priests and at least four Mass centres were closed, but this was the last major disruption faced by the community before the Relief Act of 1778. The Act itself, however, was the occasion for further harassment when the Protestant Association, led by Lord George Gordon, sought its repeal in 1780. A large rally at the beginning of June got out of hand and a week of violence and rioting, in which Catholic property and places of worship in the capital were destroyed, ensued.

The 'Gordon riots' marked an end rather than a beginning, and were expressive of social antagonism against wealthy Catholics and the embassy chapels as much as of religious bigotry. The community continued to grow in the industrializing parts of the kingdom; chapels, supported by wealthy businessmen, were built in Birmingham in 1786 and 1809, and at Newcastle there were Mass houses both in the town and nearby at Blyth, Gateshead, North Shields and Hexham. The greatest growth, however, was to be found in the traditional stronghold of Lancashire, where strong roots enabled the Church to build in the face of massive population increase, especially among the Irish, who sometimes threatened to overwhelm the native tradition. In the four towns of Wigan, Liverpool, Manchester and Preston the number of Catholics attached to the eight chapels which existed in 1810 was about 22,000, a fivefold increase on the figure of thirty years previous. By 1820 that figure had increased by another 10,000 and estimates for 1834 suggest a total of 51,000, of which over 30,000 were Irish or of Irish descent. In London also the proportion of Irish within the Catholic community grew in the years following 1800. This influx followed a half-century of native growth and retrenchment based on the town missions and, though in the years after 1770 the community was expanded and transformed by the Irish, it was never overwhelmed by them. It was on its own foundations established over 200 years that the English and Welsh Catholic community built its future, secured by the Emancipation Act of 1829.

13

The Evangelical Revival in Eighteenth-Century Britain

W. R. Ward

L IKE THOSE OTHER good products of the eighteenth century,
Enlightenment and political economy, religious revival was to be far
more influential in the nineteenth century than ever it was in the
eighteenth; and its origins, like theirs, illustrate British involvement in a
much wider world. The Orthodox parties, Lutheran and Reformed, and
their Tory High Church counterparts in England, clung to the delusion
that they could go it alone and drive the confessional state harder. But by
the eighteenth century the confessional state was falling upon hard times.
Kings and courts everywhere were turning to new methods; and so did
men of faith, not least men of revival. Religious revival began, indeed,
among the Protestant minorities of the Habsburg lands which, under the
arrangements of the Westphalia settlement, mostly had no Church, and felt
the full force of a hostile State. They had no option but to innovate or go
under, and their efforts set the timetable for revival in the English-
speaking world. Yet in England as in central Europe, innovation thrived on
one of the oldest of confessional fears, that of the armed triumph of Roman
Catholicism. Germans were on tenterhooks as to the outcome of the
Jacobite rebellion of 1745, for Britain was one of the guarantors of their
peace settlements of Ryswick and Utrecht; and if at the beginning of the
Seven Years War in 1756 Howel Harris raised a company of volunteers for
the defence of the east coast of England, the town council of Zurich closed
the gates and brought out the cannon and munition trains, convinced that
the survival of Frederick the Great was all that could save them from
invasion by the Catholic powers and the long-delayed vengeance of the
Catholic cantons. The very durability of the Catholic bogey, the visible
evidence that reliance on the arm of flesh in the shape of international
guarantees had not solved the problem, was an invitation to men of faith to
seek new strategies.

Certainly the politicians were fertile in bringing forth new strategies to get up the gross national product, to deal with poverty and disorder, to assimilate national, provincial and religious minorities, and all these policies had important religious consequences, most of them unpalatable, for the orthodoxies of the Counter-Reformation period. In Britain the capacity of a weak state for forward action had been further restricted during the Interregnum and Revolution, but the same needs made themselves felt; and when the Protestant succession was endangered, members of the Church of England had shown a capacity for informal action by societies for every purpose. In societal action the principle of contract, which had already triumphed in business, and was beginning to interpret the State, began to leave its mark on the Church. This was not welcome to high-fliers who regarded the Church as a *societas perfecta*, but formed the basis of new machinery indispensable when Church and State began to co-operate in tackling fairly severe problems of assimilation in Wales and Scotland.

Welsh Wales occupied a curious position halfway between that of the Protestant Poles of Silesia, subject to both German and Catholic oppression, and that of the enserfed Sorbs and Wends of Upper Lusatia, whose German and Pietist masters were determined to put them to rights – both the continental causes were supported with ideas, propaganda and religious inspiration from Francke's great foundations at Halle. The Welsh Church was poor, ill-organized and, at the end of the seventeenth century, increasingly English in both hierarchy and parish preaching. Of this latter, unpalatable, alien commodity, there seems to have been in the early eighteenth century an increasing supply; the long Welsh memory reacted with the view that the only preaching worth having was the Welsh itinerant sort associated with the legendary Puritans John Penry (1563–93) and Vavasor Powell (1617–70) and their like. The early eighteenth century saw the emergence of another Puritan, Griffith Jones (1682–1761), who in 1716 became rector of Llanddowror. Jones had difficulty in securing ordination, and in his early appointments was fairly constantly in trouble for preaching to huge crowds in the open air and relentlessly beating the drum about man's sin and need for repentance. In important respects, however, Jones was a Puritan with an eighteenth-century difference. He encouraged Welsh preaching to admit the Lockean requirements of simplicity and lucidity; he was an active member of the Society for Promoting Christian Knowledge (SPCK) and supported efforts to get it to produce a new Bible in 1720 and 1727; he applied to join the mission at Tranquebar, and was familiar with the work of the Halle foundations. One of the big efforts of the SPCK had been to create schools in Wales, and when, by the early 1730s, the impulse had faded, Griffith Jones began to create 'circulating schools'. Like the great Communion seasons in Scotland, these were adapted to rural underemployment and met for three months at a time, generally in winter, with evening classes for those at work in the day. Pupils were taught to read the Welsh Bible and to learn the Church Catechism. Between 1731 and 1737, thirty-seven of these schools were created, with 2,400 scholars, the masters being trained at Llanddowror by Jones. In 1761, the year of his death, *Welch Piety*, the annual report of the schools with its self-conscious echoes of *Pietas Hallensis*, recorded that 3,495 of these schools had been set up and that over 158,000 scholars had passed through them. Moreover, Jones's patron (and later brother-in-law), Sir John Phillipps of Picton Castle, Pembrokeshire (1666?–1737), who was the most influential member of the SPCK from its beginning to his death and was active in many of the religious societies, took Jones on a preaching tour in Wales, England and Scotland in 1718, kept him in touch with his international circle – Francke at Halle, Ostervald at Neuchâtel – with A. W. Boehme at court, and later on with the Oxford circle of the Wesleys and Whitefield, to whom he gave financial support for a time. In 1735 Jones assisted at the conversion of Daniel Rowland, but within a short time it was clear that both Rowland and what was becoming a Welsh Great Awakening were not quite what he had bargained for; and to the background of this we must briefly return.

The schools were not the sole, nor perhaps even the chief, vehicle of the effort of the SPCK to civilize, Christianize and assimilate Wales. There was a great crescendo of Welsh-language publishing. From 1546 to 1660 about 108 separate Welsh books had been printed; from 1660 to 1730 the minimum reckoning is 545, no fewer than three-quarters of which were published after 1700, a combined result of output by the SPCK and from presses at Shrewsbury (from 1696), Trefedhyn (from 1718) and Carmarthen (from 1721). Almost half the books were translated from the English, and this harmonized with the SPCK view that Welsh publishing might in the short term save the souls of the monoglot Welsh, while the charity schools raised up a new generation whose heavenly pilgrimage should follow the broader and safer paths of English civilization. The bulk of the output was devotional prose or verse, and the bulk of both the religious and secular works (including the inevitable almanacs) was directed towards the family, and especially the head of the family. This was a point of importance. In England the parish still engrossed most of the official religious effort, but in Wales the propaganda was directed to a much less artificial community, and one in which the head of the family (44 per cent of whose members were supposed in 1695 to be under sixteen) had a prospectively priestly position of great significance. In 1809 Jabez Bunting received a letter from the Durham coalfield describing how the Methodist revival there was bringing in new members '*per stirpes* and not merely *per capita*', and by 1730 it was possible to imagine a Welsh revival in which the same might be true; indeed, when revival came its first effect was to strengthen the centrifugal forces in Welsh life by adding public worship to the functions of the farm kitchen, and its second to contribute to the curious distribution of Welsh rural chapels: what appears now as a site of gaunt isolation was often the intersection of routes linking the farms and avoiding the nuclear village at the parish centre.

This propaganda deluge, loyally supported by the London Welsh, the principal beneficiaries of the Union, had mixed fortunes. It included plenty of anti-Catholic polemic, but was directed mainly against the magic, astrology and witchcraft which still made up much of the popular *mores*; there was little to choose here between the Establishment and the later evangelical Dissent. But where the one failed the other in a measure succeeded; this side of Welsh life was part of the past it sought to blot out. On the other hand, the quantity of religious verse now poured into the country corresponded to a genuine Welsh genre, which had its counterpart in Gaelic Scotland. The sneer of the Methodist Robert Jones of Rhoslan, that in Wales before the revival a religious verse or carol was reckoned to be the equal of a sermon, hit the nail on the head. The outcome was full of paradox. A sustained campaign to assimilate Wales to the English language, culture and religious establishment generated by way of reaction a religious revival which was Welsh, evangelical and dissenting, though as in England the largest organization it produced sprang from within the establishment, and hoped to hold its ground there.

What could and could not be accomplished by the old Dissent speaks volumes about the situation in Wales in the two generations before the revival. As a proportion of the total population, the Welsh Dissenters were not much below the strength of the English, but in absolute numbers they were very thin on the ground, and were hardly represented at all in north-east Wales, interestingly enough the very last area to feel the pressure of the revival. What they achieved was achieved mostly by gentleman preachers with private resources, and achieved mostly on the fringes of the country and in the main area of Dissenting strength in south and south-west Wales; it consisted chiefly of itinerant preaching, the gathering of new congregations on a sort of circuit system, and (like the New Divinity parishes in later New England) ministerial training. Thus Stephen Hughes, the 'apostle of Carmarthenshire' (1622–88), kept eight Independent churches under his own charge, but his great work was in training half a dozen or more significant preachers to follow him, and in encouraging his public to stick to the Welsh language. Henry Maurice, another indefatigable Independent in Brecknock, like some of his contemporaries in England, showed how the Puritan heritage was being adapted to the religious affections; he retained 'a wonderful skill in unravelling the very thoughts and inward workings of men's hearts, and was very particular and convincing as well as affectionate in his applications to the consciences of his hearers'. Philip Pugh (1679–1760), another Independent of Cilgwyn, gathered five churches in the region of the upper Aeron and Teifi and was credited with 1,000 hearers by 1715; but more than anyone he illustrates the limitations of the old Dissent, for he achieved maximum gearing to his effort by influence in the Established Church. If there was one preacher of the younger generation who harrowed his flock with the old Puritan jeremiad, it was Daniel Rowland (1713–90), curate of Llangeitho, who had been converted through the agency of Griffith Jones in 1735, and was only one stage removed from monoglot Welsh. Pugh's advice to Rowland was: 'Preach the gospel to the people, dear Sir, and apply the Balm of Gilead, the blood of Christ, to their spiritual wounds . . . If you go on preaching the law in this manner, you will kill half the people in the country, for you thunder out the curses of the law, and preach in such a terrific manner, that no one can stand before you.' This advice, given about 1737, transformed Rowland's preaching, and marks the real beginning of the Welsh revival.

Later in 1737 Rowland made the acquaintance of Howel Harris (1714–73) who had undergone much the same kind of conversion as himself, at about the same time, in 1735, and had begun to evangelize the neighbourhood of his Brecknock home. Refused ordination, Harris too was advised by Griffith Jones to cool his proceedings; and, overwrought curmudgeon as he could easily become, Harris for many years formed an effective partnership with Rowland and did his best not merely to keep the movement within the Church, but to secure the co-operation of the sympathetic English clergy, the Wesley brothers and Whitefield. Whitefield helped to supply organization in the Calvinistic Methodist Association, and a leadership which both Rowland and Harris could accept. But before long the Welsh Calvinistic Methodists cut their ties with their English brethren, and went their own way; the protest against assimilation was not to be denied. The doctrinal differences between Calvinist and Arminian divided the religious societies even more sharply than the evangelical leaders; so Wesley, who was prepared to preach and travel in Wales, but not to organize societies against those who invited him, was left with a tiny handful of exclusively English-speaking and anti-Calvinist societies. Rowland and Harris quickly secured the conversion of other lads like themselves – Howel Davies, William Williams of Pantycelyn, John Thomas – and by the time they split up in 1750 there were 433 religious societies in Wales and the borders. It was now left to Rowland to hold this flock together until a fresh tide of revival set in with the war crisis in 1762. There could now be a great harvest for the old

Dissenters as well, but the Calvinistic Methodists never lost their lead. The Welsh sees proved unable to absorb this movement any more than the English sees could in the end absorb either variety of English Methodism. The Calvinistic Methodists nevertheless retained the signs of their establishment origins: an allegiance to the Thirty-Nine Articles, men in holy orders at the helm, the enduring contempt of the more fastidious Dissenters for their 'eagerness of zeal, devoid of the light of knowledge, [producing] a fondness for crude, allegorical interpretations of the sacred Scriptures, which gained them, among the raw disciples whom they called out of the world, the reputation of wonderful men, at the cheap rate of a wild imagination, and a voluble tongue'.

In post-Revolution Scotland, despite the creation of a Presbyterian establishment ultimately guaranteed by the Act of Union, the problem of assimilation was oppressively and ubiquitously felt. In the Highlands the Kirk had to get Episcopalians out of the parishes, and, long before the Jacobite clan chiefs had expended their power in a series of vain rebellions, the Kirk understood its business to be to break the hold of Gaelic culture, the notions of chivalry which propped up the chiefs, and the mass of what they took to be primitive superstition which constituted the Highland religion. If the English Bible was good enough for the Lowlands, they did not doubt that it was good enough for the Highlands. But if assimilation and modernization were the Kirk's recipe for the Highlands, both the Kirk and the parties within it were very suspicious of both when applied to themselves. The General Assembly deplored the Toleration Act put through in 1712 by a London government known to have backstairs relations with the Jacobites; the oaths required under it harrowed ministers who had to take them, and still more congregations who did not. Worse in the longer run was the Patronage Act of the same year. This restored to ancient patrons – non-jurors and Roman Catholics alone excepted –the presentation to parishes. There had been a long history of patronage in Scotland before 1690, but then in practice the people elected their ministers without much dispute, and for a long time after the Act of 1712 most parishes were filled up by presbyteries. There was a deep-rooted feeling, relentlessly fanned by men of Cameronian heritage, that the Patronage Act was contrary to the spirit of the Reformed Church, and there was no disputing the facts that the new Act was the work of the United Kingdom Parliament, and that the active exercise of patronage rights to which it eventually led was part of the process by which British governments mobilized interest in their own support. Every approach to this problem was beset with difficulties. The doctrinaires were avid to take popular election and the Crown rights of the Redeemer under their sole protection, regarding the Moderates as the Trojan horse of English, even

Arminian, influence; the Moderates fairly replied that to contest the Patronage Act was to contest the civil constitution, and to put a weapon in the hands of the Jacobites. The Kirk was tugged both ways. By the mid-century the Moderates had built up a dominance in the General Assembly which was to last over a generation; but a dismal series of secessions had set in which enabled the sponsors of the Overture on Schism at the General Assembly of 1766 to claim that there were now 120 meeting houses in Scotland attended by over 100,000 people. It looked as though in Scotland, as in the continental churches covered by the Westphalia settlements, to rely on the arm of flesh was a recipe for the blues. New strategies were called for. Among these was religious revival, and it was characteristic of Scotland that this took different shapes in the Highlands, where it first began and where there was least dispute about ends or means, and in the Lowlands, where these disputes were hottest.

The problem of the Kirk in the Highlands was similar to that of the Church establishment in Wales, but more acute. For the problems of a primitive society whose separateness was underpinned by a language with little prose literature were compounded by the facts that at first many parishes were in the hands of Episcopalians, that the allegiance of the upper classes was Episcopalian where it was not Roman Catholic, and that these confessional differences were an element in persistent rebellion. Jacobitism threatened not only the constitutional position of the Kirk but the international confessional balance generally. The work of the Kirk was independent of, but no less important than, the economic developments which were transforming Highland life, for better or worse, at another level; but to an average Highlander the Kirk must have appeared an ally of the Whigs. Newly inducted Presbyterian clergy were often rabbled like the later Methodists south of the border. In the lands lately dominated by the Seaforth family, it was 1730 before Presbyterian ministers could gain access. But at least the enemy was clear to all, the Kirk fought hard to get its machine in place, and it had no trouble in the Highlands with Presbyterian Dissent. By establishing Sabbath discipline it created a public benchmark distinguishing the loyal from the disloyal, and by using preaching, in the north German Reformed manner, to address the regenerate and the unregenerate separately, it created another of potentially great importance. The General Assembly treated the area north of the Tay as a mission area, catechists reinforced the efforts of the ministers on one side, and, on the other, the schools, ineffective as they were, created a class of children, indispensable to Highland worship in an age when even ministers were not literate in Gaelic, who could give current translation from the English Bible into spoken Gaelic.

This artificial exercise shows how urgent was the need to find some other method of penetrating Gaelic society from the inside. Not surprisingly this was developed in that part of the Highlands with memories of a covenanting tradition and of recruiting for the Protestant crusades of Gustavus Adolphus, Sutherland and Easter Ross. It was in Ross-shire, too, that the bitterest post-Revolution struggles between Episcopacy and Presbyterianism took place. In Sutherland, the clan MacKay was headed by General Hugh MacKay whose piety was of the Dutch evangelical type. In 1724 the Presbytery of Tain appointed meetings for prayer and fasting in three of their parishes, and, at the same time, the people of Nigg, led by the 'elders and serious people', did the same. The Nigg meetings multiplied over the next fifteen years in both numbers and intensity. Above all, in 1730, John Balfour became minister of the parish and began systematically to develop the eldership. He formed a fellowship meeting of his elders and a few others. This fellowship not only gave an impulse to all the other meetings, but provided an invaluable training ground for the elders, the characters who became known as 'the Men', in prayer, Scripture exposition and experimental religion. The fellowships, moreover, developed public functions, and on the Fridays of Communion seasons, when people had flocked in from all parts and all parishes, fellowship meetings were held at which 'the Men' resolved cases of conscience, and determined who might communicate and who might not. This situation was clearly open to abuse, and in 1737 the Synod of Caithness and Sutherland attempted to suppress it, only to be required by the General Assembly, after a 21-year conflict, to give way.

'The Men' had won a resounding victory over the clergy. But they had also provided an indispensable means of planting Presbyterianism within the Gaelic community and sustaining its distinguishing features: the Sabbath, family worship and the like. Balfour created the whole apparatus of additional instruction and devotion which Spener recommended (on the whole unsuccessfully) against Lutheran decline, and found (as the Protestant minorities of the Habsburg lands found, when for lack of a church system they employed them not as a supplement to, but as the substance of their corporate religious life) that they issued in a deep and genuine religious revival. This had the usual contagion effect and from 1739 onwards was affecting a whole series of neighbouring parishes. Moreover, the revival among the Ross-shire 'Fathers' provided the power and set the standard for the evangelical conquest of the Highlands as nothing else could have done. The Highlands of Scotland were won for the Kirk as the Highlands of Wales were lost to the Church. While the battle for supremacy was on, the pioneers of revival were not parochial in their views. They saw to the appointment of David Brainerd as missionary to the Red Indians, and had an impact on revival in the Netherlands. And though in many respects resembling the revival in New England and in the Lowlands at Cambuslang, their work differed in two important respects. There is no evidence of the psychological abnormalities generated in the other places; and, still more important, the revival in north-east Scotland was not a convulsive and short-lived affair, but, like the English revival, a gradual work which lasted well into the next century. It had two other peculiar characteristics. It was in the main managed by the ministry, though 'the Men' early served notice of how damaging their truculence might become in the nineteenth century. The ministry also imparted a distinguishing feature to the piety of 'the Men' and, after them, the flock. The best of them had New Testament Greek and a substantial body of Reformed divinity at their elbow from Switzerland, the Netherlands and Puritan England; in 1729 the Presbytery of Gairloch resolved to discuss the main heads of doctrine in Latin. In most parts of the Protestant world revival offered some release and relief from the niceties of confessional orthodoxy, but in the Highlands it helped to root them in a popular milieu. In 1717 the Presbytery of Tain could initiate proceedings against the modernizing Professor Simson of Glasgow, and in due course 'the Men' kept their scruples alive in the flock long after the ministry had moved on to something else.

In the eighteenth century the Highlands accounted for one-third of the population of Scotland, but even then the destinies of nation and Church were decided in the Lowlands. Here revival took another shape, and almost more than one. In the Lowlands the patronage question became entangled with others arising from changing currents of thought and feeling. Early in the eighteenth century Thomas Boston of Ettrick rediscovered an old book, Edward Fisher's *Marrow of Modern Divinity*, first published in London in 1646. It soon caught on with a number of Scots clergy seeking to improve their religious experience, and was republished with a preface by James Hog of Carnock in 1718. The attraction of the *Marrow* was that it admitted a tenderer kind of piety than had been in vogue, and took seriously the missionary vocation of the Church and offers of grace. But Hog and three of his colleagues were examined by a commission of the Assembly, and in 1720 the book was savagely condemned as heretical by the Assembly itself. If the proto-rationalists exemplified by Professor Simson had been laxly handled, the proto-evangelicals whose banner was the *Marrow* received very rough treatment. It was not therefore very surprising that the *Marrow* men found support in congregations which missed the fire-eating of the past and detested patronage, nor that the man who led the defence of the *Marrow* in the Assembly, Ebenezer Erskine, clashed with that body at the end of 1732 on the question of patronage without any intention of compromise. In the following year he seceded, with Ralph Erskine and Thomas Mair, to form the Associate Presbytery.

The Assembly now trod cautiously, but the Seceders had little inducement to return, for they found a highly satisfactory response to their proselytizing. Everywhere in the west of Scotland they were welcomed, and welcomed especially by members of the Praying Societies. These Praying Societies went back to the first great revival in Scottish history which took place at the Communion season at Kirk o' Shotts in 1630. They had since been transplanted to America, and one of the spiritual second generation of Kirk o' Shotts had been with Jonathan Edwards in the New England revival of 1734, the news of which was now having its impact upon Scotland. The Praying Societies, often composed of people discontented with their ministers and the patronage by which they were appointed, welcomed the Seceders and formed the core of their new congregations. The experience of growth convinced the Associate Presbytery that they were in the company of those promoting renewal or revival in Germany, England, Ireland and America, and, when Whitefield came back from his triumphant American tour in 1741, Ralph Erskine invited him to evangelize in Scotland in their company. How deceptive appearances were, was revealed in the event. Whitefield arrived in Leith in July 1741; almost at once the Seceders broke with him, and denounced him as 'a wild enthusiast . . . engaged in doing the work of Satan'. The Seceders, it appears, tried to tie him to a strict Presbyterianism and to maintain that they alone were the Lord's people. On the first point there were limits to what could be expected from Whitefield, who was in Anglican orders; on the second, he had made no secret in his correspondence with Ralph Erskine that he wished to promote revival in every denomination. The result was that Whitefield preached to others, and was not alone in discovering possibilities of revival in the Established Church. Another chain of events produced a replica of Kirk o' Shotts at Cambuslang, and the Praying Societies were shown to be capable of operating in more ways than one. The Associate Presbytery, on the other hand, turned away from converting sinners from the world to hunting out the true saints in the country, from revival to secession. But it had been a close call, as their relations with Whitefield showed.

Cambuslang was a parish which encapsulated many of the problems of the Scots establishment as a whole, being challenged to pull itself together before the insidious threats of rationalism, upper-crust patronage and schism. After the Toleration Act, the minister of the parish, Archibald Hamilton, refused to take the oaths and the Perthshire itinerant catechist Addison passed through it, rousing the restless Covenanting element with sermons on the blind man who came to Christ and cast away his garments.

He 'began with the garment of the Union, that of the Patronages, that of the Toleration, that of the Oath of Abjuration'. This produced a 'Protest and Testimony' to the kirk session from Hugh Cumin, inveighing against 'all defections contrary to the Word of God and our Covenant engagements'. Addison eventually turned Independent, but as late as 1739 Cumin was a trouble-making elder in the parish. Archibald Hamilton died in 1723, and it took the patron, the Duke of Hamilton, a long time to replace him. By the time he presented Thomas Findlater, the Praying Societies had had ample opportunity to get up opposition, and at one point troops were called in to keep the peace. In 1731 Findlater left for another parish, pursued by unproven charges of misconduct. The Duke now presented the kind of minister the parishioners wanted in William McCulloch, forty years old, but receiving his first parish. McCulloch was bred in Galloway of a strong Covenanting tradition, the spirit of which was now his worst problem. In 1739 Cumin got up a faction in the kirk session against an apparently blameless elder, which made it impossible for him to exercise his Communion functions, and took another stand on the Covenant. This came just two months after the Seceders of the Associate Presbytery had been condemned by the Assembly; and Seceders were what Cumin's party became. Most members of the kirk session were suspended.

McCulloch was one of those much moved by the news of the revival in New England; he read accounts of it to his congregation and preached on conversion and the experience of regeneration, an experience no parish needed more than Cambuslang. He was more than informed about the revival in America. In December 1741 a Whitefieldite newspaper reporting the revival on both sides of the Atlantic was begun in Glasgow; it was Scotland's first religious periodical, *The Weekly History*, and McCulloch was its editor. This journal provided a model for the *Christian Monthly History*, begun by James Robe in 1743, and for John Gillies' *Historical Collections Relating to the Success of the Gospel*, in which ministers of the Kirk took up a central position in the international dissemination of information about the revival. The first impact of the journal, however, was on the parish of Cambuslang. Ninety heads of families asked McCulloch to hold a weekly weeknight lecture. At the third of these meetings there were strange spiritual signs, and fifty people came for counsel. McCulloch preached daily, the crowds flocked in, and the following June the greatest awakener of them all, Whitefield, now reviled by the Seceders, arrived to try his hand at the moment of destiny in Cambuslang. Whitefield's influence had, however, preceded him in the parish. When McCulloch began to collect information from converts in the summer of 1742 he found that many had been present at Whitefield's Glasgow services and had been impressed by his preaching of the New

Birth. But the scenes after his arrival had no parallel in Scottish history. He began by preaching to 20,000 the day before Communion. The sacrament was perforce celebrated in the fields, rousing nostalgic memories of the days of persecution. 'People', he noted, 'sat unwearied till two in the morning to hear sermons . . .' and, he remarked, in self-conscious emulation of the Saviour in Luke 12: 1, 'you could scarce walk a yard, but you must tread upon some.' The one sensation generated another; the kirk session decided to hold another Communion the following month, and this time 30,000 people turned up while Whitefield and other evangelical ministers preached in turn, 3,000 receiving Communion in tents. There were reminiscences of the French Prophets – bodily agonies, faintings and cries – which were uncommon in the ministry of Whitefield, and the young John Erskine, later the famous minister of the Old Greyfriars Church, Edinburgh, splashed *The High probability that the present appearances in New England and the West of Scotland are a prelude of the Glorious Things promised to the church in the latter Ages* across the title of a pamphlet.

Massachusetts and Scotland were equally avid for news. Events in Cambuslang had by contagion an important effect upon all the parishes within a dozen miles, and by the transmission of news and movement of preachers, at a distance also, most notably in James Robe's parish at Kilsyth. Kilsyth in its turn influenced other local parishes, and Muthill in southern Perthshire, where the trouble had been not Cameronianism, but violent Episcopalianism. Contact was made with the north-east. John Sutherland, minister of Golspie, visited Cambuslang, Kilsyth and Muthill in 1743, and the news he brought back stimulated revival in his own parish. Careful recording by McCulloch and Robe made it plain that those who actually professed conversion held their ground. Hostile criticism helped. The Associate Presbytery could hardly have incited revival more wantonly than in its fast day statement that

it is no wonder that the Lord in his righteous displeasure, left this church and land to give such an open discovery of their apostacy from Him, in the fond reception that Mr George Whitefield has met with, notwithstanding it is notoriously known that he is a priest of the Church of England, who hath sworn the oath of supremacy, and abjured the Solemn League and Covenant, and endeavours by his lax toleration principles to pull down the hedges of government and discipline which the Lord has planted about His vineyard in this land.

Events in Scotland had their effect in England. William Darney, an eccentric convert at Kilsyth, played a notable roving part in the

Lancashire–Yorkshire border country, was instrumental in the conversion of Grimshaw of Haworth, and embarrassed the Wesleys by, among other things, perhaps the worst religious verse ever produced. On the institutional level the work of the Praying Societies was formalized by agreements between Jonathan Edwards and the Scots evangelicals into the Concert of Prayer for the revival of religion and the extension of God's kingdom upon earth. This system caught on in England, especially in the south midland country of evangelical Dissent, and was developed into regular prayer for overseas missions. Out of this movement sprang, among other things, the Baptist Missionary Society, and a reverse impulse into Scotland in the 1790s when foreign missions became one of the causes round which party organization polarized.

Yet in Scotland the convulsive excitements of the summer of 1742 were not the prelude to the glories of the last days. Even in Cambuslang the church was able to hold the congregation by November. The Evangelical party remained a minority in the Church, and secessions continued. The patronage question was still painfully divisive, and the next vacancies in the parishes of Cambuslang, Kilsyth and Nigg alike were the signal for dreadful conflicts. Without the elemental simplicities of the struggle in the Highlands, the Lowland Church could neither sublimate its policy differences in revival nor even sustain revival itself. And a revival movement which had been a valuable check to secession forfeited at the outset the liberty to develop its own impulse which secession might have given. Like the revival in New England to which it was so closely linked, the revival in the Lowlands bloomed for a day. And in so far as the Lowland revival succeeded in a milieu distracted by the results of perceived assimilation, it integrated Scotland into a wider unity, not of confessional solidarity, but of unconfessional and international revival. On this point the Associate Presbytery spoke more truly than they knew.

If Scotland could produce more than one kind of revival, it was certain that England could do likewise, and these differences underlie the apparently opposed explanations which have been suggested for its outbreak. One view is that the heartland of the Church of England was in the south-east of the country, that its influence spread outwards from there and never effectively reached the fringes in the west and north. On this basis the Methodist movement was another version of the great Anglican effort in Wales, another attempt to make good age-old weaknesses, and it was the sudden shock of a full-blooded Christian appeal upon the systems of men not inoculated against it by small doses that produced the abnormal psychic phenomena which accompanied Wesley's early preaching. This view helps to explain why revival began inside the establishment, and why Methodism struck deep roots in many (though not all) of the fringes of the country and among many (though not all) of what have become known as the 'marginal' classes. The other line of explanation follows a totally opposed argument. It points out that in the west and south midlands, the Puritan movement of the previous century had left behind bodies of Dissenters strong enough numerically to be cushioned against the threats of imminent demise which vexed the history of small Quaker and Dissenting meetings; that their open geographical situation guaranteed exposure to new ideas; and that new ideas ensured that the conservatives who threw up barriers against change would not triumph in the movement, and would in the end make room for the allied forces of religious revival and missionary enterprise which before the end of the century transformed the whole milieu. (This perspective has some bearing even upon Methodism; for both friend and foe, high and low, were very apt to construe the enthusiastic preaching of the New Birth in the light of Puritan models. English High Churchmanship left no such standard in the public mind.) Both views underestimate the widespread sympathy in England, constantly refreshed by the newspapers, with the Protestant cause in Europe, and the influence this had on people's reading of the situation at home.

By 1730 plenty of Englishmen knew that the day of the confessional state was in fact past, that many of the established Protestant churches abroad could not solve their problems, and that the affairs of the Protestant minorities in Salzburg, the Habsburg lands, Poland and Lorraine were approaching a crisis. The High Church party under Queen Anne had venomously advocated a policy of going it alone, only to find that the Church, energetically reconstructed with gentry backing during the Restoration, could, in Hanoverian England, no longer raise that essential support for Church mobs of the old lethal kind, for planting out the Church (as in the 1740s even Lutheranism was planted out) in the American colonies, nor yet, in the north-west, raise enough in church rates to keep church towers upright. Toleration was followed by a public surge of Dissent, and left canon law awkwardly out of phase with the statutory law of the land. The possible policies to mend this unhappy state of affairs were not more than four, and all were familiar from continental experience.

The first was to seek a vigorous cultural impulse by relying on the pure streams of modern knowledge, and, in particular, on reason as understood by Newton and Locke. In the generation which followed the Revolution all parties had naïvely appealed to rational criteria, and had encountered fearful embarrassments in relation to the doctrine of the Trinity. Moreover, lurking under the stone of reason were some strange little creatures which boded no good in politics or religion. The second policy, much associated with Archbishop Wake, but canvassed by the SPCK from its early years, was that of international Protestant union. The SPCK had corresponded with the rational orthodox of Switzerland who had aspired to soften the high orthodoxy of the Formula Consensus and to find common ground not only between the confessions, but also between religion and a culture dominated by French names. To Wake, Protestant union offered a way of shoring up the Protestant succession in Britain and a means of strengthening a Church which had failed to achieve comprehension; and, still more, it embodied a Latitudinarian principle and a means of escape from damaging controversy which on religious grounds it would be foolish to forgo. But Protestant union required action by princes; by the mid-1720s the princes knew that the great Catholic forward move which had brought the Empire to the brink of confessional war in 1719 was over. Within a few years Emperor Charles VI was buying Protestant support for the Pragmatic Sanction, and Wake's policies were clearly dated.

There were, thirdly, the policies associated with Bishop Gibson. Gibson's premiss was that the Church had no option but to act with the Whig party as the only reliable defenders of the Protestant succession, and organize clerical patronage to create a party for them in the Church. The Church, too, needed a new broom; non-residence should be restricted or abolished, discipline tightened up, canons revised. But these policies also required the sympathy of a government able to give parliamentary assistance; in 1736 Gibson bitterly concluded that Walpole lacked that reciprocal sympathy, there was a breach between them, and in the following year, when Wake's successor at Canterbury was chosen, Gibson was passed over. Of all the policy failures of the early eighteenth century, Gibson's was the most public, and it came at a very telling time. For behind all the factious and factitious confrontations of Walpole and the opposition, there was a deep and genuine revulsion against what he had done with English politics – a revulsion which powerfully reinforced a conclusion that the clergy should have drawn long since, but had been pathetically unwilling to contemplate. If, despite fresh pressure from the bishops on the parish clergy, the Church as a machine was not equal to what was required of it, the State, from an ecclesiastical point of view, was a lost cause. If salvation there was to be, it must be the fruit of private enterprise, the fourth policy to which we turn.

There was indeed a history of private action to draw upon. In Restoration England the sensitive had been aware of the uncomfortable contrast between the Church's claim to have realized primitive Christianity and the realities of the national life. In 1678 a religious society was created in London to do something about this, on the initiative, incongruously enough, of Anthony Horneck, the minister of the German congregation in the Savoy. One has the feeling that this owed something to fears for the

Protestant succession and to the prospective need to keep Protestantism alive in a very adverse climate. In the next generation these societies spread in considerable numbers in London and the provinces, and many of their members reappeared in the Societies for the Reformation of Manners which began on a big scale after the Glorious Revolution, seeking to enforce the laws relating to the collective regulation of morality in a way now clearly beyond the Church courts. The working ideal of these societies, including the most famous, the Society for the Propagation of the Gospel (SPG) and SPCK, was again the recovery of primitive Christianity. Not much is known about the history of these societies in early Hanoverian England. But by the 1730s it was clear that the gap between their aspirations and their achievements was enormous, that they imposed a heavy burden on conscience and that their frame of mind was dated. The primitive Church had certainly been pre-Newtonian, the doctrine of the Trinity had become a matter for *Angst*, and Bishop Hoadly had exposed the Achilles heel of Church authority.

Perhaps the last important representative of the piety of the societies was John Wesley, 'Mr Primitive Christianity' as he was known. When he, fresh from a bizarre attempt to impose that ideal upon hard-pressed Georgia settlers who wanted a familiar *Kulturprotestantismus*, underwent conversion in 1738, he shed the burdensome part of his inheritance in favour of the New Birth, and freed his hand to develop new techniques of societal piety. In one sense the English revival, prepared by laborious but unsuccessful efforts by the establishment to make up for lost time, can be regarded as an attempt to achieve the survival of Christianity and the salvation of the common man by applying private enterprise to a new field. It was most likely to be undertaken by someone within the establishment who had a residual sense of responsibility for the welfare of the nation as a whole, and who recognized that all else had failed. And that recognition was easiest in the milieu of the opposition to Walpole. It was not for nothing that the Holy Club had been gathered in the University of Oxford, the centre of diehard ideological opposition to the Court, that Wesley had toyed with the idea of securing the succession to his father's parish by the interest of Lord Bolingbroke, that Pulteney dabbled with Whitefield and the Countess of Huntingdon, and that the Methodist movement, beginning from bases in London, Bristol and Newcastle where anti-Court sentiments were strong, should entrench itself most deeply in the fringes of the country. Like Württemberger Pietism (on the work of whose hero, Bengel, Wesley based his *Notes on the New Testament*) it was part of the syndrome of 'country' politics.

The Wesley of these years took into himself not merely his parents' Dissenting past, but much of the current crisis in the Protestant world.

Converted (in the meeting of a religious society) 'where one was reading Luther's preface to the *Epistle to the Romans*', as was now very nearly obligatory in the pietist world, he had made contact with Salzburger refugees in Georgia, with Moravians on the way out, in London, and then on a visit to Herrnhut itself, and his most striking conquests in Ireland were among the Palatines who in due course carried the Methodist message to the American colonies. The varied sources of his inspiration, and the very varied contexts into which Methodism found its way, are crucial to the understanding of the man and his movement; for they intensified as nothing else could have done the empiricism which he absorbed from the Enlightenment. Single-model accounts of Methodism – such as that constructed in authoritarian terms by Jonathan Clark in his *English Society 1688–1832* (1985) – ignore the breadth of its origins and the breadth of the problems it encountered. In England Wesley at least professed to have a mission to the poor, even 'the outcasts of men'. But in Scotland he looked to work with the Kirk and was a darling with a section of the aristocracy. In Ireland he worked downwards and outwards from the Protestant gentry class and the garrison to a degree which would have been unthinkable in England, yet the wider story of even Irish Methodism hardly fits Clark's model. Like other men of country sympathies, Wesley, while sympathetic to the lot of the American colonists, was jolted sharply to the right by the outbreak of actual rebellion, his denunciation of which was enormously profitable to him in England, and did more than anything to establish him as the popular public institution he became in his later years. By the same token, however, he was in difficulties in both America and Ireland. The tradition in the connexional management was that he had almost wrecked nascent American Methodism; certainly after independence the American Methodists proved entirely dissatisfied with the limited ecclesiastical self-government he had in mind for them, and even left his name out of their Conference minutes. Moreover, underlying the breakneck expansion of American Methodism was the fact that the English in America were an ethnic group as much as any other, and Methodism offered them a way of affirming their Englishness without being Anglican, the last thing Clark's model permits. In Ireland Wesley had set himself against the Catholic community, and the vivid Irish response to the destruction of the American part of the old colonial system set him against all those Anglican and Presbyterian forces which wished to use the war crisis to reduce the disadvantages of colonial status. Before Wesley's death the situation could be foreseen in which, in southern Ireland, Methodism would retain little but its urban redoubts in Cork, Bandon and Dublin, and its powerful strongholds among the unassimilated foreign, and especially German, minorities. It was, paradoxically, these (who had caught in the Wesleyan preaching the whiff, not of English divine right, but of Luther) who conformed most nearly to Clark's model. Barbara Heck took Methodism to America and, when the crisis came, became a United Empire Loyalist, emigrating to Upper Canada. In the war of 1812 Methodists shed each others' blood along the Canadian frontier. But as soon as the war was over, the Canadian offspring of the Loyalists reintegrated themselves into the American Methodist Episcopal Church, notwithstanding that 'the government of the Methodist Episcopal Church was American and therefore un-English, if not anti-English'. What enabled Wesley's followers to pick their way through minefields of this complexity was a large share of the empiricism Wesley himself had perforce shown; the ability to recognize 'our' doctrines, i.e. doctrines which Methodists did not create but found profitable, to produce forms of discipline and administration which met a need, unimpeded by a sense that past models were normative, to think in terms of policy.

English Dissent was not immune from the international tremors we have noted. Whig Dissenters had long been alive to the need to sustain the Protestant interest in Europe; no less a man that Philip Doddridge was the grandson of an émigré Czech Protestant, and used willingness (or unwillingness) to support the Reformed congregation in Breslau as a touchstone to assess the bishops. But Dissent had several handicaps in entering the world of revival. Its constituency was small; few Englishmen had ever cherished the scruples which sent the Dissenters into the wilderness, and, despite the multiplication of chapels, their numbers probably diminished throughout the first half of the eighteenth century. Still more inhibiting were the habits of mind bred by Dissenting discipline; in the interests of the 'pure' church, Dissenters had sought to keep people out rather than to welcome them in. Moreover, the initially largest group of Dissenters, the Presbyterians, retained a paradoxical commitment to comprehension, and spent much of the century seeking to broaden the basis of subscription to the Toleration Act. This led them into important intellectual issues and to views of Church growth diametrically opposed to those of the revivalists. While Presbyterians of this kind moved steadily towards Unitarianism, there were always others attracted to High Calvinism by its system; they so went overboard in the cause of sovereign grace as to leave no room for human co-operation. Baxter had sought to keep up a middle way between what in seventeenth-century terms was called Arminianism on the one hand and Antinomianism on the other. But the internal mechanics of survival made it difficult for even Baxterian Dissenters to maintain this fine balance in the Restoration period.

The temperature may be tested by a generational inquiry. Philip Henry (1631–96), one of the ejected ministers of 1662, possessed many of the characteristics which Pietists and evangelicals came to prize in the Puritan literature. As a young man 'he had often sweet meltings of the soul in prayer, and confession of sin . . . and many warm and lively truths came home to his heart'. But his view of faith was more that of assent than that of the New Birth and, though he preached a good deal by invitation, he regarded himself so much as an auxiliary to the parish ministry that he would never serve as a pastor to a Dissenting congregation. Where his son Matthew Henry (1662–1714) stood is shown by his heavy dependence on Baxter, and by the continuing authority of his Bible commentary among those who came to regard themselves as Evangelicals, i.e. occupying the Baxterian middle way. Yet Matthew Henry was not quite as Baxter was, nor yet as his own father was, if only because the going for true religion was now much harder. He found the heathenism of villages round Chester at the turn of the century so oppressive that he established an itinerant evangelistic ministry there. 'The vehemency of his affections both in prayer and preaching was such as, occasionally at least, to transport not himself only, but his auditory, to tears,' and he was solemnly warned to go steady with small beer and sack when 'warmed with preaching'. He lacked his father's deference to public authority – 'He would call no man *master* . . . He regarded implicit obedience to human dictates . . . as in direct hostility to the claims both of revelation and reason.' This was a response to a pastoral situation rather than an accommodation to Enlightenment, but his Augustan style partook 'largely of the improvement of the times' and 'triumphed over the forced conceit and deformities' of his predecessors. In the next generation Matthew Henry's mantle was inherited by Philip Doddridge. Here the element of Enlightenment and of deliberately seeking to get behind denominational difference was much larger; and, as an enthusiast for foreign missions, Doddridge had lost altogether the old oppressive sense of the imminence of the end of the age. Yet the Doddridge who preached on regeneration, whose works were translated into all the great European languages for the use of Pietists, belongs also to the prehistory of revival. Of him it might be said, as Isaac Watts said of Jonathan Edwards, that he stuck to the Baxterian middle way, 'the common plain protestant doctrine of the Reformation'; and it was out of Doddridge's open south midland nonconformity that Dissenting evangelism, at home and abroad, arose – not to mention undenominational 'catholic Christianity' to which that movement gave birth. Of course the process was a painful one. When Presbyterians became hooked on reason, hyper-Calvinists raised their barriers, and often retreated into Independency. When Independents showed a propensity to follow Doddridge, the barriers went up again, and many retreated to a Baptist profession. When Fullerism, 'moderate Calvinism', found its way among the Baptists, they in turn suffered losses to newly formed Strict Baptist churches. But by the end of the eighteenth century, when the social barriers impeding the Dissenters were much less severe, their numbers had increased out of all proportion to anything which might have been anticipated in the age of Walpole, and the balance among them changed out of recognition. The old princes of Dissent, the Presbyterians and Quakers, had been pushed to the fringe, the Independent and Baptist denominations had been broken and reconstructed in a very different shape, and the old Puritan belief that conversion was the work of the Holy Spirit, while sanctification was the work of the Church, had metamorphosed into a working assumption that conversion was the work of the Church while sanctification was a matter of the Holy Spirit or of chance. The worst fears of the Hypers, now tucked away in Strict Baptist Zions, were confirmed.

The Hypers might be without policy, but their scruples were an index of important changes. The revival had purchased a new lease of life for Reformed denominations at the expense of their Calvinism. The moderate Calvinists could show that the doctrine of the Hypers was not that of Calvin himself, but they could not alter the fact that in the bumper years of the revival, when the harvest was limited only by the number of reapers, it was hard to envisage the process in terms of a limited atonement. Particularly hard for the Hypers was the fact that that the doctrine which went with a swing in the revival was salvation by the blood of Christ, and an unsung process of backing favourites in the Trinity began which has continued to the present day. Similarly with the symbolic aspects of Church life. Wesley could regard the Eucharist (and even baptism) as a converting ordinance, because in the eighteenth century it so frequently was a converting ordinance. But to the devotees of the missionary Church, bent on the business of conversion, ordinances which did not convert (as by the end of the eighteenth century they mostly did not) were a matter of diminishing interest. There was the same problem with history and the Church. The Hypers understood history through the symbols of the book of Revelation; the revivalists were empiricists who collected archives. In the early eighteenth century the Church itself had been a symbol, episcopalianism symbolizing one view of the Church's essence, the Dissenting meeting where the saints gathered out of the parish to meet their God symbolizing another. But the missionary Church was a purposive organization, a 'rational' one in Weberian terms, and the geopolitical approach which characterized Carey's plan for a Baptist missionary society (or indeed the connexionalism which was the new development in all the churches) turned on analysing the purpose to be achieved and contriving an organization which would bring to bear the manpower and other resources necessary to achieve it. The churches assumed their modern shape of vast and rambling machines, capable of being assessed in terms of their efficiency for their policy objectives, but not reasonably to be discussed in terms of symbols (notwithstanding the vigour of contemporary attempts so to do). This in turn set a theological problem. For those who most beat the drum about the total depravity of mankind and the all-sufficiency of grace were now the most committed to hectic programmes of works and to the construction of rational organizations for their accomplishment. Works-righteousness might in the jargon of that day be filthy rags, but that is what the religious community was being adapted and devoted to. In this respect the Great Awakening bequeathed a problem in theology and pastoral psychology which is still with us.

Plate 3   Caledonia Road Church, Glasgow (architect Alexander Thomson, 1956;
photograph Thomas Annan, c.1860)
Reproduced courtesy of Dr Gavin Stamp.

PART III
Industrialization, Empire and Identity

14

Church and State since 1800

Edward Norman

DESPITE SOME residual traces of the old relationship of religion and
government in England, the last century and a half has in practice
seen their effective separation. In Ireland and in Wales there have been, in
this period, formal disestablishments; in England itself, as in Scotland, the
remaining establishments of religion are highly anomalous. The theory and
practice of the constitution, viewed from each end of the time-scale,
disclose an extraordinary transformation, remarkable in one perspective
for the peculiar elasticity that has allowed the persistence of legal forms
within a collapsed framework, and in another for the practicality of the way
in which patently outmoded arrangements have been accommodated to
change in political management.

In 1800 the State was confessional: the United Church of England and
Ireland, just consolidated by the Act of Union between the two countries,
and the Presbyterian Establishment in Scotland, were accorded exclusive
endorsement as the spiritual and theological basis in the ordering of
society. Political groups saw it as their highest duty to maintain the union
of throne and altar. The Church established by law was, at least in
England, effectively governed by Parliament as a kind of lay assembly, and
had been ever since the suspension of the Convocations in 1717. As the
'bulwark of the Reformation' the Church was regarded, both popularly and
by ruling opinion, as the repository of Protestant virtue, the guarantor of
order and morality, and – a strange notion to modern understanding – as
the guardian of political liberty. This last role derived from the enduring
conviction that Roman Catholicism was inherently hostile to free
institutions and demanded of its adherents a 'dual allegiance', to the Pope
as well as to the sovereign. It was a conviction which, far from diminishing,
actually grew in the nineteenth century as anti-Catholic fervour was
reinforced by reaction to the Syllabus of Errors, by Protestant endorsement
of the *Risorgimento*, by the *Kulturkampf*, by the Vatican Council and by the
proto-Weberian supposition, fed by an examination of what were thought
to be the facts of Irish life, that Catholicism was detrimental to material

progress. In 1900, however, it was a very different landscape of state policy which lay before the observer. Governments by then acted as a sort of neutral arbiter between the various Christian denominations, and non-Christian belief, too, had been formally admitted to the evolving scheme. The Religious Disabilities Removals Act of 1891 removed the requirement of any kind of religious subscription from those who sat in Parliament. It was a concluding stage in the century-long process of piecemeal and practical dismantling of the old confessional state, and what was born out of it was considerably less coherent and therefore awkward to categorize: it was the liberal, modern, collectivist state, recognized in its liability to treat society as a religious pluralism, with each of the components legitimately able to seek the protection of government but with none entitled to special privilege.

Yet the Church establishments in England and Scotland were still clearly possessed of a number of formal advantages at law. In scale and political significance, however, these survivals were a poor remnant – an anomaly within the practice of the constitution which even the more militant of militant Free Churchmen began to tire of assailing. Eventually restricted virtually to the question of education, the old clash of Church and Dissent, which had accompanied the relative separation of Church and State in the Victorian era, and had on so many occasions provided the actual levers of destabilization, began to move to the periphery of religious as well as of secular public concern. Unlike the experience of most parts of the Christian world – and especially the experience of Europe and Latin America – the separation occurred in Britain without cataclysmic upheaval, and without a party victory for the enemies of religion. For the separation was not the result of increasing realization of secular orientations of life and thought, nor of the obvious decline in support for organized religion. 'The dominant force in favour of disestablishment is a religious force,' the Liberation Society, the agency of militant Dissent, correctly pointed out in 1884; 'it may be safely assumed, therefore, that in putting an end to the political ascendancy of a particular Church, care will be taken, possibly at the expense of some logical consistency, to do nothing that will be prejudicial to the religious interests of the nation.' That is as good a summary of the nineteenth-century transformation as it is possible to get.

At the start of the nineteenth century the Church of England had assumed a settled relationship with the State. There were good reasons why this should be so. The practical utility of the union of throne and altar had just been demonstrated in reaction to the ideals of the French Revolution; Protestant Dissent appeared to have declined as a possible threat to the State; and concessions to Catholics were already being made as an indication that they, too, had established their pedigree of good citizenship. The repeal of the Test Act and Corporation Acts in 1828, and Catholic emancipation in 1829, seemed to many in public life to be the laying of old ghosts – not, as they in reality turned out to be, the beginnings of a constitutional upheaval. The suddenness and sharpness of the ensuing assault upon the Church of England's position by the Protestant Dissenters took churchmen by surprise. How did it happen?

Dissent was not a very formidable force in the 1830s, the crucial decade in the transformation of the constitution. It is easy to transfer the buoyancy of Nonconformity in the later nineteenth century, after the success of the great pressure groups in which it articulated itself, and after the revelations of the Religious Census of 1851, to the first half of the century, and this is sometimes done unconsciously by historians. Dissent in the 1830s still lacked national coherence. The most expansive of its components, the Methodists, had a strong Tory leadership and were still in many places hardly distinguishable from the Church of England itself. The family of Hugh Price Hughes, the great Methodist spokesman of later Victorian England, was in the 1840s still attending Holy Communion at their local Welsh Anglican church as well as resorting to a Wesleyan chapel. The Baptists were the most militant of the Dissenters, but their numbers were comparatively small. Unitarianism had infiltrated many Presbyterian congregations, prompting local disputes about property ownership. Centralization was weak in all the denominations. Yet as a spearhead of assault upon the privileges of the national establishment of religion the Dissenters were taken very seriously indeed by the political groups of the 1830s. The reason for this lay partly in the Dissenters' rediscovery of their own seventeenth-century role as the upholders of political doctrines hostile to aristocracy, both in the social structure and in religion; hence the newly expressed alliance of Dissent and radicalism of the 1830s. That, however, was the work of comparatively narrow elites within Dissent – though it was finding resonances further down the scale. The reason lay also in the unpreparedness of the leadership of the Church of England to counter the assault. Having just assisted the repeal of the Test and Corporation Acts, as a reward to the Dissenters for their political responsibility, the ferocity of what followed took them unawares. The reason lay mostly, however, in the method used by the Dissenters' leaders themselves in their attack upon the old confessional State. Instead of a frontal ideological assault they projected a series of 'practical' grievances, and it was this pragmatism, so well attuned to the style of English political discourse, and so easily portrayed as a matter of ordinary justice without any ulterior constitutional objective, that proved effective. There was no 'conspiracy' about this: planning was short-term, and the degree of support the leaders could expect from their own religious constituents was always uncertain. It is, again, only too easy to over-emphasize the coherence of Dissent in the first half of the nineteenth century. The alliance with radicalism was distrusted in many places; in others relations with the Church of England were, for local reasons, traditionally good; in still other parts of the country the pattern of political deference spilled over to inhibit some Dissenters from assailing the religious preferences of established groups in their area.

For all that, however, the general projection is still of Dissent achieving a significant harmony between the kinds of demand for 'religious equality' made at the centre and the expectations of local congregations. Those expectations had changed during the eighteenth century, as Dissent gradually ceased to regard itself, and to be regarded by the parsons and the squires, as outside local society. The Evangelical revival had done much to transform Dissent religiously: old Calvinist orthodoxies were blunted and in part discarded by the new styles – styles which had as great an impact inside the State Church. The new Christianity of hymn-singing and sentiment was a significant dissolvent of denominational differences. Now that all changed again. The rise of 'political Dissent' in the 1830s was the symptom of a new consciousness of denominational diversification, marked on the side of the Church of England by the High Church movement, on the side of Dissent by the claims for 'religious equality', and evident even within the English Catholic Church in the popular Italianate devotions. Between 1830 and 1870 there was a rally of most parts of Dissent to the militant leaders: attitudes which at the start had characterized only the Baptists became widely diffused. The renewed emphasis on denominationalism, and the acceptance of religious pluralism in society, produced a sense that the future lay with those churches that were truly free of traditionalist, aristocratic and state control. Religious pluralism itself, the 'free trade in religion' which so typified the era, had the paradoxical consequence of uniting the Dissenters in their consciousness that a foe required defeating. 'Denominationalism' itself gave the competing denominations something in common, at least for defined political objectives like disestablishment or education freed from Anglican control. Between the leaders at the centre and the congregations in the country there came into existence an uneven but reasonably clear unity of purpose.

The same could not be said of the Church of England. There the assault upon the confessional State brought varied responses. The leaders, both lay and episcopal, were internally divided about appropriate action, unable collectively to decide exactly how far concessions should go in order to preserve the substance of the constitution, and some objected to any change. Among the lower clergy and the laity in the parishes, however, there was much less ambivalence: most were quite unable to accommodate any of the 'practical' modifications to the operation of the confessional State that the Dissenters demanded. This division of opinion within the Church leadership weakened the effectiveness of the Church at the centre, where it was unable to defend itself without the fatal appearance of allying itself to a political party; it also accounts for the extreme bitterness of the political rift between the Church of England and Dissent in the localities, where opposition to change encountered opposition to perceived privilege. It was in these local exchanges that the popular politics of the middle decades of the nineteenth century were fashioned.

Despite all these considerations Dissent itself remained internally divided in a number of ways, and a general pattern of response to the crisis in the relations of Church and State in the middle years of the nineteenth century did not clearly emerge. Dissent was also, of course, not the only – perhaps not even the decisive – force making for a redefinition of the religious parts of the constitution. A whole amalgam of traditional hostilities, some expressed within ordinary political radicalism (itself no less divided than Dissent) was in the later 1820s and 1830s pressing to achieve the dismantling of the old Church-and-State system. The Dissenters' agitation, that is to say, coincided with pressure for the reform of all institutions – including the Church – from within the existing, traditional political classes. In selecting 'practical' grievances for the centrepiece of their assault upon the privileges of the Church of England, therefore, the Dissenting leaders were self-consciously selecting tactically sound options. By avoiding large general principles they least divided their constituents, at both central and local levels. This approach also placed their opponents at an ideological disadvantage, by initiating a public debate which deliberately avoided ideology. The bishops recognized this at once. 'Under the plea of seeking the redress of practical grievances,' declared the Bishop of Lincoln, 'they demand concessions in which the very principle of a Church Establishment is involved.'

The pragmatic style of English parliamentary debate was ideally suited to further the Dissenters' schemes. It was usually noted by observers that the conduct of public affairs and the legislative processes were characteristically promoted on grounds of 'expediency'; that 'philosophical' discussions of politics were what happened on the continent – or perhaps among Scottish thinkers. This phraseology, however, disguised a long and persistent tradition of actually raising fundamental questions of political association, not in the secular language which later interpreters expected and failed to locate, but in religious discourse. The nineteenth-century debates about Church and State, for all their 'practical' exterior, were the places where English political theory was laid out and adjusted. And so the long discussions about ecclesiastical endowments, and such seemingly surface issues as church rates, educational finance, the admission of Dissenters to the ancient universities, burial rights in parochial church-yards and marriage registration, in reality had a profoundly important function as the occasions for basic redefinitions of the nature of the State. Defenders of the Church of England replied in kind. The whole debate, on the face of it, eschewed theoretical explanation. Indeed, the few who attempted to support the continuation of the old confessional state on ideological grounds – Coleridge, the young Gladstone, and Maurice – were not, at least in that particular aspect of their work, influential. Their ideas were taken up by a few other thinkers, but were never central to the kind of parliamentary and public discussions in which the transformation of the state actually proceeded.

The main Church defence was very traditional, emphasizing as it had always done the advantages to the state of a moral diffusion, achieved through official religion, which promoted order and furnished a basis for the foundation of law less controversial than conceivable alternatives; for the Church itself there was the advantage of a territorial structure which provided the services of religion for an entire society. A national establishment of religion, according to Anglican apologists from Bishop Blomfield in the 1830s to the Chadwick Report of 1970, continued to echo widely felt if inarticulate assent to Christianity in the life of the nation. When the attack showed signs of pressing to far-reaching success, as it did already by the 1840s, churchmen in Parliament, in a characteristically English pragmatism of response, proposed 'concurrent endowment' as a settlement: the public resources for religion should not be abolished, as the Dissenters argued, but rather be redistributed among the denominational components of the *de facto* religious pluralism. By the 1860s it became clear that this was not a possible solution except in the educational field. The Maynooth grant for the training of Irish Catholic priests, the payment of the *Regium Donum* to the English and Irish Presbyterians, and the *ad hoc* financial allocations to the various denominations in the overseas colonies had furnished good precedents, but the rising tide of militancy among the Dissenting leadership swept these away too. When the Irish Church was disestablished under the terms of the 1869 Act it was disendowed at the same time – in response to the joint agitation of Irish Catholics and English Dissenters. The whole purpose of the British Anti-State Church Association (1844), renamed the Society for the Liberation of the Church from State Patronage and Control in 1853, was to end *all* connection of Church and State, and so to procure 'religious equality', by the dismantling of government subvention. It viewed concurrent endowment as no less evil than the exclusive endowment, through the ancient ecclesiastical revenues, of the Church of England establishment. The last direct parliamentary support for the provision of public worship by the State Church was made in 1824. In the 1840s Peel thought of some kind of grant for religion but the weight of hostile opinion, at least as it presented itself to the perspective of Westminster politics, induced him to hold back, and none of his successors has ever regarded it as a possibility. With the advent of the Nonconformists' great campaign against parliamentary support for the Church of England's educational facilities, the National Education League of 1869, it became additionally clear that even in specialist areas of social service the application of 'religious equality' was intended to dismantle confessional evidences within the State.

Although contemporaries were periodically given to declaiming a belief that revolution was as possible in England as it was in the European countries, what impressed observers from overseas was the fundamental stability of English political institutions. The observers were correct: even the most radical English politicians still assumed the maintenance – or restoration – of the general fabric of the constitution. The reform process, in the minds of radicals as well as of public men in the traditional governing groups, was about the removal of 'accretions' from the machinery of the constitution. It was about returning to a condition once supposed to have existed (in a series of not very historical tableaux) when a 'natural' harmony of social interests produced good government. This rather conservative centre of the reform impulse meant that political parties were not clearly defined around policies for change. Until well into the century, and until after the main episodes in the dismantling of the old confessional state had already occurred, politics at the centre still tended to be formulated around an old-fashioned balancing of interests. Politicians pursued an order which minimized, not enhanced, the entry of the state into the nexus of contractual relationships that comprised the social fabric. In practice this meant that neither Church in defence, nor Dissent in assault, needed to redefine its role around rival ideologies of government. Dissent, it is true, had a traditional distaste for regarding the state as a divine institution, a stance which certainly divided it sharply from the Church Establishment, and from the English Roman Catholics, who adhered strongly to the belief that government represented a providential ordering.

In the nineteenth century the Dissenters went on to express their conviction within the popularized practices of political economy: the slogan a 'free church in a free state' was raised to dogmatic proportions that were never fully explored; a 'free trade in religion' presupposed a low-level definition of the state. Without an alternative political order in mind the Dissenting leaders were in fact attacking the state itself when they assailed the 'aristocratic' management which was the only *apparat* they knew. Like the Anti-Corn Law League, the Liberation Society and the rest of the

Dissenters' associations for public agitation promoted views about government which identified existing grievances and alleged evils pretty thoroughly, but which declined to describe an alternative order.

Early in the century only a handful of London radicals had spoken about the desirability of 'secular' institutions, and they used the word almost exclusively in relation to education; in the second half of the century the leaders of Nonconformity were calling for 'secular' government without any precise or intended notion of real secularization. Their solution to the existence of a religious pluralism within the state was a complete severance of formal links between the churches and government. That was what they meant by a 'secular' polity. In exactly the same years, as it happened, they were also increasingly involved in agitations over issues of public morality – especially the temperance question – which required legislative regulation. The 'Nonconformist conscience', that is to say, sought the enforcement of Christian morality by law but denied the capability of the state to recognize and promote particular religious bodies as the agents of public policy.

The Dissenters' leaders themselves looked overseas, to the United States and to those British dependencies where there had been separations of Church and State, to prove their theses. There they beheld plainly Christian governments passing Christian laws without the encumbrance of state churches.

Why should this not happen in England? In fact the disestablishments in those countries had produced constitutional inconsistencies which began to show up in the middle years of the twentieth century. A series of cases in the American courts in the 1950s and 1960s began to test and to overturn laws requiring specifically religious practices – such as Bible reading in the schools – and it has become clear that the issues the English Dissenters of the nineteenth century presumed solved were certainly far from being so. Their grand vision of a Christian State without a state recognition of official religion merely postponed decisions of weight to another generation and time. They had attacked the Church Establishment in a manner which resulted in the partial displacement of one anomaly by another. The chance survival of the State Church in England did little to make the reality of the changes that were occurring much different from the experience of the United States, with its constitutional severance of Church and State and what Jefferson once called 'the wall of separation' between them. The English Dissenters had attacked the Church establishment from the ground of 'voluntarism' in religion, from the lower ground, therefore, of endowments and practical grievances: they mistook these things for the essence of establishment status. But an establishment of religion exists where there is a connection between law and religious opinion. In contending for such a connection the Dissenters were seeking a constitutional recognition of Christianity that was very far indeed from a separation of religion and the state.

The Dissenting assault, anyway, operated at a time when changes in the function of the state itself were beginning to occur, and these were in themselves so far-reaching as to account for a radical redefinition of the relationship between religious bodies and public policy.

The very limited functions of government at the start of the nineteenth century allowed, still, a reasonably coherent understanding of the relationship between the Church and the State. It was a relationship of mutual dependence: the Church promoted morality and education, the State preserved order and guaranteed the maintenance of institutions. The rise of political economy to a prominent position of intellectual respectability in the first half of the century reinforced this limited view of the competence of the State. With the entry of government into new areas of social regulation, in the piecemeal accumulations of 'exceptional' powers to deal with particular social evils, the old definition of the state was gradually laid aside. At the same time the trauma to the constitution induced by the reforming outburst of the 1830s made men conscious that, despite the continuation of much that was still familiar and traditional, a new order was being put together in the management of government. By the end of the nineteenth century the essentials of what was, forty years later, to be recognized as the 'welfare state' were already in existence. But the *ad hoc* nature of the responses of government to the various social issues that had been intruded upon the public realm by expert opinion, and by philanthropic bodies, had produced no consistency – no theory of parliamentary intervention. The growth of the State was pragmatic and non-ideological, just as the vocabulary of politics tended to be.

This meant that Church leaders, though they were often found at the centre of the reforming dialectic, had no doctrine of the collectivist state, and when they became aware of just how extensively government was beginning to enlarge its sphere were as alarmed as other men were at the potential threats to individual liberty. The absence of a theoretical basis for legislation helped to domesticate the massive changes that were impending, however, and religious opinion, like opinion in general, accommodated itself to the expanding functions of the state without too much difficulty.

Yet the effect on the social and public role of the Church was very marked. Functions like education and care of the sick, for centuries the preserve of religious bodies or trusts under their direction and control, were passing to the State. The reason was the sheer scale of the work to be undertaken. Confronted with the need to extend church building into the vast new urban complexes, the ecclesiastical authorities were neither constituted for the national operation of social relief agencies nor capable of financing them. Truly heroic efforts were indeed made in the attempt to keep up with the pace of change: enormous sums were raised by churchmen to found more schools and to finance hospital trusts, and so forth. The work was nevertheless too great for their resources, and the State gradually took over a large, and increasing, part of the duties of welfare and education. The rise of the modern State in practice disestablished the Church.

What the Dissenting attack contributed was the superstructural loosening of many traditional ties. Is it conceivable that a confessional State could have come through the process of collectivism, had there been no Dissenting assault, no existence of a religious pluralism in society? There was nothing about collectivism that was inherently secularizing. Some Catholic states have offered twentieth-century examples of a collectivist order with a confessional basis. But they were countries which had always had strong traditions of ideological conflict. England's nineteenth-century political pragmatism was ideally suited to the Dissenters' ideological innocence: in England the growth of the modern state and the acceptance of religious pluralism went hand in hand.

The Established Church was slow to arrive at a *collective* response to the sort of public issues which the agents of change were forcing upon government. It was ill-suited to determine a national attitude to such issues as factory reform, public health legislation or slum clearance – the kind of issues around which the growth of the state was actually occurring, as legislative regulations stacked up increasing powers of intervention. Even in the area of education, in which the Church was particularly well qualified as the chief provider until far into the second half of the nineteenth century, coherent and united responses to modern needs were not always forthcoming. This was not through lack of will. The Church took an enormous interest in the existence of social evils, and attempted solutions: but in the end it was usually individual churchmen who were effective, rather than the corporate ecclesiastical body itself.

There were a number of reasons for this. A lack of adequate financial resources, as in the case of education, was one. Another was the distrust of centralization, and the growth of bureaucracy; these tendencies seemed to undermine the traditional relationships of the parishes and offended the paternalism of the parsons and the squires. Then there was the problem of ecclesiastical particularism. From the self-conscious independence of the bishops to the parsons' freehold in the parishes there was a reluctance to concede initiative to outside bodies. In addition, the Established Church had no official machinery by which to arrive at collective decisions on public issues, even had they been considered desirable. In the 1850s a movement, eventually successful, for the revival of the deliberative functions of the two Convocations of Canterbury and York had rather limited objectives: there was no intention that the resuscitated assemblies should encourage discussion of public issues. From the 1860s there were annual gatherings of 'Church Congresses'. These bodies, though influential, were completely unofficial and tended to be easily captured by pressure groups – some of which, in fact, were concerned with social questions and did valuable service in establishing a Church voice in the matters under discussion. In 1903 the Church Representative Council was set up, and in 1919 the Church Assembly.

In the recovery of ecclesiastical autonomy the Church was in practice recognizing the extent of its separation from the State. As government had come to exercise increasingly specialized functions which left little space for ecclesiastical issues (its will anyway sapped by the agents of the religious pluralism in the society it governed), so the Established Church developed its own means of internal administration, as its functions, too, grew in relation to its own constituents. When the system of synodical government emerged in 1970 the process of ecclesiastical autonomy was virtually (though not constitutionally) complete. By the time the Church had achieved a coherent collective voice – around the time of the Enabling Act (1919), creating a new Church Assembly – the independent evolution of the collectivist State had already gone too far for the Church to have any other than a marginal influence on the sort of issues with which government was by then concerned. Parliament was plainly no longer suitable as the lay government of the Church, and although lingering and rather popular erastianism has been slow to pass from the national scene, and still periodically gets up minor demonstrations in Parliament, the Church's independence of government is more or less effective. Its collective voice on public issues, however, now looks rather like those of the other pressure groups in society: it has achieved a measure of internal coherence but has lost a national means of giving it substance.

Another reason for the decline of the Church as a vehicle of national concern in public issues was the nineteenth-century practice of avoiding partisan politics. Episcopal charges were constantly urging the clergy to attend to their duties and to eschew 'politics'. It is true that by 'politics', at least in the first third of the century, the bishops commonly meant 'faction', but they also clearly intended that a distinction should be made between religious and moral questions, which were the proper concern of the clergy, and affairs of public governance, which were not. They tried to apply the same kind of definition to their own conduct in the House of Lords. But the distinction soon began to break down. Reform itself, in the first instance, caused this. Many of the bishops felt obliged to oppose the reform of Parliament – not because they were reactionary upholders of the old order (though some were certainly that also) but because Parliament was the government of the national Church and they could not conceive of an assembly opened up to new classes without hazard to the ancient relationships. The same problem had obtruded itself over the question of Catholic emancipation in 1829: here the difficulty had been the changed *religious* composition of the legislature, making it, to the understanding of many churchmen, wholly unsuited for its ecclesiastical function.

These sorts of issue placed the Church in a position that was unavoidably partisan in politics. In the first part of the century this did not matter too much, since the novelty of the reforms themselves, the fact that parliamentary activity was still not regarded as primarily to do with reform, and the fact, also, that parties still did not define themselves around policy issues, allowed Church leaders to appear no more than participants in a general political fabric of interests which managed to persist. The Dissenting assault, in alliance with political radicalism, began the process of forcing the Church leaders into reluctant political affiliations. At the time, in the 1830s and 1840s, this was still not a partisan association, since both Whig and Tory politicians continued to regard the maintenance of the Established Church as a major duty. In the second half of the century that all changed. The emergence of the Gladstonian Liberals, with a popular basis in some large measure furnished by militant Nonconformity, meant that the Church's adhesion to its traditional role increasingly made it appear as part of the 'aristocratic' state system that was under fire. When the Liberals took up Irish and Welsh disestablishment and, above all, when they showed hostility to the Church's monopoly of education, the establishment was forced into a more articulate alliance with the Conservative Party. It was from this period that the expression 'the Tory Party at prayer' derived. The old distinction of religious and public issues was washed away by the Dissenters' claims, and the growth of the machinery of the State left the clergy with diminished public functions. Together they rendered the Church considerably reduced in national effectiveness. The tradition of avoidance of partisan politics persisted, and is still to this day the normal behaviour of the clergy and Church leaders – joined in this by the Free Churchmen, whose long and extremely active relationship with popular politics declined in the twentieth century with the decline of the Liberal Party, changes in the nature of the popular parties themselves, and the ebbing away of the old tides of bitterness between church and chapel.

The clergy of the Church of England have retained a deceptive proximity to public life through social class. Throughout the nineteenth century, and until the last three decades of the twentieth, they were drawn from the same social classes, and were educated in exactly the same way, as the men who governed. As William Temple noticed early in the 1940s, 'It is not legal bonds that make the Church too closely to follow the State; it is personal ties and economic interests.' The clergy have tended to reflect the shifts of emphasis and the major preoccupations of the secular intelligentsia, and it has been these, and not any residual constitutional links or public functions, which have allowed them to suppose that the Church retains a significant place in the evolution of opinion.

In all these adjustments and changes the one influence which has taken surprisingly little part is secularization itself. The separation of Church and State in modern English society has occurred at the promptings of Christian opinion. Even in government, where the number of those who actively subscribe religious formularies has not been great, especially in the twentieth century, there has never really been any inclination to espouse secular ideologies or to treat the churches with any other than benign regard. In some ways this merely reflects the ideological inconsequence of English popular religion itself – a centuries-old phenomenon, which certainly antedates the Reformation. There is a passage in Newman's *Grammar of Assent* where he points to 'Bible Religion' as 'the best description of English religion'. Despite its benefits, he contended, popular English religion 'professes to be little more than thus reading the Bible and living a correct life'. It has been 'comparatively careless of creed and catechism'. The Church, that is to say, has never really succeeded in conveying the notion that it has a teaching office, that religion constitutes a structure and not mere moralism or sentiment. Evangelicalism had enormously sustained this national inclination; the Oxford Movement was a reaction against it. From the perspective of the present question, the relative absence of a popular structured religious presence in England made the progressive elimination of the Church from public life all the more easy.

What was being marginalized by a series of developments was anyway fairly indistinct. Secularization in England was an existing disposition, a practical orientation of life and habit of thought, not an ideology. The small groups of intellectual secularists, with their perhaps large band of fellow-travelling *de facto* agnostics within educated society, and the Secularist elite within the skilled working class, led by men like Holyoake, took almost no part in the changes which transformed the English constitution from confessionalism to liberalism.

Thirty years ago Will Herberg noticed that American society was simultaneously secular and religious, and regarded this as a unique phenomenon; it was explained by the churches' role as social integrators, their very success an indication of loss of authentic religious content. England has actually had, in modern times, a strongly parallel experience. Here, however, the churches have not had a function of social integration except at the margins of social change – among Irish immigrants within Catholicism, for example, or the contemporary black sects in areas of heavy urban concentration, where the churches help to overcome the social *anomie* of first- and second-generation citizens from the West Indies. America at the time of the Revolution had church attendance figures which were not unlike England's at the end of the eighteenth century: perhaps 12–15 per cent of the population. During the nineteenth century, with westward expansion and with the integration of mass arrivals from Europe, American experience departed from the English pattern, and, by voluntary means, without the assistance of the State, one of the most successful penetrations of culture in religious history occurred: by the middle decades of the twentieth century over 60 per cent of citizens were church-related. In England the Victorian boom in religion was largely restricted to the intelligentsia and to sections of the middle classes, who for a time employed organized Christianity as the vehicle of their moral seriousness. They began to cease to do so sometime in the 1860s and 1870s, and the rise in Church support which was the evidence of this temporary enthusiasm has been subsiding, extremely slowly, ever since. Yet England, like America, has in these years been characterized by voluntary religion: the State has withdrawn its support, except in matters like the provision of military and institutional chaplains, and subsidies to Church schools.

The nineteenth-century Dissenters were wrong in their claim (often based on the example of America, of which they were acutely conscious) that voluntarism in religion was itself a stimulus to vitality, and that state support sapped the authority of religion. Both in England and in America men supposed that the diminution of the public functions of religion would oblige the state to discover some alternative cohesion as the basis of society. Yet in neither place did that in practice happen, partly because of the unpopularity of secular alternatives, and partly because of the incoherence surrounding the actual separations of Church and State that had occurred. 'It is in our judgment', said Cosmo Lang, in the House of Lords discussion of the Welsh Disestablishment Bill in 1913, 'a very serious thing for a state to take out of that corporate heart of its life any acknowledgment at all of its concern with religion.' This opinion unquestionably reflected a widespread and enduring popular conviction, which time has done surprisingly little to diminish. The English do not like their religion to be expressed within precise formulations or to be obtrusive, but if they sense it is not there at all their regret, if inarticulate, is real enough.

15

The Church of England in the Nineteenth Century

Sheridan Gilley

THE CHURCH of England in the nineteenth century presents a paradox. On the one hand, its established position as a uniquely privileged corporation with a central official role in the nation's life was eroded, though not abolished, after 1830. Yet the forces of renewal and revival, many of them of a voluntary kind, both greatly extended the actual fabric of the Church, making the era a golden one for church building and church restoration, and gave it a massively extended function as an agent of popular and middle-class education and philanthropy. Much of this church building was undertaken to accommodate a fast-increasing population. There were over nine million people in England and Wales in 1800 and thirty-seven million in 1900. Indeed, Anglican church building never caught up with the expansion in numbers which had already occurred during the eighteenth-century era of pastoral neglect, a neglect compounded by the soaring population figures in the first half of the nineteenth century. The major concerted Anglican attack on the problem came as late as 1820, and had to wait upon the growing demand for change from among the ranks of churchmen themselves.

The Church in 1800 was an outwardly imposing institution. Its twenty-six bishops in the House of Lords exercised an influence at the highest level. Its cathedrals and ten and a half thousand parish churches were the dominant buildings in the landscape. Its clergy conducted the two universities, which existed principally to provide a curiously informal and non-professional training for future clerics; subscription to the Church's own Thirty-Nine Articles was required of all students on matriculation at Oxford and on graduation at Cambridge. Most public employments were closed to Dissenters and Roman Catholics, and while the former could gain admission to Parliament under annual Indemnity Acts, the surviving Test and Corporation Acts maintained a virtual Anglican stranglehold on central and local government.

The Anglican influence was both defined and circumscribed by the class-bound character of the Church's ministry. Although since the Reformation ecclesiastical income from the great tithes had usually been impropriated by lay or institutional landowners, the changes and chances of the agricultural and industrial revolutions, improvements in farming methods, rising property values and increasing income from bounties on coal enriched the revenues of some livings and made the Church ever more attractive as a place of employment for the sons of noblemen and gentlemen. Half the advowsons or rights of presentation to livings were held by laymen, and in much of rural England there was a close connection between the gentry families who owned the right to appoint to parishes and the appointees to the richer ones. It was generally the younger sons of a genteel family who went into the Church, but there was also the figure of the 'squarson', the local parson who was also a leading local landowner.

This clerical influence flowed into other positions of authority; the proportion of magistrates who were also priests reached its peak in 1830. Only in Cumbria and Wales was there anything like a peasant clergy recruited from the mass of the population, and despite the establishment of numerous theological colleges in the first half of the nineteenth century – the first was St Bees, for non-graduates, in 1816 – the great majority of clergymen throughout the Victorian era remained the products of the education for gentlemen provided by Oxford and Cambridge. There were more aristocratic bishops in 1800 than in 1700, and the sins of pluralism, absenteeism and non-residence, consequences of the need to finance a pleasant lifestyle in pleasant places, had fatally impaired the Church's pastoral effectiveness and its will to respond to the crisis of the age. It is difficult to distinguish technical non-residence, in which the incumbent lived near the parish, from actual absence, but in 1827 only four parishes in ten had resident incumbents, and a minority of these non-residents did not even employ a curate to do duty for them. The cathedral canonries were well-endowed sinecures – the golden prebends of Durham required residence for only one month in the year – and these highly lucrative stalls functioned as a convenient subsidy for less substantially funded bishoprics or deaneries elsewhere. Nepotism was especially rife among the bishops, who enriched their male relations with the better livings in their gift.

The Church's weaknesses, however, were profounder still. Its parishes were most numerous where the population had been most concentrated in the middle ages, in the rural south and midlands. In northern England, large parishes ministered to a scattered population, and in Lancashire and the north-east a substantial number of Roman Catholics remained. A new inadequacy appeared in this traditional pastoral provision in the north as some parishes between 1780 and 1830 became cities, with little new church building to meet the need, so that the Church of England could be said to have lost the modern urban working class in the very decades of its formation. The widespread building of proprietary chapels limited attendance to those who could afford to rent a pew. There was a great increase in chapelgoing after 1790 among the Protestant Dissenters, especially the Methodists, though it was not until the unique experiment of a national religious census in 1851 that it was known that in terms of the number of actual worshippers, Nonconformity enjoyed near parity with the Church of England. Anglican rigidity over sub-dividing parishes and keeping to the letter of the *Book of Common Prayer* stood in contrast to the flexibility of the Nonconformist methods of itinerant evangelism, non-liturgical worship and emotional preaching of conversion, which were made the more effective by the establishment's political unpopularity. It was the Church's tragedy that the fastest-growing religious body after 1790, the Wesleyan Methodists, created by Anglican clergymen like the Wesleys to strengthen the Church of England, should have been driven into separate communion as much by Anglican hostility as by the desire for a distinctive Wesleyan Church.

A further source of Anglican weakness lay in the Church of England's union with the Church of Ireland when the two parliaments were united in 1800. The population of Ireland was then five million to a population in England and Wales of something over nine million, but the Church of Ireland was an ecclesiastical slum, with four archbishops and eighteen bishops sustained by the tithes of the overwhelmingly Catholic peasantry. Though the Irish Church could boast the allegiance of only a tenth of the population, its following was outnumbered even in the north by the Presbyterians, and in nationalist eyes it shared in the lack of legitimacy of the English State itself. Significantly, Church reform in England was to be prefaced by Church reform in Ireland in 1833, but the Irish Church was to remain a target vulnerable to the opponents of the principle of Church establishment until its disestablishment by Gladstone in 1869.

Yet for all these structural weaknesses, the Church of England had at first been only strengthened by the French Revolution's attacks on official ecclesiastical regimes throughout Europe, making it ever more important to the Tory Party and to the propertied classes as a breakwater against the revolutionary tide. In the early 1790s, the Church was even popular for a time with the anti-revolutionary mobs who attacked the conventicles of Dissenters accused of revolutionary sympathies, and the High Church party wanted to tar all Dissenters with the Jacobin brush. For all the opposition of the non-jurors to the Revolution Settlement, traditional High Churchmanship had been sometimes associated with an erastian attachment to the union of Church and State; among the 'two bottle orthodox' it was synonymous with hatred of Dissenters and love of tithes. But even in the eighteenth century, it could boast an intellectual tradition among the 'Hutchinsonian' disciples of the anti-Newtonian John Hutchinson and the allegiance of as great a Christian layman as Samuel Johnson, while Samuel Horsley, Bishop of St Asaph, was the leading exponent of orthodoxy as well as the most distinguished spokesman for the Church in the decade of the French Revolution.

Indeed, Church–State relations in the early years of the nineteenth century appeared to be at their most harmonious and most favourable to the interests of the Church for centuries, while High Church influence was at its height during the long administration of the Earl of Liverpool (1812–27), partly through the activities of the Hackney Phalanx or Clapton Sect, a body of clergymen and laymen centred on the north London suburbs of Hackney and Clapton and led by a wine merchant, Joshua Watson, and Henry Handley Norris, later the rector of South Hackney. They dominated the older Anglican societies like the Society for the Propagation of the Gospel and the Society for Promoting Christian Knowledge. In 1811, the Hackney churchmen founded the National Society for Promoting the Education of the Poor in the Principles of the Established Church, which over the next half-century oversaw a huge extension in popular education. In 1818 the Phalanx inspired the creation of the Church Building Society for the construction and repair of churches, and in 1818 and 1824 secured Acts of Parliament under which the government gave a million and a half pounds for the same purposes, the first such grants since the reign of Queen Anne.

These High Churchmen did not lack religious spirit, but despite exceptions to the rule, it was a spirit tightly bound by Prayer Book formality, and one which understood reform in institutional terms of strengthening the political and ecclesiastical status quo. The High Churchmen's Toryism was shared by the Evangelicals within the Church (the term 'Evangelical' is sometimes restricted to Anglicans), but it was the Evangelicals, broadly defined, who more clearly than the High Churchmen had a Gospel to proclaim, and held the religious initiative in England and Wales in 1800 both within the Church and outside it. The Rome of Evangelical churchmen was Clapham, where the rector, John Venn, presided over a congregation which included the leading saints of the movement, most notably William Wilberforce, whose campaign against slavery led to the abolition of slave trading in 1807 and of slave owning in British possessions in 1833. Wilberforce was the embodiment of the national conscience, and the prophet of the solid sub-stratum of what became Victorian Protestantism: a religion centred on the hearth, on daily family prayer, Bible reading and Sabbath observance, and upon a spirit of 'holy worldliness'. This was a faith requiring self-sacrifice and the conscientious discharge of social obligations to dependants and inferiors, professing its belief in sin, heaven, hell and judgement, and taking a restrained delight in the sober enjoyment of the innocent pleasures of this world.

Evangelicals also ushered in the golden age of voluntary religious association, through their innumerable societies to convert, educate and reform the world, which met in London at 'May meetings' from the early years of the century and found a symbol and centre in 1831 in Exeter Hall in the Strand. The May meetings involved co-operation between Evangelical Anglicans and Dissenters, as in the British and Foreign Bible Society, established in 1804, and in the 1830s in the city missions created to evangelize the urban poor through the agency of professional lay missionaries. The strains in such interdenominational co-operation can be seen in the creation of separate denominational missionary societies: the greatest of the Evangelical societies, the Church Missionary Society, was a purely Anglican institution from its foundation in 1799. There were strong Evangelical Anglican loyalists, like the Pope of the Evangelical movement, Charles Simeon, who was for more than half a century from 1782 incumbent of Trinity Church, Cambridge, and who trained up a large body of undergraduate 'Simeonites' in his own image. Simeon influenced the preaching of the wider Church through his 'sermon skeletons', made Cambridge the Evangelical university and Jerusalem of the movement, and guided his followers on a moderate course, taking a proper account of the Calvinist and Arminian extremes in Evangelical theology.

The Evangelical programme as a whole was summed up in William Wilberforce's *Practical View* of 1797. Wilberforce exploited the popular reaction against the atheistic impieties of the French Revolution by offering Britain a moderately conservative reforming path between the extremes of Revolution and black reaction, and reasserted the necessity of the central dogmas of the Evangelical Gospel–especially the death of the Incarnate God on the Cross for human sin – against the powerlessness of the eighteenth-century public religion of mere moral exhortation based on prudential reason alone.

In this, Anglican Evangelicalism was part of a popular Protestant culture much wider than the Church of England, a culture which was to flourish and expand for the remainder of the century. A characteristic figure was the great church builder and educational reformer Francis Close, who dominated the life of Cheltenham through his auxiliary cohort of clergy and retired army and naval officers. Even in its more secular reaches, popular Protestantism sustained the Puritan ethic of industry, sobriety, thrift, and suspicion of godly pleasure, and disapproval of the cruel sports of the eighteenth century and of the theatre and of novel reading, though the objection to the last was weakened by the emergence of the religious novel itself.

This Protestant culture could degenerate into sexual hypocrisy, concern for respectable appearances and the crusade to police the casual amusements of the semi-pagan working class. More positively, it inspired the idealism of Wilberforce's successor as the leading saint of the Evangelical movement, Anthony Ashley Cooper, seventh Earl of Shaftesbury, whose campaigns to improve the working conditions of women and children bore fruit in the Ten Hours' Bill of 1847 and the Factory Act of 1874. Shaftesbury was the symbolic figurehead of a pan-Evangelical crusade to the Godless cities of Great Britain which included among its agencies the 'ragged school' movement (founded in 1844), Mrs Ellen Ranyard's Biblewomen nurses (1857) and the deaconess movement (1861) founded on the German Lutheran model of Kaiserswerth. As the chief ecclesiastical adviser after 1855 to the Prime Minister, Lord Palmerston, Shaftesbury also secured the appointment of a number of Evangelical bishops. He lacked, however, Wilberforce's blithe spirit; his literal belief in the prophecies concerning the premillennial return of Christ to usher in the millennium in a darkening world, and his fierce hatred of Roman Catholicism and of the papacy as the Beast and Scarlet Woman of the Book of Revelation, were typical of the more otherworldly Evangelicals of his generation. These otherworldly convictions captured the young Evangelicals who came together for the prophetic conferences at Albury Park from 1826; one of them, Hugh M'Neile, precipitated the conflict between the Protestantism of the Orange Order and the Catholicism of the largely Irish immigrant population of Liverpool, which passed into a century of sectarian war. Anglican and Dissenting Evangelicals joined together at a national level to oppose the menace of Rome in the Evangelical Alliance in 1846 and the Protestant Alliance in 1851, but such co-operation, even against a common foe, was bedevilled by the opposition of church and chapel.

It was this fiercer, darker Evangelicalism in the 1820s and 1830s which produced both John Nelson Darby's Plymouth Brethren and Edward Irving's Catholic Apostolic Church. The oddity was that the heart religion and the tensions within Evangelicalism were partially responsible for the Catholic reaction in Anglicanism. This reaction was, however, also a consequence of Romanticism; the Lake Poets, William Wordsworth, Robert Southey and Samuel Taylor Coleridge, had by the 1820s all outgrown their radical youth to become defenders of the Church, and though Southey retained in private his Unitarian opinions, Wordsworth's *Ecclesiastical Sonnets*, originally published as *Ecclesiastical Sketches* (1822) and Southey's own prose *Book of the Church* (1824) defended the historic *Ecclesia Anglicana* as part of the nation's ancient constitution against Romanism, radicalism and Dissent. Coleridge's *On the Constitution of the Church and State* of 1830 offered a profounder philosophical apology for the national Church as the mediating force between the major and minor barons in agriculture and commerce, and as the guardian of the nation's civilization and culture, as well as the God-given local embodiment of the Catholic Church of Christ. The Romantic impulse was, however, given a more explicit ecclesiastical statement in the High Churchman John Keble's *Christian Year*, published in 1827, containing one poem for each Sunday, fast day and feast day of the Anglican *Book of Common Prayer*, by which the Prayer Book was invested with the Romantic associations of awe, mystery, tenderness and love, and was assigned a central role within the mainstream culture of the age.

It was one of Keble's disciples, a young ex-Evangelical Calvinist and fellow of Oriel College, Oxford, John Henry Newman, who combined the dogmatic conviction and deepest feeling of the Evangelical movement with the doctrines of the older High Churchmanship to revolutionize the character of the Church of England. The catalyst was the 'crisis of the Church' of 1828–33: the full formal admission of Nonconformists into Parliament with the repeal of the Test and Corporation Acts in 1828, the admission of Roman Catholics with the passage of the third Catholic Emancipation Act in 1829, and the election in 1830 of a Whig government apparently resolved to reform the Church if not to plunder it. The Bill to suppress ten Church of Ireland bishoprics in 1833 drew from Newman, Keble and their followers a protest against what they perceived as the State's erastian oppression of the Church, which did not owe its foundation to the State but was a divine society founded by Christ. This 'Oxford Movement', so called from the university where it originated, began in a reaction to the onslaught on the properties and privileges of the establishment and in the resistance to liberal political reform in the university, especially to the admission of Dissenters, but quickly adopted the paradoxical conclusion that the freedom of the Church to exercise its own Christ-given authority was worth infinitely more than worldly privilege or power.

The Oxford Movement continued in the weak position of opposing the necessary reforms of the Church which stemmed from the government-appointed Ecclesiastical Commission of 1835–6 and from a succession of Acts – the Established Church Act of 1836, the Pluralities Act of 1838 and the Dean and Chapter Act of 1840 – which over the next generation remedied the worst aspects of absenteeism, pluralism and non-residence. Within the framework of such institutional reform, however, the Oxford

Movement greatly enhanced the spiritual substance of the Church. Its initial novelty lay in its willingness to surrender the erastian and Protestant elements in the High Church tradition and to redefine the Church of England as a *via media* between popery and Protestantism rather than, as traditionally, between popery and radical Protestantism or Puritanism. The movement was called Tractarian, from its ninety 'Tracts for the Times', published between 1833 and 1841; it was called Puseyite, after Edward Bouverie Pusey, the Regius Professor of Hebrew in Oxford, who abetted Newman in his aspiration to remake Anglican theology in the image of the teachings of the Fathers of the Early Church; and it was called Anglo-Catholic, to indicate its English and national character against the foreign internationalism of Roman Catholicism.

In Newman's hands, the movement found a spokesman of genius celebrated for the clarity and beauty as well as the occasional violence of his language, but in the last of the 'Tracts for the Times', *Tract 90*, published in 1841, he sought to show that the Thirty-Nine Articles of the Prayer Book could be reconciled with a true Catholicism, at the expense of the Protestant meanings intended by their authors. The result was the virtual excommunication of Newman by most of the bishops of his own Church, and his subsequent conversion to Rome in 1845 deprived the modern Anglican tradition of its only thinker of international stature. Pusey, however, had a spiritual greatness as a preacher and shepherd of souls, and encouraged the extension of the movement's high conception of the pastoral office into the parishes, where it supplemented the work of Evangelicalism in the partial professionalization of the clerical office.

Pusey also established the first Anglican sisterhoods, which were active and charitable rather than contemplative, dedicated to teaching, nursing and the reclamation of prostitutes, and took as their model the burgeoning new female religious orders of Rome. The first woman to take religious vows was Marian Hughes in 1841. The best-known of the new orders were those of the Society of the Most Holy Trinity or Devonport Sisterhood, founded in 1848 by the remarkably strong-minded Priscilla Lydia Sellon; the Communities of St Mary the Virgin, Wantage (1848) and of St John the Baptist, Clewer (1851); and the Society of St Margaret, East Grinstead (1855). The quixotic Joseph Lyne, 'Father Ignatius' in religion, failed in his attempts at Llanthony in Wales to establish the Benedictine Order in the Church of England, while Dom Aelred Carlyle's later Benedictine abbey on Caldey Island seceded to Rome in 1913, leaving the nucleus of the later Anglican Nashdom Abbey. There was, however, to be a large number of successful active religious orders for men, including the Society of St John the Evangelist, established in 1865 at Cowley, Oxford, by Richard Meux Benson; the Community of the Resurrection, established in 1892 by

Charles Gore, now at Mirfield, Yorkshire; and the Society of the Sacred Mission, dating from 1894, which had its centre at Kelham in Nottinghamshire, and which pioneered the training of non-graduate clergy.

The other major Tractarian influence was on the form of worship itself. The Gothic neo-medieval movement in church architecture and art deriving from the work of the Catholic convert Augustus Pugin achieved its widest outreach in the Church of England, through the Camden Society, later the Ecclesiological Society, founded in Cambridge in 1839 by two undergraduates, John Mason Neale and Benjamin Webb. It has been said that as the Cambridge equivalent of the Oxford Movement it gave that movement its clothing. The society made middle-pointed or decorated Gothic *the* central Anglican style, the authoritative basis for the church building and restoration which craved just such an authority, and enriched the religious culture with new realms of symbolism in stained glass, pointed arches, brassware and coloured encoustic tiles. By 1900 there was hardly an Anglican church in the country unaffected by the change, which thrust the pulpit from its central position to the north side, restored chancels to full use with a central altar, and introduced robed or surpliced choirs and organs to replace the rustic west-gallery orchestras of flutes and fiddles. The musical models were suggested partly by the English cathedral tradition, partly by medieval monastic plainsong. The cathedrals themselves were gradually restored after 1850, while at Truro the architect J. L. Pearson built the first new Anglican Gothic cathedral since the Reformation. Of the main Gothic revival architects, Sir George Gilbert Scott did his most considerable work for the Church of England, while G. E. Street and William Butterfield were, like Pearson, devout High Churchmen.

These were some of the elements in the mainstream recovery in institutional Anglicanism which resulted in the creation of a new Church culture with the imaginative power to rival popular Protestantism. Other evidences of the Church revival were the restoration of the representative institutions of the clergy themselves, the Convocations of Canterbury in 1852 and of York in 1861; the institution of diocesan synods, conferences and Church congresses; the great urban ministries of clergy like Walter Hook at Leeds; and the emergence of the much higher standards of pastoral and administrative oversight set by bishops like Samuel Wilberforce of Oxford and Edward King of Lincoln. Diocesan subdivision began with new sees at Ripon in 1836 and Manchester in 1847. At an international level, the Church's self-confidence was confirmed by the spread of Anglicanism by English colonists through north America, Australasia and southern Africa. There were seventy-six bishops at the first

Lambeth Conference in 1867; the number of ordinations peaked in 1886, and though the 1880s saw the first notable urban declines in church attendance, there were very high rates of middle-class Anglican religious practice until the First World War.

The price of such vigour was controversy. Both Church and State had difficulty in policing the wilder fringes of the Catholic revival, as the affection for medieval models overflowed at the movement's extreme into the desire for Roman Catholic ritual in Anglican churches – sometimes, as in Father Charles Lowder's East End church of St Peter's, London Docks, in an attempt to evangelize the unchurched poor through a non-verbal symbolism of coloured vestments, banners, candlelight and incense. The outcome was often Protestant violence aided and abetted by a drunken conservative mob. Even the attempt by the High Church Bishop of Exeter, Henry Phillpotts, to compel the wearing of the surplice in the pulpit caused riots in his cathedral city in 1845. A dispute between Phillpotts and one of his clergy in 1843 resulted in the establishment of the small schismatic Free Church of England. A loftier ritual, ridiculed by Shaftesbury as the worship of Jupiter and Juno, aroused popular fury in 1859–60 in the church of St George's in the East, where local public house and brothel keepers might have had reason to fear a more effective kind of religion. There was controversy over the introduction of private confession, while between 1854 and 1858 the west country priest George Anthony Denison was unsuccessfully prosecuted for teaching Christ's real presence in the Eucharist.

The Anglo-Catholic reaction to militant Protestantism included the favourite Victorian resort to voluntary association, in the formation of the English Church Union of 1860. Anglican Protestants responded with the Church Association in 1865 to combat Catholic ritual irregularities, and after the Public Worship Regulation Act of 1874 five priests were gaoled for offences against the law. The principles involved were important ones – whether the senses could be fully explored in 'spiritual worship', and whether the Catholic sacramentalism taught in this visual and olefactory symbolism was Christian or idolatrous – but the amount of controversy and parliamentary time devoted to ritualism was out of all proportion to its incidence, even while it sharpened dissatisfaction among the ritualists with State influence upon the Church, especially with the authority, in internal Church affairs, of the Judicial Committee of the Privy Council. The Archbishop of Canterbury took the initiative in 1890 in substantially acquitting the saintly Bishop of Lincoln, Edward King, of ritual offences, but the heightening of ritual was ultimately beyond control by either Church or State, and the ritualist clergyman who disobeyed his bishop became a familiar figure in the Church. There was also a creeping

Catholicism in hymnody, as one of the leading ritualists, John Mason Neale, translated large tracts of the Byzantine Greek and medieval Latin hymnals into English, translations which reached a much wider audience with the publication of *Hymns Ancient and Modern* in 1861.

Above all, the Oxford Movement inspired the creation of a new clerical pride in caste. The Tractarians taught a heightened doctrine of the Church, so that the opposing term 'Low Church', hitherto liberal or Latitudinarian in its connotations, acquired strongly Protestant ones. Against a low doctrine of the Church, the Oxford Movement re-emphasized the High Church tradition's insistence on the necessity of the apostolic succession from Christ and the Apostles of the bishops, who were, with their auxiliary orders of priest and deacon, the only God-guaranteed and appointed dispensers in England of the grace given in the sacraments. This principle implied that the Church survived in those three 'branches', Roman, Orthodox and Anglican, which were ruled by bishops, so that other churches, whether Lutheran, Calvinist or Dissenting, which lacked bishops were not churches, a judgement which sharpened the Anglican hostility to Dissent without improving Anglican relations with Rome.

There were already profound social as well as religious differences between church and chapel, but the Oxford Movement compounded them, and after 1850 the difference was increasingly reflected in the gulf between Liberal Nonconformists and Tory Anglicans, even though the longest-serving and greatest leader of the new Liberal Party was also the greatest of lay Tractarians, William Ewart Gladstone. There was violent controversy over the Dissenting determination to refuse church rates for the upkeep of the parish church (the compulsory rates were abolished in 1868), and to be buried by their own ministers in Anglican churchyards (conceded in law in 1880), but the worst of the conflict was over education. Despite the introduction of state schools in 1870, and the erosion of the Church's network of poor schools thereafter, the Church retained an extensive body of schools with a government subsidy towards them, a position confirmed by the Balfour Act in 1902. The reform of the older public schools and the foundation of new ones, especially by the Woodard foundation, the creation of Nathaniel Woodard, actually strengthened the Church's role in secondary education, even while its poor school system was in decline. This public-school role was embodied in the substantial persons of the many great clerical headmasters who well into the twentieth century supplied the bench of bishops. The abolition of undergraduate subscription to the Articles in 1854 and 1856 and of religious tests for university teachers in 1871 still left the Church with a powerful presence in Oxford and Cambridge including the possession of college chaplaincies and chapels.

The partial educational unsettlement was also a consequence of a more fundamental unease about Christianity itself. One aspect of this unease was obvious in the 1820s, a distrust of the suspect morality of the Calvinist system of the fewness of the elect, the substitutionary theory of the atonement and everlasting punishment. This would have been sufficient in itself to create a 'Victorian crisis of faith' without the further dissolvents of warring theologies. The Enlightenment attack on Christianity had been repulsed with the weapon of the science of Christian evidences wielded by the Reverend William Paley – the evidence of Christ's divinity in miracle and in the fulfilment of prophecy in Scripture, and the evidence of God's existence in divine design in creation – but the appeal to reason ran counter to the Romantic mood, and some of the most orthodox, like Newman, were uneasy about attempts to rest Christianity upon external demonstrative proof, when the decisive witness was that of the believer's heart and conscience. An unambiguous appeal to scriptural proofs was disturbed by the growing influence, if only upon a learned minority, of the historical findings of German biblical criticism, which sought to demonstrate the complex processes of formation of the biblical text, while the appeal to proofs from nature was increasingly doubtful in an age of scientific revolution.

The challenge to Christian scientism was on one level addressed simply to biblical literalism, like that of biblical criticism itself. The uniformitarian geology of Charles Lyell vastly extended the age of the earth beyond the biblical time-span of about 6,000 years. Far more controversial was the consequent revolution in biology as a result of Charles Darwin's hypothesis of the evolutionary development of one species from another through a struggle for resources in which the fittest survived. This cast doubt not merely on the biblical account of the special divine creation of fixed species but on the alleged benevolence of a nature red in tooth and claw, as well as on the special creation of man in the divine image and the whole theology of fall and redemption built upon this.

The eighteenth-century liberal or Latitudinarian tradition in Anglican theology never wholly succumbed to the Evangelical and Tractarian tides, and the Church of England already possessed clergymen of a suspect 'liberal' cast of mind, like the notorious supporter of Catholic emancipation the Reverend Sydney Smith, and the 'Noetics' Richard Whately and Renn Dickson Hampden at Oriel College, Oxford, who had influenced and were later denounced by the Tractarians. The intellectual refounder of liberal Protestantism was arguably Coleridge, and in the 1850s some commentators identified a 'Broad Church' party to balance the parties of High and Low Churchmen, including clerics like F. D. Maurice, whose eirenic theological system strove to transcend Church parties, and who was deprived of his professorship at King's College London in 1853, ostensibly for denying the doctrine of everlasting punishment. The quintessential Broad Churchman A. P. Stanley wanted a less dogmatic Christianity open to the objections from criticism, science and moral doubt.

The premature effort to come to terms with this challenge was undertaken by the seven liberal Anglican contributors to *Essays and Reviews* in 1860, but their work was denounced as that of 'Seven against Christ', and united the High and Low Churchmen to oppose it in the courts. The older generation of High Churchmen, like Pusey himself and his biographer-disciple H. P. Liddon, remained firmly opposed to such Germanizing, and the subsequent rather ham-fisted assault on biblical literalism by J. W. Colenso, Bishop of Natal, resulted in a minor schism in the South African Church and was more productive of heat than of light. The outcome was the failure of liberal attempts to provide a convincing restatement of the Christian faith. The authors of the *Essays* included two eminent Oxford academics, Mark Pattison and Benjamin Jowett, who, though clergymen, were supporters of the reform which was largely to secularize the universities, and neither of whom achieved the task of theological construction which they had thought essential to the survival of Christianity.

In fact, in the following generation, the wilder speculations of German biblical criticism received a convincing refutation in the careful commentaries and textual criticism of a distinguished triumvirate of Anglican scholars, J. B. Lightfoot, B. F. Westcott and F. J. A. Hort. Moreover, the optimistic German cosmic idealism stemming from G. W. F. Hegel and mediated to Oxford by T. H. Green could be employed to recast evolutionary theory and a developmental view of Scripture in a neo-Christian form, and the younger High Churchmen like Charles Gore and Henry Scott Holland carried the honey of idealism to their hive to reformulate a 'liberal Catholicism' which was both orthodox and critical. Their manifesto, *Lux Mundi*, published in 1889, sought to place Anglican theology on firm sacramentalist and incarnational foundations and to come to terms with Darwinism and historical enquiry after a fashion which was largely uncontroversial even in its generation. What turned *Lux Mundi* into an ecclesiastical typhoon was Gore's 'kenotic' theory that in the Incarnation, Christ was deliberately restricted in his natural knowlege. Gore, however, insisted on the Virgin Birth and the bodily resurrection as credal cruxes of Christian believing, and it was arguably his classic *via media* between tradition and criticism which ensured the Church's intellectual survival.

Indeed, the most fundamental challenge to the Church came not from biblical scholarship or science but from social criticism. An active late

Victorian Anglican parish like St John the Divine in Kennington, south London, boasted ten curates, twenty-five district visitors, 150 Sunday school visitors, 170 other volunteer workers, one paid and nine voluntary bell-ringers, two lay readers, one paid nurse and eight voluntary sisters. There were two and a half thousand children in the parish schools, fifteen hundred in the Sunday schools and fifteen hundred communicants. The result of such an enormous effort can be seen in the volumes devoted to 'Religious Influences' in the celebrated survey of *London Life and Labour* by Charles Booth. The churches arguably remained the most vital and important of late Victorian voluntary institutions, and respectable public opinion regarded them as central agencies for helping the poor and preserving social and moral order. The difficulty was that this function defined the Church of England's influence as a middle-class institution, ever more unwearied in well-doing, but acting on rather acting through the urban poor themselves.

It was this lack of a popular following which characterized the various Anglican attempts to create Christian Socialist movements. The first, between 1848 and 1854, was a reaction to the last phase of Chartism, and was led by F. D. Maurice, the priest and novelist Charles Kingsley and the barrister J. M. Ludlow. Maurice's conception, of realizing the Kingdom of Christ, was in practice paternalist, undemocratic and educational – workmen should be allowed the vote when they were informed enough to use it wisely – and found expression in his Working Men's College. Ludlow established English equivalents of the French co-operative societies, but these had the merit of bypassing the need for an extensive legislative programme. The neo-medieval idealism of the Reverend Stewart Headlam's Guild of St Matthew of 1877 bore the radicalism of its founder, who was prepared to stand bail for Oscar Wilde, but it had only about 400 members, while the much larger, more respectable and very moderate Christian Social Union, established in 1889 by Westcott, Charles Gore and Henry Scott Holland, took no particular party line in its vague if lofty vision of Christian brotherhood, and was probably better at interesting Christians in socialism than socialists in Christianity.

None of these movements had a working-class leadership; the Guild of St Matthew and the Christian Social Union were clerical and middle-class. Large claims have been made for the Anglican Christian socialist role in inhibiting the development of a full-scale anticlericalism of a continental kind. At least as much credit, however, must go to a more old-fashioned Anglican paternalism, to Liberal Nonconformity and to working-class Roman Catholicism and its great radical guardian Cardinal Manning, as well as to the predominantly empirical and undogmatic temper of English socialism itself. In any case, the well-meaning Anglican contribution to socialism did not do more than dent the political conservatism of the Church and clergy as a whole.

In all, the Church of England had been offered a devastating challenge and had undergone a remarkable recovery, which has preserved its established role to the present. That Victorian recovery, however, had its limitations, which lie behind the Church's decline in the twentieth century.

16

Religious Life in Industrial Britain, 1830–1914

David Hempton

THE YEAR IN which Charles Dickens opened his novel *Hard Times* with the words 'now what I want is Facts . . . nothing but Facts' (1854), Victorians were obligingly given a feast of statistics with the publication of Horace Mann's report on the census of public worship carried out three years before. No document could more graphically highlight those characteristic Victorian preoccupations with fact gathering, urban growth and religion. Among the myriads of facts processed by contemporaries, and by ecclesiastical historians since then, two stand out with particular clarity. The first is that more than five and a quarter million people had chosen to stay away from public worship on census Sunday and it was alleged that most non-attenders were to be found among the working classes in Britain's most populous cities. A second, and from a modern perspective more striking fact was the sheer scale of voluntary religious activity designed to convert the heathen at home and abroad. Besides the continuous work of churches, chapels and mission halls, over thirty million pieces of cheap religious literature were distributed by an army of domestic missionaries and enormous sums of money were raised for church extension, clerical support and charity. Victorian Britain was thus at the same time remarkably religious and disturbingly irreligious.

The facts presented in the census report, whatever may have been the methodological weaknesses and administrative frailties in the gathering of them, have served for more than a century as a basis for investigating nineteenth-century urban religion. Indeed, statistical surveys of religious practice, as distinct from investigations of attitudes, beliefs, rituals and behaviour, still have their allure for sociologists and historians and it is worth pausing for a moment to summarize the results of such enquiries. As Coleman has stated, 'the larger the town, the faster its growth rate and the more industrial its character, the lower its level of religious practice – and particularly Anglican practice – was likely to be.' Attendances were lowest of all in London, south Lancashire and west Yorkshire, and in the great provincial capitals of England's industrial expansion. Conversely, Anglican attendances held up well in southern agricultural counties and in towns with fewer than 25,000 inhabitants while Nonconformity scored spectacular success in Wales, Cornwall and Lincolnshire, and in the smaller industrial communities of the west midlands, the Potteries and the north-east.

Aside from the well-known national patterns, a plethora of local studies have shown up considerable variations within regions, counties and even census registration districts. It has become clear that patterns of religious practice must be closely related to the diverse economic, occupational and denominational characteristics of specific regions. Local studies have shown, for example, how religious practice could vary enormously within a small cluster of industrial villages in a single county, or even how the fortunes of two churches of the same denomination in the same town could fluctuate dramatically in the course of half a century. The social geography of nineteenth-century religion cannot, then, be traced without an acute awareness of wider social and economic changes; but neither ought it to be drawn without an appreciation of those who forged new religious cultures, often in the most unlikely of places. Consequently the relationship between personal motivation and underlying economic structures in the religious life of Victorian Britain is deserving of the most sensitive treatment.

The religious census is useful chiefly as a means of comparing the relative strength of religious denominations in early Victorian England and Wales, and as such came as a disappointment to the Church of England which accounted for only half of the worshipping population. But it showed, too, that all denominations found it hard to sustain high levels of attendance in the larger cities, a problem which became more pronounced as the pace of urban growth remained unpredictable throughout the century. According to recent estimates the urban population increased almost tenfold between 1801 and 1911 and the percentage of the population living in cities of over 100,000 people increased from 11 per cent in 1801 to 43.6 per cent in 1901. Urban growth was most rapid in the 1820s and 1830s when a predominantly youthful migration from the countryside reached its peak before going into decline in the second half of the nineteenth century. Cities also had a significantly larger share of people in their twenties and thirties than the countryside.

The real test for churches and voluntary religious organizations in the first half of the nineteenth century, therefore, was how well they could adapt to the realities of urban living and, more particularly, how much support they could attract from a predominantly youthful and mobile working class. There is need for care here, because urban and rural Britain were not as separate as is conventionally assumed. Not only was the demographic growth of Victorian cities sustained by substantial migration from the surrounding countryside (and from Ireland), but most urban populations contained a circulating medium of domestic servants and casual labourers who sometimes returned to the countryside in later life. Not surprisingly then, most towns reflected the religious characteristics of their surrounding regions, and there were more links between urban and rural churches and chapels, albeit not altogether harmonious, than was once thought.

In coping with urban expansion, churches not only faced financial and logistical problems in supplying enough clergy, buildings and facilities, but also had to consider how older forms of religious organization could be made to work in a new environment. The former required energy, which the Victorians did not lack, but the latter demanded a flexibility of mind and imagination which were not always equally forthcoming. Mr Rigby's opinion in Disraeli's *Coningsby* that 'want of religious faith was solely occasioned by want of churches' is indeed absurd; but equally, churches needed suitable buildings close to the centres of population. By 1820, for example, the Church of England in cities such as Birmingham, Sheffield, Leeds, Nottingham and Bradford was still relying on ancient parish boundaries and church buildings long after the first dramatic phase of urban growth had taken place. The Church of England, as a recent study of Bradford has shown, was at its most vulnerable in the fastest-growing towns and cities in the fastest-growing decades of the nineteenth century. Bradford's growth rate in the 1820s and 1830s was between 5 and 6 per cent per annum, which was not only double the average for British cities in the nineteenth century, but is even faster than the remarkable growth rates of third world cities in the 1960s and 1970s. On the day of the religious census in 1851 less than 5 per cent of Bradford's population showed up for Anglican morning service and Nonconformist attenders outnumbered Anglicans by a ratio of three to one. Not only did Nonconformist chapel-building reach its peak in the two decades it was most needed, but the Anglican population was not availing itself of the sittings already in place. According to Theodore Koditschek, 72 per cent of Bradford's population did not attend church on census Sunday and he thinks it unlikely that more than 20 per cent of the working-class population attended any service. Koditschek's conclusions match those of other predominantly left-wing historians who have generally concentrated their work on Britain's fastest-growing and most capitalistic cities. These historians have not found it difficult to marshal evidence to support the conclusion that the vast number of early industrial workers in rapidly growing towns 'did not avoid church or chapel because there was no room for them, but because the religious culture of the mainstream denominations was alien to their experiences and needs'. Moreover, non-attenders were not necessarily irreligious; they simply avoided the kind of religion that was on offer to them, with the notable exception of the well-attended Sunday schools.

Ground lost by the churches in the urban demographic expansion of the early industrial revolution was not easily recovered, despite the remarkable Victorian contribution to church building and restoration which Samuel Butler in *The Way of All Flesh* regarded as the most characteristic feature of the Victorian era. Even this monumental achievement has received a recent dose of cold water in the shape of the longitudinal measurements of church accommodation and attendances in the second half of the nineteenth century carried out by Robin Gill. In a study of London, Liverpool and eleven other major towns he concludes that both Nonconformist and Anglican church building, especially in the last two decades of the century, was too successful for its own good. Overcapacity and emptier services carried their own secularizing dynamic in the shape of crippling debts and the emotional unattractiveness of half-empty buildings. Furthermore, he suggests that the combination of free market Nonconformist and subsidized Anglican church-building was disastrous for the proper regulation of supply and demand. Simply having the right facilities for the right people in the right place at the right time was therefore a formidable task for nineteenth-century churchmen of all persuasions; but as they soon came to understand, buildings alone did not create religious cultures, they merely serviced them.

The more difficult task of forging a closer relationship with working-class communities was a much-discussed topic in the nineteenth century, but few had any profound understanding of the issues at stake, much less the capacity to make the kind of changes which would have made any difference. From Mann's report on the census to conferences on working-class attitudes to religion, and from working men's diaries and autobiographies to the comments of foreign observers, the same reasons for the non-participation of the poor in official religion appear again and again. Pew rents, poor preaching, dull services, lack of suitable clothes, fatigue, poverty, inequality, illiteracy and the appeal of counter-attractions all find a place and should not be lightly dismissed. A study of pew renting in Glasgow, for example, has shown how increased rents and higher-paid clergy went hand in hand with disapproval of an unhygienic and uncultivated working class. Pew renting was part of the *business* of church management, but it was also, as Brown suggests, a device 'for creating and sustaining social exclusivity'. Remarkably, the much admired Thomas Chalmers, whose parochial management schemes were so influential among nineteenth-century churchmen, presided over the church with the highest pew rents of the ten Church of Scotland congregations in Glasgow. Evangelical paternalism was by no means as sacrificially populist as its exponents sometimes claimed.

Next to pew rents, the most common cause of working-class complaints about church services was dull and irrelevant preaching. 'What could our young heads or hearts make of the mysteries and creeds of the pulpit?' wrote Samuel Bamford; 'they were strange certainly; wonderfully incomprehensible were these matters the preachers tried to impress on us.' A recent survey of the social origins of Nonconformist preachers in the nineteenth century helps show why. Recruitment to the ministry increasingly came from the lower middle-class ranks of teachers, white-collar workers and clerks, a high percentage of whom were from the Celtic fringes and the English countryside. Inadequately trained and poorly prepared for the stress of the job, the leakage rates in the first four years of ministry were remarkably high. It seems that the great pulpit orators and civic leaders of nineteenth-century Nonconformity were a tiny minority. Most lacked the talent, training and experience of English urban life to make much of an impression. The growing tendency of ministers of all denominations to come from clerical families is itself an indication of a ministerial sub-culture at home with theology and church business, but, in George Eliot's words, 'somewhat at a disadvantage during the week in the presence of working-day interests'.

To concentrate on specific working-class criticisms of organized religion, important though they may be, is, however, to miss the fundamental point that there was a gap, in part cultural and in part one of social class, between the 'respectably' religious regular churchgoers and those whose religion was expressed outside the confines of official denominations. Separated by urban geography, cultural values, social status, wealth and, at times, feelings of resentment, the unskilled urban working classes were not attracted by forms of religion that seemed to exacerbate rather than diminish such distinctions. The very ethos of much Victorian and Edwardian Christianity, with its emphasis on sabbataria-nism, temperance and self-help liberalism, undoubtedly appealed to an upwardly mobile minority of the working class, but it almost certainly alienated as many as it attracted. Similarly, the weekly and annual rhythms of working-class life came to diverge more sharply from those attached to religious institutions as churches steadily lost control over leisure. Public houses and emerging popular sports, especially football, were formidable competitors for the weekly attention of male urban labourers, whatever advantages the Church continued to enjoy through festivals, rites of passage and influence over women and children.

There were, of course, energetic and imaginative attempts to bridge this cultural divide by all kinds of religious traditions, including Anglo-Catholicism, Christian socialism and the Salvation Army. The Salvationists in particular (along with other undenominational missions) made striking gains in English cities in the last quarter of the nineteenth century. With citadels not unlike music halls, the Army made contact with working-class culture through its vernacular music, wide-ranging social concern and straightforward message. But despite its compelling mixture of energy and sentiment, entertainment and military discipline, the Salvation Army's war was not just against sin but against aspects of working-class life it defined as sin. Ultimately it was as culturally dissociated from labouring life as the churches it replaced. Essentially, the main difficulty facing official religion in the nineteenth century was that the 'respectability' of churches came across more as a cultural badge of middle-class values of success and sobriety than as an attractive picture of religion as a way to a better life on earth as in heaven.

It would nevertheless be a mistake to conclude that urbanization and industrialization effectively excluded Christianity from an entire social group, for there is much evidence to the contrary. Churches made most impact on the labouring classes when they either provided facilities of agreed social utility or enjoyed the kind of relationship in which religion helped express a particular culture rather than wage war against it. An example of the former is education, over which the churches, despite being in competition with one another, enjoyed a virtual monopoly until the State began to assume responsibility at the end of the century. Apart from the myriad of elementary schools in which the Church of England, with State support, enjoyed a preponderance, the most striking contribution made by the churches to the education of the people came through Sunday schools.

Professor Laqueur has estimated that by 1851 over two million pupils, representing 75 per cent of working-class children between the ages of five and ten, were enrolled in Sunday schools. While not a monopoly of any one region, religious denomination or social class, Sunday schools were particularly important in northern cities where they frequently 'replaced church or chapel as the focus of working-class religious life'. As they were cheap, and did not affect children's earning power during the week, they were well patronized by those in search of basic literacy and who either valued or tolerated the religious content of the teaching. Debate still rages about whether Sunday schools were predominantly instruments of social control, and taught by social superiors, or whether they were largely run, financed and taught by the workers themselves. The evidence is inconclusive because examples of both are common, but what one can say with confidence is that since, according to Ward, the Sunday school 'was the only religious institution which the nineteenth-century public in the mass had any intention of using', control was a prize worth fighting for. The subsequent battles reflected many of the tensions in nineteenth-century English society including class conflict, anticlericalism, anticentralization and sectarianism. But Sunday schools not only occasioned disputes, they also made a distinctive contribution to working-class culture through their anniversary celebrations, street parades, Whitsun outings, book prizes and benefit societies. Moreover, these activities attracted a loyal band of supporters whose lives were transformed by the weekly rhythms of preparation, prayer and planning. What Sunday schools did not do, however, was solve the recruitment problems of churches and chapels in working-class communities, for only a small minority of Sunday scholars graduated into committed church membership.

If holding the keys to elementary education gave the churches a limited and transitory hold on working-class children and their teachers, holding the keys to heaven and hell opened up more dramatic possibilities. Revivalism, for example, which had flourished in Methodist environs in the late eighteenth and early nineteenth centuries, especially in cohesive mining communities and among rural migrants to the manufacturing towns, offered quick rewards to Victorian Nonconformists. (Anglicans, incidentally, were never much impressed.) Apart from Cornwall, Wales and Ulster and parts of Scotland, old-style community revivalism gave way to new measures in the course of the nineteenth century. Revivals moved from outdoors to indoors, were often led by the Americans Finney, Caughey and Moody, and were made more palatable to respectable churchgoers. They were advertised, planned and orchestrated for maximum emotional appeal, but their long-term impact on the religion of the poor was limited. They did more to persuade church members that they were indeed urgent in reclaiming the lost than they did to persuade the lost to embrace church membership.

While control of education along with the apparently inexhaustible evangelism of Victorian churches and voluntary agencies gave organized religion a foothold in working-class communities, longer-term patterns of working-class religiosity were based on a symbiotic relationship between religious loyalty and other kinds of allegiance. The Roman Catholic revival in nineteenth-century Britain, for example, at first paralleled the expansion of English Nonconformity, but from 1830 the Roman Catholic Church in England acquired a new character under the influence of Ultramontanism from the continent and mass immigration from Ireland. By 1860 there were some three-quarters of a million Irish-born inhabitants, most of them living in the industrial towns of Lancashire, western Scotland, the north-east of England and London. The majority were at least nominally Catholic, but it was a Catholicism 'rooted in an ancient Gaelic-speaking tradition of native Irish spirituality and in a pre-Tridentine popular peasant culture of the home and the pilgrimage, rather than in Mass-going in a new shrine church'.

The ethos and atmosphere of this humble Irish culture of 'belligerent fidelity' have been vigorously brought to life by Sheridan Gilley and Raphael Samuel. Separated by their nationality, religion and poverty, the Irish initially clustered together in tight slums in which survived a patriotic religiosity 'which was heartily popular because it was heartily vulgar'. Primitive violence and drunkenness were rarely far from the surface in such communities, but there existed also warmth and generosity, humour and faith. There was, moreover, a gregarious familiarity between some priests and people, in marked contrast to the stiffer relationship – made so by respectability and clerical professionalism – between clergy and laity in the Protestant denominations. Equally important in cementing community solidarity were the valuable welfare and educational facilities offered by the Catholic Church and its lay organizations. Despite these advantages, however, and despite the emotional power of the close relationship between Celtic nationalism and Catholicism, only a minority of Irish migrants conformed to the prescribed devotions of official Catholicism. Not only did many come from parts of rural Ireland where Mass-going was a minority pursuit, but the Irish settlements in England were occupation-ally transient and relatively starved of ecclesiastical resources until later in the century, when more stable conditions prevailed. The Catholic Irish were nevertheless better church attenders then their English working-class counterparts, for, as Hugh McLeod's study of late Victorian London has shown, Roman Catholicism was the only form of religion that integrated its adherents into a working-class environment instead of making them stand out from their neighbours. One unpleasant by-product of Irish immigra-tion to British cities, for which the Irish were not entirely responsible, was the outbreak of sectarian violence, especially in Liverpool where Orangeism gained a foothold early in the century. Religious conflict subsequently dominated Liverpool politics from the Great Reform Act of 1832 until after the First World War, and the Labour Party did not finally capture the Liverpool city council until 1955. Sectarian conflict may have been bad for working-class unity and labour politics, but it kept religious issues, if not religious devotion, to the forefront of civic life in Liverpool, Glasgow and Belfast throughout the Victorian period.

Ethnicity, then, was the cultural bedrock upon which many of the socially disadvantaged Irish maintained their devotion to Roman Catholic-ism, but this was not a unique pattern. The remarkable growth of Welsh Nonconformity in the same period, for example, had its origins in the religious and social protest of tenant farmers and smallholders in the countryside, and among the proto-industrial workers of Glamorgan and Monmouthshire against predominantly Anglican landowners and entrepreneurs. By 1860 to be Welsh was largely to be a Nonconformist as the Established Church struggled for survival in the industrial parishes of south Wales. Welsh Nonconformity was also (as it was in Ulster, the Scottish Highlands and Cornwall) characterized by frequent pulses of revivalism, especially in the south Wales coalfield where danger and disease threatened mobile populations in search of a sense of community and neighbourly support. With its male voice choirs and 20,000 deacons and elders, Nonconformity offered working-class Welshmen a religious and political creed which matched their economic and social status. Yet even this seemingly impregnable fortress began to crumble in the early twentieth century as revivalism waned after 1904–5 and social inequality disturbed the cohesion of Welsh chapels. Ironically, the Established Church won back some lost ground and was then disestablished, leaving the Welsh Free Churches unsure of what they were free from. Unfortunately, as time proved, they were not free from the same secularizing forces that affected all parts of the British Isles in the course of the twentieth century.

The well-integrated religious cultures forged by the Irish and the Welsh were by no means absent from English society, particularly in the first half of the nineteenth century when a cottage-based evangelicalism spread rapidly in areas where control by squire, parson and employer was weakest. Initially, Wesleyan Methodism was both a stimulus for those popular religious energies and the vehicle by which they were expressed, but as it became more formal and chapel-based, non-Wesleyan Methodism became the dominant expression of cottage religion. Based in the home and serviced by lay preachers, including women, such religion was genuinely popular because it helped re-create a disappearing world of cottage industry, village familiarity and household unity. Anticlericalism and antiauthoritarianism were rarely far from the surface in cottage religion, and not surprisingly it threw up more than its share of colourful religious eccentrics. The groups they serviced flourished during a period identified by Valenze as 'a specific preindustrial phase of popular evangelicalism, when public and private converged within the domestic framework of labouring life', but its heyday was shortlived. By the 1850s cities, institutions and railways had brought a degree of national integration to English society and cottage religion all but disappeared with the household economy that had sustained it. The scores of 'little bethels' in late Victorian cities nevertheless testify to the persistence of lower middle- and working-class attempts to forge their own religious communities in the midst of a bleak urban environment. But by then the rigid sectarian temper of some kinds of evangelical pietism was more apparent than the more flexible domestic religion of the earlier period.

The same quality of cultural resonance and social utility, exemplified in cottage religion in the first half of the nineteenth century, was evident also in many of the mining communities of industrial England. Sensitive studies of the role of Methodism (especially the Primitive variety) in the northern coalfields have pointed to the importance of religion in creating a sense of community and psychological reassurance for the people at the raw edge of industrial England. In villages that were intimate and conforming, yet subject to scarcity and disaster, Methodism fulfilled many needs. It helped explain, and took the sting out of, suffering and death. It offered an agreed moral and religious framework for the education of the young. Its individualistic conversionism and corporate expectancy in prayer meetings brought drama and a sense of importance to otherwise humdrum lives. Its emphasis on music and song, even to the extent of appropriating local tunes and dialects, both chimed in with, and offered a religious alternative to, the local tavern culture. For women, who were largely excluded from that culture, Methodism offered new opportunities for service and social intercourse outside the domestic tedium of the house as well as giving a religious sanction to the daily battles against poverty, illness, scarcity and filth. For men, chapel offered a congenial environment for the nurture of civic abilities, including an entry into the political arena of trade unionism and wage negotiations with employers. But, far beyond the realm of social utility, the truly significant feature of Methodism in many mining communities was the way in which its language and hymns, its images and values, its festivals and celebrations, its emotions and disciplines, and its earthly concerns and heavenly aspirations became the very essence of life for large numbers of people. This cultural exchange between religion and the everyday life of working people was a rare achievement in Victorian England where so much religion was mediated through paternalism and respectability (however well-intentioned), in which appearances counted for as much as reality.

What the preceding examples of popular religion have in common is an element of cultural harmony between working-class communities and the kind of religion that took root in them. This harmony had less to do with dogma or doctrine than with social utility and popular accessibility. The novels of William Hale White are the clearest literary expression of the view that religion, to be of any use to working people, had to have a tangible social function. For those who gathered in the little meeting in Drury Lane, 'their trouble was not the forgiveness of sins, the fallacies of Arianism, the personality of the Holy Ghost, or the doctrine of the Eucharist. They all *wanted* something distinctly. They had great gaping needs which they longed to satisfy, intensely practical and special' (*The Deliverance of Mark Rutherford*, 1893). The cultural accessibility of religion to the poor was equally important. Leslie Stephen wrote in 'Religion as a Fine Art' that 'a religion to be of any value must retain a grasp upon the great mass of mankind and the mass are hopelessly vulgar and prosaic'. Vulgarity was not an easy notion for religious Victorians to embrace, whatever twentieth-century critics might think of their ecclesiastical architecture and ritualistic controversies. J. C. Miller, the Anglican clergyman who tried to stem the tide of secularization in early Victorian Birmingham, confessed that 'we have a morbid horror of being vulgar'. Instead, as students of the stained-glass windows of the period will know, the Victorians preferred to portray religion as a civilizing, ennobling and cultivating force in which the values and images of the Anglican public schools were conspicuous. But those within the Church of England with the closest experience of the urban poor, whether Evangelical, ritualist, Christian socialist or Broad Church, recognized that Anglicanism would never make much of an impact on the cities while it was wedded either to a rural vision of how parish life should function or to a paternalistic mentality. Robert Bickersteth, the long-serving Evangelical Bishop of Ripon (a see created in 1836 to cope with the manufacturing population of the West Riding of Yorkshire), made frequent appeals for working-class Anglicans to take more responsibility for church extension. Predictably, he found that working men were more eloquent in their criticism of the Church of England's shortcomings than they were desirous of reforming them. Bickersteth nevertheless did much to improve the pastoral efficiency of the Established Church in his diocese in the mid-Victorian period, a contribution that was by no means uncommon in the last quarter of the nineteenth century when Anglican communicants increased quite significantly. Unfortunately, the role of the Church of England in the industrial north from 1850 to 1900 still awaits proper historical investigation.

Although the suggestion made by Currie, Gilbert and Horsley that 'a church's power to recruit arises from its proximity to, congruity with, and utility for those whom it recruits' is generally correct, it would be a mistake to reduce urban religion to a crude social, economic and ethnic determinism in which personal motivation had no place. The plethora of studies of individual towns and cities now available for the nineteenth century make it clear that in each city there were intense pockets of religiosity carried there by zealous evangelicals, slum priests, Christian socialist missions, voluntary societies, the Salvation Army, independent Methodists, unorthodox sects and dutiful Anglicans. Even within the mainstream denominations the personality and flexibility of the clergyman or minister could make a decisive difference to the fortunes of urban congregations. But there is, nevertheless, a distinction between pockets of urban religion, sustained by unusual zeal but unable to attract more than a committed minority, and the long-term strength of religious cultures which helped express the very heart and centre of community life. The former often depended on regular stimuli from outside, and were therefore vulnerable to allegations of paternalism and social control, whereas the latter was an indigenous religious species. A sense of identity and social utility were therefore more important long-term factors than zeal alone in sustaining the popularity of religious cultures.

The emphasis so far has been on explaining patterns of religious practice in Victorian Britain, with particular reference to the urban working class, but that in itself is not very revealing of the beliefs and experiences of ordinary people, especially non-churchgoers. New light has been shed on this dark corner of religious history in the past decade through the admittedly risky use of literary evidence, oral history and the accumulated impressions of a great army of city missioners, Scripture readers and domestic visitors. Despite the teeming variety of opinions reflecting different regions, different methods of investigation, different perspectives of social class and the more obvious differences of age, gender and occupation, there exist the beginnings of a rough consensus on the prevailing religious attitudes of the urban working classes in the nineteenth century.

Outright scepticism and militant infidelity were rare, and the general level of religious knowledge, if anything, was improved, not diminished during the course of the century, partly because of a more pervasive national integration of British society and partly because of the indefatigable efforts of city missioners of all persuasions. Non-churchgoers were therefore not necessarily irreligious or even hostile to official Christianity. Describing what they were not is, of course, easier than capturing what they were, and the catchphrases used by contemporary observers and subsequent commentators have not been very helpful. 'Unconscious secularists', 'habitual neglecters', 'practical atheists' and practitioners of a 'diffusive Christianity' are all terms insufficiently flexible to describe a complex range of beliefs and experiences. In general, ordinary people appropriated from Christianity the view that religion was primarily about doing the best one could and doing no one else any harm. This ethical and community-based definition of Christian living has a long history in English religion and proved to be equally resistant to Puritan preachers and nineteenth-century Evangelicals. Justification by faith, irrespective of the attractions of making a fresh start and having a second chance, was not a doctrine well understood by English workers. Their vague belief that a generally well-intentioned life, lived free of the worst debaucheries, would be rewarded was both more prevalent than open scepticism and more difficult for the churches to counteract. Even hell, the ultimate in doctrinal terrors, lost its grip on the urban poor who seemed more concerned with temporal inequalities than with eternal punishment.

Oral evidence, in the shape of taped interviews with controlled samples of people brought up at the beginning of the twentieth century, for all the obvious limitations of such evidence, has helped fill out the religious attitudes of town and city dwellers. The preliminary results of completed oral history projects tentatively suggest that the churchgoing minority of working people may be larger than conventional statistics indicate. In addition, even non-churchgoers sent their children to Sunday school, dressed up on Sundays, used religious affiliations to obtain jobs and welfare relief, sang hymns as a means of cementing community solidarity, respected 'practical Christian' virtues, relied heavily on Christian sexual ethics (not least as a point of departure), derived comfort from religion in times of suffering or disaster, accepted that church and chapel or Protestant and Catholic were fundamental social divisions, and used the churches' social facilities without feeling any need to attend more overtly 'religious' activities.

One important, but often neglected, aspect of popular religion amplified by oral evidence is the emotional resonance achieved by the religious music of hymns and choirs, and the happy memories of seaside treats and social gatherings organized by church or chapel. Hymns in particular, so central to the Methodist revival in the eighteenth century, became the common currency of nineteenth-century Protestantism, reaching the peak of their influence in the 1850s and 1860s when 400 collections appeared in England alone. 'If there has been a common religion in England in the last hundred years', Obelkevich has said, 'it has been based not on doctrine but on the popular hymns.' Characterized by earnestness, self-absorption, sentimentality and images of military might and family bliss, hymns offered both emotional satisfaction and a shared religious language to those who found the theological abstractions of the pulpit too impenetrable. With the formation of the great choral societies, as in Huddersfield in 1836, sacred music was combined with civic pride to express Victorian Protestantism's confidence in its own culture. But ultimately the music of organs and choirs was more the vernacular of the middle and 'respectable' working classes than it was of the unwashed and the unchurched. The emotions generated by hymn-singing could, however, be transported outside church services into the home, the workplace and, on occasions, even the public house.

Oral evidence also highlights a complex range of relationships between religious employers and their workforces in Victorian Britain. In the great age of family businesses and voluntary initiative, employers used varying degrees of paternalism and coercion in providing religious facilities for their workers, but while deference could bring tangible rewards for obedient employees, it was never absolute or unconditional. As the explosion of sectarian urban religion illustrates, there were generally alternative congregations available to those workers who were either sufficiently independent or sufficiently disaffected to search them out. But this should not detract from the convenient harmony of factory, church and political allegiance achieved by many employers in this period, nor from their immense contribution to church building in the high Victorian era, when supply outstripped demand. Never again in British history, as Stephen Yeo has shown, did liberal capitalism, civic pride and religious duty combine so effectively to give urban culture such a pervasive religious character, especially in its middle-class strongholds.

Above all, what the evidence from domestic visitors, novelists and taped conversations has shown is that the religious beliefs and experiences of ordinary people were not prescribed by convocation or conference, nor enforced by priests and deacons; they were not codified into a systematic theology nor recited in creeds; they were not consistent from day to day, far less over an entire life-span, nor were they the same for men and women or for parents and children. Ultimately, they were determined more by social function than by metaphysical speculation.

For churches trying to convert such belief into more distinctively Christian forms 'the change from zeal to routine, from confident aggression to worried organizational concern', as Yeo puts it, betrayed an institutional introversion which boded ill for the future. They also increasingly surrendered the community ideal of the Church in favour of organizations designed for a specific age and gender. This was done with the best of intentions to withstand secularization, but probably only hastened it. Outside the churches even more portentous changes were occurring in the early twentieth century. The growing power of the State was chipping away at the educational, charitable and institutional importance of the churches at the same time as their declining control over leisure was further eroded by the emergence of national sports and a new entertainment culture. Moreover, the growth of socialism and the labour movement finally gave political expression to the problem of class separation which had motivated, divided and ultimately weakened the churches during the course of the nineteenth century. But even here religion was far from buried. Early socialist campaigns were conducted with all the idealism, missionary enthusiasm and self-sacrifice of a Gospel crusade. In addition, early leaders of the Independent Labour Party in English and Welsh counties, as with Chartists in an earlier period and trade unionism throughout the century, were by no means all committed secularists. Many were from Nonconformist or Roman Catholic backgrounds. Indeed, the kind of Chartism and trade unionism that emerged in many parts of England not only relied on religious personnel and organizational structures, but was also shaped by a distinctive brand of biblical radicalism combining warnings against the rich with a desire for better social relations. Christian imperatives, based upon particular scriptural interpretations of Christ's special love for the oppressed and special hatred of oppressors, led to distinctive forms of religio-political radicalism in nineteenth-century Britain. For a significant, but often neglected, minority of those involved in the familiar radical campaigns for parliamentary reform and factory reform, the relief of poverty, trade unionism and the People's Charter, their radicalism was fired by their Christianity and their Christianity was enlivened and shaped by their radicalism.

This symbiosis threw up an array of colourful characters in the industrial environs of Britain. Although they transcended the conventional denominational boundaries, many of them seem to have cut their teeth as lay preachers in the manifold popular Protestant sects before denominational alienation accelerated their commitment to radical causes. Religion, therefore, as much shaped working-class politics as it suffered from their growth. Thus, whatever ground was lost by churches in the late nineteenth and early twentieth centuries was lost not primarily because they were challenged and found wanting by a vigorous labour movement, nor even because they were threatened by the ineluctable secularizing dynamics of urban life as diagnosed by some sociologists, but because of the inexorable diminution of the churches' sphere of public influence through suburbanization, State welfarism and the attractiveness and greater accessibility of leisure alternatives. These changes were all facilitated by a rise in living standards which as much as anything led to the ascendancy of material over more directly spiritual values.

In retrosect, what is remarkable about religion in urban Britain in the nineteenth century is the extent to which a predominantly evangelical pietism managed to spread its values and preoccupations far beyond the doors of the churches it controlled. Its power lay not so much in its theology or dogma as in its energy and its ability to mobilize the middle-class laity – men, women and children – in an unremitting war against urban vice and irreligion. Women, in particular, were both used as collecting boxes in the countless local auxiliaries of the popular evangelical societies, and appealed to as national custodians of the evangelical virtues of temperance, charity and pious family life. Evangelical energy was also at the root of many of the great 'anti' movements of the century, from slavery to alcohol, whose values formed the backbone of the Nonconformist

Conscience and Free Church Liberalism in English cities. But evangelicalism was only the noisiest element in a revival of many religious traditions in Victorian Britain, the most notable of which was the recovery of Roman Catholic fortunes with the unlikely help of the pauper Irish. In addition, the Established Church, eclectic as ever, was administratively reformed and then spiritually enlivened by both Evangelicals and High Churchmen. What gave Victorian Britain its religious temper, by comparison with some other west European states, was the sheer strength of its middle-class religiosity together with a much greater acceptance of religious values among the working classes than social historians have been prepared to acknowledge. Thus, industrialization and urbanization, far from being the nemesis of British religion, probably stimulated greater religious enthusiasm in the short term while eroding its popularity in the long term. In the light of these suggestions, secularization theory is not only in need of fresh analysis, but also requires a considerably revised time-scale.

17

Hebrews Hellenized? English Evangelical Nonconformity and Culture, 1840–1940

Clyde Binfield

IN 1978 AN INTERNATIONAL consultation of 'theologians, anthropologists, linguists, missionaries and pastors', convened in the aftermath of the Lausanne Congress on World Evangelization (July 1974), produced this definition of culture: '. . . an integrated system of beliefs . . . , of values . . . , of customs . . . , and of institutions which express these beliefs, values and customs . . . , which binds a society together and gives it a sense of identity, dignity, security, and continuity'. This definition speaks pointedly to the condition of English evangelical Dissenters between 1840 and 1940. Theirs was a society within a society. It was localized and it was atomized. It was a negation. Its accents were provincial. It was diluted and sidelined as much by its disintegrative polities as by its largely self-chosen exclusion from the norms of national culture. Yet theirs was also a society which transcended society. Its pacesetters were as often British as English and its horizons easily encompassed the Empire and great tracts beyond, for their limits were bounded only by eternity. Its exclusion was increasingly more apparent than real and its polities had their own integrative force. Each had its core of professed believers. Each had its hinterland of clients and family, held together by commerce and politics and education. Affection came into it too. What to outsiders was destructive, to Dissenters was dynamic.

It was a negation all the same, for how might Dissent succeed and remain dissenting? Three things prevented Dissent from being wholly negative: its beliefs, its standing and its prospects. There was little doctrinal difference between the generality of Nonconformists and the generality of Anglicans; Dissenters too were established, for they were recognized by law and they had never quite lost their place within the pale of the constitution; and they saw themselves as the chief beneficiaries, indeed as the prime movers and moulders not only of the new Britain, but also of the new world. There was, in fact, a relationship between Dissent and the establishment which was not necessarily always to Dissent's disadvantage; and given the encouraging conviction of many that the world was renewing itself with Britons at its head, it was natural for pace-setting Dissenters to see themselves as midwives of the new culture. The next generation, their generation, would inherit that culture. Previous generations of their sort had contributed to it in testing times, now they, in bringing it to birth, had an opportunity to evaluate what had made them and to assimilate what was rightfully theirs in the national culture. They had a particular investment, therefore, in the dissemination of knowledge, the shaping of education, the study of history. Consequently they were inveterate wordsmiths and they had a peculiar interest in politics. Did they assimilate or were they assimilated? That is probably an academic question. Midwives are not indispensable but they can be vital. Lives depend on them. Dissent is neither a necessary nor a permanent condition, but it can direct as well as affect a community's health.

This chapter first considers a representative midwife of early Victorian Dissenting culture and then explores London suburban chapel culture between the 1890s and the 1920s. What still seems in retrospect to have been a golden age for such communities was quite as deceptive as golden ages usually turn out to be. Even so, these scenes from Edwardian life offer a summation of what constituted Victorian urban Nonconformity, while remaining surprisingly accessible to those who recall the Nonconformity of the 1950s and 1960s. Their representativeness might be called into question since they are metropolitan and concern large and prosperous chapels. Their 'growth' should certainly be called into question, for was it not in fact 'decline'? So might their Dissenting authenticity, for who was assimilating whom? On the face of it there can be no doubt as to the answers – Dulwich is not Dewsbury, and the numerical decline has been all but total – and yet Dulwich's pioneering Edwardian Congregational minister came straight from a Dewsbury pastorate where he had used very similar techniques, and what follows etches out a distinctive culture which was nationally, congregationally and even transdenominationally representative. If it is true, as they liked to believe, that Victorian Nonconformists most truly represented the best of the middle classes, then to that extent the matter of assimilation is almost settled (for are not all British Christians dissenters now, as well as middle-class?) and the matter of decline becomes irrelevant. The midwives had done their job.

The period's principal cultural midwife, whom most contemporaries would have recognized as such, must be Robert Vaughan. Vaughan epitomizes the social mobility of his age in one often understated aspect: that clerical underworld or intermediate intelligentsia which composed the Dissenting ministry. He was an under-educated, therefore self-educated, west country son of the (Anglican) Welsh diaspora who caught the eye of a Bristol Dissenting pulpiteer and entered the Congregational ministry. Two eligible pastorates followed, the first in Worcester and the second in Kensington which he held latterly in tandem with the chair of history at University College London. That was a useful break for a man whose earliest significant purchase had been Raleigh's *History of the World*. It introduced him to Whig circles. It enlarged his influence as preacher, author (the ages of Wyclif and the Stuarts were, predictably, his fields) and occasional pamphleteer. It made his a reliable wrist for any Whig who needed to test a Dissenting pulse. It also made him the ideal president for his denomination's theological college in Lancashire, newly removed in Tudoresque grandeur from Bury to Whalley Range, which was perhaps the Kensington of Manchester. The year of Vaughan's removal (1843) saw the publication of his *Age of Great Cities*, among the first and most significant celebrations of life's new urban facts. As president of Manchester's Lancashire Independent College, Vaughan was a weightier person than as professor of history at London's University College. In role, residence and rhetoric he encapsulated the dynamic, the tensions and the compromises which announced the Dissenting mind.

Vaughan's imperative was evangelical certainty. He was theologically conservative and his retirement in 1857, the year which saw the death of his only son and the murder of a missionary son-in-law, was understandably attributed to ill-health. That, however, can only have been intensified by the Davidson affair, a heresy hunt directed at an awkward colleague. Heresy hunts are occupational hazards for college principals. In retrospect they seem more often to have been personality hunts, but their focus is words and Vaughan's mastery had depended on words, spoken and written. His strength had been the skill with which he had reasoned his evangelical's conscience through and into words, at once traditional, up-to-date, canny and credible.

The author of *The Age of Great Cities* knew his age: 'While the social system of England shall be what it is, and while the prevalent feeling in favour of an Established Church shall be what it is, there ought, as I conceive, to be such a church.' He wrote those comfortable words for a Wesleyan readership in 1838, the year in which he also published his three-volume *Protectorate of Oliver Cromwell*. But within those facts of contemporary life, which he explored with a logic that exasperated Dissent's Young Turks, Vaughan steadily advocated more radical things. One of these was the role of the university as centre for research and discovery as well as for the transmission of knowledge. Vaughan criticized current methods of imparting knowledge (and saw more professors as one answer to that problem); he championed the proper and productively utilitarian place in university life of such disciplines as law or medicine. And he did this with the orator's sense of moment and audience. Paxton Hood, that contemporary connoisseur of pulpiteers, studied Vaughan carefully. Here was a man 'essentially born an Orator. But then . . . His sermons . . . how much more like the voice from the Professor's chair!'

> See him on the platform yonder! his head thrown back, his eyes and his voice directed to the farthest extremity of the spacious building, his grey hair plentifully falling from the back of his head; his voice not shrill nor full, its tones, however, though occasionally thick, answering well to that countenance and mouth so capable of expressing either smiles or frowns – and there are few speeches in which they do not chase each other rapidly over the face.

Vaughan's credibility lay in his constituency. 'The civil magistrate', he told Huddersfield, 'can indeed lay your property and person under interdict and death in this world, but the *priest* can follow you with unswerving malignity and fellness of purpose into the life to come.' And there was the 'wonderful moment' in Manchester's Free Trade Hall when, reading the 'Prayer of Kossuth', he extended his hand to the freedom fighter himself: 'What a thunderpeal was that which shook that renowned though ephemeral building to its foundations. Never was an audience more completely transfigured by the simple grandeur of unadorned and probably unstudied, but most highly-finished, rhetoric.' To attack the priest in Yorkshire and to welcome the free-born hero in Lancashire before audiences which contained the first generation of Dissenting magistrates, and to do this with such stirring moderation that Whigs could sleep soundly at night, suggests the truly representative assurance of a man at one with his auditory. But then, of Vaughan's closer family circle, a brother-in-law, a son, two sons-in-law, a nephew, a great-nephew and a great-nephew-in-law were Congregational ministers, two of them in the Worcester church where Vaughan had first ministered; a third son-in-law was a Congregational missionary, while a fourth son-in-law and a grandson were Anglican clergymen. This family predilection for ordination was, moreover, permeated with pedagogy. The nephew became principal of a London Congregational college and second dean of the university's faculty of theology. A son-in-law ('worthy descendant of a good old Nonconformist ancestry') ran a school in St John's Wood with the suggestive name of Hampden House. The missionary son-in-law, a Westphalian who had become a Congregationalist in St Petersburg, ended up as principal of the East India Company's college at Bareilly. Here, rippling from the Free Trade Hall through the cousinhoods, the schools, the theological colleges, the missionary society with its outposts in every continent, were the nerves of a whole culture. Here too was the context for that culture's *beau idéal*, Vaughan's only son, that raven-locked 'Arthur Hallam of Nonconformity', Robert Alfred ('Alfy') Vaughan.

The younger Vaughan expresses the swift completion of the cultural transition within the tradition. For him there was a formal education – University College School followed by University College, London, with a year at Halle and five months in Italy. For him there was choice ('He wrote verses, drew landscapes and thought of taking to art as a profession'), which boiled down in theory to 'the life of a lettered divine' and in fact to the pulmonary martyrdom of one pastorate thwarted in Bath and another shortened in Birmingham. Even so, the letters flourished. The father wrote on Wyclif or Cromwell. The son called his child Wycliffe but wrote *The Witch of Endor and Other Poems* (1844) and *Edwin and Elgiva*, a 'dramatic piece' (1846). His ambition was Shakespearean – to write the history of the Church as drama; and his first step in this direction, *Hours with the Mystics*, secured him his place, Hallam-like, in the *Dictionary of National Biography* and ensured his fame among Victorians. To write it he learned Dutch and Spanish in addition to his French, Italian and German: 'It has proved an introduction . . . to a class of writers and thinkers never before presented to the English mind in such lifelike tints.'

In part at least, *Hours with the Mystics* owed its audience, if not its fame, to one influential medium exploited by the older Vaughan. Robert Vaughan founded the *British Quarterly Review* in 1845 and edited it for twenty years. It was in the *British Quarterly* that he outlined his views on education and it was for the *British Quarterly* that he persuaded his son to write pieces on Origen or Schleiermacher or Savonarola, coaxed an aspiring Lancashire banker to write on Handel or Mendelssohn or Tonic-Sol-Fa, and generally provided 'as serious and sensible reviews of fiction . . . as any Victorian periodical.'

It was the *British Quarterly Review* which best displayed the compatibility of Nonconformity and culture. Here was a world which responded to words with the rhythm of music and the power of picture-painting, life-like rather than counterfeit, the week-day outworking of a preached and therefore shared theology, educated but not academic, and well into its stride when Matthew Arnold took it on in *Culture and Anarchy*. It was a world accessible to organists turned composers, mutual improvement society debaters turned essayists (or journalists), builders or estate agents turned architects, cabinet-makers turned arts-and-craftsmen, engravers turned artists, ushers and governesses turned educationists, mechanics turned engineers, and all of them turned social engineers. Here the world which had formed Ruskin and Browning had them restored to it.

The *British Quarterly* ceased publication in 1886. It had served its purpose as the nobly severe face of high Dissenting culture and was now too redolent of the manse study for a much enlarged constituency eager for encyclopaedias. It had moved from south-west Manchester to north London where Henry Allon, its third and last editor, reigned in the architecturally grand and musically celebrated Union Chapel, Islington. Among Allon's protégés in the *Quarterly*'s last decade was a young barrister, a Balliol man with some ability as an adult educationist and obvious political ambitions, whose mother was one of Allon's church members. This man, Herbert Asquith, earned some necessary guineas by writing useful articles for Allon. The network worked on. Emily Asquith's special friend – and distant family connection by marriage – was another widow, Susan Willans, 'Alfy' Vaughan's sister and Robert Vaughan's daughter, whose husband's family had been prominent in the Leeds chapel where the *Quarterly*'s second editor had ministered. That editor, Henry Robert Reynolds, had been proposed for the Athenaeum by Matthew Arnold in 1869 – the year of *Culture and Anarchy*, that notorious volume first essayed in a rival journal, the *Cornhill Magazine*. Arnold outlived the *British Quarterly* by two years. Since he died of a heart attack induced by running for a tram after morning service at the Liverpool Presbyterian church made famous by John Watson, 'Ian Maclaren' of *Beside the Bonnie Brier Bush* fame, it might be felt that he too had succumbed to the rising tides of a discreetly popular Dissenting culture. Those tides were at their height between 1890 and 1925, not least in London's suburbia.

A Dissenting church is a self-conscious church. Hampstead Garden Suburb Free Church was unusually self-conscious. 'It must still be many years before the Hampstead Garden Suburb Free Church can cease to be regarded as an experimental church in an experimental neighbourhood,' stated its secretary in 1913.

Services had begun in May 1909. A church had been formed in February 1910 and a building opened in October 1911. 'God is larger than the Creeds' announced the stone laid by Henrietta Barnett. The Free Church elders, though wedded to the union principle, had paused at such Free Church wording, but the Anglican Mrs Barnett, backed by Queen Mary, proved larger than the elders. It was exciting to pioneer so. 'I suppose the road is sufficiently good for my car to traverse it without breaking the springs?' wrote the London Baptist Association's Revd. Thomas Greenwood to the church secretary. 'The car's width is 6 ft., it will not do to leave it all day in the road and if there is no shelter in the courtyard I think I shall dispense with it.'

It was in that letter that Greenwood commended a Bethnal Green railwayman's son who shortly became the new church's first minister. J. H. Rushbrooke was pacifist, politically radical and upwardly mobile. His railwayman father became a stationmaster in Essex. He himself had civil engineering in view until he sat under John Clifford at Westbourne Park Baptist Church. The first sermon of Clifford's that he recalled hearing was in memory of Lord Shaftesbury. It had the remarkable title, 'A Typical Christian Socialist'. Rushbrooke turned from civil to spiritual engineering.

Like many bright Baptist ordinands of his generation (and like the Presbyterian John Watson or the Congregational R. A. Vaughan before him), he studied in Germany. He married a German. They spoke German at home. Rushbrooke incarnated the social and cultural fusion which Henrietta Barnett sought for her garden suburb.

By 1914 the Free Church's membership was 250. A decade later and with another minister it was Ramsay MacDonald's administration at prayer, with a membership above 450 and a rhetoric to match:

It is time that the intellect of the Christian Church began to reject the sophistries of the natural man . . .

It is time that the Church told the business man that he is but a steward and distributor of God's gifts – that increased prices should only follow increased service to the community, and not be imposed merely because of temporary shortage of supply. The church needs to realise that the callous rise in coal prices in bitter weather means that the poor must buy less food if they are to be able to cook it when bought! We have scarcely begun to learn in this and many another church that service to others is the first consideration for the businessman and not his private interests . . .

. . . It is time we believed more in the efficacy of the commands of Jesus for all purposes, personal, national and international. God will not refrain from helping those who believe the Sermon on the Mount to be a finer defence than thousands of aeroplanes, just because a rear-admiral on the retired list is of a contrary opinion. Yet what a lot of Church members agree with the rear-admiral!

We have had enough trimming of the Sermon on the Mount to suit social fashions and political creeds. It is time the followers of Christ comprehended the platitude that He was the greatest revolutionary the world has ever seen . . .

But if Christ's followers failed to realize that:

then we shall fail as a church, though North Square on a Sunday should be one large park of motor cars.

Hampstead held back when it came to revolution, at least where it concerned the fittings for the Free Church's new Sunday schools. Though these were as up-to-date as tile-hung cottage suburbia could wish, their managers preferred straw-coloured glass light shades to their architect's rose-pink art silk ones and green curtains to his dark 'butcher blue'.

Social conscience cottage-styled in art silk, rose pink and butcher blue, or even in more workaday green with straw-coloured glass, is a harsh encapsulation of these garden-suburban Free Church folk as they acclimatized themselves to the acoustic horrors of Edwin Lutyens's interpretation of what a Free Church should look like – a domed domesticity, part Dutch, part American, across the high green from the Byzantine ship at anchor which was his spired St Jude's. But it will serve, for the Free Church, with its membership drawn from all denominations, from all parts of Britain and from all sections of the middle classes, was the stuff of which instant myth is made. Where else could it be recalled how once, at morning service, the minister announced a new poem, read it and then left the pulpit, for the service was over? But then John Masefield's *The Everlasting Mercy* was prayer, praise and Word in one.

Clearly the Garden Suburb's Free Church was the crucible for the firing of a culture, but none of the elements in that culture was foreign to any of the Protestant ecclesiastical traditions which fused within it.

Highbury Quadrant, south and east of Heath and Suburb, was more obviously in the suburban mainstream although its heady days, which had seen their peak in 1911, the year of *The Everlasting Mercy*, were already passing by 1925. The cause dated from 1878. A temporary chapel was secured, a church quickly formed. The site was good: a triangular public garden on high ground in the centre of Highbury Quadrant. The ambitions were considerable: a building to hold 1,200 rising to 1,500, and a lecture hall for 250 enclosed by twenty-six classrooms in two tiers. It was all to cost £10,000. By 1912 those ambitions had been met and justified. The church was into its fourth pastorate; its membership was 611 (with a further 166 in two missions); there were 361 children in the Sunday schools (with 985 in the missions) and fifty-two teachers (eighty-six in the missions).

The Manchester Guardian had called the Garden Suburb's Free Church 'the most original Chapel in or near London'. Highbury's Quadrant was by then nearly thirty years old but it too had claimed originality, or at least unusual aptness for purpose. The *Congregational Year Book* was careful to explain how this was so:

The architect [John Sulman of Furnival's Inn, a good chapel practitioner] has boldly diverged from the traditional church arrangement of Western Europe, with its numerous columns and long-drawn aisles, which, however beautiful and appropriate to the ritual of the Church of Rome, is no better than an anachronism when pared down to suit the Free Church worship of the present day.

In such worship preaching has taken the place of ritual and it is therefore of the first importance that all shall 'see and hear'. The effect of the 'sympathy of numbers' both on preacher and people has also to be considered, and it naturally follows that numerous columns are inadmissible. In large buildings internal supports are an absolute necessity, if economy is studied, and any regard is paid to aesthetics. They should, however, be as few as possible, but of sufficient size to satisfy the eye as well as serve their structural purpose.

Sulman's solution was novel but not unique. His Highbury Quadrant, like James Cubitt's Union Islington, Alfred Waterhouse's Lyndhurst Road Hampstead, Bickerdike and Paull's Christ Church, Westminster Bridge Road and T. Lewis Banks's St James's, Newcastle, all built within a decade of each other, was to be a Greek cross. There were to be four columns in the area, with seating so arranged that the pulpit was clearly visible from almost every sitting, each hearer thus individualized in close community. The church was more gothic in spirit than detail, grey-slated, red-brick and stone-dressed externally, with cream bricks inside. The accent was on utility:

The satisfactory external treatment of this type of building with a due regard for economy is a problem somewhat difficult of solution, but, as the most natural is also usually the most successful method of proceeding, the spirit of the internal arrangement has, in the present instance, guided and moulded the external design, and even the subsidiary features, valuable for giving scale to the principal masses, have their origin in the practical requirements of the structure.

No attempt has been made to follow any specific example, ancient or modern, the scheme having been worked out, on a logical basis, to meet the practical needs of modern worship in an aesthetic spirit, and the author adds this design as a contribution towards the solution of the problem how best to provide modern churches suited to modern congregations at a moderate cost.

A modern church for this particular modern congregation meant sensitively designed pews, easy and unobtrusive access and plenty of stairways and doorways, some of them with swing doors. It meant an organ unencumbered by chamber and recess yet 'half concealed by a screen, so as not to attract too much attention'. The organ console was among the sittings in front of the pulpit, so that 'the organist has the choir grouped round him as part of the congregation'. A modern church also meant daily activity – parlours and vestries and lavatories and a 'roomy kitchen . . . with coppers for boiling water, gas stove, sink, and cupboard for urns, china, etc. and a serving door is not forgotten'; neither was a caretaker's flat – living room, scullery, pantry, two bedrooms and 'a large store cupboard'. Thus the carapace for the Congregational mind and soul.

Their medium was not the least of this modern church's modern institutions – a thoroughly professional monthly magazine. The issue for February 1909 contained not just the necessary details of new members or the serial accounts of the two Boys' Brigade companies, the Literary Association and the Britannia Row Mission, but also a sermon, an editorial and two heated correspondences, one socio-literary and the other socio-political, all of them of high and combative quality. The sermon, naturally, sets the tone. It is a Sunday morning sermon on 'Immortality', preached by the minister. The Literary Association and the Britannia Row Mission encompass the vernacular Quadrant life. The correspondences sketch the further shores of its mentality. The whole expresses its culture.

'Immortality' announces the Quadrant tradition: ' "Now are we the sons of God: and it doth not yet appear what we shall be". I delight in that phrase. It is the New Testament doctrine of the other world at its highest and best.' The minister, Harold Brierley, had read his T. H. Green. Here, in commendably plain and simple English, was the liberal voice of Christian idealism, hot and strong on character and the actuality which releases the eternal:

It is the larger life (the larger life rather than 'the other life' – for all life is one: 'Shall make one music as before, but vaster,'), stated in terms of character 'What we shall be'. That is Heaven . . . And character is the first condition of Immortality . . . And the change has not been in the direction of destroying the political world, but rather of actualising and realising it . . . what some short-sighted folk are inclined to call the secularisation of the other life is really the spiritualisation of this. People who are living the immortal life do not trouble about immortality, just as the healthy man never troubles about his heart, though all his life hangs upon it.

Being hot and strong on actuality meant being hot and strong on context. It forced the historical sense upon people:

What we need in reading the New Testament is not merely a translation of words, but a translation of ideas. If this very serious historical rule had been observed we should have been saved the torture and the shame of crude materialistic dogmas of a Hell of never-ending flame. We should never have heard of Jesus at all if He had not employed the language and familiar figures of His day. His was the voice of all time speaking in the tones of a narrow age. *To hear the Voice* we may have to neglect the tone.

Like many of his hearers Brierley knew his Italy, so he brought Dante into play to demonstrate the 'relativity' of those concepts of heaven which were so naturally and so accurately coloured by the contemporary constraints of mentality and geography:

Surely . . . Immortality must be the fulfilment of our own individuality . . . There are only two things that we carry with us into the unseen . . . They are just the things that make us, *us* . . . Individuality and Character. The consciousness that we are: and the quality of our being. Immortality is not something bestowed: it is something realised and developed. First brought to birth in us, then perfected. Its perfection is Heaven.

That was the trouble. Such arguments were all very well for the Balliol minds of T. H. Green's latest posterity, some of them in Brierley's pews, Asquiths-in-embryo if not already -in-waiting, but how might they speak to the half-formed and vulnerable who crowd so loyally at a congregation's periphery and are in fact at its heart? To their aid Brierley called in a long quotation from John Watson. To the whole man's gospel, ever Green, that 'Every man makes his own Heaven' and that 'Knowledge begins with self-consciousness . . . The end of knowledge is God.' Brierley added the maimed man's gospel, the 'infinitely varied capacity of Heaven, for bringing to fulfilment all the broken strivings, the half-lights, the painful beginnings of Earth':

Does not this conception of the future solve a very dark problem – the lives that have never arrived? . . . They are the reserves of the race, kept behind the hill till God requires them. They will get their chance: they will come into their Kingdom.

These Sunday words broke with a more weekday tone in the Literary Association and with fuller emotion in Britannia Row's Children's Treat.

The former had met three times since the magazine's last issue, once to follow Arthur Malden on 'A Tour through the Italian Cities', once to hear G. H. Radford, East Islington's MP, read a paper on 'John Ball and the Peasants' Insurrection of 1381', and once to hear Miss Madeleine O'Connor lecture 'with vocal illustrations' on 'some Emotions and a Motor'. Mr Malden's tour ('a most exquisite series of lantern slides and animated pictures') began in Dover harbour and culminated with 'bioscope films of Messina after the earthquake'. Miss O'Connor's was more a *tour de force* in which she described her adventures 'while motoring in wild parts of Ireland and Scotland', taking in *en route* 'two quaint old songs describing the joys of a beggar's life . . . delightful ballads embodying the deeds of Dick Turpin and his companions . . . an old ditty about two lovers in a riverside garden . . . that old favourite, "Love the Pedlar", in which Miss O'Connor's beautiful voice showed to the best advantage' and the first verse of the National Anthem, which 'the lecturer kindly sang.' That was indeed 'an eloquent defence of the motor', or so reported Edna Smallwood, whose Progressive father represented East Islington on the London County Council as G. H. Radford had represented West Islington, and would succeed Radford in the Commons as East Islington's MP.

Edna Smallwood's great friend was Ella Torrance, whose father had also been a Progressive on the London County Council, becoming its chairman as well as Islington's mayor. He too had been an MP – for Glasgow, where he had business interests, since East Islington had rejected him. Miss Torrance transmitted the spirit of Madeleine O'Connor's highwaymen, beggars and pedlars to the sober realities of Britannia Row, whose children's horizons it was her mission to enlarge:

> Every Christmas, *somehow*, it seems our Children's Treat grows happier than the one before – hearts grow kinder – little members of God's great family wind golden threads of love more closely around our tiny brothers and sisters and shield them from the cold. Go on, little comrades, wind closer, closer yet, stretch out the golden cord, and gather in till *none* are left outside!

If this was the world of Palgrave's *Golden Treasury* as illustrated by Eleanor Fortescue Brickdale, its force should not be underestimated, and what truly distinguished the mind of Highbury Quadrant glows in the two correspondences, one on 'The Church and the Drama', the other on 'Women's Suffrage'.

The former grew from an epistolary clash between two Quadrant young men, H. Woodward Aston, who took an advanced line, and George Hartley Holloway, whose safer views were more fitting for a future

Congregational minister. The debate focused on whether the church should publicize plays. Hartley Holloway's stance had provoked six letters, three in his support and a fourth largely so.

Charles Rae Griffin of Lordship Road, who was in publishing, took the common 'weaker brethren' view, popular in temperance circles:

> It must be admitted by all that there can be no more wrong in a person 'dressing-up' and so acting a character not their own, than, say, anyone who gets up at a concert and informs the audience that he is a 'Warrior Bold', etc.; but the case appears in a very different light to any like myself, who have often to pass through any place where actors and actresses 'most do congregate', and sees and hears things which are anything but what they should be. I would no more think of supporting such, than order, say, cases of lemonade from a publican.
>
> As regards the suggestion that the Church should advertise the 'clean' plays, when once you have given a young fellow the taste for such, how are you going to guarantee that he will stop there?
>
> After all, there is nothing like the old saying, 'when in doubt, don't'.
>
> Let Mr Aston put himself in the position of a Sunday school teacher at one of our Schools, and what answer will he find for the boys who habituate 'Collins's' or the Holloway 'Empire'? Does he think they can discriminate between the 'Third Floor Back' and 'Salome'? Speaking for Highbury Vale School I know that the worst (*not* the high spirited) boys we have to deal with are the ones who scoff at such entertainments as we can offer them – and go to the Empire.
>
> No, let the Church attend to her own business of saving the people, and a 'freeze-out' of all that is offensive in theatre and music hall will follow.

Falkner Lee of Stamford Hill agreed. He took such arguments a stage further:

> . . . To say that the Church above all institutions should act as an 'advertising centre' in the interest of a community which, according to evidence which is common knowledge, seethes with immorality and artificiality, seems to me to be the height of folly.
>
> Although I admit that the Stage by means of some play or other may sometimes point a moral effectively, I take exception most strongly to Mr Aston's description of the Stage as that of 'the handmaid of the Church'. How, I say, can such a community lay claim to such a title

when a large majority of its members are leading grossly material, irreligious and worldly lives? We know that the preaching of the Gospel has saved thousands of souls. Sport does not profess to teach or preach – the Theatre does. Has it fulfilled its claims? Do we, any of us, know one soul who has been saved, not reformed only, but *saved* by the preaching of the Stage, its influences and associations?

Why then, choose a long and doubtful method of doing good or becoming good when a short and sure one is within our reach? One word more. It is *so* hard for young men to-day to keep straight as it is; let no Christian make it still harder by throwing the weight of his or her influence on the side of temptation and the world . . . I should like to express in conclusion my regret that the spirit of the age makes such a subject as this debatable in a Church Magazine.

And Emily Gough, who lived on Highbury Quadrant itself, added her conviction 'that not only "plays" but semi-public dances and whist drives should neither be reported nor advertised in a *Church* Magazine'.

That left a riposte from Woodward Aston and cross-questioning from Irene Ofverberg, Ella Torrance's main standby at Britannia Row. For Aston, 'the histrionic instinct is one of the most primal instincts in man'. It could be ignored neither as a talent to be used to the full nor as a factor in the ennoblement of mankind:

I take it the chief function of the Church is the ennoblement of mankind and, as part of this, the ennoblement of those pursuits which make up the life of the people. The drama is one of these . . . Am I to mortify one of my instincts by disuse because my neighbour disgraces the same instinct in himself by abuse?

As an immediate practical measure I am only urging that the Church should do its share to support the efforts of those who, always at great financial risk, and often at great financial loss, are catering for the still small, but happily increasing, body of playgoers and occasional playgoers who want the 'best' . . .

. . . may I mildly point out that my way was Christ's way? – 'And the Pharisees and Scribes murmured saying, This man receiveth sinners and eateth with them.'

For Irene Ofverberg there were four questions which Hartley Holloway ought to answer:

(1) Does he really believe that 'in the end the regular theatre-goer becomes the non-Church-goer'? I very much doubt it.

(2) Does he think it at all probable that someone, even though he might be 'lacking our Church-fellowship or home influence', on going to see such a play as 'The Passing of the Third-Floor Back', would be thereby encouraged to hurry off to a Music Hall? He might just as well argue that it is risky to read a good book because you might not be able to stop at the good books!

(3) What does he think the Church is for? Is it to be a narrow sect of Pharisees, saying, 'This thing, with all its associations, is not fit for me to touch, therefore I will condemn wholesale all that is good and bad in it'? What would be the condition of our places of amusement if all professing Christians suddenly remarked, 'Well, though this is a good play, still there are bad ones, and I am encouraging them indirectly, so I had better condemn them all'? The effect of this would be simply to put a premium on plays that would lower instead of uplifting in order to attract that class of the public which will go to see anything. Surely it is better to support those entertainments which provide good healthy amusement or real lessons, such as all of Shakespeare's plays do. Besides which the whole idea of refusing to see a good play because it might lead you to enter a Music Hall, seems to me rather cowardly. If we are to flee from everything which might possibly be a temptation, our characters won't be worth much in the long run.

(4) To look at another side of the question. I suppose that Mr Holloway, while admitting that the talent for music, art, etc. . . . is God-given, that for acting is not. Apparently some of the great lights of the stage, such as Mrs. Siddons, Sir Henry Irving, etc., would have done better to have 'hid their talents in a napkin'. The dramatic art is one of the oldest in the world, and while human nature remains it will never fail to respond to the call of the make-believe. The art that can carry one completely away for the time being from this prosaic world, that can blot out the furrows of care and anxiety for a few brief hours, and that can for a little span make the old young again, is not one to be lightly dismissed as worthless.

Thus, one feels, had such young communities in earlier generations chipped and smoothed away their Calvinism.

The second correspondence, to do with women's suffrage, had been provoked by Arnold Freeman, one of the Quadrant's young men at Oxford. That rankled with Sidney Shortland, 'one of those unfortunates who are still hard at work while the élite of Highbury Quadrant and Oxford are debating all and sundry' and with Thomas Hughes, who wrote in from Essex to say that, while he did not know Mr Freeman, 'his letter . . . seems to have been written hot after a debate on the subject at the Oxford Union

Society . . . Down here in Thundersley we . . . found we were able to answer, at any rate, some of these same arguments. But I am not able to speak for the intellectual quality of Oxford.'

Mr Shortland, from Digby Road, Finsbury Park, and Mr Hughes, of 'Hazelwood', Thundersley, were the heavy essence of conventional Dissenting wisdom on such matters, the one an old-guard radical, the other just old guard.

> First let me say [wrote Shortland] that I concede the justice of the claims of women to the Franchise *on the same terms as men.* Why do not women make a greater use than they do of the measure of Franchise which they already possess? What guarantee have we that women will take any more extended interest in the larger questions of the Imperial Parliament than they do at present in those municipal matters lying at their doors and which closely affect their immediate interests?
>
> . . . The year 1906 witnessed the return of a Parliament more democratic than any of our time. It was pledged up to every moment of its time and opportunity to pass into law or to attempt to pass into law, measures making for the good of the community at large and the masses in particular, and involving many much overdue reforms.
>
> Why, then, is such a Parliament to let all this go by the board and to place first and foremost, as the only vital thing that matters, the granting of Votes for Women? . . .
>
> As for the 'tactics', I can neither trust my vocabulary nor demand your space to comment upon [them], save to say that no one who was present at the Liberation Society meeting at the City Temple could pronounce a benediction upon either the tactics or the tacticians. As to the Albert Hall — !!

Thomas Hughes was a not-so-closet anti. He began with calm suspicion: 'Suppose we admit for a moment that this Votes-for-Women question has anything in common with the life of the Church, surely then as members of the Church we should approach the subject only in a perfectly fair, calm and unbiased manner . . .' But there could be no doubt as to his drift. He spoke, and Thundersley spoke with him, 'for the women of this country': 'I think still that the welfare of the children and the homes of England may be best assured by women not being brought into the demoralizing atmosphere of political life.'

No editor could let matters rest there. The *Quadrant Magazine*'s J. T. Hosking reminded his correspondents and his readers that such issues were entirely within the magazine's churchly purview and to urge otherwise was heresy: 'Is the Christian Church so lacking in vitality that its life will be extinguished if a breath from the great pulsating world, God's world by the way, blows upon it to disturb its serene and saintly atmosphere?' He called to aid both Bible (Christ 'discussing things with the woman at the well, or with the guests at the house of Simon the Pharisee') and tradition ('our rough and ready forefathers, whose strange and lawless doings brought about the freedom of speech and action we now enjoy') and tied them to the forward march of history:

> Suffice it to say that the Franchise for Women is an economic necessity. Women are, through no fault of their own, but as one of the developments of modern civilisation, now standing side by side with men in the daily business life of the world, and in the near future they are sure to win their rightful place in the Councils of the nation.

By 1909 Highbury Quadrant might justifiably feel that it had its own modest access to those councils. The Smallwoods, Edmondsons, Torrances and Freemans, whose young people wrote letters to the chapel magazine, spoke at the chapel literary society, played tennis at chapel tournaments, swam in chapel galas and taught unruly children in chapel mission halls, and whose elders sold coal (the Smallwoods), made cigars (the Freemans), merchandized textiles (the Torrances) or tea (the Lees), or were building a brighter suburbia (the Edmondsons), had political ambitions. Ella Torrance married Peter Freeman, who became a Labour MP; Elsie Freeman married Albert James Edmondson, who became a Tory MP. Arnold Freeman struck out far into the idiosyncratic left. Their spiritual paths lay with Theosophists, Anthroposophists and Anglicans rather than with the Congregationalists and Baptists of their upbringing, but in 1909 they were still Congregationalists and Liberals; and theirs, though he had turned his back on it for all save electoral purposes and the occasional sermon-tasting, was Asquith's first constituency and the one most worth nurturing. Hartley Holloway, like Asquith, was an Old Citizen; Edward Smallwood, Sir Andrew Torrance, G. H. Radford, counted in the lobbies at least. In his Union Chapel schooldays Asquith had lodged with the Whittinghams on Liverpool Road. Now there were Highbury Quadrant Whittinghams, living in Brownswood Park, one of them about to marry a Finnish Lutheran. It was a broad constituency.

Highbury fed Hampstead. South of the Thames there was Dulwich. Emmanuel Congregational Church, Dulwich, was either twenty or thirty-three years old in 1909. It descended from an iron chapel erected on a site 'which for position is almost unrivalled in the suburbs of London', purchased in Barry Road in 1876 by the London Congregational Union. A church was formed in 1889 at the point when the iron chapel's congregation was ready for the Kentish Rag, Bath, Farleigh Down and Corsham stone with which W. D. Church interpreted 'the early decorated style of English Gothic architecture, of the purest type'. Church's church was to be massively towered and spired and conventionally shaped. It was to seat 900. And from that point it was a success story to parallel the Quadrant's. Its new minister, A. A. Ramsey, stayed on for nineteen years. In that time he received 1,200 into membership. By 1912 the church was into its second minister and the Irish Adam Ramsey had been succeeded by the Scottish Maxwell Kirkpatrick. In twenty-three years the church had grown tenfold, from 57 to 573 members, with 493 Sunday scholars and 100 teachers. Ramsey had retired to Enfield. His son Arthur was by then a fellow of Magdalene College, Cambridge, and soon to be deacon of Cambridge's Emmanuel Congregational Church. Arthur's son Michael would become Archbishop of Canterbury.

So it was with many Edwardian suburban Nonconformist churches. And like many, this one marked the *Titanic* disaster with a special service. The service was full, its order set out and explained in a printed programme. It included three hymns ('Eternal Father, strong to save', 'Lead, kindly Light' and 'Abide with me'), two anthems (one by Mendelssohn) and a chant. It began with the slow movement from Beethoven's Fifth Symphony and it ended with the Dresden Amen. There was no sermon. Where the sermon would have been there was instead a performance of the Brahms Requiem (soloists: Miss Marie Beech and Mr T. J. Morgan; leader of the orchestra: Miss Clara Hutchinson; conductor: Mr Martin Klickmann). Hence the programme, largely taken up with the conductor's explanatory notes.

He was careful to explain for those 'who are listening to it for the first time this evening' that 'this *Requiem* has nothing in common with the ordinary Roman Requiem Mass'. Its words, for example, were well known. They were from the Bible and Apocrypha. Its music was in memory of the composer's mother and perhaps of his devoted friend Schumann. Klickmann told an anecdote of the first performance in Vienna. He stressed how the chorus, 'How lovely are Thy dwellings fair', 'should appeal to everyone, even at a first hearing'. He alerted his readers, who were of course his hearers, to the soprano solo, 'remarkable for its difficulty', observing that 'the music lies very high, and the long phrases make it a heavy tax on the voice even of an experienced singer. But we would not have a note of it altered.' Here, then, was the highest and best in music, for here a great composer 'has revealed to us his innermost soul'. And for conclusion Klickmann quoted Ernest Newman: 'A work such as this seems to voice all our own profoundest thoughts upon life and death. The appeal of such a work cannot diminish until humanity itself alters; philosophy of this kind endures like the noble metals and the hills.'

From Hampstead Heath to Dulwich Common, from dome to spire, from *The Everlasting Mercy* to the Brahms Requiem via *The Passing of the Third Floor Back*, the culture was the same. What were its distinctive elements?

W. J. Dawson, H. E. Brierley's predecessor at Highbury Quadrant, called his memoirs *The Autobiography of a Mind*. This chapter has explored some external expressions of a collective cultural mentality, shared but never uniform and consequently never static. There were all the social, intellectual and political tensions to be expected in separated communities of men and women who had been spiritually trained to think in individuals. Theirs were societies which encouraged their members to aspire but which held back from individual excellence. They were commonwealths. Just as their businessmen popularized for the many what had previously been for the few – shirts and shoes, packaged soap, carpets, jams, cigarettes – so, by the same token, their communicators popularized the arts – foreign towns, encyclopaedias and pocket classics, the tonic sol-fa – and if the *Bonnie Brier Bush* beat the *British Quarterly* in the popularity stakes, how else could the way have been prepared without scandal for a poem or a requiem to take the place of a sermon? In 1915 J. M. Dent brought out a new edition of Anna Sewell's *Black Beauty* with illustrations by Lucy Kemp-Welch. Dent was a Free Methodist turned Congregationalist whose family's church membership embraced Woodford Green, Enfield and Purley, and whose business acumen early saw the promise of Letchworth; Anna Sewell's background had been Quaker; Lucy Kemp-Welch's was Congregationalist. Neither the art nor the literature was great, but their joint impact was profound. It was popular, wholesome, distinctive – and suburban. This popular middle-class culture was as much a levelling-up as it was a lowest common denominator. It was an extraordinary achievement. And it was a collective achievement. Chapel buildings like Emmanuel, the Quadrant, or the Garden Suburb Free Church issued from decisions reached in committee, however powerful the personalities of individual committee members. Their quality gains rather than is diminished in the light of those constraints. Chapel politics, like the chapel's polity, was representative. Chapel literature was compendious. Chapel art was practical – it concerned the telling of story or the moralizing of the romantic moment. Chapel was a good training ground for critics.

All these things were deeply rooted. Although W. J. Dawson's major pastorates were English Congregationalist and American Presbyterian, his formation was Wesleyan Methodist. St Albans in 1862 was still cushioned from the age of great cities and its Wesleyan circles were some distance from the Congregational circles of Robert Vaughan, but its terrain was ripe for acculturation:

> I can remember no library of any sort; books were hard to come by and were expensive. A daily newspaper was a luxury known to few . . . The only paper my father took was a weekly semi-ecclesiastic journal, 'The Watchman' . . . And there were virtually no magazines . . .
>
> From these facts, no doubt, the modern reader . . . will infer that we were a very barbarous and illiterate race. But the inference would be quite wrong, and for this reason, that having few books, we read with great delight those we had, and the word of the Lord – which is an admirable phrase for good literature – was precious in those days, just because there was no open vision. My grandchildren will never read Sir Thomas Browne or Raleigh; I doubt if they will even read 'Robinson Crusoe' . . . But I had to read the immortals, because they were the only writers whom I knew . . .
>
> And there is another thing . . .: simply because our area of vision was so constricted, what we saw was registered with a peculiar intensity. I have seen my mother's face express real horror at a reported crime; it was something not to be spoken of, or only in awe-struck whispers, and with a shrinking sensitiveness of apprehension. No audience in the great days of Drury Lane was ever moved to more profound emotion by the murder of Duncan and Lady Macbeth's horrible soliloquy than were we by the recital of the story of Tawell the Quaker, who killed his mistress at Slough, and was promptly arrested an hour later as he stepped off the train at Paddington, the first instance in which the electric telegraph had been used in the detection of crime . . .
>
> This acuteness of feeling arose from an acute sense of the diabolic nature of sin, for in those days no one had learned to think of sin as 'error'; 'guilt' and 'punishment', 'shame' and 'hell' were real words, charged with immeasurable meanings. But it also owed itself to the uneventful nature of our lives: when life is uniformly gray, a sudden burst of colour seems violent, a small event enacts itself upon the stage of Aeschylus or Sophocles and has the pomp and proportion of immortal tragedy.

Dawson's ministry, whether Wesleyan, Congregational or Presbyterian, thus formed, was strenuously literary. His books had such titles as *The Makers of Modern Poetry*, *The Makers of Modern Prose*, *The Makers of Modern Fiction*. They were received with a carefully judged enthusiasm.

'Dickens himself might have wept over it,' remarked the *Dundee Advertiser* of Dawson's *London Idylls*. The *Sheffield Independent* found his *The Story of Hannah* 'not far behind any of the minister-novelists'. He had a mission to set puritanism within the world of popular letters. While still a Wesleyan he appropriated Cromwell's England and wrote 'A Sermon by Oliver Cromwell'. This was an apologia in verse for Roundhead vandalism:

> Into the city at dawn of day,
> Oliver Cromwell, stern and gray,
>
> Rode at the head of his saints, and said:
> 'This city must find me money and bread.'
>
> A grim smile ran like a flash of light
> Down the ragged lines in their famished plight.

So the musketeers march four abreast through empty streets until they reach the cathedral, where the purple-robed mayor, 'Plump with three sumptuous feasts a day', stops their passage. Cromwell looks about him:

> Twelve silver statues, six in a row,
> Stood in the sunlight's softened glow,
>
> And the quiet of God was in the place,
> And the smile of God on each lifted face.

The outcome is predictable. The city is silent, the mayor is atremble, the Roundheads are pinched with hunger. Cromwell's gray eyes flash:

> 'Apostles of silver I never heard
> Could comfort the sick, or preach the Word.
>
> 'They must be tired of service and psalm,
> Of indolent peace, or impotent calm.
>
> 'Kindle a fire, and drag them down;
> An idle saint is not worth a crown,
>
> 'But put to the uses of human need,
> A saint is God's servant in truth and deed'.
>
> And then he added in kindlier mood,

'A saint should go about doing good;

'These gentlemen coined into money will make
The world somewhat happier for their sake;

'And so will perform, by deed if not lip,
The duties of their Apostleship.'

That indifferent verse triumphantly serves its purpose. A story is told. A heritage is reclaimed. A moral is drawn. A picture is painted which puts art in its place. It is all done as poem, not as hell-fire tract; or rather, it is a tract, but it is one for citizens and not lost souls, for young chapelgoers from St Albans who might find themselves at Highbury Quadrant one Sunday evening.

The core of this essay has concerned the representative culture of three suburban churches as it had accumulated on the eve of the Great War. It ends on the eve of the Second World War, in the City of London's last major surviving Congregational church. In 1938 the City Temple was arguably Britain's most famous Free Church pulpit, sustaining a fame which it had held in varying degrees since Joseph Parker's arrival from Manchester in 1869. Although its Congregationalism came a poor second to the requirements for filling its pulpit on the proper level, the church faithfully reflected the elements which announced Nonconformist culture. Its architects, Lockwood and Mawson, had been the sound provincial team which had put Victorian Bradford on the architecturally up-to-date map. It was, none the less, literally a city pulpit, since the City of London had given the City Temple its 'great white pulpit', a rostrum, apparently in multi-coloured marble, 'which is a copy of an Italian *ambon*, or elaborate reading-desk often found in medieval churches in Tuscany and the Marches'. It was the first London church to be lit by electricity and the first church in Britain to be nationally known for the preaching of a woman minister.

In 1938 its minister was a Methodist, Leslie Weatherhead, and it was the preferred London church of the American Baptist, J. D. Rockefeller. There were 640 members, with sixty children in the Sunday school. When the *Daily Mail* columnist, Norman Hillson, visited it on the round of sermon and service tastings which he subsequently collected into a series of Sunday impressions of England's year of crisis (September 1938 to September 1939), the preacher was not Weatherhead but his assistant. She was Dorothy Wilson, a Liverpool Presbyterian barrister's Oxford-educated daughter, 'with a mass of dark hair and a fair complexion'. In her black gown and graduate's hood she 'looked definitely sombre by contrast with the almost gay appearance of the choir of women in the gallery a few yards away in white cassocks and dark blue overalls. Above her head was a dark lantern with a plain cross picked out by a red light.' She faced 'a huge congregation in which men easily outnumbered women'. She did so a shade too conscious of the occasion, but she impressed the *Mail* journalist, almost despite himself:

> There is always something refreshing about the homely illustrative way which the typical Congregational minister, man or woman, utilizes in bringing home the lesson he – or she – desires to teach. The Minister is never dependent on abstruse theology or liturgical arguments. On the contrary. It is a method which relies for its force on its utter simplicity.

Dorothy Wilson began with two illustrations. The first was the release felt by the Canadian physician, Sir William Osler, when as a young man he determined to live in 'day tight compartments'. The second was about the ocean-going liner which could be divided by safety doors into separate compartments as a protection from total disaster, at an order from the master:

> We are all on the voyage of life. We must learn to control our lives, to close the bulkheads when need arises. Remember always that you will not be asked to bear more than one day's burden in one day. For each day's burden there is the strength for that day. You are not asked to take on the anxieties of the future before they come. Those of the past are in the hands of God. I remember walking years ago on Ilkley Moor among the rocks and bogs where the path meandered over dale and plain and lost itself in the rising ground. You could only remotely tell where it was leading. But you had to follow it for all its twists and turns for if you decided to take a short cut, then soon your shins would be barked against the crags and you might conceivably get lost in the marshland. That walk was a lesson to me. I began to realise that I could only see the next bend of the road when I came to it. It is the same with life. If only we would realize that the injunction 'Sufficient unto the day' is one of the greatest of all the many messages of Jesus Christ. God will look after the future and the past. But to-day is ours to make what we can of it.
>
> This day, this Sunday, what is it? It is the latest and most glorious work of God. This day has grown out of all the yesterdays which have gone before. To-day, well lived, will make yesterday a memory of happiness and the idea of tomorrow a thing of hope. We can reach that

stage if we begin each day with the thought of God and end the day with the same thought. There would never be a crisis in the world if the nations looked on life in such a way.

Such was the deceptive simplicity of Hebrews Hellenized: carefully crafted, knowingly directed, culturally contexted, for all the questions that it begs.

18

The Roman Catholic Church in England, 1780–1940

Sheridan Gilley

THE NINETEENTH CENTURY was the great, the imperial century of English history, when England was ruler of the seas and workshop of the world. It was also the great century of English Protestantism, the era of the Evangelical and Nonconformist revivals, when the religion of the Reformation influenced and moulded the lives of as high a proportion of the population at as deep a level as in any previous era of English history. To Britons of the time, these two facts were connected: Britain was great because, in adopting the Reformation, it had become a favoured nation like the Jews of old, a people blessed by Providence and chosen by God to do his will. Britain was great because Britain was Protestant; and even Protestants who sat lightly to their religion believed devoutly in the congruity between the Protestant ethic of industry, sobriety and thrift and the heroic spirit of progress and enterprise which carried British goods and soldiers and sailors as well as missionaries to the remotest corners of the earth. Moreover, the mass of Englishmen defined these national virtues as the antithesis of Roman Catholic poverty and dirt, summed up as popery and wooden shoes. Protestantism was patriotism, and popery was the religion of England's enemies, France and Spain, and of the despised sister-kingdom of Ireland. Popery was tyranny, and Protestantism was liberty. Popery was bound up with passionate historic memories of Mary's burnings, of the defeat of the Armada, of the expulsion of James II at the Glorious Revolution, and with a whole internal history of national liberation from Rome, in which a popish England had become Protestant and free.

In the twentieth century, however, Protestant nationalism has faded, and Britain has ceased to be great as it has ceased to be Protestant. Even the Church establishment has been partly Catholicized from within, while the largest English Church as measured by the number of its worshippers is now the Roman Catholic. The transformation of English public religion in two hundred years has been extraordinary. England in 1800 was becoming more Protestant, not less so, and its Catholic population of about a hundred thousand people was an inconsiderable minority – a minority regarded with superstitious awe. When the Catholic convert Augustus Pugin crossed himself on a railway journey, a lady passenger cried out, 'You are a Catholic, sir! – Guard, let me out – I must get into another carriage.' 'No Popery' was renascent, as the liberal tradition of the eighteenth century suffered eclipse in the face of a new Evangelical fervour, and the radical Evangelicals revived in the national imagination the old Protestant apocalyptic images of Rome and the Pope as the Beast and Scarlet Woman of Revelation, as the Antichrist and Man of Sin of St John and St Paul. By 1900, this Protestant apocalyptic tradition was in eclipse. Catholicism was clearly on the march, and until 1960 it enjoyed a better fortune than its Protestant rivals, as a direct outcome of its nineteenth-century history.

There has been a recent debate among Catholic historians, stimulated by John Bossy's trail-blazing *English Catholic Community*, as to whether the modern Roman Catholic Church in England was a medieval survival or a modern revival. The new sixteenth-century Church undoubtedly looked back with nostalgia to the medieval Church, but as an underground, illegal, evangelistic and missionary body it was a very different sort of organization. Papal authority was remote, and the disastrous papal initiatives of the sixteenth century – above all Pius V's excommunication of Elizabeth as a heretic and a usurper – bred a Gallican reserve towards Rome. Apart from a brief period in the 1620s, it had no bishops before 1685; and when the Pope appointed four bishops for England during the brief reign of James II between 1685 and 1688, these bishops were not diocesans in ordinary but were merely Vicars Apostolic to the Holy See.

From 1688 until 1840, the Vicars Apostolic nominally ruled a Church divided up into four Vicariates, the London, Northern, Midland and Western Districts; the last also included Wales. But the Vicars Apostolic counted for little in the Church. A disproportionate number of the missionary clergy were members of religious orders answerable to their own superiors, the largest of these orders being the Jesuits and Benedictines. Moreover, the same spirit of independence from episcopal authority developed among the secular clergy, who had their own separate organization, the Old Chapter, set up by a bishop in the 1620s but largely independent of the bishops thereafter, so that large parts of the Church were virtually Presbyterian. The Counter-Reformation Church was a battleground of competing jurisdictions, and any delver into Roman Catholic archives will be impressed at the energies which English Catholics devoted to fighting one another. Yet there is a certain especial impressiveness to the evidences of warfare and bad feeling between the

Vicars Apostolic on the one hand, and the regular and secular clergy on the other, and between the seculars and regulars. These animosities were to last for three centuries, and it was only in the course of the nineteenth century that the bishops got the upper hand and brought their clergy under their control. The Apostolic Constitution *Romanos Pontifices* of 1881 was to curb the independence of the religious orders, especially the most powerful, the Jesuits, at the behest of Archbishop Manning, but Rome's Sacred Congregation for the Propagation of the Faith, which had England under its jurisdiction as a missionary territory until 1908, found all this conflict sadly puzzling.

The real power in the Church lay in the hands of the aristocratic or gentry families who sent their sons and daughters into the ministry or the religious life and maintained an extensive network of colleges, convents, monasteries and schools upon the continent. But as they paid the piper, so they called the tune, hiring and firing their chaplains with scant reference to the bishop. On this basis the faith survived best in some of the remoter, what the Puritans called the 'darker', corners of the kingdom, especially in parts of north-east England and Lancashire, where one village, Little Crosby, remained wholly Catholic, and one town, Preston, remained perhaps a third so. The penal laws against Catholics were designed to beggar them by recusancy fines for avoiding the parish church, but Catholicism survived the early modern period as the religion of the quality. As one might put it, Catholicism is the only religion fit for a gentleman, and that has given popery a certain social chic which has lasted in England ever since.

That upper-crust lay element in Catholicism became less important in the eighteenth century, with the lightening of persecution and the growth of urban missions outside gentry control. Many English Catholic country folk migrated to the towns; but this was only one aspect of the transformation of a rural upper-class institution into a wholly different kind of Church. The Evangelical revival among Nonconformists had its Roman Catholic parallel in a new political activism and middle-class religious seriousness, encouraged by the Emancipation Acts of 1778 and 1791 which legalized Catholic worship. Many lay Catholics acquired the taste for politics, and the failure of the Jacobite cause and the hostility of anti-Catholic High Church Tories shifted Catholic politics to the left, from Jacobite to Jacobin. In their claim for emancipation from the Anglican confessional State, Catholics were allied to the radicals and Whigs, and Bossy has suggested that around 1800, English Catholics formed with the Quakers and the Unitarians the radical non-Protestant wing of English religious Dissent. In the 1780s, the influential Birmingham priest and writer Joseph Berington was a good friend to the leading English

Unitarian, Joseph Priestley. The first passenger railway line in the world, the Stockton–Darlington line, was a Catholic–Quaker enterprise, with two priests present at the laying of the first rail.

Indeed, some radical Catholics wanted a semi-democratized Church; but the days of lay power were passing. The new model bishop was the intransigent John Milner, Vicar Apostolic of the Midland District, a writer, fighter and biter, christened 'the English Athanasius' by Newman. Where most of the Old Catholics wanted good relations with tolerant Protestants, Milner signalled the rise of a more militant Catholicism by smiting the Protestants hip and thigh; his work *The End of Religious Controversy* turned out to be its beginning. Milner also wanted clerical power over the laity, episcopal power over the clergy and papal power over the bishops. He fought the tendency towards ecclesiastical democracy, and in the event, the French Revolution was to bring about a conservative reaction in Catholicism which resulted in a far more clerical, episcopal and papal Church, a Church asserting its own authority over its faithful as well as against its enemies.

The immediate consequence of the French Revolution was to send to Albion seven thousand French priests and religious, who became, with thousands of lay *émigrés*, pensioners on English charity and the English State. The first refugee bishop, of St Pol de Léon, arrived in a cargo of brandy, and when the emigration was at its height, there were a thousand priests in the King's House in Winchester who raised the roof every night with their singing of 'God Save the King'. The Church of England deplored their popery, yet gave them charity as ministers in a sister Church, and the Protestant University of Oxford printed their Latin Vulgate Bibles. French Trappists established a monastery at Lulworth, French Carthusians went to Wardour, and one French nunnery, complete with a Bourbon princess, put down its roots into English soil, and was still keeping its records in French a century later. Most of the Gallican clergy returned to France after Napoleon had restored the French Church in 1801, but some remained to found missions and to do work of lasting pastoral effectiveness. They encouraged devotion to the Blessed Sacrament and to the Sacred Heart of Jesus, and were to be the first of an invasion of England by continental Catholic priests, who were to play an important role in the internal transformation of English Roman Catholicism.

Even more important was the flight back to England of around thirty English Catholic convents, monasteries and seminaries from the continent. Benedictine monks from Douai and Dieulouard and the prince-abbey of Lampspring in Germany eventually established new houses at Downside and Ampleforth. The Carmelites of Lierre received a pension from the Bishop of Durham at Bishop Auckland; the English Benedictine convents of Brussels, Cambrai, Ghent, Paris and Dunkirk were ultimately re-established at Stanbrook, Oulton, Colwich and Teignmouth. The only medieval religious order to have survived the Reformation intact, the Bridgettine nuns of Sion, ended in Devon their four centuries of exile in Antwerp, Rouen and Lisbon. The surviving ex-Jesuits settled at Stonyhurst, while the seminary at Douai gave rise to new Catholic colleges at Ware and Ushaw. With freedom of worship and a new institutional vitality on English soil, Catholics saw the dawn of a Catholic revival in England.

What transformed the English Church's fortunes, however, was the influence of Catholic Ireland. The parliaments of both countries and their Protestant Church establishments were united in 1800, at a time when the population of Ireland was five million and the population of England and Wales was something over nine million, a far closer ratio than today. Three-quarters of the Irish population were poor Catholic peasants, who were organized in the 1820s by their priests into a Catholic Association, the first democratic mass movement in the modern world, under the leadership of a Catholic lawyer, Daniel O'Connell. O'Connell's Association forced the English Tory administration in 1829 to pass the third Emancipation Act admitting Roman Catholics to the British Parliament and to most public offices under the Crown. From 1830, there was a body of Irish Catholic MPs at Westminster, and a small but significant number of English Catholic peers with seats in the Lords, so that the Catholic interest had henceforth a definite say in the government of Protestant England.

The Irish economy, however, was already in crisis, and was subject to periodic famine. Even by 1790, Irish peasants were beginning to migrate in large numbers to England, some as seasonal harvesters, some to remain in the poorest and most squalid quarters of the English towns. There were three main routes of emigration: from Ulster to western Scotland, from Cork to London direct by sea or via Bristol, and from Dublin to Liverpool. But while the three largest concentrations of Irish settlement developed at the ends of these routes in London, Liverpool and Glasgow, there were a great many smaller centres of Irish settlement, and by the 1830s the Catholic Church in much of northern England was in a state of crisis, as young priests shortened their lives in ministering to huge new Catholic populations for whom no proper pastoral provision was yet possible.

Irish immigration was a trickle in the 1790s. It was a stream in the 1820s, but by the 1840s it had become a flood, as the Irish potato harvest failed, a million people died of starvation and more than a million emigrated, mostly to North America. Many of the poorest, however, came to Britain, nearly doubling the number of Irish-born people in England from 291,000 to 520,000 between 1841 and 1851, so that by 1850, with the children of the

Irish in England, the English Church had the task of evangelizing a nominally Catholic population of well over half a million people.

This was, moreover, a Catholic population with a rather different understanding of Catholicism. The immigrants were much more willing than the English Catholic gentry to defer to the priest in matters of religion, and so reinforced the rise of English Catholic clericalism, but it was unwise for an English priest to foist his political views upon them. The English priest, unlike his Irish brethren, could not become a political leader by appealing to the Irish blend of radical nationalism and religion, and by invoking the intermingled loves of faith and fatherland. Where the Irish were Gaelic-speakers, the English clergy were ignorant of their language, and some English bishops were reluctant to import Irish-speaking priests from Ireland. The Irish were still attached to customs like the wake for the dead, and their religion was permeated by an ancient pre-Christian folklore driven underground in much of Catholic Europe by the Counter-Reformation. Moreover, in parts of rural Ireland, especially in the west, perhaps as few as 40 per cent of the population went to Mass every Sunday, and the practice of the faith was centred not on the scattered priesthood and weekly Mass attendance at a distant chapel, but on family prayer and the local shrine or holy well and the pattern or pilgrimage, in a rural landscape which had not yet lost its sacred character. Weekly Mass-going was a habit which some of the immigrants in England would have to acquire, together with a religion centred on the priest, the Mass and the chapel, for the chapel would be the only holy place in an English urban slum.

Thus the English Catholic Church had one overwhelming task on its hands: the provision of priests and churches for the immigrant Irish, and the re-education of some at least of them in the modern norms of English Catholicism. But its leaders had still bigger fish to fry, in the opportunities opened up by the dramatic impact of Romanticism on the English cultural stance towards the Catholic Church. The novels and poetry of Sir Walter Scott created a new fascination with the religion of the middle ages, while Wordsworth wrote a sonnet teaching the doctrine of the Immaculate Conception:

> MOTHER! whose virgin bosom was uncrost
> With the least shade of thought to sin allied;
> Woman! above all women glorified,
> Our tainted nature's solitary boast;
> Purer than foam on central ocean tost;
> Brighter than eastern skies at daybreak strewn
> With fancied roses, . . .

The study of Anglo-Saxon and medieval history aroused a new interest in the ancient English Church in communion with Rome. A young historian from Ushaw, John Lingard, wrote first on the Anglo-Saxon Church and then a restrainedly Catholic history of England, to challenge the pre-eminence of Hume and later of Macaulay. The most virulently pro-Catholic work came from the pen of a great Protestant radical journalist, William Cobbett, who extolled the loving charity of the medieval monks and described the Reformation as the plunder of the patrimony of the poor by violent and unprincipled barbarians. Antiquarian-minded architects like Thomas Rickman identified the various styles in medieval building, and when the Houses of Parliament burned down in 1834, they were rebuilt in true Gothic style by the brilliant young architect Augustus Pugin, the son of a Swiss-descended Protestant *émigré* and a convert to Catholicism.

Pugin was a revolutionary of genius. He insisted that as there is an intrinsic connection between a religion and the culture it produces, so classical architecture was pagan, and only Gothic was Christian. He called St Peter's in Rome the 'upas-tree' of Christendom, a pagan building which should be pulled down and rebuilt in a Christian style. Pugin found two great church-building patrons: the Earl of Shrewsbury, whose strangest public production expresses his enthusiasm for young north Italian ladies with the stigmata, and a Leicestershire squire called Ambrose Phillipps, later Phillipps de Lisle, who had been converted to Catholicism by a divine revelation that it was the Turk and not the Pope who was Antichrist. Pugin designed hundreds of churches, gave away a fortune in charity, married three times and died of madness and exhaustion at the age of forty, having accomplished in two decades the work of several lifetimes. It was his circle which produced one of the profoundest revolutions in English religion, out of the belief that the only proper religious atmosphere is one created by stained glass, pointed arches, pipe-organs, all-male choirs, central marble altars, brass eagles, crocketed choir stalls, encaustic tiles, stone fonts and all the other paraphernalia of neo-medieval devotion.

> The Catholic Church, she never knew
>   Till Mr Pugin taught her,
> That orthodoxy had to do
>   At all with bricks and mortar.

At its most successful, as in Pugin's gorgeous church at Cheadle, the Puginesque church is a riot of light and colour, and makes worship as much a matter of the eye as of the ear. Pugin also taught the ritually illiterate English religion its love of ritual:

the stoups are filled to the brim; the rood is raised on high; . . . the lamps of the sanctuary burn bright; the saintly portraitures in the glass windows shine all gloriously; and the albs hang in the oaken ambries, and the cope chests are filled with osphreyed baudekins; and pix, and pax, and chrismatory are there, and thurible and cross.

Medieval Catholic art and architecture had been widely considered barbarous: the word Goth was close cousin to Vandal. Now, it was the only Christian style. Catholic chapels built before 1840 were plain rectangular ballroom type buildings, and even when they had architectural pretensions, these were usually classical, not Gothic. The music, if available, as in the Catholic embassy chapels in London, was provided by a very unmonastic operatic choir containing women from the Italian opera, and one London chapel was called the shilling opera house. To Pugin, this was pure secularity.

The *Zeitgeist* was clearly moving in a Catholic direction, towards an interest in forms of worship and in an artistic and architectural symbolism invested with a sense of awe, and tenderness, and mystery, and wonder, in qualities lacking both in the eighteenth-century preaching of a reasonable religion and in the emotional but aesthetically barren presentation of the atonement theology of popular Protestantism. There was a sense of the need for a symbolism of the spirit that neither Protestantism nor rationalism could command, and that symbolism was Catholic.

Some of the most radical Protestants felt this. One of the premillennial sects of the 1830s, the ex-Presbyterian Edward Irving's Catholic Apostolic Church, adopted a hierarchy of angels and Apostles and an externally splendid liturgy, at the very time that the same enthusiasm for a higher doctrine of Church, ministry and sacrament appeared among the new High Churchmen of the Church of England. Their theology at first appeared in 1833 as a reassertion of their Church's religious authority against the radicals, Dissenters and Roman Catholics who were attacking the power, privileges and properties of the Church as an establishment controlled and supported by the state, so that the High Church reaction began by being bitterly anti-Roman Catholic. By 1838, however, the leading High Churchmen were calling themselves Anglo-Catholic, were denouncing the Church of England's Protestant tradition and were actually accused by the liberals and Evangelicals in the Church of being secret Roman Catholics themselves.

By 1845, however, the Anglo-Catholics were dividing into two groups. One remained Anglican, and set out, with considerable effect, and under Protestant and liberal persecution, to Catholicize the worship, doctrine and devotion of the Church of England. The other group, which included three of the four sons of William Wilberforce, followed the lead of the only great theologian whom modern England has produced, John Henry Newman, and became Roman Catholics. The result was a considerable influx of educated men and women into the Roman Catholic Church, most of them the refined and genteel offspring of the landed aristocracy and gentry, among whom the High Church revival was strong. It is notable that Newman, another former Evangelical from the commercial middle class, converted no one in his family, reminding one of the remark that Protestants should only be worried when the shopkeepers showed signs of becoming Catholics. Gordon Gorman's work on Roman Catholic converts indicates that about 450 nineteenth-century Anglican clergy became Catholics, and Vicary Gibbs' appendix in *Cokayne's Complete Peerage* suggests that there were over seventy convert peers and peeresses, though some of these were in traditionally Catholic households. As W. H. Auden said, Baptists were people who came to the back door, but conversion to Catholicism was a disaster that might happen in the best of families.

The nineteenth century was, however, the golden age of the ecclesiastical gypsy of no fixed abode, and not all the converts stuck. There was Richard Waldo Sibthorp, a member of an old Lincoln family which also produced his mad brother Colonel Sibthorp MP, a man who opposed the Great Exhibition as calculated to attract wicked foreigners to England. Richard Waldo Sibthorp figures as a saintly radical Evangelical in Newman's early history. He became a Roman Catholic, went back to the Church of England, and then became a Roman Catholic again. He died a canon of Nottingham Cathedral, having asked for the Prayer Book service at his grave. Another clerical convert was the American Episcopalian Pierce Connelly. As he wanted to become a priest, he persuaded his wife to become a nun. Reverting to Protestantism, he sued unsuccessfully in the courts for the restoration of his conjugal rights, but seized custody of his children. His wife remained true to her vows, and is now venerated as the foundress of the Society of the Holy Child Jesus.

A significant number of the converts were women. Many of these became nuns, and not the least of the attractions of Catholicism was the fact that it gave women's work a degree of autonomy in its religious orders, which initiated massive new works in the realm of education, nursing and charity. It is notable that Florence Nightingale was attracted to Catholicism, and the converts included some Protestant women who had gone with her to the Crimea, and had worked there with Catholic nursing nuns. Again, Catholicism was a sanction for both outraging and defying the authority of the Victorian paterfamilias; there was no more dramatic way of breaking free from parental authority than converting to Catholicism. One old naval captain settled in Brompton in order to combat the sinister influence of its Roman Oratory; his son was to become its superior. Many fashionable conversions owed nothing to Roman missionary enterprise. Newman knew hardly any Roman Catholics before he became one himself, and Rome's puzzlement about these odd convert *Inglesi* is reflected in Pope Pius IX's remark that Pusey was like the bell which calls the faithful to church but never enters itself.

The well-known conversions were not typical of converts as a whole. Most Roman converts were humble folk who were converted on marrying a Catholic as poor as themselves. But the movement attracted visionaries, and one of these, a member of the Shrewsbury circle, the Honourable and Reverend George Spencer, the nephew, brother and uncle of successive Earls Spencer, began in 1839 a Crusade of Prayer among both foreign and British Catholics for the conversion of England. Spencer was opposed by the more conservative Old Catholics, even by as imaginative a man as Bishop Peter Augustine Baines, a renegade Benedictine who had converted the old mansion of Prior Park above Bath into a Catholic college with nearly a quarter of a mile of façade, through grand arcades connecting the main house to two pavilions. In quite correctly pouring contempt on the prospects of converting England, Baines did not recognize that Rome now had the fascination of forbidden fruit, and was again an influence on the national culture.

The outcome of the Catholic cultural influence in the long term was a succession of conversions of novelists, poets and painters to Catholicism: Gerard Manley Hopkins, Coventry Patmore, Edward Caswall, Lionel Johnson, Aubrey de Vere, Frederick Rolfe and Robert Hugh Benson, the last a priest-novelist with two equally distinguished literary brothers and son of an Archbishop of Canterbury. The more wayward or eccentric left conversion to their deathbeds, like Robert Hawker of Morwenstow, Aubrey Beardsley and Oscar Wilde. It is notable how many literary figures, not all of whom remained Catholic, received in the later Victorian period a Catholic education: Alfred Austin, Wilfrid Scawen Blunt and George Moore at Oscott; Arthur Conan Doyle at Stonyhurst; Lafcadio Hearn and Francis Thompson at Ushaw.

This was in spite of the failure of Newman's Catholic university in Ireland to attract English Catholics, the defeat (in part because of Archbishop Manning's hostility) of his plan to found an Oratory in Oxford, and the failure in turn (because of the hostility of Newman and the Jesuits) of Manning's Catholic university at Kensington. Catholicism had an intellectual cutting edge; and the pattern established itself whereby the public defence of Christianity to the literate English public increasingly fell into Roman or Anglo-Catholic hands. The best-known Christian apologists in the first half of the twentieth century were to be Anglo-Catholic poets and novelists, such as T. S. Eliot, C. S. Lewis, Charles Williams, Dorothy L. Sayers and John Betjeman, and Roman Catholics like Chesterton and Belloc, Monsignor Ronald Knox, Wyndham Lewis, Edith Sitwell, Evelyn Waugh, Graham Greene and J. R. R. Tolkien. There are no professional theologians in the list, but then they have been generally marginal to English culture anyway. The historiography of the Catholic revival in its English aspect was put on a sound footing by the members of a single family, Bernard, Wilfrid and Maisie Ward. The odd result has been a twofold Catholic culture in England: an aristocratic, convert and literary culture on the one hand; and an Irish proletarian culture on the other. Here, then, were the two strands to the Church's mission: to reclaim Irish Catholics and to convert English Protestants; to convert Protestants who were mostly educated or rich and to reclaim papists who were mostly poor.

There were some odd encounters in consequence. One convert, W. G. Ward, recalled a priest who read his pauper parishioners the French court sermons of Bourdaloue. Ward and a fellow-convert Grafton were the only gentlemen in the midst of a rough Irish congregation as the priest thundered out: 'Hear this, you young voluptuary! Hear this, you butterfly of fashion! Hear this, you that love to haunt the antechambers of the great!' 'I looked at Grafton,' the burly Ward added, 'to see how we could divide the parts – which was the butterfly and which was the voluptuary. For myself, I didn't think I looked much like a butterfly.' There was the fastidious Newman encountering bugs for the first time in the confessional while hearing the confessions of 'dirty Paddies'; an aristocratic novelist, Lady Georgiana Fullerton, practising holy poverty by wielding an Irish crossing-sweeper's broom; the Countess de Stacpoole founding the poor Battersea mission in the teeth of opposition from the Bishop of Southwark by pulling rank to get at the Pope, and gravitating between a caravan on the site of the new parish and the Dorchester Hotel. Many poor missions were founded out of just such an accident of upper-crust charity, and while weak in the middle class who were the backbone of English religion, Romanism in England enjoyed something of the advantage of a poor following below and a rich leadership above.

One thing, however, was clear to Rome at an early date: there was a boom in Catholicism in England. In 1840 the Pope doubled the numbers of Vicars Apostolic from four to eight. In 1850, he restored the hierarchy proper, with twelve bishops of full territorial dioceses under the primatial authority of the Cardinal Archbishop of Westminster. The measure was announced to a startled nation by the new primate, Nicholas Wiseman, in a flamboyant pastoral letter from out the Flaminian Gate of Rome, which produced the last great outbreak of popular 'no popery' sentiment in England, over the 'Papal Aggression' of the restoration of the hierarchy, fuelled by a letter to the Bishop of Durham by the Prime Minister, Lord John Russell, who as a Whig had always supported the Catholic claims, but now seemed to be opposing them. Out of the furore came a last piece of anti-Catholic legislation, an Ecclesiastical Titles Bill of 1851 denying the new Catholic bishops the right to use the names of their sees; but the Act was a dead letter, and was quietly repealed by a later Liberal Prime Minister, Gladstone, in 1871. Indeed, just as Lord Russell conceded in his Durham letter the Roman Church's right to minister to its Irish poor, so the decades from 1850 saw a kind of official endowment of Catholicism: an increase in government aid to Catholic schools and the appointment of Catholic chaplains in the army, which was about a third Catholic, and to the workhouses and prisons, which contained many Irish paupers and criminals, together with the concession of their right to worship as they pleased, a right for long denied to them.

It was Wiseman who was the architect of the new Church. A flamboyant purple figure, born to be a cardinal, he was the son of an Irish merchant family long settled in Seville, but was educated at Ushaw and then in Rome, where he became an internationally famous Syriac scholar in his twenties, and then rector of the English College. Rome has a weakness for clever English aristocrats – there were several English curial cardinals in the nineteenth century, including Weld, Acton and Howard – but Wiseman was determined to return to England to push forward the English Catholic revival, and in the 1840s he made Oscott College near Birmingham, where he was the Bishop-President, the centre of the English Catholic world. Wiseman was incredibly facile in everything except administration, and even wrote a popular novel, *Fabiola*, about a girl-martyr of the early Roman Church; at one time the prize possession of every Catholic schoolchild, this work has included among its twentieth-century schoolgirl readers such famous lapsed Catholics as Mary McCarthy and La Pasionaria. It was Wiseman's combination of personal friendliness and doctrinal intransigence that made possible the Anglican conversions, and he was the patron of those converts who followed his lead in making the English Catholic Church more Roman than Rome.

The heart of the matter was the transformation of English Catholic devotion. English Catholics used as their manual of prayer the eighteenth-century Bishop Richard Challoner's *Garden of the Soul*, a work instinctive with a sober piety stemming from the English medieval mystical tradition. This was in keeping with a reserve of feeling natural to an intensely private faith which had of necessity dispensed with the public ritual and extravagant aids to worship of the Counter-Reformation baroque. Until the nineteenth century, the Mass was called 'prayers'. Priests were plain 'Mr', not Father, and had nothing intrinsically sacerdotal in their demeanour and dress. They were a sad disappontment to poor Pugin: 'What's the use of decent vestments with such priests as we have got? a lot of blessed fellows! Why, sir, when they wear my chasubles, they don't look like priests, and what's worse, the chasubles don't look like chasubles.'

English Catholic decorum was reinforced by Augustan formalism, but it succumbed to the religious excitements of the age. Wiseman wanted nothing less than the full Roman ritual, including Roman architecture, vestments and art, to the fury of Pugin and his Goths. Wiseman introduced the Roman devotion of the *Quarant' Ore* or forty hours' adoration of the Blessed Sacrament, and in his enthusiasm for warm Italianate devotions to the Sacrament, the Virgin and saints, he was seconded by the new revivalist religious orders of Italian origin, Rosminians, Redemptorists and Passionists. Newman himself preferred Italian classical to Gothic, as a style better suited to the modern Church, and introduced into England the Oratory of St Philip Neri, the apostle of Counter-Reformation Rome. The spiritual leader of Wiseman's 'Devotional Revolution' was one of Newman's followers, the son of a Bishop of Durham's secretary, Frederick William Faber, brought up at Auckland Palace. Like Newman, Faber was of Huguenot descent; he had been an Evangelical in his youth, and as a Roman Catholic pioneered the new kind of Catholic revivalism. He also called the Virgin Mary 'Mamma', and liked nothing better than a procession with a Madonna in petticoats. He is, however, a great and now greatly neglected spiritual writer, and two of his works, *The Creator and The Creature* and *Growth in Holiness*, are two of the Catholic Church's modern spiritual classics. Newman himself came to prefer the restraint and reserve of the older English Catholics, but it was Faber who made the spirituality of the younger generation more Roman than Rome.

Faber was in part responsible for the tension and conflict between the Old Catholics and the new Roman converts which boiled over in the 1850s into a celebrated row between, on the one hand, Wiseman and his loyal convert assistant Henry Edward Manning, and on the other the predominantly Old Catholic Westminster Cathedral Chapter, of which Manning was Provost, and Wiseman's coadjutor Archbishop George Errington. Wiseman accused his enemies of Gallicanism, and got Errington dismissed by Rome; when Wiseman died in 1865, he was succeeded by Manning as Archbishop of Westminster. Here was speed indeed: Manning had gone from being an Anglican archdeacon to a Roman archbishop in fourteen years, and he set out to complete the Ultramontanization and Romanization of the Church in England. Manning had influenced Wiseman to get a ban on a joint Anglican–Roman Catholic prayer organization, the Association for Promoting the Unity of Christendom. Manning was also a leading proponent of the measure to define papal infallibility at the Vatican Council in 1870, where he was the 'chief whip' of the infallibilist majority among the bishops. In this, he was assisted by the sharpest mind converted by Newman, one of the ablest philosophers of his generation, William George Ward. The son of the owner of Lord's cricket ground and himself the owner of much of the Isle of Wight, Ward was an intellectual extremist, with the blundering body of a rhinoceros and the mind of an archangel. His solution to the problem of religious doubt was an infallible papal encyclical on the breakfast table with his *Times* every morning. Yet he was regarded with enormous respect by T. H. Huxley and John Stuart Mill, who declared Ward's reply to him on the subject of free will as the best that could be said, and whose death in the midst of the controversy Ward described as a severe controversial disappointment. It is in Ward that one can see most clearly the attraction to minds beset by the characteristic forms of Victorian doubt of an infallible Church, and the especial attraction of this idea to former members of the Church of England.

Newman's theology is the greatest of nineteenth-century responses to the problem of doubt, but he found himself in the odd position of becoming the totem and figurehead of the more reserved and liberal or Gallican Old Catholics against the fiercer neo-Ultramontanes like Ward and Manning. Manning and Ward thought Newman a heretic, and Manning seems to have tried to prevent the grant of Newman's cardinal's hat by a none too clever piece of trickery. The personal dispute, however, reflected a conflict of international importance. The Roman Catholic Church was confronted in the Latin nations, and especially in Italy, by liberal anticlerical movements intent on secularizing education, public morality and charity, and on seizing the monastic lands and properties of the Church. The result was Pope Pius IX's condemnation in the Syllabus of Errors in 1864 of 'progress, liberalism, and modern civilization'. The neo-Ultramontane movement to define papal infallibility was the Church's response to liberalism, especially to the seizure by Italian nationalists of the Papal States themselves. Of course, the reaffirmation of Church authority in the face of liberalism also took place in some Protestant churches, but to Newman, Manning's Ultramontane crusade was a refusal of the intellectual challenge and opportunities of the age.

Manning, however, also has his greatness. Much more effectively than Wiseman, the old parson, as Manning was called, threw himself into the crusade to reclaim the Irish for the Church, by building up a chain of poor schools in his diocese, by his temperance crusade, the League of the Cross, and by identifying himself, with some reservations, with the moderate expression of Irish political aspirations to home rule for Ireland. In the 1870s, Manning's social activism expanded into an attempt to reclaim the

English working class to Christianity by placing the Catholic Church at the forefront of the movement for social and political reform. Conservative Catholics shuddered when Manning appeared on a largely Protestant platform to endorse the Primitive Methodist Joseph Arch's Agricultural Workers Union, when he denounced the pogroms against Russian Jews, when he applauded the social activism of the Salvation Army, when the notorious journalist W. T. Stead arrived at Archbishop's House to apprise the cardinal of the horrors of the white slave trade in under-age girls, and when leading labour agitators like Horace Mann and Ben Tillett advised him on the progress of the dock strike, in which his successsful mediation won him a place beside Marx on the trade union banners in the world's first May Day procession.

Manning's archiepiscopate did something to bridge the gap between the English Catholic bishops and their Irish flocks, and it was a loss to the Church when his social policies were abandoned by his successor Herbert Vaughan. Vaughan was one of the eleven children of a Welsh gentry border family to become priests or monks or nuns. He was as Ultramontane as Manning, and he placed the keystone on the arch of Catholic triumphalism in building Westminster Cathedral, but as a strong Tory, he was probably nearer the politics of most of the higher clergy in England. English priests were opposed to revolutionary Irish nationalism, and were even uneasy about the involvement of their Irish faithful in a succession of nationalist organizations that supported the Irish MPs in the Commons and sent to Westminster one Catholic nationalist MP, T. P. O'Connor, member for more than forty years from 1885 for the Scotland Road division in Liverpool. The only other social activist and militant Hibernophile among the English Victorian bishops was Edward Bagshawe, who tried to ban Catholics from joining Disraeli's Tory Primrose League on the ground that it was a secret society of the type condemned by the Holy See.

Yet most nineteenth-century English priests were probably Liberals, like their flocks, and their successors in the twentieth century blessed the departure of those flocks into the Labour Party, which formed some of its great redoubts in the Catholic strongholds of northern England and western Scotland, where the collective faiths of socialism and Catholicism have reacted on and reinforced each other. The most extraordinary example of such Irish Catholic political influence was in inter-war Stepney, where an Irish–Jewish condominium in local government was ruled by an Orthodox Jewish socialist crook, Morry Davis. The general ecclesiastical approval of the Irish Catholic alignment with Labour rather contradicts the impression of ecclesiastical conservatism given by the condemnation of the general strike in 1926 by Vaughan's successor Francis Cardinal Bourne, and it is difficult to say how far the conservatism of many of the Roman clergy lost it the following of some of its Irish faithful. More Irish bishops might have made a difference. There were only two in England in the 1870s and only three in the 1920s, though some parishes continued to import Irish priests even when the Irish-born had become a small element in the congregation. England was never wholly part of the Irish ecclesiastical empire that embraced millions of Catholics in North America and Australasia, an empire which has decisively shaped Rome's power in the twentieth century, and many Irish Catholics may have failed to identify with English Catholicism in consequence.

The number of Irish-born in England peaked at 602,000 in 1861, and the English Church's mission was assisted by the steady rise in the number of priests and churches after 1860 as immigration from Ireland fell away. From 392 in 1771, the number of priests had more than doubled to 826 by 1851, but it then underwent an astonishing near-fourfold increase to 3,298 by 1901, and was 5,652 by 1940. The increase in the size of the largest of the orders, the Society of Jesus, formally restored in 1829, was nearly as remarkable: from 100 members, including novices, in the unrestored society in 1826 to 507 in 1885 and 807 in 1925. This steady growth in clerical manpower permitted the steady consolidation of congregations. In 1850, the Redemptorist missioners were preaching to the unchurched poor; by 1900, their role was to strengthen church attendance in existing parishes in which the Catholic population had settled down to a regular pattern of religious practice and non-practice. The Church seems to have held on to the active allegiance of only about a third of the nominal Catholics in Secularist London. This figure rose to over 60 per cent in sectarian Liverpool, which reproduced the sectarian antagonisms of Belfast and erupted in 1909–10 in some spectacular sectarian rioting over the setting up of a street altar for a public procession. Rates of churchgoing were higher among the Irish than among the English working class, but compared poorly with the very high rates of practice among the native English Catholics. What helped the Church in the long term was the emergence of partly Irish Catholic neighbourhoods, settled peacefully in the midst of the British working class, but with their own pubs, schools and churches, and with a large core of committed churchgoers and a large fringe of 'bad Catholics' who might be reclaimed for a time by a mission, who would despatch their children to the Catholic school and send for the priest when dying. By the 1920s, these Catholic neighbourhoods were ready for the more public display of their faith, with public street processions like the Corpus Christi procession in Middlesbrough or the Whit walks in Manchester, where the Labour councillors walked behind their priests, so that as the loyalty to Ireland faded, it was Catholicism that provided the social cement for a flourishing communal life. Just as striking was the extension of the Church by post-war demography into new areas in southern England where Catholics had traditionally been few.

It was, however, arguably the Ultramontanization of the Church that made it a success, as the new gaudy shrine chapels with their altars and statues and smells of incense and melted beeswax projected a sense of the sacred with a visual and olefactory power increasingly lacking in the tabernacles of Nonconformity. Moreover, Ultramontane clericalism gave the Church a firm dogmatic structure that underpinned its pastoral success. The suppression in 1907 by Pope Pius X of the Modernist movement led by the Anglo-Irish Jesuit priest George Tyrrell and the Scoto-Austrian Baron Friedrich von Hügel was the expression of an authoritarianism welcome in its day and generation to most Catholics. The priest, garbed in the Roman collar that was spreading through all the churches, was a figure of authority, and the immediate servant of higher authorities, His Lordship the bishop and His Holiness in Rome, whose picture stared from hundreds of thousands of domestic, classroom and presbytery walls. In a sense, that authority was popular and voluntary. Manning not only strengthened Roman authority in England over bishop and priest and layman; he also helped to create the ethos of the priest as the remote and awesome but compassionate representative on earth of the most high God. Manning's most influential work was *The Eternal Priesthood*, which is notable not only for its high Ultramontane doctrine of the authority of the priest, but for its uncompromisingly otherworldly demand that the priest lead a life of utter dedication and holy poverty like his Lord. Most priests lived better than their parishioners; hence the not wholly true remark ascribed to the Roman priest that if Anglicans had better halves, he had better quarters. Yet the demands upon the Roman clergy were there, to be available at any hour of the day or night to console the sick or to administer the last rites to the dying, whatever the cost. The outcome of this dedication was the only substantial working-class Church in the country. Outside St Patrick's Church in Toxteth, there is a memorial to the ten Liverpool priests who died ministering to the typhus- and cholera-ridden refugees of the great Irish famine, in an epidemic in which not a single Anglican incumbent lost his life. The Church of England did produce many devoted slum priests and pastors, but they were not so typical of the system that produced them; and the difference in fortune between the Anglican and Roman Churches for most of this century arises in part from that comparison.

19

Religion and Community in Scotland and Wales since 1800

Keith Robbins

CHURCHES ALWAYS exist in ambiguous relationship with the society in which they are set. Their members both reflect and reject the values of the wider community to which they belong. They owe allegiance, but not exclusive allegiance, to the State which preserves and protects the common life. They also know that their faith imparts a wider perspective. The tension that results is both inescapable and insoluble. Since 1800, the churches in Scotland and Wales have had to grapple with this central issue in a context of unusual complexity.

The religious development of Scotland and Wales since 1800 cannot be regarded as quite distinct from that of England. The two countries have been part of the wider political, social and cultural entity of 'Great Britain'. Naturally, English influences have been very powerful in Scotland and Wales, though they have been matched by strong Scottish and Welsh influences on various facets of English life. The word 'British' is difficult to handle and its significance has been variously interpreted since 1800. The political structures appropriate to the British State have been thoroughly, though intermittently, debated. It follows that the institutional and administrative system that has evolved over nearly two hundred years cannot be easily summarized. There has been, in different aspects of life, an emphasis upon both the centralization and the diffusion of power. It has not been an easy matter to reconcile the unity of the kingdom with its diversity.

We should recognize, however, that although it can be important to stress the distinctive place of Scotland and Wales within Britain, the twinning of these two countries within the same chapter represents little more than editorial convenience. Scotland and Wales differ from England, but they also differ from each other. Nothing can be more misleading than to posit some common Celtic self-consciousness which binds them together in contradistinction to England. In so far as we can speak internally of

Scotland and Wales as single 'communities' (a term which itself poses a major problem of definition), they are different communities and the links between them, while not non-existent, are less strong than either possessed with England. For much of the period since 1800 their constitutional positions have also been different. Briefly stated, while the 1707 Act of Union can be said to have consolidated the British State, Scotland retained a distinctive place within it, chiefly in the spheres of the law, the Church and education. By the end of the nineteenth century, the political distinctiveness of Scotland was also recognized by the appointment of a Scottish Secretary in government. From time to time, there has been a demand for 'home rule'. Although the political parties operating in Scotland have been largely 'British', their fortunes have differed significantly from their counterparts south of the border. In recent decades, a Scottish National Party has been spasmodically successful in certain parts of Scotland. By comparison, during most of the nineteenth century, Wales did not possess most of the external badges of nationhood which Scotland had retained. Within the British State, it had no separate legal, educational or ecclesiastical system. There was no Secretary of State for Wales, nor even a recognized capital city to give the country some kind of focus. These developments did not come until after the Second World War. A national party, Plaid Cymru, has had occasional successes but has fallen far short of its aim of self-government. Neither in Scotland nor in Wales were the requisite majorities obtained within the countries in 1979 for the introduction of devolution schemes.

It is against this background that the place of religion must be seen. The churches have been, to a fluctuating extent, expressions of a national consciousness which has stopped short of a demand for political independence. It is a role they have sometimes consciously sought and by which they have sometimes been embarrassed. It has sometimes brought them allegiance and support which they have welcomed, but it has equally made them liable to offer little more than a spiritual endorsement of 'our way of life'. Of course, churches in England have not been immune from the same pressures; but, because 'English nationality' has been more self-confident, the need for reinforcement has been less acute. Both Scotland and Wales have been felt to be communities 'under threat'. Industries have risen and fallen, creating alternating moods of exhilaration and depression. Since 1800 the populations both of Scotland and Wales have greatly expanded, but the population of England has grown even more. There have been decades in the twentieth century when both Scotland and Wales have been unable to retain their populations. To some extent, it is possible to speak of a 'culture of emigration'. Of course, these are broad statements, and it would be misleading to suppose that there have not been substantial improvements in living conditions and personal welfare between the second half of the nineteenth century and the second half of the twentieth. Nevertheless, in all these matters there was no uniform British development. These facts must be kept in mind if we are at all tempted by the notion that late-twentieth-century 'consumer prosperity' is a powerful solvent of institutional religion. Speaking generally, Scotland and Wales tended not to prosper at the same rate and to the same extent as southern England. This case cannot be argued out fully here. It would be as misleading to exaggerate the contrasts in economic and social development as it would be to pretend that they did not exist at all.

Similarly, we must not suppose that religion in Scotland and Wales constituted a totally different phenomenon from English religion, despite the political, social and economic facts mentioned above. In 1800, an acute foreign observer travelling throughout Britain would have noticed many differences between parts of the country, but he would also have noticed that there was within the diversity a uniformity; or perhaps he would have recognized many similarities but noticed within the similarities a certain irregularity. England, Scotland and Wales were all 'Protestant' countries with insignificant Roman Catholic minorities (of the order of two or three per cent).

SCOTLAND

Scotland in 1800 was overwhelmingly Presbyterian in allegiance. The Church of Scotland claimed to be the 'national' Church and it was 'established'. However, just what 'establishment' meant was one of a number of issues connected with Church government and relations with the State which had led to defections in the late eighteenth century and was to continue to cause tension in the nineteenth. Presbyterian Dissenters went under a variety of names, the Secession Church and the Relief Church being two of the most important of these bodies. Their appeal varied greatly in different parts of Scotland but it was undoubtedly growing. The Church of Scotland was still the largest single church, but in the Lowlands Presbyterian Dissenters may have attracted about a fifth of the population. The Established Church also contained various 'parties', chief among them being the Moderates and the Evangelicals, and the annual Assembly in Edinburgh was often the scene of stirring debates on constitutional and theological issues. The Presbyterian divisions were deeply felt, but the points involved were apt to seem obscure to commentators from south of the border. Particularly in the countryside, however, the issue of patronage reflected the social and economic tensions that existed.

Very small numbers of Baptists, Congregationalists, Wesleyan Methodists and Quakers could also be found, chiefly in the bigger towns. It appeared unlikely that these groups would grow very rapidly, but the presence of their evangelists broke up the totally Presbyterian image which Scotland otherwise presented. The only other denomination of note was the Episcopalian – accounting for perhaps 1 per cent of the total population but relatively strong in the north-east – bitterly divided in the eighteenth century by divisions between Hanoverian and Jacobite clergy and congregations, but recovering a greater unity.

Fifty years later, the picture was markedly different. In 1843 there occurred the 'Great Disruption' within the Church of Scotland. The complex legal and ecclesiastical issues which led up to it have been frequently described, but the affair has not received the attention it deserves from modern historians. The climax, when it came, was not unexpected. The respective rights of patron, kirk session and congregation had been in dispute for many decades. In the early 1830s, when the Evangelical party was growing in strength, attempts were made to insist that no pastor should be intruded on any congregation contrary to the will of the people. When the Assembly did pass this veto, there was then dispute as to whether it was legally empowered to do so. In turn, the 'claim of right', passed at the Assembly in 1842, stressed that Christ was head of the Church and insisted upon its spiritual freedom. It was clear that a substantial portion of the Church would leave rather than accept the jurisdiction of the State in this matter, particularly when the State was British. It was equally certain that a substantial section of the Church had no wish to defy the State. Of course, there had been many Scottish precedents over two centuries on which spokesmen from both camps could draw. The issue could easily be turned into a legal dispute of baffling density. There is the story of a mother who asked her child, over its porridge, for a statement of the true relation between Church and State. She was given the satisfactory reply: co-ordinate jurisdiction with mutual subordination.

The dispute had its Scottish peculiarities, but in one form or another it afflicted many other European states at this time. It could have happened in England. Indeed, ironically, one of the reasons for parliamentary unwillingness to yield to the claims of the Evangelical Non-Intrusionists was that it might give encouragement to the Tractarians within the Church of England. When 474 out of a total of 1,203 ministers solemnly left the Assembly and the Church of Scotland in May 1843, they set in train a momentous sequence of events. The best-known figure was Thomas

Chalmers, who set about the work of establishing the 'Free Church' with such energy that it must have contributed to his early death. There was, of course, a vast amount to be done in seeking to build up a parallel presence throughout Scotland. The Free Church did spread throughout the country, though not evenly: its appeal was greatest in urban districts and in parts of the Highlands and Islands. In these latter areas, enrolment in the Free Church was also often a way of registering protest at the agricultural change that was taking place. Recruitment was weak in the Borders where the Secession Church was already strong. There is, however, no accurate measure of the transfer of the laity from one Church to the other across Scotland as a whole. Great efforts were made to provide the new body with adequate central finance. In this and other respects, the Free Church has been characterized as 'bourgeois', but its membership was not restricted even to this ample category.

The term 'Free Church' was adopted but in fact Chalmers himself stated that, in principle, he and his supporters were not 'voluntaries'. A formal connection with the State was not anathema, provided it was on an acceptable basis. In practice, however, they were becoming 'voluntaries'. On the other hand, in the year of Chalmers's death, 1847, the Secession Church and the Relief Church came together under the name of the United Presbyterian Church. Its polity was more 'democratic' and its appeal was particularly strong in Edinburgh and Glasgow, though like the Church of Scotland and the Free Church of Scotland it aimed to operate nationwide.

Scottish Presbyterianism in the second half of the nineteenth century was therefore divided into three sections. In the initial decades after the Disruption much effort was necessarily expended by the three churches in obtaining a truly national coverage, with the erection of new churches and the provision of separate colleges for ministerial training. The rivalry which developed was no doubt in a certain sense beneficial to all parties. Group loyalties were reinforced and many examples of self-sacrificing devotion can be found. It is difficult to judge how far rivalry was accompanied by asperity. Generalizations are inevitably hazardous. Many instances can be found where personal relations on a local basis survived division, but in other cases rigid walls of separation were erected. Circumstances varied enormously between different parts of Scotland and different types and sizes of community. It was also the case that, despite variations in matters of government, about which church members felt strongly, these were still family disputes, with all the peculiarities that such a description entails. It was never inconceivable that they could be overcome and, whatever office-bearers might say, there remained members in all three churches who were relatively indifferent to the great principles allegedly at stake.

It occurred to some church leaders that there was nothing intrinsically close to the heart of the Gospel in the spectacle of corporate competition for market share. That realization might have gathered force as it began to become apparent that the market as a whole was not proving as responsive as all churches hoped. The social and economic transformation of central Scotland during the course of the century could not but be disruptive of modes of behaviour and belief which had hitherto seemed both normal and Christian. It was not yet a struggle for survival, but it was a challenge to adapt and innovate within a social framework still permeated with Christian assumptions.

The first challenge was posed by the nature of the city itself. Glasgow, for example, gave grounds for both optimism and pessimism. Its dramatic transformation in the course of the nineteenth century had led to enormous social problems. But alongside poverty there existed wealth and conspicuous public signs of material progress. The churches straddled the resulting social divisions in an uneasy fashion. No denomination can be firmly located in a particular social class, though certain correlations and alignments are possible. The unsurprising discovery has been made that the leadership exercised by elders within congregations was heavily male and 'middle-class'. The emphasis on individual responsibility and probity, within a congregational setting, duplicated 'middle-class values' – or perhaps moulded them. The development of the temperance movement was one illustration of the stress placed upon self-discipline. It seemed to many ministers and congregations to be the answer to the conspicuous alcohol abuse they observed around them. It was alleged at the time that kirk sessions were more keen to discipline members for intemperance than, for example, for reckless commercial speculation. If that was the case, and historians do not agree on this point, then it could be taken as another example of the way in which the moral judgements of the kirk tended to be more severe on the working class. The notion that it was the middle-class character of the Presbyterian (and Dissenting) congregations which alienated the working class from organized religion became increasingly attractive to many middle-class churchmen. That alienation was neither complete nor ubiquitous but it was sufficiently apparent to make such an explanation appear plausible. Even supposing the analysis to be correct, however, it was not easy to discover a remedy, except by embarking on a general critique of prevailing social and economic doctrines in society at large. Socialism might usher in a more Christian order. Those who agreed called the spokesmen of this view prophets. If only there were more of them, it was said, Scottish workingmen would see that the churches wished to escape from their middle-class captivity. It was equally apparent, however, that many church members neither believed the analysis nor found the 'captivity' particularly dispiriting.

The 'Condition of Scotland' question was linked to other cultural and intellectual developments. An educated ministry had been a source of national pride in a country which had four ancient universities. Reformed Scotland had always emphasized the exposition of the Word. A minister who could not preach a sustained sermon was scarcely a good minister. By the end of the century, however, it was clear that, in the body of the kirk, the appetite for a lengthy sermon was diminishing. Alongside this burgeoning feebleness there emerged a small but vocal 'High Church' movement which was distressed at the extent to which a kirk was thought of as a large preaching-box and little more. It was true that the singing of hymns in services had been introduced and that, amid some controversy, organs were allowed to provide accompaniment. Even so, there was a call for greater liturgical formality and more frequent celebration of Communion. However, infrequent Communion remained the norm, though it was still celebrated in some areas as a major communal experience. A renewed, though still modest, interest in the forms of worship stemmed from a variety of influences. It may be taken, however, to be related at a deep level to the need to find a new balance in Scotland between head and heart, reason and emotion. The exposition of the Word was still fundamental; but how far and in what way was the Word to be equated with the Bible? An article in 1875 from the pen of William Robertson Smith, professor of Old Testament at the Free Church College, Aberdeen, which put forward novel views on the composition, authenticity and authorship of Scripture, caused great controversy. Smith was put on trial and deprived of his Chair. There were other less celebrated cases. However, in practice, 'higher criticism' became increasingly acceptable, particularly when it became clear, with the passage of time, that there was nothing sacrosanct about the findings of that criticism. Even so, it is probable that a substantial section of churchgoers still yearned for fundamental certainties.

Such developments, of course, were not peculiar to Scotland, but they did have a particular intensity there because of a national educational mould which still placed emphasis on ratiocinative ability. Religion was something to be reasoned about; and it might simply be the case that it was not true. Gilbert Murray, professor of Greek at Glasgow University at the end of the century, was able to rid himself of the embarrassment of a prayer before he began his lecture. It was a sign of the times, though that does not mean that Scottish philosophers and theologians, among whom we may number A. J. Balfour, could not find reasons for believing that Christianity was, in some sense, true.

A combination of these social and intellectual pressures pointed in the direction of ecclesiastical reunion. The twentieth century began with the union of the United Presbyterian and Free Churches, under the title United Free Church. There was a celebrated legal wrangle over the assets of the Free Church, initiated by the Free Church minority which opposed the union. Within a few years, there were informal steps, subsequently made official, to seek a union between the Church of Scotland and the new United Free Church. The First World War delayed these discussions but also gave them greater urgency, in so far as the war showed chaplains how far removed from church life many Scottish soldiers were. Despite this revelation, union was not straightforward. There were complex legal problems to be resolved relating to endowments, and it was also necessary to find a formula to deal with 'establishment' in such a way that a national recognition of religion and the spiritual freedom of the Church could be mutually accommodated. In 1929, in the presence of the Duke of York (later King George VI), the Assemblies of the two churches came together under the name Church of Scotland.

Superficially, Presbyterian reunification returned Scotland to the ecclesiastical condition which had existed at the beginning of the nineteenth century. There were some congregations which had declined to join the union and now carried on independently under various titles but, with this exception, and that of the still small Baptist and Methodist communities, the Church of Scotland was the national Church of the Scottish people to which, with greater or lesser degrees of commitment, they all belonged. Quite apart from the fact that the link was manifestly tenuous for many mid-century Scots, this conception ignored the presence of the Roman Catholic Church in Scotland. Many Scottish Presbyterians were able to do this with equanimity because they took the view that while there were indeed signs that the Roman Catholic Church existed in Scotland, its members, with few exceptions in insular or Highland regions who had contrived to resist the Reformation, were not Scots. They were Irish. It was indeed beyond question that the growth of the Roman Catholic Church had been made possible by the very substantial Irish immigration into urban Scotland, particularly in the west. This was initially a poor population with its emotions still primarily engaged by events in Ireland. Even inside the Church, Archbishop Manning of England was not alone in noting the unhappy discord between the Scottish and Irish clergy. The reserve of the Scots, he noted, did not react sympathetically to the Irish temperament. It was in such a context that a hierarchy was restored to the Roman Catholic Church in Scotland in 1878.

The complex interplay between the Irish and Scottish communities cannot be easily or effectively summarized. It is perhaps most accurately characterized as a condition of subdued tension. Its ramifications were manifest in all communal activities – politics and sport as well as religion itself. The fact that not all the Irish immigration was Catholic further complicated the picture. The bonds across the Irish Sea remained strong and were deliberately maintained; but, on the other hand, by the end of the century, the majority of west-of-Scotland Catholics were Scottish-born. The community could not be thoroughly Irish, attached though it still was to various symbols of Irishness, but neither was it fully or 'authentically' Scots. Whether the condition of being 'Scoto-Irish' was permanent or merely a transitional stage before the attainment of full integration was a matter of opinion and argument, among both the Irish and the Scots. Either way, for Roman Catholicism in Scotland there was a risk. The preservation of 'Irishness' over generations might reinforce the position of the Church, in so far as it would continue to be the major agency for transmitting that communal identity. On the other hand, to follow this course could only confirm the notion of an 'alien wedge'. It would hinder and delay the conversion of 'true' Scots, who would be reluctant to denationalize themselves, in effect, in their own country. Yet to loosen the Irish link by deliberate act might jeopardize the allegiance and loyalty of a Catholic population which was still Irish-descended, at whatever removes. On the other hand, to stress that Catholics were Scots would assist Catholics to claim a full rather than a marginal place in Scottish life and institutions. There was also the risk that Catholics who particularly sought such acceptance would give up their faith if that was the only way it could be attained. In the last decades of the nineteenth century and the first half of the twentieth, bishops and clergy sought to guide their flocks in an appropriately tortuous fashion. The result was a clear cleavage running deep through Scottish life. The theological and ecclesial claims of the Church of Scotland and the Roman Catholic Church in Scotland still seemed fundamentally antagonistic. Opportunities and indeed desire for social or intellectual intercourse scarcely existed. The fears and hopes engendered by the successive phases of Irish political history, culminating in the establishment of the Republic of Ireland, also cast a long shadow over Scotland.

That shadow still exists and still manifests itself in public rituals of allegiance, such as Orange marches, in Glasgow and elsewhere. In other respects, however, the closing decades of the twentieth century have seen some unexpected transformations, though it would be wrong to see these as directly arising from Scotland itself. Indeed, one might say that there is a time-lag before ideas and practices promulgated elsewhere come to find their particular Scottish expression. It was not easy for the teaching of the Second Vatican Council, and all that has ensued from it, to take root in a soil conditioned to a rather different expression of the faith. Yet the logic has ultimately been irresistible, uncongenial though some might still find it. It has produced an uneasy openness as individuals and churches with little previous intimacy stumble towards a mutual Christian understanding which might produce a unity at once comprehensive and comprehensible. The structure of the Church of Scotland made a comparable dramatic change of emphasis unlikely, but it too has responded to Roman Catholic overtures, though in a tentative manner. It would be foolish to expect too rapid a change in relationships given the historical background that has been outlined in this chapter. The Episcopal Church in Scotland, though small in numbers, has been able to act as a bridge between the two major churches, but only to a modest extent. Whatever its theological and ecclesiastical insights, it is still widely regarded as an 'English' church. As elsewhere on the European mainland, ecumenical relations have to develop without the aid (or complication) of a *via media*.

It would be a rash historian (though they do exist) who ventured to be dogmatic about the reasons for the Ecumenical Movement. It might be said, in the Scottish case, that the two churches need and complement each other to a remarkable degree. Only by working together can they now relate to a Scottish society which has become less segmented than at any time since the beginning of Irish immigration. The numerical strength of the two churches may now be approximately equal – it is not necessary to spell out the difficulty in comparing figures – and Scotland is now neither 'Protestant' nor 'Catholic' in predominant character. The contrast with 1800 is a remarkable one, but Roman Catholic statistics now indicate that the apparently inexorable growth of the community is at an end. The situation is also being affected by the more or less complete detachment of previously loosely connected members that has severely afflicted the Church of Scotland in the decades since 1945, and particularly latterly.

It is, indeed, the Church of Scotland whose position appears serious, though not yet parlous. Youth organizations, like the Boys' Brigade, with which the Church of Scotland has been closely linked since its foundation in 1883, have similarly had to struggle against the blandishments of a youth culture not sympathetic to its ideas or activities. The Church of Scotland's decline may indeed be caused solely by the disappearance from its ranks of those whose connection with it rested upon a social convention of regular churchgoing which no longer obtains. It may be being reduced to a committed core undismayed by the indifference or hostility of society at large. On the whole, the small Scottish denominations – Baptists, Episcopalians and Methodists – seem in the very recent past to have been holding their own and even, in some cases, showing a slight increase in membership. The Church of Scotland's decline may therefore stabilize at an appropriate 'committed' level. However, in its case, the erosion of its support sits awkwardly with its continuing aspiration, through the General Assembly and the Church and Nation committee, to speak, in some sense, for Scotland. The complex relationship between Church and State, which we have seen erupting at various times over a 200-year span, remains a problem. The Scottish Sabbath, so widely remarked on by foreign observers even a century ago, has all but disappeared. It is significant that Sunday trading had been legalized in Scotland but has only just been legalized in England and Wales. Even so, 'Presbyterian atheists' sometimes remain attached to the notion that the Church of Scotland should remain part of their landscape. That is not because they are attracted to the idea of a vibrant Christian community but because its disappearance would remove a very important, perhaps still the major, expression of distinctive Scottish identity. It is an anxiety which also afflicts active Christians as they contemplate ecumenical adventures which could conceivably lead to a 'Church of Britain'.

The import and explanation of these developments can be variously explained: wickedness, prosperity and unbelief all have their exponents. All that can be said with any certainty is that the place of religion in the Scottish community in subsequent centuries is likely to be as different from the present as the present is from 1800.

WALES

The place of religion in Welsh society has as many points of contrast with Scotland as it has points of similarity. It was often supposed by outside observers that both Wales and Scotland in the nineteenth century were more 'religious' than England. It is difficult, however, to evaluate such observations, though we may conclude that they derived from the signs of conspicuous chapel and church building, from observed high attendance at services, from the high public profile of ministers, and from the importance apparently attached to issues of Church and State in both countries. The level of popular interest in these matters seemed greater than in England. Such are the complexities attached to the social expression of Christian belief that we may well wonder how far these indicators do take us to the heart of the matter.

However, it was also often observed that the character of religious observance and practice differed strongly between Scotland and Wales. It was claimed that Scottish religion was cerebral whereas Welsh was emotional. Again, we may be reluctant to accept such generalizations. Religious belief involves both head and heart in a balance which is more often personal than national. There had been notable 'revivals' in eighteenth-century Scotland and such phenomena did not disappear. On the other hand, the Welsh were lucid in biblical exposition and theological argument. The contrast, clearly, cannot be pushed too far. Nevertheless, the pulpit tone of the Scottish churches was the expression of a nation with four universities and a home-produced theological/philosophical culture. Although the precise meaning and implications of Calvinism were much debated in the nineteenth century a kind of Calvinism was pervasive, notwithstanding ecclesiastical divisions.

At the beginning of the nineteenth century, religion, theology, education and society did not stand in such a close relationship in Wales. There was no national Established Church, there was no university, and there was no distinct educational system. At first sight, it might seem that the religious picture in Wales was little more than a variant of that which obtained in England. The Established Church was the Church of England, which existed in Wales alongside the Dissenting denominations which existed contemporaneously in England: Baptists, Independents or Congregationalists, Methodists and a few Unitarians and Quakers.

What made the picture rather different in practice was the numerical balance among these churches and the question of the language used in their communal life. Dissent, in its various expressions, showed a remarkable growth in the first half of the nineteenth century. In 1800 there were more than twice as many Anglican places of worship as Nonconformist. Half a century later there were two and a half times as many Nonconformist chapels as Anglican churches. Furthermore, it was claimed that the 1851 religious census showed an even larger Nonconformist preponderance of worshippers. It could not be disputed that Nonconformity had been much more successful than the Established Church at least in accommodating the growing population of the principality. More than that, however, ministers and congregations saw their advance as a sign of national as well as religious renewal.

This was particularly true of the Calvinistic Methodists, a denomination unique to Wales. The mid-eighteenth-century Evangelical revival in Wales had flowed into many channels but, under the guidance of Howel Harris, its predominant form was Calvinist. Wesley preached and had some success, but in Wales 'Methodist' was normally taken to refer to the Calvinists rather than the Wesleyans. Like the Wesleyans in England, they had initially existed within the Established Church, but a formal break was made in 1811. The polity that governed the new denomination was basically Presbyterian but it was indigenous rather than imported from Scotland. By the time we reach the twentieth century the term Presbyterian Church of Wales was coming into use and stronger links with the Church of Scotland were being cultivated. In the nineteenth century it became the largest denomination in Wales, though with a marked regional preponderance in the north-west as contrasted with the south-east. It is no accident that this difference also reflected the fact that it was predominantly a Welsh-speaking body; indeed, controversy had frequently attended moves to dilute this Welshness by conducting additional services in English or establishing wholly English congregations. It set up its own institutions for training its ministers and for other educational purposes. As the decades passed its adherents came to have a vital role in the preservation and transmission of Welsh language and culture. To a lesser extent, that role was also played by Baptists and Congregationalists. Both of these denominations, however, had matching counterparts in England. They also – particularly the Baptists – had many English-speaking congregations in south Wales.

Notwithstanding the differences among them on points of polity and doctrine, collectively these bodies were able to assert that their beliefs and practices were those of the majority of religiously committed Welsh people. Precisely how large the majority was admitted of a variety of answers and on occasion not a little chicanery. English Nonconformists could not claim to have achieved such a position. It followed that Dissenters in Wales could either commit themselves to a joint campaign with their minority English cousins against the maintenance of an Established Church of England in England and Wales or go their own way. There was little doubt that the latter course offered at least the prospect of success. The Irish Church Act (1869) seemed to offer a precedent. Disestablishment became the goal of most Welsh Nonconformists, though they were to find that the citadel did not crumble immediately.

The campaign derived added impetus from the identification of the Anglican Church in Wales as the 'English' Church. It was indeed the case that it had been substantially served in the first half of the century by a largely English episcopate and had failed to develop a Welsh-medium religious press to stand comparison with the major activity in this field of the Nonconformist denominations. It had looked for support from the Welsh English-speaking squirearchy and had not coped adequately with the rapid industrialization of south Wales. In some areas, English incomers specifically built English-medium churches alongside existing parish churches. Thus it was not difficult to polarize the issue, for political purposes, into the appearance of a struggle between radical/participatory/chapel 'Wales' on the one hand and conservative/hierarchical/church 'England-in-Wales' on the other. There were elements of truth in this picture, but it was always a caricature. Even though it was in a numerical minority, the Church's parochial structure gave it a better claim to be truly representative of the diversity of Wales than any single Dissenting denomination – Dissenters had marked regional allegiances. Nor was it in practice monoglot English. Three strong English bishops – Thirlwall of St Davids, Ollivant of Llandaff and Short of St Asaph – were by no means insensitive to Welsh needs and aspirations and contributed greatly in the mid-century to the revival of their dioceses. A Welsh-speaking Welshman was appointed Bishop of St Asaph in 1870. Over subsequent decades the cymricization of the episcopate continued apace.

Nevertheless, the campaign for disestablishment was unmoved. It was the principle that counted. Whether the campaign could be successful depended not only on feeling within Wales but, more importantly, on the configurations of British politics as a whole. Gladstone shifted from his conviction that the Church in Wales had a complete constitutional, legal and historical identity with the Church of England to the view that the Welsh Church, like Wales as a whole, could be treated as a separate entity in certain circumstances. Between 1894 and 1914 four Welsh Disestablishment Bills were placed before Parliament and only in the latter year did one reach the statute book. There still remained some difficulties to be resolved concerning the accompanying disendowment and it was with distress that some of those engaged in the dispute came to accept the temporary disruption of their discussions caused by the outbreak of the First World War. The political argument had occasioned considerable heat and a little light. The possible implications of what might happen in Wales for the principle of establishment in England and, in its different form, in Scotland, had weight with some MPs. Nonconformists were adamant in their refusal to accept that the Church was the national Church. Between 1906 and 1910 a Royal Commission tried to get to grips with supposedly hard statistics on the entire issue and found, like many ecclesiastical historians before and since, that different church bodies attached different importance to the same signs (baptism and Communion for example). People liked to be married in church; did that mean that they were Church people? Was the number of sittings relevant, or should the commissioners only take note of members? And how were they to define members? The supposed ecclesiastical allegiance of between half a million and a million Welsh people could hang upon how these questions were answered.

It is not surprising that by the time disestablishment reached the statute book a certain aridity had entered into the entire debate. When success was finally achieved, social and economic issues in Welsh life were coming to the fore in a fashion which made disestablishment seem largely irrelevant. Notwithstanding their hostility to the privileged position of the Church, some Nonconformists were not altogether happy that certain of its revenues were going to be disbursed for purposes which had no direct link with religion of any kind. In addition, while church and chapel leaders were squabbling over the rightful attribution of their adherents it became increasingly apparent to them that there were some hundreds of thousands of Welsh people who had no significant allegiance to any religious body – who either had never had such a connection or were extracting themselves from it. This discovery was not highlighted because it conflicted with the national stereotype of the religious Welshman or Welshwoman. Nevertheless, for good or ill, after the First World War, Wales, unlike England or Scotland, had no Established Church. All Christian denominations were now on a par in the eyes of the State.

In one sense, the achievement of this constitutional position was a triumph, but it proved to be a hollow one. Whatever the strength of the argument for equity, the spectacle was not in itself religiously edifying. It was obvious that on both sides synthetic emotions were being generated by men, like Lloyd George, who appear to have had no religious convictions. It was also apparent that a 'victorious' Nonconformity was at a crisis point in its own development. It might appear strong on paper but, roughly from the beginning of the century, it might be best characterized as one force among many in Welsh life. Some historians have seen this development as the collapse of a hegemonic power which had dominated Welsh society and arrogantly equated itself with 'Welsh culture'. On the other hand, Nonconformists were themselves only too aware of their limited capacity to control the mores of their compatriots, even at the height of their influence. It follows that some historians have seen the enthusiasm of the Welsh revival of 1904–5 as 'encapsulating the crisis of the Nonconformist conscience in an increasingly secular world' (Tim Williams), while others have seen in the efforts of Evan Roberts and his female associates in particular an explosion of fervour which bypassed ministers and deacons who had allowed their faith to become a kind of professional occupation. In the short term, the increased membership reported as a result of the work of the revivalists was striking, but it did not last.

The 'eclipse of Nonconformity' was to be a feature of subsequent decades, though to use that term was inaccurate in any constitutional sense. In a cultural sense, indeed, it might be said that the Calvinistic Methodists, the Baptists and Congregationalists constituted a Welsh 'Establishment'. Their problem was that Welsh-speaking Wales was itself in crisis. The 1921 census showed an absolute drop in the number of Welsh-speakers for the first time; just over a third of the population could speak the language. The interlinking of religion, language and culture posed a problem which has remained to the present. How far was the survival of the denominations dependent upon the survival of the language? Or should the question be posed the other way round? Both the chapels and the language seemed vulnerable to the same economic and social pressures. From the standpoint of religion there was the clear danger that the Gospel would become fossilized and its institutional manifestation would be merely a cultural ghetto cut off from a 'modern' and increasingly 'English' way of life. It was noted on some occasions that even those who had attended a service in Welsh began to talk in English to each other as they left. From the standpoint of the language, the erosion of the support still offered by the chapels might be catastrophic. On the other hand, in a more general social sense, Nonconformists could be said to be victims of their very success in bringing about greater recognition of a Welsh identity within Britain by the creation of such institutions as the University of Wales and the National Library of Wales. Nonconformists could no longer claim to be the sole 'carriers' of Welsh identity. And, if those who founded the Welsh Nationalist Party in 1925 had their way, Wales would go on to full political independence and would therefore have even less need of religion as an institutional barrier against anglicization.

These pressures must be seen in the context of the general economic crisis which Wales experienced between the wars, in both rural and industrial areas. In the prevailing circumstances it became clear that, in financial terms, congregations had often over-extended their commitments. The maintenance of large buildings became an increasing burden. Migration away from particular areas, and away from Wales altogether, strained the viability of many chapels. In the decade up to 1935, for example, it was found that 8,867 members of Nonconformist chapels in the Rhondda had moved away. For many who remained it seemed easy to believe that socialism offered a solution to the stricken valleys. It would be wrong to picture too catastrophic a decline, however, and equally wrong too posit too fundamental a confrontation between old chapel ways and socialism. Many ministers were persuaded of the necessity for left-wing politics and many socialists were perhaps less agnostic in their souls than they proclaimed publicly.

The Church in Wales (as the disestablished Church was called) was not immune from these tensions. However, it survived its own internal reorientation with a success that some found surprising. It set up its own Representative Body and its members responded well to the financial demands which its new position required. As time passed, the loss of privileged status frequently came to be seen as an advantage. It contributed further to the removal of the suggestion that it was an alien ecclesiastical interloper. Slowly, church–chapel relations improved. It was in the inter-war period, too, that the Roman Catholic Church came to be noticed as a factor in Welsh life. The Irish had not migrated into Wales on the same scale as they had into Scotland. Nevertheless, an Irish and Irish-descended population in Cardiff and elsewhere enabled the Catholic Church to establish a presence. Its growth was also helped by a number of prominent converts to Roman Catholicism, among them the writer Saunders Lewis, of impeccable Nonconformist descent. It was indeed sometimes suggested that Roman Catholics were colonizing the Welsh Nationalist Party. We are not here dealing with a large movement, but there was a body of opinion which argued that both in religion and in politics Wales had come to a dead end. It was time to make a fresh start with a new 'old' religion which would have more to contribute to the vitality of the nation than a moth-eaten puritanism struggling to keep alive enclaves of sabbatarianism, teetotalism and absence of gambling in a country which was moving on beyond that phase in its cultural development.

In general, it was not until several decades after the end of the Second World War that an ecumenical mood appeared. Until this point, and indeed beyond it, all the denominations inevitably still carried the legacy of their nineteenth-century history about with them. The myths surrounding Welsh old-time religion still tangled awkwardly with the present. 'Nonconformity' still seemed inextricably bound up with a certain conception of Welshness. The chapels were still bastions of the language in Welsh-speaking areas, but the walls were crumbling and a certain despair of the future was pervasive. On the other hand, there still appeared individuals, like Gwynfor Evans, the first Plaid Cymru MP, who were capable of projecting a nationalist vision in which the Independent religious tradition, to which he belonged, was still a vibrant factor. And, in dioceses where there was a substantial presence of Welsh-speaking Anglicans, there was also considerable support, at least among the clergy, for ideas of Welsh self-government. At the time of the 1979 referendum on devolution for Wales the Church in Wales Archbishop of Wales strongly identified himself with the cause on public platforms. Such gestures appeared to support the view that the church/chapel communal divide had lost its resonance. But, of course, even in a Welsh-speaking area like Gwynedd, devolution failed to carry majority support. The reasons for this failure cannot be discussed in detail here, but one aspect would appear to be an apprehension on the part of the non-Welsh-speaking majority that Welsh-speakers would have a privileged position under devolved government. Whether or not that fear was misplaced, it would also seem to have been present among English-language congregations in denominations whose official leaders supported devolution.

In any event, the Wales of the 1970s and 1980s had moved on, in both social and economic terms. The image of industrial south Wales was ceasing to bear much relationship to reality. Amid the pain of change, there was a new prosperity, adjustment to which seemed to cause the denominations as much difficulty as depression had done. In the eyes of some commentators, 'Welsh religion', like so many other aspects of Welsh life, was ceasing, perhaps had ceased, to be distinctively Welsh. Chapels and coal mines alike were becoming things of the past, whose only future would be as pieces of heritage. Visitors would walk round uncomprehendingly as they listened to the recorded voices of actors pretending to be ministers caught up in the ecstasy of *hwyl* as their sermons reached their climax, or listened to male voice choirs pretending to be chapel male voice choirs. That there was a stark 'secularization' was incontestable, at a certain level. Even so, there was abundant evidence that it remained a Welsh kind of 'secularization'.

It was also possible to wonder whether much that had apparently been lost was of the essence of 'religion' anyway. Stripped of their pretensions and humbled into awareness of each other's strengths and insights, all the denominations began to grapple together with Wales's rich mixture of faith and fiction. The poet-vicar R. S. Thomas, shepherding his flock in the Lleyn peninsula, felt all these tensions as past and present mingled in his writing. There were regions of the mind and spirit which could not be satisfied with the heaven promised by Vernon's Pools (Cardiff). Another poet, Idris Davies, had written between the wars a dramatic poem in which he captured 'Capel Hebron' surging with the sound of praise. Such singing could still be heard; but in Wales, as elsewhere, it was perhaps now a matter of listening for a still small voice after so much noise and passion. There has been loss and gain in the troubled relationship between religion and community in Wales since 1800.

20

British Religion and the Wider World: Mission and Empire, 1800–1940

C. Peter Williams

BISHOP STEPHEN NEILL, looking at missionary prospects in the non-European world from the perspective of the eighteenth century, concluded that 'the omens' for Christianity 'might be regarded as being distinctly unfavourable'. Yet the next century and a half was to see perhaps the greatest outburst of missionary activity since the period of the Early Church. Much of the energy for this emanated from Great Britain. In seeking an explanation, it is obviously tempting to see this expansion as a religious expression of the increasing western involvement with Africa, Asia and South America, and there is a sense in which this is so. Exploration widened horizons and secular settlement in distant lands provided a model and a challenge. It could be, and sometimes was, argued that missionaries were useful handmaidens to the imperial undertaking. This is not, however, the whole explanation. The missionary impulse was often independent of imperialism, indeed not infrequently opposed to it, particularly to the aspirations of the British colonists, traders and adventurers. It will be the contention of this chapter that the phenomenon requires a range of explanations including the theological conviction of those concerned.

Britain's missionary activity before 1800, like that of most Protestant countries, had been very limited. The Society for Promoting Christian Knowledge had a small operation (mainly using German Lutheran missionaries) in south India, and the Society for the Propagation of the Gospel in Foreign Parts devoted its energies primarily to the American settlers but also, to a much smaller extent, to the American Indians and the black slaves. Both societies had been established under royal charter. Within the space of about twenty years from 1792 a wholly new instrument for missionary work was formed: the voluntary missionary society. These bodies showed themselves able to tap considerable resources of previously unfulfilled energy and enthusiasm and revealed that a significant number of people were willing to devote themselves to the immensely hazardous and largely unregarded life of a missionary. Of crucial importance in effecting this change was the growth in awareness of a wider world, particularly through the publications of Captain Cook's voyages; through the dawning realization that countries such as India were of interest and importance, not only as places to trade with, but as areas to rule over and therefore to live in; and finally through that releasing of creative potential among quite ordinary people undoubtedly stimulated by the French Revolution.

The new enthusiasm for mission cannot be explained in terms of these factors alone. The Evangelical revival of the second half of the eighteenth century, with its commitment to conversion and its instinctive rejection of those forms of hyper-Calvinism which emphasized God's role in evangelism at the expense of man's, widened the horizons enormously. It was mixed with strains of millennialism, most of which in the late eighteenth and early nineteenth centuries emphasized that God's kingly rule would come before the second coming (postmillennialism), but as the nineteenth century progressed increasingly affirmed that it would happen thereafter (premillennialism). Either form could and did motivate the new missionary concern. Jonathan Edwards, the theologian of the Great Awakening in America, well illustrates the earlier view. He anticipated the gradual introduction of God's kingdom by way of preaching and prayer for the ingathering of the nations. Consequently he went to work among the Massachusetts Indians and called for 'concerts for prayer' for the con-version of the nations. His advice was influential far beyond America: one such concert was formed in Northamptonshire and was attended by the Baptist shoemaker William Carey (1761–1834). That very great future missionary was clearly stirred by the movements of the period, particularly the French Revolution and the Romantic Movement, and, like many Dissenters, fitted them into an eschatological framework and developed a critique of the old order which also provided an incentive for radical action.

There is no doubt that the revival was most influential among those groups who looked for change in society. That was as true in the commercial world of upper-middle-class Evangelicalism associated with William Wilberforce and the Clapham Sect as it was among the deprived working class who so eagerly responded to the message and methods of John Wesley and of those who emulated him among Congregationalists and Baptists. At both extremes, what the revival did was to emphasize the need for and the fact of redemption in Christ; it highlighted the value of lay involvement and the possibility of creating new initiatives for evangelism and religiously motivated social action. It also proclaimed the worth of every 'soul', whether Hindu or Negro or European. Such convictions provided the religious motivation of the Abolitionist movement and, at the same time and often through the same people, prompted the determination to carry the Gospel to the ends of the earth. It is, then, not so remarkable that those who formed the new missionary organizations were not the official religious leaders but enthusiasts who found themselves bonded together by a common emerging commitment.

It is not possible here to describe in detail the formation of the missionary societies in this period. Fortunately, William Carey was not only the most important catalyst to the missionary process but also, in the forces which shaped him and in the convictions which he formed, typical of many who, though less talented and less influential, were no less committted. Carey found himself driven to a passionate theological belief that the Great Commission to preach the Gospel in all the world applied not only to the Apostles, as the hyper-Calvinism of some Particular Baptists taught, but to all Christians. This he argued in his famous *Enquiry* (1792). It so echoed popular Evangelical convictions (significantly already given a missionary interpretation by the Wesleyan leader Thomas Coke) that within a few months the Baptist Missionary Society (BMS) was formed, followed within a few years by numerous other societies with missionary objectives – perhaps most importantly the largely Congregational London Missionary Society (1795), the Evangelical Anglican Church Missionary Society (1799) and the Methodist Missionary Society (1819). A whole cluster of questions confronted these new voluntary societies: Where to go? How to recruit? How to train those selected? What missionary policy to pursue? What degree of authority to exercise over far distant missionaries?

The question of where to go immediately raised the problem of India. British India was governed through the British East India Company, which though it had been prepared to allow the German missionaries of the SPCK to work in the south, was much more cautious about the north. Consequently the first Baptist missionaries settled outside British India. In 1808 the Court of Directors of the company declared its intention of protecting Indian religions and taking care 'that they are neither harassed nor irritated by any preacher or over-zealous attempts to convert them to Christianity'. This statement reflected the company's long-standing opposition to missionaries, motivated more by commercial self-interest than by any respect for the religions concerned – as had been demonstrated in the 1793 parliamentary debate over the renewal of the company's charter, when William Wilberforce and the Clapham Sect were unable to overcome the forces arrayed against their proposal that the company should send missionaries to India. This defeat was arguably, as Neill observes, a 'great advantage to the cause for which they stood', as it prevented the possibility of missionaries being appointed by governments. When the charter was again presented to Parliament for consideration in 1813 any idea of the official sponsorship of missionaries had been dropped; but the pressure for opening up access to India was even more intense, coming now not only from Evangelicals but also from Utilitarians who were concerned that India should not be closed to western education. The pressure achieved its end and also offers an illustration of what was to become a recurrent phenomenon – the influence of a missionary cause on the metropolitan Church – in that it gave Evangelicals a uniting purpose and popular cause perhaps greater even than that of Abolition. While India was regarded as the greatest prize, missionaries also went to other areas – chiefly the South Sea Islands and west Africa. The South Seas had been made popular through the romantic interest in Cook's voyages, and west Africa had achieved prominence because of an increased conviction of the obligation to make reparation for the horrors of the slave trade.

The missionary was a full-time Christian worker, and it might have been thought that ordained men would have been recruited from the start. This did not happen immediately, for two reasons. First, those who were involved in the establishment of the early missionary societies were not convinced that the pioneer work required the normal theological training. Second, they had a shrewd suspicion that they would find it very difficult to recruit from the ordained ministry or from ordinands in training. Consequently the London Missionary Society (LMS) called in its initial appeal for 'Godly men who understand mechanic arts'. The first LMS missionaries were almost all from an artisan background with little formal training. The results were mixed. Missionaries of great calibre and commitment emerged, but the majority found that they did not have the personal resources and training for the role demanded of them. The consequences were twofold. Critics, such as Sydney Smith, sought to ridicule the missionary venture by establishing that it was undertaken by 'a nest of consecrated cobblers' and 'didactic artizans'. Though 'consecrated cobblers' such as Carey proved that clever satire based on the conventional social stratification could fall very wide of the mark indeed, it was soon agreed that missionaries could not be sent out without some academic and theological training.

The Church Missionary Society (CMS), with its establishment background, decided not to rely on lay catechists. A missionary should be ordained. Lest he regard missionary service as a back door to ministry and social elevation in England, it was important that he should be acceptable for ordination in the Church of England before going abroad. As there were virtually no volunteers with such a background, the society relied first on German Lutherans and then, increasingly, on training its own candidates.

They seldom had the middle-class, university or professional background normal for English ordinands. The training was therefore concerned to establish comparability and to remove the consequences of a 'defective education'. Its end was to provide, as the CMS Secretary, Henry Venn, explained, 'such a training as would be given to men preparing for Holy Orders at home'. They emerged consequently with a sound grounding which, he boasted in 1846, made them 'fully on a par with the best men from Cambridge'. That was its single rationale. There was no concern with the cultural and linguistic questions which they would face in a totally new environment.

The majority of the missionaries in the first half of the century came from backgrounds not dissimilar to that of Carey, and even those from more professional occupations seemed to have been concerned to achieve more recognition in the increasingly industrialized world. They were, it has been argued by Piggin, from what R. S. Neale calls the 'middling class' – a group lying between the middle and the working classes, composed of the *petite bourgeoisie*, aspiring professional men, literates and artisans, characterized by the 'individuated or privatized' attitudes of the middle classes but 'collectively less deferential' and more concerned to attack privilege. They were, in other words, part of a wider grouping that sought escape from the stratification of traditional English life. The fact, however, that the societies were keenly and critically aware of the possibility of self-advancement as a motive, together with the immense danger and uncertainty of life in the tropics, suggests that this impulse was normally accompanied by other motives judged to be more acceptable.

Questions of policy cannot be explained in detail here, but it is sufficient to say that the early Protestant missionaries, particularly in India, established methods which became extremely influential for the future, very largely because of the work of four remarkable missionaries in Bengal. Carey, Marshman and Ward, the famous Serampore Trio, are best known for their extraordinary linguistic achievements in translation, and as grammmarians, dealing with perhaps thirty-four languages or dialects. Historians are divided as to how profound a commitment to indigenous culture they had. Some would argue that it was deep, though always with their proviso that no human system, however much it evidenced genius, was of ultimate worth without saving (that is, Christian) faith. Others see their motivation, while undoubtedly more culturally aware than that of most missionaries, as being primarily concerned with the overthrow of the Hindu religion and much of its associated culture. If Hinduism was better known, it could be more effectively routed. They do not, then, represent 'fundamental exceptions' to a pattern of western cultural domination. That they sought to advance a knowledge of Hindu culture is not in question.

Carey and Marshman gave a great deal of time to translating the *Ramayana*, and Ward became massively learned about Hindu culture. Undoubtedly they were driven by their convictions that the saving truths of the Gospel were crucial to any culture and should be presented, as much as possible, through the representatives of that culture. Undoubtedly, too, their early attitudes to Hinduism and Islam were harshly condemnatory; but they learned to curb their negative comments and even discovered common insights in the religious systems which they sought to replace. Their mature vision of the value of other cultures does seem to the present writer to be more than propagandist. It was not merely that Christianity should be provided with more effective instruments for evangelism, but that it should be allied with a culture which deserved to be compared with the Graeco-Roman. Like that culture, it was defective because it was pagan. It should not therefore be rejected; rather, the objective should be the cultivation of the 'the oriental classics . . . in subservience to divine revelation'. They were able to look forward to the day when 'the splendid imagery of the great national poets shall be employed to elucidate and adorn Christian truth'.

It was in keeping with this vision that they emphasized the importance of developing an Indian Church and that in 1818 they founded Serampore College to be open to all, irrespective of their religion, with the objective of providing instruction 'in every branch of knowledge peculiarly suited to promote the welfare of India'. The brave intention was in fact to teach Indian literature and western science. Sanskrit was to be given the role in India occupied by Greek and Latin in Europe. This never became a reality, partly because of the difficulty of staffing, partly because the BMS did not support such wide-ranging objectives and partly because other missionaries, the government and ambitious Indians became increasingly convinced of the value of English as the main medium for modern education. Despite this, the Serampore Trio had a much more crucial role in building up indigenous culture than was generally to be the case among their missionary successors in India – or, indeed anywhere else.

The case for the so-called 'Anglicist' position (as opposed to the 'Orientalist' objectives of the Serampore Trio) was best put by the brilliant Scottish Presbyterian missionary, Alexander Duff (1806–78). He arrived in India in 1830 and opened a school targeted on the children of high-class Brahmins. He believed that Hindu culture was too deeply impregnated by Hindu religious ideas for it to be an appropriate vehicle for a Christian or indeed a modern scientific education. By contrast, in the very act of learning English 'the mind . . . is perpetually brought in contact with the *new ideas*, the *new truths* . . . so that, by the time the language has been mastered, the student must be *tenfold less* the child of Pantheism, idolatry and superstition than before'. In government circles, too, the influence of the 'Orientalist' position was on the wane, and Duff became a leading figure in persuading the Bengal authorities to change to an 'Anglicist' position in 1835.

This conceptual debate highlights key missiological issues concerning the relationship of the Christian Gospel to indigenous and European cultures. The 'Orientalist' policy, even when interpreted as being less appreciative of Hindu culture than we have argued, makes it evident that all missionaries were not in any simple sense cultural imperialists on behalf of European civilization. The 'Anglicist' position was certainly one of cultural imperialism, and it encouraged the general movement in that direction. It did not, however, reflect either territorial imperialism or racial superiority. It is significant to note that many of the most educated Indians in fact supported Duff rather than the Serampore Trio, and that Duff was as committed as Carey to the evangelism of India through Indians. If there was an identification with Indian culture in the 'Orientalist' position which seems much more in tune with late twentieth-century perceptions, it is important to understand that neither approach reflected an unthinking Europeanization determined to sweep all before it and to plant a church which was but a clone of its parent. What was similar in both approaches was a commitment to evangelism through education. This was to be a dominant characteristic of missionary work, becoming increasingly energy-absorbing and decreasingly productive in terms of converts.

This picture of quite sophisticated and independent missionary action is reinforced in south India, the West Indies and South Africa. In south India, where the CMS encountered the ancient Syrian Church, its instructions to its missionaries were remarkably unimperialistic in intent. The objective was to be reformation rather than proselytization:

> The Syrians should be brought back to their own ancient and primitive worship and discipline, rather than be induced to adopt the liturgy and discipline of the English Church; and should any considerations incline them to wish such a measure, it would be highly expedient to dissuade them from adopting it, both for the preservation of their individuality and entireness, and greater consequent weight and usefulness as a Church.

Even allowing for the fact that the Society had a rather romantic view of the primitive purity of the Syrian Church, this was an attitude notably at variance with any simple desire to spread English political or ecclesiastical influence. It is a further qualification to the sweeping judgement that the 'essence' of the missionary movement was 'cultural imperialism'.

It is no more accurate to see it as invariably supportive of the European political establishment. As Piggin argues, missionaries were not themselves from the governing and commercial classes, and such considerations seem to have had little weight with them. Indeed, their background inclined them to be critics of the status quo. Thus Willam Knibb (1803–45) and the BMS became highly unpopular with colonial whites in Jamaica for their support of the emancipation cause. Missionaries were suspected of complicity in the slave revolts between 1823 and 1832 and in the negro insurrection of 1865. One, John Smith, died in prison under a death sentence for his alleged part in rebellion. Similar identification with the cause of the underprivileged people to whom they ministered was evident in South Africa. There the LMS missionaries, particularly J. T. Vanderkemp (1747–1811), John Philip (1775–1851) and David Livingstone (1813–73), laid the foundations of Christian opposition to white settler ambitions. It was Philip, for example, working with William Wilberforce, T. F. Buxton and English philanthropic opinion, who was most instrumental in securing the House of Commons resolution of 1828 which declared equality for the indigenous Africans. It asked that 'directions be given for effectually securing to all the natives of South Africa the same freedom and protection as are enjoyed by other free persons residing at the Cape, whether they be English or Dutch'. This of course, together with the abolition of slavery in 1833, led to the Great Trek of Boers beyond the sphere of British rule. The conviction that the will of the colonists needed to be opposed for the sake of the indigenous African population led Philip to a 'fervent belief in the benevolent purposes of British imperialism', as this was the only force which seemed capable of protecting their interests – a good example of the perception, frequent among missionaries, that imperialism was the most humanitarian and Christian option available.

At times, then, missionaries could be as strong, strident and persistent in their criticism of the political establishment as they were radical in their ecclesiastical polity. It has become too common to dimiss these early missionaries as clumsy paternalists, uncritically promoting the interests of their own kith and kin. Many, of course, were. Many had no sense of indigenous capacity. Most had little interest in the cultures they met. Frequently their linguistic attainments were limited. There were political conservatives, such as Robert Moffat, critical of the commitment of the radicals like Philip, or, like the Wesleyans in South Africa, quite sympathetic to the settler outlook. The missionaries' natural inclination was generally to eschew politics but often, whatever their political position, they were close to people among whom they worked. Later, when missionary work began to expand, when (perhaps above all) mission stations became large and elaborate, missionaries slowly became the servants of the ever more complex institutions they had created and needed to govern, and consequently more remote from those they sought to serve.

It would be easy to exaggerate the scale of the missionary operation in the first half of the nineteenth century. Between 1789 and 1858, 559 missionaries went to India from the thirteen main Protestant societies working there. In Sierra Leone, the biggest of the CMS missionary areas in Africa, there were perhaps twenty missionaries in the 1850s. It was calculated in 1860 that there were 112,000 Protestant Christians in India and 250,000 in Africa. However, the second half of the century was to see a phenomenal growth in missionary commitment. The number of mission-aries increased dramatically. Many new societies were formed, among the most influential being the Anglo-Catholic Universities' Mission to Central Africa (1857), the inter-denominational China Inland Mission (1865) and the Roman Catholic Mill Hill Fathers (1866). There were dramatic changes in recruitment patterns, with more from the middle classes, more women and more laymen. Missionary thinking moved from a position in which the orthodoxy was self-governing churches at the earliest possible moment to one where full integration between European and indigenous members became the ideal.

In explaining why there should have been an advance on this scale at this time, there are a number of obvious factors. Improvements in communica-tions – by rail, sea and telegraph – made distant parts of the world accessible. It took Hudson Taylor six and a half months to get to Shanghai in 1854; by the early twentieth century the journey could be made in six weeks. In 1850 many parts of the world remained unexplored and inaccessible. By the end of the century, most of the great geographical puzzles had been solved. It was a period of comparative peace; what wars there were were settled reasonably quickly and were not large-scale. If, as far as the Church in Britain was concerned, it was a time of heightened acrimony because of the sharp divide between Catholic and Protestant (both within and beyond the Church of England) and because of the increased competitiveness of the major Protestant denominations, it was also a time of spiritual vitality, often expressed in energetic and self-giving evangelism. It was also the age of imperialism and this raises again the question of the relationship between empire and mission.

By the mid-nineteenth century the link between Christianity, commerce and civilization had been formed in the minds and policies of at least some missionary thinkers. It received its most famous articulation from David Livingstone. We need not here enter into the debate about the role of Providentialist theology in forming the links. Cairns is no doubt broadly right in asserting that there was an 'unquestioning identification, or intermingling' of Christianity and civilization in the minds of missionaries.

Stanley likewise argues that 'for most of the nineteenth century, British Christians believed that the missionary was called to propagate the imagined benefits of Western civilization alongside the Christian message.' The question remains whether the link was ever quite as absolute as this. Porter maintains that 'the association of commerce and Christianity was *never* complete,' and indeed was often actively resisted in the first half of the century and again in its last quarter. Into this more varied pattern what we have argued above about the Serampore Trio fits easily. We would also question whether there was any such unquestioned identification between Christianity and western civilization in the minds of the more thoughtful administrators and missionary thinkers over the mid-century period. Henry Venn (1796–1873) of the CMS, undoubtedly the greatest British missionary thinker of his period, spoke out against the 'bewitching' idea that 'we must settle and civilize in order to convert'. Civilization was an advantage but not a necessity and, in itself without Christianity, could not teach moral principles. He consequently never used the Livingstone slogan, nor did his equally perceptive American missionary administrator friend Rufus Anderson. Thus Venn was always ambivalent about education, fearing that it might be divisive, drawing the educated converts away from their compatriots into a European world. In his analysis of Francis Xavier, the great Jesuit missionary, he argued that he had failed precisely in this way.

That is, however, by no means to say that civilization and commerce were not valued among the missionaries. They were, particularly in relation to developing a trade which would undermine that in slaves, which, it was feared, could not be truly suppressed until there was a viable alternative, until, that is, 'the Natives had learned through Christian civilization the true value of agriculture and commerce'. It is to say that the Christian missionary was warned against drawing the links with a particular form of western civilization too closely. To say that Christian morality ruled out certain 'heathen' practices or to see a role for trade was not, at any rate to the perceptions of the mid-Victorian, a call for a root and branch introduction of western civilization. The LMS secretary, Mullens, could declare in 1860 at a very representative missionary conference that all were agreed that 'in their dress, manners and style, native pastors and missionaries should continue to live like their countrymen'. The aim was 'not to make them hybrids, but to Christianize their own native life'; not to build 'grand and capacious Gothic churches', but rather to encourage designs which would be, in the words of Dr Trestrail, the General Secretary of the BMS, 'conformed to the native idea of size, cost and general structure'; not, Trestrail also argued, to reproduce British ministerial hierarchy and pomp, but rather for pastors to discover titles which would 'harmonize with the customs, habits of thought and expression' which prevailed locally. It was firmly believed that, in the words of another speaker, Christian truth could be 'naturalized'; in other words, that it could become in 'look, tone, word, imagery, idiom' appropriate to the people, 'even the most degraded', to whom it was being presented. The 'higher Christian civilization' of the missionary was therefore seen by many as a positive hindrance, likely to produce dependency, and consequently active measures, such as discouraging missionaries from being pastors and encouraging 'native' pastors, practices and institutions, were demanded.

This amounted to the official orthodoxy of the 1860s. The goal of self-supporting, self-propagating and self-governing churches was widely accepted and by 1861 there were sixty indigenous clergy working under CMS auspices. In no sense was it intended that these should be socialized into the forms of western civilization. It was argued that the great weakness of the Irish and Welsh Churches was that they had been 'denationalized', and the challenge facing Christianity in India, for example, was whether it could find an expression appropriate to a Hindu culture. The logical extension of this line of thought, for Venn, was the establishment of an indigenous liturgy, the organization of the Church '*as a national institution*', and the appointment of an independent native bishop. The last aim was first partially realized in the consecration in 1864 of the ex-slave Samuel Crowther (*c*.1806–91), who was given responsibility for 'the countries of Western Africa beyond our dominions'. It was a deeply symbolic step indicating a very considerable commitment to a prominent role for non-Europeans. Indeed, Venn is credited with 'originating Nigerian nationalism, ideologically'. It was, however, a fatally flawed step, because Venn was unable to persuade his European missionaries to accept Crowther's authority. He became a bishop, therefore, not of a mature and well-developed Church but of a pioneer mission. The self-governing status which his title and position represented was consequently not the crowning mark of a natural progression of a native Church to independence. It was rather a compromise agreement which created an odd diocese with numerous holes, where a different and European episcopal jurisdiction prevailed because European missionaries worked in those areas who were disinclined to accept the rule of an African. But if the flaws have seemed more important to historians in search of an explanation for Crowther's later 'failure' on the Niger, the significance of the symbol should not be ignored. His elevation to the episcopate was a declaration that a mission Church should and could move to a substantial independence in a comparatively short time.

It was a declaration the more notable because it was not the vision of a man much ahead of his times. The idea of an independent Church with institutions and liturgies derived from the indigenous culture was shared not only by other Protestant societies, but also by Anglo-Catholics such as Bishop Steere (1828–82) of the Universities Mission to Central Africa (UMCA). He believed that each nation should have 'its own Church and its own bishop and clergy'. Like many who shared this vision, he was suspicious of European civilization, and confident of indigenous capacity. It is the existence and influence of such ideas that must significantly qualify blanket charges of paternalistic imperialism or of the automatic association of Christianity and western civilization.

Such charges cannot, however, be avoided altogether because the accepted orthodoxy of most missionary strategists was not the accepted practice of most missionaries. Many believed in the superiority of the white man as a present reality, though not as a biological fact. The reality was, said Henry Townsend, a CMS missionary in west Africa, in 1858, that as 'white merchant and civilization . . . go hand in hand with Missionary work', the changes brought about would be revolutionary at every level and must include 'foreign elements'. Furthermore, as religious change is 'a revolution of the most extensive kind . . . the commanding minds' who had introduced it must 'become leaders'. It is 'a law of nature and not contrary to the law of God'. All shared the prevailing low view of non-Christian religions: they were in 'darkness'; and many missionaries were convinced that the overcoming of this darkness had huge cultural implications which effectively justified westernization and which would ensure their dominance for many years. To Venn such missionaries suffered from 'a tendency to under-rate the social and intellectual capabilities of the native races'. Steere had similar difficulties with his missionaries, who were often paternalistic and were, for example, convinced (against Steere) that potential African leaders should spend longish periods of training in England. It was such problems which drove Venn to push even more strongly for separate national Churches and led him to declare, rather bleakly, that 'the *proper position of a missionary is one external to the native church*'. In other words, the missionary, because he could not work with the 'native' Church without dominating it, would be best left out of the emerging structures even though, in areas where there was a considerable number of Europeans, this would mean overlapping dioceses – in effect, one for Europeans and one for indigenous Christians. That was not a solution which commended itself as it seemed to divide according to race. The strategists (based mainly in Britain) were thus frequently frustrated by the hesitations of the missionaries on the ground. They were not, however, without success. There were many ordinations. If ultimate power was generally denied, penultimate power was sometimes given. If Crowther was the only diocesan bishop, there were other indigenous leaders who achieved substantial influence and prominence. If Venn, Steere and others were limited in what they could persuade their missionaries to implement, their conclusions were, and remained, very subversive of missionary paternalism.

Many historians, drawing almost exclusively on west African evidence, have argued that Venn's ideas were quickly abandoned by a society caught up in the racialism of the last decades of the nineteenth century. It can be argued that the picture is more complex. The CMS, and with it much Victorian missionary thinking (for example Steere's episcopal successor, Bishop Smythies), retained Venn's ideals until the early 1890s. The creation of an 'independent Native Church' remained the objective. If this meant that the English in India, and wherever else they formed a sizeable minority, would have to have separate provision made for them, so be it. Thus the CMS declared in 1877:

> Where the Anglo-Saxon cannot be at home, there neither can his Church . . . While the English wish to enjoy the order and discipline of their Church exactly as in England, the Native Christians already show signs of desiring for themselves a Church modified to some extent in its forms, its ceremonies, and its organization, to suit their oriental nature and their oriental life.

Thus there were a number of attempts to appoint indigenous bishops in India, Ceylon and west Africa between 1877 and 1888. All these foundered. Gradually in the 1890s and explicitly in the early twentieth century Venn's aspirations were abandoned, as were Steere's in the UMCA. The convictions which replaced them had a much greater confidence in European leadership and influence which was, it was almost universally accepted, certain to be a reality for the forseeable future.

In place of the principles of such as Venn and Steere, the inevitability of a long missionary presence slowly became the orthodoxy. This cannot be explained solely with reference to the missionary opposition to sharing and handing over power. That had always been a factor, but previously it had frustrated yet not defeated the official commitment to self-governing Churches in the near future. Nor was it due to an ever-closer partnership between commerce, civilization and Christianity. There was rather widespread disenchantment about this relationship in the 1880s and the early 1890s. Confidence in the progress of civilization was being replaced by 'social Darwinism', which posited a racial struggle in which the whites were clearly superior. That is not to say that talk about civilization ceased. It did not, and it continued to be useful in imperialist apologetic. It became, however, less central as an aim. As far as missionaries were concerned, we have seen that the extent to which they were ever committed to the Christianity–commerce–civilization link can be exaggerated.

If the likes of Venn, Anderson and Steere were ambivalent, a new breed of missionaries, nurtured in a Romantic culture and in the holiness, revivalist and premillennialist themes to which it gave rise within Evangelicalism, were becoming increasingly influential. Their world-renouncing premillennialism ensured that they had no great optimism for, or indeed great interest in, contemporary western civilization. Their precursor and guru was Hudson Taylor (1832–1905), the founder of the China Inland Mission (CIM). This was a 'faith-society'. He depended on God, rather than on the wisdom and strategy of man. He felt that missionary societies were too rationalistic, too compromised with the 'world' (and therefore with western culture) and insufficiently prepared to commend their missionaries to live as the people, casting aside the support of western civilization. Such ideals were attractive to many. Many of Taylor's principles were echoed in the spirituality of the Keswick Convention, an annual Evangelical gathering with a strong holiness emphasis. They were given a respectable Anglican face through Handley Moule (1841–1920) who, as Principal of Ridley Hall, Cambridge, did much to channel the new spiritual enthusiasm of his confident, able and sometimes wealthy ordinands. Much of this enthusiasm was mission-orientated – some to the CIM but also to other societies. The CMS, in response, deliberately changed its image to attract those with the sort of 'ideal' background from which it had previously recruited only with difficulty.

Recognizing this, a number of historians have seen a connection between the new 'Keswick'-shaped and often Cambridge-educated missionaries and the racialist ideas of the period, and this would of course explain their commitment to a long-term and dominant missionary presence. Porter and Hansen have questioned this. Much of the evidence on this point lies in the conflict between missionaries in the Niger Delta and the aged Bishop Crowther. Porter points out that in fact the hostility of these missionaries was focused on missionary methods and not on Africans as such. Indeed, they were often more critical of the European missionaries and the structures in which they worked. They disliked particularly the connections drawn between Christianity and commerce. Nor does the accusation of racialism nurtured by 'social Darwinism' square with the evidence. There was a genuine desire for identification with Africans, seen for example in a desire to live and dress in a 'native' way, and this was sometimes achieved. What brought about the confrontation were perfectionist theological convictions which produced intolerance with the sort of ordinary Christian living which the missionaries found in west Africa, but which they might as easily have discovered in Weston-super-Mare. Paradoxically, Porter suggests, it may have been the belief in the equality of European and non-European and in the similarity of their response to the same revealed truth 'which exacerbated the clash of culture'. There was a resort among those faced by the clash to racialist explanation, but this was a consequence not a cause of the conflict. In other words, the explanation for the conflict lies more in religious ideas in Britain than in the influence of secular thinking, though this of course cannot be discounted as an element.

Hansen also rejects any simple racialist explanation, but is more sceptical about the influence of a European cultural and theological background and, taking his evidence from Uganda, sees the local context as decisive in framing missionary attitudes. Certainly positions were, for some, changed utterly by the mission-field experience, but others seemed largely unaffected by their context. It was not a time when the British were particularly noted for their cultural sensitivity, and it seems perverse to discount the metropolitan influence altogether, though Hansen is surely right to indicate that it was not necessarily decisive. Returning to the theological context, it is important to note that the concentration on a simple primitive Gospel with the central emphasis on evangelism prevailed beyond the CIM and CMS, and indeed beyond Evangelicalism, and can be seen in the Anglo-Catholic UMCA, the Oxford and Cambridge Missions in India, the Methodist 'Joyful News' evangelists and the Salvation Army, and in a quite general stress on asceticism.

At the same time, there was a change of fundamental importance in the metropolitan understanding of imperialism. The emphasis moved from 'the informal imperialism of collaboration' to a 'new imperialism' which had as its objective colonial control. Generally very reluctantly, and for reasons which had more to do with weakness than with strength, Britain came to accept that its overseas possessions needed to be increased or strengthened. In this context there was a reassessment of the traditionally hostile secular attitudes to the missionary. Men such as the colonial administrator Sir Harry Johnston (1858–1927), while remaining totally sceptical about the truth of Christianity, began to argue for its value as 'the preparer of the white man's advent'. Should not the very fact that missionaries 'live in a European manner, in a house of European style, surrounded by European implements, products and ornaments . . . open the eyes of the brutish savages to the existence of a higher state of culture, and prepare them for the approach of civilization?' Indeed, concluded an article in the *Quarterly Review*, 'the extension of Christianity means the extension of civilization'. The missionary, Johnston acknowledged, often opposed the harsher expressions of imperialism, but even this could be seen as a benefit because it disciplined and controlled 'the ruthless proceedings of the unscrupulous pioneers of the white invaders'.

Does this more positive assessment of the missionary role help in explaining missionary attitudes in this period? If the argument thus far is correct, then their putative role in relation to civilization can have been of small attraction to many of them. It is indeed a curious fact that those most anxious to reject the effete contemporary civilization were often most proud to be involved in planting the flag. Temple Gardiner was one of the able young middle-class missionaries thrown up by the climate of the 1890s. On the one hand, he regarded 'the full blaze of modern life, with its competition and seething ambitions' as a temptation he was well rid of as a missionary. On the other, he was glad to discover that, as a missionary, he could still have a role to play for his Queen. Thus he recounted his emotions as he watched the Diamond Jubilee proceedings of 1897 and contrasted Victoria's procession with that of Jesus' 'poor little procession' into Jerusalem:

> To my joy I found that He does not *despise* all this earthly glory, but is going to make it swell the glory of His triumph. Not every monarch's glory will seem glorious in Heaven. But my Queen's will, because the glory of this day was not the procession of the soldiers but a people's love. I should like to serve my Queen. Can I do that better than by taking Christ to her Empire? She would like that, I think.

There was, then, no fundamental contradiction in feeling guilty about, and indeed rejecting, the trappings of prosperity and civilization and simultaneously feeling pride and superiority in being European and British. There was, moreover, a positive moral role for European involvement in Africa in that it could be presented as part of the battle against slavery. So General Gordon was a hero figure to many would-be missionaries. He provided a telling example of someone who was prepared to fight for what was right. Those less influenced by premillennialism began to believe in an optimistic vision of God's kingdom through the empire. So the CMS longed 'that the English speaking race may have the honour of leading the way in a policy of Christian Imperialism, which shall have no other object than to bring nearer the fulfilment of the divine promise that the Kingdom of this world is to become the Kingdom of our Lord and His Christ'. It was an optimistic postmillennial view likely to be associated with considerable confidence in western civilization. The sense of being able to serve justice, country and God, all at the same time; of (for some) advancing the kingdom of God in this world; and of fulfilling a role which could win some of the recognition accorded to a brother making a name for himself in the colonial services or the army was surely a factor in the burgeoning middle-class recruitment of this period. It was a factor too in producing missionaries more naturally disposed to govern than to work for the independence of the young Church.

Changes in the metropolitan world-view are not the only explanations of the demise of the commitment to self-government. It may be doubted how far the African and Indian Churches wanted self-government if the price was self-support. There is some evidence that when, in the 1870s and 1880s, there were serious attempts to establish indigenous episcopates, 'native' reluctance was one factor in their rejection. There were, as Moriyama indicates, 'concrete visible signs, i.e. power, authority, and material gains, from Christianity' which would be lost if the missionaries were to leave. Collaboration with the missionaries brought benefits and avoided difficult decisions about the elevation of one or two indigenous Christians above their fellows.

We have also seen that as imperialism became more popular, so did the missionary cause. We must then again, in a context where the evidence is more telling, face the question whether the missionaries were agents, or tools, or at any rate abettors of imperialism. Certainly the connections could be very close. Johnston declared that 'the negro potentate was scarcely unjust when he complained that "first come the missionary, then the merchant, and then the man-of-war" '. Cairns underlines the missionaries' role in pressing humanitarianism and thus in 'associating the right to power with moral fervour; in effect, with being British'. There are obvious examples – Bechuanaland (1885) and Uganda (1894) – of the missionary urging the government to closer involvement. Occasionally missionaries even acted as temporal rulers themselves, and they often had consular or vice-consular status. Yet close examination defies any simple categorization.

There was a great variety in the attitudes of missionaries to imperialism even at this time and even within particular mission fields and churches. When, moreover, the missionaries argued for British annexation, it was generally in a context where some sort of annexation was inevitable. The LMS pressed for a British protectorate in Bechuanaland, but in order to help Khama, the Chief of the Ngwato, to survive a threat to his territory from Cecil Rhodes. Likewise, the CMS urged a comparable case in Uganda, but because they regarded British Protestant imperialism as preferable to French Catholic or, to them far worse, Arab Islamic imperialism. In no sense were the missionaries making a choice between self-government and imperial government. They were seeking what, from their perspective, was the best form of imperialism. They were sometimes bitterly hated by arch-imperialists such as Rhodes. They sought 'justice and humanity' every bit as much as twentieth-century anti-colonialists, argues Stanley. Johnston saw them as 'tribunes and advocates' on behalf of 'the scared and bewildered savage' and argued that they 'by their fearless clamour compel the reluctant intervention of higher authorities'. Professor Ayandele, commenting on the consequences of their prohibition from Muslim areas of northern Nigeria, noted that 'the poor, often oppressed, people could not enjoy the political services of missionaries as tribunes of the oppressed'. In Kenya, in the early 1920s, it was the missionary pressure, exerted through Archbishop Randall Davidson (1848–1930) and J. H. Oldham (1874–1969), which led to a famous government declaration that where there was a clash between the interests of the African races and 'the immigrant races . . . the former should prevail'. It is a particularly good example of the missionaries appealing to the sense of trusteeship which was basic in at least some of the rationales for empire.

The picture, then, is of qualified missionary support for imperialism. Yet, though qualified, the overall identification made 'a powerful moral impact'; and although it often sought to control and alleviate the harsher aspects of imperialism and was inspired by a genuine concern for the welfare of people who were, or were likely to be, oppressed, it is difficult to avoid the conclusion that the connection altered missionary attitudes, and the way missionaries were generally perceived, significantly. It encouraged a cast of mind which assumed not only European superiority, but the likelihoood of a long-term European presence. The reaction was often bitter, particularly because mission-inspired expectations, training and ministerial promotion had had as their open premiss a vision of progression from trusted local leadership to independence sooner rather than later. The most articulate protestors did not hesitate to quote their heroes from the past, such as Henry Venn, but, in the new climate, such uncomfortable parts of the heritage were subject to creative reinterpretation. Self-government became a distant dream and this, in turn, was a major factor in giving rise to separatist churches in Africa (and to a much lesser extent in India), and to the anti-foreign and anti-missionary actions in China culminating in the Boxer risings of 1900. China illustrates how, in a setting where passions were roused, even those missionaries who had no commitment to western civilization could have a role in heightening local fears and hatreds. Hudson Taylor, for example, was a passionate advocate of identification with Chinese culture and opposed to any appeal to the British authorities for compensation or redress on behalf of missionaries or their property. He was equally committed to an uncompromising, and somewhat confrontational missionary approach – for example, cere-monially destroying Buddhist images and ancestral tablets. Such actions certainly played a role in rousing the anti-foreign emotions of 1900. Yet this position was no more motivated by racialism or any developed doctrine of cultural imperialism than the attitudes of the Nigerian missionaries considered above. The explanation is rather to be sought mainly in unbending theological convictions nurtured in a particular metropolitan centre, no doubt strengthened by the general sense of European superiority.

It was typical of this understanding that the missionary message preached was largely a challenge to the individual to acknowledge his sin and to accept Christ's redemption. The challenge was then to conversion and membership of the Church through baptism. This would be presented in different ways and with varying nuances – the more Protestant and Evangelical societies emphasizing faith in Christ, the more Catholic baptism into Christ – but what united Protestant and Catholic was a concern primarily for the individual, what McGavran calls 'the one-by-one-against-the-current process'. Latourette comments on Roman Catholicism, which had often in the past been associated with mass conversions, that its spread 'was more by individual and less by group conversion than in any period since the fourth century'. Consequently missionaries had considerable difficulty in coping with anything approaching a mass movement of a people to Christianity. Mass movements, which happened quite often, were deemed suspect because the converts could not have made the individual decisions which were expected and because the size of the movements of often poor people threatened to alter radically the balance of the Church. What these mass movements represent is the decisions of societies accustomed to act in a unified way. They may also represent the impact of particularly able and charismatic indigenous evangelists. Certainly it is true to say that one of the great, and still largely unexplored, areas of missionary work was the ministry of native catechists and evangelists. If missionaries provided the organization, the education and the expertise in translating the Scriptures, it may well be that it was their army of catechists who provided the real local impact. So Bishop Tugwell of the Niger admitted candidly in 1895 that the

> only work for which Europeans are really qualified is to train and direct African Agents: as Evangelists we are a failure: I do not know of one successful European Evangelist either in the Niger or in the Yoruba Missions. Mr Harding most nearly approaches the ideal: but a junior African agent could do better work in this direction than dear Mr Harding.

An estimate of the importance of 'native catechists' remains to be undertaken across missions, but where there has been analysis, as in

Uganda, they emerge as a major force in Church expansion. Because such expansion was genuinely indigenous, Pirouet concludes, it 'gives the lie to the idea that Christianity was more or less forcibly imposed on unwilling subject populations'. Further support is given to this thesis by the remarkable fact that some of the most notable advances of Christianity took place where missionaries were excluded – as in Madagascar in the first half of the century and in Buganda for periods in its last decades – or were greatly reduced in numbers, as during the First World War.

While, therefore, the missionary achievement was immense in the educational field, in the laying of organizational structures and in providing an orthodox faith, doubts remain as to how close the majority of missionaries in this period ever got to the people to whom they ministered. Samuel Azariah (1875–1945), later to become the first Indian bishop, in a famous speech at the World Missionary Conference at Edinburgh in 1910, acknowledged the great deeds and sacrifices of the missionaries but tellingly concluded: 'We also ask for *love*. Give us FRIENDS!' Moreover, the increasingly elaborate 'mission-station', often with a commitment to education and thus inevitably to an elitist minority, further separated missionaries from the people they served and drew them ever more tightly into 'a secular web of their own creation'.

An added reason for the ever-increased complexity of the 'secular web' was the acceptance of medical work as a major instrument of missionary advance. With a few exceptions, medical missionary work had been resisted in the first half of the century, partly because it was seen as a distraction from the real task, and partly because the medical profession was only beginning to take the steps which were to raise it high in public esteem. The few doctors who were sent out were ordained to indicate their real role. The professionalization of medicine occurred rapidly in the second half of the century, and the process was accompanied by a considerable increase in the numbers of lay medical missionaries. The developing rationale for their presence is instructive. The duty of providing missionaries with proper medical care was urged as a first priority, but the reality that medicine broke down barriers in areas of hostility was also persuasive, and the contention that Christianity should be concerned for the body as well as the soul, particularly as healing played such an important role in Christ's ministry, began to carry weight. These arguments were given the greater strength as philanthropy was extremely popular in Britain in the 1880s and 1890s, and many doctors and medical students were applying to the societies to serve, significantly, as doctors and not as clergy who happened also to be doctors. Ironically, though Hudson Taylor (a doctor himself) had considerable reservations about the distractions of medical work, the premillennial enthusiasm he represented had influential strands which were quite committed to philanthropy and therefore to the cause of the medical missionary.

The employment of lay missionary doctors was one sign of the breakdown of the clerical domination of missionary work. Hudson Taylor, again something of a pioneer as far as missions were concerned and much influenced by the revivalist stress on lay evangelism, was convinced that, though God could use a Paul as well as a Peter, he 'more commonly speaks by an unlettered Peter at a Pentecost'. Consequently he employed mainly laymen and, even more significantly, laywomen. In 1867, at a time when women were still very infrequently recruited, he declared that they were 'the most powerful agency we have at our disposal'. Gradually the other societies followed, strongly pressed by the impact of the general expansion in the roles open to women on their supporters and potential recruits. Women undoubtedly strengthened greatly the work among women and children and also began to minister to men, but they were another and very significant factor in greatly increasing the size of the missionary operation and hence of creating institutions where the symbols were of permanence, and where Venn-like talk of 'the euthanasia of the mission' seemed wholly inappropriate.

This chapter has looked at the missionary achievement of the period with a critical eye, and that may easily obscure the scale of Christian advance in this period. It was, in terms of numbers of converts made and churches established, quite simply immense. Geographically Christianity was spread more widely than ever previously. In most of Asia and Africa the Christian Church had established itself and gained a following which, though often modest in relation to the traditional religions, was very significant. It had also through its social services, particularly education, made a contribution which, though it often stopped far short of conversion, was of inestimable importance.

There had also been advances in the mutual understanding of the Protestant missionary societies. Working in a non-Christian environment had made co-operation across denominational and theological boundaries desirable. Many so-called 'comity' agreements had been made which, in effect, controlled where the various societies worked. There was, too, an increasing recognition of the value of regular meetings at regional, national and international levels. The first real international conference was in Liverpool in 1860, and that trend had its best known outcome in the World Missionary Conference at Edinburgh in 1910. This huge conference, with 1,200 delegates, was broadly based and organizationally and ecclesiastically ambitious, including for the first time Anglo-Catholic societies and missionaries. In many ways the climax of the nineteenth-century missionary movement, it displayed many of that movement's weaknesses.

It exuded confidence and aggression to the point of triumphalism. As in all
the previous international and national conferences, there were very few
indigenous representatives – only seventeen. Yet there were also signs that
the missionary movement was coming to terms with the new century.
There was a degree of commitment to taking other religions seriously,
sympathetically and respectfully which had not previously been in
evidence. The conference threw up talented young leaders who were to be
very much in the forefront of the missionary and Ecumenical Movement
for the next three decades. It gave itself, through a Continuation
Committee and through what was to become a widely respected journal,
the *International Review of Missions*, a permanent organization and means
of communication.

That element of continuity was to be very important, because the First
World War on the one hand brutally challenged confidence in western and
Christian superiority, and on the other greatly broadened the horizons of
the many non-European and non-Christian combatants. Organizationally
the pre-war move towards greater unity among Protestant missions
continued, and was reflected in the formation in 1921 of the International
Missionary Council. Theologically the combination of the post-war loss of
confidence in traditional Christianity, accentuated by Russia becoming
communist, and the impact of theological liberalism, led to a much more
hesitant tone about the uniqueness of the Christian message and to a
greater emphasis on uniting religions against the advances of secularism.
This trend reached something of a high point in the late 1920s at the
Second World Missionary Conference at Jerusalem (1928) and especially in
a report entitled *Rethinking Mission*. The Jerusalem conference in fact
reaffirmed the distinctiveness of Christianity, but this was given a much
more robust assertion at the Third World Missionary Conference at
Tambaram (1938). Here the key figure was Hendrik Kraemer (1888–1965)
who was, in turn, much influenced by the neo-orthodoxy of Karl Barth.

Meanwhile the pressures towards political freedom grew apace.
Missions were not in the vanguard in understanding and creatively
interpreting these changes. Pirouet's judgement of missionaries in Uganda
in this period – that they were in a state of stagnation, that they had
largely abandoned the traditional aim of developing self-supporting, self-
propagating and self-governing churches and that they considered
themselves 'a permanently necessary scaffolding' – is probably true of most
areas. Thus the Church lost potential leaders to other careers, including
politics, because they found in them 'that independence of action which
the missionaries seemed determined to deny to them for ever and a day'.
Though there was the beginning of a much stronger theology of the
Church, and occasionally very forceful bishops could shake themselves free

of the still all-pervasive missionary societies, generally speaking the judgement on the CMS that its policies acted as 'a powerful braking-system on devolution from mission to diocese' probably applied to most of the societies. Certainly there were very few appointments of even suffragan indigenous bishops; indeed, the commitment to training indigenous ordinands if anything declined.

Clearly missionaries, in the main, reflected uncritically their often very comfortable colonial setting. They remained, of course, different from the colonists and much closer to the 'natives' than other whites thought appropriate, but they accepted the inevitability of imperialism (and colonialism) which theoretically in any event, still retained a high sense of moral purpose to which missionaries could appeal as they worked through the implications of trusteeship. Even those from conservative, 'Keswick' backgrounds seemed more positive about the advantages not only of British imperialism but of western civilization. It had been much easier to dissent at times of rapid change than from within the seemingly well-established regularity and order of inter-war life. Theological liberalism, now more dominant, often took a much more sanguine view of western civilization than had been the case in the late nineteenth century. Thus in China it played a primary part in presenting Christianity 'as the central ingredient of an integrated package of Westernization'. This was a dangerous policy and the disastrous consequences were reaped in China in the anti-Christian reaction of the post-1949 period. The dangers, however, seemed remote in large missionary and European settlements – which in turn fostered a greater distance from the people to whom they ministered. It is ironical that the high point of missionary identification with imperialism came when it was in terminal decline.

Yet one constant strand of this chapter has been that it is difficult to generalize about missionary attitudes. Different settings, or personalities with unusual insight and force, could produce very marked variations. Thus Roman Catholicism, having been noted during most of the nineteenth century for a paternalism even more pervasive than that of Protestants, under the impact of enlightened and prophetic encyclicals from Benedict XV (*Maximum Illud*, 1919) and Pius XI (*Rerum Ecclesiae*, 1926) and of a far-sighted Prefect of Propaganda, Cardinal van Rossum (1918–32), made very rapid advances in the appreciation of other cultures and nationalities and in the appointment of Asian and African priests and bishops. So in 1933 it was said that 60 per cent of Roman Catholics in Asia worshipped under indigenous clergy and 20 per cent under indigenous bishops. By 1939 there were seven Roman Catholic Indian and twenty-three Chinese dioceses under indigenous diocesans and, in the same year, Pius XII consecrated twelve missionary bishops including four non-

Europeans or non-Americans. There was the beginning, too, of a movement away from the earlier period's individualistic approach to evangelism, with its tendency to assimilation to western models, towards an emphasis on planting the Church in every area; this, it can be argued, made adaptation to local culture more likely. It was not, in any sense, that the Catholicism of this period was particularly radical or open, but it had leaders with a passionate commitment on this issue and they made their mark.

Despite a missionary effort which was less certain of its proclamation because of liberalism, and which had become more comfortable with colonialism because both had become part of the fabric of the accepted world, the Church continued to grow enormously. In India its members doubled in number during the thirty years up to 1941. In Africa numbers quadrupled between 1900 and 1930 and then more than doubled again in the next twenty years – greatly outstripping the population rise for the half-century of 88 per cent. This growth did not all take place in a European mission context. Now, in Africa at any rate, the independent churches began to flourish. They had come into existence partly as a reaction to European superiority – what Barrett calls 'a failure in love'; partly as a declaration of the need for an African, non-western expression of Christianity (significantly, often concerned with eschatology and healing); partly as a response to the appeal of a number of charismatic, 'prophetic' indigenous leaders who were marginalized as extremists by the missionaries; and partly as a consequence of the Christian message being heard in areas where the missionary effort did not have the resources adequately to follow up initial interest. Their adherents began to show up in indices measured in millions. They were an indication that Christianity could be expressed in forms very different from those thought appropriate by most Europeans.

If most of the growth was within the context of European missions, it remains probable that indigenous evangelists continued to be its most important instruments. Occasionally, as in the east African revival which began in the 1930s, indigenous Christians found dramatic new ways of expressing the reality of their faith. The followers of the revival differed from the independent churches in that they remained just inside the mission churches, though largely outside of missionary control. This freedom, within constraints, was surely more important than the fact that they were often spiritually arrogant, narrow and very negative towards their own culture. They were an indication that the missionary could quite quickly become, perhaps already was, despite all appearances to the contrary, rather peripheral to the Church his fathers had established.

In the next forty years Britain was to take a lesser part in missionary work as its empire rapidly diminished. In 1940 British missionaries still appeared to be a major force. Estimates of the significance of their contribution remain almost impossible without placing them against a subsequent history. If many of those they sought to convert had discarded their message because of the trappings of the west, many others had accepted it for that very reason, while yet others had accepted it because they discerned a relevance behind the trappings which they had never really made their own or perhaps had never faced because they had met the Church through indigenous evangelists and priests. Many who discarded it continued to be influenced, in different degrees, by the missionaries' message and civilization. What would the next half-century reveal? Would Christianity, planted by Europeans, influenced in varying degrees by colonialism and imperialism, and often regarded as being even more inextricably bound up with them than it actually was, outlast their demise? Would the young churches, by and large denied genuine self-expression, ever be granted it and, if they were, would they have lost the capacity to act vigorously, creatively and in a way which was culturally appropriate? The fact that by the 1970s observers were talking of 'the most radical shift in the centre of gravity of the Christian world for at least a millennium' – from the northern to the southern continents – suggests a more lasting, if less controlled, influence than many predicted. In 1940, however, there were no more than scattered clues. The missionaries, more rather than less than formerly, governed their converts like potentates in a rigidly hierarchical society. Newbigin, having indignantly described examples of missionary distance and overlordship in relation to Indian Christians, concluded in 1936: 'But one thing is as sure as death: surely they won't stand this sort of thing from the white man much longer.'

21

Secularists and Rationalists, 1800–1940

Edward Royle

FREETHOUGHT, AS IT developed in the eighteenth century, was largely a matter for philosophers, scholars and theologians. Confident in the powers of human reason alone, men like John Toland (1670–1722), Anthony Collins (1676–1729) and Thomas Woolston (1670–1733) went beyond the classical synthesis of rational and revealed truth as expounded by the Natural Theologians to adopt the theology of Deism or even, in a heavily disguised and ironic form, outright atheism. Occasionally such ideas were carried beyond the narrow circle of intellectuals to the wider world of artisan anticlericalism and unbelief, but it was only at the very end of the eighteenth century, during the crisis in Church and State engendered by the French Revolution, that critical freethought in religion and politics merged with the nascent class consciousness of the artisans to produce a radical attack on the established order. Freethought in the nineteenth century was not simply a philosophical position but a social and political movement.

The context within which this radical freethought spread was defined by the political and religious establishment. A close alliance between religion and politics lay at the heart of the constitution – as Chief Justice Raymond stated at the trial of Thomas Woolston for blasphemy in 1728, 'Christianity in general is parcel of the common law of England.' In particular, the Established Church of England enjoyed a privileged position in law, society and politics. It was, as contemporary radicals put it, a part of 'Old Corruption'. Christianity underpinned the political establishment and was the basis of both law and morality, so those who lacked religious beliefs were deprived of their civil rights. But, as radicals argued in response, if it were true that civil society rested on religious belief, then a thorough reform of society would depend upon the eradication of that belief. Radical reformers lent a ready ear to those who proclaimed the very basis of religion to be a cheat and a fraud.

The one man who, above all others, helped to consolidate this radical critique of establishment politics and religion was Thomas Paine (1737–1809), who had made his revolutionary reputation in America with the publication in 1776 of *Common Sense*. During the 1790s he confirmed his position in Britain as the principal enemy of exclusive politics and revealed religion in two major works, *Rights of Man* (1791–2) and *The Age of Reason* (1794–5). Though the latter was intended as a defence of Deism against atheism, it contained a complete rejection of revealed religion and biblical Christianity and soon acquired the reputation of being the major work of popular atheism. Nourished on these writings, and others such as William Godwin's classic of utilitarian materialism, *Political Justice* (1793), and cheap translations of French Enlightenment texts, an extreme form of artisan radicalism developed which looked forward to a democratic state in which authority would be de-mystified and the powers of organized religion broken for ever.

The irony of this development is that anti-religion took on a very religious appearance. Paine and Godwin were avidly studied on Sundays (the one day free from labour) in what might otherwise have been called Bible classes. When larger meetings became more formalized they moved to tavern upper rooms or, later, separate lecture halls not unlike Nonconformist chapels. Radical freethought can, indeed, best be understood as an anti-religious sect, an extreme form of Nonconformity within which many of the emotional and social satisfactions of the religious life were met without the burden of a dogma based on revealed religion. Intellectually and socially, freethought held a position a little beyond Unitarianism, being more anti-metaphysical in its theology than the latter and also more plebeian in appeal.

Radical discussion groups in the 1790s were dispersed by an alarmed government anxious to preserve internal security while the country was at war with France, but after the return of peace in 1815 the ideas of the previous generation were revived by what was termed 'the blasphemous and seditious press'. Probably only a minority of radicals at this time were outright atheists, but a common bond of anticlericalism brought atheists and others together to denounce 'priestcraft' in all its forms. One of the most influential editors to republish Paine's writings and to spread the twin doctrines of republicanism and materialistic atheism was Richard Carlile (1790–1843), whose reissue of Paine's *Age of Reason* in 1819 led to his conviction for blasphemous libel and six years in Dorchester gaol. While there he encouraged his followers to form local Zetetic or Free Enquiry societies: the first societies of their kind to be formed by members of the lower classes – artisans, tradesmen and lesser shopkeepers in the main – explicitly to oppose the Christian religion.

By the later 1820s Carlile had fallen under the influence of the Reverend Robert Taylor – the so-called 'Devil's Chaplain' – a former Anglican who preached a variety of mystical Christianity heavily influenced by eastern religions and comparative mythology. The ease with which Carlile was able to adopt this new ground, taking some of his followers with him, is an indication of the fluidity of doctrine on the frontiers of belief. In the London of the early 1830s the adventurous lecture-goer or sermon-taster could pass from Carlile and Taylor with their allegorical Christianity to the Southcottian teachings of John 'Zion' Ward and James 'Shepherd' Smith, and so on to Edward Irving's millenarian Apostolic Church or Robert Owen's utopian socialism and back again without leaving the shared mental world of seekers after a new truth not imposed by the educated and the orthodox.

Within this world, Robert Owen (1771–1858) was rapidly emerging as a leading influence. Owen had made his fortune and his reputation as the benevolent factory master of the New Lanark mills in Scotland, where he had developed progressive views on education and had championed the cause of factory reform. He has frequently been portrayed as a labour leader and inspirer of co-operative trading and trade unionism in the early 1830s, but this is to misunderstand the man. He saw himself as the prophet of the new age – an age in which the divisiveness of religion would be swept away to permit a rational reordering of human society. Though Owen was a Deist (and in old age became a spiritualist) he was – like Paine – treated as an atheist because he had no time for existing institutions and the beliefs which sanctioned them. In a notorious speech delivered in frustration at the City of London Tavern in 1817, after he had failed to win a hearing for his plan to replace the discredited poor laws with self-supporting pauper colonies, he denounced 'the fundamental notions of every religion that has hitherto been taught to men'.

Owen was an environmentalist, believing not in original sin but in the innate goodness of mankind. Salvation therefore lay not in faith, but in the perfect environment of 'the new moral world' which Owen planned to demonstrate with the erection of huge utopian communities, initially on an experimental basis financed by private capital. Later, as his idea worked its peacefully revolutionary way across the world, these 'communities of united interest' would become self-supporting. The millennium would thus be commenced on earth; but the saviour who would defeat at the last the forces of evil would not be some transcendental God but the power of human reason following the science of society (or socialism) as revealed by its prophet, Robert Owen.

To implement his plan, Owen began in May 1835 a propagandist organization grandly entitled 'The Association of All Classes of All

Nations'. By the time of its second annual congress, meeting in Salford in 1837, Owen's message had begun to attract considerable support among artisans who in the previous decade had been drawn into the co-operative movement as a means of raising funds to build, if not an Owenite community, then at least a self-supporting haven for artisans threatened with increasing capitalistic control over their work processes. Many of these members of the working classes were politically conscious and thinking men (and occasionally women) who saw in Owen's Association of All Classes a propagandist vehicle for the realization of their own dreams – an onslaught on the corrupt, selfish, hypocritical, old immoral world of Christians and capitalists.

In Owen's view, the Association was to prepare public opinion for the commencement of his millennium. Accordingly a structure was created appropriate to a religious sect. The country was divided into districts, to each of which a social missionary was allocated, rather like the early Methodist 'rounds' with their travelling preachers. Locally, social institutions or, more grandly, halls of science were built like chapels, the larger ones being cared for by their own stationed lecturers. Some lecturers were even persuaded to register themselves as Protestant Dissenters under the Act of Toleration, to secure their right to hold meetings on Sundays. A hymn book was issued for use at these Sunday meetings, at which readings from Owen's *Book of the New Moral World* were rendered. A Rational Tract Society was also formed along the lines of the Religious Tract Society. This local activity was in danger of becoming an end in itself for many Owenites, but officially the true end was to be the building of an experimental community: not accommodation to the world, but sectarian withdrawal from the world. So the 1837 congress also approved the creation of a National Community Friendly Society to look for a site and to collect funds.

By the time of the 1839 congress there were over fifty branches of the Association in existence, mainly in the industrial areas of Lancashire, Cheshire, Yorkshire, the midlands, the Clyde valley and London, with a membership of several thousands; moreover, a property had been found for lease at Queenwood Farm in the parish of East Tytherly, Hampshire, on which a community could be commenced. As industrial depression bit deeply into living standards in the late 1830s, the Owenites looked forward eagerly to the promised land which was described with Old Testament fervour. Owen now began to subordinate the propagandist organization to the task of building the community. The Association and the National Community Friendly Society were amalgamated to form the Universal Community Society of Rational Religionists – later shortened to Rational Society – and antireligious lecturers were ordered not to offend against public opinion at a time when capitalist backers were being sought to provide the thousands of pounds required for the proper implementation of Owen's grand plan.

Those members of the working classes who had hoped to find in Owenism a democratic and militantly anti-Christian propagandist organization were angry and felt deceived. The social missionaries were now told to concentrate on the positive side of Owen's message and to cease their attack on the evil of the divisive, sectarian religion of the Christian Churches. One man who resented this attempt to curb his anti-Christian and democratic instincts was Charles Southwell (1814–60), a social missionary in Bristol, who in November 1841 started a new periodical in which to expound his own uncensored views. This was the *Oracle of Reason*, a self-proclaimed weekly periodical of militant atheism. Within a month, Southwell was prosecuted for a blasphemous denunciation of the Bible, which he described as 'that revoltingly odious Jew production'. He was sentenced to a year in gaol. George Jacob Holyoake (1817–1906), a Birmingham whitesmith and stationed lecturer in Worcester, then stepped forward to take the editorial chair. Stung by the prosecution of Southwell, he abandoned the last vestiges of his own Unitarian religion and adopted the full-blooded creed of materialistic atheism. Within six months, he too was in gaol for blasphemy. Martyrs, a cause and a movement were thus born.

Meanwhile, the official Owenite cause was struggling. Starved of capital and incapable of demonstrating the truth of Owen's system for regenerating the world, the Queenwood community was foundering. It closed amid acrimony in 1845. Yet despite this there remained in the country many branches of the Rational Society, some of which were capable of maintaining their own social missionaries and advocating those democratic and anti-religious aspects of Owenism which had always been most popular among the rank and file of Owenites. Charles Southwell had no difficulty making a living as a freelance anti-Christian lecturer and dramatic actor among such people in his native London, while Holyoake was employed in Glasgow and Paisley, and another like-minded missionary, Robert Cooper (1819–68), worked in Edinburgh and then Huddersfield.

Holyoake decided to try to organize these remnants of the Rational Society, and in 1845 issued a pamphlet entitled *Rationalism, a Treatise for the Times*, in which he summarized the essential features of Owenism as he saw it, shorn of its now discredited communitarianism. This new creed he called simply Rationalism:

Rationalism advises what is useful to society without asking whether it is religious or not. It makes morality the sole business of life, and declares that from the cradle to the grave man should be guided by reason and regulated by science. It looks on man, to all practical purposes, as a purely material being – other systems have chiefly spiritualised him.

The full programme was later summarized in the sub-heading of the *Reasoner*, a periodical begun by Holyoake in 1846 which was to appear weekly for the next fifteen years: 'Communistic in Social Economy – Utilitarian in Morals – Republican in Politics – and Anti-Theological in Religion'. Holyoake experimented with various names for his followers: after Rationalism he tried in 1847 Theological Utilitarianism, before settling on Secularism in 1851.

Secularism was therefore a new name, but not a new movement, having inherited much of its philosophy, organization and membership from the Owenite propagandist organization which in its prime in the early 1840s had established a national network of over a hundred branch societies and classes, many of them in the chapel lands of Lancashire and the West Riding where Secularism also was to be at its strongest. At first Holyoake and other ex-missionaries were unable to halt the decline and decay of the organization. Only a few of the larger local societies were able to maintain an active presence and lecture programme. Most could not afford the mortgage payments on their halls of science, which had to be disposed of. Local Owenites put their efforts into other things: some, as at Rochdale, took up retail co-operation, at first to build up their own funds to found a genuinely working-class community, later simply to make life better for themselves in their own local communities; some, as in Northampton, formed freehold land societies and building societies to realize their dreams of independence on a smaller scale; some threw in their lot with the political agitation for the People's Charter which reached its climax in 1848; some continued their anti-Christian propagandism. Holyoake attempted to hold them all together with his *Reasoner*.

Slowly, in the 1850s, he began to make headway. Secularism caught the public imagination. Ministers of religion, led by a Congregational minister called Brewin Grant, sought to make names for themselves in public debate with Holyoake. All they succeeded in doing was making a name for Holyoake and his movement. The sales of his paper rose from under a thousand to over five thousand. The number of local societies reporting activity rose to over fifty. By the end of the 1850s, huge rallies in the north of England were drawing ten thousand or more supporters. Secularism as a movement had become a fact of some significance in the life of Victorian Britain. Politically radical, the Secularists supported calls for an extension of the franchise, and as republicans they sent subscriptions to the cause of European freedom as personified by the Italian nationalists, Mazzini and Garibaldi. Economically they were keen co-operators. Religiously they criticized biblical Evangelicals, sabbatarianism, and such privileges of the Established Church as tithes, church rates and church schools.

But as the movement grew, all was not well within it. In his youth, when he had rushed to edit the *Oracle of Reason* for Charles Southwell, Holyoake had appeared an extremist and an outspoken advocate of materialistic atheism. This was not his true character. In fact he was a rather mild man, with a weak voice, poor eyesight and a pedantic, scholarly manner. Though largely self-taught, he thought himself the equal of his betters and the better of his equals. In London he fell in with the radical, literary middle class: men like the liberal philosopher and economist, John Stuart Mill; Henry Atkinson, friend of Harriet Martineau; Thornton Hunt, journalist; Francis Newman, deistical brother of the Catholic convert John Henry Newman; W. J. Fox, minister at the radical Unitarian South Place Chapel where the literary intelligentsia worshipped if they worshipped anywhere at all. These people, and the money they gave Holyoake to subsidize his publications, helped modify his views. They introduced him to the Positivist ideas of Auguste Comte. Secularism became a more rounded and sophisticated philosophy than that which had been advocated in the halls of science by men like Charles Southwell. To the latter, atheism was a clear statement of truth; to Holyoake it was no more than an unprovable theological position. In concentrating on this life, Holyoake was agnostic about the next; Secularism was, strictly speaking, neutral on the matter of religion, not hostile to it.

This subtle change in outlook did not meet with the approval of those more rugged individuals who had kept the Owenite flag flying. Lecturers like Southwell and Robert Cooper felt that religion had to be destroyed if Secularism were to flourish; neutrality was not a practicable position to adopt in the face of militant Christianity. Furthermore, Holyoake's attempt to identify the movement with himself did not go down well with many who had earlier resented Owen's own dictatorial approach to their movement. Southwell emigrated to Australia; Cooper started a periodical named the *London Investigator* after the leading American freethought paper, the *Boston Investigator*. Secularists who wished to proclaim their atheism rallied to Cooper, and it was from among this group of malcontents in the late 1850s that a new star appeared – Charles Bradlaugh (1833–91).

Bradlaugh was born in Hoxton, north-east London. He was too young to have been an Owenite or a Chartist, but as a youth he had lodged for a time with Eliza Sharples, widow of Richard Carlile, and had imbibed a radical anti-clericalism from lecturers in Victoria Park and at Sharples's Warner

Street Temperance Hall. A powerfully built youth with a loud voice, he was a natural orator and quickly made his mark. By 1860 he had been invited to edit a new national radical/Secularist paper, the *National Reformer*. He soon quarrelled with his co-editor, the more experienced West Riding radical, Joseph Barker, and then fell out with Holyoake too when he became associated with the paper. Bradlaugh and Holyoake were never to be wholly reconciled. They represented different temperaments and different aspects of the movement: the one cautious, scholarly, compromising in politics and theology alike, and (it appeared at the time) increasingly ineffective; the other exciting, positive, dogmatic, and apparently capable and worthy of leading a radical onslaught on established religion and undemocratic politics. Most of the movement in the country followed Bradlaugh. He could fill their lecture halls. But pockets of support for Holyoake remained, especially in places where more positive memories of Owenism were long, such as Glasgow, Failsworth (near Oldham), Huddersfield and Leicester.

In the 1860s, political concerns came to the fore in the popular mind, with the agitation to secure an extension of the franchise to working men. Although both Bradlaugh and Holyoake were involved, it was the militant Bradlaugh who took the more prominent part in the agitation of the Reform League leading up to the Reform Act of 1867; and in the first general election under the new Act, which had extended the franchise to the better-off sort of urban working men, he stood for Parliament at Northampton. He was to nurse this candidacy for twelve years before finally being elected in 1880. Before then much else was to happen. In 1866 he signalled his leadership of the Secularist movement by announcing the creation of the National Secular Society, with himself as president and his paper, the *National Reformer*, as its official organ. Charles Watts (1836–1906), son of a Wesleyan minister from Bristol, was his sub-editor and secretary of the National Secular Society. Gradually, independent Secular Societies affiliated to the National Secular Society, which became the principal national organization for Secularism. In the early 1870s, though, the movement fell into decline and even decay as Bradlaugh devoted more and more of his energies to the republican cause which was enjoying a brief upsurge of popularity in Britain and in which he took (as ever) a leading part. It was not until 1875 that he turned again to devote his energies to the revival and propagation of Secularism. Almost at once he acquired a new lieutenant, the separated wife of a rather priggish clergyman, Mrs Annie Besant (1847–1933).

Every bit the match for Bradlaugh in energy, oratorical powers and uncompromising idealism, Mrs Besant became the major influence in his life for the next ten years. Her rise in the movement caused raised eyebrows and resentment in some quarters. Kate Watts, wife of Charles, resented her loss of position as first lady of the movement and her husband's downgrading for the new favourite, and when in 1876 Watts declined to defend the publication of an early birth-control work, Charles Knowlton's *Fruits of Philosophy*, of which he was the nominal publisher, Mrs Besant insisted that she and Bradlaugh would republish the work and defend it in the courts. Watts was sacked from the *National Reformer* and drummed out of the National Secular Society. He naturally gravitated towards the elder statesman of Secularism, George Jacob Holyoake, who had quietly been pursuing his own minority way, largely through journalism. Watts was given a part in, and eventually took over, Holyoake's latest effort, the *Secular Review*.

Secularism was now divided into two camps, centred respectively on the *National Reformer* and the *Secular Review*. The former controlled the National Secular Society; the latter formed a new organization, the British Secular Union. Holyoake strongholds, such as Huddersfield and Leicester, sympathized with the latter. Several towns had rival organizations. The division was not simply over personality, but also over policy. Bradlaugh had long been an advocate of birth control – neo-Malthusianism as it was then known. Indeed, it was over Bradlaugh's support for another birth-control work, George Drysdale's *Elements of Social Science*, that Bradlaugh had split with Joseph Barker and Holyoake back in 1860–1. The economic thinking behind neo-Malthusianism was individualistic: it argued that poverty is caused by the poor having too many children. But for many old Owenites, poverty was caused by the maldistribution of wealth in the capitalist system. Although Bradlaugh could pose as the great defender of freedom of publication, the split of 1877 showed his opponents to be potentially the more radical in social terms, and in the 1880s it was the *Secular Review* which was to be most open to new ideas including revived socialism, while the *National Reformer* remained the champion of an increasingly old-fashioned individualistic radicalism. When Annie Besant became a socialist in 1884, she had to find another outlet for her views.

However, this is to anticipate developments. In 1880, an event occurred which greatly strengthened the Bradlaugh camp and regained him the support of many opponents, for in that year Bradlaugh was at last elected to represent Northampton in Parliament. He applied to make an affirmation rather than take the oath of allegiance, on the grounds that he did not believe in the oath. A Select Committee of the House of Commons ruled that the Affirmations Act of 1855 allowed only for religious objections to legal oaths, such as those held by Quakers. Bradlaugh's irreligious objections were not acceptable. He therefore asked to take the oath, but this was refused on the grounds that he had acknowledged it had no meaning for him. So he was not allowed to take his seat. This 'Bradlaugh Case' rolled on for years, and was not fully cleared up until a new Parliament met in January 1886. But as Bradlaugh was time and again chosen in by-elections by the electors of Northampton (many of whom were Nonconformist Liberals) only to be refused by the House of Commons, he became a national celebrity, the personification of radicalism and popular democratic rights. And, despite the fact that he tried not to make his Secularism an issue, inevitably it became one and the movement benefited greatly from its association with his name. The number of branches affiliated to the National Secular Society rose to over a hundred in the early 1880s and, although the total paid-up membership at any one time probably never exceeded 4,000, those who came under the general influence of Secularism and attended lectures may have numbered ten times that figure, or more.

One man who moved from the *Secular Review* to the *National Reformer* camp as a result of the Bradlaugh case was George William Foote (1850–1915), the son of a customs official from Plymouth, a cultivated young man with literary tastes and ambitions. Angered by the treatment of Bradlaugh he threw caution to the wind and in May 1881 began a new periodical, the *Freethinker*, a scurrilous monthly and later weekly publication which attacked Christianity with barbed wit and savage humour. Foote was soon the subject of two blasphemy prosecutions and in 1883 was sentenced to a year in gaol. The circulation of the *Freethinker* topped 10,000. This was the high point of Secularist achievement, as the movement became identified in the public mind with the struggle for the democratic right of constituents to select their own MP, and with the liberal right to freedom of expression in a free country.

During these years, local Secularism continued to display many of those semi-religious characteristics which had been such a feature of Owenism. Some local societies arranged themselves into lecture circuits. The more prosperous groups acquired their own lecture halls which became centres for leisure-time activities. Sunday lecture meetings were enlivened with music – even singing from the old Owenite hymn book or more recent compilations such as *The Secularist's Manual of Songs and Ceremonies* (1871) which included a form of words for the commemoration of the various rites of passage. Sunday schools were opened, choirs formed, outings organized, sewing meetings and bazaars held – all the trappings of chapel life were to be found in the local Secular hall. By the mid-1880s the local Secular Society was serving four functions within its community:

1 It provided a focus for radical political activity, both in the local community and constituency, and in rallying public opinion to support

Bradlaugh's struggle, a further extension of the franchise, and other topics of the day.

2 It acted as a centre for the leisure-time recreation of its members. Summer outings and picnics were organized to local scenic beauty spots; concerts, amateur dramatics and soirées occupied dark winter evenings.

3 It served a quasi-religious function, providing for non-believers many of those services and emotional satisfactions which were traditionally supplied by the churches. Music played an important part in meetings. The Stalybridge Secular Choir became quite a feature of northern Secularism – they even rendered a secular version of Mozart's *Gloria in excelsis Deo*!

4 It served to focus the energies of a pressure group striving to challenge religious influences in society, especially as they affected the local community in such matters as restrictive Sunday legislation and religious education.

From the mid-1880s a decline set in. With Bradlaugh accepted in Parliament and Foote's *Freethinker* deprived of the publicity of further blasphemy prosecutions, Secularism sank into the background and the support which had gathered in the heat of controversy slipped away again. More broadly, fundamental changes were occurring within British society which were challenging the traditional functions of Secularism. Both Bradlaugh and Foote were Gladstonian Liberals – strong individualists with no sympathy for socialism. As the nineteenth century drew to a close that natural and assumed relationship between Secularism and 'advanced' political opinion was for the first time broken. While some of the more enterprising of individual Secularists devoted their energies to socialism, others became such extreme individualists as to verge on Conservatism. By the Edwardian years, the old radical consensus had been shattered. At the same time, alternative opportunities for leisure activities were drawing people away from both chapels and Secular Societies. As G. W. Foote remarked, after he had succeeded Bradlaugh as president of the National Secular Society in 1890, in the old days 'Unless you went to the dram-shop or the gospel-shop, it was "Bradlaugh or nothing" on a Sunday evening.' The truth was that both politics and leisure were now breaking free from the religious framework within which they had traditionally been conceived: they were becoming secularized. The irony is that Secularism was as much a victim of this process as religion. 'When . . . "God is dead", Atheism dies also,' quipped George Bernard Shaw. By the outbreak of the First World War, many branches of the National Secular Society and local Secular Societies had closed, or were so shrunken in membership that they were no longer able to maintain their halls and a regular programme of events. What activities they did pursue were more narrowly focused on specifically religious issues, such as campaigns against religious education and for the abolition of the blasphemy laws.

The National Secular Society continued into the twentieth century, but less as a national movement than as a pressure group, with few branches and a membership counted in hundreds rather than thousands. The *National Reformer* closed in 1893, two years after Bradlaugh's premature death, but G. W. Foote's *Freethinker* continued not only until his death in 1915, but also under his successor, Chapman Cohen (1868–1954), a Jew from Leicester, and under his successors too. Though reduced to monthly publication in 1973, it still survives, along with the National Secular Society. The society has, since the 1960s, operated as a centralized pressure group interested in a variety of humanistic and libertarian causes. Fortunes have fluctuated, with some expansion in the 1960s before a renewed period of contraction in the 1970s. Locally, only a few Secular Societies survived into the second half of the twentieth century to maintain continuity with the golden age of Secularism in mid-Victorian Britain.

With the decline in Secularism, other freethinking approaches enjoyed greater success. The *Secular Review* passed under the control of an idiosyncratic Scot, William Stewart Ross (1844–1906), after Charles Watts had temporarily emigrated to Canada in 1884, and became the *Agnostic Journal* the following year. Ross's policy was to denounce the hypocrisies of the modern age (among which he included 'Knowltonian filth', dogmatic atheism and Charles Bradlaugh), but at the same time he was open to a discussion of socialism and the 'new morality' associated with writers such as Grant Allen. Charles Watts's publishing business was continued in his absence by his son, Charles Albert Watts (1858–1946). In 1890 the latter launched a Propaganda Press Committee in association with G. J. Holyoake, F. J. Gould and a number of other writers and intellectuals. Two years later the name was changed to the Rationalist Press Committee and, in 1899, to the Rationalist Press Association. This organization aimed to disseminate the ideas of intellectual freethought as widely as possible through the issue of inexpensive editions of both Rationalist classics and modern works. Watts's market was the expanding lower middle class of the first generation to have received compulsory state education after the Education Act of 1870. One of the earliest publications of the Rationalist Press Association, a translation of Ernst Haeckel's *The Riddle of the Universe*, sold over 100,000 copies by 1905. This level of success was maintained up to the First World War, with Watts issuing his 'Pamphlets for the Million' series in 1911, providing twenty-four-page works for a halfpenny. The war and its aftermath proved difficult times, but an even greater success was achieved in 1929 with the start of the

'Thinker's Library' series which brought freethought works into many homes for the first time.

Other freethinkers in the later nineteenth century sought to bring new life to the practice of their unbelief by adopting more overtly religious forms. If Secularism can be called the freethought of the chapel, Positivism and the Ethical Movement were the freethought of the Church – even of the High Church. Dissatisfaction with what appeared to some to be the arid rationalism of traditional freethought led to the demand for more emotion, ritual and music in services. Holyoake had not been immune from these influences in the 1850s, and had justified his adoption of Secularism with the phrase from Comte, 'Nothing is destroyed until it is replaced.' Secularism never became the English equivalent of Positivism, but some of its adherents made the transition from the one to the other.

The leading English Positivist was Richard Congreve (1818–99), a clergyman of the Church of England and tutor at Wadham College, Oxford. After resigning his fellowship to get married in 1854, he devoted himself to the dissemination of Comte's views and in May 1867 established the London Positivist Society. His leading disciples were former pupils at Oxford, Frederic Harrison (1831–1923), Edward Spencer Beesly (1831–1915) and John Henry Bridges (1832–1906). Together they established the Positivist School at Chapel Street in London in 1870, but eight years later a schism occurred between Congreve, who continued with a more churchly form of Positivism at Chapel Street, and his disciples, who formed a less priestly meeting at Newton Hall, Fetter Lane. The split was not healed until 1916. The total number of Positivists in the late 1870s was probably no more than about two hundred. Their leaders were intellectuals and professional men but their 'Religion of Humanity' had some attraction for moderate Secularists with their wider social appeal. In Leicester, where Holyoake's version of Secularism was dominant, a few members of the Secular Society led by Malcolm Quin and George Findley formed a Positivist Society. When Quin moved to Newcastle upon Tyne in 1878 he took his enthusiasm with him and established a church in the Congreve tradition of worship. Despite the formation of several other churches in the north-east, Birmingham, Manchester, Liverpool and Leicester, the Religion of Humanity remained of strictly limited appeal and that little support faded in the inter-war years. The London Positivist Society closed in 1934. Nevertheless, English Positivism exerted a widespread though diffuse influence as an intellectual movement out of all proportion to its limited numbers.

Despite the attractions of Positivism for some Secularists, the Ethical Movement with its less ritualistic approach to worship proved more congenial to their way of thinking. The Ethical Culture Movement was founded in New York in 1876 by a former Jewish rabbi, Felix Adler, to promote a non-theistic and non-credal education movement; but there were in England separate roots in the South Place Chapel in London. Here, William Johnson Fox (1786–1864) had gradually led his flock from Unitarianism to a liberal Theism which by the 1850s came close to being a middle-class version of Holyoake's Secularism. The trend was continued under Fox's successor, Moncure Daniel Conway, an American who ministered at South Place from 1865 until 1885 when he retired to write what is still a standard biography of Thomas Paine. Stanton Coit (1857–1944), another American who was a close associate of Adler, then took charge and converted South Place into an Ethical Society. He went on to form the Ethical Union in 1895, which had a peak of twenty-six affiliated societies in 1906, many of them in and around London but not including South Place. After the First World War, the Union fell into decline and most societies closed. The strongest remained South Place, which moved to new premises – Conway Hall – in west London in 1929. Here the South Place Ethical Society remains in the 1990s as an active participant in various agitations for freedom of thought and expression.

The history of this freethought denominationalism is as hard to interpret as its Christian equivalent, and the social bases of unbelief are as obscure as those of belief. Class is clearly an important factor. As with the Dissenting churches, most of those attending Secularist meetings were, broadly speaking, of the working classes – this is not surprising, since over three-quarters of the population fell into this category – but those working people who bothered with religious or anti-religious organizations were outnumbered by those who did not. Moreover, though artisans have traditionally been regarded as 'infidels', there were undoubtedly far fewer Secularist artisans than there were Christian. Similarly, the appeal to the upper element within the working classes was common to both Nonconformist and freethought organizations. These were the people with some degree of social and economic independence, who resented the patronizing control exerted in particular through the Church of England and had sufficient educational and economic means to do something about it. They gravitated, if they were interested in religious matters at all, towards the chapel and the secular hall – but why the one rather than the other?

Here we reach the limits of social explanation. Individual choice and belief, accident of influence or experience at a critical point in youth or early adulthood appear to have been the significant factors. For many Secularists the decision to become a Secularist was a positive one, involving a rejection of sincerely held Christian beliefs and a 'conversion' experience as compelling as that which had brought them and thousands like them to Christianity in the first place. The Secularist conversion, though, appears frequently to have occurred in adulthood rather than in adolescence, and was often the result of solitary reading and reflection rather than attendance at a revivalist meeting. In the nineteenth century, when militant Christianity was represented by a biblically based Evangelical Protestantism, the Bible seems to have been the single most common book to have turned people to freethought. Secularist arguments emphasized the immorality of the Bible (particularly of the Old Testament) and its inconsistencies, which belied the claim of Evangelicals that it was the Word of God. Next to the Bible, Thomas Paine's work, itself strongly critical of the Bible, was often cited as a major influence on the formation of opinion. It may be significant that scientific developments do not seem to have played a large part in the making of freethinkers. Darwinism – or, more usually, a Lamarckian evolutionism – was taken up as a confirmation of a position rather than as a cause of it. More important was the association between freethought and popular science: phrenology, mesmerism, even spiritualism. These were the interests of the self-taught, whose democratic intellects were pitted against the received ideas and academic wisdom of those who were termed 'authorities'.

In the twentieth century the pattern has varied. With the decline in biblical literalism and the wider acceptance within the churches of liberal Protestant theology, the Roman Catholic Church has become more important as the epitome of authority to be rejected and attacked. By the late nineteenth century Secularists were dismissing a Protestantism which appeared to be abandoning its old defences and accepting views for which freethinkers had earlier been derided or even persecuted. The division of the modern world was increasingly expressed in the phrase 'Rome or Reason'. The product of the Methodist Sunday school was in the twentieth century replaced by the child from the Catholic day school as the 'typical' potential freethinker.

As with the Christian denominations, so also with the divisions between Secularists, Rationalists, Positivists and Ethicists: class could be an important factor in the distinction between 'chapel' and 'church'. Generally speaking, the appeal of the latter at the end of the nineteenth century was to the 'middle class' and to women more than men. The Secularist Movement, on the contrary, was overwhelmingly male – perhaps as few as 10 per cent of the membership was female – while the Ethical Movement claimed 'a very large proportion' of women members. According to the *Daily News* census of worship, Ethical services were held on Sundays at nine locations in inner London during 1902–3, attended by 463 women compared with 507 men on typical Sundays. At South Place, the women outnumbered the men by almost two to one.

To this extent, generalizations from the sociology of religion can apply equally to the sociology of irreligion. Reason was seen as a male characteristic; emotion as female. Religion was therefore a concern for women. Secularists, most of whom were advocates of female emancipation, attributed the thraldom of women to the Bible and sought to cultivate female and family membership in their societies by introducing music into their Sunday meetings and making them more like 'services'. At a time when the churches were debating their lack of appeal to men, the Secularists had the opposite problem. The sociology of religion can also be applied to an interpretation of the development of freethought organizations, using the 'sect', 'denomination' and 'church' typology. Owenism assumed many of the characteristics of a millenarian sect. The leader, Robert Owen, was a detached and autocratic figure who inspired his followers from the wings of the day-to-day organization. He drew to himself supporters who had a previous history of sectarian involvement and offered them a new life through withdrawal from the corrupt world. But even in the heyday of Owenism, other followers in local halls of science were creating a reformist denomination located firmly in the old world. The strength of the boundaries between these Owenite, and later Secularist, societies and the wider world varied according to both external and internal factors. Their emphasis on a rejection of orthodox religion always meant they would remain something of a sect, cut off from and disowned by the mainstream of nineteenth-century religious life; but the policy of accommodation adopted by Holyoake led in some cases to coexistence with and even acceptance by local and predominantly Christian communities. The disputes between the Bradlaugh and Holyoake schools of Secularism can in part be interpreted as a difference between sect and denomination, advocates of the former campaigning by emphasizing their distinctiveness, and of the latter by seeking to influence by playing down differences.

Other forms of freethought, of a Positivist and Ethical nature, with their more middle-class and conformist religious appeals, were always more acceptable and denominational in outlook, although the existence of an overlapping membership in practice breaks down some of the sociological types when applied to individuals. In the twentieth century, as the religious form of organization has declined in significance, the shape of freethought organization has also changed. The Rationalist Press Association in particular, as a publishing company, is different from the classic form of nineteenth-century religio-political organization, although it did experiment with touring lecturers as part of a wider propagandist effort before the First World War, rather like the *Clarion* socialists. The Association took to its logical conclusion the freethought of the individual mind and had more in common with a book club than with a church; while the National Secular Society in the twentieth century might be compared to a campaigning charity, except that it was and is denied charitable status. Meetings of freethought societies in the twentieth century look less like religious services and more like political gatherings.

Much of the significance in studying freethought organizations lies in the perspective which they give to religious forms. When so much of religious practice in fact takes its nature not from belief but from human need and social practicalities, a study of antireligious organizations can suggest what is of the essence of belief and what derives from social form. The Secular Societies of the nineteenth century sometimes parodied Christian ceremonies by way of propaganda, but more often they did so because there was a clear social need for such forms of behaviour. The decline of such need is reflected in the changing forms which rational freethought has taken in the twentieth century, as well as in the absolute decline of nineteenth-century models, both religious and otherwise.

A study of freethought in its various manifestations is also important to an understanding of nineteenth-century religion because many nineteenth-century Christians thought it important. Some were obsessed with the evils of 'infidelity' – the lack of religious faith. They saw the fabric of their society being threatened by it. One would not imagine, from some of the more colourful sermons on the topic, that the Secularists were such a small and relatively uninfluential band. Their importance lies in the way they exposed a raw nerve in Victorian religion. Christians needed 'the infidel' to define themselves and their purpose; they also needed him both to explain their failures and to provide an enemy in whose defeat their own doubts could be allayed and the superficial optimism of their age reinforced.

A study of freethought also shows up for the historian of Christianity its weaknesses and blemishes – the intolerance, narrow-mindedness, bigotry and anti-intellectualism of many nineteenth-century (and later) Christians. One who at the time felt more sympathy with Bradlaugh than with his fellow-Christians was the Reverend Stewart Headlam, Christian socialist, priest extraordinary and unpaid chaplain to Bradlaugh's notorious Old Street Hall of Science which so filled the neighbouring London City missionaries with alarm. There was little doubt in Headlam's mind as to who the 'true' Christians were.

To view the Secularist, Rationalist and Ethical movements purely in this negative light, however, is rather like writing a history of Methodism only for what it reveals about the Church of England. The task is a useful one – but partial. The freethinkers are worth studying also in their own right as a legitimate part of the spectrum of belief. In their sincerity and honest doubt, their belief in rational and scientific progress, and their conviction that religious issues really mattered, they were eminently Victorian.

Plate 4 Pope John Paul II meets Salvation Army Commissioner Eva Burrows at the house of Cardinal Gray during his visit to Great Britain in 1982

Photograph: The Press Association.

PART IV
Modern Britain

22

The Jewish Community in Britain

Jonathan G. Campbell

THE FIRST JEWS to enter Britain were those who followed William the Conqueror into England after 1066. Initially they flourished, but the growth of hostility towards them in the twelfth and thirteenth centuries culminated in the expulsion of the Jews from England by Edward I in 1290. However, the Jews were readmitted under Cromwell and have remained ever since, resident mainly in the cities, especially London, and increasing in numbers particularly during the second half of the nineteenth century. The 1800s also saw the firm establishment of Scottish and Welsh Jewries, there being little evidence for a Jewish presence in Scotland or Wales in the medieval period.

Since the seventeenth century, British Jews have generally experienced a greater and more consistent degree of freedom than their counterparts in other European countries. Incidents of antisemitic violence have been rare and the nineteenth century saw the erosion of most restrictions on full Jewish involvement in society and politics. Further, the United Synagogue, the office of Chief Rabbi and the Board of Deputies of British Jews, all essentially nineteenth-century in origin, are three of the main enduring institutions of British Jewry with official status. Britain's Jews should not, however, be thought of as a single entity; on the contrary, there are important divergences in matters of practice and belief, as well as in demography, which must be taken into account in order to avoid oversimplification. In particular, an increasing antagonism marks relations between the representatives of Orthodoxy on the one hand and Reform and Liberal Judaism on the other. Informing the background of such differences is the fact that in recent generations the number of Jews in Britain has declined, especially in provincial towns and cities. The reasons for this are complex, one being that many Jews, either by necessity or by design, remain outside any specifically Jewish institution and marry outwith the community. In any case, London, Manchester, Leeds, Glasgow and the Brighton area are left as the main centres of Jewish population. Current estimates of the total number of Jews in Britain stand at approximately 330,000; around one-third of these are resident in north-west London.

Clearly, a history treating the whole of British Jewry as one phenomenon is out of the question. This chapter is accordingly divided into sections on the following areas: Jews in medieval England; Jews in England from Cromwell to the First World War; Jews in Wales; Jews in Scotland; and the Jews of modern Britain.

JEWS IN MEDIEVAL ENGLAND

As noted above, the first Jews to settle in England came into the country after 1066 in the wake of William the Conqueror. Most of them were financiers and in the main came from France, although others arrived from elsewhere in Europe as well as from Muslim countries. Thus, during the twelfth century Jews came to reside in a number of important towns in medieval England: Bristol, Lincoln, Norwich, Oxford, Winchester, York and, of course, London.

While William's immediate successors appear to have treated their Jewish subjects reasonably well, this tolerance gave way to antisemitic sentiment as the twelfth century unfolded. In particular, the first recorded 'blood libel' in Europe was made in Norwich in 1144, followed by similar accusations in Bury St Edmunds, Bristol and Winchester in succeeding decades. The charges centred on claims that Jews ritually murdered Christian children, especially as Easter approached, in order to re-enact Christ's Passion and to use the victim's blood in the preparation of unleavened bread for Passover. In the Norwich case, the body of a boy was found on the town's outskirts; the Jews were blamed for his death and witnesses were produced who claimed to have seen the alleged abuse taking place. Although there were no immediate repercussions, attacks were made on Norwich's Jewish community in the 1230s. The caricature underlying these accusations, which assumed that Jews knew the truth about Christ but stubbornly rejected it, became ingrained in popular European Christian culture, where it persisted until recent times (a case was brought to trial as late as 1911 in Russia and the Nazis revived the 'blood libel' in their war against the Jews). Moreover, as far as medieval England is concerned, the crusades did not help matters. After the first crusader preaching and massacres in the Rhineland during the First Crusade (1096–99), the Jews of England suffered violent attacks at the time of the Third Crusade (1189–92). At the coronation of Richard I in 1189, Jewish notables attending the ceremony were assaulted and the Jewish quarter of London was sacked, followed by similar incidents in other towns in 1190. The Jews of York committed suicide *en masse* rather than be maltreated or forcibly converted.

Inseparable from these developments were monetary matters. Jews had entered England as capitalists, and it was often in the interests of petty barons indebted to them to encourage animosity towards them. At the same time, the Crown was aware of the financial muscle of the Jews and not infrequently imposed arbitrary, excessive tax demands, or tallage. In 1188 one-quarter of the movable property of London's Jews was levied; similarly, after the death of the great financier Aaron of Lincoln (*c.* 1125–86), his monies were declared to be the property of the Crown. The royal authorities also knew, however, that it was in their own interests to protect Jewish affairs, and so instituted the Exchequer of the Jews (*scaccarium Judaeorum*) and the office of Jewish Archpresbyter (*presbyter Judaeorum*). The former may be described as a government department for Jewish affairs, probably originating with the Crown's desire to manage the estate of the abovementioned Aaron of Lincoln. Although Jews were involved, it was ultimately controlled by Christian justices or keepers of the Jews, and it held responsibility for the administration, justice and finance of the Jewish community; this included charge over the *archae* or chests located in various towns in which Jewish moneylending activities were recorded. The role of the office of Archpresbyter, although unclear in its precise origin, was that of official representative of the Jews of medieval England; the incumbent was supposed to be a pious Jew who was also a skilled financier. We are fortunate in knowing the names of six of them in the decades leading up to the expulsion: Jacob of London (until 1207), Josce son of Isaac (1207–36), Aaron of York (1236–43), Elias le Evesque (1243–57), Hagin son of Moses (1258–80) and Cok Hagin son of Deulecresse (1281–90).

It would be wrong to interpret the establishment of these two institutions as a sign of growing security for the Jews of England. Indeed, the reign of Richard I (1189–99) marked the beginning of the end for medieval English Jewry, whose position declined throughout the thirteenth century, especially under the lengthy rule of Henry III (1216–72), culminating in Edward I's order expelling the Jews in 1290. As a prelude to this, in 1253 Jews were forbidden to dwell in towns where there was not already an organized community, and during the Barons' War (1263–66) the Jewish quarters of various towns were attacked: Cambridge, Canterbury, Lincoln, London, Worcester. Overall, the deterioration in the position of the Jews can be attributed to a number of factors: excessive taxation, causing poverty; various enactments by the Church against the Jews (as at the Council of Oxford in 1222 which, implementing the decisions of the Fourth Lateran Council of 1215, required Jews to dress distinctively); and continued accusations of ritual murder. In addition, by the late thirteenth century, the financial services of the Jews were no longer required, since other banking means were available. Indeed, in 1275 King Edward I issued the *statutum de Judaismo*, forbidding usury and trying to alter Jewish occupations. The attempt failed, however, largely because Jews did not have the right to join the merchant guilds. As a result, some continued to occupy themselves illegally, hangings ensued and, finally, Edward I issued a decree on 18 July 1290 ordering all Jews out of England by All Saints' Day (1 November) that year. Most of the Jews who left, probably no more than 3,000, went to France, Flanders or Germany. Only a handful of Jews – the occasional itinerant, or a physician whose services were specifically invited – are recorded as having entered the country from this time until the readmission of Jews into England in the seventeenth century.

Two further Jews in medieval England are worthy of note. Elijah Menahem ben Moses (*c*.1220–84), whose father was one Rabbi Moses of London and whose brother was an archpresbyter (1258–80), gained a reputation as a sound financier and wrote a commentary on parts of both the Mishnah and the Passover Haggadah. Jacob ben Judah, who also lived in the thirteenth century but whose precise dates are uncertain, was the author of a comprehensive guide to Jewish law entitled *Etz Hayyim* ('Tree of Life'); he drew on other medieval European Jewish writers, including the abovementioned Rabbi Moses and the famous medieval Jewish philosopher and commentator Maimonides. Finally, we must mention the *domus conversorum* ('converts' house'). This was a residence in London for converted Jews, set up in 1232 by Henry III in what is now Chancery Lane. It was able to accommodate some forty persons and, even after the expulsion of 1290, continued to be used by Jewish converts to Christianity who had recourse to it from elsewhere in Europe. Residents are recorded as late as 1609, and the office of keeper was eventually married to that of Master of the Rolls.

JEWS IN ENGLAND FROM CROMWELL TO THE FIRST WORLD WAR

Some Jewish refugees from Spain and Portugal (which expelled Jews in 1492 and 1496, respectively), as well as from the Spanish Inquisition, entered England in the sixteenth and early seventeenth centuries during the reigns of Henry VIII (1509–47), Edward VI (1547–53) and Elizabeth I (1558–1603). Some of these immigrants were marranos – Jews who had succumbed to pressures to embrace Christianity during the time of the Iberian expulsions. In spite of their conversion, however, life had become extremely difficult for many of them, who were suspected of remaining secret Jews and, as a result, suffered under the activities of the Inquisition in the sixteenth century. Although the number of marranos and other Jewish refugees coming into England was small, they were sufficient to form semi-covert congregations in London and Bristol; these managed to function intermittently but were suppressed under Mary, a pro-Spanish Catholic who succeeded to the throne in 1553. One noteworthy marrano from this period was Roderigo Lopez, physician to Elizabeth I, who was executed in 1594 for supposedly plotting against the life of the sovereign.

Jews began to collect in London more conspicuously and in greater numbers when Cromwell was in power (1649–58). This was due in large measure to an increased toleration towards them arising out of a growing Christian interest in the Old Testament and in what were thought to be the biblical grounds for readmitting the Jews into England. After the Reformation, Jewish and Christian interest in the Bible overlapped; indeed, those who produced the Old Testament for the Authorized King James Version of the Bible early in the seventeenth century had drawn on Jewish interpretative traditions. More particularly, many Puritans thought that the end of the world was near but that, before the Second Coming of Christ could take place, the Jews had to be scattered over the whole world, including England. Of a similar persuasion during the 1650s was a rabbi from Amsterdam called Manassah ben Israel, who believed that the Bible showed that Jews had to spread throughout the earth before the advent of the Messianic era would be possible. Appeal was made to Deuteronomy 28: 64 and Daniel 12: 7, the former referring to the 'end of the earth' (Hebrew *qetzeh ha'aretz*, also the medieval Hebrew term for England) which was thought to apply to 'Angle-terre' or England. With such ideas in mind, Manassah petitioned the authorities to readmit the Jews formally, visiting London to that end in 1655. A conference in Whitehall considered the matter and held there was no law keeping Jews from settling in England, since the 1290 decree applied only to the individuals expelled at the time; but otherwise no conclusion was reached. When London Jews again in 1656 applied for permission to run their own burial ground and for freedom of worship, their requests were granted by the Council of State, although the record of that decision has since mysteriously disappeared.

None the less, this semi-official permission allowing Jewish settlement in England remained in force after the Restoration of the monarchy in 1660. This rendered the Jewish situation in England during the mid-seventeenth century qualitatively different from that in other states across Europe: there were fewer legal restrictions and no ghettos. Indeed, in the face of some petty agitation against the Jews, the Crown gave an official guarantee of its protection of them in 1664 and of freedom of worship in 1673 and again in 1685. Further still, the Act for Suppressing Blasphemy of 1698 indirectly gave legal status to Jews. In view of this generally favourable climate, the number and wealth of Sephardi Jews (i.e. Jews originating from Spanish and Muslim lands) in England increased, especially under William and Mary (1689–1702) in view of contacts between the emergent community and the Jews of Amsterdam. A building leased in London's Creechurch Lane became England's first synagogue in 1656; in 1701 it was moved to Bevis Marks, where it is still functioning today. Ashkenazi Jews (i.e. Jews originally from central and eastern Europe) from Amsterdam and various German towns began to enter the country in the wake of Sephardi success. The first Ashkenazi synagogue was established in Duke Street in 1690 and, after internal disputes, others were formed in 1706 and 1761. These Ashkenazim tended to be of lower social and financial standing than their Sephardi co-religionists, many of them travelling salesmen – pedlars or itinerant traders.

Evidence suggests that from the 1720s Jews began to settle in English towns outside London, where they had previously been seen only as visitors or travellers; this was preceded by moves into the areas immediately around the capital earlier in the eighteenth century. Thus, over the next hundred years or so, Jews were to leave their mark in many places further afield, too numerous to list, from Newcastle and York in the north to Lincoln and Shrewsbury in the east and west and to Cornwall and Kent in the south. At first, most of the Jews concerned must have led fairly isolated lives, going to London for high holy days, since only from the 1740s can evidence be found for more organized Jewish life outside London. But by around 1800 there were organized Jewish communities in Bath, Birmingham, Brighton, Bristol, Cambridge, Canterbury, Coventry, Dover, Exeter, Falmouth, Gloucester, Ipswich, King's Lynn, Liverpool, Manchester, Norwich, Penzance, Plymouth, Portsmouth, Sheerness and Sunderland.

Most of the towns listed here, and others where communities were established by the time of Victoria's accession to the throne, were sea-ports or market towns, where Jewish traders and merchants from London settled with their families, joined by others from elsewhere in continental Europe. By the 1730s there were an estimated 6,000 Jews in England; by 1800 the total was probably around 30,000. Overall, therefore, the eighteenth century can be characterized as a time of quiet consolidation for the Jews of England. Nevertheless, in 1753 the proposed Jewish Naturalization Bill, intended to render the parents of British-born Jews equally as British, was rejected by Parliament because of the outcry it caused in some Christian quarters. One lasting effect of this was that representatives of both Sephardi and Ashkenazi communities came together in the form of a committee to keep a watchful eye on matters of interest to English Jews. In 1835 this body became the Board of Deputies of British Jews, recognized by the government as representative of the interests of the country's Jews at large. The Board has continued to function to the present day and consists now of some 600 members representing various religious denominations and other interest groups; it meets regularly throughout the year, although most of its work is done through committees.

As the establishment of the Board may suggest, and partly due to its efforts, the position of Jews in England, already comparatively better than that of most in Europe, improved in the nineteenth century as it did elsewhere. In view of Emperor Joseph II's edict in 1782 allowing Austrian Jews various domestic and economic freedoms, and with the French National Assembly's decision in 1791 to give equal citizenship to Jews in the wake of the French Revolution, some were keen for similar changes for English Jewry, especially after the emancipation in 1829 of British Catholics. This trend was encouraged by expressions of sympathy for the Jews in the work of Byron, as well as by translations of the writings of such as Moses Mendelssohn (1729–86) and Theodor Lessing (1872–1933), with their arguments for Jewish emancipation. Not surprisingly, the House of Commons passed the Jewish Emancipation Bill of 1833, although it was rejected for some time by the House of Lords. This and other measures relieved Jews of many of the restrictions that had been placed upon them. Acts of Parliament passed in 1854 and 1856, respectively, allowed Jewish students to enter the University of Oxford and the University of Cambridge as undergraduates, while from 1871 Jews could take higher degrees and fellowships.

An exception to these new freedoms was membership of Parliament itself, as illustrated in the case of Lionel de Rothschild. From 1847 he was repeatedly elected member of Parliament for the City of London but, unable to submit to the required Christian oaths, he could not take up his seat. Fortunately, in 1858 a compromise was reached in which each House adopted its own revised oath. Thus Nathaniel de Rothschild, Lionel de Rothschild's son, became the first Jew to receive a peerage. Sir David Solomons was appointed Lord Mayor of London in 1855, Sir George Jessel became Solicitor General in 1871, while Herbert Samuel was made the first Jewish cabinet minister in 1909. Such appointments demonstrated that nearly all restrictions on the involvement of Jews in public life had been removed.

The nineteenth century also saw many internal changes for England's Jewish community. By the early 1800s, Ashkenazim predominated over Sephardim and the rabbi of London's Great Synagogue in Duke Street became their spokesman. One of them, Nathan Marcus Adler, can be viewed as the first Chief Rabbi from 1844; he was succeeded by his son, Hermann, in 1891 and has since been followed by four more: Joseph Herman Hertz (in office 1913–46); Israel Brodie (1948–65); Immanuel Jakobovits (1966–91); and Jonathan Sacks (from 1991). In 1870 the Jewish United Synagogues Bill was passed by the House of Commons. There were two main reasons for this official sanction of the formation of the United Synagogue, as it was thereafter called. First, it was in the interests of the government, as well as of the Jewish community at large, to ensure that there was a suitable religious and social structure which would secure the peaceful and controlled integration of the considerable number of Jewish immigrants who had already begun to enter the country by 1870; this applied not least to arrangements for legal marriages. Second, there were Jewish and non-Jewish Liberal parliamentarians who saw in the Act, itself only one element of nineteenth-century legislation on behalf of the Jews, both an assertion of the priority of the House of Commons over the more traditional House of Lords and another sign of an increasing distinction between Church and State.

At the practical level, the aim of the United Synagogue was to consolidate the Ashkenazi communities of London centred on the Great Synagogue and the Chief Rabbi; it has remained the largest Orthodox body to the present day, with many affiliated congregations throughout the country. However, it should be remembered that, strictly speaking, the Chief Rabbi represents this organization only and not English or British Jews as a whole. Another and, to some extent, competing body called the Federation of Synagogues was formed in 1887 by Samuel Montagu. Because of the large numbers of Russian immigrants who began to arrive in London from 1881, it was intended to organize under a single umbrella the *stieblach* (European-style religious gatherings) of these newcomers, who were unable or unwilling to fit into the worship of the United Synagogue. Montagu intended that his organization should work to improve the health and safety of the buildings in which the immigrants worshipped and to discourage socialism among them, while simultaneously becoming integrated with existing structures. But, due to tensions with the United Synagogue, the Federation eventually broke away after his death in 1912 and, in effect, constituted a competing denomination.

Two other Orthodox institutions, both associated chiefly with the United Synagogue and still functioning in the 1990s, should be touched upon at this point: the *Jewish Chronicle* and Jews' College, London. The former, founded in 1841 and based in London, became and has remained British Jewry's main weekly newspaper (although mention should also be made of Glasgow's *Jewish Echo*, which began publication in 1928 and is still published). It has played an important role in debates within the community on various matters at different times – emancipation in the nineteenth century, for example, and Jewish responses to Zionism or antisemitism in the twentieth. Jews' College, established under Adler in 1855, had a narrower task. While the then Chief Rabbi (and his successors) was adamant that he alone was and should remain the sole rabbinic authority for Ashkenazim in Britain, it was clear that synagogues throughout the land urgently required competent teachers and pastors. To meet that need, Jews' College began to train such ministers, who were to be addressed as 'reverend', not 'rabbi', and wear dog-collars. Anyone desirous of a thorough rabbinic training, however, travelled to centres elsewhere in Europe to study (as did Adler's son Hermann), although it did not take long for Jews' College to produce some noteworthy preachers.

In contrast to these Orthodox developments, 1840 saw the establishment of the first Reform synagogue in London, despite considerable opposition. None the less, the fact that British Reform Judaism was not very radical led others, notably C. J. G. Montefiore (1858–1938) and Lily Montagu (1873–1963), to form the Jewish Religious Union, which in turn became the basis for the Liberal Jewish Synagogue, founded in 1911. Despite their success, both of these have remained minority movements in Britain in terms of numbers, and have been considerably less influential than parallel institutions in the rest of Europe and America.

Two further important changes took place during the second half of the nineteenth century. First, there was a general tendency for Jews to move into large towns and cities away from the smaller communities prominent earlier in the century, many of which declined or disappeared; one of the main reasons for this was increasing industrialization. Second, from 1881 large numbers of immigrants fleeing Russian persecution or seeking economic opportunity flooded into London. Even by 1881 there were 60,000 Jews in Britain; between then and 1905 some 100,000 of the one million Jews to leave Russia in those years came to Britain. Such large-scale immigration was to be the most important factor shaping the demographic future of Britain's Jewish communities. Indeed, combined with the nineteenth-century industrialization already mentioned, it led to a massive growth in London Jewry; several provincial communities also flourished in England and, to a lesser extent, Scotland and Wales. But in London, many of the Jews who had become thoroughly anglicized by this stage and who had moved to wealthy suburbs (like St John's Wood, Dalston or Islington) found it difficult to relate to the poor, Yiddish-speaking immigrants from eastern Europe who were pouring into Spitalfields and Whitechapel; some even questioned whether further immigration should be permitted. However, after reports of vicious pogroms in Russia during 1903 and 1904, such doubts diminished.

Unfortunately, for many of the immigrants, among whom there tended to be a rather narrow range of skills, the only hope of employment was to be found in sweatshops. Resultant over-crowding in the East End of London led to public unrest, including antisemitism on the part of the British Brothers' League. Founded in 1900 by W. Evans-Gordon, MP for Stepney, the League sought the restriction of alien immigration, thought by many to be responsible for the social ills of the East End, where large numbers of the incomers were settling. Moreover, a general anti-Jewish feeling, reflected in the country as a whole, blamed such troubles (manifest in unemployment, poor housing and disreputable working practices) on the flood of immigrant Jews. While the overall phenomenon of Jewish immigration must have contributed to the hardships being experienced by many, both Jews and non-Jews alike, the accusations were exaggerated, unfairly linked to the immigrants and levelled more or less *in toto* against the recently arrived Jews by the British Brothers' League and their supporters. Such widespread resentment, however ill-founded, struck fear of wider antisemitism into the hearts of many comfortable, anglicized Jews already established in Britain, who therefore responded to the League's campaign by acquiescing in or even supporting its arguments and the measure that was subsequently enacted by the government, the Aliens Immigration Act, passed in 1905 and intended to hold in check the numbers of Jews entering the country. It succeeded to an extent, but none the less immigrants from Russia continued to find their way to Britain. In fact, only nine years after the passing of the Act the total influx had reached around 150,000. Even in the provinces, the 20,000 Jews of 1881 had increased fivefold by 1911, and in London alone there was a total of some 180,000 Jews by 1914.

JEWS IN WALES

There is virtually no evidence for the presence of Jews in Wales during the middle ages. They are alluded to in the definitions of the privileges of some newly formed boroughs in north Wales during the thirteenth century, but only inasmuch as such boroughs had the right to exclude Jewish persons from their borders. However, there is mention of some individual Jews living in medieval Chepstow and Caerleon, both of which had come under English influence.

Otherwise, the earliest recorded Jewish settlement in Wales was in eighteenth-century Swansea. According to tradition, one David Michael came to the city as a refugee from Germany in 1741, along with a certain Nathaniel Philips. They were joined by two others and began to gather for prayers in a small building employed as a synagogue. In 1780 the modest community was granted a piece of land to be used as a cemetery, the oldest recorded burial being that of a Jew from Carmarthen twenty-five miles to the north-west. After some years in another building, a synagogue for around seventy persons was constructed in 1818 on a plot of land with a 99-year lease. By this time, David Michael's sons, Levi and Jacob, were among the leaders of the community. Levi's son, Francis, established the Swansea Savings Bank, while others were engaged in the jewellery and watchmaking trades, as were Jews in many other provincial towns in Britain. Since a record survives of its presentation of a silver goblet to Solomon Hirschell, rabbi of London's Great Synagogue 1802–42, and of its contribution to the fund for the first Chief Rabbi in 1844, the Swansea community must have been thriving in the 1830s and 1840s; by 1850 there were approximately 100–150 members. Numbers continued to grow until 1914, when it is estimated that the community was some 1,000 strong. Since then, however, the population has declined, with 418 recorded in 1969 and only a few families by the early 1990s.

Although there is evidence for a small Jewish presence at the end of the eighteenth century, tradition states that a certain Mark Marks founded the Cardiff community in 1840 and that by 1847 there was a synagogue in the city. In the late nineteenth and early twentieth centuries the population increased dramatically, particularly after 1881 when some of the refugees fleeing persecution in Russia made their way to Wales. At this time Cardiff took over from Swansea as the main centre of Jewish population in the country and has remained so ever since. It is estimated that by 1968 Cardiff was home to 3,500 Jews.

The second half of the nineteenth century also saw smaller communities forming elsewhere in the principality. Thus, from the 1840s Jews were to be found in Aberdare, Llanelli, Merthyr Tydfil, Newport, Porthcawl, Pontypridd, Tredegar and Tonypandy in the south, as well as Bangor and Llandudno in the north. The latter groups were made up from Jews moving westwards from the north-west of England with the industrialization of north Wales, while in the south Jewish traders were attracted to the growing number of Welsh mining towns. As with Cardiff, Swansea and elsewhere in Britain, the population was increased in the 1880s and 1890s with the arrival of refugees from Russia, some of whom settled in the environs of Ebbw Vale. However, the numbers of Jews living in all these towns outside the two main Welsh centres would rarely rise above 200.

In view of this fact, one unpleasant incident is of especial note. In August 1911 there were anti-Jewish riots in towns around Tredegar in the western valleys near Ebbw Vale. These took place against a general background of social and industrial unrest, manifest in strikes both on the railways and in the collieries, as well as in confrontations between rioters and the authorities. On 19 August 1911, Jewish shops in Tredegar were looted; similar episodes followed during the next seven days in surrounding towns and villages, including Bargoed, Cwm, Ebbw Vale and Rhumney. Many of the Jewish residents of these places fled to nearby larger settlements: Aberdare, Merthyr, Newport and Cardiff. Immediately afterwards, Jewish leaders played down the specifically Jewish aspect of these attacks, arguing that the economic distress of the rioters was their chief cause and pointing to the fact that non-Jewish property had also been damaged. However, it became clear that there was a premeditated element to the violence – it was reported that some Jews had been receiving threats for months and that others had been warned before the violence began. This shows that the attacks were directed against Jews as Jews, as is confirmed by a revealing, if minor, occurrence on 6 September at a meeting of the Monmouthshire Welsh Baptist Association near Bargoed: a motion supporting the local Jewish population in their recent distress was dropped, since some present took exception to the proposal, while others thought it would only encourage more Jews to settle in the area. At the same time, such hostility must be understood against a wider backdrop, in which over one-third of the population in the area were immigrants. Half of these were from outside Wales, and the sort of Russian Jew who settled in the western valleys after 1881 must have seemed particularly alien and, therefore, vulnerable to attack in a volatile situation such as that pertaining in the autumn of 1911. Even so, contemporary reports compared this show of anti-Jewish feeling with Russian and Polish antisemitism. Combined with the economic downturn that was soon to follow, the shape of the Jewish population in Wales would never be the same again.

Indeed, towards the end of the twentieth century, it is difficult to be hopeful of the survival of the Swansea community, and even the capital's long-term future is far from secure. In 1988 the Orthodox community in Cardiff sold one of its two buildings, leaving three functioning synagogues in the whole of Wales: one Orthodox in each of Swansea and Cardiff and one Reform synagogue in the capital city.

JEWS IN SCOTLAND

Several individuals in seventeenth-century Scotland are worth mentioning, as a number of converted Jews then entered the country. Two of these, J. C. Otto and A. Amidei, were the first and third professors to occupy the Chair of Hebrew in the University of Edinburgh in 1641–9 and 1679–81 respectively. Otto, the author of several grammatical works with a mystical bent, came from Germany, while Amidei heralded from Florence. Another Italian, P. Scialitti, is recorded as entering the city in 1665 as a tutor in oriental languages. It is clear that all three had been converted to Christianity before being allowed entry to Edinburgh. The sincerity of such conversions is, by nature, difficult if not impossible to ascertain, but it appears that Otto had left Germany in some haste after writing a work entitled *Gale Razayah* (Aramaic for 'the Revealer of Mysteries' as in Daniel 2: 29) which others had understood to make fun of Christians. Otto seems to have been successful in Edinburgh, and his work was appreciated.

The first practising Jews were permitted to settle in Scotland towards the end of the eighteenth century. An important point of departure was a dispute among members of the Edinburgh town council in 1691 concerning permission to work in the city requested by a Jewish trader called David Brown. Despite some opposition, one of the councillors, Hugh Blair, argued that Brown should be allowed to do so, especially since, reflecting the language of Paul's letter to the Romans, the Jews constituted 'the ancient people of God of the seed of Abraham of whom as concerning the flesh Christ came'. For this and other reasons, Blair maintained, 'they are allowed the libertie of trade in places of greatest trade wher the reformed religione is professed'. His argument won the day, and this marked the start of Jewish settlement proper in Edinburgh and in Scotland more widely. Jews, however, were not able to become burgesses of the city, as this required Christian allegiance; they were either given or had to purchase their freedom to trade. Nevertheless Blair exemplified a spirit of tolerance towards the Jews that was to become characteristic of Scotland in general. Indeed, in 1712 it was further pronounced that Jews should be able to give evidence in court. One individual from this period deserves mention: Dr J. H. Myers. Although born in New York in 1758, he studied medicine at Edinburgh in 1775–8, receiving the degree of MD in 1779 as the first Jewish graduate of a Scottish university. He proceeded to London in 1787 where, although of Ashkenazi origin, he was made doctor of the poor for the Sephardi Bevis Marks synagogue. Later he became president of the Great Synagogue's Talmud Torah (which in 1817 formed the Jews' Free School, still flourishing today as one of London's Jewish secondary schools).

It was not until the early 1800s, when numbers began to increase, that the Jewish presence in Edinburgh became more than that of a few individuals. The community's first minister was Moses Joel of London, and in 1816 the first synagogue was opened off Nicholson Street, with some twenty families attached to it. In 1825 it moved to Richmond Court, where it stayed for twenty-five years (although a splinter group formed in 1833 which lasted until 1840). Also, in 1816, the Braid Place cemetery was

consecrated and used for some sixty years thereafter until part of Echo
Bank cemetery was purchased by the community. Subsequently, other
synagogues were consecrated in 1898 and 1932. Records concerning the
election to the rabbinate of 1844 show a Jewish population in Edinburgh of
107. Only in the late nineteenth century did this expand further, with
immigrants from Russia entering the Dalsay area of the city. By 1957,
Edinburgh was home to some 1,500 Jews. However, by the late 1980s this
had dropped to around 1,000.

The other main centre of Scottish Jewry is Glasgow. As in the capital, an
organized community here goes back to the early 1800s, although before
this we know of no individual Jews living in the city as Jews. The first
settler was Isaac Cohen, a hatter from Manchester, who moved to Glasgow
in 1812. He was given the status of burgess of the city; presumably, the
Christian oath required for this was viewed as a matter of form rather than
confession. This did not, however, make him a freeman of the city. In 1823
Glasgow Jews obtained their first synagogue in a building on the High
Street near Trongate. After several moves, the community consecrated a
purpose-built synagogue on the corner of George Street and John Street.
Another move, this time to Garnethill, took place in 1879 – not before a
visit from the then Chief Rabbi, Nathan Marcus Adler, who came to
oversee a dispute which had arisen the previous year. In view of the poor
Russian immigrants coming into Glasgow from 1881, a branch of the
Garnethill synagogue was formed in the Gorbals, where most of the
newcomers settled; it opened in 1887. It became autonomous in 1898 but
joined with the Garnethill congregation to form the United Synagogue of
Glasgow. In 1899 a new synagogue was built in Portland Street, while
before this, in 1881, a separate congregation established its own synagogue
in Commerce Street. Between 1832 and 1851, part of the Glasgow
Necropolis was used by Jews as a cemetery, but a new plot was obtained in
the Janefield cemetery from 1853.

Three nineteenth-century Jews from Glasgow are worthy of mention:
Jonas Michael, David David and Asher Asher. The first headed a firm of
auctioneers and dealers in the wood and furniture trade, while Davis's
family were jewellers (more generally, evidence shows that a good number
of other Glaswegian Jews were involved in the fur trade). David Davis, also
a maker of mathematical and optical instruments, was the first leader of the
Glasgow community, which he served for some twenty years, although his
descendants assimilated to the dominant culture. Asher (1837–89) was the
first recorded Jewish graduate of Glasgow University; he went to practise
medicine in London, where he was an almoner to the Rothschild family
and was involved in the parliamentary Bill that established the United
Synagogue as the Jewish equivalent of the Church of England.

In 1831 a certain J. Cleland carried out a census of Glasgow, in the course of which he learnt that there were forty-seven Jews in all in the city. Of these, twenty-eight were male and nineteen female; twenty-eight were over twenty years old, leaving nineteen under the age of nineteen years. Over half of the Jewish community had originated from continental Europe, fifteen had come from England, while a mere six had been born in Glasgow. According to the record of the election of the Chief Rabbi in 1844, the total figure had increased to 128 (compared to Edinburgh's 107); by 1850, there were 200. However, with large numbers of immigrants entering Scotland after 1881, as elsewhere in Britain, some 5,000 Jews were resident in Glasgow by 1900, with 6,500 in 1902. By 1957, Glasgow was home to 50,000 Jews, but since then the numbers have declined, with just over 13,000 Jews present in the city by the early 1970s and a mere 9,000 by the late 1980s.

It is not possible to leave consideration of Glasgow without mentioning one other of its Jewish offspring: Sir Isaac Wolfson (1897–1991). Growing up in poor circumstances, he became a successful businessman and philanthropist as an adult. Formerly chairman of Great Universal Stores Ltd, in 1955 he set up the Wolfson Foundation, which has since donated millions of pounds to various charitable and educational causes, including a gift of £2 million towards the establishment of Wolfson College, Oxford in 1966. He has also contributed considerable amounts to building and educational projects in Israel, such as the construction of the Supreme Rabbinical Centre in Jerusalem. In 1962 he became president of the United Synagogue, encouraging further its shift to the religious right begun after the Second World War.

Outside the two main urban centres, the only other place of significant Jewish settlement in Scotland has been Dundee, although historically there have also been small communities in Ayr, Aberdeen and Inverness. Dundee obtained its first synagogue in 1874 and most of the community's members thereafter hailed from Russia or Poland. There is no evidence for organized or widely supported anti-Jewish sentiment in Scotland from the time of the earliest settlement till the present day. This situation is portrayed vividly in the recent autobiography, *Curriculum Vitae* (1992), of the contemporary writer and Catholic convert Muriel Spark (perhaps best known for *The Prime of Miss Jean Brodie*, published in 1961), who was born in Edinburgh and whose father was Jewish. Of course, there must have been individuals hostile to Jews and Judaism throughout the history of the Jewish community in Scotland, as would be the case anywhere else. But Scotland, even more than England and Wales where violent expressions of antisemitism have been rare, has the best record of tolerance in this regard in Britain.

THE JEWS OF MODERN BRITAIN

More than 41,000 British Jews fought in the First World War, suffering thousands of casualties and earning over 1,500 decorations. In view of this, as well as linguistic and cultural anglicization, ordinary Jews in Britain began to feel less conspicuous and more settled after the war than before. During the 1920s significant numbers of Jews were in a position to move out of poor areas – like the Gorbals of Glasgow and London's East End – to the prosperous suburbs; and there was a concomitant shift away from skilled manual labour to the professions. Thus Golders Green in north London and Glasgow's South Side became and remain important centres of middle-class Jewish life in Britain.

As the 1930s unfolded, two closely related new factors arose: an influx of refugees from European countries plagued by fascism on the one hand, and manifestations of a similar right-wing extremism within Britain itself, in the form of the British Union of Fascists founded by Sir Oswald Mosley (in 1932), on the other. The Blackshirts, as Mosley's supporters were known, organized processions through the East End of London and encouraged violence against Jews and their property; they used popular prejudice about 'unfair' Jewish business practices to fuel antisemitic hatred at a time of economic hardship and depression. Although the tense situation was, to a large extent, defused by the Public Order Act of 1936, which outlawed the wearing of political uniforms, this unsavoury episode left a deep scar upon the hearts and minds of London's Jewish population. Of course, Jews in Germany and elsewhere in Europe found themselves in a much worse predicament in the 1930s, and consequently, by the outbreak of the Second World War in 1939, some 55,000 had sought refuge in Britain. Given the enormity of what was happening to Jews on the continent, this was a relatively small number. A reluctance to admit more, on the part of both British Jewry and the British government, can be explained thus: the former were fearful of provoking further antisemitism through another flood of immigrants, while the latter resented the exacerbation of problems in the Middle East by the Jews of Palestine in their struggle for independence from British rule during the 1930s and 1940s.

Nevertheless, given that only 10,000–15,000 of those Jews who fled from Nazism to Britain left after the war, the impact of those who remained was almost as great on the wider Jewish community as the influx of Russian immigrants had been in the late nineteenth century. In particular, Liberal rabbis trained in Germany strengthened British Reform Judaism, with the foundation in 1956 of Leo Baeck College as a centre for the training of Reform rabbis. Simultaneously, Orthodox refugees from Hungary and

Germany were to have a competing impact, encouraging a new religious conservatism in the United Synagogue.

Another important development took place in the 1940s and 1950s: British Jewry and its leadership became in the main pro-Zionist. In the late nineteenth and early twentieth centuries the heralds of this movement for Jewish nationalism, most notably Theodor Herzl (1869–1904), received a mixed response from world Jewry, depending on religious and political affiliations. This applied to Jews in Britain, even after the government's so-called Balfour Declaration of 1917:

> His Majesty's Government view with favour the establishment of a national home for the Jewish people, and will use their best endeavours to facilitate the achievement of this object, it being clearly understood that nothing shall be done which may prejudice the civil and religious rights of non-Jewish communities in Palestine, or the rights and political status enjoyed by Jews in any other country.

However, the period between the two world wars saw the standing of the old leading aristocratic families within the Jewish community, like the Rothschilds and Montagus, enter into a terminal decline. This was because of changes taking place at the time throughout British society in the form of a steady move away from the dominance of paternalistic hierarchies; it was also due to the gradual assimilation to the dominant culture of such Jewish families. The latter had in the main been anti- or non-Zionist but, with the effectual demise of their influence in the 1940s, the majority of Britain's Jews came out on the side of Zionism. In 1943 this included the Board of Deputies, with its mixed membership of Orthodox and Progressives; it began to reflect popular anger at the reluctance of the representatives of British Jewry to push the government into action, even after the full horror of what was happening in Nazi Germany had been revealed earlier that year. Support for Zionism continued even after antisemitic riots in London, Liverpool, Glasgow and Manchester in 1947, sparked by the hanging of two British sergeants in Palestine by Zionist militia (this incident being part of a continuing battle between Zionists and the British Mandatory authorities, in which three Zionist activists had just been executed). With the formation of the State of Israel in 1948, however, the situation improved, and the Zionist cause became a focus of unity for Jews in Britain and throughout the world in succeeding decades.

The 1950s and 1960s saw a further shift, this time in the political leanings of many, if not the majority, of Britain's Jews. Given their socio-economic position and the interest shown by socialists in the Jewish working classes during the 1930s, most Jews after the Second World War were probably Labour voters. But this characteristic feature of the Jewish community gradually altered in the post-war years. In the first place, increasing numbers of Jews found themselves entering into the ranks of the middle classes, a social move accompanied frequently by a general switch in political allegiance. Secondly, reflections of popular anti-Jewish sentiment among Conservative politicians diminished and eventually disappeared in the decades after the war. Most importantly, however, early Labour support for the Zionist cause turned into antagonism during the same period. This change was especially marked after the Six Day War of 1967, when socialist opposition to Israel's military action appeared in certain quarters alongside antisemitic caricatures of Jewish involvement in capitalism and imperialism. Labour maintained an anti-Zionist stance right into the 1980s when, in contrast, there were several Jewish ministers in the Conservative cabinet of Margaret Thatcher, who seems to have deliberately set out to attract the Jewish vote during her time as Prime Minister. In any case, as in the late 1980s, so now there are more Jewish Tory MPs than Labour MPs, a situation which is more or less the opposite of what would have been found forty years ago.

After the Second World War, and more particularly after the Six Day War, there were very few Jews in Britain (or anywhere else, for that matter) who would not count themselves as Zionists – even if they might be critical of the Israeli government of the day or of Israeli government policy at any given time. Such a new focus of unity for Britain's Jews, although creating a different set of problems, has been beneficial in the past three or four decades, given the evidence since the late 1950s of increasing hostility between the various religious denominations within British Jewry. Not least among the causes of this friction was the abovementioned injection of new life into the Reform movement, as well as the shift to the right within Orthodoxy. A useful illustration of the resultant religious sensitivities within the community can be seen in a dispute surrounding Rabbi Louis Jacobs. In 1959 Jacobs, a minister of the New West London Synagogue, was appointed tutor at Jews' College, London – now more conservative than in its earlier days and engaged in the training of fully fledged rabbis. But the then Chief Rabbi, Israel Brodie, subsequently blocked both Jacobs' appointment as principal of the College and any return to his former congregation, because Jacobs, while Orthodox in practice, held modernist views, arguing that moderns could not accept that God had dictated the Pentateuch *in toto* to Moses on Mount Sinai in one act of revelation, as traditionally held. Supported by his former congregants, Jacobs had no choice but to set up the New London Synagogue in St John's Wood which, outside the organizational umbrella of the United Synagogue, has flourished for the past thirty years or so. Similar to American Conservative Judaism in its approach, if not in its size, the New London

Synagogue, together with a few sister congregations in the same area of London, encourages orthopraxy on the one hand and intellectual honesty in relation to matters of biblical criticism and Jewish history on the other. More broadly, in the three decades since this episode, the rift between Orthodoxy and the Progressive wing of Judaism in Britain has unfortunately widened. It will be useful, therefore, to sketch an outline of each of these two main denominational groupings within British Jewry.

The United Synagogue in England and Wales, incorporating virtually all Orthodox congregations and headed by the Chief Rabbi, constitutes the largest Jewish denomination in Britain; although Scottish Orthodoxy is theoretically independent, it too is supported by and supportive of the United Synagogue. Orthodox teaching holds that the Torah was revealed by God to Moses in both its written and its oral form, that is, as now found in both the Pentateuch and the Talmud. Its divine legislation has binding authority on the individual Jew and on the community at large as an inexhaustible and self-consistent resource. Although there may be room for manoeuvre in how precisely it is to be related to everyday life, the basic authority of the tradition cannot be questioned. To that end, the Bet Din or rabbinical court (especially that of the Chief Rabbi, but others elsewhere also) exists to oversee correct interpretation of the Law in, for example, cases of divorce. At the same time, what may be characterized as the 'progressive conservatism' of the United Synagogue has traditionally been able to turn a blind eye to the fact that, even according to its own criteria, the observance of many ordinary Orthodox Jews leaves much to be desired. The increasing religious conservatism among the leadership of the United Synagogue since the Second World War has meant, however, that rabbis of a younger generation have been less prepared to accept this state of affairs. This is often due to the influence during training of hasidism or ultra-Orthodoxy, which has inculcated a sense of the indissolubility of religious observance and Jewish identity which was not so rigidly maintained even a generation or two ago.

A rather different view has been taken by Progressive Judaism, which may be used as an umbrella term for what in Britain are actually two denominations: Reform Judaism (named the Reform Synagogues of Great Britain in 1958) and Liberal Judaism (institutionalized as the Union of Liberal and Progressive Synagogues in 1944). These movements have made a conscious effort to absorb the results of academic study of the Bible and Jewish history, as well as the need to reconcile Judaism with life in the modern world. As a result, belief that God directly revealed the whole compass of Jewish law to Moses on Sinai is rejected, as also the binding authority of every element in the legal system. Instead, Progressive Judaism has tended to stress the prophetic and ethical side of the tradition.

The first reformers in nineteenth-century Germany, whose movement was dubbed Liberal Judaism, implemented such changes to stem the tide of Jewish assimilation to the dominant Christian culture in the wake of the Enlightenment and Jewish emancipation; this was also the aim of the Reform Judaism that subsequently flourished in America. However, early Reform in Britain during the 1840s was rather conservative, and a separate and more radical attempt at reform emerged, culminating in 1911 in what was called Liberal Judaism under C. J. G. Montefiore and Lily Montagu, as previously mentioned. Still, the need to modernize Judaism in terms of practice and belief has remained central to both institutions, although with differing emphases on the exact nature and extent of such modification. In practical terms, the Reform and Liberal movements in Britain, both with headquarters in London, are very much intertwined nowadays; they share facilities for the training of rabbis who tend to fill vacancies wherever they occur, whether in Reform or Liberal congregations. As will be clear, when compared to Orthodoxy, Progressive Judaism remains a minority movement in Britain, representing some sixty-five active synagogues in the country in the early 1990s, including only one in each of Wales (Cardiff) and Scotland (Glasgow), or roughly 22 per cent of Britain's religious Jews. In contrast, mainstream Orthodoxy accounts for around 68 per cent, while the ultra-Orthodox represent approximately 6 per cent; Sephardi Jews currently make up some 3 per cent of the total.

Unlike the main Christian institutional divisions, denominational groupings within Judaism are all modern (i.e. post-Enlightenment) in origin. Therefore, notwithstanding the acceptable fluctuations within each camp, Orthodoxy on the one side and Progressive Judaism on the other can be characterized in terms of an overall fissure between liberals and traditionalists. Members of the New London Synagogue fall somewhere in between these two poles, while those who take the Orthodox position to its extreme make up hasidic or ultra-Orthodox groups. The latter, although numerically small and concentrated in parts of north-west London, have had considerable influence among the leadership of the United Synagogue in recent decades. More generally, it is important to remember that the split between the conservative and the liberal within Judaism is at base concerned with orthopraxy – the status and observance of Jewish law – rather than assent or otherwise to a set of traditionally accepted credal propositions. In other words, Orthodox Jews, at least in theory, will eat only kosher food and refrain from driving to synagogue on the Sabbath. Progressive Jews, in contrast, argue that such legalities are a matter for individual choice – only the person who finds them helpful to his or her spiritual growth should be concerned with them.

None the less, within this basic divergence of opinion over the continued validity of those matters of law which have historically marked Jews out as distinctive, a number of practical issues similar to those facing contemporary Christians come to the fore: the role of women, the goodness or otherwise of homosexual relationships, and the definition of Jewish status. The first of these only came to be discussed seriously in the 1960s and 1970s. The Orthodox argued and continue to maintain that women have their God-given role in the home and that they should be separated during services in the synagogue. They are obliged to keep all negative commandments (e.g. against theft) but, unlike men, are exempt from positive commands pertaining to set times (e.g. spending time in booths during the feast of Tabernacles). Clearly, the ordination of women makes little sense within such a Torah-centred framework, but this is thought to reflect difference, not inferiority. In contrast, Progressive Judaism has acknowledged that the tradition has tended to discriminate against women, not least of all by excluding them from public ritual. This has led to the introduction of a *bat mitzvah* ceremony for girls, parallel to that of the male *bar mitzvah*; even the Orthodox have now started to make moves in this direction. More strikingly, Progressives now ordain female rabbis which makes more sense for them, given their attitude to Jewish law. A similar division along denominational lines can be seen concerning the status of gay and lesbian relationships: Liberal and Reform Jews in Britain have just begun to recognize the place of such people within the divine order, while, given the importance of the traditional family unit within historic Judaism, it is difficult to see how such recognition could ever be forthcoming from the Orthodox.

A third and more pervasive issue divides religious Jews in contemporary Britain: namely, the definition of Jewish status. Traditionally, Jewishness is passed on solely through the mother; those without Jewish mothers who are attracted to Judaism are obliged to convert. The Orthodox and, thus far, the Reform movement continue to hold this view of the matter. Liberal Jews, on the other hand, maintain that anyone with a Jewish parent (and a Jewish upbringing or reasonable amount of knowledge about Judaism) can be considered Jewish; Liberal Judaism is, therefore, in a better position to cope with mixed marriages and the offspring of such unions, although Reform Jews are also keen not to lose contact with such families. This contrasts again, however, with the prevailing attitude in the United Synagogue: Orthodox Jews are expected to marry other (preferably Orthodox) Jews and those who do not can find themselves, to one degree or another, rebuked or rejected.

Despite the divergence between Orthodox and Progressive Judaism on this issue, the overall problem is symptomatic of the situation of the Jewish community in contemporary Britain. In other words, large numbers of

Jews are untouched by either major denominational grouping, except perhaps for attendance at high holy day services in the autumn when some will make the annual trip to their local synagogue. The antagonism between the Orthodox and the Progressive wings of British Judaism, evident chiefly in the movements' leadership rather than the laity, is the product of a competing attempt by each side to gain the attention of the average Jew, who is becoming increasingly secular. The latter trend is due in part to the Zionist factor, especially since the Six Day War of 1967, which has dislodged religious commitment as a focus of the unity and expression of Jewish identity for many. Indeed, since the end of the Second World War not a few Jews have left Britain for Israel or have joined strong Jewish communities abroad. Other people of Jewish origin, while certainly not adopting any specifically non-Jewish identity, are not particularly interested either in their Jewish roots or in a contemporary Jewish identity; as with other segments of British society, they are shaped by the dominant secular individualism of western Europe.

This and the assimilation that goes with it, as much as a general decrease in the Jewish birth-rate since the 1950s, explains the reduction in Britain's Jewish population from around 450,000 in 1955 to perhaps something under 330,000 by the early 1990s. Despite the efforts of a number of Jewish schools in some towns in recent decades and their limited success in inculcating a stronger sense of their Jewishness among the children they teach, it is difficult to see how this basic trend can be reversed. In any case, given the decline in provincial communities in the post-war decades, many individual Jews in affected towns are not in a position – even if they so wished – to participate in any specifically Jewish institution or activity without travelling a considerable distance.

Nevertheless, there have been some positive signs of late that the situation is at least stabilizing, in terms of the overall Jewish birth-rate in the country at large and in the number of adults remaining active within the community as a whole. Indeed, some communities, such as that in the Brighton area and others in north-west London, are actually growing. If so, this has a number of implications for the position of Jews in Britain as we approach the year 2000. It may be projected that the Jewish population will level at approximately 300,000, although provincial communities will continue to decline. This will leave London, Manchester, Leeds, Glasgow, and Brighton and Hove – and probably a few other towns like Liverpool, Birmingham and Cardiff – as the main centres of Jewish life in the country. The resultant communities, with their usual mixture of religious and non-religious concerns, may be leaner than they have been for many decades but, with a renewed sense of commitment and purpose, will be more vibrant and better able to look forward to the twenty-first century.

23

Religious Life between the Wars, 1920–1940

Stuart Mews

'THE HORROR WAS over, a brighter dawn was breaking like the sun on the lilies in the Easter Garden. Surely a new world lay before us and a new pattern of brotherhood in freedom sealed by all that agony and sacrifice. Any further war seemed unthinkable. An age – almost a Messianic age – of creative reconstruction beckoned us.' Almost half a century later Bishop F. R. Barry, having been a chaplain on the Western Front, could still recapture the joyous exhilaration of the silencing of the guns, and the ending in 1918 of what was to be known, all too briefly, as the Great War.

To a young Cambridge undergraduate, H. K. Luce, who went up in 1918, 'Christianity there was vigorous, and very much on the offensive.' It was, he felt, 'a going concern – it had nothing to fear from new knowledge, or from the loosening of old-established traditions and standards which the war had caused. The churches were advancing and the future was bright.' That was certainly how it looked to young optimists. Among them were many army chaplains who returned from the war with a burning desire and determination to reform the Church and rethink its teaching.

Their experience had been horrific. The war had come as a tremendous shock to the churches, and especially to the clergy. Religious leaders had thrown themselves into support of the British cause with few if any reservations. The nation under arms had presented a quite extraordinary challenge which chaplains had tried to meet, but it had to be ruefully admitted that their ministry had been appreciated only by a minority; services had not been as popular as concerts. The war not only revealed the extent to which the churches had been marginalized, but accelerated those long-term social trends which undermined religious institutions. The *Army and Religion* report, based on questionnaires drafted by D. S. Cairns and the Bishop of Winchester, E. S. Talbot and answered by soldiers of all denominations, attempted in 1919 to alert church leaders to the seriousness

of the situation, and to the existence of a popular religiosity which was
failing to find expression in organized Christianity. But there was little
agreement about the best way forward. For some, the great lesson of the
war was that Roman Catholic priests seemed to have a greater hold over
their men than Anglicans and Nonconformists. Therefore the future lay
with sacramental religion and Catholic teaching. Others were impressed by
the impatience evoked by denominational exclusivity and wished to
develop a common Christianity in a reunited Church.

In the aftermath of the war all the denominations attempted to
reconstruct their polity and broaden their appeal. A crisis can provoke
opposite reactions: retreat into more rigid and authoritarian positions, or
attempt at radical reconstruction of the faith. Traditional Catholicism,
whether Anglican or Roman, had an obvious appeal in a world which had
thrown off the shackles of restraint. Anglo-Catholicism reached its zenith
in the inter-war years. The Catholic Congresses held in 1920, 1923, 1927,
1930 and 1933 were exuberant, triumphalist spectacles. Attendances
snowballed to 70,000 in 1933. Bathed in the limelight of the 1923 congress
was Bishop Frank Weston, heroic African missionary and determined
defender of the Catholic faith. His rousing call for deeper devotion to
Christ, in the Sacrament and in the slum, became part of the folk memory
of Anglo-Catholicism. 'The New Reformation' was a phrase on many lips,
but had many meanings. Experience in the trenches had given many
chaplains their first real insight into the thinking of men normally beyond
the reach of the churches. To F. R. Barry had come an appreciation of the
basic goodness and courage of ordinary people. God needed to be
presented, he thought, 'as the source and architect of the great soldier
virtues'. He expressed his eagerness for a form of Christological radicalism.
'I am quite prepared to see such large developments in the coming form of
Christianity that the religion of our sons and daughters would seem to be
almost another faith if it were witnessed by our grandfathers.' Such brave
words could have been sure of rapturous applause in the optimistic glow
after the victory. This was the climate in which liberalism thrives, as it was
to do in both Anglicanism and the Free Churches.

At a popular level, T. R. Glover, Baptist layman and Cambridge don,
sought to identify Jesus with humanity in *The Jesus of History*, published in
1917, with a forward by the Archbishop of Canterbury. Within ten years, it
had gone through nineteen impressions. Hastings Rashdall, Dean of
Carlisle, explained his own controversial contribution to the 1921 Girton
Conference of the Modern Churchmen's Union as a response to difficulties
reported by army chaplains in presenting the manhood of Jesus in a
credible way. Some Congregationalists, like Frank Lenwood and the south
London group dubbed 'The Blackheathans', seemed close to Unitaria-

nism. In the Church of England, men like V. F. Storr and Guy Rogers championed a liberal Evangelicalism which had cut loose from the biblical literalism and credal crudities of their Victorian forebears. There even emerged a new breed of liberal Catholics such as Eric Milner-White, E. G. Selwyn and Will Spens, the last-named of whom in 1920 launched the journal *Theology*.

An American minister was ridiculed by Hensley Henson, Bishop of Durham, for proposing that the Church of the future should include spiritualism, socialism and faith-healing. In Britain all three of these fads had their champions, but they were rarely advocated in the mainstream churches as part of the same package. In working-class popular religion, the links were more obvious and acceptable. The desire to seek the spirit of a departed loved one was hardly surprising in view of the enormous premature loss of life. What perhaps was surprising was the support given to spiritualism by such eminent people as Sir Oliver Lodge and Sir Arthur Conan Doyle, and the fact that such a prominent High Church leader as Edward Talbot, Bishop of Winchester, could write a letter to Lodge on the matter covering six printed pages. But Talbot had lost a soldier-son and his wife had been to a seance. Acording to the Wesleyan travelling apologist, Frank Ballard, 1920 was the year in which he received most invitations to speak on the spiritualist threat.

At first the prospects for change in the Church of England seemed bright. For a short period, the initiative seemed to rest with a new breed of younger people. Dick Sheppard, William Temple and Maude Royden kicked off with Life and Liberty, a campaign to secure self-government for the Church of England through a national assembly which would include both laymen and women. Strenuous campaigning by Temple and his team forced the pace to secure the passing by Parliament of the Enabling Act in 1919. Some indication of the dead weight of the fossilized ecclesiastical machine can be glimpsed from the immense excitement and enthusiasm evoked by this achievement. William Temple's wife, Frances, recalled how a normally quiet and serious churchwarden ran from the Commons, and, bursting into the house, managed to gabble, 'It's passed – it's passed!' Nothing seemed to be able to stop the tide. Even Charles Gore, Bishop of Oxford, whose threats of resignation had previously been sufficient to block any changes which he disliked, had to accept the inevitable: in March 1919, the most distinguished High Church bishop in the Church felt compelled to retire on the question of the franchise condition of the national assembly. Gore need not have bothered. The dire consequences he foresaw did not happen. Things hardly changed. Maude Royden saw more clearly when she wrote to Dick Sheppard, 'When Life and Liberty chose wise, able, prudent Temple instead of you, it lost its soul.' She knew that

Sheppard had not intended to start a pressure group which would stop only at administrative reform but saw it as part of a great movement for the quickening of religion in the Church.

Maude Royden's patience with the Church of England was by now wearing thin. An ardent advocate of, among many things, women's suffrage in pre-war days, pacifism during the war and the ministry of women afterwards, she was a persuasive and scintillating champion of progressive causes. Quick to reach conclusions and make up her mind, she did not suffer fools gladly, and was temperamentally unwilling to wait for slower and more cautious spirits to catch up. 'You cannot write anything that is worthwhile if it is not also dangerous,' she once warned. She did nothing to dispel the image of a fast woman by listing her recreations in *Who's Who* in 1931 as 'bathing and motoring'. At the Guildhall in the inter-war years she created a parallel Church of like-minded people who gathered to hear her candid comments on religious aspects of contemporary concerns. Harold Begbie described her in 1922 as 'at once a true woman and a great man'.

The Lambeth Conference of Anglican bishops met in 1920, in the full flood of post-war idealism, to consider 'The Faith and Witness of the Church to this Generation'. Its 'Appeal to all Christian people' seemed to suggest a new willingness to explore reunion. When the Free Churches responded in a constructive spirit, it looked as if a great breakthrough in inter-church relations was possible. The wartime thaw seemed about to pass into a warm summer of mutual repentance and reconciliation. Harmony was in the air. In addition to their dialogue with the Anglicans, the Free Churches were pressing ahead with their own scheme of mutual co-operation, the Federal Council of the Evangelical Free Churches having come into existence in 1919. Though the Wesleyan Methodists held back from this movement, they were themselves deeply involved in talks with the other branches of Methodism, the Primitive and United Methodist churches, which were to culminate in union in 1932.

The Lambeth Appeal of 1920 was significantly and deliberately addressed to all Christian *people*, not to sister churches or denominations. It manifestly did not envisage any response from the Pope! Indeed, it can be seen more as an acceptance of international ecclesiastical leadership by the Archbishop of Canterbury, now the undisputed religious leader of a victorious world power. When the World Alliance for the Promotion of International Friendship through the Churches met after the armistice, only one name was considered for the presidency. But Archbishop Randall Davidson was too cautious to exploit to the full the new potential of his office. He quailed before the Anglo-Catholic assault of the 1920s. It would have been better if he had resigned in 1924, when he had already been archbishop for twenty-one years and was seventy-six years old. He might even have persuaded Ramsay MacDonald to appoint William Temple as his successor and saved the Church from the burnt-out Cosmo Gordon Lang, chosen without a moment's hesitation by the Conservative premier Stanley Baldwin in 1928. Within three weeks of his enthronement, Lang had a succession of illnesses from which he was rescued only by two Mediterranean cruises on the yacht of the American billionaire, John Pierrepoint Morgan.

Partly to keep alive the Anglo-Catholic dream of reconciliation with Rome, the Anglican lay leader, Lord Halifax, W. H. Frere of the Community of the Resurrection and Armitage Robinson, Dean of Wells, began an unofficial exchange of views with Roman Catholics, led by the Belgian Cardinal Mercier, in Malines. Between 1921 and 1926 five meetings took place. The atmosphere changed, however, with Mercier's death, and the growing suspicions of those English Catholics and Protestants who relied on hearsay and imagination.

The Roman Catholic Church had had a good war and, despite such potential disasters as the Protestant suspicion that the Vatican was pro-German, the consummate political skill of Cardinal Bourne at Westminster and the robust English patriotism of Cardinal Gasquet in Rome ensured that there were no reasonable grounds for any accusations of lack of patriotism. But then there was Ireland. The execution of those who had taken part in the Easter Rising in 1916 was a blunder of incredible magnitude and detonated a time-bomb which was to transfer the killing fields to the Emerald Isle. The British government had claimed to have been fighting the Great War on behalf of small nations: gallant little Belgium, plucky Serbia, and the rest. At the peace conference, President Wilson had promoted the principle that nationality should be related to ethnicity. So what about Ireland, squawked a bruised and embittered nation of Catholic Irishmen? To maintain its authority the Tory-dominated coalition government relied on an army brutalized by wartime active service, and in so doing destroyed any lingering loyalty to the British State. Irish nationalists moved from obstinacy and insolence to guerilla warfare. When arrested they perplexed their persecutors by resorting to the strategem of the hunger strike, an action which seemed to stem from Gaelic Catholic ascetic spirituality. When the Lord Mayor of Cork, Terence MacSwiney, vowed to hunger-strike till death in 1920 he became not only a nationalist martyr but also a serious obstacle to Cardinal Bourne's attempts to overtake the Church of England as the national Church. 'Murders, suicide and endless crimes seem mixed up with masses, rosaries, Holy Communion and the sympathy and help of the clergy,' complained a lady from London to Cardinal Bourne. With MacSwiney to the end was his local priest from Cork; after a hunger strike of seventy-four days, the emaciated corpse was taken to Southwark Cathedral for a Requiem Mass held in the presence of two bishops and Archbishop Mannix of Melbourne. Overnight the coffin was opened and an Irish Republican uniform placed on the body. Opinion in England was divided between those disturbed by the callous refusal of the government to bend, and those irritated by the unwillingness of the Roman Catholic Church to regard MacSwiney's refusal of nourishment as suicidal, and therefore as sinful. Father Charles Plater, who devoted his life to the promotion of a non-socialist welfare programme through the Catholic Social Guild, observed that 'our working people being mainly Irish are incensed against the Government because of its treatment of Ireland'. He worried that their hostility might extend to making common cause with communists. 'If it were not for the aggravation of the Irish question the masses of Catholic workers would be a solid conservative force.' Perhaps this was wishful thinking, but the removal of Ireland from the English political agenda after 1921 did create a new fluidity which had not been there before.

At home, the post-war economic boom reached its peak in 1920. In the decade ending in 1924, the average earnings of full-time workers rose by 94 per cent. Abroad, peace for all time seemed to be guaranteed by the League of Nations, which was backed by an immense amount of goodwill from the churches, especially the Free Churches. In 1922 alone, over 500 Free Church Councils organized demonstrations in support of the League. Never had most people been more comfortable, and never had there been a greater yearning for new sources of inspiration and stimulation. A constant moan of many preachers was that the average middle-class family now took a Sunday newspaper, had a gramophone, wireless, telephone and motor car, and even went to the theatre, cinema and possibly dance-hall. With fewer drunks in the streets as a consequence of wartime licensing restrictions, ecclesiastical moralists switched their attention to gambling. The report of the House of Commons Select Committee on a Betting Duty in 1923 drew attention to this 'new' problem. In 1924 the alarm bells were sounded by Peter Green, a High Church vicar in a Salford slum, and the Irish archdeacon R. H. Charles. The Nonconformist conscience was focused by Wesleyan ministers such as E. Benson Perkins, Cecil Rose and John Bretherton. Green, Rose and Bretherton drew on pastoral perceptions in Lancashire, while Benson Perkins conducted his own surveys in Sheffield and Birmingham which encouraged him to persevere in his lifelong campaign to ban betting. When a committee of the churches on gambling was set up in 1933 Perkins was made chairman, which gave him some standing in his stalwart opposition to every form of gambling: football pools, premium bonds, lotteries, sweepstakes, a flutter on the

Grand National. Though the findings of historian Ross McKibbin suggest that working-class gambling in this period was affordable, indeed a manageable portion of family expenditure, gambling practices emerged as one of the areas in which middle- and working-class attitudes were divided. Many clergy clung to an image of a feckless working class which squandered dole money in the hope of something for nothing. The Methodist Benson Perkins was dismissive of Anglican moral hauteur as expressed by an Oxford don, Dr Robert Mortimer, in his 1933 pamphlet on *Gambling*, where he wrote of 'surplus money' which could be safely lost for amusement. This was a language which Free Church ministers rarely understood. The post-war world had indeed changed, and too many churches had been left behind.

One Free Church grouser commented in the 1920s about the habits of young people on Sundays: 'They don't want rest – they want zest.' That same critic, who sheltered under under a pseudonym but dedicated his book to the editor of the Free Church *British Weekly*, particularly had it in for the new youth, the new women, make-up and dancing. The dance craze had been given respectability by Victor Silvester, who had learned to dance because the Bishop of London held a ball for the Sons of the Clergy, of which young Victor was one. He went on to win the World Professional Ballroom Championship in 1922. 'Can Methodists dance?' was a question put to Samuel Chadwick, Wesleyan President in 1918. 'Some can; most can't,' was the reply.

Many clergy were eager to take bold steps to react to the competition and brighten their services. Dick Sheppard's lively services at St Martin's-in-the-Fields set the pattern for the popular services which became the vogue. In Sheppard's congregation in 1922 was the young John Reith, a Scottish minister's son, who four months later was to be appointed managing director of the newly created BBC. The alacrity with which the churches responded to the new possibilities of broadcasting, pressed upon them by Reith, was one sign of the new mood for experiment and innovation. A Religious Advisory Committee with Anglican, Free Church and Roman Catholic representatives was formed in 1923, and Dick Sheppard conducted the first church service to be broadcast in January 1924.

The campaign to brighten religion and to give it more meaning and relevance for the public provided an extra stimulus to the efforts of those who urged the necessity of revising the Church of England's *Book of Common Prayer*, and the replacement of the solemn Victorian music which contributed to the general atmosphere of gloom which pervaded so many services. In 1923 an archbishops' committee on 'Music in Worship' proposed sweeping reforms which led, among other things, to the foundation of the School of English Church Music. The compilation in

1926 of *Songs of Praise* – described by Erik Routley as 'breezy, zestful, youthful and fresh in its approach' – marked a significant stage in the effort to enhance the quality of religious worship. So too, did the Liturgical Movement, which sought to establish the Parish Communion as the central act of parish worship, and was pioneered in churches like St John's, Newcastle upon Tyne, by Noel Hudson and Henry de Candole. The battle for Prayer Book revision was to consume much time and energy as the various factions in the Church tried to introduce their own liturgical changes – or, more accurately, tried to prevent others from sneaking in their party preferences. Eventually the considered judgement of the overwhelming majority of bishops, clergy and lay representatives was overturned by the ecclesiastically unrepresentative House of Commons in 1927 and 1928.

The war had been primarily a time for action, not for words. Effort had gone not into thinking but into actually doing things. B. H. Streeter, an eminent New Testament scholar, was critical of Life and Liberty for the very reason that it attached too much importance to the Church's body and not enough to its soul. He believed that the movement was beginning at the wrong end, and that the spiritual and intellectual condition of the Church was in more urgent need of attention. This was not, however, a retreat by Streeter from action into the realm of mind. Though not now physically strong, he valued energy. As an undergraduate he had rowed for his college, and for the rest of his life showed an enthusiastic interest in rowing and in students. He was strongly representative of many people in the inter-war period in being fascinated by the interaction of spirit and mind with the body, by power and pain. In 1919 he collaborated with Lily Dougall and Archbishop Charles D'Arcy of Dublin in writing *God and the Struggle for Existence* for the Student Christian Movement. Writing for those for whom the war had led to Nietzsche's conclusion that 'God is dead,' the trio argued, in Streeter's words, that 'God is alive, and from Him we may get power ourselves to really live.' It was this quest for vibrant power which led to Streeter's interest in the 1920s in the 'new psychology', Pentecostalism, spiritual healing and the spiritual teachings of India. In 1920 he collaborated with A. J. Appasamy in writing an account of the teaching of Sadhu Sundar Singh, the Indian mystic who combined Christian devotion and Hindu asceticism. In his saffron robes and turban, the Sadhu found himself to be a star turn in Europe and America. Then Streeter turned to the study of the Buddha. Even after his election as Provost of The Queen's College, Oxford, Streeter never ducked the forces of change blowing in the religious world. There was even symbolism in his death in 1937: his plane crashed in a fog.

While cloistered in Queen's, Streeter joined the movement known as the

Oxford Group, whose founder, Frank Buchman, a tall, well-scrubbed American Lutheran, had settled down to work in Oxford in 1922. His movement began with the name of 'The First Century Christian Fellowship'. His followers had to agree to live by the 'four absolutes' of honesty, purity, love and unselfishness. Importance was attached to 'guidance' and 'sharing'. Great efforts were made to attract gifted young people to house parties where famous people might be addressed by their Christian names. There were worries about what seemed to be an appetite for salacious personal revelations, but this seems to have been more anticipatory than experiential. Many critics, including Bishop Henson of Durham, rose to the bait and denounced the new movement, especially after the acceptance of the name 'the Oxford Group', applied in error in South Africa in 1929. Use of this title particularly annoyed A. P. Herbert, Oxford's MP; but then, there was political cunning in Herbert's echoing of an old buffer's rage. He was already championing the cause of divorce law reform which, with some clerical hostility, reached the statute book in 1937 as the Matrimonial Causes Act. In 1939 Buchman changed the focus and name of his movement to Moral Rearmament.

Another group which claimed to have rediscovered the atmosphere of the first century was the Christian Healing Mission. In England this new phase in the resurgence of spiritual healing began in 1924 when an Anglican layman, James Moore Hickson, held a mission at Frizinghall, Bradford. For twenty years Hickson had pioneered this forgotten form of ministry in relative obscurity. Now, in the post-Great War world, his time had come. The formation of the first Labour government in 1924 created something like an apocalyptic atmosphere in many areas, and especially in Bradford where socialism was a force to be reckoned with and had claimed the allegiance of many former chapelgoers. The Christian Healing Mission maintained that the signs and wonders displayed at their services were signs of the last days and looked for the return of Christ. In the context of the anti-Bolshevik hysteria of the 1924 general election, the conditions were ripe for a localized revival which took the form of spectacular supernatural phenomena. 'CRIPPLE WHO PUSHED HER BATHCHAIR' announced the *Evening Argus* on its front page. For three days the 'miracles' were splashed over the press. Hickson became a signicant figure in the Anglican *demi-monde*. The controversy he ignited only increased the demand for his services. His next healing mission, in Paddington, prolonged the debate. Bishop Henson again came forward as the critic of what he saw as a surrender to superstition, while W. R. Inge, Dean of St Paul's, denounced episcopal collusion with 'the craze for miracle-mongering'. The Archbishop of Canterbury, who was sceptical, being himself frequently confined to bed as a consequence of a shooting accident while a student, appointed a committee which, after enquiring from doctors in the places where Hickson had held missions, concluded that there was no evidence that physical healing had occurred. None the less, it admitted in a footnote that there were sufficient grounds for concluding that many had been cured of functional disorders. By 1925, Hickson had come to resent the glare of publicity and the snide carpings of the press. He retreated to conduct his work in a more private setting at Crowhurst in Sussex, where the rector, Howard Cobb, opened his home to those seeking spiritual and physical wholeness.

The social and political witness of the churches received new prominence in the years after the Great War. The heightened political consciousness aroused by the industrial unrest of 1917 and 1918, the catapulting of Labour into the role of main opposition to the Conservatives, and the rumbling antireligious threat of Russian Bolshevism presented a new minefield through which the clergy had to tiptoe. Henson complained that at Lambeth the speeches in the industrial affairs debate were uniformly 'socialistic'. The Industrial Christian Fellowship, which had been formed just after the war by the merging of the Christian Social Union and the Navvy's Mission, was assured of better publicity when Geoffrey Studdert Kennedy, the blunt and unconventional 'Woodbine Willie' of the trenches, was appointed chief missioner. Backed up by an elaborate organization headed by P. T. R. Kirk, the ICF went into action with an ambitious programme of open-air 'crusades', factory and street-corner meetings, correspondence courses and study circles. Something of the old wartime spirit of brotherliness and sacrificial service was promoted in Toc H. Founded by an ex-chaplain, P. B. 'Tubby' Clayton, this organization spread with amazing rapidity throughout the land.

In this atmosphere of brave idealism, combined with a keen sense of social responsibility, plans were laid in 1919 for an interdenominational Conference on Politics, Economics and Citizenship (COPEC). Though the Roman Catholics withdrew before the conference, it met in a blaze of publicity at Birmingham in 1924 with Temple as its chairman. COPEC gave new impetus and sense of direction to Christian social witness. Like sparks flung from a catherine wheel, the burning fervour of COPEC set hearts ablaze in many parts of the world. Under its influence, a bureau of social research was set up on Tyneside. Overseas delegates returned home and drummed up support for the idea of a great universal Christian conference to link the movements for social witness and Church unity. In the following year, 1925, the Life and Work conference was held, on Archbishop Nathan Söderblom's initiative, in Stockholm. There the great clash on social questions came between proponents respectively of German pietist non-intervention and of American Protestant activism, with the

British delegation led by Bishop Frank Woods of Winchester closer to the Americans.

Ecclesiastical intervention in industrial disputes would, therefore, be a reasonable expectation; however, when the TUC called a general strike in 1926, one immediate effect was to paralyse most Christian thinking. All that the COPEC movement could contribute was a rambling meditation on the strike as a symptom of alienation from God. Christian compassion aroused sympathy for the locked-out miners, but the use of the strike weapon looked like revenge taken on the rest of the nation. Both Tory and Labour leaders agreed, in theory, that the Archbishop of Canterbury should attempt to break the deadlock, but unhelpfully refused to give the green light. Eventually, after some prodding from the mine-owner, Lord Londonderry, and persuasion from Wesleyan leaders, the archbishop agreed to act. With the help of a group of experienced clergy, an 'appeal' of three points to be acted on 'simultaneously and concurrently' was produced. It was really a plea for both sides to pull back in the hope that some less painful solution could be found. With the newspapers on strike, the only way to publicize the archbishop's intervention was to include it in a wireless news bulletin. The archbishop was mortified when John Reith refused, on the insistence of a government official, to sanction the transmission. Asa Briggs, the historian of the BBC, considered this the 'low-water mark' of the company's power and influence.

If the appeal had been broadcast, it is doubtful if it would have attracted much notice, but the banning of an Anglican archbishop by a Conservative prime minister had obvious news value. The story soon found its way into the *British Worker* and the provincial press, and (much to his own surprise) Archbishop Davidson was cheered in the streets. But if the people cheered Canterbury, the peers applauded Westminster. When Cardinal Bourne denounced the strike as a sin, he earned the gratitude of an anxious establishment, from which, later that year, he was able to extract the valuable prize of a Catholic Relief Act. For Bourne the new Act was the fulfilment of a dream going back to 1908. The 1930s were an unusually fruitful period for Roman Catholic writers, thinkers and publicists. The world of Hilaire Belloc and G. K. Chesterton moved on into the realms of Christopher Dawson and Evelyn Waugh. Fathers Ronald Knox and Martin D'Arcy exercised a magnetic appeal at Oxford on those who had cut loose from traditional family moorings. Arnold Lunn, a ski-ing and mountaineering enthusiast, born in India where his father was a Wesleyan missionary, went through an aggressive Rationalist phase as a student at Balliol. Irritated by one of Ronald Knox's polemics, he attempted a demolition, and in the debate which followed came to the bewildering conclusion that truth lay more with Rome than with rationalism. He was received by Knox into the Roman Catholic Church in 1933 and devoted the rest of his life to the twin claims of the ski slopes and Catholic apologetics.

The post-war economic boom had been followed by the onset of a long and severe depression, the slump, mass unemployment, and the cost-cutting National Government. Attention was focused on the inadequacies of housing in both town and country by the Bishop of Southwark, Cyril Garbett. Direct action was taken by Father Basil Jellicoe with the St Pancras Church Housing Society, and indirect action by Charles Jenkinson, a vicar in Leeds who secured election to the city council as a representative of the Labour Party and became chairman of the housing committee. By 1939 over a million new houses had been built in Britain, and a start had been made on slum clearance. Overcrowding was much reduced in the inter-war period – not just because of the erection of new council house estates like Wythenshaw in Manchester or Quarry Hill Flats in Leeds, but also through the reduction of family size. Families shrank from a norm of five or six children before the war to an average of 3.2 in 1939.

The causes and consequences of this change have been much debated. It largely depended, of course, on knowledge of effective methods of contraception. This could lead to changes in attitudes to sex, the role of women and the concept of the ideal family. Improved health care made it more likely that babies would survive and grow to maturity. Women, having gone out to work in the Great War, were reluctant to return to the traditional routine of children, kitchen and church. When Marie Stopes unleashed *Married Love* on the British public in 1919 it was to the secret satisfaction of many junior clergy, who wrote to her to express their reaction, and the disapproval of most bishops. She followed up the book with an unnecessarily forthright declaration to the bishops attending the Lambeth Conference in the following year. Her efforts were rebuffed and the bishops came out decisively against 'the open or secret sale of contraceptives' and teaching which 'encourages married people in the deliberate cultivation of sexual union as an end in itself'. Such old-fashioned notions were effectively demolished in 1921 by Maude Royden in *Sex and Common Sense*. Though the Roman Catholic bishops never reconciled themselves to birth control, and indeed financed a court case against Marie Stopes, the Anglicans took a small step forward at the 1930 Lambeth Conference, when they sanctioned contraceptives where another pregnancy could damage a wife's health. Effectively, they were responding to what was clearly current practice by many couples.

The bishops' decision also represented acceptance that the needs of an existing family should be put first. The 1930s were a family-oriented decade. Gathering round the radio, especially for the King's Christmas Day broadcast, took on an almost quasi-religious significance. The nuclear family was valued as never before and the possibility of dispersing its members was a terrifying prospect. In King George V the nation had a respected and respectable sovereign, a family king, whose programme of civic visits transformed the image of aloof Victorian monarchy and aroused that popular interest in the royal family which has from 1910 to the present absorbed some of the devotion which previously had religious outlets. It was the painstaking construction of that image of royalty which was threatened in 1936 when the new king, Edward VIII, wanted to marry an American woman who had divorced two husbands. An Anglican bishop, the Christian socialist A. W. F. Blunt of Bradford, inadvertently detonated the abdication crisis, which was insensitively handled by Archbishop Lang. The King's decision and Lang's sanctimonious comment provide a classic confrontation between the Anglican ethic of self-denying responsibility and the personal happiness ethic being increasingly dispensed through the cinema.

After 1931 the publication of a spate of books by ex-soldiers contributed to disenchantment with war. Robert Graves's *Goodbye To All That* (1929) fed a market which instinctively felt that it had not been told the whole truth about the war, and was ready to believe that army chaplains were too often inadequate fools. Mahatma Gandhi's passive resistance campaign in India powerfully reinforced the conviction that mobilizing popular opinion was more important than marching with tanks and guns. The Japanese invasion of Manchuria in 1931 had produced the naïve but magnificent possibility of the 'Peace Army', summoned by Maude Royden and Dick Sheppard to interpose themselves between the invaders and their prey. Not surprisingly the 'Peace Army' was never called to turn its plans into performance, and it remains a romantic relic of proffered Christian self-sacrifice. The British public had demonstrated by their votes in the Peace Ballot of 1934 that they were in no mood for another war. Also in 1934 the National Secular Society had printed *Arms and the Clergy (1914–18)*, a mélange of quotations from sermons and writings which, divorced from time and context, made ministers sound like whirling dervishes.

In Italy, Germany and Spain new forces had begun to emerge which alarmed many but gave hope to some. Their British counterpart, Sir Oswald Mosley, had some Anglican and Catholic admirers. But it was Henson, the angular Bishop of Durham, who spoke out in the House of Lords for the plight of German Jews, and it was a Methodist minister, Henry Carter, who masterminded refugee relief. At the ideological level, it was again an Anglican and a Methodist who took the lead. The Anglican, James Parkes, sought to understand Judaism and remove Gentile prejudice, while the Methodist William Simpson gave his energies to the Council of Christians and Jews.

Two men who could never be called typical none the less can be seen as representative in the range of ideas which influenced them. W. E. Orchard and D. R. Davies came from similar Free Church backgrounds. Both preached the social gospel and liberal theology before 1920, and they became firm friends, but though subject to the same sense of disillusionment, they sought very different paths of escape. For both of them the war and subsequent social unrest were profoundly disorienting. Orchard had been deeply impressed by Pope Benedict XV's Peace Note of 1917 and looked to Rome to provide a supranational organization which could umpire disputes. But things were not so simple. Joining Rome in 1935 meant having to field for Bourne's successor, Arthur Hinsley. When asked what the Pope was doing to stop Mussolini's invasion of Abyssinia, Hinsley could only plead pathetically that the Supreme Pontiff was only 'a helpless old man'. That was not what Orchard had expected from Rome. In 1938 he could only lament privately, 'Our Catholic papers are tying their hopes far too much to Franco and to the sword generally. See if it does not put our convert numbers down again this year.'

Spain also became crucial in the experience of D. R. Davies. The spiritual peaks and troughs of his life are graphically described in his aptly titled autobiography, *In Search of Myself*. The years 1914 and 1926 brought events which had a massive impact on his thinking. In the aftermath of the general strike he transformed his Congregational chapel in Southport into a Labour church dedicated to the brotherhood of man. Three hyperactive years led only to spiritual collapse. Resigning his ministry, he moved to London where, after eking out a precarious existence addressing envelopes and teaching musical appreciation for a record company, he was swept up by the fervour of the hypnotic Serb, Dimitrije Mitrinovic, to campaign for a New Europe. But even this vision gradually faded, to be replaced by an increasingly desperate sharing with people struggling and searching for new beliefs and ideologies to bring meaning and purpose to their spiritually barren lives. It brought contact with the guild socialism of G. D. H. Cole, A. R. Orage and G. H. Penty with its rejection of the bureaucratic features of State socialism; also with the even less plausible social credit theories of C. H. Douglas, which for a time interested William Temple and a future Labour leader, Hugh Gaitskell. In 1936 Davies broke with New Europe and transferred his energies to the Socialist League, which under the chairmanship of the ascetic Anglican and former Labour cabinet minister, Sir Stafford Cripps, was swayed by the seductive simplicities of pseudo-scientific Marxist solutions.

Davies may have been an idealist, but he was never for long naïve. When he became conscious of the German, Italian and Japanese threats to peace, he preceded Cripps into a 'People's Front against Fascism', which brought him into the company of the Marxist Anglican clergy in Islington. At their centre was Father Bill Iredell, vicar of St Clement's, Barnsbury, who at the time had two like-minded curates, Stanley Evans and Leonard Schiff. Services at St Clement's at that time always closed with the People's Front sign, a right fist being raised before the altar. It was to Father Iredell that the Spanish Republican government turned when it wanted a British delegation to report on allegations from the Franco rebels that atrocities were being committed against Catholic priests and nuns. Iredell's great coup was to get the Dean of Canterbury to agree to lead the delegation. Though he had been attracted by social credit ideas, Hewlett Johnson had not yet acquired the notoriety which followed the publication in 1939 of his best-selling *The Socialist Sixth of the World*. His delegation, which included the philosopher John Macmurray as well as D. R. Davies, produced first-hand evidence to refute pro-Franco claims. For Davies, it provided the moment of personal crisis which led to a deep spiritual reassessment of his life. Watching the pitiful procession of homeless refugees fleeing from a bombarded Spanish town, sheltering in the ruins of Bilbao, and walking the wards of a military hospital at Guernica with its mangled bodies, moans of agony and screams of pain, Davies was thrown back on discarded fundamentals. It was, he recorded, 'the end of the faith' – humanist, self-sufficient – by which he had lived since 1928. Now he was face to face with the grim consequences of human ambition, folly and sin. Now he was ready for a spiritual reconversion. Eagerly, he devoured the writings of the American exponent of theological realism, Reinhold Niebuhr. It took him back to his earlier life-goals. It was to the Christian ministry that he now felt drawn again – but eventually to the ministry, not of Congregational-ism, but of the Church of England.

After sitting for sixteen years, the committee appointed by the Archbishops of Canterbury and York produced its report: *Doctrine in the Church of England*, published in 1938. So different was the intellectual climate from that of 1922 that the chairman, Archbishop William Temple, said that if they were to begin their work again, 'its perspectives would be different'. In dealing with the credal statements about the Virgin Birth and physical Resurrection of Jesus, the 1938 report looked back to the intellectual climate of the 1920s – or perhaps forward to the intellectual climate of the 1980s as set forth by Bishop David Jenkins. Either way, it did not address the state of mind of the 1930s. 'It came upon us like a flood after 1931,' recalled George Every: 'Liberalism of every kind became open to attack, in philosophy, in politics, in theology, in general culture.' Charles Raven, Regius Professor of Divinity at Cambridge from 1932, could only deplore what he regarded as the blight which infected theology with the spread of the transcendentalism of Karl Barth, the rejection of natural religion, the assertion of biblical authority and the pessimism created by the fear of a second world war.

That foreboding created a mood of anxiety which pervaded the late 1930s. No one wanted another war, and its apparent prevention through the personal initiative of the British Prime Minister Neville Chamberlain at Munich seemed a divine deliverance. When asked for a contribution to a volume called *If I Had One Sermon Only to Preach*, Archbishop Lang offered a paean of praise for the Birmingham Unitarian. Between the two men, both destined to be eclipsed by their successors, was a mutual regard verging on sycophancy. For Lang, British foreign policy was safe in the hands of Neville Chamberlain, who had placed its direction in the hands of Lang's fellow High Churchman Lord Halifax, a friend at All Souls and a near neighbour in Yorkshire for over thirty years.

In this climate, some Catholics were especially wary because of the popular suspicion that Catholic beliefs somehow were conducive to totalitarian systems. Cardinal Hinsley had the difficult task both of defusing that anti-Catholic sentiment which still lingered in the subconscious mind of John Bull, and also of earning the government's trust by helping in neutralizing Spain without arousing Protestant hackles. In August 1939 the archbishop approached Lord Halifax with the suggestion that British Catholics should raise money to help repair the damaged churches of Spain. It was an obvious propaganda ploy which was matched by a similar move on the part of German Catholics. With a hidden donation of £500 from the Foreign Office, a respectable sum was raised and handed over to the Archbishop of Toledo by Peter Amigo, the Gibraltarian Catholic Archbishop of Southwark.

The outbreak of war on Sunday 3 August 1939 coincided with the opening of the Methodist connexional new year. At Westminster Central Hall, Dr W. E. Sangster was about to open a distinguished London ministry which would involve sleeping during the blitz in the underground with hundreds of tired but resilient cockneys. The City Temple, where F. W. Norwood had enlivened a pre-war sermon with the dramatic flourish of 'Heil Hitler', was destroyed. In June 1940, after the invasion of France, Britain stood alone. Every potential source of assistance had to be deployed to maintain morale and build up the nation's resolve to fight the foe. The battle for the mind seemed to assume a new importance: 'Consideration has to be given to the part that religion can play in the crisis,' noted the BBC's controller of programmes. It was not so much the positive power of religion which engaged attention so much as forming a response to its negative aspects. Anti-Catholicism could be fuelled by allegations that Catholicism bred fascism. Protestantism could be tarnished by the slur that Hitler was in some sense Luther's spiritual heir. Both traditions had, however, formidable defenders. The cultural historian Christopher Dawson stood up for the democratic credentials of Catholicism, and the Methodist expert on Luther, Gordon Rupp, with wit and learning made short work of Lord Vansittart. Regrettably Rupp's balance seemed to desert him on the possibility of cinemas and theatres in London being allowed to open for the benefit of servicemen and women on leave: in April 1941 he claimed to see parallels between the Nazi political incursion into church hours through their demonstrations and youth activities, and the British government's willingness to sanction entertainment on Sundays.

But these were all matters of minor significance compared with the need for a Christian clarion call to rouse the nation. Who would come forward and give a lead? The Archbishop of Canterbury was irritated by calls for strong leadership. 'I am conscious of a certain lack of pushful ardour,' he wrote in his diary. His colleague at York chose, instead of filling the gap and beating up patriotic fervour, to concentrate on long-term goals and write to the *Daily Telegraph* about war aims. For some, this war was qualitatively different from anything that had happened before. Maude Royden was felt by some to have gone back on a lifetime's testimony for peace when in June 1940 she announced in pained words her support for the war against Hitler.

It was Barbara Ward, the 26-year-old assistant editor of *The Economist*, who took the initiative by putting before Hinsley the fears of younger Catholics. They had noted with alarm Nazi methods for undermining national morale. These were believed, probably wrongly, to have destroyed the will of the Dutch and French to resist. According to Ward, Britain was now in the front line and about to be subject to subtle and sinister techniques which could bring about social disintegration by accentuating every difference of opinion and class interest. British Catholics were particularly vulnerable, a possibility which was not lost on Hinsley. In a bold pre-emptive strike, he announced a new Catholic-inspired cultural crusade, 'The Sword of the Spirit', at a public meeting held on 1 August 1940. This time it was the Catholic archbishop who spoke for Christian England and had his efforts recognized by a German complaint to the Vatican. Though organized and led by Catholics, the 'Sword' was initially open to all, a fact strikingly emphasized by the unprecedented willingness of Cardinal Hinsley to invite everyone present to join in the Lord's Prayer. Perhaps the most dramatic achievement of Dr Josef Goebbels was to get the Catholic Archbishop of Westminster and the Anglican Bishop Bell of Chichester to pray together – though only once. In the view of Hinsley's biographer and eventual successor, Cardinal Heenan, it was 'the opening chapter of the modern history of religion in Great Britain'. That was making too great a claim. But if that historic 1940 meeting did not attract a Pentecostal dove, it at least called up an ecumenical swallow.

The inter-war years cannot be treated as a single period. In the optimistic early 1920s there seems to have been a new buoyancy in Church circles as efforts were made to pick up the threads and return to normal. But there could be no going back. People had been through too much; minds and attitudes had changed. It was not just experience of war which undermined faith, but also experience of peace in a country where many had grown used to living now, for tomorrow may bring death. The craving for vitality and sensation, though an intelligible reaction, also challenged convention. The collapse of deference was one of the lasting legacies of the First World War and was bound to undermine religious authority. But 1926 and 1929 brought the roaring twenties down to earth with a bump. The general strike and Wall Street crash demonstrated that the pillars of society had no solid foundations. The churches were revealed as unable to prevent war or mass unemployment. They had been marginalized from national and international affairs, and marginalized themselves from domestic and personal concerns. They frowned upon many popular pleasures. The Free Churches were out of step when they distanced themselves from dancing and football pools, the Roman Catholics when they opposed contraception; the Church of England contained those who shared both points of view and neither.

Churchgoing slumped in the 1930s and left those who remained either turned in upon themselves, clinging grimly to selected Victorian beliefs and values, or waiting doggedly for a revival, usually conceived along essentially Victorian lines. The 'new Reformation' was postponed.

24

The Christian Churches in England since 1945: Ecumenism and Social Concern

Alan M. Suggate

In its crudest form, in the politics of our day, the pagan dream of human power has turned once more into a nightmare oppressing men's outward lives. That will pass, because it is too violent a disorder to be endured. But elsewhere and less vulgarly, as a *mystique* of technical and scientific mastery of men's environment, it is swiftly replacing the old materialism as the prevalent anti-christianity of the twentieth century. In this subtler form it will more secretly but even more terribly oppress the human spirit.

These words, which exactly capture the mood of thoughtful Christians during the Second World War, appeared in January 1945. It is significant that they are to be found not in a book on Christian social ethics, but in *The Shape of the Liturgy*, written by Dom Gregory Dix, monk of the Anglican Nashdom Abbey. The easy-going modernism fashionable in the 1920s had overplayed its hand and been falsified by world events. The poet T. S. Eliot made a vigorous plea for a return to Christian foundations in *The Idea of a Christian Society*. V. A. Demant typified the mood when he scrutinized the ideologies of the late 1930s in *The Religious Prospect*. What, he asked, could prove a match for fascism and communism? Not liberalism; not even Christian liberalism. For though it correctly adhered to certain doctrines, such as the dignity of the individual and the objectivity of truth and goodness, its own dogma or presupposition that human beings were to be understood in purely historical terms, without any anchorage in a transcendent reality, only eviscerated those doctrines. Furthermore, liberalism's trumpeting of individual rights could pose no threat to regimes which catered effectively for people's basic craving for community.

Demant's plea was that Christians move away from moralistic idealism and recover their hold on Christian dogma. At the heart of the Christian faith was good news, not good advice.

The threat of continental totalitarianism had already given a strong impetus to the quest for Christian unity. The Ecumenical Movement had in effect begun with the Edinburgh Missionary Conference of 1910. The ensuing International Missionary Council, which first met in 1921, aimed to promote co-operation and avoid undesirable overlapping and rivalry between the churches in the mission field. It arranged world missionary conferences at Jerusalem in 1928 and at Tambaram, in India, in 1938. At Tambaram the model of churches in Christian countries and mission fields in heathen lands was abolished. Instead, the churches in different parts of the world were simply to be distinguished as older and younger, and all had a problem of mission on their doorstep.

In parallel with this ecumenical missionary movement there developed a concern for world problems, which were the focus of the first World Conference on Life and Work, held at Stockholm in 1925. The English contribution was a pastiche of the social idealism which had prevailed at the Conference on Christian Politics, Economics and Citizenship held at Birmingham in 1924 under William Temple's chairmanship. The mood of the second World Conference, held at Oxford in 1937, was very different. Faced with the challenges of secularism and totalitarianism, the guiding committee, admirably served by J. H. Oldham, ensured a thorough process of research and consultation, and the resulting volumes on *Church, Community and State* (1937–8) were of a very high order. The conference was determined that the full resources of the Bible and Christian tradition should engage with the desperate contemporary situation, and the impact of biblical theology (especially that of Karl Barth), with its accent on sin, judgement and grace, is evident.

The Missionary Council and the Life and Work Movement had both tried to avoid doctrinal issues. Faith and Order became a third movement and held its own first world conference at Lausanne in 1927. But the deeper reflection of the 1930s showed that doctrine could not be thus isolated, and one of the objects of the timing of the second World Conference on Faith and Order at Edinburgh in 1937, in the same month as the Oxford conference, was to secure the adoption of proposals for the foundation of the World Council of Churches. It was an indication of the collapse of modernist liberalism that the subsequent deliberations at Utrecht in 1938 affirmed the Nicene faith as the basis of the future Council. A provisional committee later appointed W. A. Visser't Hooft as the general secretary of the World Council of Churches in process of formation. Its offices in Geneva, London and New York kept Church leaders in touch with each other during the war, and were well placed to organize relief and reconstruction work in its aftermath.

This interrelating of faith, life and mission is apparent also in the setting up in 1942 of the British Council of Churches, as a fellowship of churches in the British Isles 'which confess the Lord Jesus as God and Saviour'. It represented the Church of England, the Church in Wales, the Church of Ireland, the Free Churches, the Salvation Army and the Society of Friends, with departments for faith and order, education, social responsibility, international affairs and youth, as well as a committee on evangelism. It was particularly active through its Inter-Church Aid and Refugee Service, which later became Christian Aid. Local councils were rapidly formed, and an early activity was the sponsoring of Religion and Life weeks to promote the concerns of the 1937 Oxford conference.

Into this ecumenical stream there also flowed the Liturgical Movement. Its origins lay in the life and work of Dom Guéranger (1805–75) a French Benedictine monk who re-established the Abbey of Solesmes on the basis of a medieval religious community. Though marred by a backward-looking romanticism and ecclesiasticism out of touch with society, his work inspired Dom Lambert Beauduin in Belgium and Abbot Herwegen and Dom Odo Casel at the German Abbey of Maria Laach. Beauduin emphasized that the liturgy was not something to be seen and heard alone, but rather a corporate activity – 'the bringing to God of the whole individual man in the whole Christian community'. Casel stressed the dimension of mystery in the liturgy.

In England the Liturgical Movement was given enormous impetus by the work of the Anglican Father Gabriel Hebert SSM. His translation of the Swedish Lutheran Archbishop Ingve Brilioth's *Eucharistic Faith and Practice, Evangelical and Catholic* (1930) brought to the English an ecumenical and historical perspective on the Eucharist and taught them to contemplate it as a 'polished jewel, each of whose facets shows some different and beautiful refraction of one and the same light'. Brilioth presents five such facets of the Eucharist: thanksgiving, communion, commemoration, sacrifice and mystery. Hebert himself in his *Liturgy and Society* (1935) deplored the fragmentation of life and the easy-going materialism depicted satirically in Aldous Huxley's *Brave New World*. He exposed the widespread liberal and humanistic assumption that religion is a matter of mere individual opinion, an option for those who feel the need for it. Such private beliefs could not of course influence social life. Hebert looked for deeper foundations and found them in the Eucharist. The Eucharist is fundamentally something done. The commemoration of Christ's saving work is an objective remembrance by means of a ritual, which binds together past, present and future. It is moreover an action which is social. Hebert demonstrates the truth of this for the Early Church and particularly Augustine.

> To worship God in church is not a substitute for the service of God in daily life: rather, it is that which makes the service of God possible by bringing the things of daily life into the light of eternity. And as the Christian redemption is not merely individual but social, so the normal type of Christian worship is not the individual's meditation, but the common worship of the Body, when the members are met together to learn the meaning of the common life which is in Him.

It was chiefly Hebert who inspired the translation of these convictions into the practice of the parish, and he edited a book of essays entitled *The Parish Communion* (1937). Meanwhile, A. M. Ramsey in his work *The Gospel and the Catholic Church* (1936) argued that the liturgy declared the whole meaning of the Gospel and of the one Body of Christ, and was a key to the meaning of all life.

Among Free Churchmen a significant work was *Christian Worship* (1936). Edited by Nathaniel Micklem, Principal of Mansfield College, Oxford, it comprised essays by Congregationalists, Presbyterians and Baptists (among them H. Wheeler Robinson, T. W. Manson, C. H. Dodd, James Moffatt, C. J. Cadoux and J. S. Whale) on worship in the Bible and the Christian tradition, and indicated its primary importance for the contemporary life of their communions.

The chronic task of mission, reinforced by the power of the new ideologies over the minds of whole cultures; the recovery of a strong biblical accent, especially on redemption; the drive for the reunion of the Church and for the reintegration of social life; the recovery of the central place of the Eucharist – these are the interwoven strands of the outlook of thoughtful Christians in 1945.

Mission was the subject of *Towards the Conversion of England* (1945), the report of an Anglican committee chaired by the Bishop of Rochester. It rightly saw that 'evangelization of those without' was inseparable from the spiritual renewal of the Church within. But it spoke as if the Church had little need to listen to the world and as if the Gospel had only to be taught and understood to be effective. Many, however, realized that the issue was much more complex. The Lambeth Conference of 1948, pondering the vulnerability of cultures and the attractiveness of totalitarianism, diagnosed a spiritual soil erosion which prevented Christianity from taking root. A rebirth of religion would require the preparation of a cultural soil for its nurture. Thus alongside the more traditional understanding of mission (another example was Dr Billy Graham's nationwide crusade in

1954) other approaches were being considered more in tune with the insights of Demant and Eliot.

Archbishop William Temple had worked closely with R. A. Butler on the Education Act of 1944, taking advantage of the vastly improved relations between the Church of England and Nonconformists. The dual system of State schools and Church schools was preserved, the latter category involving a partnership of Church and State. There was to be a daily act of worship, together with religious instruction according to an agreed syllabus, subject to rights of conscience of parents and teachers. Both Church and State were agreed that the worship and the teaching should be Christian – a plain reflection of the sense of cultural crisis engendered by fascism. Dr Spencer Leeson, in *Christian Education* (1947) and *Christian Education Reviewed* (1957), slated any attempt to separate Christian ethics from Christian faith and wanted to arrest the process of secularization. The task of Church schools was to initiate children into membership of the Church; the State, he noted with satisfaction, was recognizing that it was in idea and intention Christian and had the task of contributing to the nurture of the nation's children in the faith. For Leeson, as for Temple and Eliot, the critical question was the purpose of education. This must involve the full development of personality and training in citizenship. Only Christianity had the right understanding of personality, and it alone could supply the power to fulfil the purpose. Whether British society was in a frame of mind to make Spencer Leeson's aspirations capable of fulfilment remained to be seen. In the virtual absence of scientifically acquired data, Christians hazarded guesses about England's spiritual state, and varied in their attitudes, depending whether they focused on the Englishman's abiding disinclination to abandon his attenuated Christianity or on his polite refusal to embrace a more vibrant form.

The victory of the Labour Party under Clement Attlee in the 1945 general election ushered in a government which carried out an extensive programme of social control and welfare. The Bank of England, gas, electricity, coal and transport were all nationalized. The Beveridge Plan of 1942 was largely implemented in the National Insurance and the National Health Service Acts of 1946. Christians mainly welcomed the welfare state. Archbishop Garbett saw it as the embodiment of the principle: 'Bear ye one another's burdens and so fulfil the law of Christ.' Yet several feared an excessive growth of State control and the erosion of personal and local responsibility. Moreover, while a reasonable degree of material security was part of God's will, the State could easily foster materialistic attitudes to the neglect of spiritual needs. A similar fear underlay the negative attitude of the churches to the creation of premium bonds in 1956 and a vast increase in gambling generally. Caution was also expressed over sterilization in a Moral Welfare Council report, *Human Sterilisation, Some Principles of Christian Ethics* (1951). While legitimate if it was the only means of curing disease, it was deemed totally unacceptable for eugenic purposes, or as a punishment for crime. A committee appointed by Archbishop Fisher sought to protect the sanctity of marriage by distinguishing sharply between artificial insemination by the husband, which could be justified, and insemination by a donor, which could not, in *Artificial Human Insemination* (1948). The integral relation of spiritual and physical was emphasized in the Churches' Council of Healing, which aimed to co-ordinate the work of spiritual healing and to encourage the co-operation of doctors and clergy. The British Medical Association nominated three representatives, and later backed a commission, which in a report entitled *The Church's Ministry of Healing* (1958) carefully assessed all aspects of spiritual healing and gave much helpful guidance.

Another way of preparing the cultural soil was being pioneered in some of the big cities. Coventry Cathedral, devastated by German bombing in 1940, was rebuilt and became a centre not only for reconciliation, but for engagement with contemporary society. In Sheffield Bishop Leslie Hunter appointed E. R. Wickham in 1944 to pioneer industrial mission. Wickham not only established good relations with many industrial firms, but also carried out a piece of sociological research into the fortunes of the churches in Sheffield. This was embodied in what became the charter document of industrial mission, *Church and People in an Industrial City* (1957). Wickham exposed the long-term intractability of the problem of mission in Sheffield. The churches had never succeeded in attracting the working class in substantial numbers, and the flight of the middle classes in the twentieth century, particularly through the upheavals of war, secularization and material seductions, had completed the collapse. The churches could not recover lost ground by enervating spurts of evangelism. They needed to face the conditioning of entire social groups, to understand the social shaping of the culture pattern of the working class, whose habits were closed to organized religion, and find secular modes of conveying the meaning of the Christian faith. Further, the churches still thought of the parish as the centre of influence on the community. Yet people were now far more mobile, living in one district, working in another, and taking their leisure in a third. Further, society was shaped for good or ill by industrial and political forces of great magnitude, which were no respecters of local or even regional boundaries. The Church therefore needed a specialized ministry which would enable those working within these 'principalities and powers' to get some purchase on them in the light of Christian and humane criteria. The chief work of mission therefore devolved upon the laity.

Wickham's success was followed by the planting of industrial missions in many other conurbations, including London and Teesside. All have endeavoured to be thoroughly ecumenical. Their pattern of work has been to seek permission for regular visits to a factory, and to build up personal contacts at all levels. Most missioners have been full-time, simply in order to give them time to acquire an understanding of industry – its human relations as well as its technical processes – so that they can contribute responsibly to the exploration of personal and collective issues on site. The work of industrial mission has been an added impetus to the growth of industrial committees of the various churches and the British Council of Churches, which enable the churches to keep abreast of developments in industry and commission reports giving guidance on specific issues. Particularly distinguished work has been done by the Methodist Luton Industrial College under the leadership of William Gowland.

Complementary to industrial mission have been interesting experiments within city parishes to work out the relationship of communion and community. At Darnall, Sheffield, a parish of 14,000, Alan Ecclestone encouraged visual aids to the Parish Communion to bring home the concerns of the members. Inseparable from the Communion was the parish meeting, which translated some of the concerns into action. For example, it initiated a community association, sponsored work for the elderly, and organized public meetings and deputations on issues such as world peace. Ecclestone noted that a more disciplined congregation emerged, capable of understanding how faith and life related and of undertaking tasks in the local community.

In Halton, Leeds, Ernest Southcott was vicar of a slum clearance area with five estates which lacked any sense of community. The Parish Communion on Sunday was the centre of worship, true to the insights of the Liturgical Movement. Southcott and the parish meeting were keen to emphasize mission and the fullness of initiation into a teaching, worshipping and caring community. He therefore created as a supplement (not a substitute) two kinds of house churches. The first was 'intensive', for those who were more fully instructed and committed, where Holy Communion was celebrated. The second was 'extensive', for the less committed, consisting normally of prayer, study and discussion. Hundreds of parishioners were helped to discover the presence of Christ in the midst of the ordinary, and to offer prayers for home, work and neighbourhood. The story is told by Southcott in *The Parish Comes Alive* (1956).

Dom Gregory Dix's *The Shape of the Liturgy* was a major influence at all levels of church life from national to local (for example in the Parish and People Movement, pioneered by Henry de Candole, Bishop of Knaresborough). Dix's chief contribution was to show that the liturgy is constructed not round a pattern of words but round the fourfold action of Jesus at the Last Supper: he took, he blessed, he broke, he gave. John A. T. Robinson acknowledged Dix's illumination in his *Liturgy Coming to Life* (1960), an account of an experiment at Clare College, Cambridge, while Robinson was Dean. The Prayer Book order was accompanied by a manual which brought out the meaning of what was said and done. Above all Robinson stressed the integral relation of liturgy and life. 'The offertory starts where the bread and wine start, where our lives are rooted in the everyday world of everyday relationships, of family and society, work and leisure.' The corporate nature of the liturgy was expressed by the participation of the congregation not only in the offertory, but also in the readings and intercessions. And the outward movement at the end of the service was shown by the rubric: 'The ministers go out, a deacon carrying the remainder of the loaf not set apart for the Communion, to be shared at the breakfast,' and by the gloss: 'The sharing of bread, now concluded sacramentally, must be continued socially – and then economically and politically.'

The Liturgical Movement was given more official recognition within the Roman Catholic Church by Pope Pius XII's *Mediator Dei* (1947), the first encyclical wholly devoted to liturgy. Meanwhile Free Churchmen were also showing a deep interest in the question of how they could contribute from the riches of their own tradition to the Liturgical and Ecumenical Movements. J. E. Rattenbury wrote a study called *The Eucharistic Hymns of John and Charles Wesley* (1948). Nathaniel Micklem, J. S. Whale and Bernard L. Manning all enabled Congregationalists to recover the High Genevan tradition, and John Marsh, Romilly Micklem, John Huxtable and James Todd prepared a *Book of Public Worship Compiled for the use of Congregationalists* (1948), which drew extensively on the wider Reformed tradition, including the Scottish Presbyterian. The influence of the Liturgical Movement is also plain in *Call to Worship* (1960) by the Baptist Neville Clark. Further impetus was given by the rising interest, particularly among young people, in the Taizé Community, the first Protestant monastic community on the continent since the Reformation. *Eucharist at Taizé* (1959, translated 1962) is the fruit of wide ecumenical study and experimentation, and Brother Max Thurian has made a distinguished contribution to the understanding of liturgy. Moreover the Community, as it has spread worldwide, has impressively served alongside the very poorest in areas of desperate need.

The search for Christian unity, already in full swing in India (the Church of South India was born in September 1947), was given further momentum with a sermon in November 1946 by Archbishop Fisher of Canterbury.

Frankly recognizing that the divisions of Christendom were a scandal, he discountenanced organic unity, but did suggest the churches should move 'towards a free exchange of life in worship and sacrament'. He wondered whether the Free Churches could 'take episcopacy into their system' and explore its nature and value. The archbishop had already convened a group of Catholic Anglicans to consider the causes of differences between Catholics and Protestants. He later invited a group of Evangelical Anglicans and some leaders of the Free Churches to tackle the same issues independently. In 1950 the Joint Conference of the Free Churches and the Church of England, taking account of the three reports – respectively *Catholicity: A Study in the Conflict of Christian Traditions in the West* (1947), *The Fullness of Christ: The Church's Growth into Catholicity* (1950) and *The Catholicity of Protestantism*, ed. R. N. Flew and R. E. Davies (1950) – published *Church Relations in England*. They considered six conditions which would have to be met if negotiations were to be successful. Each church would have to be satisfied with the others' loyalty to the apostolic faith; a Free Church would take episcopacy into its system, provided that each church had the same liberty of interpretation of the nature of episcopacy and priesthood as already obtained in the Church of England; the Church of England would agree to intercommunion of baptized and communicant members; the Church of England would hope that episcopally administered confirmation would become the norm; the Free Churches which became episcopal would retain the fellowship and intercommunion they already enjoyed with non-episcopal churches; and each church would agree that the continued existence of two parallel churches in the same area was only a temporary stage on the road to full unity. As Paul Welsby has pointed out, these conditions set out the basis of conversations between the churches in the next thirty years, and revealed some of the rocks on which many hopes were shattered.

The first official conversations on this basis were between the Church of England and the Methodist Church. They began in 1955, and the interim report of 1958 not only set out the common ground between them, but also envisaged full communion as soon as the ministries were unified: 'The final goal should be nothing short of organic unity.' Meanwhile conversations between the Church of England and the Church of Scotland extended for twenty years, incorporating the Episcopal Church of Scotland and the Presbyterian Church of England. However, the General Assembly of the Church of Scotland dissented from its own representatives and declined to ingest episcopacy in the form of 'bishops-in-presbytery'.

Relations between the Church of England and the Roman Catholic Church before the Second Vatican Council were rather frigid. The only exception was over questions of social order, where there was good co-operation ecumenically with the Catholic group Sword of the Spirit. The Instruction of the Holy Office in 1949 *On the Ecumenical Movement* did allow Roman Catholics to take counsel with others 'concerning joint action in the defence of the fundamental principles of Christianity and the natural law' or 'to deal with the rebuilding of social order and similar questions'. But Anglican orders were still null and void, and the dogmatic definition of the Assumption of the Blessed Virgin Mary in 1950 could only exacerbate relations, since the Church of England could not accept as necessary for salvation a dogma which it thought had no warrant in Scripture.

Relations between the Church of England and the Eastern Orthodox Church were much more cordial, largely owing to the flourishing Fellowship of St Alban and St Sergius, founded in 1928, which through its programmes of events, its journal *Sobornost* and especially its annual conference enabled ordinary Anglicans and Orthodox to spend time together and appreciate the others' worship and ethos. Many Anglicans came to realize that the Eastern churches had preserved a religious way of life with deep roots in the early centuries of the Christian Church, and had been spared acrimonious and arid Western controversies. Insights recovered through the Liturgical Movement were seen to be a normal feature of Eastern Church life, especially the concept of community enshrined in the word 'Sobornost'. Moreover, Eastern Orthodoxy had produced a succession of theologians of high calibre, many of whom had come as refugees to the West and whose works were therefore widely accessible: Sergei Bulgakov, George Florovsky, Nicholas Berdyaev and Nicholas Zernov.

In the immediate post-war period the international questions which most concerned the churches were nuclear power and communism. The war had ended with the dropping of atomic bombs on Hiroshima and Nagasaki. The British Council of Churches was quick to appoint a commission to consider atomic energy and the atomic bomb. Its exploration of the issues of power, law and democracy led it to set out in its report *The Era of Atomic Power* (1946) the dilemma posed to the Christian conscience by modern warfare. The commission was divided between those who believed that in no circumstances should atomic bombs be used and those who stressed a Christian responsibility for defending the fundamental rights and liberties of people and institutions, if necessary by nuclear deterrence. The Church of England appointed its own commission to study the British Council of Churches' document. Its report, *The Church and the Atom* (1948), rejected the justification offered for dropping atomic bombs on Hiroshima and Nagasaki, but also employed the concept of the just war to defend the retention of such weapons, and even said that in certain circumstances necessity might justify their use for defence against an unscrupulous aggressor. The report was heavily criticized for conceding too much by its use of the concept 'necessity' and for failing to give distinctively Christian guidance. The mounting frustration of Christians and non-Christians over the growth of nuclear arsenals and the waste of resources led to the founding of the Campaign for Nuclear Disarmament in 1958 under the chairmanship of Canon John Collins of St Paul's Cathedral. It called on Britain to declare that it intended to abandon the military use of nuclear power, and began its Aldermaston marches.

Those who had fought to defeat fascism had to define their attitude to another ideology, as the Soviet Union imposed communist governments across most of eastern Europe and blockaded Berlin, and in the Far East Mao Tse Tung established a People's Republic in China in 1949 and South Korea was invaded by communists from the North in 1950. By 1949 the Soviet Union had the knowledge to conduct atomic tests. Attitudes formed against fascism were now directed to the new threat. A balanced assessment of communism appeared in 1953. Edited by Donald Mac-Kinnon, *Christian Faith and Communist Faith* was heavily critical of communism's subordination of morality to the class struggle. However, it did not merely condemn communism, but attempted to understand it. At least communism did seek to uncover the dynamic of modern economics and had given its supporters hope within history. Several of the contributors recognized that in some respects Christianity had more in common with Marxist materialism than with the philosophical idealism which had been in the ascendancy fifty years before. For Christianity, with its doctrines of human nature, the Incarnation and the Resurrection of the Body, plainly took matter seriously and also gave a primacy to certain events in history. The connection with liturgy was drawn out by MacKinnon: 'It is by the action of the Eucharist that the life of the individual is in its daily movement rooted in and held to the source of its redemption, the action of Calvary and the empty tomb.' The materialist aspirations of Marxism could be met only by a faith which proclaimed a deed done in flesh and blood and offered a vision of cosmic redemption. The appearance of this book coincided with the death of Stalin. Within three years Khrushchev had exposed his tyranny, and though the west roundly condemned the suppression of the Hungarian bid for independence and neutrality in 1956, the tension between east and west gradually eased.

The first Assembly of the World Council of Churches was held at Amsterdam in 1948, the second at Evanston, Illinois, in 1954. Both continued the offensive against totalitarian communism, but allied this to a concern to mitigate the worst effects of *laissez-faire* capitalism and find a juster economic order. The umbrella concept of the 'responsible society' plainly reflected the outlook of Christians of the west. But in the 1950s membership of non-western churches grew apace, and it was significant that the third Assembly was held in New Delhi (1961). It was also at this Assembly that the Eastern Orthodox churches were welcomed to membership of the Council. Criticism of Communism became more muted, and attention focused much more on colonialism and neo-colonialism, and on racism and racial equality. The vivid writing of Trevor Huddleston in *Naught for your Comfort* (1956) and of Alan Paton in *Cry the Beloved Country* (1948) turned the spotlight on apartheid in South Africa.

When Arthur Michael Ramsey was enthroned as the hundredth Archbishop of Canterbury in June 1961, he singled out in his sermon, 'Whose Hearts God has Touched', three priorities: the quest for unity; 'greater freedom in ordering and in the urgent revising of our forms of worship'; and involvement of the Church in the community: 'We shall strive to penetrate the world of industry, of science, of art and literature, of sight and sound, and in this penetration we must approach as listeners as well as teachers.' Above all, the context for these pursuits should be 'a constant detachment, a will to go apart and wait upon God, in silence, lest by our very busyness we should rob ourselves and rob others of the realization of God's presence'.

In 1952 at Lund, Sweden, the third World Conference on Faith and Order had focused on what united rather than divided the churches, and propounded the principle that churches should act together in all matters except where deep differences of conviction compelled them to act separately. In 1964 the Faith and Order Conference of the British Council of Churches, held at Nottingham under the theme 'One Church Renewed for Mission', was sanguine enough to challenge the British churches 'to covenant together to work and pray for the inauguration of a union' by Easter 1980. The most promising area was Anglican–Methodist relations, where a report on the conversations published in 1958 had suggested two stages to full unity. The first stage would be inaugurated by a Service of Reconciliation, involving the integration by reciprocal action of the respective ministries, and the acceptance of episcopacy by the Methodists, provided that this did not imply any defect in their ministry and gave Methodists as much freedom of interpretation as Anglicans enjoyed. The second stage of complete union would follow within a generation. The two churches agreed to commission a body to clarify certain issues and draw up a detailed scheme, including a revised Service of Reconciliation and a common ordinal. The intention of the Service was that at the laying-on of hands every minister should receive whatever he might lack of the gifts and graces bestowed upon the ministers of the other Church. There was thus a deliberate and almost inevitable ambiguity over the significance of the laying-on of hands. Some Methodists already objected to the admission of a view of episcopacy and priesthood which would allegedly undercut the priesthood of all believers. Now Anglo-Catholics and Evangelicals attacked the ambiguity from diametrically opposite standpoints. In July 1969, though the Methodist Conference accepted the scheme by a small margin, the Church of England Convocations failed to reach the required 75 per cent majority. A further attempt in 1972 fell even further short.

One of the criticisms of the Anglo-Methodist scheme was that it was too much an affair of the higher echelons of the Church. A strong impetus to the development of ecumenism at a local level was given by 'The People Next Door', a study programme promoted by the British Council of Churches in 1967 'to test the relevance of the ecumenical insights in the local church situation'. It did much to increase understanding and friendship across denominational boundaries. In 1968 the Church of England voted to admit to Holy Communion communicant members of other churches who were in good standing – a practice long accepted among Nonconformist churches. There was also a growing tendency for joint churches among Nonconformists, and, in 1969 the Church of England joined in through the Sharing of Church Buildings Act. The British Council of Churches in 1969 published *The Designation of Areas of Ecumenical Experiment*, offering guidelines, and by 1973 all the main churches joined to set up a Consultative Council for Local Ecumenical Projects in England. Meanwhile the British Council of Churches was drawing together various renewal groups across the denominations – the Anglican Parish and People Movement, the Methodist Renewal Group, and a Baptist Renewal Group and Congregational Church Order Group – into a movement called ONE for Christian Renewal, whose members committed themselves to mutual acceptance, to renewal as a prerequisite for reunion, and to social witness.

Among the participants in the first Conference of ONE for Christian Renewal were some Roman Catholics, a sign of the immense change which had been brought about in ecumenical relations by the Second Vatican Council (1962–5), called by Pope John XXIII. A Secretariat for the Promoting of Unity among Christians was set up as part of the preparations, and after a visit to Rome in 1960 by Dr Fisher (the first by an Archbishop of Canterbury since 1397), a representative of the Church of England lived in Rome during the Council, which invited non-Roman churches to send observers with the right to make comments. Among the sixteen documents of the Council was a Decree on Ecumenism. Although it restated the exclusive claim of the Roman Catholic Church to be the source of the fullness of the means of salvation, it did positively recognize that all the baptized stood in a special relationship, enjoyed a common inheritance in the Scriptures, and a bond in the celebration of the Eucharist. In March 1966 Dr Ramsey visited the Pope officially as head of the Anglican Communion, and together they declared their intention to inaugurate dialogue which might lead to unity. This led to the establishment of an Anglican Institute at Rome and eventually to the creation of the Anglican-Roman Catholic International Commission (ARCIC) which first met in 1970, and a specifically English ARCIC (1974). The two communions begged to differ in their attitudes to birth control following Pope Paul VI's Encyclical *Humanae Vitae*, but this did not prevent the growth of cordial relations. In a set of essays prepared for the Lambeth Conference of 1968, *Lambeth Essays on Unity* (1969), Dr Ramsey set out principles of Christian unity, stressing that ecclesiastical negotiations were 'but a fraction of the total work of Christian unity, for it includes all that happens in the renewal of churches in holiness in worship, in theology, and in mission, and in the involvement of Christians with one another in this'. And the Roman Catholic Gregory Baum outlined the changes brought about by Vatican II, both in the acknowledgement of other Christian churches as ecclesial realities and in the affirmation of the collegial nature of the Church, and he endorsed the experience of the Ecumenical Movement that Common Prayer, dialogue and joint projects could lead to deeper self-understanding and to reinterpretation of doctrine in greater fidelity to the Gospel.

Another major document of Vatican II was the Constitution on the Sacred Liturgy, which in laying down guidelines for the reform of the Roman rites endorsed the insights of the Liturgical Movement. The liturgy is Christ's act, and the whole public worship is performed by the head and members of his Body. The laity are therefore to be actively engaged in the rite and be fully aware of what they are doing. To this end 'the rites should be distinguished by a noble simplicity. A warm love for Scripture should be promoted, and there should be more readings from Scripture in the mass.' Emphasis was also laid on the importance of the sermon. The fruit of this document was to be the *Missa Normativa* in the vernacular, which first appeared in English in 1969.

Liturgical revision proceeded apace in most denominations during the 1960s. The Church of England set up its Liturgical Commission in 1964, and the Prayer Book Measure of 1965 authorized experimentation with alternative services. Anglicans were soon offered three series in succession. The Methodist Church experimented with a new Sunday service from 1968, and approved a definitive version in 1974 which now appears in a single volume with other offices. Also in 1968 the Presbyterian churches in England and Wales produced a Service Book with three orders of Holy Communion. Here a formative influence was the experience of the Iona

Community, founded by George MacLeod, which has emphasized the primacy of worship as the mainspring of mission, and has followed the insights of the Liturgical Movement in clearly connecting sacrament and social justice. Among the Baptists, Ernest A. Payne and Stephen Winward compiled a manual of *Orders and Prayers for Christian Worship* (1960) which contained two orders for the Lord's Supper. They affirmed it was 'a departure from apostolic worship to celebrate the Lord's Supper infrequently, or to regard it as an appendage following another service'.

Ecumenical co-operation over worship also flourished in the 1960s. The Joint Committee on the New Translation of the Bible embraced almost all the denominations in Britain, including the Society of Friends, and the British and Foreign Bible Society. The *New English Bible* appeared in two stages, the New Testament in 1961 and the Old Testament and Apocrypha in 1970. It has taken its place alongside the older versions, the Roman Catholic *Jerusalem Bible* (1966) and *The Bible in Today's English Version* or the 'Good News Bible' (1976). In 1963 a Joint Liturgical Group was created, again representing most British churches, which published an agreed *Daily Office* (1968) and *Holy Week Services* (1971). A volume of essays published in 1965, *The Renewal of Worship*, revealed how much common ground there was among the group on the fundamental principles of liturgy and their application in public worship. Particularly striking is Stephen Winward's exploration of the relationship between the outward and the inward in worship, and the balance between hearing and seeing ('the ear-gate' and 'the eye-gate' as Horton Davies once put it). The longest essay (by the Presbyterian R. Aled Davies) explores the integral relationship of liturgy and mission. Another joint venture was the International Consultation on English Texts, which embraced the major churches throughout the English-speaking world, including the Roman Catholic. They produced for experimental use an agreed set of texts on the Lord's Prayer, the Creed, the *Te Deum*, and the congregational parts of the Communion service, in *Prayers we have in Common* (1970).

Good news is no news, and this ecumenical and liturgical work (much of it under the wise guidance of Dr R. C. D. Jasper) passed largely unnoticed by the public. It is however much more germane to the strength and vitality of the contemporary Church than the more ephemeral gambits which attracted the lion's share of media attention. The easing of international tension and the growing prosperity under the premiership of Harold Macmillan were partly behind the burst in religious questionings in the 1960s. Throughout the decade there was a spate on books on secularity. In 1939 T. S. Eliot had advocated a return to a Christian society as the only alternative to an ultimately pagan society. By 1963 D. L. Munby was pleading in *The Idea of a Secular Society* for the idea of a secular society, neutral, pluralist, tolerant, pragmatic, as more consonant with the way God deals with human beings than attempts to impose Christian ideals on the mass of society. To many there seemed to be no problem whatever in reconciling the Christian faith and the secular; indeed, what was the message of the Bible if it was not the abolition of the distinction between the sacred and the secular?

Public debate was fired by John Robinson's *Honest to God* (1963), partly because of his rash speculations and partly because by now he was Bishop of Woolwich. He rejected what he called a supernaturalist ethic, replete with absolute rules decreed by God 'out there', on the grounds that it could cut no ice with a secular society and was inconsistent with the teaching of Jesus. He drew on Paul Tillich to appeal to the claim of the sacred and the absolutely unconditional encountered in, with and under all finite relationships as their ultimate depth and meaning. The only absolute in Christian ethics was love, which he claimed had a built-in moral compass, enabling it to home in intuitively upon the deepest need of the other, and to allow itself to be directed completely by the situation. He thus offered an existentialist ethic for 'man come of age', using ideas from Bultmann and Bonhoeffer.

Robinson undoubtedly struck chords in a large number of people, and the mood of the whole decade was in favour of liberalization. Following the Wolfenden Report of 1957 the law on homosexuality was eased, and suicide and attempted suicide ceased to be criminal offences in 1960. The abortion law was liberalized in 1967, and by an act of 1969 irretrievable breakdown of marriage became the basic ground for a divorce petition, replacing the concept of a matrimonial offence. In the shaping of this legislation the churches contributed substantially through various reports, for example, *Ought Suicide to be a Crime?* (1959), *Abortion* (1965), and *Putting Asunder* (1966). It was generally only with hindsight that they realized that a secular society would exploit their best intentions, particularly over abortion and divorce.

The revolt against standards and conventions was particularly strong among the young, and there was a considerable growth of a counter-culture. Though this contained genuine elements of disenchantment with the materialism of the age, there is no doubt there were many casualties, especially through drug addiction. Christians closely involved with the exploited knew that a 'situation ethic' was no match for the exploiters. It was heavily criticized by a succession of writers for its lack of clarity, its preoccupation with sex, its utopianism and its individualism.

In religious education, the failure of the 1944 Education Act to produce a generation of Christian citizens precipitated a deep questioning of the aims of teaching religion. For a time it looked as if a liberal teaching about religion and handling of ethical issues would carry all before it, but by the time of *The Fourth R* (1970), produced by a commission chaired by Bishop Ian Ramsey, there was a concern that children should understand what it was like to adhere to a religion in all its facets, so that they could find for themselves a faith to live by. *The Fourth R* was concerned with the specific contribution of Christianity to education. Ramsey also promoted corporate approaches to ethical issues, involving people of various disciplines, experience and expertise. He played a leading part in bringing together clergy, doctors and others to study health and healing in an Institute of Religion and Medicine created in 1964.

Several Christians devoted their energies to working with drug addicts and the unattached. They detected in the counter-culture a search for an authentic spirituality. The trek east to sit at the feet of Indian gurus made Christians ask about the resources of the tradition of Christian spirituality. Kenneth Leech, who worked among drug addicts in Soho, saw *Honest to God* as 'the lowest point of collapse of the spiritual tradition' of Christianity. Through books such as *Soul Friend* (1977) and *True God* (1985) he has himself played an important part in the revival of an interest in Christian spirituality. Michel Quoist's *Prayers of Life* had a considerable vogue in this country from their publication here in 1963. There has been a renewed appreciation of the place of monastic communities in society, and large numbers have found inspiration in the treasures of the Eastern Orthodox spiritual tradition, mediated in particular by Metropolitan Anthony Bloom.

Particularly striking from the 1960s onwards has been the broadening of the outlook of English Evangelicals. A National Evangelical Congress at Keele in 1967 issued a statement which stressed the need for social responsibility, for ecumenical attitudes, and for a weekly celebration of the Sacrament as the central corporate service of the Church. For this historic shift in direction the chief credit must go to John Stott, Rector of All Souls, Langham Place. The series of Grove booklets has been one fruit of this movement.

At the close of the 1960s A. M. Ramsey's little book *God, Christ and the World* (1969) reviewed the theology of the decade. It had been an era without affection for past tradition or concern for a world beyond this. There had been a rejection of authority in morality, a dimming of the sense of history, and a belief in the omnicompetence of the technological sciences to explain human beings and serve their needs. Ramsey called for a recovery of the sense of transcendence and adoration. 'There is the danger of theology becoming assimilated to the world's wisdom in a false secularity . . . It is when we have lost the attitude of the worshipper, of awe and reverence in the presence of the Other, and when we have ceased to ask forgiveness for our sins, that the line has been crossed. It is on this line that the crisis for secular Christianity is located.' But Ramsey also lived by the advice of his enthronement sermon: 'There is the danger of theology becoming meaningless through not learning from the world which it sets out to teach.' The book ends with a plea for openness – openness not just to the contemporary, but also to the past and to the eternal. And 'nowhere more vividly than in the sacrament of the Eucharist do Christians find Christ through an openness to the past and to the present, to heaven and to the world . . . The Eucharist is a prophecy and a prayer for our coming to the vision of God and for the coming of God's reign in the world.'

In 1972 the Presbyterian Church in England and the Congregational Church merged to form the United Reformed Church. The fact that the union of two contiguous churches encountered such difficulties did not bode well for more far-reaching reunion. Following the merger the new Church proposed talks to discover how wider unity could best be fostered. The Churches Unity Commission (including the Moravians and the Roman Catholic Church) was formed in 1974, and issued a report, *Visible Unity in Life and Mission*, in 1976 containing ten propositions as an acceptable basis for continuing the search for unity. The responses of the churches revealed either outright rejection or deep internal divisions, or at best heavy qualifications in accepting; not surprisingly by 1982 the scheme had failed.

Meanwhile there have been many bilateral discussions between the churches, Protestant, Orthodox and Catholic. Perhaps the best known are the Anglican–Roman Catholic International Commission (ARCIC), which has produced agreed statements on the Eucharist (1971), ministry (1973) and authority in the Church (1976, 1981). These are gathered and elucidated in the final *Report* (1981). From the World Council of Churches has come the Lima text on *Baptism, Eucharist and Ministry* (1982) and the mass of Christians have been invited to share in the process of reception and enquiry.

Back in 1950 Leonard Hodgson wrote: 'It is only through personal intercourse that one begins to learn what other ways of holding and practising the Christian faith look like and feel like from within. It is only by learning that one can begin to understand them. And it is only by growth in such understanding that we can begin to find the way to that Church unity for which we hope and pray.' There is far more fraternization nowadays at the local level. Lent radio courses like 'What on Earth is the Church For?' (1986) have proved an important stimulus. Many have found denominational boundaries crumbling through participation in the charismatic movement. There has also been a growth in alternative churches to the mainstream, usually committed to social action and critical both of society and the existing churches, and there have also been many experiments in house churches and community living. Another recent phenomenon has been the growth of black-led churches, which have met the spiritual and cultural needs of Christians of Afro-Caribbean roots. The British Council of Churches (recently renewed as the Council of Churches for Britain and Ireland) has been involved in discussions with them, and many were involved in a three-year process of ecumenical consultation ('Not Strangers but Pilgrims') to see what patterns of common life and witness were called for.

A striking development in British society has been the growing tide of feminism. This fundamentally concerns the claim by women to a full recognition of their human dignity. They are highly critical of the way in which throughout history men have structured every aspect of society to ensure their dominance and women's subordination. There has been a good deal of theological backing for this movement. The implications for the place of women in the life of the Church are still being drawn, but the obvious focus has been women's ordination. Nonconformist churches have found no difficulty in the concept of women ministers, but the Roman Catholic and Orthodox churches adamantly oppose the ordination of women. The Church of England has unsurprisingly been racked by division – a situation complicated by divisions within the Anglican communion as a whole. The vote for the ordination of women to the Anglican ministry in November 1992 has inevitably not resolved this problem. Schemes for unity are therefore faced with an additional obstacle.

Most of the British churches have now completed a lengthy phase of liturgical revision. For example, in 1980 the Anglican Church produced its *Alternative Service Book*, which was definitive for the rest of the decade. While many have deplored the displacement of the *Book of Common Prayer* in most churches, and the alleged poverty of the language in the new rites, there are undoubtedly great gains. It is increasingly difficult to tell, without already knowing, which rite stems from which Church (or which church building one is in). This is not a testimony to universal mediocrity, but rather to the far-reaching dissemination of the insights of the Liturgical Movement, which are based not only upon extensive research into the history of the liturgy, but also on a deep pastoral concern for mission and the equipping of Christians for engagement with contemporary society.

The quality of the churches' social thought and action has generally been very high. Most of them now have boards of social responsibility which keep abreast of developments, draw on people with relevant experience, and produce reports which guide the response of the churches.

The churches have been deeply unhappy about the working of the

Abortion Act of 1967, but no attempt at substantial modification has yet succeeded. They have, however, been successful in staving off the liberalization of the law on euthanasia, not only through documents like *On Dying Well* (1975) but also through the loving care shown to the terminally ill in the hospice movement. There has also been a deepening understanding of the needs and capacities of the mentally handicapped. The churches have all wrestled with the problem of how to maintain a Christian insistence on life-long monogamous union and also show compassion to those whose marriages break down. *Marriage, Divorce and the Church* (1971) and *Marriage and the Church's Task* (1978) are two Anglican examples.

Race relations in Britain have been a major topic, and many churches now have special units on race. They supported the Race Relations Act of 1965, which created the Race Relations Board to hear complaints of discrimination and find ways of alleviating racial tension, and later the Act of 1976 by which a Commission for Racial Equality could act directly against discriminatory acts and speeches and ensure equality of opportunity. While superb work is done by the churches in very difficult situations, many Christians remain ignorant of it and of the latent racism in themselves. In society as a whole discrimination remains rife and the task is monumental, as Kenneth Leech's *Struggle in Babylon* (1988) shows.

The economic difficulties which followed the boom years of the 1960s have led to a wide range of responses from the churches to issues of industry, work, unemployment and leisure. Some have focused on job creation; others have diagnosed a technological revolution which will keep jobs at a premium, and are pioneering new lifestyles to take over from those associated with the dominant work ethic. The issues here have led to Christian critiques of economic systems. It is significant that contemporary industrial mission has been discussing its orientation, and tackling these wider structural questions while maintaining its practice of factory visiting.

The persistence of poverty and deprivation has attracted the attention not only of pressure groups but of church leaders. The Methodists launched their Mission Alongside the Poor before the Church of England produced the report *Faith in the City* (1985), which addresses itself to Church and nation. It asks critical questions about its own performance in urban priority areas and makes a large number of recommendations for a strategy for the Church, as far as possible on an ecumenical basis. The issues of the environment, nuclear power and nuclear weapons all figured prominently in Church discussions during the 1980s, largely because of the failure of governments to make any substantial progress. For the same reason the churches kept pressing the issue of southern Africa (both apartheid in South Africa and the policy of total security practised by the

South African government against neighbouring states). Particularly notable work has been done by CAFOD (Catholic Fund for Overseas Development) and the Catholic Institute for International Relations, which have drawn heavily on Pope Paul's encyclical on development *Populorum Progressio* (1967), and were very ably served until their deaths by the distinguished economists Barbara Ward and Fritz Schumacher.

A striking feature since 1979 has been the number of occasions on which the churches, including the Established Church, have been at variance with the Conservative government. Their stance on poverty and the inner cities, on nuclear weapons, on the Falklands service in St Paul's Cathedral, and on South Africa, have all brought sharp exchanges. The Conservatives themselves have enjoyed widespread support among Christians and powerful Christian voices have been heard within the 'new right'. However, much of their theology is very thin, and savours too much of the convenience of the well-to-do in a country of growing divisions.

On the whole the churches in England to-day, while they may exercise very little power in a highly secularized society, are widely respected. Their social concern is well informed, thoughtful and sometimes costly, their ethics no longer a captive of passing fashions but closely related to a deeper theology and spirituality. They are far more united than ever before, and if ecumenism still has difficult waters to cross, their common recovery in the field of liturgy gives them a solid craft for the journey. And if they are wise, they will not succumb to a careless amnesia, but cherish such wisdom as they have received during the upheavals of the last fifty years.

25

Religious Pluralism in Modern Britain

Paul Badham

ONE OF THE most striking features of late twentieth-century Britain is the extent of religious and ideological pluralism. There seems no longer to be any agreed consensus, or even a framework of reference within which such a consensus might be sought. In a democratic society, it seems axiomatic to many people that 'everyone is entitled to believe what they want', and that 'anyone's beliefs are as good as anyone else's'. In part, of course, such views are entirely appropriate. Freedom of religious belief is a freedom which was won at a heavy price in earlier ages, and the difficulties in the way of seeking to 'grade religions' are widely recognized. From an academic perspective one faces the lack of any generally agreed criteria. From the point of view of racial and ethnic harmony, or even simply as a matter of good manners and human sensitivity, it seems boorish even to suggest that grading religions might be possible. And yet it cannot be the case that all belief-systems are equally well founded, or that all moral systems are equally beneficial to human society. In principle evaluation ought to be possible, and from the perspective of eternity it must be. However, the point has to be acknowledged that in our present state we do not possess that perspective, and can only marvel at the diversity which is within our midst.

Some scholars suggest that the extent of religious pluralism is overstated, for all polls show an overwhelming majority of British people 'profess and call themselves Christian'. It is important not to ignore such self-descriptions, and I shall argue later that 'residual', 'folk' or 'diffusive' Christianity does significantly affect the structure of British life. However, for some judgements about religion it is more helpful to look at religious practice, and if we do this then the religious map of the British looks like this: non-churchgoing Christians 55 per cent; atheists or agnostics 27 per cent; churchgoing Christians 10 per cent; and religious non-Christians

8 per cent. If the way we behave is taken as reflecting what we 'really' think, then it might be argued that the lifestyle of the non-churchgoing Christian could have more in common with the lifestyle of the agnostic than with that of the devotee of another faith, while in terms of practice the worshipping Christian might have more in common with other worshippers than with contemporary secularists. On the other hand, if affirmations of belief are treated independently from practice of worship the situation becomes more complicated. For there is abundant evidence that some regular churchgoers, including clergy and ministers, have a thoroughly secular world-view, while many who never attend church affirm traditional beliefs, and indeed are anxious that state schools should teach these beliefs to their children. The situation is therefore exceedingly complex and any generalizations need to be treated with great caution. There does, however, appear to be evidence that a wide pluralism of belief and practice exists, but they do not necessarily overlap.

One useful starting-point for looking at the religious pluralism of modern Britain is to look first at the range of religious practice which exists among committed adherents of the various denominations and faith communities. Other contributors to this volume have discussed the recent history of the Established Church, mainstream Nonconformity and Roman Catholicism. My brief is with all that lies outside that range. This category will include the Independent, the Afro-Caribbean and the Pentecostal churches, the sects and new religious movements, and the non-Christian religions represented in Britain, including Jews, Muslims, Sikhs, Hindus and Buddhists.

The first point to make about the groups listed together under this head is that once one takes these groups into account, one has to change radically the verdict one might wish to give concerning the progress of secularization in modern Britain. If attention is confined solely to the traditional churches the picture is one of steady and, until recently, of seemingly inexorable decline. Numerous surveys have shown that from 1910 to 1970 both the Anglican and the historic Free Churches went into a spiral of decline. Roman Catholicism went against this trend with a record of steady growth until 1962, but since then it has suffered an annual decline which gathered pace after the proclamation of *Humanae Vitae* in 1968. Whatever statistics are chosen for the mainstream churches – baptism, confirmation, marriage, ordination, Sunday school membership, electoral roll membership or church attendance – all show a fairly steady downward drift, for more than than seventy years in the case of the Anglican and Free Churches and for approximately thirty in the case of Roman Catholicism. Most recently the figures appear to have stabilized, and there are some signs of new growth. But as a generalization, the history of religion in twentieth-century Britain makes depressing reading for any religious believer who confines his attention only to the mainstream Christian churches.

However, the secularization thesis looks very different if one looks more widely at the religious scene in Britain. The first consideration is that the new Free Churches are rapidly becoming in numerical terms at least as significant as the traditional Free Churches, if not more so. The second is that heterodox sects such as the Jehovah's Witnesses and Mormons are expanding rapidly. The third is that new religious movements, though attracting small memberships, are contributing in important ways to religious awareness through the dedication of their members. Fourth, Muslims, Sikhs and Hindus now represent numerically significant faith communities which are increasingly demanding appropriate recognition in public life, Buddhism is making converts and Judaism maintains its historic place within our society. Finally, we must note the continued existence of a diffuse Christian religiosity among the broad mass of the populace, even though this religiosity does not extend to church membership or attendance. Once these diverse groups are taken into consideration the estimate one forms of the place and future of religion in contemporary society is significantly changed.

According to the 1989 English Church Census the Free Church community in that year was comprised of the following percentages: Methodist 32 per cent, Baptist 16 per cent, United Reformed 9 per cent, Independent 23 per cent, Afro-Caribbean, Pentecostal and other Free Churches 20 per cent. Moreover, since the latter three categories have been steadily expanding over the past ten years while the traditional churches have declined, the census compilers extrapolated forward to the year 2000 and forecast that by then the new Free Churches would have overtaken the traditional ones in terms of their overall support and become the third largest 'denominational grouping' after the Anglican and Roman Catholic Churches. Since their membership is significantly younger than the membership of other churches, such extrapolations may be made with reasonable confidence on demographic grounds as well as on the assumption that present trends in attracting new members will continue.

The main characteristic of the new Free Churches as described in the census is that they are overwhelmingly evangelical, and within that category they are predominantly charismatic evangelical. In other words they stress the features of biblical certainty, moral order and religious enthusiasm which were the formerly the hallmark of the older Free Churches during their days of expansion in the late eighteenth and early nineteenth centuries. In fact, a church historian who surveys the present scene will have a strong sense of *déja vu*. During the eighteenth century,

'Old Dissent', the heirs of the ancient Puritan tradition who dissented from the imposition of the 1662 Prayer Book and were consequently 'ejected' from the establishment, became increasingly moribund. Their numbers dropped away, and their former enthusiasm waned under the influence of the Enlightenment. The historic Presbyterian churches and the Baptists of the Old Connexion began to fade away into Unitarian rationalism. By 1740 the future for Dissent looked extremely bleak. Then with the birth of Methodism and other kinds of evangelical revival, the 'New Dissent' emerged consisting of Methodists (Wesleyan, Primitive and Free), New Connexion Baptists, revived Congregationalists, Calvinistic Methodists in Wales and new Trinitarian Presbyterians linked initially to Scotland. These churches were primarily responsible for the thirty-fold increase in Nonconformist strength between 1740 and 1910. Now it seems that these churches themselves have lost momentum, and the baton has been passed to the new Independent, Afro-Caribbean and Pentecostal churches which appear to possess the expansionist dynamism, evangelical zeal and internal discipline which formerly characterized the churches they appear in many ways to be supplanting. Another, lesser, parallel is that it is only through the statistical surveys of the Marc Europe 'Prospects' series, culminating in the English Church Census, that information on the new developments has reached public consciousness.

Most Christian opinion in the 1950s and 1960s placed its hope in the Ecumenical Movement leading to Church unity and consequent renewal. It is ironical that the liveliest growth in Christian membership has come from outside this area, from churches characterized by a bewildering diversity of organization, and by a constant tendency to split and split again, and in many cases to function as entirely independent congregations working on their own. In particular it is notable that the United Reformed Church, which drew together Congregational and Presbyterian Churches in the one real instance of unification across a former denominational devide, has subsequently steadily declined (from 150,000 members in 1975 to 114,000 in 1989), while independent Congregational churches have been the most dynamic in the Free Church sector. The Congregational Federation, consisting of those which did not join the URC, expanded by 8 per cent between 1979 and 1989, the same percentage as the various Pentecostal churches. The Afro-Caribbean churches, consisting of 949 congregations in 164 separate mini-congregations, grew by 25 per cent, and the Federation of Independent Evangelical Churches by 46 per cent in the same period, while the largest growth came from the most disunited group of all, namely those churches loosely defined under the umbrella of the house church movement, which increased from 44,000 members in 1979 to 108,500 a decade later, a growth rate of 144 per cent.

A theologian whose intellectual formation was shaped by the 1960s might find these developments hard to understand. One had supposed that the way forward for Christianity was to modernize, and to seek for ways to articulate faith in terms which were more in accord with the intellectual life and thought of today's world. But what is distinctive of the new growth area is precisely that it is largely fundamentalist and treats as axiomatic patterns of thought which theologians from Bultmann onwards have assured us are no longer possible for people living in today's world. For the flourishing new churches not only accept almost totally a very traditional understanding of Christian doctrine, but have also revived such phenomena as exorcism, prophecy, speaking in tongues and the expectation of answer to petitionary prayer.

A readiness to accept doctrines which do not accord with those commonly accepted in the world of academia is even more pronounced when one moves beyond the frontiers of what would generally be recognized as Christian into the domain of the sects and new religious movements, and the even more diffuse world of 'the new age'. The largest and most rapidly growing sects are the Jehovah's Witnesses and the Mormons. Few homes are unvisited by enthusiastic members seeking to make converts. In the case of Jehovah's Witnesses, the convert will be expected to accept their very distinctive interpretation of the Bible and biblical doctrine, to believe in an imminent premillenial Advent, and to adopt a strictly disciplined way of life. In the case of the Mormons, the convert will be expected to accept the teaching of the Book of Mormon, which purports to give supplementary information concerning an American history of both the people of Israel and of Jesus Christ. The Mormon will also abstain from alchohol, nicotine and caffeine, and live a respectable and ordered existence. That the Jehovah's Witnesses' idiosyncratic interpretation of biblical texts, or the Mormon's beliefs about American history, lack any kind of supportive evidence has no bearing on the fervency with which their beliefs are held, or the change in life which accepting them brings about. In numerical terms, the Jehovah's Witnesses' membership doubled in the 1950s and the Mormons increased sixfold between 1957 and 1967. In both cases the progress of expansion continues unabated. In the *UK Christian Handbook for 1992* the Jehovah's Witnesses are credited with 116,612 members and the Mormons with 149,000. These figures place them almost in the same numerical league as major historic denominations; given a steady increase in the number of their full-time ministers and church buildings, their further growth seems very likely.

When we turn to the so-called new religious movements, the most surprising thing to be discovered by sociological research is that some of them are so small. According to Eileen Barker, 'The more successful of the alien, innovative, new religious movements gained a few hundred full-time members each.' The difference between media sensitivity and reality is most clearly evidenced by the case of the Unification Church (the Moonies). Throughout the 1970s and 1980s this sect was constantly making headlines in the press and television for its allegedly dramatic success in winning converts. These successes were credited in dozens of news stories as the product of a highly developed process of brainwashing which made the sect's appeal irresistible to the wavering convert. Yet at its peak the total British membership was only 570, far less than the membership of one successful mainstream congregation. There can be few evangelists who have ever had such poor results in proclaiming their message. It is therefore extraordinary that for a decade they were a media sensation for their work in this field, until the myth of Moonie brainwashing was demolished by detailed sociological study and first-hand investigation. The reason the Moonies appeared so formidable was the bewildering number of ventures the movement initiated. Their primary goal was presumably to win converts for the view that their Korean leader was really the Messiah or Christ, in his Second Coming, and to this end students were targeted throughout the higher education system. Their secondary aim was to seek to bring unity throughout the world. This goal was pursued by a succession of conferences on interfaith dialogue, on the unity of science and value, and the pursuit of world peace. Such conferences certainly encouraged a great deal of holistic thinking without necessarily advancing the wider aims of the sect itself, but the long-term effect of establishing such contacts remains to be seen.

The second most newsworthy sect was the Hare Krishna movement. This also has attracted substantial negative publicity for its activities. Its habit of soliciting contributions from travellers at airports and stations, together with its colourful robes, unusual hairstyles and habit of chanting an Indian mantra, have made it very noticeable. In reality it is a movement devoted to applying Hindu insights and practices to western life, largely as a product of western eclecticism drawing on a few Hindu traditions. Yet it has also more recently come to attract some younger members of ethnic communities who find in it a form of Hinduism in which they can participate without distancing themselves from their sense of belonging to the western world which they also want to embrace as part of their overall heritage. This dual role has significantly increased its membership to 50,000 which makes it, in terms of numbers, the most important of the so-called 'new religions'.

The public interest in these and other sects indicates one difficulty in talking about modern Britain as a secular society, namely that there appears to be a religious vacuum in the lives of numerous young people.

One of the most intriguing features in Eileen Barker's investigation of the Moonies was that virtually all who attended one of their workshops had recently tried to find help through one of the mainstream churches but had failed to find satisfaction there. Such failure is far more widespread than the tiny handful who do think they can find what they want in a new religious movement. A far larger number continue to search for truth and meaning in what is loosely referred to as 'the New Age movement'. In one sense there is no such thing, but the term remains useful to cover the spectrum of ideas and thoughts of a quasi-religious kind which manifests itself on shelf upon shelf of books, often classified as 'occult' by the bewildered bookseller. These books will discuss such things as 'the ancient wisdom', 'theosophy', 'reincarnation' and the 'paranormal'. In such works there is a sense that outside the traditions of Christianity, but perhaps from past paganism, modern parapsychology or exotic eastern religions, some vital truths may be rediscovered. This field is a fascinating new research area. I offer no assessment here except to say that we are far from being a secular society when such books proliferate in such numbers, and clearly outsell the more traditionally religious books, if displays in ordinary bookshops are any guide to actual demand.

One of the most important features of modern British religious and cultural life derives from the long-term impact of immigration from countries of the former British empire. On a large scale this began from the Indian subcontinent after the granting of independence in 1947 and the subsequent communal violence that followed, and from Jamaica in 1948. Thereafter, throughout the 1950s, massive immigration took place from many areas of the former British empire. The 1962 Immigration Act put a brake on the process, but the numbers of immigrants continued to rise throughout the 1960s as dependants joined the men who had gone ahead in search of work or safety. In the 1970s and 1980s the number of people of Commonwealth extraction grew primarily through births in Britain to earlier immigrants.

One impact we have already noted is the significant growth of the Afro-Caribbean churches. Essentially the existence of these churches is a sad reflection on the endemic racism of British society. Ninety-two per cent of the immigrating Jamaicans were Christian, and 54 per cent had been church attenders in Jamaica. Shocked by the hostile reaction they received from white Christians and depressed by what they saw as the lifeless character of normal worship, the immigrants set up their own churches which grew rapidly. The main leadership of these churches tended to be Pentecostal and drew in not only immigrants who had been Pentecostal before, but also other Jamaican immigrants who were attracted by the warmth and vitality of the worship which had far more in common with the 'black' worship of their own churches in Jamaica than the staid dignity of typical English worship.

Of even greater significance for religious pluralism in modern Britain has been the influx of people of other faiths from the Indian subcontinent, as well as people of Asian descent expelled from Uganda and Kenya. As a consequence of this there are now at least a million Muslims, 400,000 Sikhs and 300,000 Hindus in Britain. The significance of such figures can be seen if one thinks back to the 1989 English Church Census. On one reading of these figures, one could conclude that there were almost as many Muslims as Anglicans, as many Sikhs as Methodists, and as many Hindus as Baptists and Reformed put together. Such a reading would of course overstate the case, for it compares churchgoing figures on the one side with total figures on the other. Yet this is not wholly misleading, because for the ethnic minorities membership of a faith community is not the optional extra that it is perceived to be by the nominal Christian. Instead, membership of a faith community is for most Muslims, Sikhs and Hindus constitutive of both individual and communal identity. Moreover, whatever else may happen the relative proportion of the population committed to such faiths seems bound to increase simply on demographic considerations derived from the median age of the membership of the various groups and of the typical family size.

Buddhism differs markedly from all other non-Christian religions in Britain in that its primary impact comes not through immigration but through western conversions. Deirdre Green points out that there is some evidence that Buddhism is 'the fastest growing religion in Britain at the present time'. It must be admitted that this growth is from a small base. One hundred and twenty Buddhist centres does not compare with 39,000 Christian churches, and their total UK membership of 27,000 is half that of the Hare Krishnas. However, it is significant that Buddhism is increasingly attracting intellectual interest among both philosophers and theologians as well as the religiously minded but metaphysically sceptical inquirer. Don Cupitt explicitly described his own position at one stage as being a form of Christian Buddhism, and in the philosophy of mind, Buddha's denial of the substantial self has been seen as anticipating many of the insights of post-Wittgensteinian philosophy. In a department of religious studies, Buddhism appears to be the only other faith to exercise a significant intellectual pull on Christian or post-Christian students. As Deirdre Green comments, 'its relative lack of dogmatism and its emphasis on personal experience and experiment appeal to those who have become disillusioned with the institutionalized forms of Christianity and yet still feel a need for spiritual meaning and fulfilment'. However, Dr Green rightly goes on to question whether the interpretation of Buddhism that is being purveyed in the west represents more a 'selling out' of authentic Buddhist insights rather than a 'skilful means' of interpreting it to a new culture. For Buddhism in its historic form in unequivocally committed to a doctrine of rebirth and a transcendent understanding of reality. If western forms of Buddhism dispense with such belief, the question of their real continuity with the ancient tradition does arise.

Judaism differs from other non-Christian religions in being longer established in British life, and better integrated with structures of power and responsibility. It also shares with Christianity the phenomenon of a largely non-practising membership, with many who regard themselves as Jewish and yet adopt a predominantly secular world-view with little involvement in acts of worship other than the observance of rites of passage. The Jewish community, like other non-Christian religions, has greatly increased by immigration in the twentieth century, though in the Jewish case this happened at least two generations earlier than in that of Commonwealth arrivals. In 1880 there were 60,000 Jews in Britain. This rose to 300,000 by 1920 and to 450,000 today. The Board of Deputies of British Jews has long had a recognized voice in society, and there was widespread approval when the former Chief Rabbi was nominated to the House of Lords and his incoming successor was invited to give the Reith Lectures. Jews are well represented in Parliament, government and business, and integrated into the life of the whole community. Antisemitism, which was common in the 1930s, is now wholly repudiated, and there is a growing sense among many Christians that it is particularly inappropriate for a Christian to seek to convert a Jew away from his ancestral faith. This view was endorsed by the decision of the Archbishop of Canterbury, Dr Carey, in 1992 to withdraw his primatial patronage of the Church's ministry among the Jews, though his decision has been bitterly criticized by some members of his Church.

The growing strength of non-Christian religions in Britain has profound educational, cultural and social implications. Its most immediate impact has been in the world of education, because the impact of immigration in the 1950s and 1960s has produced a growing proportion of non-Christian school-age children in the 1970s and 1980s, many of whom are now moving on into the sphere of higher education. This will inevitably affect the nature of religious education and stimulate the trend towards neutral multicultural presentations of the various beliefs and practices of the world religions. This trend will not be reversed by government decisions that such education must be 'mainly Christian', because even if teachers themselves supported the policy (which increasingly they do not), teachers cannot deliver a policy of Christian nurture in a classroom environment where many, perhaps the majority, are adherents of non-Christian religions. It seems invevitable that such changes will also affect the structure of departments of theology and religious studies in higher education and the university world. An environment in which there are as many committed Muslims as committed Anglicans provides a context in which an exclusively Christian department of theology will be seen increasingly as an anachronism. On the other hand, if more committed Christians come forward from the new churches they will continue to need teaching in Christian theology, even if, in state-financed universities, such teaching may in future be given in departments featuring both theology and religious studies.

The changes that have been perceived in the world of education will also have an impact in the wider society as the proportion of second-generation members of ethnic groups grows. Those who entered Britain to seek employment tended to accept that they were entering an alien culture in which it was appropriate that they should not expect their own customs and laws to influence society. Those who are born in Britain will tend to have a much greater expectation that their values and ideals should be respected and protected. The 'Rushdie affair' is perhaps the first example of what may well come to be a recurrent phenomenon. In this instance Muslims insisted that society ought not to allow a work of blasphemous pornography to be directed against everything their faith holds most dear. In this particular instance their campaign did not succeed, but it has fired an important warning shot over the bows of those who believe that a free society can allow anyone to say anything. A pluralist society can flourish without hostility only if conventions of politeness and common sense protect the susceptibilities of significant portions of society. Just as it becomes increasingly accepted that anti-feminist and racist smears are unacceptable, so too it will need to become accepted that religious groups have a right not to be disparaged or insulted in a genuinely open and pluralist culture. In the world of multicultural and religious education, this is increasingly normative. It seems bound to become normative also in the wider world of the media and entertainment, though tensions are likely to exist permanently in such areas.

One such tension has of course already surfaced, and this is a tension within Christianity as how to respond to such diversity. In 1991, one-fifth of the clergy in England and Wales signed a petition opposing any coming together in worship between people of different faiths. According to the petitioners, 'Salvation is offered *only* through Jesus Christ' who is 'the only Saviour' and 'the only way to God'. According to this group, 'Interfaith relations is the issue of the decade.' If this view became common it would be clear that we were moving, not to a pluralist society of mutual toleration and understanding, but to a divided society of uncomprehending and antagonistic religious groupings. However, this outcome seems unlikely because the two thousand clergy who signed the petition can be contrasted with what may well be the majority Christian view which sees Christ as the Saviour of all, regardless of their attitude towards him or knowledge of him. In this inclusive vision other religions are viewed as partially correct in that they tend to have some points in common with Christianity. The third Christian response is that of theological pluralism, which sees all religions as a response to a single transcendent reality, though understood differently as a result of the influence of different human cultures and world-views. It seems likely that only if inclusivism and pluralism come to be accepted will society escape the tensions of religious antagonism and bitterness which have had, and continue to have, such serious consequences in so many human societies.

Inclusivist or pluralist responses seem to have gained substantial support from the managers and teachers of denominational Church schools. Increasingly they appear to be interpreting their modern role as helping to foster good relations between religions rather than remaining havens of a distinctively Christian culture. It is for this reason that many argue against the setting up of Islamic schools on the older denominational model, because these would almost inevitably be seen as a force for separating religious and ethnic groups, rather than as a means for preparing children for life in a multicultural and pluralist society.

The most common response in British society as a whole to the existence of growing religious diversity seems to be general acceptance on the grounds that religion is essentially a private matter for the individual or the individual's family or group. This viewpoint is influential in the secular world, which tends to see religion as a hobby for those who happen to like it. It is also influential in evangelical circles, which interpret Christianity primarily as a matter of a personal relationship with God through Christ. In so far as Christian growth today seems confined to the evangelical churches with this perspective, a privatized view of religion may well become increasingly dominant. Given that the sects tend to encourage withdrawal from an evil world, and that members of other religions in Britain characteristically avoid any kind of involvement in political or social issues, including voting at elections, this privatization of religion is further endorsed.

Such views, which Professor Moyser has shown to be very widespread, clash significantly with those Christian insights which see an important prophetic role for the Church as a living community and as the Body of Christ. Throughout this century Christian leaders such as William Temple or Robert Runcie have felt themselves compelled to speak out on social and political issues, and there is a long-established tradition of social critique in all the main churches. Political theology is a popular option in university departments, and the theology of liberation in Latin America is often held up as a model which should be followed by western thinkers. This tradition of prophetic critique was very much to the fore in the debates associated with the *Faith in the City* report of 1985, and indeed the Church of England under Robert Runcie and David Jenkins was widely perceived in the media as a significant locus of opposition to Mrs Thatcher's policies.

This does not, however, affect my argument on the essentially private nature of most religion today, since the majority of Christian believers distance themselves from the collectivized political stance of many church leaders. A comparison between attitudes towards the State and religious affiliation shows that majority support for the prophetic critique is to be found only in the category self-described as 'atheist or agnostic'. Professor Moyser comments: 'It is noteworthy that theologically inspired political dissent, with its illustrious line of ecclesiastical exponents, should in fact be most typically associated at the mass level with those most unsympathetic to traditional religious values'. In my own book *Religion State and Society* I argued that the *Faith in the City* controversy should be seen more as a symptom of unconscious secularism within the Church than as an application of theological insights to contemporary life.

So far this chapter has focused on the faith communities of modern Britain, and we have seen that diversity has become the norm. The Church of England is no longer the Church of the English people, but in terms of active membership ranks behind both Roman Catholicism and Nonconformity. We noted also that other major world faiths have numerical strengths which put them on a par with individual Christian denominations. This is a context quite different from that which has prevailed in the last thousand years and indicates a significantly new situation. However, this argument has not yet come to terms with the fact that many people in England and Wales do identify themselves with Christianity, without church involvement or participation. The English Church Census of 1989 claimed that 55 per cent of the population identified themselves as Christian believers but non-churchgoers, and indeed 47 per cent as Christian believers but as neither going to, nor being a member of, any Church. It is extremely difficult to know how to interpret such figures, and indeed significantly different results will be obtained by asking the question in different forms. George Moyser obtained much higher figures by asking not about membership or attendance but about 'belonging'. His questions related to Britain as a whole (England, Scotland and Wales, but not Northern Ireland). In 1979, 55.6 per cent claimed to 'belong to' one of the Christian churches when asked the question. 'Do you belong to any Church or religious group?' Of these, 31.2 per cent identified themselves as

Anglicans. In 1985 the question was put in the form. 'Do you regard yourself as belonging to a particular religion?' This drew a response of 73.2 per cent as belonging to the Christian religion, of whom 43.8 per cent were Anglican. What this tells us, of course, is not that there was a dramatic revival of Christianity between 1979 and 1985, but rather that more people are ready to identify with the Christian religion than with the Christian Church, even though the respondents were almost always ready in a supplementary answer to name a denomination as the locus of their religious identity. (Only 2.2 per cent of the adherents to the 'Christian religion' were unable to name a denomination through which their adherence was expressed).

Moyser suggests that focusing only on church attendance may be misleading, for, 'so far as being open to corporate religious influence and cues is concerned, the strength of an individual's denominational self-image might be just as significant as the number of times he attends a religious meeting'. Hence Moyser asked people claiming a religious commitment whether they felt 'very strongly, fairly strongly, not very strongly, or not at all, attached to people of the same religious background and belief'. He found that one-fifth described themselves as 'very strongly attached' and one-third as 'fairly strongly attached', which means that more than half the population were in one of these two categories. In other words, in terms of how people see themselves, half the population are fairly or very strongly attached to the Christian Church. Much more weight needs to be given to such findings if we are really to understand our present society.

For the past two hundred years many scholars have been aware of what they discuss as 'diffusive' or 'folk' Christianity. It is quite clear that this is still a significant factor in our present society. Christian beliefs and moral principles continue to enjoy widespread support, and in many and various ways non-churchgoers continue to see themselves as participating in the 'Christian religion'. Most parents of children at primary school will expect a nativity play, celebration or concert which they will be glad to attend. There is a widespread wish for religious education to continue and indeed to be definitively Christian. Strong public pressure for this influenced the drafting of the 1988 Education Act. At university level, applications and admissions for degrees in theology and religious studies have risen steadily, and the subject is increasingly becoming available in other areas of higher and further education. In terms of corporate worship, any national disaster will call forth a televised funeral or memorial service which prominent politicians will be expected to attend. A royal wedding or funeral will impose virtually a public holiday throughout the whole society. It is axiomatic that religious festivals, synods and controversies should be covered by television, radio and press. A bishop who makes a controversial comment on a major political or social issue will be reported throughout the media, and, as we have already noted, many people saw the Church of England under Runcie as offering an important focus of opposition to Mrs Thatcher's principles and policies. A significant proportion of the population want Christian baptism for their children and are genuinely wounded when their sincerity in asking for this is called into question. Weddings are very frequently religious events, and funerals almost always so. These factors all indicate a very much wider concern for Christianity than would be the case if churchgoing alone were considered as the sole criterion for Christian participation.

It is extrordinarily hard to know how one is to evaluate the validity of extra-ecclesial 'Christianity'. When a music society sings a Mass or an oratorio, is this in any sense a religious activity? Should the 10 per cent of the population who attend at least one carol concert during the Christmas season be included in the total number of Christmas worshippers? Yet for at least some, these events are at least as real as regular church attendance. Most difficult of all is to know how to evaluate television religion. The importance of this may be gauged by the fact that twice as many people will watch a Communion service on Sunday morning on television as will attend in person, and more people will watch *Songs of Praise* than *Match of the Day*. To some this cannot be considered to be a religious activity, but there is a real problem in saying why this could not be so, if the viewer perceives it to be so.

One problem with evaluating the secularity of our present society is that there has been a steady decline in all aspects of participation in public life. Societies of all kinds have lost ground steadily throughout the century as people's interests and concerns have become increasingly home-based. But this does not necessarily mean that their wider interests have been lost. Drama societies may have died out through lack of support, not because interest in good theatre has declined, but because the local amateur group cannot compete with the televised version. No one would suggest that there is little interest in politics today because few leave their homes to attend the meetings organized by their local political party. In part this may also be true of religion. At least some people watch televised services and talks because the standard is just so much better than what is available locally. This may show a misunderstanding of what it means to be part of the Body of Christ, but it could not be identified as equivalent to a wholly secular pattern of living.

On the other hand explicit atheism, genuine agnosticism and uncon- scious Secularism are significantly present in modern Britain. According to the English Church Census, 27 per cent identify themselves as atheists or agnostics. This is broadly similar to the 25 per cent 'no religion' response in Professor Moyser's survey, and we can safely conclude that approximately a quarter of the British do not believe in God. This atheism tends not to be very dogmatic, and some of it may even be churchgoing. Little anti-clericalism exists and correspondingly there is no longer any concern about the religious views of people in public life. Hugh Gaitskell's agnosticism was not widely known until after his death, but no secret is made of Neil Kinnock's, and in neither the 1987 nor the 1992 election was it considered an issue. It is also accepted as entirely appropriate that despite his scepticism he should attend public worship and join enthusiastically in the singing of hymns when a religious service is part of his expected role. In a way this highlights the present state of religion in modern Britain. By 1992 Britain (outside Northern Ireland) had become a pluralist society with a wide diversity of religious points of view. Those who are strongly committed can be found in a number of different religions, but there is a strong consensus that religion should be perceived as a private option which should not affect public life. When a public event such as a terrorist massacre or a royal wedding occurs, a religious ceremony should be held which is of as representative a type as possible to ensure maximum participation and goodwill. This does not mean that religion has ceased to matter, for it clearly does matter to many individuals. It is simply that the public response to religion has become pluralist and has come to place a premium on everyone living together in harmony and toleration.

26

Secularization and the Future

Alan D. Gilbert

IN *THE HERETICAL IMPERATIVE*, written in 1979, Peter Berger cited the 'debate over secularization' as evidence that students of religion were finding 'the present situation . . . hard to read, confusing, and full of contradictory possibilities'. He observed that 'Historians and social scientists find it hard to agree on what secularization has been in the past and on what it is today, let alone on what its future course will be.' Recognizing these conceptual difficulties as part of a wider problem, he added: 'The same goes for every other manifestation of modernity.'

Coming from one to whom it seemed, only a decade earlier, 'among the safest of sociological generalizations' that the process of secularization would continue, such remarks confirm that this chapter ventures into difficult territory. Empirical evidence about religion is always slippery. Experts differ not only about what counts as religious belief and behaviour, but also about the relative significance of different manifestations of religiosity. So to explore any aspect of religion raises problems at once theoretical and practical. Questions of definition are inevitable, and conclusions often must be regarded as tentative. These qualifications are especially pertinent in a chapter which attempts to understand secularization and to anticipate its future significance.

Etymology, which often provides illumination in the history of ideas, is a good starting-point for a study of secularization. Language echoes consciousness. Words and concepts etch themselves into the landscape of human discourse by meeting important cognitive needs, and this makes etymology at once an aspect of cultural history and a guide to the character and significance of cultural phenomena. The idea of 'secularization', rooted in the medieval Latin concept of the 'world', especially as opposed to the 'Church', has had a long history in the English language, but its meanings and nuances have undergone considerable evolution since the late thirteenth century, when the adjective 'secular' was first used simply to distinguish clergy living and working in the wider medieval world from 'religious' clergy who lived in monastic seclusion.

By the late fourteenth century, Wyclif was using both adjectival and adverbial forms of the word to distinguish institutions and functions concerned with temporal matters from others which were clearly religious or spiritual. By the sixteenth century, the noun 'secularization' was widely used in legal and ecclesiastical circles, where it described the transfer of a religious institution or its property to lay ownership or temporal use. Samuel Richardson still used it in this sense in *Pamela* in 1742. The narrow, legal boundaries of the concept were, however, by then being extended. 'Secularization' was being used to describe a certain kind of social or cultural reduction of religion. There had been a reference in 1711 to ministers of religion becoming ' "secularized" in their conversation', and in 1755 Samuel Johnson defined 'secularize' as 'to make worldly'. This secondary meaning became dominant in the eighteenth century, and as its narrow legal and ecclesiastical application was extended 'secularization' evidently gained a more general currency. In 1831 Robert Southey expected his *Quarterly Review* readers to understand a character whose 'worldly-minded husband might have secularized and deadened her heart'.

On the eve of the Victorian era the established usage of 'secularization' thus carried the notion of someone or something becoming less religious in any of a number of senses: the conversion of the clerical to the laic, the sacred to the profane, the sublime to the mundane, and so on. There was as yet no clear implication of a general social or cultural trend. 'Secularization' described certain regrettable vicissitudes in the unceasing struggle between the 'Church' and the 'world', but without implying that worldliness might be getting the upper hand. By the late 1830s, however, this important new element was beginning to attach itself to the word.

In a sermon preached at Chichester in 1842 the young Tractarian, Henry Edward Manning, warned his congregation that the temper of the age was increasingly irreligious. He referred to 'the secularizing action of worldly things' not as an ancient, familiar threat to spirituality, but as a prevailing tendency – a trend towards a more 'secular' culture. If his early Victorian audience found such a usage novel, theirs would be the last generation to do so. 'Secularization' was soon being used to describe a perceived decline of religious influences in art, literature, education, philosophy, ethics and culture generally, and William Lecky wrote in his *History of the Rise and Influence of the Spirit of Rationalism in Europe* (1878) of a 'general secularization of the European intellect'.

Victorian authors, publishers and readers were fascinated by the recurrent spectacle of devout men and women losing their faith, believers becoming unbelievers, people formerly religious ending up with 'secular' ways of understanding reality. In themselves, such instances did not point to a general decline of religion, any more than the existence of illness among some individuals necessarily implies that a society as a whole is becoming less healthy. But for the Victorians, loss of faith by individuals had begun to look less like normal, though regrettable, casualties in a healthy Christian culture and more like a spreading epidemic. They spoke of a crisis of faith. The 'supernatural Christianity' which traditionally had been the basis of European culture was 'certainly going', Matthew Arnold wrote in 1882. Herbert Spencer agreed. 'Now that moral injunctions are losing the authority given by their supposed sacred origin,' he argued in *Data of Ethics*, 'the secularization of morals is becoming imperative.' And as the century closed the Baptist theologian and preacher W. K. Clifford, evoking Nietzschean images, called his generation the first to have seen 'the spring sun shine out of an empty heaven, to light up a soulless earth', and to have 'felt with utter loneliness that the Great Companion is dead'.

'Secularization', as such people now used it, not only described this process, but implied an explanation. In the idea of secularization emerging during the Victorian period a perceived trend towards spiritual infidelity and apathy was linked inexorably to the nature of modern civilization. Modernity was seen as intrinsically secular, and 'secularization' as an aspect of 'modernization'. In a typical elaboration of this idea an Anglican clergyman, H. H. Snell, explained that 'unparalleled' advances 'in knowledge, in wealth, in invention, in convenience,' were creating a culture in which 'All our senses seem occupied to their fullest with momentous incidents of the *outer* world. But the most momentous incident after all is the evolution of the inner world of civilization. And the greatest question – how fares the soul of man in all this?' The answer, repeated in countless tracts, sermons, articles and private exchanges, was that the social, psychological, intellectual and material forces creating the modern world were somehow subversive of religious faith and spiritual devotion. Arnold, whose poem 'Dover Beach', written in 1851, had evoked the 'melancholy, long, withdrawing roar' of the sea of faith before the 'night-wind' of modernity, wrote later in *Culture and Anarchy* of Christianity as part of a traditional culture threatened by the spiritual inertness of modern civilization, a civilization already in the 1880s 'mechanical and external' and tending 'constantly to become more so'.

Among those dedicated to traditional orthodoxies and values, this understanding of modern society as intrinsically counter-religious, not just in its beliefs, values, symbols and rituals, but also in the basic cognitive processes through which knowledge and opinion were fashioned and evaluated, encouraged a religious reaction against modern tendencies. The Oxford Movement was, among other things, an anti-modern movement, as were various fervent sectarian bodies which subsequently broke away from the mainstream churches. Other Christians reacted to secularization by compromise. At once more liberal and more pragmatic, they concluded that religion could survive only by adapting theological beliefs to the inevitable realities of modern, secular culture. They accepted accommodations of the kind Charles Hennell anticipated in his pioneering *Inquiry Concerning the Origin of Christianity* (1838), which envisaged the future of religion in terms of a transition from 'Christianity as a divine revelation to Christianity as the purest form yet existing of natural religion'.

Both resistance and accommodation were, however, perilous paths. Resisting the norms and values of modernity threatened the more conservative elements within Christianity with increasing marginality, and even before the end of the Victorian era the dangers of accommodation were also apparent. In his *Theory of the Leisure Class* the pioneer sociologist, Thorstein Veblen, remarked that in religious bodies which had compromised traditional 'beliefs or observances' even the clergy were becoming indistinguishable from 'secular-minded persons' in the wider modern world. Secularization, in short, threatened either to marginalize religion or to subvert it.

As twentieth-century sociology built on the Rationalist principles of pioneers such as Comte, Spencer and Veblen, the Victorian idea of secularization was elaborated into a sophisticated social theory. A long-term decline of religion was implicit in Max Weber's understanding of modernization as a process involving rationalization, desacralization and disenchantment, and implicit also in the quite different sociological tradition of functionalist theory influenced by Emile Durkheim's *The Elementary Forms of Religious Life*. It also fitted readily into Ernst Troeltsch's theories of sectarianism and Marxist interpretations of religion as social and psychological compensation. The idea of secularization, although not initially the term itself, became a preoccupation of liberal theologians even before the First World War; and by the closing years of the Second World War, in Dietrich Bonhoeffer's later work, a call for 'religionless Christianity' could be coupled with an impressive understanding of how 'secularization' might be applied historically and sociologically as well as theologically. Throughout all such elaborations the link between secularization and modernization remained intact. One of the fundamental characteristics of 'modernity', Harvey Cox has concluded in a recent survey of modernization theory, is 'the trivializing of religion and the harnessing of the spiritual for patently profane purposes'.

Until around the end of the 1960s secularization theory remained entrenched as the conventional wisdom among scholars studying religion in modern societies. This was as true of scholars such as S. S. Acquaviva who, along with Weber, regarded with dismay the seemingly inevitable triumph of modern consciousness over traditional values and concerns, as it was for those who celebrated the spiritual and cognitive results of modernization, such as Bishop J. A. T. Robinson in *Honest to God* (1963), Paul van Buren in *The Secular Meaning of the Gospel* (1963), Harvey Cox in *The Secular City: Urbanization and Secularization in Theological Perspective* (1965) and Ronald Gregor Smith in *Secular Christianity* (1966). In one of the more depressing elaborations of the link between modernization and secularization, Acquaviva wrote in 1966:

> From the religious point of view humanity has entered a long night that will become darker and darker with the passing of the generations, and of which no end can yet be seen. It is a night in which there seems to be no place for a conception of God, or for a sense of the sacred, and in which ancient ways of giving a significance to our own existence, of controlling life and death, are becoming increasingly untenable.

It was at this time that, in much more neutral vein, Berger accepted the prospects for continuing secularization as 'among the safest of sociological generalizations'.

Even those unhappy about the conventional wisdom found the theory indispensable. David Martin, a leading English sociologist of religion, expressed irritation as well as scepticism about secularization in an article written in the mid-1960s. 'Towards Eliminating the Concept of Secularization', he called it. Yet Martin found his own advice hard to follow. When in 1969 he entitled a book *The Religious and the Secular*, he subtitled it 'Studies in Secularization'; and a major work he published nine years later was given the title *A General Theory of Secularization*.

Since the end of the 1960s, however, persistent theoretical and empirical queries have weakened the previously dominant position of secularization theory in the sociology of religion. American scholars have been in the vanguard of this reaction. Andrew M. Greeley's *Unsecular Man: The Persistence of Religion*, published in 1972 and reissued with a new introduction in 1986, trenchantly attacked the idea of secularization by arguing that what the theory portrayed as the diminution or marginalization of religion was nothing of the kind. What modernity produces, according to Greeley, is not the decline of religion, but its metamorphosis. 'The fundamental argument of this book has not changed,' he explained in 1986; 'people will need religion as long as they need meaning. Whatever may be their ultimate explanation for the meaning of life, that is their religion.'

Such attacks turn on questions of definition. Greeley feared that an uncritical acceptance of secularization was diverting scholarly attention

from contemporary evidence of religious growth and vitality. He pointed
out that in cases where religion was not so much 'disappearing' as
'relocating' itself in modern forms of cultural expression, definitions which
confined 'religion' exclusively to traditional types of belief and practice
could thwart proper investigation. Martin Marty, long an authority on
religion in modern America, has often made the same point. 'If used as a
paradigm rather than a hypothesis, secularization may pre-empt other
instruments and theories', he remarked in 1984, and leave an analysis
without the means 'to do justice to a variety of religious phenomena'. What
worried him particularly was the taken-for-granted nature of the paradigm
of secularization at a time of apparently increasing religiosity in America.

This argument is pertinent, but it works both ways. Greeley's inclusive
definition of religion subverts the idea of secularization, not on empirical
grounds, but by making it untestable, indeed meaningless, on *a priori*
grounds. An example of this theoretical subversion at work occurs in
Thomas G. Saunders's conclusion to *Secular Consciousness and National
Conscience* (1977), a report of a conference on secularization held in Rome
in 1976. 'Every world view or dominating concern,' Saunders wrote,

> whether it is transcendent or not, functions like a religion. That is, a
> person may have a dominating concern that shapes his thinking and
> action, which is his religion; or, if he has several such concerns, they
> constitute a form of secularized polytheism. Under such a definition,
> liberalism and Marxism are religions in that they constitute views of
> reality. Similarly, a belief in science or hedonistic consumerism can
> also be a form of religion. If we accept this reasoning, there is no such
> thing as a secular consciousness but only various forms of religious
> consciousness.

Serious obfuscation is almost bound to arise from this kind of analysis. The
easy identification of something which 'functions like a religion' with
religion itself begs a fundamental question about modern culture.
Certainly, if liberalism, Marxism and hedonistic consumerism are forms of
religion, then there can be 'no such thing as a secular consciousne'. But
that is a very important 'if'.

Redefinitions at odds with traditional usage, however valid in a logical
sense, are methodologically dangerous. This is especially true in the study
of history. The historian must respect past usage, for to use old terms in
new ways is to risk overlooking or misinterpreting patterns of change and
continuity over time. A definition of 'religion' which precludes the idea of
secularization on *a priori* grounds, for example, fails to respect a broad
stream of European intellectual history predicated, in ways often vague but

none the less influential, on the idea that religion has been declining in the face of modernity. 'But it seems that something has happened that has never happened before: though we know not just when, or why, or how, or where,' T. S. Eliot wrote in 'Choruses from *The Rock*'. 'Men have left God not for other gods, they say, but for no god; and this has never happened before.'

It is precisely because Eliot is only one of a large number of intelligent observers of modern society who have thought the same thing, that the idea of secularization has been so influential. In Britain and Europe particularly, the decline and marginalization of religion have struck them as so obvious, so important, as to require explanation. Such observers may of course be mistaken. Pessimism about the state of faith and morals has had advocates in every generation. So the historian must turn, as always, to an examination of the evidence. Like any other hypothesis, secularization must stand or fall on empirical grounds, but certainly not on the *a priori* expedient of defining 'religion' so inclusively as to make the very notion of decline meaningless.

We should therefore place less weight on Greeley's theoretical argument than on Marty's concern about the empirical evidence against secularization which he and other scholars have observed, particularly in modern American society. If secularization is a concomitant of modernity, religion presumably should have lost ground in modern America as well as in modern western Europe. Yet traditional forms of religion have proved remarkably durable in the United States, and even more problematical for the hypothesis secularization is the modern revival of conservative Evangelicalism in the 'born again' movement which has been a feature of American life in the 1970s and 1980s. Marty referred in 1984 to a survey conducted in 1977–8 by the American Institute of Public Opinion. It discovered that more Americans than ever – perhaps one in six of the total population – were claiming to have been 'born again'. American religion seemed to be thriving. In the words of Edwin Scott Gaustad, one of the most prolific of American historians of religion: 'Fundamentalism has scored many successes and may stand on the verge of many more. The airwaves are filled, and the coffers too, with radio and television versions of fundamentalism. Publishing houses, bookstores, and best-seller lists testify to its power.' The strident voice of the Moral Majority and kindred interests give the most persuaded exponent of secularization good reason to reconsider the theory in the context of American culture.

It is therefore interesting for scholars concerned primarily with British religion to note that despite a decade and a half of reappraisal, and in the midst of such buoyant religiosity, American scholars continue to find the idea of secularization illuminating. First, there is little in the persistence of mainline American religion, or in the American commitment to 'civil religion', to undermine the theory. In his classic study, *Protestant–Catholic–Jew*, published in 1955, Will Herberg wrote:

> So thoroughly Secularist has American religion become that the familiar distinction between religion and secularism appears to be losing much of its meaning under present-day conditions. Both the 'religionists' and the 'secularists' cherish the same basic values and organize their lives on the same fundamental assumptions – values and assumptions defined by the American Way of Life.

As its title implied, *Protestant–Catholic–Jew* argued that the accommodation of America's major religious bodies to the increasing secularity of modern culture had produced a generalized religiosity so expurgated of specific dogmatic content or traditional theological differentiation that an American's particular religious commitment scarcely mattered. Protestants shared with Jews as well as with Catholics a common allegiance to what Herberg called 'a secularized religion embracing the great mass of the American people.' He may have qualified the argument had he been writing a couple of decades later, but he would not have had to abandon it.

When in 1985 Robert Schuller, host evangelist on the American television *Hour of Power*, commissioned a Gallup survey of the values, religious beliefs and theological knowledge of Americans, he saw the results as evidence that 'organized religion has failed in its mission in many ways.' Gallup discovered, among other things, that while 81 per cent of Americans classified themselves as 'Christians', only 42 per cent believed that Jesus was divine 'in the sense that he was God living among men'. Similarly, American Catholicism, stronger than ever in institutional terms, has recently been confronted with a report from a Catholic researcher, John Deedy, which has been called 'a long inventory of "horror stories" of religious ignorance'. The American Catholic Church at present has 7.5 million young Americans under religious instruction, Deedy observes, 'But the fact seems to remain that by old catechism measurements the church is raising up a generation, if not of religious illiterates, then of individuals with a bare knowledge of the details of [Catholic] doctrine.' The English religious commentator, William Oddie, observed recently that the papacy has no alternative but to oppose many aspects of American Catholicism. Reporting on the papal visit to the United States in September 1987, Oddie wrote that conflicts between Pope John Paul II, concerned about 'the secularization of values' in American Catholicism, and 'ordinary [American] Catholics, more sophisticated than the run-of-the-mill Catholics in less "advanced" countries', were central to the fate of religion in the modern world. Like Dutch Catholicism, he said, Catholicism in America had failed to resist 'the absorption by secular values which has overtaken most liberal Protestant churches'.

If American evidence is to subvert secularization theory, then, it is likely to be the evidence of the conservative evangelical revival. Yet there is a sense in which both the *raison d'être* and the success of this revival depend on an evangelical vision of 'modernity' as a pernicious, counter-religious force. Indeed, while using it to explain recent scholarly doubts about the validity of secularization theory, Martin Marty himself called the religious conservatism of the past twenty years 'resurgent antimodern religion'. It was also in such terms that William McKay and George Barna, both 'born again' believers, recently interpreted the revival. In *Vital Signs: Emerging Social Trends and the Future of American Christianity*, they reported, with candid surprise, research findings indicating that even very conservative elements of Evangelical Protestantism exhibit attitudes and values highly secularized in comparison with traditional Christian beliefs and values. They arrive at conclusions expressing concern about the 'superficiality' of an apparently buoyant movement.

A more neutral observer, W. W. Wagar, one of America's leading historians of religion, remains convinced that secularization theory makes sense in an American context. There is much that is exceptional in American religious culture, he wrote in 1982, but 'the American experience is unique only in the way that secularization has occurred, and not in the thing itself'. Similarly, George A. Kelly, contributing to an important recent symposium, *Religion and America: Spirituality in a Secular Age*, notes Thomas Luckmann's much-quoted view that 'traditional church religion was pushed to the periphery of "modern life" in Europe while it became more "modern" in America by undergoing a process of internal secularization'. He concludes: 'This seems to me correct.' And despite his uncertainty about 'what secularization has been in the past and . . . what it is today', Berger himself remains able to discuss the revival of 'born again' Christianity in America in classical Weberian terms linking the ideas of secularization and modernization. 'Evangelical Protestantism', he wrote in 1984, 'is the closest we have on the American religious scene to barbarism. There is something barbaric about this kind of religion, in the sense of unsophisticated, raw, grounded in folk culture, and really not yet very much assimilated into modern, sophisticated universal discourse.' Thus even in the society which offers the most obvious contemporary evidence against secularization, much informed opinion continues to support the idea that a modern culture has proved hostile to traditional religion, and that where traditional religiosity succeeds it is as part of an anti-modern reaction within the wider culture.

British Christianity has been much less obviously influenced by a resurgence of 'unsophisticated, raw', popular evangelicalism, but there have been echoes of the American revival, and a comparable trend for theologians and church leaders, as well as sociologists and historians of religion, to use the idea of secularization with greater subtlety, and perhaps rather less confidence, than they did twenty years ago. There was a tone of considerable optimism, for example, in the response of Church leaders to the census of English religion carried out in 1979 by the Nationwide Initiative in Evangelism, and published by the Bible Society under the title *Prospects for the Eighties*. Peter Brierley, the Bible Society's programme director, noted that while the census had shown that the great majority of the English people were 'outside the regular influence of the churches', it also revealed 'an improving situation rather than a deteriorating one'. Gavin Reid of the Church Pastoral Aid Society thought that 'the size and "survivability" of Christianity in England is surely the main conclusion to be drawn from these figures'.

The figures might, however, easily have been viewed more pessimistically. The survey of 74 per cent of the Christian congregations in England showed that in an adult population growing by 0.5 per cent per annum, church membership was falling by 0.4 per cent annually while church attendance was also declining. In absolute terms, 46,000 fewer Anglicans and 108,000 fewer Catholics were attending church in 1979 than had done so four years before. The Methodist and United Reformed Churches had suffered even greater losses. Two things, however, made the authors of *Prospects for the Eighties* relatively optimistic. First, the overall rate of decline was slower between 1975 and 1979 than it had been in the first half of the 1970s; and second, some of the smaller, more Evangelical churches were actually expanding.

Both trends need to be placed in broader perspective. In Britain almost half the adult population, and fully three-quarters of younger people, never go to church at all. About one person in five attends perhaps twice a year. Only one person in ten attends regularly, whereas about half the population did so 140 years ago. In the long ensuing period of secularization, the most sustained decline has occurred since the end of the Second World War. The available evidence does not, moreover, indicate that more private forms of religious observance have replaced public worship. The electronic media have not provided a new conduit for the Christian message. Audiences of religious programmes on radio declined by two-thirds in the decade after 1945, and by a further 50 per cent in the 1960s. If the rise of television was a factor in this decline, its own religious programmes were equally vulnerable. The BBC television morning service on Sundays attracted in 1970 only 40 per cent of the viewing audience it had in 1963, and the programmes themselves were bland and devoid of either theological content or proselytizing zeal. As Charles Moore, editor of *The Spectator*, put it in 1987: 'Religious programmes are not based on the assumption that religion is true but just that it is interesting.' The head of BBC religious broadcasting, John Whale, confirmed that this was a matter of policy. 'There won't be televangelism on the BBC because the BBC isn't in the persuasion business,' he said. The more popular Independent Television Authority was even less likely to expand its religious broadcasting, having discovered in the 1960s that ratings doubled as soon as religious programmes ended.

Evidence about religious belief and devotion also indicates continuing secularization. In 1981 the Gallup organization discovered that only 13 per cent of the British public saw Britain as a Christian society, and only 23 per cent regarded the eclipse of Christianity as the dominant culture as 'bad in any way'. When asked in 1967 whether they considered 'religion as a whole' to be 'increasing its influence on British life or losing its influence', fewer than one person in ten surveyed had answered that the influence of religion seemed to be increasing. Two-thirds of the sample said religion was declining. Evidence about changing patterns of belief since 1967 supports this majority view. The proportion of Britons believing that Jesus was the Son of God declined only slightly between 1967 and 1981, Gallup discovered; but in 1981 only 36 per cent of the population accepted the existence of a 'personal God', a finding indicative of the extent to which there had been a secularization of traditional theological concepts. Moreover, by 1981 the proportion of the population willing to affirm that Jesus was 'just a man' had reached 31 per cent, almost twice the level of fourteen years earlier. The proportion denying the existence of the devil had risen meanwhile from 46 per cent to 73 per cent.

Such figures, coupled with evidence of continuing institutional decline, make it difficult to find, either in the development of the wider culture or in the performance of the major churches, any sign that the decline of Christianity since the Victorian era was beginning, in Reid's optimistic words, to 'bottom out' around 1980. Nor does the evidence available for the years since the appearance of *Prospects for the Eighties*. The Methodist Church lost almost 30,000 members, 6 per cent of the total, in the three years after 1981. An official report on Church Statistics to the Church of England General Synod in 1983 noted that numbers of full-time diocesan clergy were falling, and that new candidates for the stipendiary ministry, 605 in 1980, fell to 566 in 1981 and 541 in 1982. On confirmations the report noted: 'After a levelling out, and indeed a slight upturn, in the late 1970s, there has been a fall in the numbers of confirmations in 1981 and 1982 for both sexes and all age groups.' Its authors added bravely: 'It is too early to judge whether this is a temporary phenomenon or whether it is a renewal of the long-term trend of earlier years.' In other cases the continuation of a century-long decline was certain. The United Reformed Church, the product of a merger in 1976 of already declining denominations, saw its membership fall from 161,691 in 1981 to 136,000 in 1986, and its full-time ministry reduced from 1,747 to fewer than 1,000 in the same short period. The Catholic Church in England and Wales was also continuing to shed clergy, with numbers falling from 7,409 in 1981 to 6,768 five years later. Such figures scarcely justify even the qualified optimism with which the decade began.

It was not, however, in these major denominations that the authors of *Prospects for the Eighties* had found most hope. Despite his qualified optimism, Reid had admitted that 'these figures reveal that we are still in a spiritual drought in this country', but (evoking the Old Testament story of Elijah) he continued: 'I also believe that they reveal a little cloud coming up from the sea. The life-giving rain may well be coming. God knows, we are thirsty enough.' He was alluding to the fact that in the five years before 1980 the Pentecostal churches in England had been growing at 2.3 per cent per annum, while Open Brethren, house churches and Independent Evangelical churches had maintained annual growth rates of 5 per cent. While the leaders of the larger denominations readily attributed their problems to the secularization of the wider society, the Pentecostal theologian Julian Ward found in the 1979 statistics evidence 'that the Pentecostal and Holiness church groups have the capacity to make the Gospel meaningful within our secular culture'.

Yet the questions remain: Meaningful to whom? Meaningful in what way? For what Berger and others have observed about resurgent evangelicalism in America – that it is 'unsophisticated, raw' and 'not yet assimilated into modern, sophisticated universal discourse' – is entirely consistent with secularization theory. Perhaps, on a lesser scale, the same phenomenon is apparent in English society. Because there is no thoroughly 'modern', 'secular' culture anywhere in the world, in every culture there will be those estranged from, or at odds with, modern, secular values, beliefs, assumptions and expectations. The Pentecostals had 850 congregations totalling about 88,000 attendants in 1979, the Open Brethren were of comparable size and the house church movement was considerably smaller. Their successes had not offset the decline of the larger denominations, and much of their membership growth (Reid speculated in *Prospects for the Eighties*) had come not from the conversion of outsiders as much as from the transfer of more conservative believers from the mainstream churches.

So the secularization hypothesis holds. This kind of religious scenario might have been predicted long ago on the basis of Weber's classic understanding of the nature of religion and its fate in the modern world. As Arnold explained in 1882, the religion of pre-modern and early modern Europe was 'supernatural Christianity'. Of course, not everyone in such societies had been a sincere and literal believer. Because Christianity had been normative and coercive we can take it for granted that religious activity historically had been sometimes merely nominal and perfunctory; and despite pressures to conform, there is unmistakable evidence of the existence of scepticism and irreligion in pre-modern societies. Nevertheless, the normative culture from which irreligious people deviated had depended profoundly upon belief in the supernatural, and upon reliance on supernatural agencies to meet the exigencies of human existence. Works like Keith Thomas's *Religion and the Decline of Magic* make it difficult to argue seriously with Arnold's view.

If some kind of supernatural orientation is inherent in the idea of 'religion' as historically understood in Christian cultures, it is also present in the contemporary common understanding of the word. This is why sociologists of religion anxious to explore belief systems in secular cultures sometimes use such terms as 'religious surrogates' or 'functional equivalents of religion' to refer to the mundane preoccupations or thoroughly this-worldly 'isms' which frequently hold sway over human emotions in modern secular societies. It is also why the general public frequently is nonplussed or critical when secularized versions of Christian theology receive publicity. Thus when Bishop J. A. T. Robinson told readers of *Honest to God* that there was nothing supernatural about religion, that 'God' was simply the essence of human existence, and that traditional orthodoxy was based on myths and superstition, it became clear that many people rejected as patent nonsense the very definition of 'religion' which he implied. 'He says religion isn't necessary – it's all phoney,' was how an Anglican clergyman paraphrased the popular reaction. The philosopher Alasdair MacIntyre was blunter. 'What is striking about Dr Robinson's book,' he said, 'is first and foremost that he is an atheist.' There was a similar furore twenty years later following the appearance of David Jenkins on Thames Television's *Credo* programme. Jenkins had recently been nominated for the bishopric of Durham, and the Archbishop of York received a petition bearing 14,000 signatures from people who refused to accept that a man who denied the central supernatural tenets of Christianity should be given high office in the Church.

So a proper definition of 'religion' gives centrality to the idea of the supernatural mainly because only by so doing does it capture the authentic cultural meaning of the concept. Modern liberal theology was simply not 'religious', the *Daily Telegraph* remarked in a leading article in December 1985 prompted by the report *Faith in the City* presented to a current meeting of the Church of England General Synod. The key question, the newspaper said, was whether the document

> owes anything at a fundamental level to a supernatural understanding of human life, and whether or not precisely the same conclusions might not have emerged from a meeting of the British Humanist Association . . . The problem is whether or not such documents owe anything whatsoever to a specifically Christian understanding. Producing biblical quotations in support of secular arguments proves nothing.

It is no accident that the exclusive definition of 'religion' here implied makes the idea of secularization at once plausible and testable, for the very word 'secularization' evolved to describe perceived changes in the role and significance of religion as traditionally understood.

Max Weber called the world of so-called primitive cultures an 'enchanted garden' world. He meant that the 'breaking points' in human consciousness – the crises at which natural, empirical, mundane explanations fail to cope with human experience and understanding – are so ubiquitous in such a world that all aspects of life seem to involve supernatural, capricious forces and therefore to evoke 'religious' responses. The Weberian concept of *modernization* implied a theory of *secularization* precisely because Weber saw the making of the modern world as a process of rationalization and disenchantment. A modern culture is a garden 'disenchanted', even (it must be emphasized) for people who remain deeply religious.

There is still no better insight into why human beings are religious than that contained in the ancient biblical story of the Garden of Eden. Unlike sub-human species, human beings respond to their environment consciously and reflectively, not just instinctively. Able to stand back from their involvement in nature and see themselves objectively, they confront questions about the meaning, significance and morality of life, and aspire to know, to understand and to control their destiny in the world around them. But the very consciousness which generates these godlike aspirations also brings painful awareness of the relative ignorance, ignobility and powerlessness of humankind, and tells of the seeming brevity and triviality of mundane existence. In this profound tension between consciousness and creatureliness, 'flesh' and 'spirit', religiosity has its roots. The temptation to be godlike, the semitic story implies, is as old as the human race, but the fruit of the Tree of Knowledge is the realization that humans are vulnerable and limited. Thus if consciousness carries with it a sense of the infinite, self-consciousness brings awareness of inescapable finitude, and produces a profound hunger for some kind of transcendent knowledge, power and authority to bridge the gap between human attainment and aspiration. Religion enters human culture as human beings turn to the supernatural to find salvation from this essentially human failure to be godlike. It provides answers to questions otherwise unanswerable, promises power where human knowledge and ingenuity are exhausted, gives hope beyond human optimism, certainty beyond human powers of prediction, life (in some cases) beyond physical death.

So understood, religion operates at one or more of a variety of cultural levels. It has *cognitive* significance when natural phenomena are explained with reference to supernatural forces; that is, when supernature is made a basis for understanding and knowledge. But humankind has often sought transcendental power as well as transcendental knowledge. So religion also has *instrumental* significance. People turn to the supernatural to control or manipulate the natural order, seeking, perhaps, bounty in harvest, victory in war, recovery in illness or safety in an unpredictable world. Yet even people who have lost confidence in religion as a *cognitive* or *instrumental* factor in this world may remain deeply 'religious' at another level. For religion also can have a profound *expressive* significance, offering perhaps the only widely satisfying means of symbolizing and legitimating the hopes, fears and aspirations of individuals and social groups.

Distinctions such as these are vital in any analysis of a perceived decline of religion. 'Secularization' describes processes through which human consciousness and activity become increasingly 'secular' rather than 'religious'. But 'becoming increasingly secular' may involve one or more of several possible reductions of religious commitment. In terms of the understanding of 'religion' just adumbrated, secularization includes anything leading people to think and act without recourse to the supernatural, or encouraging them to understand their environment more exclusively in terms of natural causation, or to manipulate it more exclusively through physical agencies, human institutions and empirical logic. Secularization can therefore operate differently at different levels; indeed, the *expressive* significance of religion may actually increase during a period when religious faith is playing a greatly reduced role at the *cognitive* and *instrumental* levels. This has not, in fact, been the case in modern Britain, but it may be the case in modern America. What Robert N. Bellah calls 'civil religion' may continue to flourish, perhaps indefinitely, in a cultural climate resulting in the secularization of cognitive and instrumental activities.

Several important conclusions follow from this analysis. First, *secular-*

ization is a complex process, operating in different ways in different contexts.
Just as the decline of religion has not been a single, uniform process, so
secularization is not a simple social theory. The reappraisals of recent years
have been valuable. Introducing a recent major study to which many
leading sociologists of religion contributed, Phillip E. Hammond has
written of secularization: 'Scholars do not – and probably cannot – doubt
the essential truth of the thesis. But increasingly they are coming to doubt
its adequacy . . .' It would be slightly more precise to say that while
scholars probably cannot doubt the essential truth of the thesis, they are
coming to appreciate the complexity of the changes it addresses.
Furthermore, there are many valid and important perspectives on
contemporary religion which need take no cognizance of its decline or
metamorphosis under the influence of modern beliefs, values and
assumptions. When it comes to understanding the relationship between
religion and modernity, however, it is not the adequacy of the theory which
is the problem but the tendency, less frequent now than in the past, for
secularization to be regarded as something one-directional, irresistible and
irreversible.

The reality is that both religion and secularization are complex matters,
involving many sub-activities which are only partially interdependent.
Beliefs may persist, at least for a time, in the absence of the rituals and
practices which traditionally reinforced them, and without the emergence
of new, alternative rituals and practices. On the other hand, beliefs may
atrophy long before rituals and symbols they originally generated have lost
significance. Similarly, private devotions may survive while public
religiosity lapses, and the reverse is also true. Such cautionary remarks are
entirely consistent with the perception that religion – and secularization –
can operate at different cultural levels, perhaps even advancing on one level
while retreating on another.

Second, *secularization can never be anything other than a partial process.*
A modernity involving a complete 'autonomy of man and the world' is a
hypothetical social and cultural model, not a description of any imaginable
reality. There is not, nor in principle ever could be, a thoroughly
modernized society, because in a world where accident, uncertainty and
mortality hold sway, the inexplicable and the arbitrary will always preclude
a complete rationalization and disenchantment of the ways human beings
understand their natural and social environment. While ever there are
'breaking-points' in human understanding and control in the universe,
there will be room for religion, and where recurrent crises in human
confidence occur, and anti-modern reactions spread, religion will regain
some of its lost ground. Conversely, however, as long as the progress of
knowledge and technology provide increasing capability for humankind to

control the material environment, secularization will remain the primary long-term process in the history of religion in modern societies.

Third, *the impact of secularization on a culture is segmental rather than general.* Julian Ward was wrong to interpret the recent growth of Pentecostal and Holiness Churches as evidence of a 'capacity to make the Gospel meaningful within our secular culture'. The key word is *within*. The most likely prospects for the 1990s in Britain appear to involve the continuing decline or marginalization of those religious bodies seeking to operate *within* the secular culture, and considerable – but strictly limited – success for movements such as Pentecostalism which operate *outside* the values and assumptions of the modern, secular world.

Such a prediction must be understood in relation to the complexity of the process of secularization recognized above. For churches seeking 'relevance' by accommodation with the secular culture the future holds various possibilities. Institutional decline may slow as accommodation continues to reduce tensions between religious and secular commitments, for a drift away from secularized religious associations, when it occurs, must reflect apathy rather than any positive alienation. Indeed, a fairly secularized religion may achieve in Britain what it has retained in America – considerable expressive significance. It may serve, in a world of hasty, impersonal associations and urban anonymity, as a focus for community sense. It may continue to offer important, if residual, contact with traditional values. And even after traditional supernatural underpinnings have faded, Christian symbols and rituals may still provide the most fitting way to mark life's important rites of passage.

Sectarianism will continue to ebb and flow. As existing sects become institutionalized and begin to make their own accommodations with the wider culture, new, more pristine movements will replace them. In his classic analysis of modernization, Weber predicted that conservative elements within traditional cultures would maintain a 'heroic resistance' to the norms and values of modernity, and religious sectarianism has always been among the most effective vehicles for these anti-modern reactions. In Britain, influenced by an international Catholicism tied increasingly to 'third world' constituencies and other societies relatively little touched by modernization, the Catholic Church may opt for a sectarian orientation to the wider secular culture. Rashid Mufti, a Catholic academic sociologist and delegate to the National Pastoral Congress, recently advocated such a course. In a paper on 'Organization and Renewal' he wrote: 'Today, perhaps more than in other times, the Church as the *whole* people of God must be a 'sign of contradiction' in the world. Among those disillusioned, for whatever reasons, with the values and tendencies of modernity, or denied what they see as a fair share of its material rewards, sectarianism of all kinds will continue to find converts. A finding in *Prospects for the Eighties* that recent converts to Pentecostalism were drawn mainly from lower middle- and working-class social groups is consistent with this well-established analysis.

Finally, *secularization is not necessarily irreversible*. Counter-modern tendencies within modern cultures create or expand constituencies for traditional types of religiosity. As they wax and wane with the underlying confidence of the modern culture, such tendencies introduce cycles of resurgent religiosity as a secondary pattern within an overall process of secularization. But what if the modern culture actually collapses? Secularization certainly does not persist in the kind of post-modern culture which fundamentalist Islam has created in Iran and elsewhere in recent years.

'Desecularization' is a scenario for the future which has fascinated theologians and sociologists of religion in the 1980s. In 1983 the British Council of Churches produced a paper entitled *The Other Side of 1984: Questions for the Churches*, which sought to prepare Christians for a post-modern world. Its thesis was that 'we are nearing the end of the period of 250 years during which our modern European culture has been confidently offering itself to the rest of the world as the torch-bearer for human progress'. A long period of secularization, it argued, was about to end in an impending crisis of 'modernity'. More recently, William Oddie has edited a similar work for the SPCK entitled, significantly, *After the Deluge: Essays towards the Desecularization of the Church*. In the Introduction he wrote: 'If one thing is certain, it is surely this: that whether in the East or in the West, the world's "advanced" industrialised cultures, built on the belief that man could control his environment and his destiny, have come to the end of their belief in themselves.' He and his fellow authors called on the churches to return to a bold, uncompromising supernaturalism to meet the 'intense and growing uncertainty, even despair' of the 'post-modern' age.

The prospect of a fundamental 'crisis of modernity' is scarcely something to be welcomed, except perhaps by the most fearless, uncompromising adherents of other-worldly supernaturalism. For the values, attitudes, assumptions and knowledge underlying the growing 'autonomy of man and the world' generate not only secularization, but also the entire modern industrial civilization without which the earth could support only a fraction of its current population. The turmoil precipitated by the fundamentalist revolution which has reversed the secularization of Iranian Islam would be nothing in comparison with the cataclysm necessary to effect a major desecularization of modern western societies. Indeed, the kind of demodernization which would radically reverse the process of secularization might prove catastrophic for civilization as a whole.

In Britain, if, as is likely, secularization continues, an important consequence will be the gradual eclipse of Christianity by non-Christian traditions whose natural constituencies in the society lie in ethnic and class groupings least assimiliated into the modern culture. By 1987 perhaps a third of the Britons who practised their faith were Muslims, not Christians. Their population growth, coupled with the intensity of their commitment to Islam and the effectiveness of their family and community controls over the socialization of their children, virtually guarantee Muslims a rapidly improving position among British religious communities in the decades ahead. Yet it is a measure of the ubiquitous nature of secularization that Muslim leaders in Britain already perceive and fear its effects. In a leading article on 'Islam in Britain', *The Times* warned such leaders that they 'must not force their communities to live too inwardly, nor to indulge in the ignorant fantasy – as encouraged by the rhetoric of some Islamic axe-grinders overseas – that Western culture is somehow spiritually barren'. Plausible and sensible no doubt, this was also the voice of secularization. More significantly, so was the voice of Dr Zaki Badawi, chairman of the Council of Mosques, who had spoken a week earlier of the inevitability of a Muslim adjustment to British society. Over time, he said,

> The position of women will become different, more liberalised. We shall lose our suspicion of science and technology, fears which hold back so many Muslim nations. We shall acquire the idea of democracy, the clever balance of responsibility and freedom; we shall learn such skills, the lack of which means most of our world is governed by dictators.

Doubtless he was right. Like the flourishing Christian sects, Islam will in the long run be unable to avoid compromises with its secular environment. But the process is bound to be slow. In the second half of the 1980s a highly defensive Muslim subculture is still actively encouraging resistance rather than compromise with the host culture.

'The outstanding non-event of modern times', Paul Johnson wrote recently, 'was the failure of religious belief to disappear.' To say that is to misunderstand the decline of religion in modern societies, for secularization is not simple, one-directional, irresistible or comprehensive. In the great transformation of human culture in modern times, secularization has been among the most profound of developments. At present, as at all other periods in history, the future remains open, beckoning and threatening with a range of probabilities and possibilities. Yet the fact remains that in societies such as Britain, demodernization and desecularization are much less likely prospects for the future than a scenario in which the influence of religion continues to be eroded by secularization.

Chronology

61	Destruction of temple at Colchester by the Iceni under Boudicca
c.166	Church built at Glastonbury
c.304	Martyrdom of St Alban
314	British bishops at Council of Arles
c.432	St Patrick made bishop for Ireland
c.450	St Ninian's mission to Picts
429	St Germanus visits Britain and confronts Pelagianism
c.500	Monastic foundation at Tintagel
c.550	St David's mission to Wales; Gildas' *History of Britain*
563	Columba settles on Iona; dies 597
597	St Augustine preaches in Kent
617–54	London lost to Christianity
627	St Paulinus baptizes King Edwin at York
c.630–47	Mission of St Felix in East Anglia
c.635	Start of mission of St Aidan in Northumbria from Lindisfarne
c.657	St Hilda founds Whitby Abbey; abbess until 680
664	Synod of Whitby accepts Roman date of Easter
669–90	Theodore, Archbishop of Canterbury
681–6	Kingdom of South Saxons converted by St Wilfrid
685	Foundation of church at Winchester
687	Death of St Cuthbert
c.695	*Lindisfarne Gospels* produced
718	St Boniface starts his mission to the Rhineland
731	Bede's *Ecclesiastical History of the English People*
782	Alcuin joins Charlemagne's court
793	Lindisfarne sacked by the Vikings
c.800	St Andrew's tomb shrine
807	Iona finally abandoned after raids of 795
c.866	Destruction of the great library at York
871–900?	Alfred sustains Christianity in Wessex
943	St Dunstan founds Glastonbury Abbey; leads revival of monasticism with Oswald, Archbishop of York 972–92
973	Edgar crowned King of England by St Dunstan

*c.*993	Aelfric's *Lives of the Saints*
1014	Wulfstan's *Sermo Lupi ad Anglos*
1062–95	St Wulfstan, Bishop of Worcester
1070–93	St Margaret, wife of Malcolm III of Scotland
1093	Rebuilding of Durham Cathedral
1093–1109	St Anselm, Archbishop of Canterbury
1107	First Welsh bishop, Urban of Llandaff, to make allegiance to Canterbury
1128	First Cistercian house in England at Waverley
*c.*1131	Gilbertine order founded by Gilbert of Sempringham
1147–67	St Ailred, Abbot of Rievaulx
1154	Nicholas Breakspear elected Pope as Adrian IV
1160	Building of new cathedral at St Andrews begins
*c.*1167	English scholars at Paris migrate to Oxford
1170	Martyrdom of Becket
1190	Richard I joins the Third Crusade; massacre of the Jews at York
1208–13	Papal interdict imposed on England
1209	Some scholars from Oxford move to Cambridge
1213	England a papal fief
1215	Fourth Lateran Council; Magna Carta
1221	Dominicans in England
1224	Franciscans reach England
1250	Canonization of Margaret, Queen of Scotland
1289	Bull forbidding foreigners to be appointed as heads of religious houses in Scotland
1290	Expulsion of the Jews from England
1312	Order of the Templars expelled from England
1326–49	Richard Rolle lives life of a hermit at Hampole near Doncaster
1351	Statute of Provisors
1373	Revelations of Dame Julian of Norwich
1370s	John Wyclif preaches at Oxford, withdraws in 1381 and dies in 1384
1393	Statute of Praemunire
1400–15	Owain Glyndŵr rising in Wales
1401	*De Heretico Comburendum*, first burning of a Lollard
1412	Foundation of university at St Andrews
1413–33	Margery Kempe on pilgrimage
1437	Walter Bower's *Scotichronicon* completed
1441	Foundation of King's College, Cambridge
c. 1455	Introduction of the Observant Franciscans to Scotland
1472	First archbishopric in Scotland established at St Andrews
1480s	Franciscans and Dominicans in Scotland gain independence from the English province
1494	Bishop Elphinstone founds King's College, Aberdeen
1499	Erasmus' first visit to England

1510	Publication of the *Aberdeen Breviary*
1525	Tynedale's *New Testament* in English
1527	First attempt by Henry VIII to obtain a divorce
1528	Patrick Hamilton burnt for heresy at St Andrews
1531	Execution of Thomas Bilney for heresy
1533	Thomas Cranmer appointed Archbishop of Canterbury (to 1556); Henry VIII secures divorce
1534	Act of Supremacy
1535	Execution of Thomas More and John Fisher
1536	Suppression of smaller monasteries; Pilgrimage of Grace in the north
1538	Royal Injunctions authorize Bible in English; Henry VIII excommunicated
1539	Suppression of larger monasteries; Act of Six Articles
1543	Scottish Parliament passes Act permitting reading of Scripture in vernacular
1547	Dissolution of the Chantries
1549	First *Book of Common Prayer*; clerical marriage permitted in England
1552	Second *Book of Common Prayer*
1553	Accession of Mary Tudor and restoration of Roman Catholicism
1553–8	Many leading English Protestants choose exile, principally in Strasbourg, Zurich and Geneva
1555	Re-enactment of *De Heretico Comburendum* and revival of persecution of Protestants; burning of bishops Hooper, Latimer and Ridley and other, humbler victims
1556	Burning of Cranmer
1556–9	John Knox in Geneva
1559	Elizabethan Settlement, Acts of Supremacy and of Uniformity establish Protestant Church order; Knox returns to Scotland where reformers destroy the abbey church of Scone
1560	Reformed Calvinist Church approved in Scotland; First *Book of Discipline* drawn up; Geneva Bible published in English
1563	English edition of Foxe's *Book of Martyrs*; the Thirty-Nine Articles passed in Convocation, approved by Parliament in 1571
1566	Archbishop Parker's *Advertisements* result in conflict with radicals over vestments
1567	First Welsh *New Testament*; Separatist congregation meet at Plumbers' Hall, London; Presbyterianism established by Act of Parliament in Scotland
1568	Catholic seminary for priests to work in England founded at Douai
1569	Rebellion of the Northern Earls
1570	Excommunication of Elizabeth I by Pope Pius V
1572	Thomas Cartwright's *Admonition to Parliament*

1574	First Roman Catholic missionary priests enter England; Andrew Melville returns to Scotland from Geneva
1576	Archbishop Grindal refuses to suppress prophesyings and is suspended from office until his death in 1583
1577	Execution of Cuthbert Mayne
1578	Second *Book of Discipline* published; endorsed by General Assembly in 1581
1581	Legislation against priests; execution of the Jesuit Edmund Campion
1582	Robert Browne's first separatist tract published; *New Testament* in English published by the Catholics from Rheims (*Old Testament* published 1609)
1583	Archbishop Whitgift's Three Articles against the Puritans
1587	Execution of Mary Queen of Scots
1588	The Spanish Armada
1588–91	Puritan *classes* established in midlands and suppressed by the Court of High Commission
1592	Presbyterianism officially established in Scotland
1593	Legislation against separatists; execution of John Penry; First four books of *The Laws of Ecclesiastical Politie* by Richard Hooker published
c.1595–1620s	Separatist churches in exile in Netherlands
1598	First Catholic archpriest appointed
1603	James VI and I, union of Crowns of England and Scotland
1604	Hampton Court Conference between bishops and Puritans; Ecclesiastical Canons promulgated by Archbishop Bancroft
1605	Gunpowder Plot
1606	Imprisonment of Andrew Melville in London, and subsequent exile
1610	Episcopacy restored in Scotland
1611	Authorized Version of the Bible
1616	Henry Jacob's semi-separatist Church returns to England
1618	The Synod of Dort; Declaration of Sports issued in England; The Five Articles of Perth passed by General Assembly
1620	Mayflower takes first Puritan settlers to the new world
1623	Jesuits establish separate English Province
1624	Publication of Herbert of Cherbury's *De Veritate*
c.1625	General Baptists have rudimentary organization in England
1632	George Herbert's *Country Parson* published; Catholic chapel opened for the Queen in London
1633	William Laud becomes Archbishop of Canterbury; Book of Sports re-issued
1634	Trial of William Prynne before Star Chamber
1637	King and Laud attempt to impose Prayer Book on Scotland
1638	National Covenant formed in Scotland

1639	First Bishops' War
1640	Long Parliament; Root and Branch petition; Archbishop Laud imprisoned
1641	Abolition of the High Commission; bishops excluded from Parliament
1642	Outbreak of war between King and Parliament
1643	Westminster Assembly of Divines; Solemn League and Covenant
1645	Execution of Archbishop Laud
1646	Abolition of episcopacy in England and Wales; itinerant ministry of Vavasour Powell begins
1649	Execution of Charles I
1650	First use of term Quaker for George Fox; Blasphemy Act; adultery made a capital offence
1651	Hobbes's *Leviathan*
1652	Readmittance of the Jews to England
1653	Barebones Parliament
1656	Richard Baxter's *Reformed Pastor*
1660	Restoration of the monarchy and the Church of England
1661	Savoy Conference between bishops and Presbyterians
1662	Act of Uniformity; over 2,000 clergy refuse subscription and remove from Established Church
1664	Conventicle Act
1665	Five Mile Act
1672	Declaration of Indulgence
1673	Test Act
1674–81	Welsh Trust for the Propagation of the Gospel in Wales
1675	Rebuilding of St Paul's cathedral begun; completed 1716
1678	John Bunyan's *Pilgrim's Progress*
1678–81	'Popish plot' and Exclusion Crisis
1679	Defeat of Covenanters at Bothwell Bridge; murder of Archbishop James Sharp of St Andrews
1682	William Penn gets charter for Pennsylvania
1682–1700	Emigration of over 2,000 Welsh Quakers to Pennsylvania
1685	Accession of James II; Catholics in England organized into districts under vicars-general
1687	First Declaration of Indulgence
1688	Trial of the Seven Bishops; James II flees
1689	Act of Toleration; non-jurors, including eight bishops, refuse oath of allegiance to William and Mary
1690	Locke's *Essay Concerning Human Understanding*; Convention Parliament establishes Presbyterianism in Scotland
1698	Society for Promoting Christian Knowledge established
1701	Society for the Propagation of the Gospel established
1704	Foundation of Queen Anne's Bounty

1707	Act of Union of England and Scotland; Isaac Watts' *Hymns and Spiritual Songs* published
1709	Impeachment of Henry Sacheverell
1712	Last witchcraft trial in England (Scotland, 1722); Patronage Act in Scotland
1713	Occasional Conformity Act
1715	Jacobite rebellion
1723	Trial and condemnation of Francis Atterbury
1726–9	John Wesley at Oxford, forms the 'Holy Club'
1731	Griffith Jones establishes 'circulating schools' in Wales
1733	Seceder Church breaks from Scottish National Church
1735	John and Charles Wesley undertake mission to Georgia
*c.*1737	Welsh revival begins, led by Daniel Rowland and Howel Harris
1738	John Wesley's Evangelical 'conversion'
1739	John Wesley's preaching ministry begins
1741	Wesley employs lay preachers; George Whitefield establishes a chapel at Moorfields, Bristol; Richard Challoner leader of Catholics in London District
1742	Scottish revival starts at Cambuslang and Kilsyth; first performance of Handel's *Messiah*, in Dublin
1745–6	Jacobite rebellion
1748	Hume's *Essay on Miracles*
1753	Hardwicke's Marriage Act
1761	Relief Church formed in Scotland
1768	Methodist seminary established by Countess of Huntingdon at Trevecca House
1778	First Relief Act for Catholics
1779	Posthumous publication of Hume's *Dialogues concerning Natural Religion*
1780	Sunday school movement established in Gloucester; Anti-Catholic Gordon riots in London
1784	Wesley makes provision for the continued existence of the Yearly Conference of the People called Methodists
1791	Catholics allowed to license places of worship; death of John Wesley
1792	Religious disabilities of Episcopalians in Scotland removed
1794	William Paley's *View of the Evidences of Christianity*
1794–5	Thomas Paine's *The Age of Reason*
1795	London Missionary Society founded
1799	Church Missionary Society founded
1790–1830	Era of the Evangelical Clapham Sect
1800	Act of Union between England and Ireland and the Established Churches of England and Ireland
1802	William Paley's *Natural Theology*
1804	Foundation of the British and Foreign Bible Society

1807	Slave Trade Abolition Act; Methodist Camp Meeting at Mow Cop
1808	Foundation of Royal Lancasterian Institution (later the British and Foreign School Society)
1809	Foundation of the London Society for Promoting Christianity among the Jews
1811	Formation of the Primitive Methodists; foundation of the National Society for Promoting the Education of the Poor in the Principles of the Established Church
1813	Unitarian Relief Act
1815	Formation of the Bible Christians by William O'Bryan
1816	Foundation of St Bees Theological College
1818	Foundation of Serampore College and the Church Building Society
1818 and 1824	Church Building Acts give a million and half a million pounds in government grants
1819	Foundation of the Methodist Missionary Society
1820	Union of Scottish Old and New Light Churches to form the United Secession Church
1822	Foundation of Lampeter College
1826	Foundation of the University College, London; first conference on prophecy at Albury Park
1827	Publication of John Keble's *Christian Year*; secession of the Protestant Methodists from the Wesleyan Connexion
1828	Repeal of the Test and Corporation Acts; House of Commons resolution on African equality
1829	Third Catholic Emancipation Act; foundation of King's College, London
1830	Fall of Tory administration; return of Whigs
1831	Opening of Exeter Hall
1831–2	Slave revolt in Jamaica
1832	First Reform Bill; beginnings of Edward Irving's Catholic Apostolic Church; foundation of the University of Durham
1833	Church Temporalities (Ireland) Act; Keble's sermon on 'National Apostasy'; publication of the first 'Tracts for the Times'; Slave Emancipation Act; death of William Wilberforce
1835	Appointment of Ecclesiastical Commission; secession of the Wesleyan Methodist Association from the Wesleyan Connexion; foundation of Robert Owen's Association of All Classes of All Nations; formation of the Board of Deputies of British Jews
1836	Established Church Act; registration and Marriage Acts introduce civil marriage; Tithe Commutation Act; death of Charles Simeon; new Anglican diocese of Ripon
1838	Pluralities and Non-residence Act

1839	Foundation of the Cambridge Camden Society
1840	Dean and Chapter Act; foundation of the Roman Catholic *Tablet*
1841	Condemnation of Newman's *Tract 90* and the ending of the 'Tracts for the Times'; profession of first Anglican Sister; foundation of the *Jewish Chronicle*
1843	Nearly a third of the ministry of the Church of Scotland secedes to form the Free Church, under the leadership of Thomas Chalmers
1844	Nonconformist Chapels Act protects Unitarian endowments; publication of W. G. Ward's *Ideal of a Christian Church*; foundation of the British Anti-State-Church Association, later the Liberation Society; Nathan Adler becomes the first Chief Rabbi
1845	Secession of John Henry Newman to the Roman Catholic Church
1845	Exeter surplice riots
1846	Foundation of George Jacob Holyoake's *Reasoner*; famine in Ireland; Irish immigrants flood into Britain
1847	Union of the Secession and Relief Churches to form the United Presbyterian Church; new Anglican diocese of Manchester; death of Thomas Chalmers
1848	Foundation of the Devonport and Wantage Sisterhoods
1849	Secession of the Wesleyan Reformers from the Wesleyan Connexion
1850	Restoration of the Roman Catholic hierarchy in England and Wales with Nicholas Cardinal Wiseman as first Archbishop of Westminster; 'no popery' furore over 'Papal Aggression'
1850–1	Anti-ritualist riots in St Barnabas, Pimlico
1851	Ecclesiastical Titles Act (repealed 1871); foundation of the Clewer Sisterhood
1851	Secession of Henry Edward Manning to the Roman Catholic Church (Archbishop of Westminster 1865–92; Cardinal from 1875)
1851	Religious Census
1852	Revival of the Convocation of Canterbury
1853	F. D. Maurice dismissed from King's College, London; renaming of the British Anti-State-Church Association as the Society for the Liberation of the Church from State Patronage and Control
1854	Prosecution of George Anthony Denison; definition of the dogma of the Immaculate Conception
1854 and 1856	Abolition of student subscription to the Thirty-Nine Articles at Oxford and Cambridge
1855	Foundation of Jews' College and of the East Grinstead Sisterhood

1857	Divorce and Matrimonial Causes Act abolishes ecclesiastical jurisdiction over divorce; union of the Wesleyan Reformers and the Wesleyan Methodist Association to form the United Methodist Free Church; foundation of the Universities' Mission to Central Africa
1858	Jews admitted to Parliament
1859	Evangelical revival; publication of Charles Darwin's *Origin of Species*
1859–60	Anti-ritualist riots in St George's-in-the-East
1860	Publication of *Essays and Reviews*; foundation of the English Church Union
1861	Revival of the Convocation of York; dedication of the first Anglican deaconess; publication of *Hymns Ancient and Modern*
1862–3	Publication of Bishop Colenso's *Pentateuch and Book of Joshua Critically Examined*
1863	Foundation of the *Church Times*
1864	Judgement of the Judicial Committee of the Privy Council for Rowland Williams and H. B. Wilson of *Essays and Reviews*; consecration of Samuel Crowther as missionary-bishop; Syllabus of Errors issued by Pius IX
1865	Foundation of the Salvation Army by William Booth; of the Protestant Church Association; of the Cowley Fathers; of the China Inland Mission; negro insurrection in Jamaica; Judicial Committee of the Privy Council finds for Colenso
1866	Foundation by Herbert Vaughan of the Mill Hill Fathers, and of Charles Bradlaugh's National Secular Society
1867	First Lambeth Conference (with 76 bishops)
1868	Church Rates Abolition Act
1869	Disestablishment of the Church of Ireland (effective from 1871)
1869–70	First Vatican Council; definition of papal infallibility
1870	Forster Education Act; Jewish United Synagogues Bill
1871	University Tests Act abolishes religous tests for academic office at Oxford, Cambridge and Durham
1874	Public Worship Regulation Act
1878	Restoration of the Roman Catholic hierarchy in Scotland
1879	John Henry Newman becomes a cardinal
1880	Burial Laws Amendment Act opens parish graveyards to Dissenters
1881	Foundation of George William Foote's *Freethinker*; Russian pogroms exile Jews to Britain; Apostolic Constitution *Romanos Pontifices*
1887	Formation by Samuel Montagu of the Federation of Synagogues
1888	The Third Lambeth Conference affirms the Lambeth Quadrilateral
1889	Publication of *Lux Mundi*

1892	Foundation of the Community of the Resurrection
1894	Foundation of the Society of the Sacred Mission
1900	United Presbyterian and Free Churches form the United Free Church (the remaining Free Church stays outside the union); W. Evans-Gordon founds the antisemitic British Brothers' League
1902	Balfour Education Act
1904–5	Welsh Revival
1905	Aliens Immigration Act
1907	Union of the Methodist New Connexion, Bible Christians and United Methodist Free Churches to form the United Methodist Church
1910	First World Missionary Conference at Edinburgh
1911	Antisemitic riots around Tredegar; foundation of the Liberal Jewish Synagogue
1917	Balfour Declaration on a national home in Palestine for the Jewish people
1919	'Enabling Act' authorizes the creation of the Anglican Church Assemby
1920	Disestablishment of the Church in Wales
1921	First meeting of the International Missionary Council
1924	Conference on Christian Politics, Economics and Citizenship in Birmingham
1925	First World Conference on Life and Work, Stockholm
1927	Faith and Order Conference, Lausanne
1928	Foundation of the Fellowship of St Alban and St Sergius; Second World Missionary Conference at Jerusalem
1929	Union of the United Free Church and Church of Scotland (the remaining United Free Church remains outside the Union)
1932	Union of the Wesleyan Methodists, United Methodists and Primitive Methodists; Sir Oswald Mosley founds the British Union of Fascists
1937	Second World Conference on Life and Work, Oxford; Faith and Order Conference, Edinburgh
1938	Third World Missionary Conference at Tambaram
1939	Publication of T. S. Eliot's *Idea of a Christian Society*
1942	Foundation of the British Council of Churches; Beveridge Plan
1944	Butler Education Act; formation of the Union of Liberal and Progressive Synagogues
1946	Publication of Dom Gregory Dix's *Shape of the Liturgy*; National Insurance and National Health Acts
1947	Antisemitic riots in London, Liverpool, Glasgow and Manchester; Pius XII's *Mediator Dei*
1948	First Assembly of the World Council of Churches, Amsterdam
1950	Definition of the dogma of the Assumption

1952	Faith and Order Conference, Lund, Sweden
1954	Second Assembly of the World Council of Churches, Evanston, Illinois; Billy Graham's crusade in England
1955	Sir Isaac Wolfson founds the Wolfson Foundation
1956	Foundation of Leo Baeck College
1957	E. R. Wickham, *Church and People in an Industrial City*
1958	Foundation of the Campaign for Nuclear Disarmament and of the Reform Synagogues of Great Britain
1961	Third Assembly of the World Council of Churches, Delhi
1962–5	Second Vatican Council
1963	Publication of John Robinson's *Honest to God* and ensuing controversy
1965	Race Relations Act
1967	Abortion Act
1968	Publication of *Humanae Vitae*
1969	Rejection by the Church of England of the Anglican–Methodist unity scheme; publication of the *Missa Normativa*
1970	First meeting of the Anglican–Roman Catholic International Commission (ARCIC); creation of the Anglican General Synod
1972	Second Anglican rejection of the Anglican–Methodist unity scheme; union of the English Presbyterian and Congregational Churches to form the United Reformed Church
1974	Formation of the Churches Unity Commission
1976	Establishment of the Commission for Racial Equality
1980	Publication of the Anglican *Alternative Service Book*
1985	Publication of *Faith in the City*
1992	Ordination of women to the Anglican ministry passed by the General Synod

Selected Further Reading

INTRODUCTION

The most recent, and only modern, attempt to tell the history of religion in England within one volume is that by David Edwards, *Christian England* (London, 1986) which was originally published in three volumes; an earlier history concentrating on the Church of England, though with a still useful narrative, is W. R. W. Stephens and W. Hunt (eds), *A History of the English Church*, 9 vols (London, 1899–1910). There have been several studies of particular denominations which have spanned the centuries and these are referred to in the appropriate chapter lists, but particular mention here may be made to M. R. Watts, *The Dissenters: From the Reformation to the French Revolution* (Oxford, 1978); other minority churches are treated in P. Badham (ed.), *Religion, State, and Society in Modern Britain* (London, 1989).

Scottish religion is treated in J. H. S. Burleigh, *A Church History of Scotland* (London, 1960) and in two books by Gordon Donaldson, *Scottish Church History* (Edinburgh, 1985) and *The Faith of the Scots* (London, 1990), as well as in a collection of essays edited by D. Forrester and D. Murray, *Studies in the Hisotry of Worship in Scotland* (Edinburgh, 1984), while successive volumes in the *New History of Scotland* contain excellent chapters on religion. Religion in Wales from the earliest times until the nineteenth century forms the subject of Glanmor Williams's collection of essays *The Welsh and Their Religion* (Cardiff, 1991), while the volumes in the *Oxford History of Wales* by Rees Davies, Glanmor Williams and Geraint Jenkins include excellent material on the Church in Wales from the thirteenth to the nineteenth centuries. An overview of the impact of Celtic traditions in British religion is provided in a collection of essays edited by J. P. Mackey, *An Introduction to Celtic Christianity* (Edinburgh, 1989).

The contribution of women to the history of religion in these islands has been the subject of a number of recent studies, of which Patricia Crawford, *Women and Religion in England 1500–1720* (London, 1992), Gail Malmgreen (ed.), *Religion in the Lives of English Women, 1760–1930* (London, 1986) and several essays in W. J. Sheils and Diana Wood (eds), *Women in the Church* (Oxford, 1990) are especially valuable.

The study of religious history in Great Britain in general is fostered by the *Journal of Ecclesiastical History* and the series 'Studies in Church History', and there are also journals devoted specifically to Church history in Wales and Scotland, as well as to the histories of particular denominations.

First-person references in the following sections are by the author of each chapter.

1 Religion in Roman Britain

Religion in Britain before the first millennium BC is discussed by Aubrey Burl in a number of books: *Prehistoric Avebury* (London, 1979), *Rites of the Gods* (London, 1981) and *The Stonehenge People: Life and Death at the World's Greatest Stone Circle* (London, 1987).

The religion of the Celts before the arrival of the Romans is well understood by Anne Ross in her seminal work, *Pagan Celtic Britain; Studies in Iconography and Tradition* (London, 1967); see also, more briefly, her *The Pagan Celts* (London, 1986). Miranda Green's *The Gods of the Celts* (Gloucester, 1986) likewise covers the ground well. In my opinion neither writer takes sufficient account of the impact of Rome and the profound changes which Rome wrought in traditional religion. Undoubtedly this is a difficult area, for individuals clearly went to the same deities in diverse cultural states of mind. Graham Webster's *The British Celts and their Gods under Rome* (London, 1986) is attuned to both the British and the Roman worlds and is the best guide to popular religion in Roman Britain.

My own *Religion in Roman Britain* (London, 1984) aimed to cover non-Christian evidence (reviewed in the present chapter in greater detail), the dynamic changes which took place in everyday paganism and the impact of the 'mystery' cults. This theme is contained in a somewhat different manner in Charles Thomas's *Christianity in Roman Britain to* AD 500 (London, 1981). Much of his book inevitably deals with the continental background and with sub-Roman western Britain where, paradoxically, certain forms of evidence are fuller than they are for the Roman period. The evidence for many of the churches proposed by scholars (and I would include the famous Silchester church so often accepted as such without question) is speculative, but Professor Thomas makes an overwhelming case for Christian continuity in Britain from Roman times. Another volume, by Dorothy Watts, entitled *Christians and Pagans in Roman Britain* (London, 1991) adds to the corpus of evidence, although more caution is necessary in evaluating her judgements than is the case with Professor Thomas's great work.

The widespread interest in religious evidence among Roman archaeologists is apparent from two conference reports. Warwick Rodwell (ed.), *Temples, Churches and Religion in Roman Britain*, British Archaeological Reports, British series, 77 (Oxford, 1980) contains a number of papers specifically dealing with temple architecture. Martin Henig and Anthony King (eds), *Pagan Gods and Shrines of the Roman Empire*, Oxford University Committee for Archaeology Monographs, 8 (Oxford, 1986) ranges more widely, but over a third of the papers are specifically concerned with Britain, including Ralph Merrifield's on the London Hunter-God, Valerie Hutchinson on Bacchus and my own, further developing my ideas on the nature of upper-class paganism in late Roman Britain. Ann Woodward's *Shrines and Sacrifices* (London, 1992) gives a general account of the material remains of temples and churches. For detailed studies of specific sites and of votive offerings from them, Barry Cunliffe and Peter Davenport, *The Temple of Sulis Minerva at Bath*, Oxford University Committee for Archaeology Monographs, 7 (1985), together with Cunliffe's second volume on the finds from the sacred spring, no. 16

in the same series (1988), are of first importance, dealing as they do with a major sanctuary and how it operated. The report on the temple of Mercury at Uley by Ann Woodward and Peter Leach, *The Uley Shrines: Excavation of a Ritual Complex on West Hill, Uley, Gloucestershire 1977–9* (London, 1993) with its wealth of votive finds likewise provides important insights into Romano-British religion.

The sculpture and other major objects from the London Mithraeum are the subject of a study by the late J. M. C. Toynbee, *The Roman Art Treasures from the Temple of Mithras*, London and Middlesex Archaeological Society Special Paper, 7 (London, 1986). Finally, Catherine Johns and Timothy Potter have published *The Thetford Treasure: Roman Jewellery and Silver* (London, 1983), which does full justice to this highly important find of objects associated with the god Faunus.

2 RELIGION IN ANGLO-SAXON ENGLAND

For any serious study of early English Christianity, the oldest work remains indispensable: Bede's *Ecclesiastical History*, which may be studied in the edition of B. Colgrave and R. A. B. Mynors (Oxford, 1969) or in Leo Sherley Price's translation in the Penguin Classics (1968). In the same series J. F. Webb and D. H. Farmer, *The Age of Bede* (Harmondsworth, 1983) includes translations of the lives of Cuthbert, Wilfrid, and of the abbots of Wearmouth-Jarrow. Dorothy Whitelock (ed.), *English Historical Documents*, vol. I (London, 1955) provides a selection of primary source material.

Frank Stenton, *Anglo-Saxon England*, 3rd edn (Oxford 1971) is the standard general history; see also D. Whitelock, *The Beginnings of English Society* (London, 1952); and Peter Hunter Blair, *An Introduction to Anglo-Saxon England* (Cambridge, 1981) has an ecclesiastical section. Works specifically concerned with Church history are Henry Mayr-Harting, *The Coming of Christianity to Anglo-Saxon England* (London, 1972), William Bright, *Chapters of Early English Church History*, 3rd edn (Oxford, 1987; a classic), John Godfrey, *The Church in Anglo-Saxon England* (Cambridge, 1962), Margaret Deanesley, *The Pre-Conquest Church in England*, 2nd edn (London, 1963) and Frank Barlow, *The English Church 1000–1066* (London, 1963). For Old English paganism see Brian Branston, *The Lost Gods of England*, 2nd edn (London, 1974) and Gale R. Owen, *Rites and Religions of the Anglo-Saxons* (Newton Abbot/London, 1981). On Bede see Peter Hunter Blair, *The World of Bede* (London, 1970), G. Bonner (ed.), *Famulus Christi: Essays in Commemoration of the Thirteenth Centenary of the Birth of the Venerable Bede* (London, 1976), J. M. Wallace-Hadrill, *Bede's Ecclesiastical History of the English People: A Historical Commentary* (Oxford, 1988), George Hardin Brown, *Bede the Venerable* (Boston, Mass., 1987) and Benedicta Ward, *The Venerable Bede* (London, 1990). For Cuthbert see David W. Rollason (ed.), *Cuthbert: Saint and Patron* (Durham, 1987), G. Battiscombe (ed.), *The Relics of St Cuthbert* (Oxford, 1986) and G. Bonner, David Rollason and Clare Stancliffe (eds), *St Cuthbert, his Cult and his Community* to AD 1200 (Woodbridge, Suffolk, 1989). For Wilfrid see D. P. Kirby (ed.), *Saint Wilfrid at Hexham* (Newcastle upon Tyne, 1974). For Alcuin see Eleanor Duckett, *Alcuin, Friend of Charlemagne* (London, 1955). For the English mission to the continent see Wilhelm Levison, *England and the Continent in the Eighth Century* (Oxford, 1946), T. Reuter (ed.), *The Greatest Englishman* (Exeter, 1980), John C. Sladden, *Boniface of Devon: Apostle of Germany* (Exeter, 1980) and C. H. Talbot (ed.), *The Anglo-Saxon Missionaries in Germany* (London, 1954). On the *Regularis Concordia* see David Parsons (ed.), *Tenth-Century Essays* (London/Chichester, 1975). On Anglo-Saxon writing see E. A. Lowe, *Codices Latini Antiquiores*, part II: *Great Britain and Ireland*, 2nd edn (Oxford, 1972), E. A. Lowe, *English Uncial* (Oxford, 1960) and T. A. M. Bishop, *English Caroline Minuscule* (Oxford, 1971). On book painting see Carl Nordenfalk, *Celtic and Anglo-Saxon Painting* (London, 1977), Janet Backhouse, *The Lindisfarne Gospels* (Oxford, 1981) and George Henderson, *From Durrow to Kells: The Insular Gospel-books* (London, 1987). On the Ruthwell Cross see *The Ruthwell Cross: Papers from the Colloquium Sponsored by the Index of Christian Art, Princeton University, 8 December 1989*, Index of Christian Art, Occasional Papers I (Princeton, 1992). An Anglo-Saxon art in general see David Talbot Rice, *English Art 871–1100* (Oxford, 1952), David M. Wilson, *Anglo-Saxon Art* (London, 1984) and J. Backhouse, D. H. Turner and L. Webster (eds) *The Golden Age of Anglo-Saxon Art* (London, 1984).

The Jarrow Lectures, delivered annually at St Paul's Church, Jarrow, since 1958 constitute an important contribution to early Northumbrian studies, while the periodical *Anglo-Saxon England* (Cambridge, 1971–) covers the whole field of early English history.

3 FROM THE CONQUEST TO THE BLACK DEATH

Any serious study of ecclesiastical history in this period must begin with the original sources, recently published in Latin in good editions. *Councils and Synods*, vols 1, ed. D. Whitelock, M. Brett and C. N. L. Brooke (Oxford, 1981) and 2, ed. F. M. Powicke and C. R. Cheney (Oxford, 1964) provide essential material for the period 871–1313. Nine volumes of *English Episcopal Acta*, under the general editorship of D. M. Smith, have been published by the British Academy (London, 1980–93). For bishops' registers the volumes of the *Canterbury and York Society* and the *Lincoln Record Society* should be consulted. Other important Latin texts include *The Letters of John of Salisbury*, ed. W. J. Miller and C. N. L. Brooke (Oxford, 1979–86) and the *Letters and Charters of Gilbert Foliot*, ed. A. Morey and C. N. L. Brooke (Cambridge, 1965–7). The following volumes in the Oxford Medieval Texts series contain English translations: *The Life of Ailred of Rievaulx*, ed. F. M. Powicke (1950), *The Monastic Constitutions of Lanfranc*, ed. D. M. Knowles (1951), *Eadmer's Life of St Anselm*, ed. R. W. Southern (1962), *The Magna Vita Sancti Hugonis*, ed. D. L. Douie and H. Farmer (1961), *The Ecclesiastical History of Ordericus Vitalis*, ed. M. Chibnall (1969–80) and *The Book of St Gilbert*, ed. R. Foreville and G. Keir (1987). Biographies in translation include those of *Christina of Markyate*, ed. C. H. Talbot (Oxford, 1959) and *Wulfric of Haselbury*, ed. M. Bell (Somerset Record Society, 1932).

The series entitled *English Historical Documents*, vols 1 ed. D. Whitelock (London, 1955), 2, ed. D. C. Douglas and G. W. Greenaway (London, 1953), 3, ed. H. Rothwell (London, 1975) and 4, ed. A. R. Myers (London, 1969) contain selections of documents illustrative of ecclesiastical history, with good bibliographies up to the date of publication. Valuable general introductions include R. W. Southern, *Western Society and the Church in the Middle Ages* (London, 1970), R. and C. N. L. Brooke, *Popular Religion in the Middle Ages* (London, 1984), and B. Hamilton, *Religion in the Medieval West* (London, 1986). For the religious orders the basic works are D. M. Knowles, *The Monastic Orders in England* and *The Religious Orders in England* (Cambridge, 1940–59).

Recent publications are many, and include R. W. Southern, *St Anselm and his Biographer* (Cambridge, 1963); M. Gibson, *Lanfranc of Canterbury* (Oxford, 1978); F. Barlow, *The English Church 1000–66* (London, 1962), *The English Church 1066–1154* (London, 1979) and *Thomas Becket* (London, 1986); A. Squire, *Aelred of Rievaulx* (London, 1969); C. R. Cheney, *From Becket to Langton* (Oxford, 1956), *Episcopal Visitation of Monasteries in the thirteenth Century*, rev. edn. (Manchester, 1983) and *The Papacy and England from the Twelfth to the Fourteenth Century* (London, 1982); C. H. Lawrence, *St Edmund of Abingdon* (Oxford, 1960); R. W. Southern, *Robert Grosseteste* (Oxford, 1986); D. Owen, *Church and Society in Medieval Lincolnshire* (Lincoln, 1981); W. A. Pantin, *The English Church in the Fourteenth Century* (Cambridge, 1955); R. M. Haines, *The Administration of the Diocese of Worcester in the Fourteenth Century* (London, 1965); G. R. Owst, *Church and Pulpit in Medieval England* (Oxford, 1961). A rather wider field is covered in A. B. Cobban, *The Medieval Universities* (London, 1975), C. N. L. Brooke et al., *Church and Government in the Middle Ages* (Cambridge, 1976) and Benedicta Ward, *Miracles and the Medieval Mind* (London, 1982). Useful articles have also appeared in the *Journal of Ecclesiastical History* and 'Studies in Church History'.

4 PIETY IN THE LATER MIDDLE AGES

The best general surveys are: W. A. Pantin, *The English Church in the Fourteenth Century* (Cambridge, 1955); J. C. Dickinson, *The Later Middle Ages, An Ecclesiastical History of England*, vol. 2 (London, 1979); C. Harper-Bill, *The Pre-Reformation Church in England, 1400–1530* (London, 1989); and, most recently, Eamon Duffy, *The Stripping of the Altars: Traditional Religion in England 1400 to 1580* (New Haven, 1992). For an in-depth study of a particular place see N. P. Tanner, *The Church in Late Medieval Norwich 1370–1532* (Toronto, 1984). There is an excellent collection of documents in modern English, together with an introduction, in *English Historical Documents*, vol. 4, *1327–1485*, ed. A. Myers (London, 1969), pp. 589–922. There are useful articles on individual persons and subjects in L. Stephens and S. Lee (eds), *Dictionary of National Biography*, 63 vols (London, 1885–1900; new edn in preparation), *New Catholic Encylopedia*, 15 vols (New York, 1967) and F. L. Cross and E. A. Livingstone (eds), *The Oxford Dictionary of the Christian Church*, 2nd edn (London, 1974; 3rd edn forthcoming). England will be seen in its wider context in a general survey of late medieval

Christendom, the best being H. Jedin (ed.), *History of the Church*, vol. 4 (London, 1980).

On parishes, the clergy and religous orders see A. H. Thompson, *The English Clergy and their Organisation in the Later Middle Ages* (Oxford, 1947), D. Knowles, *The Religious Orders in England*, 3 vols (Cambridge, 1948–59), vols 2 and 3, which is a classic work, and P. Heath, *The English Parish Clergy on the Eve of the Reformation* (London, 1969).

On craft guilds and pious confraternities see T. Smith (ed.), *English Guilds*, Early English Text Society, vol. 40 (London, 1870) and H. F. Westlake, *The Parish Guilds of Mediaeval England* (London, 1919). On the mystery plays see H. Craig, *English Religious Drama of the Middle Ages* (Oxford, 1955). The texts of the plays are found in various editions. On chantries see K. L. Wood-Legh, *Perpetual Chantries in Britain* (Cambridge, 1965) and A. Kreider, *English Chantries: The Road to Dissolution* (Cambridge, Mass., 1979). On hermits and anchorites see R. Clay, *The Hermits and Anchorites of England* (London, 1914) and A. Warren, *Anchorites and their Patrons in Medieval England* (Berkeley, 1985). On pilgrimages see R. C. Finucane, *Miracles and Pilgrims: Popular Beliefs in Medieval England* (London, 1977).

On prayer and mystical writers see D. Knowles, *The English Mystical Tradition* (London, 1962). The writings of Richard Rolle, Julian of Norwich and Walter Hilton, and the anonymous *The Cloud of Unknowing* are available in various editions. On education see J. I. Catto and T. Evans (eds), *The History of the University of Oxford*, vol. 2: *Late Medieval Oxford* (Oxford, 1992), N. Orme, *English Schools in the Middle Ages* (London, 1973) and J. Coleman, *Medieval Readers and Writers, 1350–1400* (New York, 1981).

On John Wyclif and the Lollards see K. B. McFarlane, *John Wycliffe and the Beginnings of English Nonconformity* (London, 1952), A. Kenny, *Wyclif* (Oxford, 1985) and A. Hudson, *The Premature Reformation: Wycliffite Texts and Lollard History* (Oxford, 1988).

The period was largely before biographies in the modern sense, but two works stand out: *The Book of Margery Kempe*, which is available in several editions, and *The Paston Letters*, which have been edited by J. Gairdner (London, 1904) and by N. Davis (Oxford, 1971–). The *Dictionary of National Biography* (see above) is the essential secondary work of this kind.

For an excellent survey of recent literature, see P. Heath, 'Between Reform and Reformation: The English Church in the Fourteenth and Fifteenth Centuries', *Journal of Ecclesiastical History*, 41 (1990), pp. 647–78.

5 MEDIEVAL WALES AND THE REFORMATION

For the early Church history of Wales see J. E. Lloyd, *A History of Wales* (London, 1948) and M. W. Barley and R. P. C. Hanson, *Christianity in Britain, 300–700* (Manchester, 1968). The saints and their cults are treated in G. H. Doble, *The Lives of the Welsh Saints* (Cardiff, 1984) and Siân Victory, *The Celtic Church in Wales* (1977); the literary and architectural achievement can be seen in Ifor

Williams, *The Beginnings of Welsh Poetry*, trans. Rachel Bromwich (Cardiff, 1972) and in V. E. Nash-Williams, *Early Christian Monuments in Wales* (Cardiff, 1950). Wendy Davies's *Wales in the Early Middle Ages* (Leicester, 1982) fills in the background, as does R. R. Davies, *Conquest, Coexistence and Change: Wales 1063–1415* (Oxford, 1987). More specifically see Glanmor Williams, *The Welsh Church from Conquest to Reformation* (Cardiff, 1976), and for ecclesiastical administration J. Conway Davies, *Episcopal Acts Relating to Welsh Dioceses, 1066–1272* (Cardiff, 1946–8). The monastic orders are treated in F. G. Cowley, *The Monastic Order in South Wales, 1066–1349* (Cardiff, 1977) and D. H. Williams, *The Welsh Cistercians* (Tenby, 1984). The background to the Reformation period is found in Glanmor Williams, *Recovery, Reorientation and Reform: Wales 1415–1642* (Oxford, 1987) and his *Welsh Reformation Essays* (Cardiff, 1967). The cultural consequences of reform and treated by the same author in 'Religion and Welsh Literature in the Age of the Reformation', *Proceedings of the British Academy*, 69 (1983), and the Welsh Bible is discussed in Isaac Thomas, *Y Testament Newydd Cymraeg, 1551–1620* (Cardiff, 1976).

6 RELIGIOUS LIFE IN MEDIEVAL SCOTLAND

An indispensable work of reference is I. B. Cowan and D. E. Easson, *Medieval Religious Houses: Scotland*, 2nd edn (London, 1976), which also details hospitals and collegiate churches. Another is Cowan's 'The Medieval Church in Scotland: A Select Critical Bibliography', *Records of the Scottish Church History Society*, 21, part i (1981). There are remarkably few full-scale works on the Scottish medieval church, and much of the most useful commentary is to be found in the form of chapters in general textbooks, essays within general collections or articles. In the first category, G. W. S. Barrow, *Kingship and Unity: Scotland 1000–1306* (London, 1981) and A. Grant, *Independence and Nationhood: Scotland 1306–1469* (London, 1984), the second and third volumes in the 'New History of Scotland' series, contain well-written chapters on the Church. In the second category, M. Ash and I. B. Cowan contributed important essays on the Church in, respectively, N. Reid (ed.), *Scotland in the Reign of Alexander III* (Edinburgh, 1990) and J. Brown (ed.), *Scottish Society in the Fifteenth Century* (London, 1977). Two studies of belief and worship are worth consulting: G. Donaldson, *The Faith of the Scots* (London, 1990) and D. Forrester and D. Murray (eds), *Studies in the History of Worship in Scotland* (Edinburgh, 1984). An architectural historian's perspective is provided in S. Cruden, *Scottish Medieval Churches* (Edinburgh, 1986). Otherwise, much is to be found in article form, especially in *The Innes Review*, the journal of the Scottish Catholic Historical Association; a comprehensive index, published on its fortieth anniversary in 1990, is a useful tool. In that journal, there are many articles and notes by David McRoberts and John Durkan. The most important by McRoberts are 'The Fetternear Banner', 7–8 (1956–7), 'Scottish Medieval Chalice Veils', 15 (1964), 'Hermits in Medieval Scotland', 16 (1965), 'The Scottish Church and Nationalism in the Fifteenth Century', 19 (1968), 'The Rosary in Scotland', 23 (1972) and 'The Glorious House of St Andrew', in a special issue of 1974 (vol.25) on St Andrews. The most significant of many by Durkan are 'William Turnbull, Bishop of Glasgow', 2 (1951), 'Education in the Century of the Reformation', 10 (1959), 'The Cultural Background in Sixteenth-Century Scotland', 10 (1959), 'Notes on Glasgow Cathedral', 21 (1970) and 'The Observant Franciscan Province in Scotland', 35 (1984), which issue also had an article by A. A. MacDonald, 'Catholic Devotion into Protestant Lyric: The Case of the *Contemplacioun of Synnaris*'. Otherwise, both D. McKay, 'Parish Life in Scotland, 1500–1560', *Innes Review*, 10 (1959), and D. McRoberts, 'Scottish Sacrament Houses', *Transactions of the Scottish Ecclesiological Society*, 15, part 3 (1965), are essential reading.

7 The Church in Scotland from the Reformation to the Disruption

The acts of the governing body of the Church have been published as follows: *The Booke of the Universall Kirk, Acts and Proceedings of the General Assemblies of the Kirk of Scotland, 100–1618* (1839); *Acts of the General Assembly MDCXXXVIII–MDCCCXLII* (1843). Modern editions of the Books of Discipline have been provided by J. K. Cameron (Edinburgh, 1972) and J. Kirk (Edinburgh, 1979) for the First and Second Books respectively. Important materials are printed in W. C. Dickinson and G. Donaldson, *Source Book of Scottish History*, vols 2 and 3 (1952–4) and in the volumes published in *Records of the Scottish Church History Society*. Of particular value are James Kirk, 'The Scottish Reformation and Reign of James VI: A Select and Critical Bibliography', 23 (1987), pp. 113–55 and John F. McCaffrey, 'Scottish Church History in the Nineteenth Century: A Select Critical Bibliography', 25 (1989), pp. 417–36. The modern history of the Scottish Reformation begins with G. Donaldson, *The Scottish Reformation* (Cambridge, 1960) and is continued in recent studies by I. B. Cowan, *The Scottish Reformation* (London, 1982) and J. Kirk, *Patterns of Reform: Continuity and Change in the Reformation Kirk* (Edinburgh, 1989). A general account is provided by M. Lynch, 'Calvinism in Scotland 1559–1638' in M. Prestwich (ed.), *International Calvinism 1541–1714* (Oxford, 1985), and a modern life of John Knox is by J. Ridley (Oxford, 1968). W. R. Foster, *The Church before the Covenants 1596–1638* (Edinburgh, 1975) takes the story to the Covenants, which are delt with in Walter Makey, *The Church and the Covenant 1637–1651* (Edinburgh, 1979), D. Stevenson, *Revolution and Counter-Revolution in Scotland 1644–1651* (London, 1977) and I. B. Cowan, *The Scottish Covenanters 1660–1688* (London, 1977). The years after 1688 are examined by J. K. Cameron in 'The Church of Scotland in the Age of the Enlightenment', *Studies on Voltaire and the Eighteenth Century*, vol. 58 (Geneva, 1967) and in R. H. Campbell and A. S. Skinner (eds), *The Origins and Nature of the Scottish Enlightenment* (Edinburgh, 1982), pp. 116–30, by A. L. Drummond and J. Bulloch, *The Scottish Churches 1688–1843* (Edinburgh, 1973) and by Richard B. Sher, *Church and University in the Scottish Enlightenment* (Edinburgh, 1985). Church life is discussed in an earlier history, G. D. Henderson, *Religious Life in Seventeenth Century Scotland* (Cambridge, 1937) and the worship of the Church in W. D. Maxwell, *A History of Worship in the Church of*

Scotland (London, 1955). The setting of that worship forms the subject of G. Hay, *The Architecture of Scottish Post-Reformation Churches 1560–1843* (Oxford, 1957).

8 REFORMED RELIGION IN ENGLAND

The modern historiography of the English Reformation can be said to date from the publication of A. G. Dickens's *The English Reformation* (London, 1964; rev. edn 1989), which prompted several local studies of which two, C. Haigh, *Reformation and Reaction in Tudor Lancashire* (Cambridge, 1975) and D. Mac-Culloch, *Suffolk under the Tudors: Politics and Religion in an English County 1500–1600* (Cambridge, 1986) can be mentioned as representative. What many of these studies showed was that the Reformation was a more piecemeal process than Dickens had originally suggested, an argument taken up in J. J. Scarisbrick, *The Reformation and the English People* (Oxford, 1984) and in a collection of essays edited by C. Haigh, *The English Reformation Revised* (Cambridge, 1986) as well as his own *English Reformations: Religion, Politics, and Society under the Tudors* (Oxford, 1993). The enduring strength of traditional forms has recently been demonstrated by Eamon Duffy, *The Stripping of the Altars: Traditional Religion in England 1400–1580* (1992). A recent study of particular themes in Reformation history discussed in a longer temporal perspective is P. Collinson, *The Birthpangs of Protestant England* (London, 1988), and it is his work which dominates our understanding of the Elizabethan and later stages of reform, most notably in *The Religion of Protestants: The Church in English Society 1559–1642* (Oxford, 1982) and in his collected essays, *Godly People* (London, 1983). The theological and ecclesiological nature of that settlement has been most recently discussed by P. Lake in *Anglicans and Puritans? Presbyterianism and English Conformist Thought from Whitgift to Hooker* (London, 1988). Lake stressed the central role of Calvinism in the Church, a view developed by N. R. N. Tyacke in his *The Anti-Calvinists: The Rise of English Arminianism c.1590–1640* (Oxford, 1987), and earlier articles. His interpretation was challenged by P. White, 'The Rise of Arminianism Reconsidered', *Past and Present*, 101 (1983), pp. 34–54, occasioning a lengthy reply from Lake in the same journal (1984), 104, pp. 32–76, followed by a debate in vol. 115 (1987), pp. 201–29. More recently G. Bernard, 'The Church of England *c.*1529–*c.*1642', *History*, 75 (1990), pp. 183–206, has also questioned the emphasis placed on Church order by historians. That debate also looks at the early seventeenth-century Church, for which K. Fincham, *Prelate as Pastor: The Episcopate of James I* (Oxford, 1990) is indispensable; he has also edited a collection of essays, *The Early Stuart Church* (London, 1993). D. Underdown looks at regional expressions of religious and other differences in *Revel, Riot, and Rebellion: Popular Politics and Culture in England 1603–1660* (Oxford, 1985), the arguments of which he debates with J. S. Morrill in *The Journal of British Studies*, 26 (1986), pp. 451–79. Morrill's essay, 'The Religious Context of the English Civil War', *Transactions of the Royal Historical Society*, 5th ser., 34 (1984), pp. 155–78, and that of Eamon Duffy, 'The Godly and the Multitude in Stuart England', *The Seventeenth Century*, 1 (1986), pp. 31–55, are also important, as is I. M. Green,

' "For children in Yeeres and children in Understanding": The Emergence of the English Catechism under Elizabeth and the Early Stuarts', *Journal of Ecclesiastical History*, 37 (1986), pp. 397–425. Changes in worship are discussed in Horton Davies, *Worship and Theology in England from Cranmer to Hooker 1534–1603* (Princeton, 1970), and the international dimensions of the English experience in Collinson's article in M. Prestwich (ed.), *International Calvinism 1541–1715* (Oxford, 1985). Finally, the reality of Reformed religion for a self-taught artisan is movingly re-created in P. Seaver, *Wallington's World* (London, 1985), while Keith Thomas's magisterial study, *Religion and the Decline of Magic* (London, 1971) continues to inform all writing on religion in this period.

9 ANGLICANISM IN STUART AND HANOVERIAN ENGLAND

Four works can be recommended as general introductions: the essays in K. Fincham (ed.), *The Early Stuart Church, 1603–1642* (London, 1993); J. Spurr, *The Restoration Church of England, 1646–1689* (New Haven/London, 1991), an excellent monograph that ranges well beyond the Restoration; G. Rupp, *Religion in England 1689–1791* (Oxford, 1986), a sound if unspectacular survey of the major religious and intellectual figures of the eighteenth century; and the long intro-ductory essay in J. Walsh, C. Haydon and S. Taylor (eds), *The Church of England c.1689–c.1837* (Cambridge, 1993). More specialized but very wide-ranging is K. Fincham, *Prelate as Pastor: The Episcopate of James I* (Oxford, 1990). On Anglican theological method, see H. R. McAdoo, *The Spirit of Anglicanism* (London, 1965). The argument for major changes in doctrine between the late sixteenth and the early or late seventeenth century is made by P. Lake, *Anglicans and Puritans? Presbyterianism and English Conformist Thought from Whitgift to Hooker* (London, 1988) and Conrad Russell, *The Causes of the English Civil War* (Oxford, 1990); N. Tyacke, *Anti-Calvinists: The Rise of English Arminianism c.1590–1640* (Oxford, 1987); H. Davies, *Worship and Theology in England* (3 vols), vols 2 and 3 (Princeton 1975, 1961); G. R. Cragg, *From Puritanism to the Age of Reason* (Cambridge, 1966); and C. F. Allison, *The Rise of Moralism* (London, 1966). The argument for a large measure of continuity in doctrine from Reformation to late seventeenth century derives support from a number of essays in S. Sykes and J. Booty (eds), *The Study of Anglicanism* (London, 1988); A. C. Clifford, *Atonement and Justification* (Oxford, 1990); and I. M. Green, *The Christian's ABC: Catechisms and Catechizing in England c.1540–1740* (forth-coming, 1994). The idea that English Calvinists did not always speak with one voice or in the authentic tones of Calvin is developed by R. T. Kendall, *Calvin and English Calvinism to 1649* (Oxford, 1979); D. A. Weir, *The Origins of the Federal Theology in Sixteenth-Century Reformation Thought* (Oxford, 1990); and P. White, *Predestination, Policy and Polemic* (Cambridge, 1992). On Church–State relations in the Stuart period, see J. P. Sommerville, *Politics and Ideology in England 1603–1640* (London, 1986), and Spurr, *The Restoration Church of England* (noted above). N. Sykes, *Church and State in England in the Eighteenth Century* (Cambridge, 1934) retains its value, but should be supplemented by G. V.

Bennett's excellent studies of *White Kennett* (London, 1957) and *The Tory Crisis in Church and State 1688–1730* (Oxford, 1975). J. C. D. Clark's interesting insights into religious ideology in an *ancien régime* state in *English Society 1688–1832* (Cambridge, 1985) are not enhanced by his petulant tone. The European context is ably delineated in S. Gilley, 'Christianity and Enlightenment: An Historical Survey', *History of European Ideas*, 1 (1981). A survey of the printed religious literature of the period should soon be available in I. M. Green, *Religious Instruction in Early Modern England c.1540–1740* (forthcoming, 1995). There is impressionistic information on parish Anglicanism in J. Wickham Legg, *English Church Life from the Restoration to the Tractarian Movement* (London, 1914), but the following more recent works are all valuable: A. Warne, *Church and Society in Eighteenth-Century Devon* (New York, 1969); M. Chatfield, *Churches the Victorians Forgot* (Ashbourne, 1979); D. A. Spaeth, 'Parsons and Parishioners: Lay–Clerical Conflict and Popular Piety in Wiltshire Villages, 1660–1740' (unpublished PhD thesis, Brown University, 1985); B. Bushaway, *By Rite: Custom, Ceremony and Community in England 1700–1800* (London, 1982); F. C. Mather, 'Georgian Churchmanship Reconsidered', *Journal of Ecclesiastical History*, 36 (1985); and V. Barrie-Curien, *Clergé et pastorale en Angleterre au XVIIIᵉ siècle. Le diocèse de Londres* (Paris, 1992). Different aspects of the history of the parish clergy are covered by J. H. Pruett, *The Parish Clergy under the Later Stuarts: the Leicestershire Experience* (Urbana, 1978); I. M. Green, 'The First Years of Queen Anne's Bounty', in R. O'Day and F. Heal (eds), *Princes and Paupers in the English Church 1500–1800* (Leicester, 1981); G. F. A. Best, *Temporal Pillars* (Cambridge, 1964); Barrie-Curien, *Clergé et pastorale* (noted above); D. McClatchey, *Oxfordshire Clergy 1777–1869* (Oxford, 1960); and P. Virgin, *The Church in an Age of Negligence* (Cambridge, 1989).

10 Radical Sects and Dissenting Churches, 1600–1750

Two outstanding accounts are M. Watts, *The Dissenters: From the Reformation to the French Revolution* (Oxford, 1978) and B. R. White, *The English Separatist Tradition from the Marian Martyrs to the Pilgrim Fathers* (London, 1971). A useful account of the origins of Dissent can be gained from the documents in H. C. Porter, *Puritanism in Tudor England* (London, 1970), and its growth in the capital is traced in M. Tolmie, *The Triumph of the Saints: The Separatist Churches of London, 1616–1649* (Cambridge, 1977). There are some first-rate studies of individual denominations over the period. For the Presbyterians, we have the joint work by C. Gordon Bolam, Jeremy Goring, H. L. Short and Roger Thomas, *The English Presbyterians from Elizabethan Puritanism to Modern Unitarianism* (London, 1968). The Independent Congregationals are dealt with over a lengthy period in the magisterial study by R. Tudur Jones, *Congregationalism in England 1662–1962* (London, 1962). For the period of Independency's clear emergence in the Civil War decades, see George Yule, *The Independents in the English Civil War* (Cambridge, 1958) and G. F. Nuttall, *Visible Saints: The Congregational Way,*

1640–1660 (Oxford, 1957). A good way to get to grips with Independency would be to read something of one of its leading theorists, in *The Correspondence of John Owen (1616–1683) With an Account of his Life and Work*, ed. Peter Toon (Cambridge, 1970). There is a useful survey of Baptist history in A. C. Underwood, *A History of the English Baptists* (London, 1947). On John Bunyan a handy recent collection of essays is edited by Anne Laurence, W. R. Owens and Stuart Sim, *John Bunyan and his England 1628–88* (London, 1990). For the Quakers I select Hugh Barbour, *The Quakers in Puritan England* (New Haven, 1964) and Richard T. Vann, *The Social Development of English Quakerism 1655–1755* (Cambridge, Mass., 1969).

The heady years of the Puritan Revolution are brilliantly covered in Christopher Hill's masterpiece, *The World Turned Upside Down: Radical Ideas during the Revolution* (London, 1972), and in a collection of essays edited by J. F. Macgregor and B. Reay, *Radical Religion in the English Revolution* (London, 1984). For the bitterly hostile view by the contemporaneous polemicist Thomas Edwards, see the reprint of his *Gangraena* issued by the Rota at the University of Exeter (1977). An ephemeral millenarian group, the Fifth Monarchists, is ably studied by Bernard Capp in *The Fifth Monarchy Men: A Study in Seventeenth-Century English Millenarianism* (London, 1972). Fascinating light is shed on a much more enduring sect, the Muggletonians, by Christopher Hill, Barry Reay and William Lamont in *The World of the Muggletonians* (London, 1983). In *Fear, Myth and History: The Ranters and the Historians* (Cambridge, 1986), J. C. Davis attempts scepticism about the very existence of that particular movement.

The zenith and collapse of Puritan Revolution are brilliantly examined by Austin Woolrych in *Commonwealth to Protectorate* (Oxford, 1982). The story of the good old cause in defeat is told by Christopher Hill in *The Experience of Defeat: Milton and Some Contemporaries* (London, 1984). In a remarkable trilogy, *Deliver Us from Evil: The Radical Underground in Britain, 1660–1663* (New York/Oxford, 1986), *Enemies under his Feet: Radicals and Nonconformists in Britain, 1664–1677* (Stanford, 1990) and *Secrets of the Kingdom: British Radicals from the Popish Plot to the Revolution of 1688–1689* (Stanford, 1992), Richard L. Greaves examines the political fortunes of radical and Puritan dissidence after the Restoration: see also Douglas R. Lacey, *Dissent and Parliamentary Politics in England, 1661–1689* (New Brunswick, 1969). Gerald R. Cragg provides a highly readable and succinct account in *Puritanism in the Period of the Great Persecution 1660–1688* (Cambridge, 1957).

A work of surpassing scholarship now available – in ever 800 pages – is edited by Anne Whiteman with Mary Clapinson: *The Compton Census of 1676: A Critical Edition* (London, 1986), presents an unrivalled picture of the state of Dissent in the period of the Clarendon Code's full operation. For records of Nonconformity see my survey, with bibliographies, *Sources for the History of English Nonconformity 1660–1830* (London 1991). Sensitive and readable, Duncan Coomer takes us into the early eighteenth century, with *English Dissent under the Early Hanoverians* (London, 1946).

11 RATIONAL RELIGION IN ENGLAND FROM HERBERT OF CHERBURY TO WILLIAM PALEY

Although there are some fine works on individual authors and topics, a good modern overall survey of 'Rational Religion in England' in this period is much needed. Two older works are still important: John Tulloch's *Rational Theology and Christian Philosophy in England in the Seventeenth Century* (Edinburgh/London, 1874) (although, somewhat surprisingly, it does not include Herbert of Cherbury) and Leslie Stephen's *History of English Thought in the Eighteenth Century* (London, 1876) (which is admirably comprehensive but to some extent reflects its author's agnostic attitude towards religious belief). Of modern works Gordon Rupp's *Religion in England 1688–1791* (Oxford, 1986) contains many delightful cameo pen-portraits, but unfortunately the author was not sufficiently sympathetic with the intellectual debate about rational religion to enter illuminatingly into the minds of the protagonists. Gerald Cragg's studies, *From Puritanism to the Age of Reason* (Cambridge, 1950) and *Reason and Authority in the Eighteenth Century* (Cambridge, 1964) cover the ground competently and interestingly, while Basil Willey's *Seventeenth Century Background* (London, 1934) and *Eighteenth Century Background* (London, 1940), Roland Stromberg's *Religious Liberalism in Eighteenth-Century England* (Oxford, 1954), John Redwood's *Reason, Ridicule and Religion: The Age of Enlightenment in England, 1660–1750* (London, 1976) and John Hedley Brooke's *Science and Religion: Some Historical Perspectives* (Cambridge, 1991) contain valuable discussions of a number of important persons and issues. For the general intellectual background to the discussions in England, Ernst Cassirer's *The Philosophy of the Enlightenment* (Princeton, 1951) and *The Platonic Renaissance in England* (Edinburgh, 1953), Paul Hazard's *The European Mind, 1680–1715* (London, 1953) and *European Thought in the Eighteenth Century* (London, 1954) and Peter Gay's *The Enlightenment: An Interpretation* (London, 1970) are important and extensive studies.

A number of modern studies of individual issues throw valuable light on to the debate about the reasonableness of belief. They include Jamie Ferreira's *Scepticism and Reasonable Doubt* (Oxford, 1986), R. M. Burns's *The Great Debate on Miracles from Joseph Glanvill to David Hume* (London/Toronto, 1981), D. P. Walker's *The Decline of Hell: Seventeeth-Century Discussions of Eternal Torment* (London, 1964), and Henning Graf Reventlow's large, detailed but uneven study of *The Authority of the Bible and the Rise of the Modern World* (London, 1984). Peter Byrne's *Natural Religion and the Nature of Religion: The Legacy of Deism* (London, 1989) provides some useful essays on the issue of natural religion; the first volume of Isabel Rivers's *Reason, Grace, and Sentiment: A Study of the Language of Religion and Ethics in England 1660–1780* (Cambridge, 1991) is a perceptive study of some of the debates about religious belief in this period and it is to be hoped that the second volume will soon appear; J. A. I. Champion's *The Pillars of Priestcraft Shaken: The Church of England and its Enemies 1660–1730* (Cambridge, 1992) pays particular attention to the historical arguments used in the debates about the faith and practice of the Church of England.

Among works on individual authors are Robert Sullivan's magisterial *John Toland and the Deist Controversy* (Cambridge, Mass./London, 1982) (would there were more like it!), Stephen H. Daniel's *John Toland: His Methods, Manners and Mind* (Kingston/Montreal, 1984), R. D. Bedford's study of Herbert of Cherbury, *The Defence of Truth* (Manchester, 1979), Robert Todd Carroll's *The Common-Sense Philosophy of religion of . . . Stillingfleet* (The Hague, 1975), John Yolton's *John Locke and the Way of Ideas* (Oxford, 1956), and *Locke and the Compass of Human Understanding* (Cambridge, 1970), T. L. Bushell's *The Sage of Salisbury: Thomas Chubb* (New York, 1967), Robert Holtby's *Daniel Waterland* (Carlisle, 1966), Terence Penelhum's *Butler* (London, 1985), J. C. A. Gaskin's *Hume's Philosophy of Religion* (London, 1978), Robert Orr's *Reason and Authority: The Thought of William Chillingworth* (Oxford, 1967), J. P. Ferguson's *Dr Samuel Clarke* (Kineton, 1976), A. R. Winnet's *Peter Browne* (London, 1974), M. L. Clarke's *Paley* (London, 1974) and James E. Force's *William Whiston* (Cambridge, 1985). It cannot be emphasized enough, however, that there is no substitute for reading the original authors. Those considered to be major writers – such as Locke, Berkeley, Butler and Hume – are available in contemporary editions, while useful extracts of others are found in such collections as Gerald Cragg's *The Cambridge Platonists* (New York, 1968). Thanks to recent methods of reproduction, many other works have now become available. The Garland Publishing Company of New York, for example, has published a collection of *British Philosophers and Theologians of the Seventeenth and Eighteenth Centuries* in 101 volumes. Regrettably the price of editions printed in the seventeenth and eighteenth centuries has risen alarmingly in the past two decades. Finally, it may be permissible to mention a study of the ways in which the debates about reasonable religion affected and were affected by insights into other religions: David A. Pailin, *Attitudes to Other Religions: Comparative Religion in Seventeeth- and Eighteenth-Century Britain* (Manchester, 1984). Some of the issues considered in this work have now been complemented by Peter Harrison's *'Religion' and the Religions in the English Enlightenment* (Cambridge, 1990).

12 CATHOLICISM FROM THE REFORMATION TO THE RELIEF ACTS

The traditional view of recusant history was set out in D. Mathew, *Catholicism in England: The Portrait of a Minority, its Culture and Tradition* (London, 1948), and a scholarly account of the Elizabethan phase was provided in P. McGrath, *Papists and Puritans under Elizabeth I* (London, 1972). Important regional studies were conducted by H. (later J. C.) Aveling, among them *Northern Catholics: The Catholic Recusants of the North Riding of Yorkshire* (London, 1966), and the seminary priests have been chronicled in G. Anstruther, *The Seminary Priests*, 4 vols (London, 1968–77). John Bossy's major revision, *The English Catholic Community 1570–1850* (London, 1975) has been challenged for the early years by C. Haigh, 'The Continuity of Catholicism in the English Reformation', *Past and Present*, 93 (1981) and P. McGrath, 'Elizabethan Catholicism: A Reconsideration',

Journal of Ecclesiastical History, 35 (1984), and regional studies of the Reformation continue this debate. A. Dures, *English Catholicism 1558–1642* (London, 1983) is a short but sound survey of the first century and the whole period is covered in J. C. Aveling, *The Handle and the Axe* (London, 1976). Aspects of the Civil War history are found in R. Clifton, 'Popular Fear of Catholicism during the English Civil War', *Past and Present*, 52 (1971) and B. G. Blackwood, 'Plebeian Catholics in the 1640s and 1650s', *Recusant History*, 18 (1986). The political dimensions of later Stuart Catholicism are examined in J. Miller, *Popery and Politics in England 1660–1688* (London, 1973) and Bossy has written a recent account of the effects of the Revolution, 'English Catholics after 1688', in O. P. Grell, J. I. Israel and N. Tyacke (eds), *From Persecution to Toleration* (Oxford, 1991). Eighteenth-century Catholicism forms the subject of a collection of essays edited by Eamon Duffy, *Challoner and his Church* (London, 1981). Duffy's article 'Poor Protestant Flies: Conversions to Catholicism in Early Eighteenth-Century England', in 'Studies in Church History', vol. 15 (Oxford, 1978) considers the social context of converts. Provincial Georgian Catholics are the subject of J. A. Williams's *Catholic Recusancy in Wiltshire 1660–1791* (London, 1968). The Catholic Record Society has published important documents from the period and the pages of *Recusant History* are essential for local studies, while the Scolar Press published extensive facsimile editions of recusant texts during the 1970s.

13 THE EVANGELICAL REVIVAL IN EIGHTEENTH-CENTURY BRITAIN

I have attempted to establish the setting of the British revivals in that of the Protestant world as a whole (and the European Protestant world in particular) in *The Protestant Evangelical Awakening* (Cambridge, 1992). This does not mean that continued attempts to treat the revivals in the context of Atlantic civilization are not valid as far as they go; a good example is Susan O'Brien, 'A Transatlantic Community of Saints: The Great Awakening and the First Evangelical Network, 1735–1755', *American Historical Review*, 91 (1986), pp. 811–32. Studies of the revival in America, much more actively pursued than those of the British revival, continue to cast light on events in Britain, as recent works by Harry S. Stout and Michael Edwards illustrate; while Jon Butler in *Power, Authority and the Origins of American Denominational Order: The English Churches in the Delaware Valley, 1680–1730*, Transactions of the American Philosophical Society, 68, part 2 (1978) establishes an explicit and valuable English context to his story. Marilyn J. Westerkamp did likewise for the Scots-Irish in *The Triumph of the Laity: Scots-Irish Piety and the Great Awakening 1625–1760* (New York, 1988). Moravian studies also continue to illuminate the British situation, especially those of C. J. Podmore, 'The Fetter Lane Society, 1738', *Proceedings of the Wesley Historical Society*, 46 (1988), pp. 125–53, 'The Fetter Lane Society', ibid., 47 (1990), pp. 156–80, and 'The Bishops and the Brethren: Anglican Attitudes to the Moravians in the Mid-Eighteenth Century', *Journal of Ecclesiastical History*, 41 (1990), pp. 622–46; of Hermann Wellenreuther, 'Politische Patronage von John Fourth Duke of Bedford und die Stellung der Herrnhuter Brüdergemeine in dem

Borough of Bedford, 1745–55', *Unitas Fratrum*, 4 (1978), pp. 85–93; and of W. R. Ward, 'Zinzendorf and Money', in 'Studies in Church History', vol. 24 (1987), pp. 283–306. Wesley studies multiply. Henry D. Rack took a scholarly and somewhat disenchanted view in *Reasonable Enthusiast: John Wesley and the Rise of Methodism* (London, 1989); W. Stephen Gunter stated the case for Wesley's critics in *The Limits of 'Love Divine'* (Nashville, 1989); neither was bowled over by the 'warmed heart' which formed the subject of Randy L. Maddox (ed.), *Aldersgate Reconsidered* (Nashville, 1990). The grandiose *Bicentennial Edition of the Works of John Wesley* (Nashville, 1975–) is about halfway to completion; it includes the *Journal and Diaries*, edited by W. R. Ward and R. P. Heitzenrater, of which five of the projected seven volumes are completed (1988–93). A new three-volume edition of *The Unpublished Poetry of Charles Wesley*, ed. S. T. Kimborough, Jr and Oliver A. Beckerlegge, began at Nashville (1988). P. P. Streiff studied *Jean Guillaume de la Fléchère 1729–1785: Ein Beitrag zur Geschichte des Methodismus* (Frankfurt, 1984). Henry D. Rack and John Walsh contributed notably to Keith Robbins (ed.), *Protestant Evangelicalism: Britain, Ireland, Germany and America. Essays in Honour of W. R. Ward* (Oxford, 1990) with papers on 'Survival and Revival: John Bennet, Methodism and the Old Dissent' and 'John Wesley and the Community of Goods' respectively; and each independently studied the religious societies in 'Religious Societies and the Origins of Methodism', *Journal of Ecclesiastical History*, 38 (1987), pp. 582–95 and 'Religious Societies: Methodist and Evangelical, 1738–1800', in 'Studies in Church History', vol. 23 (1968), pp. 279–302. A beguiling study of the intellectual background was given by Isabel Rivers in *Reason, Grace, and Sentiment: A Study of the Language of Religion and Ethics in England*, vol. 1: *Whichcote to Wesley* (Cambridge, 1991). Evangelical Dissent appeared largely in A. P. F. Sell, *Dissenting Thought and the Life of the Churches* (San Francisco, 1990). An English version of Derec Llwyd Morgan's exuberant and often wildly inaccurate book, *The Great Awakening in Wales* (London, 1988) is eminently worth reading.

14 CHURCH AND STATE SINCE 1800

Much of the analysis in this chapter concerns political and constitutional developments, but it would not be appropriate to offer an extensive guide to historical writings in those areas since the secular caste of mind of modern historians means that the amount of space given to religious issues in them is often very economically distributed. There are some excellent works dealing primarily with religious and ecclesiastical history, however, which discuss the sort of developments in question. First in importance for providing the general context of the Church history of the period is W. O. Chadwick, *The Victorian Church* (London, Part I, 1966; Part II, 1970). Church and State issues are also discussed in R. A. Soloway, *Prelates and People: Ecclesiastical Social Thought in England, 1783–1852* (London, 1969), O. J. Brose, *Church and Parliament: The Reshaping of the Church of England, 1828–1860* (Oxford, 1959), W. G. Addison, *Religious Equality in Modern England, 1714–1914* (London, 1944), G. Kitson Clark, *Churchmen and the Condition of England, 1832–1885* (London, 1973), Adrian Hastings, *A History of English Christianity, 1920–1985* (London, 1986) and Paul A. Welsby, *A History of the Church of England, 1945–1980* (London, 1984). For the Dissenters and their critique of established religion see W. R. Ward, *Religion and Society in England, 1790–1850* (London, 1972), D. M. Thompson, *Nonconformity in the Nineteenth Century* (London, 1972), D. W. Bebbington, *The Nonconformist Conscience, Chapel and Politics, 1870–1914* (London, 1982) and W. H. Mackintosh, *Disestablishment and Liberation: The Movement for the Separation of the Anglican Church from State Control* (London, 1972). There are some distinguished works covering particular areas of this subject: H. McLeod, *Class and Religion in the Late Victorian City*, (London, 1970), G. I. T. Machin, *Politics and the Churches in Great Britain, 1832 to 1868* (Oxford, 1977); *1869–1921* (Oxford, 1987). J. P. Parry, *Democracy and Religion: Gladstone and the Liberal Party, 1867 to 1875* (Cambridge, 1986) and P. M. H. Bell, *Disestablishment in Ireland and Wales* (London, 1969).

15 THE CHURCH OF ENGLAND IN THE NINETEENTH CENTURY

The standard narrative is Owen Chadwick, *The Victorian Church*, 2 parts (London, 1966 and 1970). Also comprehensive is Horton Davies, *Worship and Theology in England*, 5 vols (Princeton, 1961–75), vol. 3: *From Watts and Wesley to Maurice, 1690–1850* and vol. 4: *From Newman to Martineau*. A valuable older work is Francis Warre Cornish, *The English Church in the Nineteenth Century*, 2 parts (London, 1910). There is also a public narrative in G. I. T. Machin, *Politics and the Churches in Great Britain, 1832 to 1868* (Oxford, 1977) and *Politics and the Churches in Great Britain, 1869 to 1921* (Oxford, 1987). For documents see David Nicholls (ed.), *Church and State in Britain since 1820* (London, 1967) and R. P. Flindall, *The Church of England, 1815–1948: A Documentary History* (London, 1972). More generally see David L. Edwards, *Leaders of the Church of England, 1828–1944* (London, 1971), David L. Edwards, *Christian England*, vol. 3: *From the Eighteenth Century to the First World War* (London, 1984). On the unreformed Church see Peter Virgin, *The Church in an Age of Negligence: Ecclesiastical Structure and Problems of Church Reform 1700–1840* (Cambridge, 1989). On Church reform see Olive J. Brose, *Church and Parliament: the Reshaping of the Church of England 1828–1860* (Oxford, 1959) and Geoffrey Best, *Temporal Pillars: Queen Anne's Bounty, the Ecclesiastical Commissioners and the Church of England* (Cambridge, 1964). On Evangelicalism see Charles Smyth, *Simeon and Church Order* (Cambridge, 1940), Arthur Pollard and Michael Hennell (eds), *Charles Simeon 1759–1836* (London, 1959), Hugh E. Hopkins, *Charles Simeon of Cambridge* (London, 1977), Michael Hennell, *John Venn and the Clapham Sect* (London, 1958), Ford K. Brown, *Fathers of the Victorians: The Age of Wilberforce* (Cambridge, 1961), E. M. Howse, *Saints in Politics: The 'Clapham Sect' and the Growth of Freedom* (Toronto, 1962), Ian Bradley, *The Call to Seriousness: The Evangelical Impact on the Victorians* (London, 1976), Michael Hennell, *Sons of the Prophets* (London, 1979) and Doreen M. Rosman, *Evangelicals and Culture*

(London, 1984). On the High Church tradition see Yngve Brilioth, *The Anglican Revival* (London, 1933) and A. B. Webster, *Joshua Watson: the Story of a Layman 1771–1855* (London, 1954). On Anglo-Catholicism see Geoffrey Rowell, *The Vision Glorious: Themes and Personalities of the Catholic Revival in Anglicanism* (Oxford, 1983), Alf Härdelin, *The Tractarian Understanding of the Eucharist* (Uppsala, 1965) and Perry Butler (ed.), *Pusey Rediscovered* (Oxford, 1983). On religious orders see Peter F. Anson, *The Call of the Cloister: Religious Communities and Kindred Bodies in the Anglican Communion* (London, 1955). On worship see James F. White, *The Cambridge Movement: The Ecclesiologists and the Gothic Revival* (Cambridge, 1962). On church architecture see Paul Thompson, *William Butterfield* (London, 1971) and Stefan Muthesius, *The High Victorian Movement in Architecture 1850–1870* (London, 1972). On ritualism see James E. Bentley, *Ritualism and Politics in Victorian Britain* (Oxford, 1978) and Lida E. Ellsworth, *Charles Lowder and the Ritualist Movement* (London, 1982). On thought see Ieuan Ellis, *Seven against Christ: A Study of 'Essays and Reviews'* (Leiden, 1980), James R. Moore, *The Post-Darwinian Controversies* (Cambridge, 1979), B. M. G. Reardon, *From Coleridge to Gore: A Century of Religious Thought in Britain* (London, 1971), J. A. Carpenter, *Gore: A Study in Liberal Catholic Thought* (London, 1960) and A. M. Ramsey, *From Gore to Temple* (London, 1960). On the social question see George Kitson Clark, *Churchmen and the Condition of England, 1832–1885* (London, 1973), P. d'A. Jones, *The Christian Socialist Revival, 1877–1914* (Princeton, 1968) and E. R. Norman, *Church and Society in England 1770–1970: A Historical Study* (Oxford, 1976). On religious practice see Robert Currie, Alan Gilbert and Lee Horsley, *Churches and Churchgoers: Patterns of Church Growth in the British Isles since 1700* (Oxford, 1977) and Jeffrey Cox, *The English Churches in a Secular Society: Lambeth, 1870–1930* (Oxford, 1982).

16 RELIGIOUS LIFE IN INDUSTRIAL BRITAIN, 1830–1914

It is probably best to start with the various statistical surveys and social geographies of nineteenth-century religion which include R. Currie, A. Gilbert and L. Horsley, *Churches and Churchgoers: Patterns of Church Growth in the British Isles since 1700* (Oxford, 1977), A. D. Gilbert, *Religion and Society in Industrial England* (London, 1976), B. I. Coleman, *The Church of England in the Mid-Nineteenth Century* (London, 1980), J. D. Gay, *The Geography of Religion in England* (London, 1971), H. McLeod, 'Class, Community and Region: The Religious Geography of Nineteenth-Century England', in M. Hill (ed.) *Sociological Yearbook of Religion in Britain*, 6 (1973) and R. Gill, *Competing Convictions* (London, 1989).

The most substantial general survey of religion in this period, including the much neglected Church of England, is still Owen Chadwick's elegantly written *The Victorian Church*, 2 parts (London, 1966 and 1970). The most recent and most accessible study is H. McLeod, *Religion and Irreligion in Victorian England* (Bangor, 1993).

Important studies of individual cities in the Victorian period include E. R. Wickham, *Church and People in an Industrial City* (London, 1957) on Sheffield; H. McLeod, *Class and Religion in the Late Victorian City* (London, 1974) on London; S. Yeo, *Religion and Voluntary Organisations in Crisis* (London, 1976) on Reading; J. Cox, *The English Churches in a Secular Society: Lambeth, 1870–1930* (Oxford, 1982); and D. Hempton and M. Hill, *Evangelical Protestantism in Ulster Society 1740–1890* (London, 1992) on Belfast. See also the chapters by D. Mole, S. Gilley and J. Kent in H. J. Dyos and M. Wolff (eds), *The Victorian City*, vol. 2 (London, 1973). On the urban working classes in particular see K. S. Inglis's pioneering book *Churches and the Working Classes in Victorian England* (London, 1963) and H. McLeod's more recent synthesis *Religion and the Working Classes in Nineteenth-Century Britain* (London, 1984), which also contains an extensive reading list.

For the particular themes highlighted in this chapter, there are more comprehensive treatments by T. W. Laqueur, *Religion and Respectability: Sunday Schools and Working Class Culture* (New Haven, 1976), John Kent, *Holding the Fort: Studies in Victorian Revivalism* (London, 1978), R. Carwardine, *Trans-Atlantic Revivalism* (London, 1978), B. Harrison, 'Religion and Recreation in Nineteenth-Century England', *Past and Present*, 38 (1967), J. H. S. Kent, 'The Role of Religion in the Cultural Structure of the Later Victorian City', *Transactions of the Royal Historical Society*, 5th ser., 23 (1973), C. G. Brown, 'The Costs of Pew-Renting: Church Management, Church-Going and Social Class in Nineteenth-Century Glasgow', *Journal of Ecclesiastical History*, 38 (1987), J. Obelkevich, 'Music and Religion in the Nineteenth Century', in J. Obelkevich, L. Roper and R. Samuel (eds), *Disciplines of Faith* (London, 1987) and H. McLeod, 'New Perspectives on Working-Class Religion: The Oral Evidence', *Oral History*, 14 (1986).

The relationship between working-class religion and popular politics is hotly contested, but the most important contributions are by W. R. Ward, *Religion and Society in England 1790–1850* (London, 1972), J. Foster, *Class Struggle and the Industrial Revolution* (London, 1974), P. Joyce, *Work, Society and Politics* (Brighton, 1980), E. Yeo, 'Christianity in Chartist Struggle, 1832–42', *Past and Present*, 91 (1981), D. Hempton, *Methodism and Politics in British Society 1750–1850* (London, 1984) and T. Koditschek, *Class Formation and Urban Industrial Society: Bradford, 1750–1850* (Cambridge, 1990).

Fertile studies of the relationship between popular religion and working-class communities include R. Colls, *The Collier's Rant* (London, 1977), R. Moore, *Pit-Men, Preachers and Politics: The Effects of Methodism in a Durham Mining Village* (Cambridge, 1974), D. M. Valenze, *Prophetic Sons and Daughters* (Princeton, 1985), Open University, *Religion: Conformity and Controversy* (Milton Keynes, 1987), J. Obelkevich, *Religion and Rural Society: South Lindsey, 1825–1875* (Oxford, 1976), a classic rural study that also raises questions about urban popular religion, R. Swift and S. Gilley (eds), *The Irish in the Victorian City* (London, 1985), D. Hempton, ' "Popular Religion" 1800–1986', in T. Thomas (ed.), *The British: Their Religious Beliefs and Practices 1800–1986* (London, 1988) and D. G.

Paz, *Popular Anti-Catholicism in Mid-Victorian England* (Stanford, 1992). Samuel Bamford's *Passages in the Life of a Radical* (London, 1841) gives valuable contemporary insights into this theme.

On clergy and ministers, Alan Haig's *The Victorian Clergy* (London, 1984) has been balanced by K. D. Brown's *A Social History of the Nonconformist Ministry in England and Wales 1800–1930* (Oxford, 1988).

There is a rich periodical literature on urban religion in this period which is well surveyed in McLeod's *Religion and the Working Class in Nineteenth-Century Britain* (see above), but four collections merit special attention: J. Obelkevich, L. Roper and R. Samuel (eds), *Disciplines of Faith* (London, 1987), D. Baker (ed.), *The Church in Town and Countryside*, 'Studies in Church History', vol. 16 (Oxford, 1979), G. Parsons (ed.), *Religion in Victorian Britain*, 4 vols (Manchester, 1988) and S. Bruce (ed.), *Religion and Modernization: Sociologists and Historians Debate the Secularization Thesis* (Oxford, 1992). The last of these collections is the most substantial contribution so far to the debate on the alleged relationship between urbanization and secularization. For a provocative introduction to the issues at stake see C. Brown, 'Did Urbanization Secularize Britain?', *Urban History Yearbook* (1988). This debate will be carried forward in a number of distinguished local studies which are due to be published in the next few years. The theses upon which they are based can be traced in H. McLeod, *Religion and Irreligion in Victorian England* (Bangor, 1993).

17 HEBREWS HELLENIZED? ENGLISH EVANGELICAL NONCONFORMITY AND CULTURE, 1840–1940

The best introductions to the context, culture and politics of Nonconformity are to be found in more general studies of the religion of the period: A. D. Gilbert, *Religion and Society in Industrial England: Church, Chapel and Social Change 1740–1914* (London, 1976), D. W. Bebbington, *Evangelicalism in Modern Britain: A History from the 1730s to the 1980s* (London, 1989), H. Davies, *Worship and Theology in England from Newman to Martineau, 1850–1900* (London, 1962) and *Worship and Theology in England: The Ecumenical Century 1900–1965* (London, 1965), G. I. T. Machin, *Politics and the Churches in Great Britain, 1832 to 1868* (Oxford, 1977) and its sequel *1869 to 1921* (Oxford, 1987), A. Hastings, *A History of English Christianity 1920–1985* (London, 1986). The whole is subsumed in G. Parsons (ed.), *Religion in Victorian Britain*, vol. 1: *Traditions*, vol. 2: *Controversies*, vol. 3: *Sources*, vol. 4: *Interpretations* (Manchester, 1988).

The social aspect of Nonconformity is localized in such pioneering studies as H. McLeod, *Class and Religion in the Late Victorian City* (London, 1974), S. Yeo, *Religion and Voluntary Organisations in Crisis* (London, 1976), J. Obelkevich, *Religion and Rural Society: South Lindsey 1825–1875* (Oxford, 1976) and J. Cox, *The English Churches in a Secular Society: Lambeth, 1870–1930* (Oxford, 1982).

For a wholly Dissenting thrust we await the sequel to M. R. Watts, *The Dissenters from the Reformation to the French Revolution* (Oxford, 1978). Meanwhile there remain two excellent volumes of documents and commentary – D. M.

Thompson, *Nonconformity in the Nineteenth Century* (London, 1972) and J. H. Y. Briggs and I. Sellers, *Victorian Nonconformity* (London, 1973) – and one suggestive essay: I. Sellers, *Nineteenth-Century Nonconformity* (London, 1977). For the Edwardian climax (and its immediate aftermath) of crotchets and conscience there are D. W. Bebbington, *The Nonconformist Conscience: Chapel and Politics 1870–1914* (London, 1982), S. Koss, *Nonconformity in Modern British Politics* (London, 1975), M. D. Johnson, *The Dissolution of Dissent, 1850–1918* (London, 1987) and J. Munson, *The Nonconformists: In Search of a Lost Culture* (London, 1991).

Munson leads on to D. Davie, *A Gathered Church: The Literature of the English Dissenting Interest, 1700–1930* (London, 1978), V. Cunningham, *Everywhere Spoken Against: Dissent in the Victorian Novel* (Oxford, 1975) and C. Binfield, *So Down to Prayers: Studies in English Nonconformity 1781–1920* (London, 1977). The whole may be localized in C. Binfield, *Pastors and People: The Biography of a Baptist Church: Queen's Road Coventry* (Gloucester, 1984) and Marjorie Reeves, *Sheep Bell and Ploughshare: The Story of Two Village Families* (London, 1978).

None of this has been better expressed than in W. Haslam Mills, *Grey Pastures* (essays from the *Manchester Guardian* evoking Albion, Ashton-under-Lyme: London, 1924) or G. Stowell, *The History of Button Hill* (a novel evoking Newton Park Union Church, Chapeltown, Leeds: London, 1929).

The seeker must then turn to the most usefully varied sources of all: the individual papers to be found in the Ecclesiastical History Society's annual series, 'Studies in Church History', vols. 1–28, and its occasional *Subsidia*, 1–9 (Oxford). Finally, but by no means least, there are the journals of the denominational societies – the *Baptist Quarterly, Congregational History Society, Journal of the Friends Historical Society, Journal of the United Reformed Church History Society, Proceedings of the Wesley Historical Society* and *Transactions of the Unitarian Historical Society*.

18 THE ROMAN CATHOLIC CHURCH IN ENGLAND, 1780–1940

There is a complete ecclesiastical narrative of Catholicism to 1890 by Bernard and Wilfrid Ward: Bernard Ward, *The Dawn of the Catholic Revival in England 1781–1803*, 2 vols, *The Eve of Catholic Emancipation 1803–1829*, 3 vols, *The Sequel to Catholic Emancipation 1830–1850*, 2 vols (London, 1909–15); Wilfrid Ward, *The Life and Times of Cardinal Wiseman*, 2 vols (London, 1897), *The Life of John Henry Cardinal Newman*, 2 vols (London, 1912). There are also more recent biographies by Meriol Trevor, Ian Ker and Sheridan Gilley. Other histories covering part or all of the period are G. A. Beck, *The English Catholics 1850–1950* (London, 1950); from a modern Anglo-Gallican viewpoint, J. Derek Holmes, *More Roman than Rome: English Catholicism in the Nineteenth Century* (London/Shepherdstown, 1978); and the sparkling Edward Norman, *The English Catholic Church in the Nineteenth Century* (Oxford, 1984). General histories of post-Tridentine English Catholicism include E. I. Watkin, *Roman Catholicism in England from the Reformation to 1950* (London, 1957), J. C. H. Aveling, *The Handle and the Axe: The Catholic Recusants in England from Reformation to Emancipation* (London,

1976) and Edward Norman, *Roman Catholicism in England from the Elizabethan Settlement to the Second Vatican Council* (Oxford, 1986). On social history see John Bossy, *The English Catholic Community 1570–1850* (London, 1975). On Jesuits see Bernard Basset SJ, *The English Jesuits from Campion to Martindale* (London, 1967) and Francis Edwards SJ, *The Jesuits in England: From 1580 to the Present Day* (London, 1985). Available on microfiche is Athanasius Allanson, 'History of the English Benedictine Congregation', MSS, Ampleforth Abbey. On Redemptorists see John Sharp, *Reapers of the Harvest: The Redemptorists in Great Britain and Ireland 1843–1898* (Dublin, 1989). On French émigrés see D. A. Bellenger, *The French Exiled Clergy in the British Isles after 1789: An Historical Introduction and Working List* (Downside Abbey, 1986). On seminary history see David Milburn, *A History of Ushaw College* (Ushaw, 1964). On the Irish see Lynn H. Lees, *Exiles of Erin: Irish Migrants in Victorian London* (Manchester, 1979), Roger Swift and Sheridan Gilley, *The Irish in the Victorian City* (London, 1985), Roger Swift and Sheridan Gilley, *The Irish in Britain 1815–1939* (London, 1989), M. Hickman and M. Hartigan, *The History of the Irish in Britain: A Bibliography* (London, 1986) and Frank Neal, *Sectarian Violence: The Liverpool Experience 1819–1914: An Aspect of Anglo-Irish History* (Manchester, 1988).

On Gothicism see Benjamin Ferrey, *Recollections of A. N. W. Pugin* (London, 1861), Michael Trappes-Lomax, *Pugin: A Mediaeval Victorian* (London, 1932), Phoebe Stanton, *Pugin* (London, 1971) and Kenneth Clark, *The Gothic Revival: An Essay in the History of Taste* (London, 1962). On Catholic architecture see Bryan Little, *Catholic Churches since 1623* (London, 1966). On conventualism see J. N. Murphy, *Terra Incognita: or, The Convents of the United Kingdom* (London, 1873) and Susan O'Brien, '*Terra Incognita*: The Nun in Nineteenth-Century England', *Past and Present*, 121 (1988), pp. 109–40. On convents and anti-Catholicism see Walter L. Arnstein, *Protestant versus Catholic in Mid-Victorian England: Mr Newdegate and the Nuns* (New York/London, 1982). On higher education see Vincent Alan McClelland, *English Roman Catholics and Higher Education 1830–1903* (Oxford, 1973). On intellectual history see Wilfrid Ward, *William George Ward and the Catholic Revival* (London, 1893) and Maisie Ward, *The Wilfrid Wards and the Transition*, vol. 1: *The Nineteenth Century* (London, 1934), and vol. 2: *Insurrection versus Resurrection* (London, 1937). On the liberal Catholic movement see Josef L. Altholz, *The Liberal Catholic Movement in England: The 'Rambler' and its Contributors 1848–1864* (London, 1962), *The Correspondence of Lord Acton and Richard Simpson*, 3 vols, ed. Josef L. Altholz, Damian McElrath and James C. Holland, (Cambridge, 1971–5). On modernism see L. F. Barmann, *Baron Friedrich von Hügel and the Modernist Crisis in England* (Cambridge, 1972) and Nicholas Sagovsky, *'On God's Side': A Life of George Tyrrell* (Oxford, 1990). On Wiseman see Richard J. Schiefen, *Nicholas Wiseman and the Transformation of English Catholicism* (Shepherdstown, 1984). On Manning see V. A. McClelland, *Cardinal Manning: His Public Life and Influence 1865–92* (London, 1962), Robert Gray, *Cardinal Manning: A Biography* (London, 1985) and John Fitzsimons (ed.), *Manning: Anglican and Catholic* (London, 1951). On Vaughan see J. G. Snead-Cox, *The Life of Cardinal Vaughan*, 2 vols (London,

1910) and Arthur McCormack MHM, *Cardinal Vaughan* (London, 1966). On Scottish Catholicism see James E. Handley, *The Irish in Scotland* (Cork, 1943), *The Irish in Modern Scotland* (Cork, 1947), *The Celtic Story: A History of the Celtic Football Club* (London, 1960) and *The Navvy in Scotland* (Cork, 1970); David McRoberts, (ed.), *Modern Scottish Catholicism 1878–1978* (Glasgow, 1979); and Tom Gallagher, *Glasgow: The Uneasy Peace: Religious Tension in Modern Scotland* (Manchester, 1987). On statistics see Jean Alain Lesourd, *Les Catholiques dans la Société Anglaise 1765–1865*, 2 vols (Lille, 1978). For the end of the period see Adrian Hastings, *A History of English Christianity 1920–1985* (London, 1986).

19 Religion and Community in Scotland and Wales since 1800

General

The section on 'Religion' in E. Royle, *Modern Britain: A Social History 1750–1985* (London, 1987) provides a useful introduction because it does take specific account of certain developments in Scotland and Wales within a general British context. Likewise there is a chapter in my *Nineteenth-Century Britain: Integration and Diversity* (Oxford, 1988) on religion in Scotland and Wales and its relationship to religion in England. I have also written an essay on 'Religion and Identity in Modern British History' in S. Mews (ed.), *Religion and National Identity*, 'Studies in Church History', vol. 18 (Oxford, 1982). It is reprinted, together with other relevant essays, in my *History, Religion and Identity in Modern Britain* (London, 1993). Statistical information will be found in R. Currie, A. D. Gilbert and L. Horsley, *Churches and Church-goers: Patterns of Church Growth in the British Isles since 1700* (Oxford, 1977). A. D. Gilbert advances a general thesis in his *The Making of Post-Christian Britain: A History of the Secularization of Modern Society* (London, 1980).

Scotland

J. H. S. Burleigh, *A Church History of Scotland* (London, 1960) is standard. There is still some interesting material in J. R. Fleming, *A History of the Church in Scotland 1843–1874* (Edinburgh, 1927) and his *A History of the Church in Scotland 1875–1929* (Edinburgh, 1933). Norman Macleod, *Reminiscences of a Highland Parish* (London, 1867) is also still worth reading. Callum Brown, *The Social History of Religion in Scotland since 1700* (London, 1987) is an admirable book with an ample bibliography. See also his 'Religion and Social Change', in T. M. Devine and R. Mitchison (eds), *People and Society in Scotland*, vol. 1: *1760–1830* (Edinburgh, 1988). There is a good chapter on 'Churchgoing' in T. C. Smout, *A Century of the Scottish People 1830–1950* (London, 1986). A. C. Cheyne, *The Transforming of the Kirk: Victorian Scotland's Religious Revolution* (Edinburgh, 1983) has many useful insights. There is also a great deal of information in three volumes by A. L. Drummond and J. Bulloch, *The Scottish Church, 1688–1843* (Edinburgh, 1973), *The Church in Victorian Scotland, 1843–1874* (Edinburgh, 1975) and *The Church in Late Victorian Scotland, 1874–1900* (Edinburgh, 1978). S. J. Brown, *Thomas Chalmers and the Godly Commonwealth* (Oxford, 1982) is an excellent biography of the outstanding Scottish churchman of the nineteenth century. There is no good treatment of the Church of Scotland in the twentieth century. Roman Catholicism is best approached through D. McRoberts (ed.), *Modern Scottish Catholicism 1878–1978* (Glasgow, 1979). M. Lochhead, *Episcopal Scotland in the Nineteenth Century* (London, 1966) opens up a not unimportant subject. D. W. Bebbington (ed.), *The Baptists in Scotland* (Glasgow, 1988) is a comprehensive account of a small minority. M. Small, *Growing Together: Some Aspects of the Ecumenical Movement in Scotland, 1924–1964* is a worthwhile initial study. Inter-communal relationships are considered in a rather different fashion in T. Gallagher, *Glasgow: The Uneasy Peace* (Manchester, 1987). See also the collection of essays edited by G. Walker and T. Gallagher, *Sermons and Battle Hymns: Protestant Popular Culture in Modern Scotland* (Edinburgh, 1990). Various aspects of the interaction between the churches and the community are considered in A. A. MacLaren, *Religion and Social Class: The Disruption Years in Aberdeen* (London, 1974), O. Checkland, *Philanthropy in Victorian Scotland* (Edinburgh, 1980), K. Boyd, *Scottish Church Attitudes to Sex, Marriage and the Family, 1850–1914* (Edinburgh, 1980), J. Springhall, B. Fraser and M. Hoare, *Sure & Stedfast: A History of the Boys' Brigade 1883 to 1983* (London and Glasgow, 1983) and A. P. F. Sell, *Defending and Declaring the Faith: Some Scottish Examples 1860–1920* (Exeter, 1987).

Wales

K. O. Morgan, *Wales: Rebirth of the Nation 1880–1980* (Oxford, 1981) places religious developments in a broad perspective. There are also helpful sections in the two books edited by Trevor Herbert and Gareth Elwyn Jones, *Wales 1880–1914* and *Wales between the Wars* (Cardiff, 1988). There are some valuable general reflections in the essays by Glanmor Williams collected under the title *Religion, Language and Nationality in Wales* (Cardiff, 1979) and his essay 'Fire on Cambria's Altar', in his *The Welsh and their Religion* (Cardiff, 1991). Articles by Ieuan Gwynedd Jones in D. Smith (ed.), *A People and a Proletariat* (London, 1980) and his collected articles published under the title *Explorations and Explanations: Essays in the Social History of Victorian Wales* (Llandysul, 1981) are invaluable. For the Church see David Walker (ed.), *A History of the Church in Wales* (Cardiff, 1976), P. M. H. Bell, *Disestablishment in Ireland and Wales* (London, 1969) and D. T. W. Price, *A History of the Church in Wales in the Twentieth Century* (Penarth, 1990). See also Price's essay 'Church and Society in Wales since Disestablishment', in P. B. L. Badham (ed.), *Religion, State and Society in Modern Britain* (Lampeter, 1989). There are denominational histories, normally written from within the denomination concerned, but there is no good recent history of Nonconformity as a whole over the period with which the chapter is concerned.

20 BRITISH RELIGION AND THE WIDER WORLD: MISSION AND EMPIRE, 1800–1940

The starting point for the modern history of missions still has to be K. Scott Latourette, *A History of the Expansion of Christianity*, 7 vols (London, 1937–45), of which vols 4–6 are the most relevant to the period under discussion. The best single-volume general history of missions is that by Stephen Neill, *A History of Christian Missions*, 2nd rev. ed. Owen Chadwick (Harmondsworth, 1986), which also contains an excellent bibliography. His *A History of Christianity in India, 1707–1858* (Cambridge, 1985) is also important. The forthcoming T. E. Yates, *Christian Mission in the Twentieth century* (Cambridge, 1994) will provide an important addition. The preparation of missionary clergy is treated by S. Piggin, *Making Evangelical Missionaries, 1789–1858: The Social Background, Motives, and Training of British Protestant Missionaries to India* (Oxford, 1984).

The various missionary societies have had their historians and the following are worthy of mention: E. Stock, *History of the Church Missionary Society*, 4 vols (London, 1899–1916), and G. Hewitt, *The Problems of Success: A History of the Church Missionary Society*, 2 vols (London, 1971–7); R. Lovett, *History of the London Missionary Society, 1795–1895*, 2 vols (London, 1899) and N. Goodall, *A History of the London Missionary Society, 1895–1945* (London, 1954); L. Nemer, *Anglican and Roman Catholic Attitudes on Missions: A Historical Study of Two English Missionary Societies in the Late Nineteenth Century, 1865–1885* (Washington, 1981), A. J. Broomhall, *Hudson Taylor and China's Open Century*, 7 vols (London, 1981–9) and, most recently, B. Stanley, *History of the Baptist Missionary Society, 1792–1992* (Edinburgh, 1992). Stanley has also written a general treatment of the subject: *The Bible and the Flag: Protestant Missions and British Imperialism in the Nineteenth and Twentieth Centuries* (Leicester, 1990).

C. P. Williams, *The Ideal of the Self-governing Church: A Study in Victorian Missionary Strategy* (Leiden, 1990) examines the attempts to develop indigenous churches. That these existed at all hints at the ambivalent impact of missions on different peoples. Aspects of this impact have been discussed in many monographs. J. F. A. Ajayi, *Christian Missions in Nigeria, 1841–1891: The Making of a New Mission Elite* (London, 1965) and E. A. Ayandele, *The Missionary Impact on Modern Nigeria, 1842–1914: A Political and Social Analysis* (London 1966) were pioneers for Africa but they have been followed by many others, including J. McCracken, *Politics and Christianity in Malawi, 1875–1940: The Impact of the Livingstone Missions in the Northern Province* (Cambridge, 1977), N. Etherington, *Preachers, Peasants and Politics in South East Africa, 1835–1880: African Christian Communities in Natal, Pondonland and Zululand* (London, 1979), G. O. Tasie, *Christian Missionary Enterprise in the Niger Delta, 1864–1918* (Leiden, 1978), M. L. Pirouet, *Black Evangelists: The Spread of Christianity in Uganda, 1891–1914* (London, 1978), B. A. Gow, *Madagascar and the Protestant Impact: The Work of British Missions, 1818–95* (London, 1979), T. O. Beidelman, *Colonial Evangelism: A Socio-historical Study of an East African Mission at the Grass Roots* (Bloomington, 1982), J. K. Agbeti, *West African Church History: Christian Missions and Church*

Foundations, 1482–1919 (London, 1986) and H. J. Sindima, *The Legacy of Scottish Missionaries in Zimbabwe* (Lampeter, 1992). Themes from these and many other studies have been brought together in the recent R. Gray, *Black Christians and White Missionaries* (New Haven, 1990). There have been comparable studies for other parts of the world, including N. Gunson, *Messengers of Grace: Evangelical Missionaries in the South Seas, 1797–1860* (Oxford, 1978), R. H. S. Boyd, *India and the Latin Captivity of the Church: The Cultural Context of the Gospel* (London, 1974), J. C. B. Webster, *The Christian Community and Change in Nineteenth Century North India* (Delhi, 1976), E. D. Potts, *British Baptist Missionaries in India, 1793–1837: The History of Serampore and its Mission* (Cambridge, 1967), M. A. Laird, *Missionaries and Education in Bengal, 1793–1837* (Oxford, 1972), G. A. Hood, *Mission Accomplished? The English Presbyterian Mission in Lingtung, South China: A Study of the Interplay between Mission Methods and their Historical Context* (Frankfurt, 1986).

There have been numerous biographies of figures connected with the emerging churches. Some of the most important of the modern period include A. Ross, *John Philip (1775–1851): Missions, Race and Politics in South Africa* (Aberdeen, 1986), T. E. Yates, *Venn and Victorian Bishops Abroad: The Missionary Policies of Henry Venn and their Repercussions upon the Anglican Episcopate of the Colonial Period, 1841–1872* (Uppsala, 1978), E. A. Ayandele, *Holy Johnson: Pioneer of African Nationalism, 1836–1917* (London, 1970), O. Chadwick, *Mackenzie's Grave* (London, 1959), P. Chiocchetta, *Daniel Comboni: Papers for the Evangelization of Africa* (Rome, 1982), P. Penner, *Robert Needham Cust, 1821–1898: A Personal Biography* (New York, 1987), W. R. Shenk, *Henry Venn, Missionary Statesman* (Maryknoll, 1983), E. J. Sharpe, *Not to Destroy but to Fulfil: The Contribution of J. M. Farquhar to Protestant Missionary Thought before 1914* (Uppsala, 1965), P. R. Bohr, *Famine in China and the Missionary: Timothy Richard as Relief Administrator and Advocate of National Reform* (Cambridge, Mass., 1972), H. Tinker, *The Ordeal of Love: C. F. Andrews and India* (Delhi, 1979), D. O'Connor, *Gospel, Raj and Swaraj: The Missionary Years of C. F. Andrews, 1904–14* (Frankfurt, 1990).

21 SECULARISTS AND RATIONALISTS, 1800–1940

The most up-to-date and wide-ranging survey is Susan Budd, *Varieties of Unbelief: Atheists and Agnostics in English Society, 1850–1960* (London, 1977), which incorporates her earlier essay on 'The Loss of Faith: Reasons for Unbelief among Members of the Secular Movement in England, 1850–1950', *Past and Present*, 36 (1967), pp. 106–25. A further general survey by a one-time president of the National Secular Society is David Tribe, *100 Years of Freethought* (London, 1967); and another centenary is celebrated in Jim Herrick, *Vision and Realism: A Hundred years of The Freethinker* (London, 1982).

The development of Secularist freethought from Thomas Paine until the First World War is the subject of Edward Royle, *Victorian Infidels: The Origins of the British Secularist Movement, 1791–1866* (Manchester, 1974) and *Radicals,*

Secularists and Republicans: Popular Freethought in Britain, 1866–1915 (Manchester, 1980). The same author has also provided a brief survey, *Radical Politics, 1790–1900: Religion and Unbelief* (London, 1971) and a collection of illustrative primary sources, *The Infidel Tradition from Paine to Bradlaugh* (London, 1976). A history of the most successful Leicester Secular Society is provided by D. Nash, *Secularism, Art and Freedom* (Leicester, 1992). Three earlier articles are still of value: John Eros, 'The Rise of Organized Freethought in mid-Victorian England', *Sociological Review*, 2 (1954), pp. 98–120, F. B. Smith, 'The Atheist Mission', in R. Robson (ed.), *Ideas and Institutions of Victorian Britain* (London, 1967) and F. H. Amphlett Micklewright, 'The Local History of Victorian Secularism', *Local Historian*, 8 (1969), pp. 221–7, which looks at the Lancashire village of Failsworth.

The prehistory of Victorian Secularism is best approached through A. O. Aldridge, *Man of Reason: The Life of Thomas Paine* (London, 1960), Iain McCalman, *Radical Underworld: Prophets, Revolutionaries and Pornographers in London, 1795–1840* (Cambridge, 1988), Joel H. Wiener, *Radicalism and Freethought in Nineteenth-Century Britain: The Life of Richard Carlile* (Westport, 1983) and John F. C. Harrison, *Robert Owen and the Owenites in Britain and America: The Quest for the New Moral World* (London, 1969). Further detail about leading secularists is provided in Lee Grugel, *George Jacob Holyoake: A Study in the Evolution of a Victorian Radical* (Philadelphia, 1977), David Tribe, *President Charles Bradlaugh, MP* (1971), Walter L. Arnstein, *The Bradlaugh Case: A Study in Late Victorian Opinion and Politics* (Oxford, 1965; 2nd edn 1984) and Anne Taylor, *Annie Besant, A Biography* (Oxford, 1992).

The other freethought movements are largely served by Susan Budd in 'The Loss of Faith' and 'The Humanist Societies: The Consequences of a Diffuse Belief System', in B. R. Wilson (ed.), *Patterns of Sectarianism: Organisation and Ideology in Social and Religious Movements* (London, 1967); Colin B. Campbell, *Towards a Sociology of Irreligion* (London, 1971); Ian MacKillop, *The British Ethical Societies* (Cambridge, 1986); and T. R. Wright, *The Religion of Humanity: The Impact of Comtean Positivism on Victorian Britain* (Cambridge, 1986).

Further references may be found in Gordon Stein, *Freethought in the United Kingdom and the Commonwealth: A Descriptive Bibliography* (Westport, 1981) and Gordon Stein (ed.), *The Encyclopedia of Unbelief*, 2 vols (Buffalo, NY, 1985).

22 THE JEWISH COMMUNITY IN BRITAIN

A brief description of the Jewish community in Britain may be found in N. de Lange, *Atlas of the Jewish World* (Oxford, 1984), pp. 168–71, part of a wider survey of world Jewry. There are a number of other one-volume works dealing with the history and religion of the Jews throughout the ages, for example, P. Johnson, *A History of the Jews* (London, 1987). For Britain's role, first as proponent then as opponent, in the rise of the State of Israel, see the relevant portions of R. Samuel, *A History of Israel: the Birth, Growth and Development of Today's Jewish State* (London, 1989).

A reasonably detailed description of Jewish settlement in England can be found under 'England' in the *Encyclopaedia Judaica* (Jerusalem, 1972), although entries under 'Scotland' and 'Wales' are less than satisfactory. Further information on English Jewry is available from C. Roth, *A History of the Jews in England*, 3rd edn (Oxford, 1964) and *The Rise of Provincial Jewry* (Oxford, 1948), although the former deals only with the period up to 1858, while the latter is concerned primarily with the eighteenth century. Nevertheless, the continuation of the story can be found in V. D. Lipman, *Social History of the Jews in England 1850–1950* (London, 1954) and H. Pollins, *Economic History of the Jews in England* (London, 1982), as also in a very recent book by Alderman described below. A useful companion to these is J. A. Romain, *The Jews of England: A Portrait of Anglo-Jewry through Original Sources and Illustrations*, 2nd edn (London, 1988), containing pictures and literary excerpts pertaining to Jewish life from the eleventh to the twentieth century.

Detailed work specifically on the Jews of Wales and Scotland is less readily available. Of interest regarding one aspect of the former is C. Holmes, 'The Tredegar Riots of 1911: Anti-Jewish Disturbances in South Wales', *Welsh History Review*, 11 (1982), pp. 214–25; more general references to the Jews of Wales in the context of the overall history of the country can be found in John Davies, *Hanes Cymru* (London, 1990). Readers should also look out for the forthcoming *The Jews of South Wales: Historical Studies*, edited by U. Henriques. As far as Scotland is concerned, the accounts in A. Levy, *The Origins of Glasgow Jewry* (Glasgow, 1949) and 'The Origins of Scottish Jewry', *Transactions of the Jewish Historical Society of England*, 19 (1955–9), pp. 129–62, are still useful, but can now be supplemented by H. L. Kaplan and K. E. Collins, *Aspects of Scottish Jewry* (Glasgow, 1987), and K. E. Collins, *Second City Jewry: The Jews of Glasgow in the Age of Expansion 1790–1919* (Glasgow, 1990).

Generally, many articles in the *Encyclopaedia Judaica* are worthy of consultation, including *inter alia* entries under 'United Synagogue', 'Board of Deputies of British Jews', 'Anti-Semitism', 'London', and various named individuals. More recent are two very helpful books, packed with information and eminently readable: S. Brook, *The Club: The Jews of Modern Britain* (London, 1987) and G. Alderman, *Modern British Jewry* (Oxford, 1992). Indeed, the present chapter has drawn not a few insights and details from both of these. The former, intended for a popular audience and incorporating the results of interviews with prominent Jews, contains sections on the religious divisions within modern British Jewry, as well as descriptions of its main institutions and concise consideration of the contemporary Jewish scene in London, Manchester and Glasgow. The book by Alderman, a weightier and more academically oriented volume, is arranged chronologically and examines the social and intellectual history of British Jews over the past 150 years; the last chapter, 'A House Divided', includes up-to-date population figures for the main Jewish centres in Britain. A number of chapters in D. Wood (ed.), *Christianity and Judaism* (Oxford, 1992) on various aspects of the Jews in Britain from medieval to modern times will also suit those seeking detailed academic studies.

Those needing to inform or remind themselves of the nature and content of Jewish religion throughout the ages might refer to either of the following in the first instance: N. de Lange, *Judaism* (Oxford, 1986) or D. J. Goldberg and J. D. Rayner, *The Jewish People: Their History and their Religion* (London, 1987). Similarly, others wishing to study Orthodox or Progressive liturgy might consult S. Singer, *The Authorized Daily Prayer Book of the United Hebrew Congregations of the British Commonwealth of Nations* (London, 1962) or J. D. Rayner, *Service of the Heart* (London, 1967), respectively. Finally, the main English version of the Bible in use among Jews in Britain is the Jewish Publication Society's *Tanakh – the Holy Scriptures* (New York, 1985).

23 RELIGIOUS LIFE BETWEEN THE WARS, 1920–1940

The essential starting-point for any study of English religion in this period is Adrian Hastings, *A History of English Christianity 1920–90* (London, 1991). The statistics of church involvement are to be found in Robert Currie, Alan Gilbert and Lee Horsley, *Churches and Churchgoers: Patterns of Church Growth in the British Isles since 1700* (Oxford, 1977).

On the churches' experience of war and peace, a good survey is Alan Wilkinson, *Dissent or Conform? War, Peace and the English Churches 1900–1945* (London, 1986). Martin Ceadel, *Pacifism in Britain 1914–45* (Oxford, 1980) has set Christian witness in a broader context. Stuart Mews discusses 'The Hunger-Strike of the Lord Mayor of Cork, 1920: Irish, English and Vatican Attitudes', in W. J. Sheils and Diana Wood (eds), *The Churches, Ireland and the Irish* (Oxford, 1989). Keith Robbins's essay on 'Britain, 1940 and Christian Civilization' in D. E. D. Beales and Geoffrey Best (eds), *History, Society and the Churches* (Oxford, 1985) draws attention to an important theme in the ideological defence of Christian Britain in its gravest hour, as also does Stuart Mews in 'The Sword of the Spirit: A Catholic Cultural Crusade of 1940', in W. J. Sheils (ed.), *The Church and War* (Oxford, 1983). David L. Edwards has provided penetrating studies of Randall Davidson, Cosmo Lang and William Temple in his *Leaders of the Church of England 1828–1944* (Oxford, 1971). Other recent studies of significant Anglican individuals include Owen Chadwick, *Hensley Henson: A Study in the Friction between Church and State* (Oxford, 1983) and Sheila Fletcher, *Maude Royden: A Life* (Oxford, 1989). A fine study which also uses government papers has come from Thomas Maloney: *Westminster, Whitehall and the Vatican: The Role of Cardinal Hinsley 1935–43* (London, 1985).

Owen Chadwick's biography of *Michael Ramsey* (Oxford, 1990) gives a good account of Cambridge and theological debate in this period. Keith W. Clements in *Lovers of Discord: Twentieth Century Controversies in England* (London, 1988) covers some of the flashpoints.

The term 'Anglo-Catholic' is carefully examined and the inter-war developments in the High Church tradition are traced by Alan Wilkinson in *The Community of the Resurrection: A Centenary History* (London, 1992). 'The Revival of Spiritual Healing in the Church of England 1920–26' was considered by Stuart

Mews in W. J. Sheils (ed.), *The Church and Healing* (Oxford, 1982). A vivid account of successive ministers of Greenfield Congregational Church, Bradford, by Clyde Binfield is to be found in Stuart Mews (ed.), *Modern Religious Rebels* (London, 1993), which also contains a discussion of Canon John Collins by Haddon Willmer. A new study of William Temple by John Kent was published by Cambridge University Press in 1993.

On the social teaching of the Church of England, a sound study is John Oliver's *The Church and Social Order* (London, 1968). A more controversial account by E. R. Norman is *Religion and Society 1770–1970* (Oxford, 1976). The biography of *Maurice B. Reckitt* (London, 1988), the inspirer of the Christendom movement of Christian socialism, was written by John Peart-Binns. Gerald Studdert-Kennedy has written a stimulating and detached study of *Dog-Collar Democracy: The Industrial Christian Fellowship, 1919–29* (London, 1982). The reaction of the churches to the general strike was examined by Stuart Mews in Margaret Morris (ed.), *The General Strike of 1926* (London 1976). An unusual study of Methodism in a mining village in County Durham has been written by Robert Moore, *Pit-men, Preachers and Politics* (Cambridge, 1974). Another important local study which challenges the conventional view of secularization is Jeffrey Cox, *The English Churches in a Secular Society: Lambeth, 1870–1930* (Oxford, 1982).

An important essay on 'Working-class Gambling in Britain, 1880–1939', which questions the accusations made by religious people, is to be found in Ross McKibbin, *The Ideologies of Class: Social Relations in Britain 1880–1950* (Oxford, 1991). The focus of *Sex, Politics and Society* (Harlow, 1981) by Jeffrey Weeks is summed up in the subtitle: 'The Regulation of Sexuality since 1800'. Kenneth M. Wolfe, *The Churches and the British Broadcasting Association 1922–1956* (London, 1984) is comprehensive and authoritative.

24 THE CHRISTIAN CHURCHES IN ENGLAND SINCE 1945:
ECUMENISM AND SOCIAL CONCERN

On the Ecumenical Movement the most readable survey with a British emphasis is John Matthews, *The Unity Scene* (London, 1986). A fuller but earlier account is Barry Till, *The Churches' Search for Unity* (London, 1972). The founding of the World Council of Churches is covered lucidly and from the inside by Leonard Hodgson, *The Ecumenical Movement* (Sewanee, 1951). R. M. C. Jeffery's *Case Studies in Unity* (London, 1972) is good on local experiments to 1972.

On worship and the Liturgical Movement, Horton Davies's *Worship and Theology in England*, vol. 5: *The Ecumenical Century, 1900–1965* (Oxford, 1965) is the very readable standard work. A useful introductory book is Alfred R. Shands, *The Liturgical Movement and the Local Church* (London, 1959). A fine example of intensive ecumenical study of liturgy is the collection of essays edited by Cheslyn Jones, G. Wainwright and E. Yarnold, *The Study of Liturgy* (London, 1978). The growing impact of the study of liturgy on systematic theology is visible in Geoffrey Wainwright's *Doxology: A Systematic Theology* (London, 1980).

Among histories of denominations it is well worth consulting Rupert Davies'

'Since 1932', in Rupert E. Davies, A. Raymond George and E. Gordon Rupp (eds), *A History of the Methodist Church in Great Britain*, vol. 3 (London, 1983). Paul A. Welsby has produced a judicious *History of the Church of England, 1945–1980* (Oxford, 1984). The most comprehensive survey and interesting interpretation of the social outlook of the leadership of the Church of England is E. R. Norman's *Church and Society in England, 1770–1970* (Oxford, 1976). Above all, Adrian Hastings' *History of English Christianity 1920–1990* (London, 1991) is a mine of information and illumination.

25 RELIGIOUS PLURALISM IN MODERN BRITAIN

The statistics cited in the course of this chapter are largely derived either from the English Church Census edited by Peter Brierley, *Christian England* (London, 1991) or from my own edited work, *Religion, State and Society in Modern Britain* (Lampeter, 1989). The latter work includes chapters on each of the major groupings in modern Britain by a leading expert on that denomination or religion. It will be apparent that my comments here owe a great deal to what I have learnt from my fellow contributors to that volume. In particular, quotations from Eileen Barker, Deirdre Green and George Moyser are from their chapters in that book, and my discussion of unconscious Secularism depends on the documentation provided in my own contribution. My historical analogies were prompted by A. D. Gilbert, *Religion and Society in Industrial England 1740–1914* (London, 1976).

The English Church Census is the latest of an ongoing series published by Marc Europe and the Bible Society, starting with *Prospects for the Eighties* and continuing with *Prospects for Wales, Prospects for Scotland,* and *Prospects for the Nineties*. This group also publishes the annual *UK Christian Handbook*. These volumes contain by far the fullest documentation of the state of the Christian churches. For insights into how the present situation came about I recommend Adrian Hastings, *A History of English Christianity* (London, 1991) and Alan Gilbert, *The Making of Post-Christian Britain* (London, 1980). The Church of England's response to the challenge of secularization can be seen in the reports of the Archbishops' Commissions on *Faith in the City* (London, 1985) and *Faith in the Countryside* (London, 1990). John Habgood provided a very perceptive analysis of the role of the Church in the modern world in his *Church and Nation in a Secular Age* (London, 1983).

Some very useful discussions of the present situation from a wider perspective can be seen in Rabbi Dan Cohn-Sherbok (ed.), *Canterbury Papers on Religion and Society* (London, 1990), in Terence Thomas (ed.) *The British, their Religious Beliefs and Practices* (London, 1988) and in Haddon Willmer (ed.), *20/20 Visions* (London, 1992). For a model of thorough research into the most controversial of the newer sects the reader is referred to Eileen Barker's work, *The Making of a Moonie* (Oxford, 1984) as well as to her wider survey on the field of *New Religious Movements* (London, 1989). On the issue of religious pluralism, Dan Cohn-Sherbok has drawn together writings by the leading protagonists in his edited volume. *Many Mansions* (London, 1992).

26 SECULARIZATION AND THE FUTURE

The essential texts for the study of secularization have been referred to directly in the chapter, but readers seeking a broad historical perspective are directed to K. Thomas, *Religion and the Decline of Magic* (1971), R. Currie, A. D. Gilbert and L. Horsley, *Churches and Churchgoers: Patterns of Church Growth in the British Isles Since 1700* (1977), S. S. Acquaviva, *The Decline of the Sacred in Industrial Society* (1979) and Alan Gilbert, *The Making of Post-Christian Britain: A History of the Secularization of Modern Society*. The essays in D. Martin, *The Religious and the Secular* (1969) represent the response of a leading British sociologist to the notion of secularization. Contemporary surveys of the churches in Britain and attitudes to religion are found in J. Cumming and P. Burns (eds), *The Church Now: An Inquiry into the Present State of the Catholic Church in Britain and Ireland* (1980), W. Oddie (ed.), *After the Deluge: Essays Towards the Desecularization of the Church* (1987), *Prospects for the Eighties: From a Census of the Churches in 1979 Undertaken by the Nationwide Initiative in Evangelism* (London, 1980) and N. Webb and R. Wybrow (eds), *The Gallup Report* (London, 1982).

Index

Aaron of Caerleon   21, 436
Aaron of Lincoln   429
Aaron of York   429
Abbot, George   168
abortion   482, 485–6, 533
absenteeism, clerical see non-residence,
   clerical
Act of Settlement, 1701   178
Act of Supremacy, 1559   157, 188, 525
Act of Toleration, 1689   4, 5, 147, 175,
   178, 199, 206, 209, 236, 251, 269,
   409, 529
Act of Uniformity, 1559   157–8, 188,
   234, 525
Act of Uniformity, 1662   204, 527
Acton, Charles Januarius, Cardinal   357
Adler, Felix   419
Adler, Hermann   434–5
Adler, Nathan Marcus   433–5, 440,
   530
Adomnan, St   99–100, 101, 103
Adrian IV, Pope   50, 524
Advent, celebration of   104
Aed   106
Aedan macGabhrain, King of
   Dalriada   99
Aelflaed, Abbess of Whitby   34
Aelfric, Abbot of Eynsham   43, 47, 524
Aelgyfu, Queen of England   42
Aethelwig   43
Aetla   37
affirmation, for objectors to oaths   414
Afro-Caribbean churches see 'black-led'
   churches
Agilbert, Bishop of Wessex   33, 37
agnosticism   8, 411, 417, 488–9, 501–2
Aidan, St   31–2, 34, 35, 38, 523

Aikenhead, Thomas   212
Ailred, St, Abbot of Rievaulx   53, 54,
   524
Alban, St   21
   cult of   21, 523
Alchfrid, sub-King of Deira   34
Alcuin   40, 524
Aldhelm, St   36
Aldwine, Abbot of Winchcombe   41
Alexander II, King of Scotland   105
Alexander III, King of Scotland   104,
   105, 108
Alexander III, Pope   50, 51
Alexander VI, Pope   63
Alfred the Great   40–1, 42, 46, 81, 524
Allen, Grant   417
Allen, William   239
Allestree, Richard   173
Allon, Henry   327
Ames, William   193
Amidei, A.   438–9
Amigo, Peter   464
Anabaptists   196, 199
anchorites   2, 54–5, 65, 69, 524
Anderson, John   394
Andrew, St, cult of   87, 101–7, 121, 523
Andrewes, Lancelot   168–9, 171, 174,
   184
Anglican Communion   299–300, 452,
   460, 470, 483
Anglicanism   60, 168, 170, 172, 174–7,
   180, 182, 187, 204, 268, 296–301,
   322
Anglican religious orders   298–9, 467,
   469, 530–2, 533
   Community of the
      Resurrection   298–9, 532

Community of St John the
Baptist 298, 530
Community of St Mary the
Virgin 298, 530
Society of the Most Holy Trinity
(Devonport Sisterhood) 298, 530
Society of the Sacred Mission 299,
469, 532
Society of St John the
Evangelist 298, 531
Anglo-Catholicism 6, 297–301, 311,
346, 353, 355–6, 390, 393, 401,
450–3, 475, 479
Anian Ddu 88
Anne, Queen 143, 177, 178, 206, 266,
294
see also Queen Anne's Bounty
Anselm, St, Archbishop of
Canterbury 49, 54, 524
Anthroposophists 340
anticlericalism 67, 124, 175, 193, 195,
197, 198, 304, 312, 316, 359, 407,
412–13
antinomianism 146, 173, 196, 197, 199,
267
antisemitism 410, 427–32, 435–8,
441–4, 461, 496, 524, 531–2
'blood libel' 428, 430
Apologists 196
Apostolic Succession 200, 301, 475
Appasamy, A. J. 456
appeal to antiquity 96–7, 99, 170–1,
188, 194, 470
Aquinas, St Thomas 63
Arch, Joseph 360
architecture, religious 14–17, 39, 42,
53, 65, 92, 100, 118, 122, 151, 181,
299, 316, 330–2, 339–40, 343,
352–3, 358
Arianism 175, 176, 196, 210, 315
Arimathea, Joseph of 96–7
Aristotle 62
Arminianism 4, 144, 149, 165, 168–9,
171–2, 175, 210, 256, 258, 267, 295
Arnold, Matthew 327, 505, 515
art, religious 15, 19, 22–3, 25, 32,
36–7, 42–3, 47, 65, 72, 81, 92,
102–3, 120–1, 151, 167, 299, 316,
340, 343

Articles of Faith
Ten, of 1536 152–3
Six, of 1539 153, 524
Thirty-Eight, of 1563 159
Thirty-Nine, of 1571 159–60,
169–70, 257, 298, 525
subscription to 278, 291, 301, 527,
530
artificial insemination 472
Ascension Day, celebration of 139
Ash Wednesday, celebration of 243
Asher, Asher 440
Asquith, Herbert 327, 339
Asser 79, 81
Association for Promoting the Unity of
Christendom 358
Assumption of the Blessed Virgin Mary
dogma of 476, 532
feast of 119
atheism 8, 146, 175, 176, 197, 212,
218, 221, 317, 373, 408–9, 412, 416,
417, 488, 501–2, 515
Atkinson, Henry 412
atomic bombs, dropping of 476–7
atonement, doctrine of 171–2, 272, 302,
353
Atterbury, Francis 179, 528
Attlee, Clement 471
Augustus Caesar 14
Augustine of Canterbury, St 28–9, 38,
48, 96, 523
Augustine of Hippo, St, in controversy
with Pelagius 23
Augustinian Canons 50, 53, 107–9, 114,
116, 130, 134, 135
aumbry, use of 119–20, 353
Austin, Alfred 355
authority of Scripture 168–9, 212–13,
216, 218–22, 224–30, 302, 464
Averroës 62
Avicenna 62
Azariah, Samuel 401

Babington plot, 1586 240
Badawi, Dr Zaki 521
Bagshawe, Edward 360
Baillie, Robert 141, 195
Baines, Peter Augustine 355
Baker, Augustine 241
Baldwin, Stanley 453

Balfour, A. J. 369
Balfour, John 259
Ballard, Frank 451
Bamford, Samuel 310
Bancroft, Richard 526
Banks, T. Lewis 330
baptism 26, 28–9, 45, 47, 58, 84, 139,
 152, 169, 174, 181, 185–6, 191, 200,
 272, 376, 399, 484, 489, 501
 believers' (adult) baptism 175, 191–3,
 199
 rebaptism 191
Baptists 149, 175, 191, 198–203, 205,
 209–10, 271–2, 279, 280, 327–8,
 340, 343, 354, 382–3, 470, 474, 479,
 481, 490–1, 505
 Baptist Missionary Society 264, 272,
 384, 387, 389, 391
 General Baptists 192–3, 198, 202,
 209, 210, 526
 New Connexion Baptists 491
 Particular Baptists 193, 197, 198,
 209, 383
 in Scotland 366, 370, 372
 Strict Baptists 271–2
 in Wales 209, 374–5, 378, 438
Barclay, Robert 205
Barker, Joseph 413, 414
Barnett, Henrietta 327–8
Barrow, Henry 189–90
Barry, F. R. 449–50
Barth, Karl 402, 463, 468
Baxter, Richard 166, 205, 210, 269–70,
 527
Beardsley, Aubrey 355
Beaton, David 131, 132
Beattie, James 148
à Becket, St Thomas 45, 51, 70, 524
Bede, the Venerable 1, 25–30, 32,
 34–7, 38, 39, 44, 101, 524
Beesly, Edward Spencer 418
Begbie, Harold 452
Bell, George 465
Belloc, Hilaire 356, 459
Benedict III, Pope 112
Benedict XV, Pope 403, 462
Benedict Biscop 35–6
Benedictines 2, 36, 41, 50, 52, 86, 88,
 103, 241, 250, 298, 347, 349–50, 355

Bennet, Thomas 175
Benson, Edward 300
Benson, Richard Meux 298
Benson, Robert Hugh 356
Bentley, Richard 176
Berdyaev, Nicholas 476
Berington, Joseph 248, 348–9
Berkeley, George 176, 223–4, 231
Bernard, St 53
Bernham, David 105
Besant, Annie 413–15
Betjeman, Sir John 356
Beuno, St 80, 82
Beza, Theodore 144, 163, 171
Bible Society see British and Foreign
 Bible Society
biblical criticism 149–50, 225, 303–4,
 370, 444–5, 531
Bickersteth, Robert 317
Bilney, Thomas 152, 525
Birinus, St 32–3, 37
Birkhead, George 242
birth control 8, 415, 418, 460–1, 466,
 480, 489
Bishop, William 242
bishoprics see diocesan system
bishops, appointment of 35, 43, 47–9,
 51, 56, 85, 89–90, 91, 93, 107, 108,
 113, 129–30, 137, 179
 resignations of Marian bishops 235
Bissett, Baldred 99
Blacader, Robert 210
Black Death 62–4, 66, 90
'black-led' churches 8, 290, 485,
 489–90, 494–5
Blackwell, George 241–2
Blair, Hugh, Edinburgh Councillor 439
Blair, Hugh, preacher 148
blasphemy 203, 212, 406–7, 411,
 416–17, 432, 497, 527
Blessed Sacrament, devotion to 119–20,
 349, 358, 450
Blomfield, Charles James 283
Bloom, Metropolitan Anthony 483
Blount, Charles 212, 222
Blunt, A. W. F. 461
Blunt, Wilfrid Scawen 356
Board of Deputies of British Jews 427,
 433, 443, 496, 529

Boece, Hector 115
Boleyn, Anne, Queen 150
Bonhoeffer, Dietrich 482, 507
Boniface 49
Boniface, St 1, 38, 523
Books of Discipline, Scottish Reformed
    First 134–6, 138, 525
    Second 138, 526
Booth, Charles 305
Booth, William 541
Boston, Thomas 261
Boudicca (Boadicea) 14, 524
Bourne, Francis 361, 453, 459, 462
Bower, Walter 116, 117, 524
Boyd, Robert 144
Boys' Brigade 331, 372
Bradford, John 190
Bradlaugh, Charles 7, 412–17, 422–3,
    531
Brainerd, David 260
Bramhall, John 168, 174, 176
Breakspear, Nicholas *see* Adrian IV,
    Pope
Brearely, Roger 193–4
Bretherton, John 454
Brethren, Christian 154
Brethren, Open 514
Brevint, Daniel 174
Bridei 101
Bridge, William 196
Bridges, John Henry 419
Bridgettines 350
Brierley, Harold 331–2
Brierley, Peter 512
British Council of Churches 469, 473,
    476–9, 483, 520, 532
British and Foreign Bible Society 296,
    512, 528
British and Foreign Schools Society 529
broadcasting, religious 455, 460, 464,
    482, 500–1, 512–13
Brodie, Sir Israel, Chief Rabbi 434, 444
Bronze Age religion 1, 13
Brown, David 439
Browne, Peter 228, 231
Browne, Robert 189, 526
Brownists 160, 196
Bruce, Robert 101, 106–7, 111
Brut, Walter 91

Brwynog, Siôn 95
Bucer, Martin 134, 155–6
Buchman, Frank 457
Buddhism 399, 456, 489–90, 495–6
Bulgakov, Sergei 476
Bull, George 173
Bultmann, Rudolf 482, 492
Bunting, Jabez 255–6
Bunyan, John 198, 527
burial 13, 16, 19, 21, 25, 46–7, 83, 84,
    169, 180, 181, 185–6, 283, 302, 431,
    440–1, 500, 531
Burkit, William 184
Burnell, Robert 56
Burnet, Gilbert 172, 179
Burroughes, Jeremiah 194
Butler, Joseph 176, 226–7, 231
Butterfield, William 300
Buxton, T. F. 389
Byron, Lord 433

Cadog, St 78, 80, 82–3, 86
Cadoux, C. J. 470
Caedmon of Whitby 30
Caedwallon 30, 33
Cairns, D. S. 449
Calvin, John 134, 144, 188, 273
Calvinism 3, 4, 7, 138, 141, 146, 148,
    162–7, 168–74, 188–9, 191, 193,
    195–8, 201, 206–7, 210, 257–8,
    271–3, 281, 296, 298, 302–3, 337,
    375, 491, 525
    hyper-Calvinism 197, 271–3, 382–4
Camden Society (Ecclesiological
    Society) 300, 529
Cameron, John 144
Cameron, Richard 143
Campaign for Nuclear
    Disarmament 477, 533
Campbell, Archibald 147
Campbell, George 148
Campion, Edmund 526
Candole, Henry de 456, 473–4
canon law, development of 2, 47, 48,
    51–2, 116, 139, 265–6
Canterbury, See of 28, 35–7, 41, 45,
    48, 50–1, 85, 180, 526
    primacy of 2, 35, 48, 85, 87, 91, 105,
    452, 524
Carey, Dr George 496

Carey, William 273, 383–8, 391
Carlile, Richard 408–9, 412
Carlyle, Dom Aelred 299
Carmelites (White Friars) 109, 349
Carter, Henry 461
Carthusians 53, 66, 349
Cartwright, Thomas 161, 163, 194–5, 525
Caswall, Edward 356
catechesis 29, 93, 164–5, 172, 181–3, 185, 242, 246–7, 255, 259
  see also education
catechisms 4, 131–2, 141, 144, 164–6, 169–70, 172, 181–2, 187, 250, 255, 290
  in Irish 182
  in Welsh 182
catechists 28, 182, 258, 385, 400–1
cathedrals 2, 46, 49–50, 65, 68–9, 76, 87–8, 105–7, 109–10, 115, 120, 169, 291–2, 300, 343, 361, 472, 477, 524, 527, 529
Catholic Apostolic Church 297, 354, 409, 529
Catholic Association, Irish 351
Catholic Fund for Overseas Development (CAFOD) 487
Catholic Institute for International Relations 487
Catholic relief *see* Roman Catholic emancipation
Catholic seminaries and colleges 235, 237–40, 244, 246–7, 247, 249, 350, 352, 355, 357, 522
Cecil, William 157
Cedd, St 26, 32
Celestine III, Pope 105
celibacy, clerical 44, 46, 57, 94–5, 104, 153, 155, 159, 525
  not the custom in Welsh Church 79, 86
Celtic Christianity 2, 30–2, 34–7, 38–40, 77–86, 89, 98, 103
Celtic religion 13–14, 15, 77
  syncretized by Romans 1, 14–17
Cent, Siôn, Welsh poet 92–3
Cenwahl, King of Wessex 33
Ceolfrith, Abbot of Jarrow 36, 38
Chad, St 32, 35, 81

Chadwick Report, 1970 282
Chadwick, Samuel 455
Challoner, Richard 249–51, 528
Chalmers, Thomas 310, 366–7, 530
Chamberlain, Neville 464
chaplains, military 290, 357, 370, 449–50, 458, 461
chaplains, prison 357
charismatic movement 8, 484, 490, 492
Charlemagne 102, 523
Charles I, King 139, 140–1, 177, 180, 195, 235, 527
Charles II, King 4, 140–2, 178, 180, 204, 235, 245, 247
Charles, R. H. 454
Châtelherault, Duke of 134–5
Chaucer, Geoffrey 67, 70
Chesterton, G. K. 356, 459
Chidley, Katherine 199, 209
Chief Rabbi, office of 427, 433–5, 437, 440–1, 445, 530
Chillingworth, William 174, 216, 231
choirs 115, 187, 299, 314, 344, 352–3, 380
  Secularist 415–16
Christian Aid 469
Christian Healing Mission 457–8
The Christian Instructor, Evangelical magazine 149
Christian socialism 304–5, 311, 316, 328, 360, 368, 451, 462
Christina of Markyate 54–5
Christmas, celebration of 28, 139, 243, 333
Chubb, Thomas 222, 231
church attendance, levels of 8, 83–4, 186–7, 290, 293, 300, 306–8, 313, 316, 318, 346, 361, 372, 373–4, 472, 489–90, 495, 500, 512–14
church and chapel building
  programmes 2, 42, 44, 46–7, 64–5, 92, 139, 285, 291, 294, 306, 308–9, 319, 352, 390, 529
  Church Building Society 294, 529
Church Commissioners *see* Ecclesiastical Commission
Church courts 45, 48, 51–2, 56, 137, 142, 178, 267

Church of Ireland   282, 293, 350, 469, 528–9
Church Missionary Society (CMS)   295, 383–4, 387, 389–91, 392–7, 403, 528
Church Pastoral Aid Society   512
Church rates   265, 282, 301, 411, 531
Church schools *see under* education; schools, Church
Church of Scotland   3, 110, 134–40, 257–64, 268, 277–8, 365–7, 370–3, 474, 475
Church Society   300
Church Union *see* English Church Union
Church in Wales   253–7, 258, 259, 264, 277, 314, 374–9
Church, W. D.   339
Churches' Council of Healing   472
churchwardens   161
Cistercians   2, 52–3, 87–8, 90, 91, 108, 115, 524
Civil War   65
Clapham Sect   294–5, 382, 383, 528
Clapton Sect *see* Hackney Phalanx
Clark, Neville   474
Clarke, Samuel   221, 223–4, 226, 231
Claudius Caesar   14
Clayton, P. B.   458
Clifford, John   328
Clifford, W. K.   506
Close, Francis   295
Cluniacs   52, 108
Cnut, King   41–3, 45, 46
Cobb, Howard   458
Cobbett, William   352
Cohen, Chapman   417
Cohen, Isaac   440
Coifi   25, 27, 29
Coit, Stanton   419
Cok Hagin   429
Coke, Thomas   383
Cole, G. D. H.   462
Colenso, J. W.   303, 531
Coleridge, Samuel Taylor   282, 296–7, 302
Colet, John   154
Collins, Anthony   212, 220–1, 231, 405
Collins, John   477
Columba of Iona, St   30–1, 34, 99–103, 105–7, 116, 523

Comber, Thomas   174
Commonwealth   141
Communion   141, 155, 157, 169, 182–3, 185–7, 243, 253–4, 259, 261–3, 369, 376, 453, 473–4, 475, 479, 500
   in both kinds   153, 181
   tables to replace altars   159
   as a religious test   235
   see also Eucharist, Mass
communism   454, 467, 477–8
   Russian, fear of   457–8
Compton, Henry   175
Comte, Auguste   411, 418, 507
Comyn, John, murder of   111
confession   55, 58–9, 89, 93, 153, 242, 244, 270, 300
Confession of Faith, Scottish   134, 136
confirmation   139, 183, 186, 250, 475, 489, 513–14
Congregationalism   6, 149, 203, 207–8, 323–6, 329–43, 382–3, 411, 450, 462, 470, 474, 479
   in Scotland   366
   in Wales   374–5, 377
   see also Independents
Congreve, Richard   418
Connelly, Cornelia   354
Connelly, Pierce   354
Conrad, Emperor   42
Constantine I, King of the Picts   102
Constantine II, King of the Picts   106
Constantine, Emperor   97, 102, 103
Continental sceptics   212
conventicles   142–3, 189, 194, 206, 293, 527
conversion
   of England   1, 25–33, 36
   of Scotland   99–101
   of Wales   77–8, 96–8
Convocations   152, 176, 178–9, 277
   revival of   287, 299, 530–1
Conway, Moncure Daniel   419
Conybeare, John   224–5, 231
Cooper, Robert   410, 411
COPEC (Interdenominational Conference on Politics, Economics and Citizenship)   458–9, 468, 532

Corpus Christi, feast of 68, 119, 120, 167, 361
Cosin, John 171, 174, 181, 184
Council of Christians and Jews 461
Council of Churches for Britain and Ireland 485
Council of Mosques 522
Counter-Reformation 75, 237–51, 253, 347, 351, 357–8
Covenants, Scottish 3, 132, 140–2, 144, 145, 148, 195, 259, 261–3, 526–7
Coventry Cathedral, reconciliation work of 472
Cowper, William 138
Crallo, St 78
Cranmer, Thomas 152, 154, 156, 162, 525
Creech, Thomas 212
Crichton, Lord 118
Cripps, Sir Stafford 462
Cromwell, Oliver 3, 7, 141, 247, 326, 342–3, 427, 431
Cromwell, Thomas 123, 152, 154
Cross, devotion to 95
Crowther, Samuel 391, 392, 394, 531
Crusades 63, 70, 259, 355, 428, 524
  attacks on British Jews at Crusade times 428–9
Cubitt, James 330
Culdees 103, 108
Culverwel, Nathanael 217, 231
Cumin, Hugh 262
Cupitt, Don 495
curates 109, 124, 185–6, 292, 304
Cuthbert, St 27–8, 36, 42, 523
Cynegils 33

Danish invasions 1, 40–2, 47, 64, 80, 84
D'Arcy, Charles 456
D'Arcy, Martin 459
Darney, William 263–4
Darwin, Charles 302, 531
Darwinism 303, 420
  social Darwinism 393–4
David I, King of Scotland 104, 105
David II, King of Scotland 105
David, St 78, 80, 81, 83, 87, 523
Davidson, Randall 398, 452–3, 459
Davies, D. R. 462–3

Davies, Horton 481
Davies, Howel 256
Davies, Idris 380
Davies, Richard 86, 91, 96–7
Davies, R. Aled 481
Davis, David 440
Davis, Morry 360
Dawson, Christopher 459, 464
Dawson, W. J. 340–3
Deaconesses, Order of 296, 531
deacons 30–1, 137, 161, 314, 339, 377, 474
Defoe, Daniel 209
Deism 4–5, 144, 146, 147, 175, 176, 220–2, 405–7, 411
Demant, V. E. 467–8, 471
Denison, George Anthony 300, 530
Dent, J. M. 340
Derham, William 223, 231
diocesan system 2, 23, 37, 56–7, 79–80, 85, 92, 107, 116, 180, 299, 529–30
  Roman Catholic 356–7, 370
  Irish Anglican 293, 297
disestablishment 167, 277, 278, 280, 282, 284, 286, 288, 530
  in Ireland 5, 277, 282, 288, 293, 531
  in Wales 5, 7, 277, 288, 290, 314, 375–8, 532
Disraeli, Benjamin 360
Dissent, Protestant 4–5, 158, 175, 177–9, 187, 188–210, 255–8, 265, 269–71, 278–86, 288, 290, 291, 293–7, 301, 322–7, 337, 374–6, 382, 409, 419, 490–1, 525–33
  Presbyterian, in Scotland 365–70
  see also Free Churches, Nonconformity
Dissenting academies and colleges 204, 324–6, 369, 375, 473, 528
dissolution of monasteries *see under* monasticism
divine right of kings, doctrine of 137, 177–8
divorce 457, 461, 482, 486, 531
Dix, Dom Gregory 467, 473–4, 532
Dodd, C. H. 470
Doddridge, Philip 210, 269–70
Dominicans (Black Friars) 58, 88, 109, 115, 123, 130, 131, 247, 524
Domnall Brec 99

Donald Ban, King of Scotland 106
Dougall, Lily 456
Douglas, C. H. 462
Douglas, John 134
Dowsing, William 65
Doyle, Sir Arthur Conan 451
druids 13, 14
Drysdale, George 412
Dubricius, St 78
Duff, Alexander 368–9
Dunbar, William 118
Duncan, Earl of Fife 106
Duns Scotus 63, 114–15
Dunstan, St 1, 41, 42, 47, 523
Duthac of Tain, St 117, 121
Dyfrig, St 88
Dyke, Jeremy 183

Eadfrith, Bishop of Lindisfarne 32
Eanfled, Princess of Northumbria 29,
    30
Eanfrid, Queen of Northumbria 34
Eanfrith, King of Northumbria 30
Easter 160, 428
  celebration of 31, 57, 59, 118–19, 139
  controversy over dating of 31–2,
    34–5, 524
Easter Rising (Ireland, 1916) 453
Eastern Orthodox churches 476, 478
Eastern religions, influence of 410, 456,
    483, 494
Eaton, Samuel 193
Ebba, St 117
Ecclesiastical Commission 297, 529
Ecclestone, Alan 473
ecumenism 8, 150, 372–3, 379, 401–2,
    450, 452–3, 458–9, 465–6, 471–81,
    483–5, 487, 491, 532–3
  bilateral conversations:
    Anglican–Orthodox 476; Anglican–
    Roman Catholic 358, 453, 475–6,
    479–80; Church of Scotland–Roman
    Catholic 372
  'Not Strangers but Pilgrims'
    process 484–5
  Roman Catholic Unity Secretariat 479
  see also British Council of Churches;
    International Missionary Council;
    Life and Work Movement; union
    agreements, Church; unity

conversations; World Council of
    Churches
Edgar, King of England 41, 42, 524
Edmund, King of East Anglia 40
Edmund, King of Wessex 42
education 408, 417, 458, 469, 471,
    531–2, 533–4
  of Christian laity 29, 39, 40–1, 57–8,
    71, 93, 95, 110, 131, 164–5, 169,
    171, 182–5, 208, 351
  of clergy 45–6, 50, 52, 55, 57, 70–1,
    90, 93, 116, 129, 131, 143–4, 158,
    171, 180, 250, 255, 291–2, 299, 367,
    369, 375
  church involvement in secular 40, 45,
    53–4, 59, 66, 70–1, 80–1, 88, 112,
    115–16, 134, 148, 180–1, 208,
    253–4, 258, 280, 282–6, 288, 290,
    291, 294, 296, 298, 301–2, 311–13,
    315, 319, 354–5, 357, 500, 528–9
  founding of schools 180, 208, 253–5,
    301
  in India and Africa 384, 386–7, 400,
    401, 529
  in public schools 301, 316
  Ragged Schools movement 296, 301
  raising of clergy standards 129, 131,
    181–3, 250
  religious education 416–17, 471,
    482–3, 489, 496–7, 500
  training of missionaries 384–5
  see also catechesis; Catholic seminaries
    and colleges; Church schools;
    Dissenting academies and colleges;
    Islamic Schools; Jewish schools and
    colleges; Sunday schools; theological
    colleges
Edward the Confessor 43, 47
Edward I, King of England 7, 45, 88,
    89, 427, 429–30
Edward VI, King of England 94, 95,
    132, 154, 156, 157, 170, 430
Edward VIII, King of England,
    abdication of 461
Edwards, John 220, 227, 231
Edwards, Jonathan 261, 264, 270, 382
Edwards, Thomas 196–7
Edwin, King of Northumbria 27, 29,
    30, 32, 33, 251

Egbert, King of Kent 35
Egbert, first Archbishop of York 35, 37
Egbert, Northumbrian abbot 38
Egyptian deities, worship of 19
elders 136–7, 161, 191, 192, 201, 259, 262, 314, 327, 368
Elias le Evesque 429
Elijah Menahem ben Moses 430
Eliot, T. S. 356, 467, 471, 481, 509, 532
Elizabeth I, Queen 94, 95–7, 133, 157–61, 162, 170, 180, 189, 194, 234–5, 237, 430–1, 525
Ellis, John 228, 232
Elphinstone, William 109, 113, 114, 115, 117, 120, 524
Emma of Normandy, Queen of England 43
emperor worship 14
English Church Union 300, 531
Enlightenment 146–9, 175, 252, 268, 270, 302, 407, 446, 491
environmentalism 408
Eorpwald, King of East Anglia 32
Episcopalianism, Scottish 145, 257–9, 263, 366, 372, 475, 528
Erasmus 115, 524
Errington, George 358
Erskine, Ebenezer 147, 260–1
Erskine, John 263
Erskine, Ralph 261
Ethelbert, King of Kent 24, 26, 28
Ethelburga, Queen of Northumbria 29
Ethelred, King of Wessex 40
Ethelred II, 'the Unready' 41, 43
Ethelwold, Bishop of Winchester 1, 41
Ethical Movement 418–21
Eucharist 8, 20, 23, 152–3, 155–60, 174, 183, 272, 469–70, 475, 484
  doctrine of 74, 153, 157–60, 174, 213, 301, 315
  see also Blessed Sacraments, Communion, Corpus Christi, Lord's Supper, Mass
Euddogwy, St 88
euthanasia 482, 486
Evangelical Alliance 296

Evangelical Revivals 5, 149, 154, 210, 252–3, 255, 259–72, 280, 346, 348, 382, 491, 511, 531
Evangelicalism 3, 5, 123, 146, 149, 151–2, 255, 259–60, 263–4, 270, 289, 294–8, 302, 314–17, 320–1, 347–8, 353, 354, 358, 365–6, 374, 382–4, 394–5, 399, 411, 420, 451, 475, 479, 483, 490–1, 498, 508–12, 514, 528–9, 531
evangelism 46, 77, 123, 149, 180–1, 261, 295, 300, 306, 312, 317, 335, 366, 382, 386–7, 389, 399, 404–5, 469, 472, 493, 512, 533
  itinerant 77, 253, 255–6, 261–2, 263–4, 270, 293, 527
Evans, Gwynfor 379
Evans, Stanley 463
Evans-Gordon, W. 435
Evelyn, John 183
Everard, John 195
Every, George 463
Exchequer of the Jews 429
excommunication 51, 57, 58, 140, 148, 165, 259, 298, 525
  of Elizabeth I 234, 347, 525
exorcisms 83, 243, 492

Faber, Frederick William 358
Familists 196
Family of Love 160
fasting 243
Felix, St 32, 523
Fellowship of St Alban and St Sergius 476, 532
feminism 485, 497
Ferneys, Richard 69
Ferrar, Robert 95
Field, John 161
Finan, Bishop of Lindisfarne 34
Findlater, Thomas 262
Findley, George 418
First World War 343, 370, 376–7, 416–18, 421, 442, 449–53, 457–8, 460–1, 466, 506
Fisher, Edward, theologian 146
Fisher, Geoffrey 474–5, 479
Fisher, St John 525
Fleetwood, William 183
Flew, R. N. 475

Florovsky, George 476
folk Christianity 289, 319–20, 488, 490, 499–501
Foote, George William 415–16
Forbes, John, of Corse 138, 144
Fothad, Bishop of Alban 107
Fox, George 202, 213–14, 232, 527
Fox, W. J. 411, 419
Foxe, John 156, 160, 525
Franciscans (Grey Friars) 58–9, 63, 88, 91, 109, 118, 122, 130, 250, 524
  Observant Franciscans 3, 118–19, 122
Fraser, William 106
Free Church of England 300
Free Church of Scotland 7, 366–7, 370, 530, 532
Free Churches 278, 288, 314, 327–30, 343, 450, 452, 454–5, 462, 466, 469–70, 475, 489–90
  see also Dissent, Protestant; Nonconformity
Free Church Federal Council 452
freethought 405–6, 415–21, 531
  see also Rationalism
French Revolution, impact of 278, 293–5, 349, 382, 405, 433
Frere, W. H. 453
friars 2, 58, 90–3, 115, 123, 153
  see also Carmelites, Dominicans, Franciscans, Trinitarians
Friends, Society of 469, 481
  see also Quakers
Fullerton, Lady Georgiana 356
fundamentals, doctrine of 171
funerals, *see* burial
Fursey (or Fursa) 32

Gaitskell, Hugh 462, 502
gambling, campaigns against 379, 454–5, 466, 471–2
Gandhi, Mahatma 461
Garbett, Cyril 460, 471
Gardiner, Stephen 155
Gardiner, Temple 396
Gasquet, Francis Aidan 453
Gau, John 130
Gaunt, Major 247
General Assembly, Scottish 136–8,

140–1, 142, 145–6, 277–82, 365–6, 370, 373, 475, 526
George III, King 180
George VI, King 370, 460–1
Gerald of Wales (Giraldus Cambrensis) 87
Gerard, Alexander 148
Germanus of Auxerre, St 23, 77, 523
Gibbon, Edward 212
Gibson, Edmund 174, 175, 179, 228, 232, 269
Gilbert of Sempringham, St 53, 524
Gilbertines 53, 524
Gilby, Anthony 160
Gildas 23, 77, 80, 83, 523
Gillespie, George 139, 141
Gillies, John 262
Gladstone, William Ewart 282, 288, 293, 301, 357, 376, 416
Glencairn, Earl of 122
Glover, T. R. 450
Glyndŵr, Owain 90–1, 524
Glynn, William 86
godparents 183, 186
Godric of Finchale 54
Godwin, William 407
Good Friday, celebration of 95, 139
Goodwin, Thomas 196
Gordon, General 396
Gordon, Lord George 251, 528
Gordon Riots, 1780 251, 528
Gore, Charles 298–9, 303–4, 451
Gother, John 248–9
Gould, F. J. 417
Gowland, William 473
Graham, Billy 470–1, 533
Graham, Patrick 113
Grant, Brewin 411
Gratian 51
Graves, Robert 461
Green, Peter 454
Green, T. H. 303, 332–3
Greene, Graham 356
Greenwood, John 189
Greenwood, Thomas 327–8
Gregory the Great, St, Pope 28, 36, 38, 48
Gregory VII, Pope 48
Gregory X, Pope 87

Grimshaw, William 264
Grindal, Edmund 158, 526
Grosseteste, Robert 56, 59, 107
Guthrie, James 142
Guthrum, leader of Danish invaders
    40
Guyse, Thomas 213, 232

Hackney Phalanx 294
Haddow, John 146
Hadrian, African missionary 35
Haeckel, Ernst 417
Hagin son of Moses 429
Haldane, James 149
Haldane, Robert 149
Haldenstone, James 116–17
Hales, John 171
Halifax, Charles Lindley Wood
    (Lord) 453, 464
Hamilton, Archibald 261–2
Hamilton, John 3, 131, 134–5
Hamilton, Patrick 130, 525
Hammond, Henry 168, 171, 173, 177
Hampden, Renn Dickson 302
Hampstead Garden Suburb Free
    Church 327–9, 340
Harding, Stephen 53
Hare Krishna movement 8, 493, 495
Harold, King of England 43
Harold Godwinson, King of England 24
Harris, Howel 252, 256, 374, 528
Harrison, Frederic 418
Harthacnut, King of England 43
Harvey, Monnox 249–50
Hawksmoor, Nicholas 181
Hawker, Robert 355
Hazzard, Dorothy 209
Heck, Barbara 269
Headlam, Stewart 304, 422
healing, spiritual 16–17, 83, 451, 456,
    457–8, 472, 483
Hebert, Gabriel, SSM 469–70
Heenan, John 465
Hegel, G. W. F. 303
Heiu, Abbess of Hartlepool 32
hell 89, 93, 186, 210, 214, 295, 302–3,
    312, 318, 332, 341
Helwys, Thomas 192–3
Henderson, Alexander 139–41
Hennell, Charles 507

Henrietta Maria, Queen 235, 238, 245
Henry I, King 49, 51
Henry II, King 45, 51
Henry III, King 49, 55, 429, 430
Henry V, King 68
Henry VIII, King 24, 68, 94–5, 113,
    130, 152–3, 156, 157, 430, 525
Henry, Matthew 270
Henry, Philip 269–70
Henson, Hensley 451, 457–8, 461
Herbert, A. P. 457
Herbert, Baron Edward 214–15, 232,
    526
Herbert, George 165, 526
hermits 2, 36, 54–5, 65, 69, 79, 524
Hertz, Joseph Herman 435
Herzl, Theodor 443
Heylyn, Peter 172
Heywood, Oliver 208
Hickes, George 175
Hickson, James Moore 457–8
Hild, St, Abbess of Whitby 32, 34–5,
    36, 37, 523
Hill, George 148–9
Hilton, Walter 72
Hirschell, Solomon 437
Hindu faith and culture 383, 385–7,
    391, 489–90, 493, 495
Hinsley, Arthur 462, 464–5
Hoadly, Benjamin 267
Hobbes, Thomas 212, 527
Hoby, Margaret 163
Hodgson, Leonard 484
Hog, James 260
Holiness churches 514, 519
Holland, Henry Scott 303–4
Holloway, George Hartley 333–6, 338
Holyoake, George Jacob 7, 289,
    410–13, 417–18, 421, 530
homosexuality 447, 482
Hook, Walter 299
Hooker, Richard 165, 168, 171, 176,
    526
Hopkins, Gerard Manley 355
Horneck, Anthony 266
Horsley, Samuel 294
Hort, F. J. A. 303
hospice movement 486

house churches   8, 21–2, 473, 484–5, 491, 514
Howard, Edward   357
Howard, Philip   247
Howell, William   184
Howie, Robert   144
Huddleston, Trevor   478
Hudson, Noel   456
Huet, Thomas   96
Hügel, Baron Friedrich von   360
Hugh of Wells   55
Hughes, Hugh Price   279
Hughes, Joshua   376
Hughes, Marian   298, 530
Hughes, Stephen   255
Hume, David   148, 212, 229–31, 232, 528
Hunne, Richard   154
Hunt, John   211
Hunt, Thornton   411
Hunter, Leslie   472
Huntingdon, Countess of   267, 528
Hus, John   64
Hutchinson, John   227, 294
Huxley, T. H.   359
Huxtable, John   474
hymns   183, 187, 209, 280, 300–1, 315, 318, 369, 474, 531
   Owenite Socialist   409, 415
   Secularist   7, 415–16

iconoclasm   65, 121, 131, 133, 153
Illtud, St   78, 80, 86
Immaculate Conception, dogma of   530
incense, use of   38, 57, 94, 300, 361
independent evangelical churches   489–90, 515
Independents   193, 194–6, 203, 205, 209, 255–6, 262, 270–1, 379, 489
   see also Congregationalism
indulgences, sale of   90, 94
Industrial Christian Fellowship   458
industrial mission   472–3, 486
Inman, Francis   166
Innocent III, Pope   50, 51
Innocent VIII, Pope   113
Institute of the Blessed Virgin Mary   241, 248
interfaith dialogue   385–6, 461, 493, 497

International Missionary Council   400–2, 468, 532
Iona   30–1, 99, 101–2, 106, 480–1, 523
Iredell, Bill   463
Irish rebellions   235
Irving, Edward   296, 353, 408, 529
   see also Catholic Apostolic Church
Islam   9, 62–3, 64, 211, 221, 352, 383, 386, 397–8, 428, 432, 489, 495, 497–8, 520–1
Islamic schools   498

Jacob ben Judah   430
Jacob, Henry   192–4, 205, 526
Jacob of London   425
Jacobite cause   145, 174, 179, 236, 249, 251, 252, 257–8, 348, 366, 528
Jacobs, Louis   444
Jakobovits, Immanuel   434, 496
James I, King of Scotland   112, 121–2
James II, King of Scotland   121
James III, King of Scotland   113, 118, 121
James IV, King of Scotland   116, 118, 119, 121–2, 140
James V, King of Scotland   112, 124
James VI of Scotland and I of England   3, 136, 138, 165, 235, 526
James VII of Scotland and II of England   143, 177–8, 206, 235–6, 242, 247–9, 346, 347, 527
James VIII, 'the Old Pretender'   145
James the Deacon   30, 31
Jansenist controversies   249
Jasper, R. C. D.   481
Jehovah's Witnesses   8, 490, 492
Jellicoe, Basil   460
Jenkins, David   463, 515
Jenkinson, Charles   460
Jenks, Benjamin   184
Jesuits   235, 237, 239–42, 347–8, 350, 361, 362, 390, 526
   establishment of English Province   240–1, 526
Jewish Archpresbyter, office of   425
Jewish–Christian dialogue   461
Jewish converts to Christianity   430–1, 438–9, 496
Jewish schools and colleges   434–5, 439, 442, 444, 448, 530, 532

Jews, British 7–8, 21, 64, 427–48, 489,
496, 529–33
  Crown guarantees to 431–2, 434
  in England 360, 417, 427–8, 437,
    439–44, 446, 448, 527
  in Scotland 427, 434, 435, 438–43,
    445–6, 448
  in Wales 21, 427, 435, 436–8, 441,
    445–6
  evangelism of 496, 529
Joel, Moses 440
John, King of England 43, 51
John XXIII, Pope 479
John Paul II, Pope 510–11
John of Leyden 199
John of Salisbury 59
Johnson, Francis 189–92
Johnson, Hewlett 463
Johnson, John 130
Johnson, Lionel 355
Johnson, Samuel 294, 504
Johnston, Archibald 140, 142
Johnston, Sir Harry 395–6, 397–8
Jones, Griffith 256, 263–4, 528
Jones, Robert 255
Josce son of Isaac 425
Jourdain, Ignatius 163
Jowett, Benjamin 303
Judaism 7–8, 20–1, 62–3, 64, 208, 346,
    419, 427–48, 461, 489–90, 496, 524,
    527, 529–33
  Liberal 7–8, 427, 436, 446–9, 532
  Orthodox 7–8, 360, 427, 435–6, 439,
    443–9
  Reform 427, 435, 442, 444–8, 533
  ultra-Orthodox 445–6
Julian of Norwich 69, 72, 73, 524
Julius II, Pope 63
Julius of Caerlon 21
Julius Caesar 14
justice system, role of Church in 45
justification, doctrine of 170–4, 273,
    317

Keach, Benjamin 205
Keble, John 297, 529
Kempe, Margery 70, 73, 524
à Kempis, Thomas 64
Ken, Thomas 169
Kennedy, Geoffrey Studdert 458

Kennedy, Walter 119
Kenneth macAlpin, King of
    Scotland 102–3
Kentigern, St 100, 107
Kiffin, William 201
King, Edward 299–300
King's College, London 302–3, 529,
    530
Kingsley, Charles 304
Kinnock, Neil 503
Kirk, P. T. R. 458
Kirkpatrick, Maxwell 339
Knibb, William 388
Knowlton, Charles 412, 417
Knox, John 121, 129, 131–3, 525
Knox, Ronald 355, 459–60
Kraemer, Hendrik 402

Lambeth Conference 299–300, 452,
    460, 470, 531
Lanfranc 44, 48, 52
Lang, Cosmo Gordon 290, 453, 457–8,
    461, 464–5
Langland, William 67
Langton, Stephen 51, 56
Lateran Council, Fourth, 1215 2, 51,
    52, 55, 56, 524
  antisemitic provisions of 429–30
Latimer, Hugh 152–3, 156, 525
Latitudinarianism 4, 169, 173, 175,
    179, 266, 301–2
Laud, William 4, 139, 165, 174, 176–7,
    181, 184, 193, 195, 216, 526–7
Lauder, William 116
Law, William 169, 176, 228
Lawson, Dorothy 244
lay preachers 314, 320, 528
lay readers 304
League of Nations, support for 454
Lecky, William 505
lectureships, endowed 162, 223
Leech, Kenneth 483, 486
Leechman, William 148
Leeson, Spencer 471
Leicester, Countess of 54
Leighton, Robert 144
Leland, John 224, 230
Lent, celebration of 104, 119, 185, 243,
    484
Lenwood, Frank 450–1

Leuthere, Bishop of Winchester 33
Levellers 198
Lever, Thomas 159
Lewis, C. S. 356
Lewis, John 182
Lewis, Saunders 379
Lewis, Wyndham 356
Lewys, Huw 96
Leyburn, John 247–8
liberalism, theological 148, 359, 402–4,
    462–3, 467–8, 509, 515–16
liberation theology 500
Liddon, H. P. 303
Life and Liberty movement 451–2, 456
Life and Work movement 458–9,
    468–9, 532
Lightfoot, J. B. 303
Lindisfarne 31–2, 36, 40, 101, 251
Lingard, John 352
liturgy 2, 4, 38–40, 61, 72, 95, 107–8,
    117, 119, 136, 139, 153–6, 159–60,
    168, 170, 174, 177, 180–1, 184, 187,
    195, 204, 339, 353, 473–4, 525, 532
    Aberdeen Breviary 117, 119, 525
    Alternative Service Book, 1980 485,
    533
    Book of Common Order 136
    Book of Common Prayer,
        English 95–6, 155, 157, 161, 169,
        174, 181–2, 184, 187, 293, 294, 354,
        474, 485; of 1549 95, 155, 157,
        182, 525; of 1552 95, 155–7, 524;
        of 1559 157–8; of 1662 491; in
        Welsh 96–8
    Book of Common Prayer, Scottish 3,
    139
    Directory for the Public Worship of
        God 141
    Joint Liturgical Group 481
    liturgical revision,
        twentieth-century 455–6, 480–1,
    485
    Presbyterian Service Book 480–1
    Sarum rite (or use) 72, 107, 117, 119
Liturgical Movement 456, 469, 473–4,
    476, 480–1, 485
    International Consultation on English
        Texts 481

Liverpool, Lord (Robert Banks
    Jenkinson) 294
Livingstone, David 388–90
Lloyd George, David 376
Lloyd, William 174
Llywelyn ap Gruffyd, Prince of
    Wales 87, 88
Locke, John 213, 218–20, 224, 227–30,
    265, 527
Lodge, Sir Oliver 451
Lollards 2–3, 72, 74, 91, 131, 151,
    153–4, 156, 189, 253, 524
London Missionary Society 383–4, 388,
    390, 397, 528
London, See of 26, 41, 49–50, 154, 251
Lopez, Roderigo, physician to Elizabeth
    I 431
Lord's Supper 169, 183, 481
    see also Communion, Eucharist, Mass
Lowder, Charles 300
Luce, H. K. 449
Ludlow, J. M. 304
Lunn, Arnold 459–60
Lutheranism 3, 130, 152, 154, 159,
    170, 172, 252, 259, 265, 268, 301,
    457, 464–5
    German Lutheran missionaries 381,
    384
Lutyens, Edwin 329
Lyndsay, Sir David 132
Lyell, Charles 302
Lyne, Joseph (Father Ignatius) 298

McCulloch, William 262–3
MacDonald, Ramsay 329, 453
Machar, St 106
MacKinnon, Donald 477
MacLeod, George 481
Macmurray, John 463
M'Neile, Hugh 296
MacSwiney, Terence 453–4
Maelgwn Gwynedd, prince of North
    Wales 81
Maimonides 430
Mair (or Major), John 115
Mair, John 261
Malcolm III, King of Scotland 103–5,
    107
Malcolm IV, King of Scotland 105
Maltby, Edward 357

Malthus, Thomas 412
Malvoisin, William 107
Manassah ben Israel 431
Mann, Horace 306, 309, 360
Manning, Bernard L. 474
Manning, Henry Edward 304, 348,
   355, 358–60, 361, 370, 504, 530
Mannix, Daniel 454
Manson, T. W. 470
Margaret, St, Queen of Scotland 103–5,
   107, 524
Margaret of Denmark, Queen of
   Scotland 121
Marks, Mark 437
marriage 24, 45, 47, 51–2, 55–6, 58,
   71, 104, 181, 183, 185–6, 199, 208,
   236, 242, 282, 355, 376, 418, 434,
   482, 486, 489, 500–1, 528–9, 531
   see also divorce
Marsh, Adam 59
Marsh, John 474
Marshman, Joshua 385–6
Martin V, Pope 112
Martineau, Harriet 411
Martival, Bishop of Salisbury 56
Martyr, Peter 155
martyrdom
   under Roman occupation 21
   of early English kings 33–4, 40
   of Becket 45, 51, 524
   of Lollards 74, 151, 153, 524
   of Protestants in Scotland 130–1,
      142, 525
   of Protestant under Henry VIII 152,
      525
   of More and Fisher 525
   of Protestants under Mary 156–7,
      189, 212, 346, 525
   of Catholics under Elizabeth I 212,
      235, 240, 525
   of Archbishop Laud 177, 529
   of Charles I 140–1, 177, 180, 200,
      527
   of Separatists 160–1, 189, 526
Marxism 360, 462–3, 477, 506, 508
Mary I, Queen of England 94, 95,
   156–8, 189, 237, 431, 525
Mary, Queen with William III 143,
   178, 218, 236, 432, 527

Mary of Gueldres, Queen of
   Scotland 122
Mary of Guise, Queen Mother of
   Scotland 130–1
Mary, Queen of Scots 99, 130–6, 234,
   527
Masefield, John 329
Mass 45, 47, 57–8, 65, 67–9, 94, 95,
   104, 117–19, 121, 153, 155, 237,
   243–6, 249–51, 313, 351, 357, 453
   for the dead 67–8, 117–18, 151–3,
      339
   proscription of 134, 234
   see also Communion, Eucharist, Lord's
      Supper
Maurice, F. D. 282, 302–4, 530
Maurice, Henry 255–6
Mayne, Cuthbert 244, 526
medical work, church involvement
   in 53–4, 67, 69, 71, 92, 185,
      285–6, 298, 304, 354, 472, 483
   in overseas mission field 400–1
Mellitus, Bishop of London 26, 29
Melville, Andrew 138, 143–4, 526
Mercier, Desire Joseph 453
Methodism 85, 187, 254–8, 264–71,
   279, 293, 312, 314–15, 318, 340–3,
   388, 395, 409, 412, 420, 422, 451,
   454–5, 459, 461, 464, 479, 490–1,
   512–13, 528–33
   American 268–9
   Free 340, 491
   Independent 314, 316
   Irish 268
   Luton Industrial College 473
   Methodist Missionary Society 383,
      529
   Mission Alongside the Poor 486
   Primitive 315, 360, 492, 529
   Scottish 366, 370, 372, 491
   Union of Wesleyan, Primitive and
      United Methodist Churches 452,
      532
   Welsh Calvinistic 7, 256–7, 374, 377,
      491
   Wesleyan 279, 293, 314, 324, 340–1,
      366, 374, 383, 388, 413, 451–2, 455,
      529–32
   Whitefield's Scottish mission 261–3

mice, church 47
Michael, St, cult of 82
Michael, David 436
Michael, Francis 436
Michael, Jacob 436
Michael, Jonas 440
Michael, Levi 436
Micklem, Nathaniel 470, 474
Micklem, Romilly 474
Mill, John Stuart 359, 411
millenarianism (millennialism) 198–200,
    203, 263, 296, 382, 394, 396, 400–1,
    408, 457, 492
  Owenite socialist 408–9
Miller, J. C. 316
Mill Hill Fathers 389, 531
Milner, John 349
Milner-White, Eric 451
Milton, John 167
miracles 78, 80, 82–4, 92, 176, 222,
    225–6, 229–30, 302, 457, 528
missionary outreach 306, 325–6, 356,
    468, 470–3, 478
  British to European continent 37–8,
    251
  to British urban poor 58, 249–50,
    295–6, 300, 304, 306, 311–12,
    316–17, 329, 332, 361, 486
  Irish to England 28, 30–2, 34,
    38
  Irish to Scotland 101
  Keswick Convention 395, 403
  Lausanne Congress 322
  Owenite Socialist 409–12, 415–16
  overseas 7, 62, 270, 381–405; in
    Africa 381, 384, 387–9, 391–401,
    403–4, 450; with American
    'Indians' 260, 381–2; in
    China 389, 394–5, 398, 403, 531;
    in India 381–7, 389–91, 393, 397,
    400–1, 403–5, 474; in South
    America 381; to South Sea
    Islands 384; to West Indies
    387–8
  Quaker in England 210
  Roman Catholic to England 236–51,
    526
  Scottish overseas 150, 259, 264
  Tranquebar mission 253

  see also Baptist Missionary Society;
    Church Missionary Society;
  industrial mission; London Missionary
    Society; Methodist Missionary
    Society; Universities' Mission to
    Central Africa
Mithraism 18, 19–20
Mitrinovic, Dimitrije 462
Moderators 161
Modern Churchmen's Union 450
Moffatt, James 470
Moffatt, Robert 388
Monasticism 1–3, 27–8, 31–4, 37, 41–3,
    46, 48, 52–5, 57, 58–9, 64, 66–7,
    69–70, 78–81, 85–6, 88–94, 104,
    107–9, 115, 123–4, 129, 353, 503,
    523–5, 531, 533
  dissolution of monasteries 94, 123,
    153, 154, 525
  re-emergence in Counter-
    Reformation 241, 242, 248, 347–8,
    358
  see also Augustinian Canons;
    Benedictines; Bridgettines;
    Carthusians; Cistercians; Cluniacs;
    Culdees; Gilbertines; Tironensians;
    Trappists; Valliscaulians; Welsh
    monastic saints
Montagu, Lady 243–4
Montagu, Lily 435, 446
Montagu, Samuel 434, 531
Montefiore, C. J. G. 435, 446
Moonies *see* Unification Church
Moravians 268, 484
More, St Thomas 166–7, 524
Morgan, William 98
Mormons 8, 490, 492
Mortimer, Robert 455
Mosley, Sir Oswald 442, 461
Moule, Handley 394
Muggletonians 201
Munby, D. L. 481–2
Mungo, St 117
Murray, Gilbert 369
music, church 115, 122, 181, 187, 249,
    299, 311, 314, 315, 339–40, 344,
    352–3, 369, 380, 455–6, 501
Muslims *see* Islam
Myers, J. H. 439

mystery cults, Eastern 19
Mystery plays 2, 67–8, 120–1, 151

National Secular Society 412–16, 421–2,
    461, 531
National Society [for Promoting the
    Education of the Poor in the
    Principles of the Established
    Church] 294, 529
Nationalism
    English 436
    Irish 350–1, 359–60, 371, 453–4
    Scottish 364, 372
    Welsh 364, 375–80
Nationwide Initiative in Evangelism
    512
Nayler, James 203
Neale, John Mason 299, 301
Neill, Stephen 381
Nelson, Robert 184
nepotism, clerical 111–12, 292
'New Age' movements 492, 494
Newman, Francis 411
Newman, John Henry 248, 289, 297–8,
    302, 349, 354–6, 358–9, 411, 530–1
Newton, Sir Isaac 227, 265, 267, 294
Niebuhr, Reinhold 463
Nightingale, Florence 354
Ninian, St 37, 100, 103, 107, 121, 523
Nominated Assembly 198, 200
Nonconformity 6–7, 206–9, 248, 250,
    279, 283–4, 288, 293, 301, 303,
    307–15, 319–20, 322–3, 325–6, 346,
    348, 361, 374–9, 407, 419, 450, 454,
    479, 491, 500
    see also Dissent, Protestant; Free
    Churches
Non-Jurors 145, 178, 257, 293, 527
non-residence, clerical 90, 92, 93, 109,
    124, 266, 292, 297, 529
Norman Conquest 1–2, 7, 30, 79, 43,
    47, 52, 84–5
Norris, Henry Handley 294
Norris, John 217
Norwood, F. W. 464
nuclear power and weapons
    issues 476–7, 486–7
Nye, Philip 196

O'Connell, Daniel 350

O'Connor, T. P. 360
Oddie, William 510, 521
Oldcastle, Sir John 74
Oldham, J. H. 398, 468
Ollivant, Alfred 376
ONE for Christian Renewal 479
Orage, A. R. 462
Orchard, W. E. 462
Osric, King of Northumbria 30
Oswald, St, Archbishop of York 41,
    524
Oswald, St, King of
    Northumbria 30–1, 33–4
    cult of 34
Oswiu, King of Northumbria 33–5
Otto, J. C. 438–9
Owain Gwynedd, Prince of North
    Wales 87
Owen, John 205
Owen, Robert 408–14, 421, 529
Oxford Movement 289, 297–303, 366,
    504, 505, 529–30

pacifism 194, 202, 203, 328, 452, 461,
    465
paganism 1, 5, 13–14, 21–3, 24–30,
    32–4, 39, 47, 58, 96, 221, 222, 352,
    386, 492
Paine, Thomas 212, 230, 232, 407–8,
    419–20, 528
Padarn, St 80
Paley, William 230–1, 232, 302, 528
Palmerston, Lord 296
Pantin, William 75
papal authority 38, 241, 277, 347, 349,
    452
    in England 33, 35, 38, 48–51, 59, 62,
    63, 150, 356–7, 359, 362, 484, 524
    in Scotland 99, 105, 111–13, 116,
    123, 132, 134
    in Wales 86–7, 89–90, 94, 97
Paris, Matthew 49
Parish and People Movement 473–4,
    479
Parker, Joseph 343
Parker, Matthew 160, 525
Parkes, James 461
parochial system 2, 39, 46, 57–8, 65,
    83–4, 85–6, 107, 111, 120, 124, 129,

151, 154, 162, 182–7, 199, 254, 266, 282, 286, 291–3, 309–10, 375, 472–4
  division of parishes   184, 293
Passion, cult of the   3, 118–20
Passion plays   119
Passionists   358
Passover   428, 430
Patmore, Coventry   355
Paton, Alan   478
Patrick of Ireland, St   23, 523
Patrick, Simon   173, 175
patristics, interest in   170, 298, 470
patronage   3–4, 46–7, 51, 108, 111, 117–18, 120, 136–7, 142, 145, 147–9, 184, 257–8, 261–2, 264, 266, 267, 292, 366, 528
Pattison, Mark   303
Paulinus, St   29–30, 523
Payne, Ernest A.   481
Peada, son of Penda of Mercia   33
Pearson, J. L.   299
Peckham, John   56
Peirce, James   210
Pelagius   23, 77, 84, 96, 523
penance   47, 48, 57, 69, 84, 152
  see also confession
Penda, King of Mercia   30, 33–4
Penn, William   206, 211, 527
Penry, John   253, 526
Pentecostalism   8, 456, 489–92, 494–5, 514, 520–1
Penty, G. H.   462
Perkins, E. Benson   454–5
Perkins, William   168, 169, 171
persecutions   84, 96, 130–2, 142–3, 146, 151, 156, 189, 190, 203–5, 212, 235–7, 240–6, 251, 263, 300, 353, 369, 405–7, 524–30
  of Freethinkers   212, 406–7, 409, 412–14
  of Irish Nationalists   453–4
  of Jews   7, 64, 427–31, 435–8, 441–3, 524, 533–4
  see also martyrdom
Persons, Robert   239–40, 243
Peter, St, cult of   82, 100, 102, 103
Peter's Pence   42, 48
pew rents   309–10
Philip, John   388

Philips, Nathaniel   436
Phillipps, Ambrose   352
Phillipps, Sir John   254
Phillpotts, Henry   300
Pilgrim Fathers   191, 526
pilgrimages   54, 70, 71, 83, 87, 94, 106, 121–2, 150, 243, 313, 351
  to Jerusalem   69, 83
  to Rome   35, 38, 42, 69, 70, 83
Pius V, St, Pope   99, 347, 525
Pius IX, Pope   355, 359, 531
Pius X, St, Pope   361
Pius XI, Pope   403
Pius XII, Pope   403–4, 474, 532
Plater, Charles   454
Platonists, Cambridge   175–6, 216–17
pluralism of preferment   90, 92, 109–10, 124, 129–30, 184–5, 187, 292, 297, 529
pluralism, religious   21–2, 26, 64, 195, 197, 203–4, 214, 278, 280, 282, 284, 286, 287, 377, 386, 392, 456, 482, 488–500
Plymouth Brethren   296
Pollard, James   244
Positivism   411, 418, 420
poverty, clerical   90, 93, 109–12, 124, 179, 184–5, 187, 361
Powell, Vavasor   253, 527
preaching, preachers   5, 38–9, 57–8, 77, 92–3, 123, 132, 148–9, 153–5, 157–64, 168, 180–1, 190, 198, 253–6, 258, 261–5, 270, 293, 298, 309–11, 314, 320, 324–5, 330, 343–5, 353, 369, 373, 382–3, 409, 435, 454, 528
  see also sermons
predestination   159, 163, 165, 168–74, 192–3, 197–8, 201–2
Premonstratensians   53, 108
Presbyterianism   3–4, 6–7, 136–8, 140–3, 144–6, 150, 161, 194–6, 203–5, 209–10, 257–64, 268–71, 277, 279, 282, 343, 347, 365–73, 470, 474, 475, 480–1, 491, 526–7
  in Ireland   282, 293
  in Wales   374–5
Price, Sir John   93
Priestley, Joseph   348–9
prostitutes, reclamation of   298

Protestant Association 251
Prynne, William 526
Pugh, Philip 256
Pugin, Augustus W. N. 299, 347, 352–3, 358
Puritanism 4, 5, 72, 138–9, 140–2, 160–3, 168–9, 175, 176, 187, 189, 194–201, 203–5, 207–8, 253, 255–6, 265, 269–71, 298, 317, 342, 348, 379, 431, 491, 526
Pusey, Edward Bouverie 298, 303, 355

Quakers 175, 200–11, 272, 340, 341, 348–9, 366, 374, 412, 527
see also Friends, Society of
Queen Anne's Bounty 187, 527
Quin, Malcolm 418
Quoist, Michel 483

Rabbi Moses of London 430
racial justice, work towards 486, 497, 533
Ramsey, Adam A. 339
Ramsey, Arthur 339
Ramsey, A. Michael 339, 470, 476, 480, 483–4
Ramsey, Ian 482–3
Ranters 201
Ranyard, Ellen 296
Rashdall, Hastings 450
Rational Society 409–10
Rationalism 3–5, 144, 146–8, 175–6, 209–32, 261, 265, 302, 353, 406–21, 459, 491
Rattenbury, J. E. 474
Raven, Charles 463–4
Rawlet, John 184
Ray, John 223, 232
record-keeping 55–6
Redemptorists 358, 361
Redwald, King of East Anglia 25, 26, 28–9
reform movements 41, 44, 48, 56, 67, 74, 86–7, 94, 114, 123–4, 131, 132, 187, 257, 283, 293, 294, 297–8, 303, 449, 451–2, 456, 479
Reformation 2–5, 50, 65, 74–5, 85, 94–8, 109, 118, 121–4, 129–44, 151–78, 180–1, 192, 195, 198, 200, 207, 235, 236–8, 270, 277, 289, 292, 346
Reformed churches 3, 144, 153, 188, 205, 257, 269, 272, 474
see also Church of Scotland, Congregationalism, Independents, Moravians, Presbyterianism, United Reformed Church
Reid, Gavin 512–14
Reid, Robert 132
Reid, Thomas 148
Reith, John 455, 459
religious orders *see under individual names; also* anchorites, Anglican religious orders, friars, hermits, Iona, Lindisfarne, monasticism
renewal movements 479
restoration of Roman Catholicism 95, 99, 156–8, 525
revivalism 5, 149, 252, 254–65, 291, 312, 346, 394, 401, 420
in England 260, 264–72
in New England 261–4
in Scotland 5, 258–64, 312, 314, 528
in Ulster 312, 314
in Wales 5, 254–7, 312, 314, 377, 528, 532
Revolution Settlement 145, 146, 293
Reynolds, Henry 327
Reynolds, John 221, 232
Rhigyfarch, biographer of St David 78, 79
Richard I, King of England 70, 428–9, 524
Richard of Lincoln 107
Rickman, Thomas 352
rites of passage 169, 181, 185–6, 310, 415, 496, 520
see also baptism, burial, confirmation, marriage
ritualist controversies 300, 316, 530–1
Robe, James 262, 263
Robert, Bishop of St Andrews 107
Roberts, Evan 377
Robertson, William 148
Robinson, Armitage 453
Robinson, H. Wheeler 470
Robinson, John 190–3

Robinson, Bishop John A. T. 474, 482, 507, 515, 533
Roger, John 208
Rogers, Guy 451
Rolfe, Frederick 355
Rolle, Richard 69, 72, 73, 524
Rollock, Robert 144
Roman occupation of Britain 13–23, 25, 29–30, 64, 77, 82
Roman religions 14–20, 300
Roman Catholicism, post–Reformation 4–6, 8, 174, 177–8, 187, 206, 213, 216–18, 234–51, 252, 257–8, 277–80, 282, 283, 286, 291, 296–8, 300–1, 304, 312–13, 320–1, 346–62, 365, 389, 399, 403–4, 420, 450, 453–5, 458–62, 464–6, 474–6, 479–80, 484, 487, 489–90, 499, 510–12, 514, 520, 525–33
    financial arrangements of 241–2, 243–4, 246–9, 282
    Irish 6, 7, 187, 268, 277–8, 282, 290, 296, 312–13, 321, 346, 350–1, 356–7, 359–61, 370–2, 378–9, 453–4
    Scottish 133, 138, 365, 370–1, 531
    Welsh 97, 251, 347, 365, 378–9
Roman Catholic emancipation 5, 187, 206, 234, 236, 247–8, 251, 278–9, 288, 291, 297, 302, 348, 350, 433, 459, 528–30
rosary, use of 95, 118–19, 246, 453
Rose, Cecil 454
Rosminians 358
Ross, William Stewart 417
Rossum, Cardinal van 403
Rothschild, Lionel de 433
Rothschild, Nathaniel de 433
Routley, Erik 456
Row, John 134
Rowland, Daniel 254, 256, 528
royal prerogatives 47–9, 93, 132, 138–40, 142, 145, 177, 206, 236
Royden, Maude 451–2, 460–1, 465
Rule (or Regulus), St 102, 107
Runcie, Robert 498–9, 501
Rupp, Gordon 465
Rushbrooke, J. H. 328
Russell, Lord John 357
Rutherford, Samuel 139, 141, 142, 144

Sabbatarianism 163–4, 207, 208, 243, 258–9, 294, 310, 373, 379, 411, 416, 465
Sacheverell, Henry 179, 209, 528
Sacks, Jonathan 434
sacraments 26, 65, 74, 93, 94, 110, 132, 152–3, 158, 167, 168–70, 174, 181–2, 301
    see also baptism, Communion, confession, Eucharist, Mass, penance
sacramentalism 300, 303
sacrifice
    animal 13–16, 19
    human 13
Sadhu Sundar Singh 456
Saeberht, King of the East Saxons 26, 28
St Andrews, See of 105–7, 109, 111, 113, 130, 524
St David's, See of 79, 87, 91
    claims to Welsh primacy 87, 91
saints, veneration of 2, 43, 82–3, 86–8, 92, 94, 95, 100–2, 104, 107, 116–17, 120–2, 152, 154, 239, 358
Sales, St Francis de 249
Salesbury, William 96, 97
Salvation Army 311, 316, 360, 395, 469, 531
Sampson, Thomas 158
Samson of Dol, St 78, 80
Samuel, Herbert 433
Sancroft, William 220
Sanderson, Robert 171
Sangster, W. E. 464
Sawtry, William 74
Sayers, Dorothy L. 356
Scheves, William 113
Schiff, Leonard 463
schools, Church 6, 412, 471, 498
    Church of England 280, 282–3, 286, 288, 290, 294, 301, 304, 531
    Roman Catholic 242, 251, 313, 357, 359, 361, 422
Schumacher, Fritz 487
Scialitti, P. 439
science, faith in 411, 421–2
Scott, Sir George Gilbert 299
Scott, Sir Walter 351
Sebbi, co-King of East Saxons 26

secessionism 3, 145–7, 160, 188, 194, 196, 258, 260–4, 365, 528–30
  Associate Presbytery 260–4
  Relief Church 6–7, 365, 367, 528, 530
  Secession Church 6–7, 145, 365, 367, 529–30
  United Presbyterian Church 7, 367, 530, 532
Second World War 7–8, 24, 343, 364, 379, 441, 442–5, 448, 464–7, 506
secularism 6–7, 289, 361, 411–21, 468, 499, 501, 531
secularization 5, 7–8, 124, 175, 199, 284, 286, 289, 314, 319–21, 359, 380, 402, 416, 471, 487, 489–90, 503–21
Seekers 200–1
Sellers, Abednego 184
Sellon, Priscilla Lydia 298
Selwyn, E. G. 451
Sensualism 196, 199
Separatism 189–201, 525, 526
Serampore Trio (Carey, Marshman and Ward) 385–7, 390
Serf, St 106
Sergeant, John 247
Sermoneta, Cardinal 123
sermons 2, 4, 43, 47, 58, 88, 92, 121, 147–9, 162–4, 180, 181, 207, 208, 220–1, 245, 248, 255, 263, 295, 332, 340, 343–5, 356, 380, 408, 422, 461, 505
Shaftesbury, Lord (Anthony Ashley Cooper) 296, 300, 328
Shakespeare, William 182, 326, 336
Sharp, James 142, 527
Sharp, John 175, 179
Sharples, Eliza 411–12
Shaw, George Bernard 416
Sheppard, Dick 451–2, 455, 461
Sheppard, William 158–9
Sherlock, Thomas 225, 232
Sherlock, William 174
Short, Thomas Vowler 376
Sibbald, James 118
Sibthorp, Richard Waldo 354
Sigeberht, King of East Anglia 32
Sigehere, co-King of East Saxons 26

Sikhism 8, 489–90, 495
Simeon, Charles 295, 529
Simpson, Sidrach 196
Simpson, William 461
Simson, John 146, 147, 260
Sitwell, Edith 356
Sixtus IV, Pope 113
slave trade, campaigns against 44, 294, 320–1, 383–4, 388, 529
  white slave trade 360
  developing economic alternatives 390
Smith, James 'Shepherd' 408
Smith, John 388
Smith, Richard 241–2, 247
Smith, Sydney 302, 384
Smith, William Robertson 369
Smyth, John 190–4, 200
Smythies, Bishop 393
Snell, H. H. 505
Socialist League 462
Society of the Holy Child Jesus 354
Society for Promoting Christian Knowledge (SPCK) 184, 253–4, 265–7, 294, 527
  Mission to south India 253, 381, 383
  Welsh-language publishing 253–4
Society for the Propagation of the Gospel (SPG) 267, 294, 381, 527
Socinianism 175, 176, 210, 218, 220
Solomons, Sir David 433
Southcott, Ernest 473
Southcott, Joanna 408
Southey, Robert 296–7, 504
Southwell, Charles 410
Spanish Inquisition 430–1
Spark, Muriel 441
Spencer, George 355
Spencer, Herbert 505, 506
Spens, Will 451
Spilsbury, John 193
spiritualism 408, 420, 451
Spottiswoode, John 134, 138
Stacpoole, Countess de 356
Stanley, A. P. 303
Starkey, Thomas 152
Stead, W. T. 360
Steere, Bishop 392–4
Stephen of Tathwell 50
sterilization, human 472

Stigand, Archbishop of Canterbury 47, 48
Stillingfleet, Edward 173, 175, 217–21, 232
Stopes, Marie 460
Storr, V. F. 451
Stott, John 483
Street, G. E. 299
Streeter, B. H. 456
Student Christian Movement 456
suicide 482
Sulien, Bishop of St David's 79, 81
Sulman, John 330
Sunday schools 6, 304, 309, 311–12, 318, 329, 334, 339, 420, 489, 528
   freethinking 7, 407, 415
surplice, wearing of 160, 161, 300, 530
Sutherland, John 266
Sutton, Oliver 56
Swiss Reformers 155, 159, 260
   see also Bucer, Martin
synagogues, British 8, 432–5, 437–41, 443–8, 531, 533
Synod of Whitby, 664 26, 34, 36, 101, 523
synodical government 55–6, 142, 176, 287, 299, 451, 532–3

Taizé Community 474
Talbot, Edward 449, 451
Taylor, Hudson 389, 394, 398, 400–1, 531
Taylor, Jeremy 168, 173, 174, 213, 232
Taylor, Robert 408
Teilo, St 78, 88
temperance 47, 164, 284, 310, 320, 334, 359, 368, 379, 454, 492
Temple, William 289, 451, 453, 458, 462–3, 465, 468, 471, 498
Teutonic religion 24–5
Thatcher, Margaret 444, 499, 501
Theism 419
Thenew, St 117
Theodore, Archbishop of Canterbury 35–6, 37, 251
theological colleges 292, 324, 325–7, 367, 529
Theosophists 338, 494
Thirlwall, Connop 376
Thomas, Archbishop of York 48

Thomas, R. S. 380
Thomas, John 256
Thomson, Andrew 149
Thorndike, Herbert 174, 177
Thraskists 195, 196
Tillet, Ben 360
Tillich, Paul 482
Tillotson, John 172, 173, 174, 176, 220–1
Tindal, Matthew 147, 222, 232
Tironensians 108
tithes 57, 58, 86, 92, 184, 197–9, 202, 292, 294, 411, 529
   in Ireland 293
   in Scotland (teinds) 109, 112, 116, 124, 135
Toc H 458
Todd, James 474
Toland, John 212, 232, 406
Tolkien, J. R. R. 356
Townsend, Henry 392
Tractarianism *see* Oxford Movement
translation of Bible 3, 155, 170
   into Asian languages 385
   into English 71–2, 74, 130, 131, 152–3, 431, 481, 525, 526
   into spoken Gaelic 258
   into Welsh 2, 89, 91, 96–8, 256, 525
   Joint Committee on the New Translation of the Bible 481
Trappists 349
Trefor, John 91
Trent, Council of 131, 241–2, 313
Trestrail, Dr 390–1
Triduana, St 117
Trinitarians (Red Friars) 109
Tuda, Bishop of Lindisfarne 34–5
Tugwell, Bishop of the Niger 399
Turgot, biographer of St Margaret 103–4
Tyndale (or Tynedale), William 130, 152, 525
Tyrrell, George 361

Ultan, Irish scribe 32
Ultramontanism 6, 312, 358–60, 361
Unification Church ('Moonies') 8, 492–4
union agreements, Church 367, 370, 474, 529–33

of Presbyterians and Independents,
    1691   205
of different Methodist traditions   452,
    532
of Scottish United Presbyterian and
    Free Churches to form United Free
    Church   370, 532
of Church of Scotland and United Free
    Church   370, 532
of Presbyterian Church and
    Congregational Church to form
    United Reformed Church   484, 533
union of England and Scotland   145,
    364, 526, 528
union with Ireland   277, 293, 350, 528
Unitarianism   209–10, 269, 279, 296,
    348–9, 374, 407, 410, 411, 419,
    450–1, 491, 529
United Reformed Church   484, 491,
    512, 514
United Synagogue   434, 440, 443–7, 464
unity conversations
    Anglican–Roman Catholic International
        Commission   480, 484, 533
    Church of Scotland–Anglican   475
    Free Church–Anglican   452, 475
    international Protestant union   264,
        265–6
    Methodist–Anglican   8, 475, 478–9,
        533
    multilateral   484–5
University College, London   324, 326,
    529
universities   3, 59, 66, 70–2, 91, 112–15,
    122, 124, 129, 130, 143, 146–8, 155,
    158, 162, 172, 185, 208, 237, 291,
    292, 301–3, 324–5, 369, 374, 385,
    497, 500
Aberdeen   113–15, 144, 369, 524
admission of Jews to Oxbridge   433
Cambridge   53, 59, 70, 112, 152,
    154–5, 161, 175, 189–90, 193, 216–
    17, 291–2, 295, 299, 301, 385, 394,
    395, 433, 449, 450, 474, 524, 529–31
continental, British attendance at   59,
    111–12, 114–15, 120, 122, 130,
    144–6, 328
Dublin, Catholic University of   355
Durham   529, 531

Edinburgh   144, 438–9
exclusion of Nonconformists from
    English universities   208, 282, 291,
    301, 530–1
Glasgow   143, 146, 369, 440
Kensington, Catholic university
    at   355
London   325; *see also* King's College,
    University College
Maynooth   284
Oxford   6, 51, 59, 63, 68, 70, 73–4,
    88, 112, 114–15, 155, 192, 254, 267,
    291–2, 297–8, 301–3, 336–7, 349,
    355, 395, 418, 433, 441, 455–9, 459,
    524, 528, 530
St Andrews   112–15, 130, 131, 133,
    142, 143–5, 146, 148, 524
of Wales   378, 529
Universities' Mission to Central
    Africa   389, 392–3, 395, 531
Urban, Bishop of Llandaff   85, 524

Vacarius   51
Valentine, Henry   183
Valliscaulians   108
Vanderkemp, J. T.   388
Vane, Sir Henry   195
Vatican Council, First (1869–70)   359,
    531
Vatican Council, Second (1962–5)   6,
    371–2, 479–80, 533
Vaughan, Herbert   360, 531
Vaughan, Robert   6, 323–7, 341
Vaughan, Robert Alfred   6, 326, 328
Veblen, Thornstein   507
Venn, Henry   385, 390–4, 398, 401
Venn, John   294
Vere, Aubrey de   355
vestments, use of   38, 57, 94, 155, 300,
    353, 358, 525
Victor I, apocryphal Pope   99
Victoria, Queen   396, 432
Virgin Birth   303, 463
Virgin Mary, devotion to   58, 82, 89,
    92, 117–19, 121–2, 154, 351, 358
Visser't Hooft, W. A.   468
Vitalian, Pope   35

Wake, William   179, 265–6
Wallensis, John   88

Wallington, Nehemiah 161
Walpole, Horace 266–7, 272
Ward, Barbara 465, 487
Ward, Bernard 356
Ward, John 'Zion' 408
Ward, Julian 515, 520
Ward, Maisie 356
Ward, Mary 241
Ward, Wilfrid 356
Ward, William 385–6
Ward, William George 356, 359, 530
Waterhouse, Alfred 330
Waterland, Daniel 176, 221, 232
Watson, John 327, 328, 332
Watson, Joshua 294
Watts, Charles 412–13, 417
Watts, Charles Albert 417
Watts, Isaac 209, 528
Watts, Kate 412
Waugh, Evelyn 356, 459
Weatherhead, Leslie 343
Webb, Benjamin 299
weddings, *see* marriage
Weld, Thomas 357
welfare state 285, 319–20, 471, 532
Welsh monastic saints 78–83, 86–8
Wesley, Charles 254, 256, 264, 474,
    528
Wesley, John 5, 149, 254, 256, 264,
    267–9, 272, 374, 382, 474, 528
Westcott, B. F. 303–4
Westminster Assembly of Divines 141,
    144, 195–6, 527
Westminster Confession of Faith 141,
    144, 146, 148
Weston, Bishop Frank 450
Whale, J. S. 470, 474
Whale, John 514
Whately, Richard 302
Whichcote, Benjamin 217
Whitefield, George 149, 254, 256,
    261–3, 267, 528
Whitgift, John 163, 237, 526
Whitsunday, celebration of 139, 312,
    361
Whittingham, William 159
Wickham, E. R. 472–3, 533
Wigheard, archbishop-elect 35
Wilberforce, Samuel 299, 353

Wilberforce, William 294–6, 353, 382,
    383, 388, 529
Wilde, Oscar 304, 355
Wilfrid, St 26, 34–6, 38–9, 523
Wilkins, John 174, 217–18
William I (the Conqueror) 43–4, 47–8,
    50, 52–3, 428–9
William II (Rufus) 43, 49, 52
William III (of Orange) 143, 145, 178,
    218, 236, 432, 527
William the Lion, King of Scotland 105
William of Malmesbury 44
William of Ockham 59, 63, 73
William of Touris 118–19, 122
William, Charles 355
Williams, John 182
Williams, William 256
Willibrord, St 138
Willock, John 134
Wilson, Dorothy 343–5
Winfrith *see* Boniface
Wini, Bishop of Winchester 33
Winward, Stephen 481
Wiseman, Nicholas 356–9, 530
Wishart, George 131, 132
Wishart, William 109
witchcraft 73, 255, 528
Wolfson, Sir Isaac 441, 533
Wollaston, William 222
Wolsey, Thomas 75
women in ministry 32, 69–70, 201, 208,
    267, 269, 296, 304, 314–15, 320,
    343–5, 353–4, 377, 447, 451–2,
    460–1, 485, 531, 533
  as missionaries 389, 401
  in religious orders 32, 34, 37, 53–4,
    66, 69, 115, 241, 298, 350, 354,
    530–1
  see also Deaconesses, Order of
women's rights 201, 208–9, 420–1, 447,
    455, 460, 485, 521
women's suffrage 333, 336–8, 452
Woodard, Nathaniel 301
Woodforde, Parson 185
Woods, Frank 459
Woolston, Thomas 212, 222, 225, 406
Wordsworth, William 182, 296, 351
World Council of Churches 468–9,
    477–8, 484, 532–3

world wars *see* First World War, Second
  World War
Wren, Sir Christopher   181
Wulfric of Haselbury   54–5
Wulfstan, St, Archbishop of
  York   42–3, 46, 524
Wulfstan, St, Bishop of Worcester   1,
  43–4, 46, 524
Wycherley, William   247
Wyclif (or Wycliffe), John   2, 71, 73–4,
  151, 189, 326, 504, 524

Wynram, John   134

York, See of   32, 35–6, 37, 40–3, 45–6,
  48
Young, Gruffydd   91

Zernov, Nicholas   476
Zetetic societies   407
Zionism   435, 443–4, 448